Advancing Criminology and Criminal Justice Policy

D1565689

Advancing Criminology and Criminal Justice Policy is a definitive source-book that comprises contributions from some of the most recognized experts in criminology and criminal justice policy. The book is essential reading for students taking upper level courses and seminars on crime, public policy, and crime prevention, as well as for policymakers within the criminal justice sphere.

There has been a growing recognition of the importance of evidence-based criminal justice policies from criminologists, policymakers, and practitioners. Yet, despite governmental and professional association efforts to promote the role of criminological research in criminal justice policy, political ideologies, fear, and the media heavily influence criminal justice policies and practices.

Bridging the gap between research and policy, this book provides the best available research evidence, identifies strategies for informing policy, and offers direct policy recommendations for a number of pressing contemporary issues in criminal justice, including:

- delinquency, intervention programs, and community crime prevention;
- problem-oriented policing and the science of hot-spot policing;
- sentencing and drug courts;
- community corrections, incarceration, and rehabilitation;
- mental illness, gender, aging, and indigenous communities.

Thomas G. Blomberg is Dean and Sheldon L. Messinger Professor of Criminology, and Executive Director of the Center for Criminology and Public Policy Research at Florida State University, USA.

Julie Mestre Brancale is a doctoral candidate and graduate research assistant for the Center for Criminology and Public Policy Research at Florida State University, USA.

Kevin M. Beaver is Professor in the College of Criminology and Criminal Justice at Florida State University, USA.

William D. Bales is Professor in the College of Criminology and Criminal Justice at Florida State University, USA.

For a quick, concise review of what is known about the effectiveness of current crime prevention practices and policies, this is your best resource.

This volume provides a much needed critical assessment of contemporary criminal justice policy and practice. For a quick overview, this is the most comprehensive review available and the focus on policy is particularly welcome, given the limited credible evaluation evidence for this type of intervention.

This scope of this volume is very broad, with short concise reviews of a wide range of current crime prevention practices and policies by the leading experts on specific types of intervention.

> **Del Elliott,** *PhD, Director, Program on Problem Behavior and Positive Youth Development, Institute of Behavioral Science, University of Colorado Boulder, USA*

The editors have assembled a veritable who's who of internationally renowned crime policy scholars for this volume, promising incisive reviews of critical issues across policing, courts, corrections, sentencing, and crime prevention. The authors deliver on that promise with precision, clarity, and insight. Skilfully weaving together theory, empirical evidence, and practical considerations to create a rich portrait of contemporary crime and criminal justice policy, each entry helps to clarify effective and cost-efficient ways forward. Notably, the essays also offer important counsel against relying on "common-sense" approaches to crime, which have often proven to be less than helpful and sometimes damaging. As the United States emerges from a period where ideology seemed to drive much of criminal justice policy, this book is essential reading for anyone who desires to have a meaningful impact on public safety.

> **Brandon K. Applegate,** *University of South Carolina, USA*

The American public's concern about crime and the criminal justice has reached unprecedented levels. Media coverage of police killings of civilians has raised awareness about police use deadly of force, and data showing that the U.S. has the highest incarceration rate of any industrialized nation has spurred calls for reform. The pressure to "do something" about crime is strong. But past policies have often been based on sound bites and not empirical evidence. This book changes that. *Advancing Criminology and Criminal Justice Policy* is a sophisticated and intelligent book that covers an impressive array of topics. Each chapter summarizes the best available evidence on crime and crime control but—more importantly—it considers how scientific knowledge can be used to design better strategies.

The contributing authors are all trusted experts, and each chapter is concise, accessible, and jargon-free. The succinct introduction to each major section makes this an ideal textbook for criminology courses. But the book isn't just for the classroom. Advancing Criminology is a must read for anyone interested in reforming criminal justice in America.

Joan Petersilia, *Adelbert H. Sweet Professor of Law, Stanford Law School, USA*

This book provides, through examples and thoughtful writings, evidence-based research strategies that can be used with policy makers to make improvements in both individual and community justice in our dynamic criminal justice system.

Patricia Brantingham, *University Professor of Computational Criminology, Simon Fraser University, Canada*

This is clearly the single best volume on the subject of evidence based criminal justice policy. It should be an indispensable resource for scholars, practitioners, and students. I recommend it without reservation.

Malcolm M. Feeley, *Claire Sanders Clements Dean's Professor, Boalt Hall School of Law, University of California at Berkeley, USA*

Advancing Criminology and Criminal Justice Policy offers a timely and important collection of essays by an internationally-renown set of scholars who are the fore of bridging the criminological/criminal justice divide. It is refreshing to see the authors demonstrate that our field cannot do one without the other. As criminologists, our main task is to conduct the most objective scientific work possible within the constraints of the data we have. Getting that material in a palpable way to practice and policy audiences is also necessary if we are to be 'at the table' when it comes to informing the policy response to crime and criminals. Blomberg and his colleagues have done our field a huge service. This book is stellar.

Alex R. Piquero, *PhD, Ashbel Smith Professor of Criminology, University of Texas at Dallas, USA*

Advancing Criminology and Criminal Justice Policy

Edited by Thomas G. Blomberg,
Julie Mestre Brancale,
Kevin M. Beaver and William D. Bales

Routledge
Taylor & Francis Group

LONDON AND NEW YORK

First published 2016
by Routledge
2 Park Square, Milton Park, Abingdon, Oxon OX14 4RN

and by Routledge
711 Third Avenue, New York, NY 10017

Routledge is an imprint of the Taylor and Francis Group, an informa business

British Library Cataloguing in Publication Data
A catalogue record for this book is available from the British Library

Library of Congress Cataloguing in Publication Data
Names: Blomberg, Thomas G., editor. | Brancale, Julie Mestre, editor.
Title: Advancing criminology and criminal justice policy / edited by
Thomas G. Blomberg, Julie Mestre Brancale, Kevin M. Beaver and William D. Bales.
Description: New York : Routledge, 2016.
Identifiers: LCCN 2015031149 | ISBN 9781138829220 (hardback) |
ISBN 9781138829237 (pbk.) | ISBN 9781315737874 (e-book)
Subjects: LCSH: Crime. | Crime prevention. | Criminal justice, Administration.
Classification: LCC HV6025 .A358 2016 | DDC 364–dc23
LC record available at http://lccn.loc.gov/2015031149

ISBN: 978-1-138-82922-0 (hbk)
ISBN: 978-1-138-82923-7 (pbk)
ISBN: 978-1-315-73787-4 (ebk)

Typeset in Sabon
by Out of House Publishing

For Jeanine's support, patience, and always meaningful insights
TGB

For my wonderful husband, John, and amazing son, Vincent
JMB

For my beautiful wife, Shonna, and my four adorable children,
Brooke, Jackson, Belle, and Blake
KMB

For my best friend and wife, Sue, who is my inspiration and guiding light
and my brothers Michael and David who always encouraged my education
and career and to our parents to whom we owe everything
WDB

Contents

Illustrations

Figures

Tables

Contributors

Celesta Albonetti is Professor of Sociology at the University of Iowa and holds a courtesy appointment in the College of Law. Her research primarily focuses on understanding the variables that influence prosecutorial and judicial discretion in felony adjudications. Most of her research examines the effect of defendant characteristics, legally relevant variables and case processing variables on sentence severity under the Federal Sentencing Guidelines. A central inquiry of her research is estimating the conditioning effect of a defendant's race/ethnicity and gender on the relationship between legally relevant variables and sources of judicial and prosecutorial discretion on sentence severity. Her current research estimates the effect of U.S. Appellate Court holding and Supreme Court decisions on federal district judges' sentencing decisions.

Thomas Abt is Senior Research Fellow at the Harvard Kennedy School of Government, where he teaches, studies and consults on the use of evidence-based approaches to violence reduction, among other topics. Previously, he served as Deputy Secretary for Public Safety to Governor Andrew Cuomo in New York and as Chief of Staff to the Office of Justice Programs in the U.S. Department of Justice.

William D. Bales is Professor at Florida State University's College of Criminology and Criminal Justice and co-editor of the journal *Criminology and Public Policy* with Daniel Nagin. He has published in *Criminology*, *Journal of Research in Crime and Delinquency* and *Justice Quarterly*, among other crime and policy journals.

Kelle Barrick is Research Criminologist in the Center for Justice, Safety, and Resilience at RTI International. Dr Barrick's current research focuses on desistance from crime and violence, jail reform and human trafficking. In 2009, she received the American Society of Criminology's Outstanding Article Award for a paper on the impact of felony labeling on recidivism.

Kevin M. Beaver is Professor in the College of Criminology and Criminal Justice at Florida State University. His research focuses on the biosocial foundations to antisocial behaviors.

Thomas G. Blomberg is Dean and Sheldon L. Messinger Professor of Criminology, and Executive Director of the Center for Criminology and Public Policy Research at Florida State University's College of Criminology and Criminal Justice. From 2008–2013 he served as Editor of *Criminology and Public Policy*. His current research is focused upon determining ways to more effectively link research to public policy and includes the role of education in crime and delinquency desistance and the identification of risk and protective factors associated with elder financial fraud. Dr Blomberg has shared his various research and policy findings with state policymakers throughout the country, the U.S. Congress, and the White House Office of Science and Technology Policy. Among his recent books are *American Penology: A History of Control* with Karol Lucken and *Punishment and Social Control* with Stanley Cohen.

Alfred Blumstein is the J. Erik Jonsson University Professor of Urban Systems and Operations Research and former dean at the Heinz College of Carnegie Mellon University. In 1987, Blumstein received ASC's Sutherland Award for his contributions to research; he was president of the ASC in 1991–92. In 2007, Blumstein was awarded the Stockholm Prize in Criminology. His criminology research on criminology and criminal justice started when he was director of the task force on science and technology for the 1965–1967 President's Crime Commission and has covered many aspects of criminal justice, including crime measurement, criminal careers, sentencing, deterrence and incapacitation, prison populations, demographic trends, juvenile violence and drug-enforcement policy.

Kate Bowers is Professor at the University College London Department of Security and Crime Science, based in central London. She has worked in the field of environmental criminology, crime analysis and crime science for over 20 years, and has published more than 80 articles. Her research has mainly involved examining spatial and temporal patterns in crime, exploring the situational context of crime problems and evaluating the effectiveness of crime reduction interventions.

Anthony A. Braga is the Don M. Gottfredson Professor of Evidence-Based Criminology at Rutgers University and Senior Research Fellow in the Program in Criminal Justice Policy and Management at Harvard University. His research focuses on improving the fairness and effectiveness of policing.

Julie Mestre Brancale is a doctoral candidate and Research Assistant in the College of Criminology and Criminal Justice at Florida State University. She is the former Managing Editor of *Criminology and Public Policy*. Her research interests include criminal justice policy evaluation and the application of criminological research to public policy.

Marilyn Brown is Associate Professor of Sociology at the University of Hawaii at Hilo. Her research specializations include: criminology; corrections; reintegration of former prisoners; mass incarceration and families; and criminal justice policy. She is the author of articles on crime and justice appearing in *Theoretical Criminology, Crime and Delinquency, Critical Criminology, Feminist Criminology,* as well as chapters in edited volumes.

James M. Byrne is Professor in the School of Criminology and Justice Studies at the University of Massachusetts, Lowell and an Adjunct Professor at the Key Centre for Ethics, Law, Justice, and Governance, School of Criminology and Criminal Justice, Griffith University. His research focuses on offender re entry, community corrections, risk classification, the link between prison culture and community culture, the effectiveness of crime control technology, and the community context of crime and crime control.

Meda Chesney-Lind teaches Women's Studies at the University of Hawaii. Nationally recognized for her work on women and crime, her testimony before Congress resulted in national support of gender responsive programming for girls in the juvenile justice system. Her most recent book on girls' use of violence, *Fighting for Girls* (co-edited with Nikki Jones), won an award from the National Council on Crime and Delinquency for "focusing America's attention on the complex problems of the criminal and juvenile justice systems." In 2013, the Western Society of Criminology named an award honoring "significant contributions to the field of gender, crime and justice" for Chesney-Lind and gave her the "inaugural" award.

Cecilia Chouhy is a PhD candidate in the School of Criminal Justice at the University of Cincinnati. Using a cross-national approach, her main research interests include testing criminological theories, the effectiveness of correctional programs, and sources of public opinion. At present, she is conducting studies on social concern theory, macro-level models of crime, and rival theories of public punitiveness in a South American context.

Francis T. Cullen is Distinguished Research Professor Emeritus and Senior Research Associate in the School of Criminal Justice at the University of Cincinnati. He is a past president of the American Society of Criminology and the Academy of Criminal Justice Sciences. His current research interests are in correctional policy, theoretical criminology and the organization of criminological knowledge.

John E. Eck is Professor of Criminal Justice at the University of Cincinnati, where he teaches police effectiveness and crime prevention. His research focuses on preventing crimes at places through a problem-oriented approach or regulation. He received his PhD from the University of Maryland.

Abigail A. Fagan is Associate Professor at the University of Florida. Dr Fagan's research focuses on the etiology and prevention of adolescent substance use, delinquency and violence, with an emphasis on examining the ways in which scientific advances can be successfully translated into effective crime and delinquency prevention practices.

David P. Farrington is Emeritus Professor of Psychological Criminology at Cambridge University. He received the Stockholm Prize in Criminology in 2013. He is Chair of the ASC Division of Developmental and Life-Course Criminology. In addition to over 650 published journal articles and book chapters on criminological and psychological topics, he has published nearly 100 books, monographs and government reports.

Nicole Frisch is a criminology and criminal justice doctoral student at the University of Maryland, College Park. Her primary research interests include translational criminology and the connection between research, policy and practice, corrections and reentry policy, and the psychological consequences of incarceration.

Natasha A. Frost is Associate Professor and the Associate Dean for Academic Programs in the School of Criminology and Criminal Justice at Northeastern University, Boston, MA. Professor Frost holds a Bachelor's degree in psychology from Northeastern University and a PhD in criminal justice from the CUNY's Graduate School and University Center. Her research interests are in the area of punishment and social control with a particular focus on mass incarceration and its impact on individuals, families and communities. Her book, *The Punishment Imperative: The Rise and Failure of Mass Incarceration in America*, co-authored with Todd Clear, was published by NYU Press (2014).

Gerald G. Gaes is Criminal Justice Consultant and Visiting Researcher at Florida State University in the College of Criminology and Criminal Justice. He was Director of Research for the Federal Bureau of Prisons and retired from government service in 2002.

Kathleen Gallagher received her PhD in 2014 from the School of Criminal Justice at the University of Cincinnati. Her current research interests include crime prevention, policing and the role of environmental criminology in practical police problem solving.

L. Sergio Garduno is a doctoral student at the College of Criminology and Criminal Justice at Florida State University. He serves as the Managing Editor for the journal of *Criminology and Public Policy*. His research interests include police corruption, jail, gangs, victimology and criminological theory.

Charlotte Gill is Assistant Professor in the Department of Criminology, Law and Society and Deputy Director of the Center for Evidence-Based Crime Policy at George Mason University. She received her PhD in Criminology from the University of Pennsylvania. Her research interests include community-based crime prevention, place-based criminology and evidence-based policy.

Marie Gottschalk is Professor in the Department of Political Science at the University of Pennsylvania. Her latest book is *Caught: The Prison State and the Lockdown of American Politics*. A former editor and journalist, she served on the American Academy of Arts and Sciences National Task Force on Mass Incarceration and the National Academy of Sciences Committee on the Causes and Consequences of High Rates of Incarceration.

Rob T. Guerette is Associate Professor of Criminal Justice in the School of International and Public Affairs at Florida International University, Miami. His research focuses on understanding the patterns and situational determinants of both domestic and transnational crimes, formulation of approaches to prevent those crimes, and the evaluation of crime reduction efforts.

Andrew J. Harris is Associate Dean for Research and Graduate Programs at the University of Massachusetts Lowell College of Fine Arts, Humanities, and Social Sciences, and Associate Professor in the University's School of Criminology and Justice Studies. His research examines the implementation of public policies at the intersection of criminal justice and human services.

Carolyn Hoyle is Director of the Centre for Criminology at the University of Oxford, UK. She has conducted research and published widely on victims, the death penalty, and restorative justice. Her work includes empirical, theoretical and normative studies of the use of restorative processes in the UK.

Roy F. Janisch was raised on the Sisseton-Wahpeton Sioux Tribe in northeastern South Dakota. While in the U.S. Army, he served as a Military Police Officer and Investigator. He has worked as a law enforcement specialist, management analyst, and federal criminal investigator throughout Indian Country. Dr Janisch received his B.S. in Criminal Justice and Psychology and Master of Public Administration at the University of South Dakota and PhD in Law and Social Sciences, Arizona State University. He is currently Associate Professor, Justice Studies, Pittsburg State University, Pittsburg, Kansas.

Shane D. Johnson is Professor in the Department of Security and Crime Science, University College London. He has published over 100 articles and has particular interests in exploring how methods from other disciplines (e.g. complexity science) can inform understanding of crime and security issues.

Kimberly Kamp is a doctoral candidate in the School of Public Affairs at the University of Central Florida working on her dissertation regarding the social media strategies employed by drug policy advocacy groups.

David Kennedy is the Director of the National Network for Safe Communities, a project of John Jay College of Criminal Justice in New York City. Mr. Kennedy and the National Network support cities implementing strategic interventions to reduce violence, minimize arrest and incarceration, enhance police legitimacy, and strengthen relationships between law enforcement and communities. These interventions have been proven effective in a variety of settings by a Campbell Collaboration evaluation, and are currently being implemented in Chicago, New Orleans, Baltimore, Oakland and many other cities nationwide.

Kimberly R. Kras is Post-doctoral Research Fellow at the Center for Advancing Correctional Excellence (ACE!) and the Department of Criminology, Law and Society at George Mason University. Her work focuses on offender reentry and community corrections. Dr Kras's work has been published in *Criminology and Public Policy* and the *Journal of Drug Issues*.

Julia A. Laskorunsky is a doctoral candidate in the Criminology program at Penn State University and a graduate research assistant at the Justice Center for Research. Her main research interests are in the areas of sentencing and corrections, with a focus on risk analysis and racial disproportionality.

Edward J. Latessa received his PhD from the Ohio State University and is Director and Professor of the School of Criminal Justice at the University of Cincinnati. He has published over 150 works in the area of criminal justice, corrections, and juvenile justice and is co-author of eight books.

Pamela K. Lattimore is Director of RTI's Center for Justice, Safety, and Resilience. Her research focuses on evaluating interventions; investigating the causes and correlates of criminal behavior, including substance use and mental health; and developing approaches to improve criminal justice operations. She is principal investigator for the evaluation of the MacArthur Foundation-funded Safety and Justice Challenge. In addition, she is leading an NIJ-funded study of reentry programs supported by Second Chance Act grants and is the principal investigator for the NIJ-funded evaluation of the Honest Opportunity Probation with Enforcement Demonstration Field Experiment. She is also principal investigator for a Department of Defense study examining military workplace violence. She has led multiple other federally funded studies. Dr Lattimore was named a Fellow of the Academy of Experimental Criminology in 2009 and received the Peter P. Lejins Researcher Award from the American Correctional Association in 2015. She is co-editor of the annual series, Handbook on Corrections and Sentencing.

John H. Laub is Distinguished University Professor in the Department of Criminology and Criminal Justice at the University of Maryland, College Park. From July 2010 to January 2013, Dr Laub served as the Director of the National Institute of Justice in the Department of Justice. Along with his colleague, Robert Sampson, he was awarded the Stockholm Prize in Criminology in 2011 for their research on how and why offenders stop offending.

Karol Lucken is Associate Professor in the Department of Criminal Justice at the University of Central Florida. She publishes in the area of punishment history, theory and policy. Her articles have appeared in *Criminology and Public Policy, British Journal of Criminology, Crime & Delinquency,* and *Critical Criminology.* She is co-author of *American Penology: A History of Control* and is currently writing a book entitled *Rethinking Punishment* with Routledge.

Arthur Lurigio is Senior Associate Dean for Faculty in the College of Arts and Sciences, and a Professor of Criminal Justice and Criminology and of Psychology at Loyola University Chicago where he is also a member of the Graduate Faculty and Director of the Center for the Advancement of Research, Training, and Education. Dr Lurigio is the current president of the Illinois Academy of Criminology.

Douglas B. Marlowe is Chief of Science, Law and Policy for the National Association of Drug Court Professionals. His research focuses on behavioral treatments for substance abusers and criminal offenders, and the effects of Drug Courts and other diversion programs for drug-addicted individuals in the criminal justice system.

Daniel P. Mears is the Mark C. Stafford Professor of Criminology at Florida State University's College of Criminology and Criminal Justice. He is the author of *American Criminal Justice Policy* (Cambridge University Press), and, with Joshua C. Cochran, *Prisoner Reentry in the Era of Mass Incarceration* (Sage Publications).

Carlos E. Monteiro is Senior Research Associate at the Institute of Race and Justice at Northeastern University. He earned a Masters of Education from the University of Connecticut and his PhD in criminology and justice policy from Northeastern University. With advanced degrees in education and criminal justice policy, Carlos's research interests have long centered on the factors affecting access to, and quality of, education for young adults of color. His scholarly interests today are still tied to race, ethnicity and educational access, but particularly as those interact to produce disparate outcomes across the criminal justice system and within corrections specifically.

George B. Pesta is the Associate Director of the FSU Center for Criminology and Public Policy Research. He served as Project Director for the Juvenile Justice NCLB National Collaboration Project and Research Coordinator for the Juvenile Justice Educational Enhancement Program. He has been the Director of Education Planning and Development at G4S Youth Services, an international juvenile justice service provider.

Laurie Robinson is the Clarence J. Robinson Professor of Criminology, Law and Society at George Mason University. Reflecting her national involvement in criminal justice policy, she twice served as the Senate-confirmed Assistant Attorney General for the U.S. Department of Justice Office of Justice Programs, and in the aftermath of Ferguson, co-chaired the President's Task Force on 21st Century Policing.

Jason Rydberg is Assistant Professor in the School of Criminology and Justice Studies at the University of Massachusetts Lowell, and an Associate with the Center for Program Evaluation. His research concerns community corrections, recidivism, sex offender management and the evaluation of criminal justice programs in these areas.

Joseph A. Schwartz is Assistant Professor in the School of Criminology and Criminal Justice at University of Nebraska, Omaha. His research interests include behavior genetics, biosocial criminology, the association between intelligence and behavior, and additional factors involved in the etiology of criminal behavior.

Myrinda Schweitzer is the Deputy Director at the Corrections Institute and a doctoral candidate in the School of Criminal Justice at University of Cincinnati. She has co-authored over 10 publications and served as a project director for several correctional projects.

Kelly M. Socia is Assistant Professor in the School of Criminology and Justice Studies at the University of Massachusetts Lowell, and a Fellow with the Center for Public Opinion. His research interests include offender reentry and recidivism, registered sex offenders, public policy-making, GIS and spatial analyses. He received his PhD from the School of Criminal Justice at the University at Albany, SUNY.

Beck M. Strah is a doctoral student in Criminology and Justice Policy at Northeastern University. His research interests include corrections, masculinity, risk assessment, recidivism and training evaluation.

Ray Surette has a doctorate in Criminology from Florida State University and is a Professor in the Department of Criminal Justice at the University of Central Florida, Orlando, Florida. His research interests include technology and its impact on community crime levels, effects on perceptions of crime and justice, and criminal justice policies. He has published numerous articles and books on crime and criminal justice topics and is internationally recognized as a scholar in the area of media, crime, and criminal justice. In addition, Professor Surette has been the PI and co-PI on a number of evaluation studies of criminal justice community based projects. Specific to this proposal, he has published research on the use of computer-aided camera surveillance systems in law enforcement and is currently studying the use of camera surveillance systems by law enforcement in neighborhoods and other public areas.

Faye S. Taxman is Professor in the Center for Advancing Correctional Excellence (ACE!) and the Department of Criminology, Law and Society at George Mason University. Her work focuses on evidence-based practices in correctional setting and implementation science. She is the author of over 150 journal articles and has received many awards for her work. She has developed translational tools including the RNR Simulation Tool (www.gmuace.org/tools).

Cody Telep is Assistant Professor in the School of Criminology and Criminal Justice at Arizona State University. He received his PhD from the Department of Criminology, Law and Society at George Mason University. His recent work has appeared in *Journal of Experimental Criminology*, *Justice Quarterly* and *Police Quarterly*.

Jeffery T. Ulmer is Professor of Sociology and Criminology at Penn State University, and also serves as Associate Department Head for Sociology and Criminology. His research spans topics such as courts and sentencing, criminological theory, symbolic interactionism, religion and crime, and the integration of qualitative and quantitative methods. He was awarded the 2001 Distinguished New Scholar Award and the 2012 Distinguished Scholar Award from the American Society of Criminology's Division on Corrections and Sentencing. He is the author of *Social Worlds of Sentencing: Court Communities Under Sentencing Guidelines* (1997, State University of New York Press), and co-author (with Darrell Steffensmeier) of *Confessions of a Dying Thief: Understanding Criminal Careers and Illegal Enterprise* (2005, Aldine-Transaction) which won the 2006 Hindelang Award from the American Society of Criminology. His most recent book (with John Kramer), *Sentencing Guidelines: Lessons from Pennsylania* was published in 2009 by Lynne Rienner Publishers.

Gordon Waldo is Professor Emeritus in the College of Criminology and Criminal Justice at Florida State University. His career covers over 50 years of university teaching, research, publication and administration and three years working in corrections. He has served on journal editorial boards and chaired or served on state, national and international criminal justice projects.

David Weisburd is Distinguished Professor of Criminology, Law and Society at George Mason University and Walter E. Meyer Professor of Law and Criminal Justice at the Hebrew University. Professor Weisburd received the Stockholm Prize in Criminology in 2010, and the 2014 Sutherland Award for "outstanding contributions to the field of criminology."

Roxana Willis is a DPhil candidate in Law at the University of Oxford, conducting ethnographic research on the role of community in restorative justice at the intersection of gender, ethnicity, and class. Before joining Oxford, Roxana obtained an LLM in International Economic Law (School of Oriental and African Studies, University of London), and an LLB in Law with European Legal Studies (University of Kent at Canterbury).

Acknowledgements

We wish to thank all of the authors who contributed a chapter featured in this volume. Each author demonstrated a strong commitment to the advancement of evidence-based research in criminal justice policy and practice. We would also like thank to Heidi Lee, Rebecca Willford and Thomas Sutton for their helpful guidance and support during the preparation of this book.

Volume introduction

Thomas G. Blomberg, Julie Mestre Brancale, Kevin M. Beaver and William D. Bales

Academic criminology's formative beginnings were at the University of Chicago at the turn of the twentieth century. In what became known as the "Chicago School," researchers conducted numerous ethnographic studies of Chicago's slum communities in the effort to guide policies and practices aimed at reducing the slum's criminogenic influences believed to be causing crime. During much of the subsequent twentieth century, criminology became less concerned with informing policy and more concerned with establishing itself as a recognized scientific discipline through the development and validation of causal explanations of crime.

Over the past two decades, however, a growing recognition of the importance of evidence-based criminal justice policies has emerged. This recognition has been demonstrated through a series of federally sponsored initiatives that include funding assistance for the implementation of particular policies that have been designated as "evidence-based." Moreover, the American Society of Criminology (ASC), the Academy of Criminal Justice Sciences, and the Association of Doctoral Programs in Criminology and Criminal Justice have formed a consortium to promote criminological research in national criminal justice policy. Additionally, in 2000, the ASC, in conjunction with the U.S. Department of Justice, established the journal, *Criminology and Public Policy* (CPP) to increase the role and prominence of research in criminal justice policy. This included the development of special issues of CPP on timely research and criminal justice policy topics that have been featured at Congressional Luncheons in DC. These initiatives have contributed to a perception among many criminologists that "the growth in applied research, scientific evidence of what works, and increased attention to evidence-based practices to be among the most positive developments in the field over the past few decades" (Baumer, 2015:8). Nonetheless, and even with these unprecedented governmental and professional association collaborations and perceptions of the value of criminological research in criminal justice policy, there remains debate among some criminologists over what criminology's priorities should be, related to a research and science versus an applied policy role.

Some criminologists, for example, claim that they cannot responsibly inform criminal justice policy with research because criminological research is largely contingent, not causally certain and, therefore, not sufficiently established as science. Specifically, Tittle (2004) contends that criminological research knowledge is shaky at best and poses more danger for policy than benefits. Wellford (2009) elaborates that criminology may have actually had too much rather than too little policy influence given its lack of scientific development. In contrast, and while acknowledging the lack of causal certainty in criminological research and the need for continuing criminology's causal quest, a growing number of criminologists share and embrace the goal of employing best available criminological research to inform criminal justice policy (Cullen, 2012). The question is: how can criminologists effectively combine their traditional research and science role with an emerging criminal justice policy role?

Clearly, the effort to combine a scientific research role with a criminal justice policy role does create challenges for criminologists. It requires them to be reflexive and responsive to pressing crime and policy questions associated with current headlines, and/or debates which can come from the public, journalists, policy makers, and practitioners. Further, they need to respond to the questions in ways that are comprehensive, understandable, and altogether objective. Because much of the research evidence produced by criminology is contingent, and involves nuanced relationships, it is not easily understood by non-research audiences. Very importantly, establishing a link between research and criminal justice policy involves a balancing process rather than an identification and advocacy for a particular criminal justice policy and practice. This balancing process can involve identifying and explaining various policy and practice options and the likely consequences based upon the best available research evidence. Certainly, there are areas of criminological research that can provide informed evidence on the likely consequences of various criminal justice policy and practice options, despite the fact that this research does not provide specific causal conclusions.

How, then, can criminology's developing research knowledge effectively inform criminal justice policy in the absence of causal certainty? *Advancing Criminology and Criminal Justice Policy* addresses this question in the effort to simultaneously advance criminology and criminal justice policy. The book is made up of five parts that include: Part I: Introduction, with chapters that address approaches to effectively integrate criminological research and criminal justice policy; Part II: Crime prevention; Part III: Policing and court sentencing; Part IV: Corrections and rehabilitation, and Part V: Conclusion, with chapters addressing the future of criminology and criminal justice policy. Virtually all of our contributing authors work at the interface of criminological research and criminal justice policy. Each of the five parts are framed by the editors with summaries of the individual chapters that are focused upon their interrelationship to the topic(s) in question, including the best research-based practices, conclusions, and policy recommendations.

Overall, the book focuses upon: (1) identifying strategies for informing criminal justice policy from research findings that are largely contingent; and (2) applying the identified research-based strategies to a comprehensive series of criminology research and related criminal justice policy areas. The underlying argument of the book is that, despite largely contingent research findings and associated causal uncertainty, criminal justice policies based upon the best available research knowledge can ameliorate the alterable conditions of the problem in question rather than eliminate its uncertain root causes. In doing so, criminologists can continue to pursue their ongoing scientific research interests in causality while simultaneously informing criminal justice policy with best available research knowledge.

References

Baumer, Eric P. 2015. Member Perspectives. *The Criminologist*, 40, (3):8.

Cullen, Francis T. 2012. Personal communication, April 3.

Tittle, Charles. 2004. The Arrogance of Public Sociology. *Social Forces*, 82: 1639–1643.

Wellford, Charles. 2009. Criminologists Should Stop Whining About Their Impact on Policy and Practice. In (Natasha A. Frost, Joshua D. Frelich, and Todd R. Clear, Eds.) *Contemporary Issues in Criminal Justice Policy: Policy Proposals from the American Society of Criminology Conference.* Belmont, CA: Wadsworth.

Part I

Introduction

Introduction

Evidence, evaluation, and strategies for moving criminal justice policy forward

Thomas G. Blomberg, Julie Mestre Brancale, Kevin M. Beaver and William D. Bales

The growing recognition of the importance of criminal justice policies that are efficient, cost-effective, and evidence-based has been reflected in the actions of local, state, and national policymakers, and researchers. With increasing frequency, especially since the economic recession that began in 2009, policymakers have sought to incorporate evidence-based research into their criminal justice policy and practice decisions. Further, a growing number of criminologists have responded to this emerging evidence-based receptivity by entering into research partnerships with practitioners, conducting evaluations of criminal justice programs, and delivering testimony to legislative bodies. While the search for causality in the field of criminology will continue, criminal justice policy can benefit significantly from the application of best available research evidence. The chapters in this section demonstrate that strategies for implementing evidence-based criminal justice should be incremental, thoughtful, and altogether scientific.

Laurie Robinson and Thomas Abt (Chapter 1) trace the growing influence of science in criminal justice policy, identify obstacles to further growth, and present strategies to overcome these obstacles and sustain progress. Although the current national nonpartisan sentiment favors evidence-based criminal justice policies, it is possible that momentum may slow due to political and social changes. Therefore, strategies to maintain the progress that has been established must focus on cultural changes at all levels of the criminal justice system. To do so, Robinson and Abt detail a series of seven recommendations that include the proactive, objective, and sensitive handling of popular and highly politicized events because they have the potential to polarize and divide the nation and criminal justice community. Additionally, the authors advocate continued federal support and leadership for science and building collaborations between researchers and policymakers. They conclude that these researcher and policymaker collaborations will help to bridge the gap between research and policy and sustain support for evidence-based policy over time; as new research is conducted and validated it can be translated directly to the researcher's partners in policy and practice.

In Chapter 2, Daniel P. Mears notes that policy evaluation and assessment is critical for developing effective criminal justice policy. Policies that are deemed to be "evidence-based" should not be equated merely with impact evaluations. Rather, they should be equated with each of the five steps of the evaluation hierarchy: (1) policy need, (2) theory, (3) implementation, (4) impact, and (5) cost-efficiency.

Francis T. Cullen and Cecilia Chouhy (Chapter 3) reflect on where the criminal justice system has been and in what direction it is headed using criminological theory, ideology, and ethics as frameworks. The authors note that the last several decades of criminal justice policies can be character-ized as overly punitive and centered on race. However, both liberal and conservative lawmakers alike have begun to realize that the punitive poli-cies of the past are no longer sustainable nor are they effective. With regard to criminal justice policy, the authors argue that criminological theory has been either ignored altogether or largely incorrect when it has been applied to policy decisions. Although changes are beginning to occur, the ideology behind many criminal justice policies has been hegemonic, conservative, and punitive. Lastly, when reflecting on the once-popular punitive criminal jus-tice policies, ethics have been disquieting and, to a degree, in the eye of the beholder. Conservative policymakers have tended to believe that it is their ethical obligation to punish offenders harshly because they owe it to victims to hold wrongdoers accountable. Conversely, criminologists tend to empa-thize more with offenders and believe they should be treated humanely.

Rather than relying on popular public opinion, or one's political ideology about crime control, Cullen and Chouhy emphasize the importance of using empirically validated theories to guide crime control policies. However, the process of applying empirically proven criminological theory to criminal justice policy is not always simple or straightforward. The authors note that even if theories are correct, they often provide little guidance for policy-makers and practitioners on the most effective means for crime control. Therefore, for the most effective criminal justice policies, it is suggested that criminologists focus on factors closer to the individual and situation in which the crime is committed. In other words, criminological theories and criminal justice policies should focus on identifying and addressing factors that can be changed. Treating the alterable conditions or characteristics of crime can be compared to addressing one's symptoms as medical doctors frequently do if the underlying cause is uncertain or untreatable.

John H. Laub and Nicole E. Frisch (Chapter 4) describe the con-cept of "translational criminology" as a way to address the disconnect between criminological research and criminal justice policies and prac-tices. Translational criminology provides a mechanism to bridge the gap by considering the processes by which scientific evidence is converted to policies and by forming interactive relationships between policymakers and criminologists. Understanding and divulging any limitations of the research and effectively disseminating findings in ways that are meaningful are important components of translational criminology. Much criminological research does not reach its intended audiences, especially if published exclusively in academic journals. Therefore, a multifaceted approach may be most effective for reaching policymakers; for example, publishing in diverse locations and developing an online and social media presence. Additionally, the authors suggest that the federal government and funding agencies should support rigorous program and policy evaluation and direct funding to programs that have been deemed effective and evidence-based. For example, the Bureau of Justice Administration's SMART programs establish researcher–practitioner partnerships to develop and evaluate data-driven programs in policing, criminal courts, and corrections. Lastly, the authors suggest that academic institutions earnestly consider the value of applied research in their graduate programs and integrate criteria to reward policy relevant work in faculty tenure and promotion decisions.

Historically, criminal justice policy and practice has been too often devoid of empirical evidence, which has contributed to expensive and ineffective policies and an unprecedented number of individuals under correctional control. However, more recent fiscal constraints and changes in public opinion have fueled calls for accountable and evidence-based criminal justice policies. As Cullen and Chouhy (Chapter 3) highlight, overly punitive polices of mass incarceration are no longer feasible or favored by the public. To sustain the current sentiment of an evidence-based criminal justice system, researchers must be transparent about what is known and what is not and provide policymakers with research that is relevant, impactful, timely, and understandable (Blomberg *et al.*, 2013; Robinson and Abt, Chapter 1). To do so, it is advisable that researchers use the evaluation hierarchy described by Mears in Chapter 2 to conduct timely policy research and follow the steps of translational criminology (Chapter 4) to deliver the best available research knowledge directly to policymakers in the most effective ways.

Chapter I

Evidence-informed criminal justice policy

Looking back, moving forward

Laurie O. Robinson and Thomas P. Abt

Criminal justice in our country defies easy description. It is a complex ecology of separate but interconnected institutions operating collectively to reduce and control criminal behavior, governed by an equally complex set of formal and informal controls. Rooted in traditions older than the nation itself, it has evolved and expanded organically over time according to the needs of history and consistent with a distinctively American brand of federalism that emphasizes local autonomy and control.

Decentralization and variability are defining features of the American system. Every one of the 50 states, 3,031 counties, and 19,519 municipalities (U.S. Census, 2012) plays a role in criminal justice, along with thousands of non-governmental organizations (NGOs) of every stripe and color. While generalizations across jurisdictions are possible, important structural and operational distinctions among them remain. As the President's Commission on Law Enforcement and the Administration of Justice observed more than 45 years ago, "All of them operate somewhat alike. No two of them operate exactly alike" (Commission Report, 1967).

Policy controls this vast and diverse system with a multitude of laws, regulations, rules, budgets, cultures, customs, and norms generated by institutions in all branches and at all levels of government, and by those outside government as well. Policy is not one thing, but a composite of many things, influenced by factors inside and outside the criminal justice system. It derives from a continuous process that is inherently complicated, messy, and erratic.

As the National Research Council has observed, "Success at promoting science depends on grasping the complexity of the policy world" (NRC, 2012). Historically, criminal justice policy has been relatively impervious to scientific inquiry. In recent years, this has begun to change. As crime rates have decreased, both the supply of and demand for scientifically sound research, evaluation, and statistics have increased. Buzzwords such as "evidence-based" and "data-driven" are now part of the policy lexicon. In short, the chasm between policy and science has begun to be bridged.

This chapter traces the growing influence of science over criminal justice policy, describes the federal, state, local, and non-governmental contributions to this trend, notes obstacles to further growth, and identifies opportunities to overcome these barriers and sustain progress. It is important to note that the objective here is not policy based exclusively on science, but instead policy that is fully informed by the best scientific theory, evidence, and data currently available (Blomberg et al., 2013). Policy should be consistently evidence-informed, if not always evidence-based. "In the domain of justice, empirical evidence by itself cannot point the way to policy." (NRC, 2014). Absolutes in this area are neither feasible nor desirable. Criminology should work to improve public policy, not replace it.

Looking back: the growth of evidence-informed policy

Just 20 years ago, 49 percent of Americans cited crime as the most important issue facing the country (Gallup, 2005). Today, only 2 percent of Americans feel the same way (Gallup, 2014). Violent crime has declined by 46 percent and property crime is down 41 percent, with current crime levels approximating those experienced by Americans in the 1960s (FBI, 2014). Despite a recent increase in homicide in several cities, the United States is a dramatically safer country than it was two decades ago.

At the same time, our scientific understanding of criminal behavior and "what works" in reducing crime has advanced significantly. For example, hot-spots policing has revolutionized our geographic understanding of crime and demonstrated how targeted police patrols can significantly reduce offending (Braga et al., 2012). DNA testing has expanded dramatically, resulting in increased convictions of the guilty, exonerations of the innocent, and – in more recent years – innovations such as identifying suspects in property crimes (Roman et al., 2008). Cognitive behavioral therapy has been proven to reduce crime, delinquency, and recidivism in a wide variety of settings (Lipsey et al., 2007). Correlation does not prove causation when it comes to crime, science, and policy, as contemporaneous increases in scientific knowledge cannot be directly linked to reductions in crime, but it is encouraging that both trends are moving in the right direction at the same time.

Landmark studies have also had impacts extending beyond academia to alter the policy landscape and shape the field. A study detailing racially discriminatory and potentially criminogenic school discipline policies in Texas, produced by the Council of State Governments Justice Center (CSG) in partnership with the Texas A&M University (Fabelo et al., 2011), helped launch the national Supportive School Discipline Initiative, led by U.S. Departments of Education and Justice, among others, to end the "school to prison pipeline." "Redemption" studies conducted by Professors Alfred Blumstein and Kiminori Nakamura have identified when ex-offenders are statistically "redeemed," i.e. no more likely to be arrested than a person without a criminal record (Blumstein and Nakamura, 2009). This work continues to reverberate in the field of reentry and was influential in the U.S. Equal Employment Opportunity Commission's decision in 2012 to advise employers against blanket exclusions of individuals with criminal records (EEOC, 2011). And numerous studies (Chandler *et al.*, 2009; Martin et al., 1995; Mitchell et al., 2012) going back some 20 years have shown the efficacy of drug treatment in reducing recidivism and drug use among substance abusing offenders, leading to support from policymakers across the political spectrum for both drug treatment courts and mandated drug treatment in prisons.

Out in the field, criminal justice practitioners and policymakers are increasingly reliant on evidence and data, with practitioners significantly more open to partnerships with researchers and policymakers consulting them far more frequently before major decisions. Key criminal justice constituencies have embraced evidence-informed approaches – for instance, in 2003, the International Association of Chiefs of Police, the largest law enforcement membership association in the world, created a Research Advisory Committee to provide guidance on law enforcement policy research and evaluation. Engagement has been deeper among police, corrections, and juvenile justice than with prosecutors or the courts, but the overall progress is real.

Several factors have contributed to the increasing influence of scientific evidence and data in criminal justice. First, as we have noted, the demand for scientific evidence and data is rising. Today's criminal justice practitioners are increasingly sophisticated and open to learning from research, evaluation, and statistics. The Center for Court Innovation recently surveyed over 600 leaders in the criminal justice field, including police, prosecutors, judges, corrections, and juvenile justice officials, and found that 89 percent "sometimes" or "always" use research or evaluation findings to guide their work (CCI, 2013).

Second, criminologists are producing more research, with more methodological rigor, then ever before. The number of Ph.D. programs and academic journals devoted to the study of crime and criminal justice has expanded, as has the use of meta-analysis and "gold standard" experimental methods. Perhaps even more importantly, this research is being presented in ways that are more accessible to those outside of academia, often by synthesizing the results of multiple studies. Recent examples include CrimeSolutions.gov, the Evidence-Based Policing Matrix, the Blueprints for Healthy Youth Development, and the Campbell Collaboration Systematic Reviews.[1] Resources like these demonstrate the practical value of science to practitioners and policymakers alike, and are especially valuable when a tight fiscal climate puts every dollar of public spending under intense scrutiny.

Third, the political climate surrounding crime issues has changed significantly in recent years. Improvements in public safety over recent decades have led to a far less politically charged environment nationally in which policymakers have more freedom to approach crime in a less ideological, more rational manner (Martin and Parker, 2014). Politicians engaging in thoughtful discussions on criminal justice are much less likely to be targeted with Willie Horton-style demagoguery than in the past. In fact, criminal justice reform has become a rare bipartisan issue in today's polarized political environment (Apuzzo, 2014). That said, in a post-Ferguson era with polarized debates about the role of police and with growing fears concerning domestic terrorism, there is always the danger of a return to a "tough on crime" posture.

A number of bipartisan bills to reform the criminal justice system have been proposed before Congress, with the support of unlikely political pairings. For example, senators Mike Lee (R-UT) and Richard Durbin (D-IL) introduced the Smarter Sentencing Act to reduce mandatory minimum sentences for certain nonviolent drug crimes. Senators John Cornyn (R-TX) and Sheldon Whitehouse (D-RI) put forward the Recidivism Reduction and Public Safety Act to allow low-risk prisoners to earn credit for early release by participating in education, job training and drug treatment programs ("A Rare Opportunity," 2014). Senators Rand Paul (R-KY) and Cory Booker (D-NJ) have also collaborated on potential legislation. Progressive institutions like the American Civil Liberties Union are partnering with conservative groups like Right on Crime, a national organization backed by former Speaker of the U.S. House of Representatives Newt Gingrich, political activist Grover Norquist, and former Governor of Florida Jeb Bush, among others. Evidence and data have played a key role in serving as a basis for finding common political ground and promoting a policymaking atmosphere of rationality and objectivity.

Fourth, states, localities, and NGOs, but especially the federal government, have demonstrated leadership and offered support for the expansion of innovative, evidence-informed approaches. These contributions are discussed further below.

Federal contributions to evidence-informed policy

While criminal justice remains mostly a state and local enterprise – 94 per cent of adult convictions are processed in state court (BJS, 2006) – the federal government has played an increasingly active role in offering leadership and a vision for the criminal justice system as a whole. Historically, the federal role was limited to the investigation, prosecution, and punishment of federal offenses. Today, the federal government often exercises leadership through strategic use of its grants, training, technical assistance, messaging, and convening power. This role has become increasingly important as the size and complexity of the criminal justice system continues to grow.

A broader federal role in state and local criminal justice was first proposed in 1967 by the President's Commission on Law Enforcement and Administration of Justice. Established 50 years ago, the Commission was the first comprehensive national effort to study and offer recommendations for improving the American criminal justice system as a whole. Composed of 19 commissioners, along with hundreds of consultants and advisors, the Commission held national conferences, conducted surveys, held hundreds of meetings, and interviewed thousands of people over the course of two years. In its report, "The Challenge of Crime in a Free Society," the Commission called for federal support for criminal justice research, statistics, and innovation at the state and local level, leading to the creation of the Law Enforcement Assistance Administration (LEAA), the predecessor agency to the Office of Justice Programs (OJP) at the U.S. Department of Justice (DOJ). These were central among the many recommendations of the report, as noted by the Commission itself: "[t]he Commission has found... many needs of law enforcement and the administration of criminal justice. But what it has found to be the greatest need is the need to know" (Commission Report, 1967).

Since that time, the role of the federal government in state and local criminal justice has evolved and expanded while remaining true to the original vision of the Commission. Today, federal leadership in this area has five critical elements. First, as the most significant supporter of research and data in criminal justice, the federal government has an important ongoing role in the development of scientific knowledge (Robinson, 2013). Second, once developed, the federal government has ongoing responsibility for the diffusion of this knowledge in a manner that is accessible to policymakers and practitioners (Robinson, 2013). Third, the federal government can offer training and technical assistance to states and localities in order to encourage the adoption of evidence-informed policies (Robinson, 2013). Fourth, federal support is critical for programs that have been proven to be effective, i.e. evidence-based, or for innovative, experimental programs that can advance understanding, as states and localities often do not have the funds to undertake enough of these activities on their own (Robinson, 2007). Fifth, the federal government can strategically use its bully pulpit and convening power to promote policy change and encourage the use of science among states and localities. Moreover, it can lead by example, modeling the behavior it wishes to see adopted.

Examples of the federal role in evidence-informed policy abound. In 1994, Congress passed the Violent Crime Control and Law Enforcement Act, an omnibus crime bill that was the largest in U.S. history. Looking for creative ways to advance the scientific enterprise, leaders at OJP, with the strong support of Attorney General Janet Reno, convinced Congressional appropriators to allow one percent of the funding for policing, violence against women, prison and drug court programs to be diverted to DOJ's research agencies in support of knowledge development and evaluation, leading to the largest investment in crime-related scientific research in U.S. history.

One of the most important studies to emerge during this time was *Preventing Crime: What Works, What Doesn't, What's Promising*, a landmark study that comprehensively reported on already existing research on a broad array of existing criminal justice programs (Sherman et al., 1997). Its publication began to change the conversation about which anti-crime programs should be funded. For example, the report cited multiple studies showing the ineffectiveness of D.A.R.E. (Drug Abuse Resistance Education), a curriculum that was in place at that time in nearly 60 percent of U.S. schools, leading to dramatic cutbacks in federal funding as well as a major effort to substantially revise the model.

Fifteen years later, the American Recovery and Reinvestment Act again provided billions of dollars in federal funding to states and localities for public safety purposes – to hire and rehire law enforcement officers, promote community policing, reduce violence against women, prevent and control crime, and improve the criminal justice system (2009). With the support of former Attorney General Eric Holder, OJP leadership looked once more to ensure that scientific research and statistics were meaningfully supported along with other priorities. Top criminologists John Laub and James Lynch were nominated to provide leadership at DOJ's science agencies – the National Institute of Justice (NIJ) and the Bureau of Justice Statistics (BJS). A Science Advisory Board was established, headed by noted criminologist Alfred Blumstein to provide ongoing scientific guidance and leadership to OJP. In addition, Congress was persuaded for the first time to provide a set-aside across OJP's entire appropriation designated for criminal justice research and statistics. Beginning in Fiscal Year 2010, one percent of all OJP funds has been allocated for these purposes (Consolidated Appropriations Act, 2010).

In addition, OJP in 2009 launched the Evidence Integration Initiative, or E2I, a comprehensive effort to improve the quantity and quality of evidence generated by the agency through its research functions and to integrate evidence more effectively into program and policy decisions (Robinson, 2011). Another key objective of E2I was to improve the translation of evidence into policy and practice, which led to the development and launch of the previously-mentioned CrimeSolutions.gov, an online clearinghouse that makes rigorous research readily accessible to practitioners and policymakers, informing them through an easily understood ratings system about what works – and what doesn't – in criminal justice, juvenile justice, and crime victim services. In addition, an initiative dubbed the OJP Diagnostic Center was also established to offer customized technical assistance to further improve state and local capacity for using evidence and data when making decisions about criminal justice policy (Robinson, 2011).

More than others before them, President Barack Obama and former Attorney General Holder have defended scientific independence and integrity and have advocated for the use of rigorous evidence in evaluating social programs. Shortly after entering office, President Obama ordered his Director of the Office of Science and Technology Policy, John P. Holdren, to issue recommendations to guarantee scientific integrity throughout the executive branch (White House, 2009). Several months later, the "Holdren Memo" was issued to ensure "the highest level of integrity" with regard to scientific and technical processes (OSTP, 2010). Beginning in 2012, the Office of Management and Budget began to push federal agencies aggressively to demonstrate the use of evidence in their budget submissions, noting that "[w]here evidence is strong, we should act on it. Where evidence is suggestive, we should consider it. Where evidence is weak, we should build the knowledge to support better decisions in the future" (OMB, 2012). Agencies were (and still are) strongly encouraged to propose evaluations, use cost-effectiveness data, and infuse evidence into grantmaking, among other activities.

In 2014, when former Attorney General Holder announced the first decline in the federal prison population in more than 30 years, he renewed his consistent support for science, calling for "the Justice Department to direct funding to help move the criminal justice field toward a fuller embrace of science and data" (DOJ, 2014). Consistent with scientific research indicating the nation's rates of incarceration are unjustifiably high, he also stated that "the United States will never be able to prosecute or incarcerate its way to becoming a safer nation" (DOJ, 2014). In a recent report entitled "The Growth of Incarceration in the United States: Exploring Causes and Consequences," the National Research Council concluded similarly that the costs of current rates of incarceration outweigh the benefits and cannot be justified on the basis of public safety (NRC, 2014).

State, local, and NGO contributions

States, localities, and NGOs have also played significant roles in encouraging the adoption of evidence-informed criminal justice policies, often working in partnership with one another. In fact, many of the strongest partnerships are the most diverse, including stakeholders from every relevant constituency group. For instance, the Pew Charitable Trusts (Pew), the Council of State Governments, the Vera Institute of Justice, and the Urban Institute, among others and along with DOJ's Bureau of Justice Assistance, have engaged with 24 states and 17 local jurisdictions to develop strategies known collectively as Justice Reinvestment. These strategies have saved millions of dollars and reduced recidivism by analyzing states' prison population data and supporting evidence-based programs to focus on high-risk individuals and improve community supervision of offenders (CSG, 2014).

In Missouri, the state Division of Youth Services has pioneered a landmark, research-based approach to juvenile justice, now simply known nationally as "the Missouri model," emphasizing small institutions that allow juveniles to remain close to home in the least restrictive environment possible, along with an integrated approach to treatment and education. With the support of the Annie E. Casey Foundation and DOJ's Office of Juvenile Justice and Delinquency Prevention, the Missouri model is now being replicated in sites across the nation (Mendel, 2010).

In New York, policymakers and researchers recently launched a major effort to reduce gun violence using strategies supported by the best evidence and data available. The GIVE – Gun-Involved Violence Elimination – Initiative, offers localities funding, training, and technical assistance to implement proven strategies focused tightly on the people and places at the highest risk for violence (Abt, 2014).

And on the West Coast, the Washington State Institute for Public Policy (WSIPP) conducts nonpartisan research with an emphasis on benefit–cost analysis in order to provide state leaders with evidence-based policies that not only work, but are also cost-effective. The WSIPP model is being replicated in 14 states with the support of Pew and the John D. and Catherine T. MacArthur Foundation's Results First Initiative (Results First, 2014).

In the examples above, states and localities serve as laboratories of innovation, adapting lessons learned from other jurisdictions and offering new strategies of their own. The federal government and NGOs play an important role in identifying promising approaches, assessing them, and then disseminating these strategies to broader policy audiences.

Moving forward: recommendations for sustaining growth

While the nation is safer and smarter than it was 20 years ago, challenges remain. Protests concerning the deaths of Michael Brown, Eric Garner, Freddie Gray, and others signal a deep resentment and mistrust of the criminal justice system among many Americans. Criminal justice institutions have been the focus of intense criticism, controversy, and debate in a manner not seen since the 1960s. Homicide remains the top cause of death for African-American young men and boys aged 15–24, causing more deaths than the nine other leading causes combined (CDC, 2010), with several large cities reporting notable increases in homicides over the past year. While the nation debates the legality of marijuana, the most recent data available indicate that the death rate from heroin overdoses doubled from 2010 to 2012 (Rudd et al., 2014). The U.S. remains the world leader in incarceration, with nearly 1 out of every 100 adults in prison or jail, a rate that is 5 to 10 times higher than the rates in other developed nations (NRC, 2014). Finally, the growth of emerging challenges like cybercrime threatens to outpace our understanding and ability to respond effectively.

The challenges above indicate not only the limits of policy, but those of science as well, both in terms of its ability to be relevant and impactful as well as its underlying substance. Continued demand for scientific knowledge will require sustained culture and systems change across jurisdictions and within institutions.

What steps can be taken to ensure that progress is sustained? First, at the national level, the emerging bipartisan consensus around criminal justice reform, especially in areas such as sentencing and juvenile justice, must be protected and nurtured carefully. The impact of traditionally hyper-partisan crime issues must be downplayed, and emerging issues like those triggered by the recent events in Ferguson, and New York City, and Baltimore must be handled proactively, sensitively, and objectively, or they have the potential to polarize and divide not only the justice community, but also the entire nation.

Second, federal leadership and support for science must also be sustained and extended. While President Obama and former Attorney General Holder have demonstrated commitment to supporting evidence-informed policy, it is unclear whether future administrations and leaders will continue to do so. In Congress, the recent switch in control of the U.S. Senate may mean less funding for scientific research and statistics. Supporters of evidence-informed policy will be under even greater pressure to demonstrate the value of sound evidence and data to leadership and staff in federal agencies and in Congress (more on this below).

Third, in order to create permanent change, scientific evidence and data-driven approaches must be embraced not just among criminal justice leaders, but also among line staff and middle managers within justice institutions at all levels. Too many practitioners continue to rely on tradition, instinct, convenience, and even guesswork as the basis for their decision-making. Support for evidence-informed policy will not be sustained unless it is institutionalized within criminal justice bureaucratic structures. Organizations – and scholars – need to focus on the importance of changing the daily habits of practitioners as part of this process, with attention paid to training, hiring, and the incentives surrounding discipline, recognition, and promotion. As Atul Gawande (2013) has noted, spreading innovation is a social process, with change spreading person-by-person, door-to-door, by means of informal communication (i.e. talking it through) and mentoring.

Fourth, academics must also continue to bridge cultural differences and increase their engagement with practitioners, as practitioner backing will be critical to sustain support for evidence-informed policy. For example, criminologists should make time not only to participate in leading academic conferences like the annual meeting of the American Society of Criminology, but also key practitioner conferences like those held by the International Association of Chiefs of Police. Academics must show policymakers how to use evidence and data in a more nuanced, sophisticated manner. Policymakers must be reminded that evidence-informed policy is about more than funding "what works," although that is critically important. This includes an appreciation of the challenges of establishing external validity, the importance of social context, and the utility of criminal justice theory (Sampson et al., 2013). It is also about raising the level of debate on criminal justice issues, synthesizing research and organizing disconnected scientific findings to advance ideas that can shape attitudes and inform public discourse (Rosenfeld, 2010).

Some researchers may be reluctant to advise policymakers, given the field's limited ability to determine cause effect relationships. Nevertheless, as former policymakers ourselves, we firmly agree with our editors that "[c]riminologists should… apply the best available research knowledge to public policy" without waiting, perhaps forever, for perfect causal certainty (Blomberg et al., 2013). Policymakers are already accustomed to making decisions in uncertain environments with incomplete information – indeed, that is what we expect our leaders to do. This does not mean that researchers should overstate their conclusions, but instead "be transparent about what [they] know and do not know," so policymakers can adjust accordingly (Blomberg et al., 2013).

Fifth, the supply of scientific knowledge must continue to rise. Policymakers need research that is relevant, accessible, impactful, and timely. If research is to be relevant to policy, the public purpose and utility of the work should be readily apparent. If it is not easily understandable and accessible to policymakers, it will not be used. While the publication of research in peer-reviewed academic journals remains important, separate products based on that research should be produced to inform these very different audiences.

As to impact, research that simply calls for more research frustrates officials looking for concrete guidance. Research should aspire for more than mere statistical significance and reach for conclusions that are clear enough to persuade legislators, budget officials, and the media, among others, of the need to take action. As Alfred Blumstein has noted, with regard to statistics, the term "discernible" may be more accurate and less susceptible to misinterpretation than the term "significant" (Blumstein, 2013). Interocular effects – meaning results that hit you right between the eyes – should be the goal.

Regarding timeliness, in today's hyper-communicative environment, social media and the 24-hour news cycle can define public debates in a matter of hours. This presents an immense challenge to researchers, who generally work more deliberatively and with longer time frames. Rather than rush new research to market and potentially compromise its integrity, research that is already completed must be identified, summarized, organized, and stored for policy purposes in case it is needed at the last minute. Moving forward, easy and timely access will continue to be a critical factor in determining the public and policy relevance of research.

Sixth, in discussions of science and policy, criminal justice statistics are often neglected, yet data is critical to the measurement of problems in order to assess their magnitude and significance. Without such data, challenges cannot be placed in context and policymakers cannot prioritize scarce public resources appropriately. In the aftermath of Ferguson, the dearth of statistics regarding lethal police use of force has inhibited our ability to respond effectively ("The country should know," 2014). The same is true of the recent heroin crisis, where policymakers have grappled with national and state data that is uncertain and several years old (Webster and Glenza, 2014).

Seventh and finally, while it is clear that public spending for research and statistics on criminal justice does not keep pace with other areas, academics must shoulder the responsibility for demonstrating the value of additional investment. The National Institute of Health has an annual budget of approximately $30 billion, while NIJ and the Bureau of Justice Statistics have a combined annual budget of approximately $100 million. Clearly this should change, but the question is how, and as criminologist Charles Wellford (2010) has noted, "money follows influence." In this time of transition and uncertainty, it is critical that supporters of research and statistics produce knowledge and information that is of use to policymakers and practitioners, as well as document the many contributions that science has already made to policy and practice with the limited funding currently provided.

Conclusion

While there is a good deal to celebrate when looking at recent progress, the current and future status of evidence-informed policy is in a precarious posture. As in other policy areas, change in criminal justice generally occurs either incrementally over time, or in a sudden burst, often spurred by outside events (and not necessarily positive – witness the rush to enact "three strikes" laws in the mid-1990s as crime rose around the nation). In the next few years, the criminal justice field may capitalize on the progress made to date and make significant positive reforms with researchers, evaluators, and statisticians contributing heavily at the policymaking table. On the other hand, momentum towards evidence-informed policy may be stopped and undone by political transitions and polarizing debates. This new, relatively nonpartisan atmosphere surrounding criminal justice over the past few years is unusual – but it is fragile, and can be easily abandoned by those at either end of the political spectrum when responding to a Ferguson-like event or terrorist incidents here at home.

Science can and should continue to serve as a bridge between policy and politics, but we must continue to build it. It is an endeavor worth the effort.

Note

1 Available at www.crimesolutions.gov/, http://cebcp.org/evidence-based-policing/ the-matrix/, www.blueprintsprograms.com/, and www.campbellcollaboration. org/lib/?go=monograph, respectively.

References

A Rare Opportunity on Criminal Justice. (March 15, 2014). [Editorial] *The New York Times*. Retrieved from www.nytimes.com/2014/03/16/opinion/sunday/a-rare-opportunity-on-criminal-justice.html.

Abt, T.P. (2014). Integrating Evidence to Stop Shootings: New York's GIVE (Gun-Involved Violence Elimination) Initiative. *Translational Criminology*, 7: 11–13.

Apuzzo, M. (2014, March 3). Holder and Republicans Unite to Soften Sentencing Laws. *The New York Times*. Retrieved from www.nytimes.com/2014/03/04/us/politics/holder-and-republicans-unite-to-soften-sentencing-laws.html.

Blomberg, T.G., Mestre, J., and Mann, K. (2013). Seeking Causality in a World of Contingency: Criminology, Research, and Public Policy. *Criminology and Public Policy*,12: 571–584.

Blumstein, A. (2013). Linking Evidence and Criminal Justice Policy. *Criminology and Public Policy*, 12: 721–730.

Blumstein, A. and Nakamura, K. (2009). Redemption in the Presence of Widespread Criminal Background Checks. *Criminology*, 47: 327–359.

Braga, A., Papachristos, A.V., and Hureau, D.M. (2012). The Effects of Hot Spots Policing on Crime: An Updated Systematic Review and Meta-Analysis. *Justice Quarterly*, 1–31.

Center for Court Innovation. (2013). Innovation in the Criminal Justice System: A National Survey of Criminal Justice Leaders. Retrieved from www.courtinnovation.org/sites/default/files/documents/Innovation_Survey_Report_0.pdf.

Centers for Disease Control and Prevention. (2010). Leading Causes of Death by Age Group, Black Males-United States, 2010. Retrieved from www.cdc.gov/men/lcod/2010/LCODBlackmales2010.pdf.

Chandler, R. K., Fletcher, B. W., and Volkow, N.D. (2009). Treating drug abuse and addiction in the criminal justice system: Improving public health and safety. *JAMA*, 301(2): 183–190.

Consolidated Appropriations Act. (2010). P.L. 111–117, Dec. 16, 2009. 123 STAT. 3141.

Council of State Governments Justice Center. (2014). Reducing Recidivism: States Deliver Results. New York: Council of State Governments Justice Center.

The country should know how many people die in police custody. (2014, December 23). [Editorial] *The Washington Post*. Retrieved from www.washingtonpost.com/opinions/the-country-should-know-how-many-people-die-in-police-custody/2014/12/23/99a343f2-86fc-11e4-a702-fa31ff4ae98e_story.html.

Equal Employment Opportunity Commission. (2011). Written Testimony of Amy Solomon, Senior Advisor to the Assistant Attorney General, Office of Justice Programs, U.S. Department of Justice. Retrieved from www.eeoc.gov/eeoc/meetings/7-26-11/solomon.cfm.

Fabelo, T., Thompson, M. D., Plotkin, M., Carmichael, D., Marchbanks, M. P. III, and Booth E. A. (2011). *Breaking schools' rules: A statewide study of how school discipline relates to students' success and juvenile justice involvement*. New York,

NY; College Station, TX: Council of State Governments Justice Center; Public Policy Research Institute of Texas AandM University.

Gallup. (2005). American Public Opinion About Crime in the United States. Retrieved from www.gallup.com/poll/15247/Crime-United-States.aspx.

Gallup. (2014). Most Important Problem. Retrieved from www.gallup.com/poll/1675/most-important-problem.aspx.

Gawande, A. (2013). Slow Ideas. *The New Yorker.* Retrieved from www.newyorker.com/magazine/2013/07/29/slow-ideas.

Lipsey, M. W., Landenberger, N. A., and Wilson, S. J. (2007). Effects of cognitive-behavioral programs for criminal offenders. *Campbell Systematic Reviews*, 6: 1–27.

Martin, J. and Parker, A. (2014, December 24). Law and Order Issues, Once G.O.P.'s Strength, Now Divide the Party. *The New York Times.* Retrieved from www.nytimes.com/2014/12/25/us/politics/law-and-order-issues-once-gops-strong-suit-now-divide-party.html?hpandaction=clickandpgtype=Homepageandmodule=first-column-regionandregion=top-newsandWT.nav=top-newsand_r=1.

Martin, S. S., Butzin, C. A., and Inciardi, J. A. (1995). Assessment of a Multistage Therapeutic Community for Drug-Involved Offenders. *Journal of Psychoactive Drugs.* 27(1): 109–16.

Mendel, R.A. (2010). The Missouri Model: Reinventing the Practice of Rehabilitating Youthful Offenders. Baltimore, MD: The Annie E. Casey Foundation. Retrieved from http://missouriapproach.org/storage/documents/aecf_mo_fullreport_webfinal.pdf.

Mitchell, O., Wilson, D., Eggers, A., and MacKenzie, D. (2012). Drug Courts' Effects on Criminal Offending for Juvenile and Adults. Oslo, Norway: The Campbell Collaboration Library of Systematic Reviews. Retrieved from http://campbellcollaboration.org/lib/project/74/

National Research Council. (2012). *Using Science as Evidence in Public Policy.* Washington, DC: The National Academies Press.

National Research Council. (2014). *The Growth of Incarceration in the United States: Exploring Causes and Consequences.* Washington, DC: The National Academies Press.

Pew-MacArthur Results First Initiative. (2014). Achieving Success With the Pew-MacArthur Results First Initiative: a State Progress Report 2011–13. Retrieved from www.pewtrusts.org/en/projects/pew-macarthur-results-first-initiative.

President's Commission on Law Enforcement and Administration of Justice. (1967). *The Challenge of Crime in a Free Society.* Washington, DC: U.S. Government Printing Office. Retrieved fromwww.ncjrs.gov/pdffiles1/nij/42.pdf.

Robinson, L.O. (2007). Testimony before the U.S. House of Representatives Committee on Appropriations, Subcommittee on Commerce, Justice, Science and Related Agencies, March 21, 2007. Retrieved from www.google.com/url?sa=tandrct=jandq=andesrc=sandsource=webandcd=1andved=0CB4QFjAAandurl=http%3A%2F%2Fwww.constitutionproject.org%2Fdocuments%2Ftestimony-of-laurie-robinson-to-house-committee-regarding-federal-role-in-reducing-crime%2Fandei=NLSZVLOfCYSgNqrEgsgIandusg=AFQjCNGBZxe22FuwtS9Pke0CL2RB6tKmpQandsig2=q7-yExlO4sFqayCzPPMslA.

Robinson, L.O. (2011). Exploring Certainty and Severity: Perspectives from a Federal Perch. *Criminology and Public Policy*, 10(1): 85–92.

Robinson, L.O. (2013). Bridging the Gap between Science and Criminal Justice Policy: The Federal Role. *Translational Criminology*, 4: 4–5, 25.

Roman, J.K., Reid, S., Reid, J., Chalfin, A., Adams, W., Knight, C. (2008). *The DNA Field Experiment: Cost-Effectiveness Analysis of the Use of DNA in the Investigation of High-Volume Crimes*. Washington, DC: The Urban Institute.

Rosenfeld, R. (2010). Raising the Level of Public Debate: Another View of Criminology's Public Relevance. Clear, T.R., Freilich, J.D., and Frost, N. (eds.). *Contemporary Issues in Criminal Justice Policy: Policy Proposals from the American Society of Criminology Conference*. Belmont, CA: Wadsworth, Cengage Learning.

Rudd, R.A., Paulozzi, L.J., Bauer, M.J., et al. (2014). Increases in Heroin Overdose Deaths – 28 States, 2010 to 2012. *MMWR*, 63: 849–876. Retrieved from www.cdc.gov/mmwr/pdf/wk/mm6339.pdf.

Sampson, R. J., Winship, C. and Knight, C. (2013). Translating Causal Claims. *Criminology and Public Policy*, 12: 587–616.

Sherman, L. W., Gottfredson, D., MacKenzie, D., Eck, J., Reuter, P., Bushway, S. (1997). *Preventing crime: What Works, What Doesn't, What's Promising: A report to the United States Congress*. Washington, DC: U.S. Department of Justice, Office of Justice Programs.

U.S. Census Bureau. (2012). 2012 Census of Governments. Retrieved from www.census.gov/govs/cog/.

U.S. Department of Justice, Bureau of Justice Statistics. (2006). Felony Sentences In State Courts, 2006 – Statistical Tables. Retrieved from www.bjs.gov/index.cfm?ty=pbdetailandiid=2152.

U.S. Department of Justice, Federal Bureau of Investigation. (2014). Unified Crime Reporting Statistics – UCR Data Online. Retrieved from www.ucrdatatool.gov/Search/Crime/Crime.cfm.

U.S. Department of Justice, Office of Public Affairs. (2013). One Year After Launching Key Sentencing Reforms, Attorney General Holder Announces First Drop in Federal Prison Population in More Than Three Decades [Press release]. Retrieved from www.justice.gov/opa/pr/one-year-after-launching-key-setencing-reforms-attorney-general-holder-annouces-first-drop-0.

Violent Crime Control and Law Enforcement Act, 42 U.S.C. § 14141 (1994).

Webster, M. and Glenza, J. (2014, May 12). Scope of nationwide heroin 'epidemic' unknown; drug-related death, overdose data lacking. *The New Haven Register*. Retrieved from www.nhregister.com/general-news/20140512/scope-of-nationwide-heroin-epidemic-unknown-drug-related-death-overdose-data-lacking.

Wellford, C.F. (2010). Criminologists Should Stop Whining About Their Impact on Policy and Practice. Clear, T.R., Freilich, J.D., and Frost, N. (eds.). *Contemporary Issues in Criminal Justice Policy: Policy Proposals from the American Society of Criminology Conference*. Belmont, CA: Wadsworth, Cengage Learning.

The White House, Office of the Press Secretary. (2009). Memorandum for the Heads of Executive Departments and Agencies on Scientific Integrity. Retrieved from www.whitehouse.gov/the-press-office/memorandum-heads-executive-departments-and-agencies-3-9-09.

The White House, Office of Science and Technology Policy. (2010). Memorandum for the Heads of Executive Departments and Agencies on Scientific Integrity. Retrieved from www.whitehouse.gov/sites/default/files/microsites/ostp/scientific-integrity-memo-12172010.pdf.

Chapter 2

Policy evaluation and assessment[1]

Daniel P. Mears

Introduction

This chapter discusses the importance and standards of policy evaluation and assessment. The salience of this topic stems from increased calls by policymakers and criminal justice officials for government accountability and evidence-based policy. Such calls appear to resonate with the public. Indeed, few would argue against the idea that government should be held accountable and implement effective policies. What, though, is meant by accountability and evidence-based policy and what counts as "evidence"?

To answer this question—and in so doing highlight the importance and standards of policy evaluation and assessment—this chapter discusses the following topics: (1) the distinction between evaluation and assessment; (2) what is meant by "policies"; (3) examples of "bad" policies and the need for research that can avoid implementing them; (4) use of the evaluation hierarchy to define, develop, and identify "good" policies; (5) benefits of evaluation; (6) the importance of institutionalizing all types of policy evaluation (needs, theory, implementation, impact, and cost-efficiency) and not just evaluation of policy impact; and (7) causal uncertainty. The chapter then concludes by underscoring the importance of evaluation in developing, implementing, monitoring, and improving policy to contribute to the goals of creating more government accountability, reducing crime, and improving justice.

Evaluation versus assessment

No established or universally agreed-upon definition of policy evaluation versus assessment exists. Some researchers distinguish between the two while others view them as synonymous. Ultimately, definitions are neither correct nor incorrect, just more or less useful. In this case, a distinction—"evaluation research" as an information-generating enterprise and "assessment" as a process of reviewing information—can be useful.

Let us define "evaluation research" as the use of social scientific methods to arrive at empirical estimates of the prevalence of certain social problems, characteristics of certain individuals, groups, organizations, or the like, associations between two or more variables (or "factors" or "forces"), and policy implementation, impacts, and costs and benefits. Such research provides information that can help to inform policy deliberations about such issues as the scope of a social problem, its causes, and what might be done to address the problem.

By contrast, "assessment" can be defined as a process in which policy-makers or practitioners deliberate about such issues as whether a policy's benefits suffice to warrant enacting the policy, the feasibility of enacting or continuing support of an existing policy, concerns about unintended effects, and whether other social problems or policies warrant more attention. The deliberations may include consideration of research findings. However, they also may include consideration of a wide range of social problems and policy options, ethical dilemmas, and the extent to which local political, organizational, social, and economic resources allow for a given policy to be well-implemented and supported in the long-term.

In short, whereas evaluation research entails collecting information, assessment involves digesting that information and other considerations to arrive at a normative judgment about which social problems warrant attention and in what way (Bardach, 2004; Welsh and Harris, 2008). Simply documenting evidence of the extent of implementation, impact, or cost-efficiency alone (i.e., evaluation) cannot substitute for effective policy-making processes (assessment). At the same time, policymaking processes devoid of reference to credible empirical research means that policies will be adopted that may be costly and ineffective.

Policies

Efforts to reduce crime and promote justice involve many activities that can be viewed as "policies" (Mears, 2010). These include the day-to-day decisions, or practices, of law enforcement and corrections officers, court personnel, criminal justice and correctional officials, and more. Some of these decisions rest on or constitute informal understandings about how certain situations or cases should be handled. Others rest on formally articulated rules. Throughout the criminal justice and correctional system, there exist administrative rules for how day-to-day operations should be undertaken. There are, too, rules or procedures that target specific behaviors and prescribe specific responses. Not least, programs exist that provide services, treatment, supervision, or various other interventions to change participants in some way. Laws constitute another form of policy, and so, too, do court decisions.

The variety of activities that can be viewed as policies is important to recognize for at least two reasons. First, many discussions of evidence-based "policies" tend to delimit our focus to a particular, formally articulated response to a problem. Discussions of evidence-based programs or evidence-based practices do the same. This tendency has the unfortunate consequence of leading us to equate something as "evidence-based" only when it is a particular law or formal rule, program, or practice. In reality, any of the above-mentioned activities can be viewed as "evidence-based." For example, a Supreme Court decision that rests in part on empirical claims that run counter to social science research could be viewed as not being evidence-based (Mancini and Mears, 2013). Similarly, an informal practice of using certain interventions with some inmates and not others is a type of policy. We might view it as evidence-based if a scientific basis exists for the differential treatment and as non evidence-based if no such basis exists.

Second, recognition of the wide range of activities that can be viewed as policies can lead us not only to focus on everyday criminal justice personnel decision-making, informal rules for processing large volumes of cases, court decisions, and more. This broader focus matters for a critical reason: The latter may have a much greater effect on public safety and justice. For example, the most effective program typically will affect only a small number of individuals. By contrast, better decision-making—such as how to classify certain inmates and assign them to specific types and levels of supervision and treatment—can affect thousands of individuals.

Of course, the broader in scope a particular activity, the less amenable it will be to rigorous impact evaluation. For example, we cannot randomly assign some states to adopt a new law and others not to adopt it. Yet, laws can affect far more individuals than can particular programs. Various quasi-experimental designs exist to assess the impacts of laws, but the credibility of the findings almost invariably will be less than what we can obtain through evaluation of particular programs. As discussed below, this situation need not bias us toward giving up the ghost on evaluating the impacts of everyday decision-making or large-scale efforts. In addition, it need not divert us from generating research-based evidence about dimensions other than impact, such as the extent to which a given policy is needed or is cost-efficient.

Bad policies: the perils of extremes, anecdotes ("evidence"), and no or weak empirical research

A central goal of policy evaluation and assessment is to promote "good" (e.g. effective and cost-efficient) policy and to avoid "bad" policy. The medical dictum, "first, do no harm," applies here. The simple act of avoiding investment in unnecessary or ineffective policies can be beneficial. Indeed, it may be one of the most important actions that policymakers, agency officials, and practitioners can take. Bad policies are harmful not only because they may be ineffective and costly. They may be harmful, too, because literally they may cause harm or because they divert us from investing in alternatives that could be effective and cost-efficient.

The seeming ubiquity of this problem justifies describing it in more detail. Here, then, three problematic situations are described: reliance on extremes as evidence to develop policy, reliance on anecdotes to do so, and development of policy without recourse to research. None of these three scenarios involve policy that is "evidence-based" because none of them involve systematic reliance on credible social scientific data or methodologies.

Extremes

The typical starting point for many policy efforts begins with lawmakers, agency officials, or practitioners focusing on extreme or non-representative cases, stories, or patterns. Extremes serve as the functional equivalent of loud, rowdy bar patrons—they command lots of attention. Sometimes that can be good. A news story might prominently feature a case in which a football player has beaten his spouse and the team appears to have down-played or ignored it. The ensuing coverage of the case might lead to greater awareness and education about domestic violence and to improved efforts to address it.

But sometimes extremes can be bad. Why? In the case of the raucous bar patron, many of the patrons' voices get lost and, indeed, many of the patrons have difficulty hearing each other. Conversation comes to a stop or is severely impeded. Similarly, when non-representative cases command headline attention, they drive discussion toward extreme cases. Policy discussions then turn to crafting legislation suited for such cases and yet end up being applied to "typical" cases. The aphorism, "bad cases make for bad law," captures this problem. In the above example, the end result might be a situation in which a football league creates tougher penalties for players who are convicted of domestic violence. Such an approach might be effective. However, it might not be nearly as effective as an effort to create a culture of awareness about domestic violence within the football league. Empirical research on the prevalence of domestic violence and its causes would help adjudicate which approach, or which constellation of approaches, likely would be most effective.

How are policies based on extremes justified? One way is through recourse to "research." For example, in the course of promoting a policy based on an extreme case, advocates may engage in a form of "confirmation bias." That is, they selectively—whether purposely or not—marshal forth theory, research, or anecdotes as "evidence" that the policy should be supported. This approach is problematic because it misrepresents extant theory and research and it creates the appearance of policy need and effectiveness where in fact neither may exist.

Extremes can be problematic, too, because they lead us away from a focus on something mundane but no less critical—systematically and empirically monitoring the prevalence and causes of different social problems, identifying different policies for addressing them, and evaluating which ones are most cost-efficient. This focus requires funding research and undertaking the hard work of carefully considering extant research on a range of social problems and policy responses. It can be far easier to work from the assumption that a particular problem exists and that the obvious solution is at hand.

Anecdotes ("evidence")

Another approach to developing policy is to rely on anecdotes. However, anecdotes are not scientific evidence. They are illustrations of one type of case, one that may be representative, but that just as easily could constitute an extreme. Typically, only research can help us to know whether an anecdote represents typical reality or an extreme case.

Anecdotes are especially pernicious because they can appeal to "common sense." Unfortunately, common sense can lead us astray and does not always accord with what theory and research tell us. The end result? A plethora of interventions that have little chance of being effective and that, when evaluated, may be found to be ineffective.

Prominent examples of this problem can be found in the prisoner reentry literature on efforts to reduce recidivism of ex-prisoners. Life skills programs illustrate the problem. They may help offenders to learn how to tackle certain life challenges, but in and of themselves such programs typically target no known causes of offending. Accordingly, as Latessa et al. (2014) have emphasized, it should be unsurprising that research does not find them to be successful at reducing recidivism. How could they if they do not target known causes of offending?

Anecdotes and a reliance on "common sense" can lead to a "quackery." This situation arises when well-meaning individuals rely on their personal experiences, views, or beliefs—and either ignore or are unfamiliar with research on the given targeted problem—to adopt a policy. Unfortunately, much quackery exists. Latessa et al. (2014:85) provide many examples in the corrections field, such as the "offenders lack creativity" theory promulgated by some policymakers and practitioners: "the theory states that if we can just get offenders interested in exploring their creative side, we can set them on the right track." Art therapy programs illustrate the idea. It is not that art therapy is ineffective or that it cannot be effective. Perhaps it helps to reduce recidivism. One certainly can find cases where a therapist or offender might testify that participation in art therapy created a life-changing experience that resulted in less offending. However, little theoretical and empirical research supports this approach to reducing recidivism. We should not be surprised: As with life skills programs, creativity-focused therapies do not typically target known causes of offending. All else being equal, when resources are scarce, we want to support efforts for which strong scientific theory and research exists that documents consistent and large improvements at little cost, not efforts with little to no empirical support.

It is not just corrections where ineffective policy and quackery exists. Crime prevention, law enforcement, and punishment policies are rife with examples of ineffectiveness and quackery. Indeed, many, though certainly not all, prominent crime policies rest on flimsy theoretical or research-based grounds (Mears, 2010).

"Get tough" sentencing provides perhaps the most obvious example. At first blush, it seems like an effective approach: Send a signal to would-be and sentenced offenders that we, society, will brook no nonsense and crime should go down. Yet, a large body of scholarship has established that there is nothing straightforward about deterrence or how it is achieved for particular offenders (specific deterrence) or would-be offenders (general deterrence) (Paternoster, 2010). A simple example illustrates the point: Studies have found that some offenders would prefer to be placed in prison for a year rather than be placed on probation for several years (May and Wood, 2010). We typically would think that prison constitutes a more severe punishment, yet these studies suggest that sometimes probation is more severe.

Another illustration—if prison exerts a specific deterrent effect, then, based on study findings to date, that effect either is weak or is offset by criminogenic aspects of incarceration (Nagin et al., 2009). Ultimately, we likely should not expect incarceration alone to have a beneficial effect. Why? Its effect likely depends on the experiences that individuals have during incarceration, the contexts to which they return, and the types of sanctions they otherwise would have experienced (Nagin et al., 2009; Mears et al., 2014).

No, or weak, empirical research

Extreme cases and anecdotes sometimes are used as "research" to suggest that "evidence" exists in support of a policy. In these cases, proponents may draw on some research to "confirm" their bias about the need for and effectiveness of a policy. Another common foundation for bad policy, however, is reliance on efforts for which virtually no research exists or where the research lacks credibility or rigor. For example, studies cited by proponents may rest on non-random samples, unreliable and invalid measures of key constructs central to a given policy, analyses that rely on no comparison groups, and so on. This situation, especially the absence of credible research, arguably characterizes the bulk of crime and justice policy, just as it characterizes the bulk of medical treatment (Millenson, 1997; Sherman, 2003). Consider the many informal policies that law enforcement and probation departments, courts, jails, prisons, and parole agencies rely on to guide their day-to-day decision-making. These decisions arguably govern the overall effectiveness of criminal justice and corrections in America, yet we know little about the accuracy of these decisions (Forst, 2004; Mears and Bacon, 2009).

Use of the evaluation hierarchy to define, develop, and identify "good" policies

What is the ideal or "good" policy? We can use different metrics to define it. For example, we might focus on the extent to which a given policy accords with certain philosophical principles. Here, it will be defined as policy that accords with the evaluation hierarchy (Rossi et al., 2004; Mears, 2010). Specifically, ideal or "good" policy is: (1) targeted toward important social problems or needs; (2) grounded in credible theory, logic, and empirical research; (3) well-implemented; (4) effective (i.e., it produces intended outcomes and avoids creating unintended harms); and (5) cost-efficient (i.e., the benefits exceed the costs). The hierarchy does not exclude consideration of philosophical principles or other considerations. Its primary relevance lies in providing a research-based foundation for determining if empirical evidence exists in support of a policy. Collectively, the five dimensions constitute can steer policymakers and practitioners towards cost-efficient allocation of scarce resources.

The logic of the hierarchy is simple: Policies should not be enacted or retained unless each step has been addressed. First, evaluate policy need. It makes little sense to adopt a new policy if no need for it exists. For example, in a county that has experienced no homicides in ten years and then experiences five, a knee-jerk response might be to assume that a problem clearly exists and that the "obvious" solution is to hire more police or enact a new gun law. What if, however, the homicides resulted from a single incident involving a relative from out of town? Perhaps the local police should undertake some new strategy, but perhaps not. The reality is that we have many crime problems that vary in magnitude and in their causes, and typically we target these crime problems through diverse efforts. Before undertaking new efforts, it is important to understand the scope of the problem, its causes, and the relative effectiveness of existing efforts.

Second, assuming a social problem exists that current policies fail to address sufficiently, then a new policy may be warranted. However, such a policy ideally should rest on strong theoretical and empirical grounds. The theory can come from existing social science, but it can involve as well a clearly articulated "causal logic," showing precisely how specific changes will result from a particular activity or undertaking. Empirical analysis is critical as well. For example, we might assume that a rise in crime results from gang activity. We certainly could find cases of gang members who committed crimes. Yet, research might reveal that gang-related crime in fact has declined and that the rise in crime stems from some other cause. Implementing a poorly designed policy makes little sense.

Third, after developing a clear policy blueprint grounded in credible theory and research, we then should implement the policy. Initially, we want to focus on taking corrective steps to adjust the policy in ways that might make it more effective. Such steps amount to the tinkering that one might do with a machine so that it runs more smoothly. Then, we want to focus on whether the policy in fact is implemented well. That is, if X, Y, and Z activities should be undertaken, are they? Is the amount and quality of implementation consistent with the blueprint?

Fourth, if the implementation appears to be sound, we proceed to evaluate a policy's impact. (If the implementation is poor, we take corrective action before evaluating impact.) A credible impact evaluation requires a credible blueprint. This blueprint describes the policy theory, or causal logic, which in turn will determine for us the outcomes that should be measured. The risk otherwise is that we willy-nilly focus on an outcome of limited relevance. If we apply to college, we do not want our grade-point average determined by just one class; similarly, if we want to evaluate a policy, we do not want to focus on only one outcome, unless the policy indeed targeted just one. Consider prisoner reentry programs. Many of them seek to improve not just recidivism outcomes but also employment, housing, drug abuse, and mental health outcomes. Failing to reduce recidivism successfully does not mean that a given program failed to achieve improvements in these other outcomes.

How do we assess impact? A multitude of approaches exists. Experimental designs can be ideal. Frequently, though, they are not possible. In these cases, a diverse range of quasi-experimental approaches exist that can yield credible estimates of policy impact (Rossi et al., 2004; Mears, 2010; Welsh et al., 2013).

In cases where a jurisdiction seeks to adopt a known policy, the question arises: How many evaluations need to exist before the jurisdiction can trust that it is "evidence-based"? Here, again, the logically prior question that should be addressed is whether a need for the policy exists and whether other policies might be better warranted. For example, just because a policy reduced recidivism with domestic violence abusers in one place does not mean that the policy is needed in another. Other efforts already under way in a particular area might simply need to be augmented. This issue aside, there is no clear answer to the question of how many studies are needed. Ideally, we have a large number of studies that consistently identify that a policy produces intended outcomes and entails few if any negative unintended effects. Even in those cases, such studies would not suffice. We also want evidence that the effects can reasonably be expected to occur in other places or with other groups or populations. For example, drug courts might be especially effective in urban areas but not work as well in suburban areas. Why? There may be too few available resources in the latter to offer sufficient drug treatment.

Fifth, and finally, if we can develop a credible estimate of policy impact, we then seek to evaluate the cost–efficiency of the policy. We can undertake cost-effectiveness analyses, which involve generating a cost-per-outcome estimate. Alternatively, we can undertake cost-benefit analyses, which involving generating cost–benefit estimates that consist entirely of monetary values. The latter approach can be especially helpful in situations where we seek to affect multiple outcomes or where we must choose between policies that target different outcomes. The central insight is that we want to obtain the most "bang for the buck." A given policy, such as a supermax prison, might improve an outcome; for example, it might reduce inmate violence. However, the cost of obtaining that benefit may greatly exceed, in monetary terms, the benefit. Cost-efficiency analyses have become more common in criminal justice in the past 20 years, but they still remain relatively rare (Mears, 2010; Roman et al., 2010). In addition, their credibility frequently rests on a shaky foundation. For example, when an impact evaluation relies on a weak research design, the resulting estimated impact carries with it considerable error. That creates attendant error in cost-efficiency estimates.

Across all steps of the evaluation hierarchy, conventional social science standards apply. That is, the standard of what counts as credible research is, by and large, the same for evaluation research as for any social scientific undertaking. We want reliable and valid measures, representative samples, information on dimensions relevant to a particular question (e.g. How large is a given social problem? What are its causes?), and study designs well-suited to answer a particular question. For example, if we want to estimate the prevalence of domestic violence or prosecutorial decision-making errors, we should not propose a randomized experiment. Similarly, if we want to estimate the effect of "hot-spots" policing on crime rates, we would not rely on a simple map of crime rates in the targeted areas. Undertaking evaluation research requires no special bag of tricks. Rather standard research methods and data sources (e.g. administrative records, surveys, interviews, observations) can be used. In contrast with typical social science research, however, they are geared to addressing the five types of evaluation questions.

Benefits of policy evaluation

What benefits accrue from policy evaluation? First, it is important for government accountability. It provides evidence that government is targeting important social problems, relying on credible policy designs, implementing policies fully and well, investing in policies that produce intended outcomes, and choosing policies that achieve these outcomes at the least cost.

Second, it can lead us to understand the relative magnitude of different social problems as well as the causes of these problems. This information in turn provides a critical platform from which to devise policies that address the most pressing problems and that do so in ways that are most likely to be effective.

Third, it can help us to identify "what works"—that is, what is effective and at what cost. Without credible research on effectiveness, policymakers, practitioners, and, by extension, society, must grasp at straws. That likely means reliance on extreme cases and anecdotes to justify particular policies.

The focus on "what works" constitutes a central benefit of policy evaluation (Lipsey et al., 2005; Welsh et al., 2013). However, it bears emphasizing that when we equate "what works" with evidence of impact, we in reality are relying on but one type of "evidence" that could be used to typify a policy as "evidence-based." Following the evaluation hierarchy, a policy can be said to be evidence-based as well if we have research that demonstrates need for the policy, credible theoretical foundations of the policy, full and quality implementation, and cost-efficiency. For example, if research establishes that a particular problem exists (e.g. violent crime, prosecutorial misconduct, gang-related drug dealing), we could view a policy that targets the problem as "evidence-based" in the sense of addressing a clear need. If research establishes that a policy is well-implemented, then we could view the policy as "evidence-based" in the sense of undertaking intended or required activities well.

Finally, we typically want evidence about dimensions of a social problem that can be changed. The evaluation hierarchy, especially needs and theory evaluations, can lead us to focus on modifiable causes. Many impact evaluations simply document whether a policy appeared to achieve an intended goal or not. We never learn whether the policy actually was needed or if other causal factors could be more readily targeted. By contrast, evaluations of policy need and policy theory can lead us to consider a broad range of potential causes and, in turn, consideration of those that might be most susceptible to policy influence (Sampson et al., 2014). That issue is critical. All else being equal, we should target policies towards those forces or factors that can be most easily manipulated to achieve the greatest gain in one or more outcomes at the least cost.

Institutionalize policy evaluation

As discussed above, ideal policies can be viewed as efforts that result from adhering to the evaluation hierarchy. That sounds simple, but achieving it is another matter. Most policy evaluation research consists of one-time studies. The studies focus on one place, policy, or time, and they evaluate policy implementation or effect. Accordingly, they shed little light on whether the policy was implemented well or achieved a similar effect at other places or times.

The alternative? Institutionalize the evaluation hierarchy (Mears, 2010) into a more general policymaking and policy monitoring process (Welsh and Harris, 2008; Bardach, 2011). Viewed in this way, evaluation research would be integrated into everyday decision-making about all aspects of crime and justice policy. Indeed, the very logic of the evaluation hierarchy requires that evaluation occur constantly. That is, a jurisdiction would continuously: (1) identify social problems and their causes, (2) design policy options, (3) implement policies that were needed and had strong theoretical foundations and then evaluate how well they were implemented, (4) evaluate policy impact, and (5) evaluate the costs and benefits of policies.

Institutionalizing policy evaluation provides one way to ensure that evaluations occur on a regular basis. It provides a way simultaneously to insulate society from knee-jerk policymaking efforts based on extremes, anecdotes, or poorly conducted research. Of course, there is no free lunch. Federal, state, and local funding for crime and justice research would need to be increased and research divisions would need to be well-integrated into the policymaking process (Mears, 2010; Blumstein, 2013). Presently, few states or local jurisdictions allow for more than descriptive empirical analysis of some parts of the criminal justice and correctional system or for contracting out specific studies. Such efforts simply cannot provide a strong empirical foundation—research-based evidence—for the vast bulk of policy.

There remains the question of where to house institutionalized research efforts. Ideally, independent research agencies would exist that were impervious to political pressure and could present research findings objectively. Such agencies—perhaps best exemplified by the U.S. Government Accountability Office—must seek both to be non-partisan and to be perceived as such. That is no easy task and requires scrupulous attention to multiple layers of review, response by different stakeholders, and further review (Basu et al., 1999). Objective and credible research can be undertaken by different government agencies, private contractors, and other groups. Yet, such groups also can undertake partisan and poorly conducted research (Farabee, 2005; Mears, 2010). No silver bullet solution exists to this problem save to ensure that processes exist to reduce the likelihood of research that is biased and that rests on weak methodological grounds.

Causal uncertainty

One of the central challenges that policymakers face is causal uncertainty. That is, they frequently do not know to what extent a given social problem results from a particular cause or set of causes or how well any of a number of policy options may address it. That uncertainty rightfully can make scholars cautious about making claims regarding the likely effects of particular policies; it should make policymakers, as well as criminal justice and corrections officials and practitioners, equally cautious. At the same time, unlike researchers, policymakers have a mandate to help society through a variety of policy initiatives. They cannot wait.

Here, again, no free lunch exists. If policymakers do not fund research that allows for more informed deliberations, then they force themselves to rely on extreme cases, anecdotes, and weak research. In those cases where a strong body of research exists, they will still confront the uncertainty problem. For example, even the best, most well-established medical treatment can fail if administered poorly or to the wrong population. Ultimately, though, uncertainty inheres to all parts of life, including policy evaluation and assessment (Blomberg et al., 2014).

An effective policymaking process would rely on the best available evidence and be explicit about the uncertainty that exists. Of course, if a more comprehensive, institutionalized approach to evaluation existed, there would be less need to be concerned about the uncertainty associated with policy impact assessments. Why? We would have empirical research continuously providing guidance about policy need, implementation, and actual impact, as well as policy alternatives that might be more needed, effective, and cost-efficient.

Consider a "black box" impact evaluation of a community policing effort. The evaluation might find that community policing reduces crime rates, but it would leave us in the dark about exactly what produced the change. A theory evaluation would lead us to consider several different activities that constitute community policing and the specific mechanisms through which these activities may lead eventually to reductions in crime rates. An implementation evaluation might uncover that one of the weaker parts of a specific community policing initiative was the undertaking of regular foot patrols in a particular neighborhood. It also might show that one of the stronger parts was the creation among residents of a sense, perhaps due to well-publicized instances of quick and courteous responses to local residents, that the police care and listen to their requests. Such information would highlight the possibility that crime rate reductions may have resulted more so from law enforcement officer efforts to engender good will and not from foot patrols. With such insights, policymakers then are armed to orient their efforts to promoting more of the activities, or parts of a given policy, that potentially are most vulnerable or amenable to policy influence and that may yield the greatest effects. (Similar examples can be found in Sampson et al., 2014.)

As can be seen in this example, reliance on multiple types of ongoing research can provide a platform from which to reduce uncertainty about policy impacts. It provides a foundation, too, for increasing the likelihood that we obtain greater societal improvements in the most cost-efficient way possible. In short, the more types of evaluation research that occur and that inform policy deliberations, the less we need to be concerned about causal uncertainty.

Conclusion

Policy evaluation and assessment is critical for developing effective public policy. Research provides but one part of an overall process for creating such policy. It is, though, a critical part. Such research should not be equated with experimental studies. Experiments can shed light on whether certain policies can be effective. However, they tell us little about whether these policies can work across a wide range of social contexts and groups. In addition, they are costly. By contrast, quasi-experimental designs can be used at far less cost for a broad range of policies.

More broadly, though, the central argument of this chapter is that "evidence-based" policy should not be equated with impact evaluations—that is, the use of experiments or quasi-experiments to assess whether a policy achieves a given outcome. Rather, it should be equated with each of the five steps of the evaluation hierarchy: (1) policy need, (3) theory, (2) implementation, (4) impact, and (5) cost-efficiency.

Institutionalizing the evaluation hierarchy into policy deliberations and reviews constitutes a critical strategy for placing more policy on an evidence-based foundation. Doing so will require a substantial investment in research nationally, at the state level, and among local jurisdictions. If, however, we want more government accountability, public safety, and justice at the least cost, the investment will be worth it.

Note

1 The author thanks Tom Blomberg and Julie Brancale for their helpful suggestions and ideas.

References

Bardach, Eugene. 2004. "Presidential address—The extrapolation problem: How can we learn from the experience of others?" *Journal of Policy Analysis and Management* 23(2):205–220.

Bardach, Eugene. 2011. *A Practical Guide for Policy Analysis: The Eightfold Path to More Effective Problem Solving*. 4th edition. Thousand Oaks, CA: Sage.

Basu, Onker N., Mark W. Dirsmith, and Parveen P. Gupta. 1999. "The Coupling of the Symbolic and the Technical in an Institutionalized Context: The Negotiated Order of the GAO's Audit Reporting Process." *American Sociological Review* 64:506–526.

Blomberg, Thomas G., Julie Mestre, and Karen Mann. 2014. "Seeking Causality in a World of Contingency: Criminology, Research, and Public Policy." *Criminology and Public Policy* 12:571–584.

Blumstein, Alfred. 2013. "Linking Evidence and Criminal Justice Policy." *Criminology and Public Policy* 12:721–730.

Farabee, David. 2005. *Rethinking Rehabilitation: Why Can't We Reform Our Criminals?* Washington, DC: The AEI Press.

Forst, Brian. 2004. *Errors of Justice: Nature, Sources, and Remedies*. New York: Cambridge University Press.

Latessa, Edward J., Shelley J. Listwan, and Deborah Koetzle. 2014. *What Works (and Doesn't) in Reducing Recidivism*. Waltham, MA: Anderson Publishing.

Lipsey, Mark, John Adams, Denise Gottfredson, John Pepper, David Weisburd, eds. 2005. *Improving Evaluation of Anticrime Programs*. Washington, DC: National Academies Press.

Mancini, Christina, and Daniel P. Mears. 2013. "U.S. Supreme Court Decisions and Sex Offender Legislation: Evidence of Evidence-Based Policy?" *Journal of Criminal Law and Criminology* 103:1115–1154.

May, David C., and Peter B. Wood. 2010. *Ranking Correctional Punishments: Views from Offenders, Practitioners, and the Public*. Durham, NC: Carolina Academic Press.

Mears, Daniel P. 2010. *American Criminal Justice Policy: An Evaluation Approach to Increasing Accountability and Effectiveness*. New York: Cambridge University Press.

Mears, Daniel P., and Sarah Bacon. 2009. "Improving Criminal Justice through Better Decisionmaking: Lessons from the Medical System." *Journal of Criminal Justice* 37:142–154.

Mears, Daniel P., Joshua C. Cochran, and Francis T. Cullen. 2014. "Incarceration Heterogeneity and its Implications for Assessing the Effectiveness of Imprisonment on Recidivism." *Criminal Justice Policy Review* (online; doi: 10.1177/0887403414528950).

Millenson, Michael. 1997. *Demanding Medical Excellence: Doctors and Accountability in the Information Age*. Chicago: University of Chicago Press.

Nagin, Daniel S., Francis T. Cullen, and Cheryl L. Jonson. 2009. "Imprisonment and Reoffending." *Crime and Justice* 38:115–200.

Paternoster, Raymond. 2010. "How Much Do We Really Know about Criminal Deterrence?" *Journal of Criminal Law and Criminology* 100:765–824.

Roman, John K., Terence Dunworth, and Kevin Marsh, eds. 2010. *Cost-Benefit Analysis and Crime Control*. Washington, DC: The Urban Institute Press.

Rossi, Peter H., Mark W. Lipsey, and Howard E. Freeman. 2004. *Evaluation: A Systematic Approach*. 7th edition. Thousand Oaks, CA: Sage.

Sampson, Robert J., Christopher Winship, and Carly Knight. 2014. "Translating Causal Claims: Principles and Strategies for Policy-Relevant Criminology." *Criminology and Public Policy* 12:587–616.

Sherman, Lawrence W. 2003. "Misleading Evidence and Evidence-Led Policy: Making Social Science More Experimental." *Annals of the American Academy of Political and Social Science* 589:6–19.

Welsh, Brandon C., Anthony N. Braga, and Gerben J. N. Bruinsma, eds. 2013. *Experimental Criminology: Prospects for Advancing Science and Public Policy*. New York: Cambridge University Press.

Welsh, Wayne N., and Philip W. Harris. 2008. *Criminal Justice Policy and Planning*. 3rd edition. Dayton, OH: LexisNexis, Anderson Publishing.

Chapter 3

The role of theory, ideology, and ethics in criminal justice policy

Francis T. Cullen and Cecilia Chouhy

Introduction

Most readers of this chapter have never lived at a time when the United States was not in the grasp of what Clear and Frost (2014) recently called "the punitive imperative." For over four decades, the nation's criminal justice system has been mired in a mean season in which one get-tough policy after another has been implemented. Elected officials at times have acted shamelessly, engaging in an orgy of punitive rhetoric and seeking to out-do one another in demonstrating who could invent the most degrading punishment to inflict on offenders. They have proudly made prison conditions more austere, denied inmates access to college courses, celebrated botched executions that made "killers suffer," embraced "scared straight" programs in which youngsters are humiliated and threatened with sexual assault should they be incarcerated, and have attached to a criminal conviction a lengthy roster of "collateral consequences" intended to exclude ex-offenders from the rights of citizenship, government benefits, and employment requiring state licensure. Too often, race has been at the center of the narrative underlying this rhetoric and policy making, with African Americans implicitly portrayed as "super-predators" and whites as helpless victims (see, e.g. Alexander, 2010; Tonry, 2011). We know of few laws passed that are named after black victims. There is often a Megan's Law but rarely a Latisha's Law (Kulig and Cullen, 2015).

Rather abruptly, however, this mean season in criminal justice policy ended or, in the least, is in the process of ending (Petersilia and Cullen, 2014–2015). A silver lining of the Great Recession that began in 2009 is that governors of states, many of them Republicans elected in 2010, discovered that mass imprisonment was a budgetary Pac-Man, gobbling up tax revenues. Locking up more and more offenders was no longer a sustainable policy; it was an unaffordable luxury that had to be curtailed. Discussions of alternatives to incarceration and of the need for rehabilitation became more plentiful. Prison populations stopped rising for the first time in four decades and started to decline in a number of states. A turning point in criminal justice policy is now upon us. It is thus an appropriate time to reflect, in terms of such policies, where we have been and where we might now head (Cullen et al., 2014).

Toward this end, we propose to examine these issues through the prism of a trinity of lenses: criminological theory, political ideology, and ethics. We will present the following conclusions about the role each of these perspectives played in criminal justice policy. Thus, with regard to policy: (1) criminological theory has been ignored, populist, and largely incorrect (when used); (2) ideology has been hegemonic, conservative, and punitive; and (3) ethics have been disquieting though, to a degree, in the eye of the beholder.

Theory

If ill and seeking treatment, patients assume that their physician's first step is to diagnose the cause of their ailment. Doctors who dispensed medications randomly would be called quacks and drummed out of the medical profession. They might end up in jail and they certainly would be sued and become much poorer. Instead of such quackery, physicians prescribe treatment based on their *theory* of why the person before them is ill. Grounded in their scientific medical training and in clinical experience, they make an informed judgment of the *set of factors causing* the sickness. If their causal theory is correct, there is a good chance the patient will recover healthily; if the theory is incorrect and the wrong causes are targeted for intervention, the patient's well-being is likely to deteriorate to the point of an acute emergency or even death. So, in medicine, theory matters.

Theory also matters in criminal justice policy—and for largely the same reason. Every policy is pregnant with a theory. Criminal justice policies have a purpose: to lower crime. When some policy prescription is applied to offenders, there is an assumption that it is targeting something about the wayward that leads them to break the law. Of course, at its most complex level, a theory can be quite formal and stated in a set of testable propositions. Typically—even in scholarly writings—they are not. Criminologists do not set the bar high in terms of what qualifies as a theory. The only requirement is that scholars say they are presenting a theory and then specify what they believe is some unique set of factors that is causing crime. The clue to what these factors are is the name given to the theory. Thus, what might Agnew's (2006) "general strain theory" argue leads to crime? If you guessed "strain," then you now understand criminological theory!

Criminological theories are often stated elegantly and persuasively. There are also a lot of them. They are difficult to prove wrong—to "falsify"— because they tend to capture a slice of life that has some role in encouraging criminal involvement. Criminology as a field keeps adding new perspectives and not discarding the older ones. Theory textbooks thus grow larger and larger with each edition, even doubling in size from the first to later versions (see, e.g. Lilly et al., 2015). But despite their immortality, criminological theories have a problem: They do not explain a large portion of the variation in offending—that is, why some people commit a lot of crime and others only a little (Weisburd and Piquero, 2008). The reality is that crime is caused by multiple factors, and each individual theory illuminates only one or a small number of them. If so, this fact makes it difficult to build policy. Thus, implementing a criminal justice intervention based on a theory that identifies only a limited cause of crime would leave all other causes "untreated."

Depressingly, matters are still worse outside academic criminology. When elected officials and their appointees develop crime control policies, their guiding theory tends to be unstated, not based on evidence, and populist. Thus, when a policy reform is rolled out, the theory underlying it is not identified and rarely is a criminologist close by to explain what causes are being targeted. To the extent that a theory is set forth, it appeals to some general understanding about crime that seems a matter of "common sense" and that "everyone knows to be true." One such theory (which we will return to shortly) is that that people will not commit crime "if it does not pay." In this sense, then, the theory is populist rather than academic.

Boot camps for young adult offenders provide an example of the role of theory in policy making. When this program was implemented, it was assumed that exposure to a tough military regime, usually from three to six months, would transform these wayward souls from undisciplined offenders into upstanding citizens. This was a questionable thesis, and one that has proven to be wrong. Boot camps do not reduce recidivism (Cullen et al., 2005; MacKenzie, 2006). More broadly, the impact of military service on antisocial conduct is uncertain at best (Sampson and Laub, 1993; Wright et al., 2005). And if such service has any crime-reducing effects, they are likely due less to surviving a boot camp and more to what takes place thereafter: full employment in the military, a life of structured activities, and constant supervision. The armed forces now reject applicants with criminal records, suggesting that they have weak faith in their ability to save offenders. These realities were ignored in the policy-making process, in large part because of an abiding confidence that boot camps "break offenders down and build them back up."

When this statement is repeated, heads bob in agreement. After all, countless movies—such as the 1982 film *An Officer and a Gentleman* starring Richard Gere—have shown it to be true! Common sense reigns. But the theory is fuzzy. What does it mean to "break down" someone? What criminogenic factors are being stripped away? It seems to be some sort of youthful rebelliousness or entitled, snotty arrogance. One wonders. And then what protective factors are then being instilled in the "building up" process? Is it self-control, moral fiber, or perhaps a healthy pride and self-esteem? One again wonders. Is there a shred of evidence that any of this is accurate or, even if so, that boot camps are capable of impacting these factors meaningfully? The answer, of course, is "no."

The more significant issue is the accuracy of the theory that guided many of the other get-tough policies over the past four decades. Again, when we say "guided," we do not mean that elected officials carefully read the criminological literature and selected the most empirically verified perspective. Policies are set forth for a variety of reasons, including political ideology and the pursuit of political capital. Still, as noted, all policies are pregnant with a theory.

In this case, the controlling perspective was, in criminological jargon, "rational choice theory." The belief existed that offenders make choices and are rational enough not to offend if the costs are high enough. If this theory is accurate, then it makes sense to increase the harshness of criminal penalties. A danger to this thinking is that it can lead to ever-escalating punishments: If offenders persist in breaking the law, then it is "obvious" that costs must be raised until they are scared straight. Because offending never stops, neither does the call for harsher penalties. In short, no matter how often it fails to produce crime-saving results, the *severity of punishment* is held to be the key to crime control. For convenience, we will refer to this variant of rational choice theory as *severity theory*.

There are two problems with this theory. First, it is a crass understanding of how people, including offenders, make decisions. The image of humans as carefully weighing up costs and benefits as they make decision after decision in their daily lives is, well, ridiculous. Much of what we do is based on habit and social learning. Social psychological research also shows that individuals use a host of "heuristics" (simple but possibly biased rules) when choosing courses of action (Kahneman, 2011). For example, some offenders appear to reset their perceptions of the certainty of punishment to a lower bar after being punished and increase their criminal participation. Similar to gamblers on a losing streak who go "all in" due to the fallacious belief that their bad luck cannot continue, some people are persuaded that "they would have to be exceedingly unlucky to be apprehended again" (Pogarsky and Piquero, 2003). But there are more factors that bound, if not undermine, notions of rationality. Thus, offenders often go into crime when their mental faculties are compromised by being inebriated or high on drugs, highly emotional, or in the company of hedonistic peers. Impulsive and risk taking, they tend to think of the benefits of crime and to ignore distant costs (Gottfredson and Hirschi, 1990). If they weigh costs, it is mainly because of their certainty, for when detection is seen as unlikely, any threats of harshness seem irrelevant. If punishment works at all, it is when it is swift and certain, not delayed and severe (Durlauf and Nagin, 2011; Kleiman, 2009). Further, offenders persist in crime because they initiated their criminal careers in childhood by engaging in antisocial conduct (Moffitt, 1993). Decisions made later in life thus reflect a life history of choices, not some isolated judgment made for the first time. Most serious offenders have been making bad choices with negative consequences since childhood. They do not suddenly wake up at age 22, do a cost–benefit analysis, and decide it would be neat to break the law. By now the point should be clear: A lot of things affect decisions, not just whether a crime pays.

Second, evaluation studies can be seen as tests of theories (Cullen et al., 2003). In this case, the policy makers' severity theory predicts that more severe or "costly" penalties will have greater success in reducing recidivism than less severe penalties. Unfortunately, this does not appear to be the case (Cullen et al., 2002). The litmus test is whether offenders sent to prison are less likely to offend than those given a non-custodial, community-based sanction. Contrary to severity theory, the evidence suggests that imprisonment does not specifically deter offenders and, in fact, might have a slight criminogenic effect (Cullen et al., 2011).

The costs of trumpeting policies based on a limited, if not faulty, theory are enormous. Lawbreakers can justifiably be sent to prison for diverse reasons—including "just deserts" and simply to keep them off the streets for a while. But many offenders have been incarcerated for sentences that were needlessly long, based explicitly on severity theory—that is, on the premise that costliness leads to godliness. Much money was wasted. But the more disquieting concern is the opportunity costs of imprisonment: Offenders who might have been given effective rehabilitation programs were not (Andrews and Bonta, 2010; Van Voorhis, 1987). Their risk of recidivism thus was not reduced, a fact that not only led them back to crime but also resulted in innumerable victimizations of the public that might have been prevented had they received a more effective correctional intervention.

Academic criminologists have no reason for hubris. As noted, our theories are not powerful and thus are problematic as guides to policy. But another difficulty exists. Although scholars articulate a host of plausible policies, they do not identify causes of crime that can be easily targeted and changed. This argument was made in 1975 by James Q. Wilson, who rightly criticized criminologists for focusing on the "root causes" of crime (e.g. socially disorganized neighborhoods, an inequitable class structure). Even if the theories were correct, claimed Wilson, they provided little guidance for how these criminogenic sources could be changed.

By contrast, criminological theories that focus on factors closer to individuals and the situations in which the choice of crime is made tend to result in more effective policies. One example is routine activity theory, which links crime to the intersection in time and space of motivated offenders and two components of opportunity—an attractive target and a lack of capable guardianship (Felson and Boba, 2010). Based on this theory, crime can be reduced by interventions that make targets less attractive (e.g. requiring bus passengers to have exact fare so that drivers carry no cash) and/or that increase guardianship (e.g. hiring a security guard). Research generally supports these predictions (Clarke, 2010; Felson and Boba, 2010).

One more example can illustrate the importance of using a theory that identifies criminogenic factors that can be changed. David Olds (2007) is well known for his Nurse Home Visitation Program (now called the Nurse-Family Partnership). Noting that early antisocial conduct problems lead to crime in the juvenile years and beyond, Olds wanted to cut off the development of criminal careers at their inception. Based on the literature, he developed a conceptual model (a theory) of the causal links that occur from the pre-natal period onward. His model recognized that newborns developed neuropsychological deficits in the womb due to mothers smoking or taking drugs (see Olds, 2007, p. 209). In a wonderful insight, Olds decided to recruit nurses—non-threatening health providers—to work with young expectant mothers to help them to refrain from ingesting harmful substances. Following birth, they also guided the mothers in positive childcare methods. The key point is that the theory illuminated causal factors that not only were salient but also changeable through a pragmatic intervention.

Ideology

Ideology is a systematic set of deeply held beliefs—or worldview—that is rooted in unstated assumptions about human nature and society and used by people to justify personal decisions and policy preferences. Ideology is often seen as a bad thing, and rightly so in some instances. But ideology also has its positive side. Strong, coherent convictions provide comfort by making sense of the human condition, and they energize political action. Most often, we decry the ideology of those we oppose and see our own ideology as nothing more than a set of truthful depictions of the world, including which policies are political nonsense and which reflect political wisdom. It is fine to have an ideology, but some reflexivity is important. We all should realize that we could be full of…blarney.

Ideology becomes problematic when closely aligned with rival political parties. Policy issues, such as global warming or immigration, are transformed from complex considerations into matters of truth and morality on which no compromise is possible. For a Republican to vote for an immigration bill, for example, is to be a traitor who should be drummed out of the party. Politics thus gives ideology power and the capacity to shape policy. Ideology also is problematic because it is impervious to evidence. Studies that confirm one's worldview are seen as brilliant, whereas those that disconfirm cherished beliefs are obviously junk science. For conservatives embracing intelligent design, no amount of empirical data will convince them that evolution is more than a theory that arrogantly allows man's science to trump God's revealed truth.

There is nothing inherent in conservative Republicanism that mandates the embrace of a theory of severity and of mass incarceration. In fact, we suspect that there are more Evangelical Christians visiting and caring about inmates than academic criminologists (see, e.g. Johnson, 2011). When Ronald Reagan became California's governor in 1967, he set about cutting costs by reducing the state's prison population from 28,000 to less than 18,000. Under other governors—including Democrats—the state's inmate count would eventually top 174,000 (Cullen and Gilbert, 2013). Be that as it may, the stubborn reality is that a number of factors coalesced in the late 1960s to lead Republicans to embrace a "law-and-order" stance and to declare "wars" on crime and drugs (see, e.g. Beckett, 1997). Rising crime rates and persistent social disorder made this appeal plausible. But it also was tied to a broader critique of the welfare state claiming that being nice to poor and disreputable populations, most of them African Americans, had simply encouraged their deviance (see Murray, 1984). These populations needed to be disciplined—to be taught that laziness and crime, as well as drug use, would not be tolerated (see, e.g. Garland, 2001). This critique was so successful that "liberal" became a naughty word. Soon enough, Democratic politicians were competing with their Republican rivals in pro-posing nasty criminal justice policies. Get-tough ideology became "hegem-onic," which is a fancy way of saying that everyone was spouting it.

Well, almost everyone. Academic criminologists were horrified by the dom-inance of punitive ideology and an ever-expanding system of mass impris-onment that eventually resulted in a ratio of one in a hundred Americans behind bars on any given day (Pew Charitable Trusts, 2008). Many books, essays, and empirical studies were published, which allowed scholars to gain tenure and become famous (well, some of them). Although exceptions exist (Cullen, 2005), these contributions, though largely correct, were ignored or simply dismissed as liberal poppycock.

Importantly, however, criminologists should not be viewed as scholarly princes (or princesses) sitting atop a sanctified throne that insulates them from the ideology that blinds lesser creatures; quite the contrary is true. Similar to other humans, scholars use heuristics to make biased, non-rational decisions and can confuse their personal beliefs with empirical reality. As members of a professional community, they are socialized into sets of beliefs that they take for granted; those who dare challenge these beliefs are, like Republicans voting for immigration, sanctioned (Cullen and Gendreau, 2001). In the 1970s, for example, it was fashionable for criminologists to say that rehabilitation did not work to reform offenders. As it turned out, this claim was empirically incorrect then and now (Cullen, 2013). However, when positive empirical results were reported, scholars would use "treat-ment destruction techniques" to question the findings—that is, such as employing such high methodological standards that no evaluation study could ever show that a rehabilitation program was effective (Gottfredson, 1979; see also Andrews and Bonta, 2010).

Today, a similar reaction is given to research published by biosocial criminologists. Most scholars were raised in academic departments in which attributing crime to biology was seen as acquitting an inequitable society of complicity in causing crime. As a result, they do not like any theory having to do with biology and reject such thinking "out of hand"—which is to say, they reject it purely on ideological grounds. Of course, crime can be due to both social inequality and biological inequality—and, in particular, to those who suffer both. Olds (2007) said as much when he noted that children born to young, impoverished mothers suffered both neurological damage in the womb and a life starting in social disadvantage. He recognized the nurses might blunt both effects—preventing biological and child-rearing deficits. If he had been ideologically opposed to a biological theory of conduct, a lot of kids would have entered the world with debilitating risk factors and now be sitting in a prison.

Ethics

Ethics generally entails whether criminal justice policies are based on sound philosophical principles and thus "moral." The difficulty is that philosophers themselves cannot agree on ethical principles and have concocted all sorts of clever arguments that leave all justifications for punishing offenders wanting. Take, for example, the principle of retribution or just deserts. It sounds nice to say that everyone who breaks the same law should be punished equally, and thus that the crime committed should govern the penalty meted out. But this principle loses its luster when it is clear that crime is not freely chosen but is at least partially determined by such things as neuropsychological deficits acquired in the womb that were not an offender's fault. Should not this mitigating factor be taken into account? Similarly, consider Anatole France's famous statement in his 1884 classic, *The Red Lily*:

> We in France are soldiers and we are citizens. Our citizenship is another occasion for pride! For the poor it consists in supporting and maintaining the rich in their power and their idleness. At this task they must labour in the face of the majestic equality of the laws, which forbid rich and poor alike to sleep under the bridges, to beg in the streets, and to steal their bread.
>
> (1884/1908, p. 85)

Punishing rich and poor lawbreakers equally—giving them each so-called just deserts for offenses such as "stealing their bread"—is thus revealed as manifestly inane.

Ethics also depends on one's point of view. For most criminologists, it is ethically troubling to place offenders in prisons that are overcrowded, unhealthy, and dangerous. But for more conservative groups (including a few criminologists), this empathy for offenders—who, after all, have harmed others—is misplaced. For them, such suffering is justified because it shows victims that offenders will be held accountable for their bad actions. In fact, a key dimension of the get-tough movement was the elevation of the victim's well-being over the offender's well-being. A genuine concern for victims is appropriate. It becomes problematic, however, when victims' rights are trumpeted disingenuously so as to secure officials' political capital. In such cases, the use of victims for their own political ends is unethical (see Garland, 2001).

Criminologists often are no better. It is part of our professional ideology to empathize with offenders and to claim that they should be treated humanely. We happen to agree with this point of view, in part because ethical practice tends to produce far better results with offenders than coercion (see, e.g. Andrews and Bonta, 2010). We also prefer to see ourselves as humanitarians rather than as punishers. The risk, however, is that we are no better than disingenuous politicians. We fear that a lot of criminologists, maybe even us to a degree, are using the plight of downtrodden offenders to say things that make us look good to others and feel good about ourselves.

Still, one of us (Cullen, 2012) has attempted to articulate one approach to ethical policy making, at least within corrections, by calling for a "Correctional Hippocratic Oath." Mirrored after the oath used in medicine, it would call for at least two core standards for intervening into the lives of criminals: first, a genuine attempt to do no harm—whether to offenders or to potential victims; and second, a genuine attempt to use the best practices available to ensure that offenders do not return to crime. Of course, those who wish to harm offenders so as to get even with them—that is, to exact retribution—will not like our preference for "doing no harm." The rejoinder is that punishment is inherent in deprivation of freedom (if in prison) or from sanctions delivered in the community. Still, an ethical criminal justice policy would not allow offenders to be placed in crowded, painful prisons where they sit idly all day and receive no rehabilitation. It would not allow young adults to be placed in boot camps that are coercive and ineffective. It would not allow interventions to be used that have not been tested and shown to be evidence based. And it would not allow quackery—the use of policies that do not reduce recidivism and lead to more, rather than less, victimization (Latessa et al., 2002).

Conclusion

We will leave you with a short and simple take-away message. When viewing any criminal justice policy, you should be sufficiently sensitized to ask three sets of questions embodied in the above essay. These questions should be part of the analytical framework used to assess whether the policy in question is defensible. Here are the three sets of questions.

- First, what theory underlies the policy? Is there any evidence to support it? Does the theory identify factors that cause crime? If so, are they important factors? Are they factors that can be changed by the policy being put into place?
- Second, what ideology does the policy reflect? Is the policy popular only because it resonates with a popular ideology? Who is profiting politically or professionally from the ideology being spouted?
- Third, does the policy cause more harm than good? If so, how might it be changed? How might the policy be implemented in a truly ethical fashion?

References

Agnew, R. (2006). *Pressured into crime: An overview of general strain theory.* Los Angeles, CA: Roxbury.

Alexander, M. (2010). *The new Jim Crow: Mass incarceration in the age of colorblindness.* New York, NY: The New Press.

Andrews, D. A., and Bonta, J. (2010). *The psychology of criminal conduct* (5th ed.). New Providence, NJ: Anderson./LexisNexis.

Beckett, K. (1997). *Making crime pay: Law and order in contemporary American politics.* New York, NY: Oxford University Press.

Clarke, R. V. (2010). Crime science. In E. McLaughlin and T. Newburn (eds.), *The Sage handbook of criminological theory* (pp. 271–283). London, UK: Sage.

Clear, T. C., and Frost, N. A. (2014). *The punishment imperative: The rise and failure of mass incarceration in America.* New York: New York University Press.

Cullen, F. T. (2005). The twelve people who saved rehabilitation: How the science of criminology made a difference – The American Society of Criminology 2004 presidential address. *Criminology, 43,* 1–42.

Cullen, F. T. (2012). Making corrections work: It's time for a new penology. *Journal of Community Corrections, 21*(Fall):5–6, 15–18.

Cullen, F. T. (2013). Rehabilitation: Beyond nothing works. In M. Tonry (ed.), *Crime and justice in America, 1975 to 2025* (Crime and Justice: A Review of Research, Vol. 42, pp. 299–376). Chicago, IL: University of Chicago Press.

Cullen, F. T., Blevins, K. R., Trager, J. S., and Gendreau, P. (2005). The rise and fall of boot camps: A case study in common-sense corrections. *Journal of Offender Rehabilitation, 40*(3–4), 53–70.

Cullen, F. T., and Gendreau, P. (2001). From nothing works to what works: Changing professional ideology in the 21st century. *The Prison Journal, 81,* 313–338.

Cullen, F. T., and Gilbert, K. E. (2013). *Reaffirming rehabilitation* (2nd ed.). Waltham, MA: Anderson.

Cullen, F. T., Jonson, C. L., and Nagin, D. S. (2011). Prisons do not reduce recidivism: The high cost of ignoring science. *The Prison Journal, 91,* 48S–65S.

Cullen, F. T., Jonson, C. L., and Stohr, M. K. (eds.). (2014). *The American prison: Imagining a different future*. Thousand Oaks, CA: Sage.

Cullen, F. T., Pratt, T. C., Miceli, S. L., and Moon, M. M. (2002). Dangerous liaison? Rational choice theory as the basis for correctional intervention. In A. R. Piquero and S. G. Tibbetts (eds.), *Rational choice and criminal behavior: Recent research and future challenges* (pp. 279–296). New York, NY: Routledge.

Cullen, F. T., Wright, J. P., Gendreau, P., and Andrews, D. A. (2003). What correctional treatment can tell us about criminological theory: Implications for social learning theory. In R. L. Akers and G. F. Jensen (eds.), *Social learning theory and the explanation of crime: A guide for the new century* (Advances in Criminological Theory, Vol. 11, pp. 339–362). New Brunswick, NJ: Transaction.

Durlauf, S. N., and Nagin, D. S. (2011). Imprisonment and crime: Can both be reduced? *Criminology and Public Policy*, 10, 13–54.

Felson, M., and Boba, R. (2010). *Crime and everyday life* (4th ed.). Thousand Oaks, CA: Sage.

France, A. (1908). *The red lily* (F. Chapman, Trans.). London, UK: John Lane. (Original work published 1884)

Garland, D. (2001). *The culture of control: Crime and social order in contemporary society*. Chicago, IL: University of Chicago Press.

Gottfredson, M. R. (1979). Treatment destruction techniques. *Journal of Research in Crime and Delinquency*, 16, 39–54.

Gottfredson, M. R., and Hirschi, T. (1990). *A general theory of crime*. Stanford, CA: Stanford University Press.

Johnson, B. R. (2011). *More God, less crime: Why faith matters and how it could matter more*. West Conshohocken, PA: Templeton Press.

Kahneman, D. (2011). *Thinking, fast and slow*. New York, NY: Farrar, Straus and Giroux.

Kleiman, M. A. R. (2009). *When brute force fails: How to have less crime and less punishment*. Princeton, NJ: Princeton University Press.

Kulig, T. C., and Cullen, F. N.(2015). *Where is Latisha's law? Black invisibility in the social construction of victimhood..* Unpublished manuscript, University of Cincinnati.

Latessa, E. J., Cullen, F. T., and Gendreau, P. (2002). Beyond correctional quackery: Professionalism and the possibility of effective treatment. *Federal Probation*, 66(2), 43–49.

Lilly, J. R., Cullen, F. T., and Ball, R. A. (2015). *Criminological theory: Context and consequences* (6th ed.). Thousand Oaks, CA: Sage.

MacKenzie, D. L. (2006). *What works in corrections: Reducing the criminal activities of offenders and delinquents*. New York, NY: Cambridge University Press.

Moffitt, T. E. (1993). Adolescence-limited and life-course–persistent antisocial behavior: A developmental taxonomy. *Psychological Review*, 100, 674–701.

Murray, C. (1984). *Losing ground: American social policy, 1950–1980*. New York, NY: Basic Books.

Olds, D. L. (2007). Preventing crime with prenatal and infancy support of parents: The nurse-family partnership. *Victims and Offenders*, 2, 205–225.

Petersilia, J., and Cullen, F. T. (2015). Liberal but not stupid: Meeting the promise of downsizing prisons. *Stanford Journal of Criminal Law and Policy*, 2, 1–43.

Pew Charitable Trusts. (2008). *One in 100: Behind bars in America 2008*. Washington, DC: Author.

Pogarsky, G., and Piquero, A. R. (2003). Can punishment encourage offending? Investigating the "resetting effect." *Journal of Research in Crime and Delinquency*, 40, 95–120.

Sampson, R. J., and Laub, J. H. (1993). *Crime in the making: Pathways and turning points through life*. Cambridge, MA: Harvard University Press.

Tonry, M. (2011). *Punishing race: A continuing American dilemma*. New York, NY: Oxford University Press.

Van Voorhis, P. (1987). Correctional effectiveness: The high cost of ignoring success. *Federal Probation*, 51(1), 59–62.

Weisburd, D., and Piquero, A. R. (2008). How well do criminologists explain crime? Statistical modeling in published studies. In M. Tonry (ed.). *Crime and justice: A review of research* (Vol. 37, pp. 453–502). Chicago, IL: University of Chicago Press.

Wilson, J. Q. (1975). *Thinking about crime*. New York, NY: Vintage.

Wright, J. P., Carter, D. E., and Cullen, F. T. (2005). A life-course analysis of military service in Vietnam. *Journal of Research in Crime and Delinquency*, 43, 55–83.

Chapter 4

Translational criminology

A new path forward

John H. Laub and Nicole E. Frisch

Introduction

The term "evidence-based policy" pervades recent discussions among academics and policymakers. President Obama's administration has demonstrated a clear commitment to improving social policies with scientific evidence in funding six large evidence-based initiatives between 2010 and 2012 (Haskins and Margolis, 2014). Furthermore, it appears that there is bipartisan support of evidence-based policies. To illustrate, in November 2014 Senator Patty Murray (D-WA) and Representative Paul Ryan (R-WI) proposed a bill that supports a committee to bring scientific evidence to bear on tax reform (Dionne, 2014).[1]

Criminologists and criminal justice policymakers are also interested in, and often dedicated to, implementing evidence-based policies in an effort to enhance the criminal justice system's capacity to prevent and respond to crime (Blumstein, 2013). Unfortunately, this rhetoric is not always realized (Tonry, 2010; Uggen and Inderbitzen, 2010). In 2012, the National Research Council released a report addressing the impact of scientific evidence on policymaking. Referencing social science research broadly, the report drew a dismal conclusion: scientific evidence could be seen to have only a minimal impact on policy decisions and it is unclear why this is the case. It is problematic that a gap exists between scientific evidence and policy decisions because each year the government allocates substantial funds to social science research in the hope that the evidence generated will inform policymaking. Accordingly, the National Research Council report called for a thorough investigation of the mechanisms underlying the use of social science research in policymaking as well as an assessment of the complex nature of the policymaking process (NRC, 2012).

The concept of "translational criminology" was proposed as a way to address the disconnect between criminological research and criminal justice policies and practices. Coined by the then-Director of the National Institute of Justice, translational criminology seeks to bridge this gap by appraising the processes by which scientific evidence is converted to policies and by forming interactive relationships between policymakers and criminologists (Laub, 2012). The fundamental belief that research evidence can improve the effectiveness, fairness, and efficiency of criminal justice policies motivates both translational criminology and more broadly the theme of the National Research Council's report. Translational criminology offers a research agenda that will allow criminologists to investigate the use of scientific evidence in criminal justice policymaking and uncover ways to improve the impact of research in a criminal justice context.

In this chapter we provide an overview of translational criminology, its goals, and offer a translational research agenda. Next, we discuss the benefits and challenges to pursuing translational criminology as a means to integrate scientific evidence into policy discussions. We end with suggestions for concrete steps moving forward.

Translational criminology

Translational criminology offers promise for unpacking the complexities of policymaking in a criminal justice context. With a research agenda that prioritizes conducting rigorous yet relevant scientific research, translational criminology seeks to understand how and when empirical findings are used or not used by criminal justice decision-makers (Laub, 2012). Translational criminology serves as a vehicle to move beyond the rhetoric regarding the lack of research influence on policy by devising innovative dissemination strategies and developing an understanding of the processes underlying program implementation.

Bringing research evidence to bear on policy decisions requires a cogent understanding of the knowledge application process (Laub, 2013). Primarily, criminal justice policymakers must be aware of research findings in order to use them in decision-making. This point may seem obvious, but a survey conducted by the International Association of Chiefs of Police in 2011 revealed that only one-third of police practitioners consult academic journals when making policy decisions (Lum et al., 2012; Alpert et al., 2013). Other studies reveal that decision-makers prioritize information produced by professional associations or interests groups over empirical evidence from academic journals (Tseng, 2012). These findings are concerning given that most criminologists aim to publish their research in refereed journals. In order to target policymakers most efficiently, it is essential to identify the sources they utilize to access research evidence. Additionally, it will be beneficial to map the social networks that provide decision-makers with empirical evidence (Tseng, 2012).

Translational criminology also calls for a thorough examination of how criminological research is converted into policies and implemented in practical settings (see, for example, Piquero, 2014). As a discipline, criminology has made strides toward identifying what works; but knowing that an intervention works does not ensure successful program delivery (Sherman, 2013). Sampson and colleagues (2013) argue that successful implementation requires knowledge of the causal mechanism underlying an intervention. Knowing why a policy is or is not successful is necessary to combat delivery challenges faced in different settings. Attention to contextual variation and outcome heterogeneity is also crucial for policymaking because policies are often implemented across multiple, diverse locations (for more details, see Sampson et al., 2013 and Granger, 2011).

Beyond knowledge application, translational criminology seeks to merge the research and policy worlds through collaboration, communication, and trust (Laub, 2012). Translational criminology aims to transcend the dichotomy of basic and applied research to produce rigorous policy-relevant research that is informed by criminological theory. Both researchers and practitioners and policymakers are essential to knowledge creation. Criminologists provide theoretical expertise to inform policies as well as knowledge of statistical or methodological techniques to determine the effectiveness of these policies. In exchange, practitioners and policymakers offer insight about the context a program will be implemented within and the organizational constraints of their agencies. Through bidirectional communication, researchers and policymakers can use criminological research to devise effective solutions to relevant problems that are feasible for the agency to implement. In doing so, basic and applied research coalesce toward creating a more effective, fair, and efficient criminal justice system.

Forming relationships that facilitate integration of scientific evidence into policy requires trust and mutual respect; however, there is a fair degree of skepticism in both camps regarding collaboration (see Laub, 2016). Researchers often do not acknowledge the professional expertise of policymakers as legitimate or relevant to scientific research. Conversely, policymakers may not see criminological research as objective or relevant to specific policy questions. Developing relationships that lead to the institution of evidence-based policies requires researchers and policymakers to view one another as equal partners in the knowledge creation process. Translational criminology can facilitate a dynamic interface between researchers and policymakers and serve as a vehicle towards the co-production of knowledge (Laub, 2013).

The National Institute of Justice (NIJ) is actively pursuing the ideas of translational criminology in a number of ways. For example, NIJ made four awards (three grants and one fellowship) directed at cultivating strategies to better understand and improve the use of research evidence in criminal justice decision-making (NIJ, 2014). The recipients will address topics including the effectiveness of NIJ dissemination efforts and the social networks through which empirical evidence is shared (Award number 2014-IJ-CX-0033), cross-sector research utilization (Award number 2014-IJ-CX-0032), the impact of collaboration between researchers and policymakers on research utilization (Award number 2014-IJ-CX-0035), and the process of defining and implementing evidence-based policies (Award number 2014-IJ-CX-0034). Moreover, each year NIJ funds multiple collaborations between criminologists and criminal justice agencies in an effort to encourage translational research (NIJ, 2014).[2] The hope is that this line of research will help us better understand both the obstacles to and facilitators of the use of evidence in the criminal justice policy world. (For research on this topic from other fields, see Oliver et al., 2014 and Kothari et al., 2009.)

Benefits of translational criminology in a policy context

The call for more thorough research on using scientific evidence by the National Research Council and the push toward translational research in criminology should not be interpreted as a claim that criminal justice agencies are ignoring science or enacting senseless policies writ large. Quite the opposite is true. In recent years, criminology as a discipline has made notable progress toward informing policy with scientific evidence (Petersilia, 1991; Petersilia, 2014). With initiatives such as the Bureau of Justice Assistance's Justice Reinvestment, the U.S. Justice Department's Violence Reduction Network, the expansion of drug courts, or the increased prevalence of researcher practitioner partnerships, the criminal justice system has clearly demonstrated a commitment to using scientific evidence to improve its practices and policies.

Now is an opportune time to pursue translational criminology. In particular, it is crucial to gauge why a program worked and how it was successfully implemented. Through this inquiry we can identify challenges that thwarted the success of evidence-based programs and discern areas for future improvement. In a time of budget deficits and limited resources, it is more important than ever to allocate funds to programs that produce desired outcomes in a cost-effective manner; therefore it is imperative that scientific evidence expose efficient and effective policies along with an understanding of the methods to deliver them. It is also essential to divert funding away from ineffective policies so that resources are not wasted.

Criminologists are often isolated from policymaking and therefore know little of the inherent complexities. Through the dynamic interface that translational criminology fosters, criminologists are exposed to the policymaking process and enlightened to the factors that affect decision-making. Direct involvement and exposure to policymaking may afford criminologists an appreciation of the policy world and steer criminologists toward investigating policy-relevant issues in the future (Petersilia, 2008; Braga, 2013). Understanding the multiple considerations that policymakers must consider will help criminologists devise feasible solutions to policy issues that are theoretically justified.

It may be challenging to bring research to bear on politically contentious issues or on policies that are highly visible in politics and the media. However, there are times when the political climate is right for change (Tonry, 2010). By pursuing the research agenda set forth by translational criminology and developing an understanding of how policies are made in criminal justice organizations, it may be possible to identify or anticipate windows of opportunity (Tonry and Green, 2003). Familiarity with policy-making may facilitate proactive strategies to capitalize on moments when change is needed.

Social scientists possess the training and expertise to conduct quality research and develop a comprehensive understanding of crime, its causes, and the potential solutions (Petersilia, 1991; Uggen and Inderbitzen, 2010). Tracing the historical development of criminology as a discipline reveals that in its earliest stage, criminology was directly linked to public policy and research focused almost solely on solving practical problems (Laub, 1983; Petersilia, 1991). Through translational criminology we can reaffirm the field's ties with policymakers and practitioners and improve the criminal justice system in tangible ways.

Challenges to translational criminology in a policy context

A prominent challenge to integrating criminological research and policy is the quality of the extant research (see Laub, 2016). Relatively few studies utilize randomized control trials, which provide the most reliable evidence as to whether an intervention has worked or not. Poor quality data and lack of data further inhibit researchers from conducting rigorous evaluations and studies. Though evidence can be used to inform and improve policies, the quality of that evidence is crucial; policy decisions should be guided by rigorous and reliable findings, which criminological research often lacks.

Regardless of whether criminological research is value-free, policymaking is inherently political (see NRC, 2012). When policies are made, parties with different values and priorities are competing for power. In this realm, criminological research provides little guidance as to which policy *should* be enacted (NRC, 2012). Instead, evidence from criminological studies demonstrates what is likely to happen if a specific option is chosen. It is up to the discretion of policymakers to determine how a certain program or intervention will be perceived in the public arena and which course of action satisfies most parties. Observational studies of policy discussions reveal that it is common for policymakers to twist scientific evidence or selectively mention research findings to support a predetermined position (Weiss, 2000; Dionne, 2014).[3]

When criminological research is considered in policy decisions, it is only one of the many factors that are discussed. Other important considerations include: financial constraints, voter preferences, the political implications of an intervention, the past experiences of policymakers, media coverage of the topic, and the positions of advocacy and/or interest groups (NRC, 2012). Policymakers are tasked with sifting through these diverse and competing factors and weighing the interests of multiple parties in selecting a course of action. As such, the view that scientific evidence is simply another opinion at the policy table rather than as an objective voice may be damaging because nothing differentiates scientific evidence from the other numerous factors. If this is the case, the intrinsic value of scientific evidence to provide information on a policy's effectiveness or to shed light on the potential implications of a particular strategy is not realized.

Very few problems within the criminal justice system are limited to one area. The causes and consequences of crime are complex, so devising an effective crime policy may require collaboration between multiple agencies. For instance, the success of Operation Ceasefire in Boston was contingent upon the collaboration between the Boston police, parole and probation departments, the faith community, federal prosecutors, youth workers, and multiple social service providers (Kennedy, 1997). Cross-sector collaboration can be challenging to initiate and sustain. Moreover, if diverse parties are consulted, research from multiple disciplines may need to be considered to fully inform policy decisions. Scholars in different fields use different methodologies and present findings in different formats. Without research training it is likely difficult for decision-makers to evaluate research from all relevant disciplines collectively (NRC, 2012).

It has been argued for a long time that academic criminology and public policy are two distinct worlds governed by inherently different values, goals, routines, and rewards (Caplan, 1979). The gap between research and policy poses two additional challenges to translating criminological research: time and reward structures. With regard to time, the research process is time consuming and demanding when executed properly (Skogan, 2010). Policymaking on the other hand happens rapidly, often in response to a crisis. Decision-makers cannot wait for criminologists to conduct an experiment or collect data on a pressing issue; they need immediate answers in order to act quickly. If relevant research on the issue at hand is not available or cannot be accessed quickly, policy decisions will be made in the absence of criminological research (see Laub, 2016).

The reward structure within academia is also not favorably disposed toward applied research. Instead, tenure review processes are governed by the quality and number of publications on an individual's CV, which often reflect a basic research agenda (Petersilia, 1991). Influencing policy decisions involves a large time commitment and goes unrewarded unless the experience results in a peer-reviewed publication. The perception that applied research will not advance an academic career deters criminologists, and younger criminologists especially, from engaging in policy-relevant research (Petersilia, 2008; Tonry, 2010).[4]

Concrete steps: moving forward

In light of the benefits and challenges to integrating policy and criminological research, how can we ensure that this translation process occurs in the future? First, we must accept that policymaking will never be based solely on research evidence. As Ron Haskins said, "Ideology will always trump evidence" (December 1, 2014).[5] Moreover, when criminological research is used in policy decisions, the influence may not be direct or apparent. Petersilia (1991) notes that untenable expectations about how policymaking should occur may distort perceptions of how research evidence has influenced policies in the past. The perspective that criminological research has not and cannot have influence on policy decisions is incorrect but also damaging because it may deter criminologists from translational research. We need to be realistic about the limitations of our findings without undermining or discrediting the value of criminological research and theory to policymaking.

Second, bringing research evidence to policy discussions will likely require diverse dissemination efforts. As mentioned above, much criminological research does not reach its intended audiences, especially if published exclusively in academic journals. A multifaceted approach may be most effective for reaching policymakers. This approach could involve publishing in diverse locations and creating more concise, "user-friendly" research products that clearly define the policy relevance of the findings.[6] Criminologists must also keep up with technological and social media advances and develop an online and social media presence (Lubienski et al., 2014; Laub, 2016). For example, NIJ could tweet a "research finding of the week" to inform others of the work they are producing. Online databases such as crimesolutions.gov are a step in the right direction toward effective dissemination, but more explicit effort to distribute information efficiently to policymakers is necessary.

Third, encourage imposed research use so that government agencies restrict funding to only evidence-based programs, which will perpetuate the influence of science in criminal justice policy. Government agencies hold the ability to divert resources from ineffective programs towards policies that are reliably effective and evidence-based. Before funding can be allocated towards effective programs it is essential to rigorously identify which programs are effective, by what standards, and under what conditions (Sampson et al., 2013; Orszag, 2014). It is also important to assess how easily programs can be implemented with fidelity. Accordingly, the federal government and funding agencies should support rigorous program and policy evaluation, coupled with implementation studies.

Many criminal justice agencies are already making strides to achieve these ends. For example, the Bureau of Justice Assistance (BJA) in the Office of Justice Programs names as two of their five strategic goals as infusing research into the agency's policies and routines and improving program effectiveness with data. A review of the policies that the BJA funded in 2014 reveals that nearly all initiatives are evidence-based and many include technical training or assistance for staff to ease implementation with fidelity. For example, BJA's SMART programs establish researcher–practitioner partnerships to develop and evaluate data-driven programs in policing, criminal courts, and probation (BJA, 2014, see also Rojek et al., 2015).

A final suggestion moving forward is for academic institutions to earnestly consider the value of applied research and integrate criteria to reward policy relevant work in tenure and promotion decisions. At present the reward structure within academia discourages applied research because it translates to fewer publications in top tier journals, which policymakers and practitioners rarely read. Moreover, graduate students should be encouraged to pursue more applied research. Perhaps as an incentive NIJ could set aside a number of dissertation fellowships for research projects that focus on translational criminology.

In sum, the criminological research community must craft research agendas that are relevant for policy and practice. This is the core idea of translational criminology. However, it is important to point out that highlighting policy and practice does not mean we are calling for an abandonment of theory (see Laub, 2004). Ideas matter and, ultimately, it is our ideas that will shape public policies moving forward.

Notes

1 There are varying definitions as to what constitutes evidence which is potentially problematic for the creation of evidence-based policies and practices. For this chapter, we define evidence as empirical findings derived from systematic research methods.
2 Another strategy used by NIJ is to provide better research synthesis to policymakers and practitioners. See www.crimesolutions.gov.
3 One should not underestimate the threat to science that exists in the United States Congress today. For example, see Prewitt (2013) for an illuminating discussion of this issue. Moreover, in the criminal justice arena ideological positions on guns have hampered basic data collection efforts (see The Editorial Board, 2014). For an illustration of cuts in data collection outside of criminal justice see Wolfers, 2014.
4 In a recent essay on his work with the St. Louis police department, Rosenfeld makes an excellent observation that age and experience are crucial for making a partnership successful. Rosenfeld states "I could not have done this earlier in my career" (2014:7). As an untenured faculty he could not have devoted the extensive time it takes to maintain an active partnership. Nor did he have the confidence in his professional judgment earlier in his career. Moving forward Rosenfeld

recommends pairing senior and junior faculty in order to enhance the likelihood of a successful partnership.

5 For an interesting discussion of the clash between scientific research and beliefs see Nyhan, 2014. He states "With science as with politics, identity often trumps the facts."

6 An example is NIJ's "Five Things" Series. This series is designed to synthesize rigorous scientific research into a one page handout. See *Five Things Law Enforcement Executives Can Do to Make a Difference* for an illustration.

References

Alpert, G.P., Rojek. J., and Hansen, J.A. (2013). *Building bridges between police researchers and practitioners: Agents of change in a complex world.* Final report submitted to the U.S. Department of Justice.

Blumstein, A. (2013). Linking evidence and criminal justice policy. *Criminology and Public Policy*, 12(4), 721–730.

Braga, A.A. (2013). Embedded criminologists in police departments. *Ideas in American Policing*, 17, 1–19.

Bureau of Justice Assistance (2014). U.S. Department of Justice's Violence Reduction Network. Accessed on December 11, 2014. www.bja.gov/Programs/VRN.html.

Caplan, N. (1979). The two-communities theory and knowledge utilization. *American Behavioral Scientist* 22, 459–470.

Dionne Jr., E.J. (2014, December 7). In politics, does evidence matter? *The Washington Post*, www.washingtonpost.com/opinions/ej-dionne-in-politics-does-evidence-matter/2014/12/07/a819969c-7ca3-11e4-b821-503cc7efed9e_story.html.

Granger, R. (2011). The big why: A learning agenda for the scale-up movement. *Pathways* Winter, 28–32.

Haskins, R. (2014, December 1). Show me the evidence: Obama's fight for rigor and results in social policy. Presentation at Brookings Institution, Washington, DC. Retrieved from www.brookings.edu/~/media/events/2014/12/01%20show%20me%20evidence/haskinsr ppt.pdf.

Haskins, R. and Margolis, G. (2014). *Show me the evidence: Obama's fight for rigor and results in social policy.* Washington, DC: Brookings Institution Press.

Kennedy, D.M. (1997). Pulling levers: Chronic offenders, high crime settings, and a theory of prevention. *Valparaiso University Law Review*, 31(2), 449–484.

Kothari, A., McLean, L., and Edwards, N. (2009). Increasing capacity for knowledge translation: Understanding how some researchers engage policy-makers. *Health Studies Publications*, Paper 8, 1–20.

Laub, J.H. (1983). *Criminology in the Making: An Oral History.* Boston: Northeastern University Press.

Laub, J.H. (2004). The life course of criminology in the United States – The American Society of Criminology 2003 Presidential Address. *Criminology*, 42(1), 1–26.

Laub, J.H. (2012). Translational criminology. *Translational Criminology*, Fall, 4–5.

Laub, J.H. (2013). Moving the National Institute of Justice Forward: July 2010 thru December 2012. Newsletter of the Crime, Law, and Deviance section of the American Sociological Association, Spring/Summer 2013.

Laub, J.H. (2016). Life course research and the shaping of public policy. In Shanahan, M., Mortimer, J., and Johnson, M.K. (Eds.). *Handbook of the Life Course: Volume II*. New York: Springer, pp. 623–637.

Lubienski, C., Scott, J., and DeBray, E. (2014). The politics of research production, promotion, and utilization in educational policy. *Educational Policy*, 28(2), 131–144.

Lum, C., Telep, C.W., Koper, C.S., and Greico, J. (2012). Receptivity to research in policing. *Justice Research and Policy*, 14(1), 61–95.

National Institute of Justice Website (2014). Fiscal year 2014 awards. *National Institute of Justice*. Retrieved from www.nij.gov/funding/awards/pages/awards-list.aspx?solicitationid=3759.

National Institute of Justice Website (2014). *Five Things Law Enforcement Executives Can Do to Make a Difference*. Retrieved from www.nij.gov/five-things/pages/law-enforcement-executives.aspx.

National Research Council (2012). *Using Science as Evidence in Public Policy*. Committee on the Use of Social Science Knowledge in Public Policy. K. Prewitt, T.A. Schwandt, and M.L. Straf (Eds.). Division of Behavior and Social Sciences and Education, Washington, DC: The National Academies Press.

Nyhan, B. (2014). When beliefs and facts collide. *The New York Times*, July 5, 2014.

Oliver, K., Innvar, S., Lorenc, T., Woodman, J., and Thomas, J. (2014). A systematic review of barriers to and facilitators of the use of evidence by policymakers. *BMC Health Services Research* 14(2), 1–12.

Orszag, P. (2014, December 1). Show me the evidence: Obama's fight for rigor and results in social policy. Presentation at Brookings Institution, Washington, DC. Retrieved from www.brookings.edu/~/media/events/2014/12/01-show-me-evidence/orszag_ppt.pdf.

Petersilia, J. (1991). Policy relevance and the future of criminology: The American Society of Criminology 1990 Presidential Address. *Criminology*, 29(1), 1–15.

Petersilia, J. (2008). Influencing public policy: An embedded criminologist reflects on California prison reform. *Journal of Experimental Criminology*, 4(4), 335–356.

Petersilia, J. (2014, November 21). Roundtable discussant: Has science taken hold in criminal justice? The Annual Meeting of the American Society of Criminology, San Francisco, CA.

Piquero, A. (2014). Moving from description to implementation of evidence-based research findings. *Criminology and Public Policy*, 13(1), 127–134.

Prewitt, K. (2013). Is any science safe? *Science* 340, 525.

Rojek, J., Martin, P., and Alpert, G. (2015). *Developing and Maintaining Police-Researcher Partnerships to Facilitate Research Use: A Comparative Analysis*. New York: Springer.

Rosenfeld, R. (2014). The St. Louis public safety partnership. *Translational Criminology* Fall, 6–8.

Sampson, R.J., Winship, C., and Knight, C. (2013). Translating causal claims: Principles and strategies for policy-relevant criminology. *Criminology and Public Policy*, 12(4), 587–616.

Sherman, L.W. (2013). The rise of evidence-based policing: Targeting, testing, and tracking. In Tonry, M. (Ed.) *Crime and Justice in America: 1975–2025*. Chicago: University of Chicago Press, pp. 377–451.

Skogan, W. G. (2010). The challenge of timeliness and utility in research and evaluation. In Klofas. J.M. and McGarrell E.F. (Eds.), *The New Criminal Justice: American Communities and the Changing World of Crime Control.* New York, NY: Routledge, pp. 128–131.

The Editorial Board (2014). Legislating ignorance about guns. *The New York Times,* June 16, 2014.

Tonry, M. (2010). "Public criminology" and evidence-based policy. *Criminology and Public Policy,* 9(4), 783–797.

Tonry, M. and Green, D. (2003). Criminology and public policy in the USA and UK. In Zedner, L. and Ashworth, A. (Eds.), *The Criminological Foundations of Penal Policy: Essays in Honour of Roger Hood.* Oxford, UK: Oxford University Press.

Tseng, V. (2012). The use of research in policy and practice. *Social Policy Report,* 26, 1–16.

Uggen, C. and Inderbitzen, M. (2010). Public criminologies. *Criminology and Public Policy,* 9(4), 725–749.

Weiss, C.H. (2000). The experimenting society in a public world. In L. Bickman (Ed.), *Validity and Social Experimentation.* Thousand Oaks, CA: Sage Publications, pp. 283–302.

Wolfers, J. (2014). Census Bureau's plan to cut marriage and divorce questions has academics up in arms. *The New York Times,* December 31, 2014.

Part II

Crime prevention

Crime prevention

Introduction

Individual, family, and community prevention programs

Thomas G. Blomberg, Julie Mestre Brancale, Kevin M. Beaver and William D. Bales

The criminal justice system is largely viewed as a reactive vehicle that typically responds to and deals with criminal offenses and criminal offenders after a law has been violated. When it comes to most aspects of the criminal justice system, this reactive approach is all that is available. In recent years, however, there has been growing interest in the ways that proactive approaches can be implemented to prevent criminal events from occurring altogether. This interest has generated a body of research evidence revealing that proactive programs and policies can be effective when used strategically by the criminal justice system. The programs and policies that focus on the prevention of crime and criminals, in particular, tend to offer some of the most effective long-term solutions for significant reductions in crime. This section of the volume contains a collection of chapters that explores in detail some of these influential crime prevention strategies.

In Chapter 5, David Farrington examines a number of delinquency prevention programs that have been shown to be effective at reducing delinquent behaviors. Given that delinquent and criminal behavior tend to show extremely high levels of stability over the life course, and given that most of the serious, chronic offenders begin to display antisocial behaviors in childhood, prevention programs that are provided early in life can be particularly effective. Farrington reviews some of the key aspects and consistent findings in delinquency prevention as related to family-based programs, school-based programs, and programs that focus on skill training. What is particularly important in this chapter is Farrington's focus upon studies that use rigorous research designs, including those that implement randomized experimental designs and those with long-term follow-up periods. Based on the best available evidence, Farrington concludes that delinquency prevention programs can be quite effective at reducing offending behaviors and they represent a cost-savings alternative to other, more punitive types of programs.

Chapter 6, by Abigail Fagan, examines in closer detail some policies that focus on strengthening the family in delinquency prevention. A focus on the family is particularly relevant because the family has taken on central importance for etiological theories of crime and delinquency, with research findings consistently pointing to the possible causal role of the family in the development of delinquent behavior. Fagan uses this body of research as a basis to examine some family-based policies that appear to reduce delinquency. Specifically, she explores the role of parent-training and family therapy as they relate to delinquency prevention. She also discusses opportunities for the enactment of public policy based on these family-based research findings. Fagan concludes by noting that family-based prevention programs have consistently been shown to be effective across a wide range of heterogeneous samples and thus these types of programs should continue to be used and expanded by the criminal justice system.

David Kennedy, in Chapter 7, focuses upon community crime prevention. As Kennedy points out, community crime prevention is frequently viewed as being secondary to crime prevention efforts employed by the criminal justice system. However, Kennedy contends that this is an incorrect view and that community crime prevention efforts should be viewed as being quite central and perhaps even superordinate to that of the criminal justice system. In developing his argument, Kennedy explores the dominant role of community crime prevention, the ways in which community crime prevention can be undermined, and reviews research findings which strongly suggest that community crime prevention is effective at reducing crime and recidivism. Based upon this research evidence, Kennedy urges more efforts and resources be funneled into large-scale community crime prevention initiatives.

This section on crime prevention concludes with Chapter 8, by Rob Gurette, Shane Johnson, and Kate Bowers, that examines some of the main facets of situational crime prevention. The authors provide a comprehensive review of the situational crime prevention approach, including its theoretical underpinnings, and a systematic analysis of the existing research literature. Their review shows convincingly that situational crime prevention efforts can achieve significant reductions in crime by removing opportunities for offending behaviors.

Proactive crime prevention approaches have received a growing amount of attention in recent years. Largely due to the fiscal crisis, policymakers have begun to look for more effective and cost-efficient means of crime prevention and control. Historically, some policymakers have been hesitant to support proactive prevention programs because of their up-front costs and the delay in observing returns. However, the available research literature has consistently shown that crime prevention programs, if implemented appropriately, are a cost-effective method of criminal justice policy and practice. As demonstrated in this section, methods of crime prevention come in many forms. Farrington (Chapter 5) presents a compelling case for the effectiveness of juvenile delinquency prevention programs, Fagan (Chapter 6) highlights the effectiveness of family-based programs for reducing delinquency, and Kennedy (Chapter 7) and Gurette, Johnson, and Bowers (Chapter 8) discuss the strengths of community-based prevention programs. For the greatest return on their investment, state and local policymakers can partner with researchers to determine which type of program or programs would be most suitable for the target population and specific crime problem(s) in question.

Chapter 5

Juvenile delinquency prevention programs

David P. Farrington

The main aim of this chapter is to summarize briefly some of the most effective programs for preventing delinquency whose effectiveness has been demonstrated in high quality evaluation research. The focus is especially on programs that have been evaluated in randomized experiments with reasonably large samples, since the effect of any intervention on delinquency can be demonstrated most convincingly in such experiments (Farrington and Welsh, 2005, 2006). There is also a focus on randomized experiments with long-term follow-ups, which make it possible to determine if effects persist or wear off over time (Farrington and Welsh, 2013).

A second aim is to review what is known about the monetary costs and benefits of these programs. The most extensive information about these has been compiled by the Washington State Institute for Public Policy or WSIPP (see Lee et al., 2012; www.wsipp.wa.gov/benefitcost, updated to December 2014). As a result of this information, the Washington State legislature abandoned plans to build two new state prisons and in their place approved a sizable spending package on evidence-based intervention programs (Drake et al., 2009). The Pew charitable Trusts then funded WSIPP to apply their cost–benefit methods to other states (Aos and Drake, 2010).

Family-based prevention

Family programs are usually targeted on risk factors such as poor parental supervision and inconsistent discipline. The most important types of family-based programs are home visiting programs (especially the work of David Olds), parent training programs (especially those used by Carolyn Webster-Stratton and Matthew Sanders), home or community programs with older children (especially those implemented by James Alexander and Patricia Chamberlain) and Multisystemic Therapy or MST (devised by Scott Henggeler).

Home visiting programs

In the most famous intensive home visiting program, Olds, Henderson, Chamberlin, and Tatelbaum (1986) in Elmira (New York State) randomly allocated 400 mothers either to receive home visits from nurses during pregnancy, or to receive visits both during pregnancy and during the first two years of life, in addition to a control group who received no visits. Each visit lasted about one and a quarter hours, and the mothers were visited on average every two weeks. The home visitors gave advice about prenatal and postnatal care of the child, about infant development, and about the importance of proper nutrition and avoiding smoking and drinking during pregnancy. Therefore, this was a general parent education program.

In a 15-year follow-up, the effects on delinquency of this Nurse Family Partnership (NFP) program were evaluated. Among lower class unmarried mothers, those who received prenatal and postnatal home visits had fewer arrests than those who received prenatal visits or no visits (Olds et al., 1997). Also, children of these mothers who received prenatal and/or postnatal home visits had less than half as many arrests as children of mothers who received no visits (Olds et al., 1998). More recently, Eckenrode et al. (2010) followed up this experiment to age 19, and found that 25 percent of the treated children were arrested, compared with 37 percent of the controls; the desirable effects were much greater for girls. (For reviews of home visiting programs, see Bilukha et al., 2005; Olds et al., 2007). The benefit–cost ratio for the NFP program is 2.77 according to WSIPP and 2.90 according to Miller (2013).

Parent management training

One of the most famous parent training programs was developed by Carolyn Webster-Stratton (1998, 2000) in Seattle. She evaluated its success by randomly allocating 426 children aged 4 (most with single mothers on welfare) either to an experimental group which received parent training or to a control group which did not. The experimental mothers met in groups every week for 8 or 9 weeks, watched videotapes demonstrating parenting skills, and then took part in focussed group discussions. The topics included how to play with your child, helping your child learn, using praise and encouragement to bring out the best in your child, effective setting of limits, handling misbehavior, how to teach your child to solve problems, and how to give and get support. An immediate follow-up showed that the experimental children behaved better than the control children, and Webster-Stratton, Rinaldi, and Jamila (2011) later found that immediate reports of child behavior problems predicted self-reported delinquency eight to twelve years later. O'Neill, McGilloway, Donnelly,

Bywater, and Kelly (2013) estimated a benefit-to-cost ratio of 1.66 for this program. The WSIPP figure is 1.19. (For reviews of parent training programs, see Piquero et al., 2009.)

Sanders, Markie-Dadds, Tully, and Bor (2000) in Brisbane, Australia, developed the Triple-P Parenting program. This program either can be delivered to the whole community in primary prevention using the mass media or can be used in secondary prevention with high-risk or clinic samples. Sanders evaluated the success of Triple-P with over 300 high-risk children aged 3 years by randomly allocating them either to receive Triple-P or to be in a control group. The Triple-P program involves teaching parents 17 child management strategies including talking with children, giving physical affection, praising, giving attention, setting a good example, setting rules, giving clear instructions, and using appropriate penalties for misbehavior ("time-out," or sending the child to his or her room). The evaluation showed that Triple-P was successful in reducing children's antisocial behavior. The effectiveness of Triple-P has been confirmed in meta-analyses by Thomas and Zimmer-Gembeck (2007), Nowak and Heinrichs (2008), et al. (2014). According to WSIPP, the benefit-to-cost ratio for Triple-P is 1.74.

Programs for older children

Another parenting intervention, termed Functional Family Therapy (FFT), was developed by James Alexander in Utah (Alexander and Parsons, 1973). This aimed to modify patterns of family interaction by modelling, prompting and reinforcement, to encourage clear communication between family members about requests and solutions, and to minimize conflict. Essentially, all family members were trained to negotiate effectively, to set clear rules about privileges and responsibilities, and to use techniques of reciprocal reinforcement with each other. The program was evaluated by randomly allocating 86 delinquents to experimental or control conditions. The results showed that this technique halved the recidivism rate of minor delinquents in comparison with other approaches (client-centered or psychodynamic therapy). Its effectiveness with more serious offenders has been replicated in many studies with high quality designs (Barton et al., 1985; Sexton and Alexander, 2000; Sexton and Turner, 2010). The benefit-to-cost ratio is 8.94 according to WSIPP, but 1.92 according to Taxy, Liberman, Roman, and Downey (2012).

Chamberlain and Reid (1998) in Oregon evaluated Multidimensional Treatment Foster Care (MTFC), which was used as an alternative to custody for delinquents. Custodial sentences for delinquents were thought to have undesirable effects especially because of the bad influence of delinquent peers. In MTFC, families in the community were recruited and trained to provide a placement for delinquent youths. The MTFC youths were closely supervised at home, in the community, and in the school, and their contacts with delinquent peers were minimized. The foster parents provided a structured daily living environment, with clear rules and limits, consistent discipline for rule violations and one-to-one monitoring. The youths were encouraged to develop academic skills and desirable work habits.

In the evaluation, 79 chronic male delinquents were randomly assigned to MTFC or to regular group homes where they lived with other delinquents. A one-year follow-up showed that the MTFC boys had fewer criminal referrals and lower self-reported delinquency. Therefore, this program seemed to be an effective treatment for delinquency. Similarly encouraging results were obtained in an evaluation of MTFC for delinquent girls (Chamberlain et al., 2007). The effectiveness of MTFC has been confirmed in systematic reviews (Hahn et al., 2005; Turner and MacDonald, 2011). Its benefit-to-cost ratio is 2.13 according to WSIPP, but 5.28 according to OJJDP Model Programs.

Multisystemic therapy

Multisystemic Therapy (MST) is an important multiple-component family preservation program that was developed by Henggeler, et al. (2009) in South Carolina. The particular type of treatment is chosen according to the particular needs of the youth. Therefore, the nature of the treatment is different for each person. MST is delivered in the youth's home, school and community settings. The treatment typically includes family intervention to promote the parent's ability to monitor and discipline the adolescent, peer intervention to encourage the choice of prosocial friends, and school intervention to enhance competence and school achievement.

In an evaluation by Henggeler et al. (1993), 84 serious delinquents (with an average age of 15) were randomly assigned either to receive MST or the usual treatment (which mostly involved placing the juvenile outside home). The results showed that the MST group had fewer arrests and fewer self-reported crimes in a one-year follow-up. In another evaluation in Missouri, Borduin et al. (1995) randomly assigned 176 juvenile offenders (with an average age of 14) either to MST or to individual therapy focussing on personal, family and academic issues. Four years later, only 26 percent of the MST offenders had been rearrested, compared with 71 percent of the individual therapy group. Later follow-ups to age 29 (Schaeffer and Borduin, 2005) and age 37 (Sawyer and Borduin, 2011) confirmed the cumulative benefits of MST. Other evaluations by Henggeler and his colleagues (1997, 1999, 2002) have also produced impressive results (see also Baldwin et al., 2012; Curtis et al. 2004). The benefit-to-cost ratio for MST is 9.51 according to Klietz et al. (2010), but 3.05 according to WSIPP.

School-based prevention

Most school-based prevention programs also had a family-based component.

Pre-school programs

The most famous pre-school intellectual enrichment program is the Perry project carried out in Ypsilanti (Michigan) by Schweinhart and Weikart (1980). This was essentially a "Head Start" program targeted on disadvantaged African-American children. A sample of 123 children were allocated (approximately at random) to experimental and control groups. The experimental children attended a daily pre-school program, backed up by weekly home visits, usually lasting two years (covering ages 3–4 years). The aim of the "plan-do-review" program was to provide intellectual stimulation, to increase thinking and reasoning abilities, and to increase later school achievement.

This program had long-term benefits. Berrueta-Clement et al. (1984) showed that, at age 19, the experimental group was more likely to be employed, more likely to have graduated from high school, more likely to have received college or vocational training, and less likely to have been arrested. By age 27, the experimental group had accumulated only half as many arrests on average as the controls (Schweinhart et al., 1993). Also, they had significantly higher earnings and were more likely to be home-owners. More of the experimental women were married, and fewer of their children were born to unmarried mothers.

The most recent follow-up of this program at age 40 found that it continued to make an important difference in the lives of the participants (Schweinhart et al., 2005). Compared to the control group, those who received the program had significantly fewer life-time arrests for violent crimes (32 percent vs. 48 percent), property crimes (36 percent vs. 56 percent), and drug crimes (14 percent vs. 34 percent), and they were significantly less likely to be arrested five or more times (36 percent vs. 55 percent). Improvements were also recorded in many other important life course outcomes. For example, significantly higher levels of schooling (77 percent vs. 60 percent graduating from high school), better records of employment (76 percent vs. 62 percent), and higher annual incomes were reported by the program group compared to the controls. The benefit-to-cost ratio of the Perry program was estimated to be 8.74 at age 27 and 17.07 (later revised to 16.14) at age 40. The WSIPP estimate for Head Start programs in general is 2.86.

School programs

One of the most important school-based prevention experiments was carried out in Seattle by Hawkins et al. (1991). They implemented a multiple component program (the Seattle Social Development Project or SSDP) combining parent training, teacher training and child skills training. About 500 first grade children (aged 6) in 21 classes in 8 schools were randomly assigned to be in experimental or control classes. The children in the experimental classes received special treatment at home and school which was designed to increase their attachment to their parents and their bonding to the school. Also, they were trained in interpersonal cognitive problem-solving. Their parents were trained to notice and reinforce socially desirable behavior in a program called "Catch them being good." Their teachers were trained in classroom management, for example to provide clear instructions and expectations to children, to reward children for participation in desired behavior, and to teach children prosocial (socially desirable) methods of solving problems.

This program had long-term benefits. By the sixth grade (age 12), experimental boys were less likely to have initiated delinquency, while experimental girls were less likely to have initiated drug use (O'Donnell et al., 1995). In a later follow-up, Hawkins et al. (1999) found that, at age 18, the full intervention group (those who received the intervention from grades 1–6) admitted less violence, less alcohol abuse and fewer sexual partners than the late intervention group (grades 5–6 only) or the control group. However, up to age 27, the beneficial effects on sexual behavior (e.g. in reducing sexually transmitted diseases) were still apparent, but the beneficial effects on offending had reduced considerably (Hawkins et al., 2008). The beneficial effects on sexual behavior continued up to age 30 (Hill et al., 2014). According to WSIPP, the benefit-to-cost ratio of the SSDP is 4.94.

Skills training

The most important prevention techniques that target the risk factors of impulsiveness and low empathy are cognitive-behavioral skills training programs, which have been recently reviewed by Zara and Farrington (2014). For example, the "Stop Now and Plan" (SNAP) program is one of the most important skills training programs for children aged 6–11. It was developed in Toronto by Augimeri et al. (2011). Children referred by the police for problematic behavior are taught to calm down, take deep breaths, and count to 10 when they are angry. They are also taught coping statements and effective solutions to interpersonal problems. Small-scale experiments by Augimeri et al. (2007) and Koegl et al. (2008) showed that SNAP was effective in reducing delinquency and aggression. This was confirmed by large-scale independent evaluations in Hamilton, Canada (Lipman et al., 2008) and Pittsburgh (Burke and Loeber, 2015). The benefit-to-cost ratio is at least 2.05 based on reduced convictions and at least 17.33 after scaling up to self-reported offending (Farrington and Koegl, 2015).

The Montreal Longitudinal-Experimental Study combined child skills training and parent training. Tremblay et al. (1995) identified disruptive (aggressive or hyperactive) boys at age 6, and randomly allocated over 300 of these to experimental or control conditions. Between ages 7 and 9, the experimental group received training designed to foster social skills and self-control. Coaching, peer modelling, role playing and reinforcement contingencies were used in small group sessions on such topics as "how to help," "what to do when you are angry," and "how to react to teasing." Also, their parents were trained using the parent management training techniques developed by Patterson (1982).

This prevention program was successful. By age 12, the experimental boys committed less burglary and theft, were less likely to get drunk, and were less likely to be involved in fights than the controls (according to self-reports). Also, the experimental boys had higher school achievement. At every age from 10 to 15, the experimental boys had lower self-reported delinquency scores than the control boys. Interestingly, the differences in antisocial behavior between experimental and control boys increased as the follow-up progressed. Later follow-ups showed that fewer experimental boys had a criminal record by age 24 (Boisjoli et al., 2007) and that the experimental boys self-reported less property crime at age 28 (Vitaro et al., 2013).

Conclusions

High quality evaluation research shows that many early intervention programs are effective in reducing delinquency. The best programs include general parent education in home visiting programs, parent management training, pre-school intellectual enrichment programs, child skills training, anti-bullying programs in schools, mentoring, FFT, MTFC and MST (Farrington, 2015; Farrington and Welsh, 2007). These programs could be implemented within a community prevention system such as Communities That Care, which is effective (Hawkins et al., 2009) and has a benefit-to-cost ratio of 5.25 (Kuklinski et al., 2012). While most is known about programs for boys, there are also effective interventions designed specifically for girls (Hipwell and Loeber, 2006). Importantly, early intervention programs often have long-lasting benefits (Dekovic et al., 2011; Manning et al., 2010).

In almost all cases, the monetary benefits of these programs have been shown to exceed their monetary costs. It is often difficult to compare different cost–benefit analyses because they take account of very different benefits. In particular, many analyses are based on reductions in officially recorded offenses, which are only the tip of the iceberg of offending. It is desirable to scale up to self-reported offenses to obtain a more realistic benefit-to-cost ratio. The great advantage of the WSIPP estimates is that all costs and benefits are calculated in a comparable way (for Washington State).

Despite this knowledge, government policymakers in many countries prefer to spend money on more police, courts, and prisons rather than on early intervention. Welsh and Farrington (2011) reviewed cost–benefit analyses of early intervention compared with imprisonment and concluded that early intervention was more likely to save money and reduce crime. Furthermore, when asked to choose, the public overwhelmingly supports the increased spending of tax dollars on youth prevention programs rather than on building more prisons.

The clear policy recommendations are:

- Implement delinquency prevention programs that have been proved to reduce crime and save money.
- Invest in early prevention rather than imprisonment.

References

Alexander, J. F. and Parsons, B. V. (1973). Short-term behavioral intervention with delinquent families: Impact on family process and recidivism. *Journal of Abnormal Psychology*, 81, 219–225.

Aos, S., and Drake, E. K. (2010). *Fight crime and save money*. Olympia, WA: Washington State Institute for Public Policy.

Augimeri, L. K., Farrington, D. P., Koegl, C. J., and Day, D. M. (2007). The SNAP Under 12 Outreach Project: Effects of a community based program for children with conduct problems. *Journal of Child and Family Studies*, 16, 799–807.

Augimeri, L. K., Walsh, M. M., Liddon, A. D., and Dassinger, C. R. (2011). From risk identification to risk management: A comprehensive strategy for young children engaged in antisocial behavior. In D. W. Springer and A. Roberts (eds.), *Juvenile justice and delinquency* (pp. 117–140). Sudbury, MA: Jones and Bartlett.

Baldwin, S. A., Christian, S., Berkeljon, A., Shadish, W., and Bean, R. (2012). The effects of family therapies for adolescent delinquency and substance abuse: A meta-analysis. *Journal of Marital and Family Therapy*, 38, 281–304.

Barton, C., Alexander, J. F., Waldron, H., Turner, C. W., and Warburton, J. (1985). Generalizing treatment effects of functional family therapy: Three replications. *American Journal of Family Therapy*, 13, 16–26.

Berrueta-Clement, J. R., Schweinhart, L. J., Barnett, W. S., Epstein, A. S., and Weikart, D. P. (1984). *Changed Lives: The effects of the Perry Preschool Program on youths through age 19*. Ypsilanti, MI: High/Scope Press.

Bilukha, O., Hahn, R. A., Crosby, A., Fullilove, M. T., Liberman, A., Moscicki, E., Snyder, S., Tuma, F., Corso, P., Schofield, A., and Briss, P. A. (2005). The effectiveness of early childhood home visitation in preventing violence. *American Journal of Preventive Medicine*, 28(2S1), 11–39.

Boisjoli, R., Vitaro, F., Lacourse, E., Barker, E. D., and Tremblay, R. E. (2007). Impact and clinical significance of a preventive intervention for disruptive boys. *British Journal of Psychiatry*, 191, 415–419.

Borduin, C. M., Mann, B. J., Cone, L. T., Henggeler, S. W., Fucci, B. R., Blaske, D. M., and Williams, R. A. (1995). Multisystemic treatment of serious juvenile offenders: Long-term prevention of criminality and violence. *Journal of Consulting and Clinical Psychology*, 63, 569–587.

Burke, J. D., and Loeber, R. (2015). The effectiveness of the Stop Now And Plan (SNAP) program for boys at risk for violence and delinquency. *Prevention Science*, in press.

Chamberlain, P., Leve, L.D., and DeGarmo, D.S. (2007). Multidimensional Treatment Foster Care for girls in the juvenile justice system: 2-year follow-up of a randomized clinical trial. *Journal of Consulting and Clinical Psychology*, 75, 187–193.

Chamberlain, P., and Reid, J. B. (1998). Comparison of two community alternatives to incarceration for chronic juvenile offenders. *Journal of Consulting and Clinical Psychology*, 66, 624–633.

Curtis, N. M., Ronan, K. R., and Borduin, C. M. (2004). Multisystemic treatment: A meta-analysis of outcome studies. *Journal of Family Psychology*, 18, 411–419.

Dekovic, M., Slagt, M. I., Asscher, J. J., Boendermaker, L., Eichelsteim, V. I., and Prinzie, P. (2011). Effects of early prevention programs on adult criminal offending: A meta-analysis. *Clinical Psychology Review*, 31, 532–544.

Drake, E. K., Aos, S., and, M. G. (2009). Evidence-based public policy options to reduce crime and criminal justice costs: Implications in Washington State. *Victims and Offenders*, 4,170–196.

Eckenrode, J., Campa, M., Luckey, D. W., Henderson, C. R., Cole, R., Kitzman, H., Anson, A., Sidora-Arcoleo, K., Powers, J., and Olds, D. (2010). Long-term effects of prenatal and infancy nurse home visitation on the life course of youths: 19-year follow-up of a randomized trial. *Archives of Pediatrics and Adolescent Medicine*, 164, 9–15.

Farrington, D. P. (2015) The developmental evidence base: Prevention. In G. J. Towl and D. A. Crighton (eds.), *Forensic psychology* (2nd ed.). Oxford: Blackwell, pp. 141–159.

Farrington, D. P., and Koegl. C. J. (2015). Monetary benefits and costs of the Stop Now And Plan program for boys aged 6–11, based on the prevention of later offending. *Journal of Quantitative Criminology*, vol. 31, pp. 263–287.

Farrington, D. P., and Welsh, B. C. (2005). Randomized experiments in criminology: What have we learned in the last two decades? *Journal of Experimental Criminology*, 1, 9–38.

Farrington, D. P., and Welsh, B. C. (2006). A half-century of randomized experiments on crime and justice. In M. Tonry (ed.), *Crime and justice*, vol. 34 (pp. 55–132). Chicago: University of Chicago Press.

Farrington, D. P., and Welsh. B. C. (2007). *Saving children from a life of crime: Early risk factors and effective interventions*. Oxford, UK: Oxford University Press.

Farrington, D. P., and Welsh, B. C. (2013). Randomized experiments in criminology: What has been learned from long-term follow-ups? In B. C. Welsh, A. A. Braga, and G. J. N. Bruinsma (eds.), *Experimental criminology: Prospects for advancing science and public policy* (pp. 111–140). New York: Cambridge University Press.

Hahn, R. A., Bilukha, O., Lowy, J., Crosby, A., Fullilove, M. T., Liberman, A., Moscicki, E., Synder, S., Tuma, F., Corso, P., and Schofield, A. (2005). The effectiveness of therapeutic foster care for the prevention of violence. *American Journal of Preventive Medicine*, 28(2S1), 72–90.

Hawkins, J. D., Catalano, R. F., Kosterman, R., Abbott, R., and Hill, K. G. (1999). Preventing adolescent health risk behaviors by strengthening protection during childhood. *Archives of Pediatrics and Adolescent Medicine*, 153, 226–234.

Hawkins, J. D., Kosterman, R., Catalano, R. F., Hill, K. G., and Abbott, R. D. (2008). Effects of social development intervention in childhood 15 years later. *Archives of Pediatrics and Adolescent Medicine*, 162, 1133–1141.

Hawkins, J. D., Oesterle, S., Brown, E. C., Arthur, M. W., Abbott, R. D., Fagan, A. A., and Catalano, R. F. (2009). Results of a type 2 translational research trial to prevent adolescent drug use and delinquency: A test of Communities That Care. *Archives of Pediatrics and Adolescent Medicine*, 163, 789–798.

Hawkins, J. D., Von Cleve, E., and Catalano, R. F. (1991). Reducing early childhood aggression: Results of a primary prevention program. *Journal of the American Academy of Child and Adolescent Psychiatry*, 30, 208–217.

Henggeler, S. W., Clingempeel, W. G., Brondino, M. J., and Pickrel, S. G. (2002). Four-year follow-up of multisystemic therapy with substance-abusing and substance-dependent juvenile offenders. *Journal of the American Academy of Child and Adolescent Psychiatry*, 41, 868–874.

Henggeler, S. W., Melton, G. B., Brondino, M. J., Scherer, D. G., and Hanley, J. H. (1997). Multisystemic therapy with violent and chronic juvenile offenders and their families: The role of treatment fidelity in successful dissemination. *Journal of Consulting and Clinical Psychology*, 65, 821–833.

Henggeler, S. W., Melton, G. B., Smith, L. A., Schoenwald, S. K., and Hanley, J. H. (1993). Family preservation using multisystemic treatment: Long-term follow-up to a clinical trial with serious juvenile offenders. *Journal of Child and Family Studies*, 2, 283–293.

Henggeler, S. W., Rowland, M. D., Randall, J., Ward, D. M., Pickrel, S. G., Cunningham, P. B., Miller, S. L., Edwards, J., Zealberg, J. J., Hand, L. D., and Santos, A. B. (1999). Home-based multisystemic therapy as an alternative to the hospitalization of youths in psychiatric crisis: Clinical outcomes. *Journal of the American Academy of Child and Adolescent Psychiatry*, 38, 1331–1339.

Henggeler, S. W., Schoenwald, S. K., Borduin, C. M., Rowland, M. D., and Cunningham, P. B. (2009). *Multisystemic therapy for antisocial behavior in children and adolescents* (2nd ed.). New York: Guilford.

Hill, K. G., Bailey, J. A., Hawkins, J. D., Catalano, R. F., Kosterman, R., Oesterle, S., and Abbott, R. D. (2014). The onset of STI diagnosis through age 30: Results from the Seattle Social Development Project intervention. *Prevention Science*, 15(S1), S19–S32.

Hipwell, A. E., and Loeber, R. (2006). Do we know which interventions are effective for disruptive and delinquent girls? *Clinical Child and Family Psychology Review*, 9, 221–255.

Klietz, S. T., Borduin, C. M., and Schaeffer, C. M. (2010). Cost–benefit analysis of Multisystemic Therapy with serious and violent juvenile offenders. *Journal of Family Therapy*, 24, 657–666.

Koegl, C. J., Farrington, D. P., Augimeri, L. K., and Day, D. M. (2008). Evaluation of a targeted cognitive-behavioral program for children with conduct problems – the SNAP Under 12 Outreach Project: Service intensity, age and gender effects on short and long term outcomes. *Clinical Child Psychology and Psychiatry*, 13, 419–434.

Kuklinski, M. R., Briney, J. S., Hawkins, J. D., and Catalano, R. F. (2012). Cost–benefit analysis of Communities That Care outcomes at eighth grade. *Prevention Science*, 13, 150–161.

Lee, S., Aos, S., Drake, E., Pennucci, A., Miller, U., and Anderson, L. (2012). *Return on investment: Evidence-based options to improve statewide outcomes* (Document no. 12-04-1201). Olympia, WA: Washington State Institute for Public Policy.

Lipman, E. L., Kenny, M., Sniderman, C., O'Grady, S., Augimeri, L., Khayutin, S., and Boyle, M. H. (2008). Evaluation of a community-based program for young boys at-risk of antisocial behaviour: Results and issues. *Journal of the Canadian Academy of Child and Adolescent Psychiatry*, 17, 12–19.

Manning, M., Homel, R., and Smith, C. (2010). A meta-analysis of the effects of early developmental prevention programs in at-risk populations on non-health outcomes in adolescence. *Children and Youth Services Review*, 32, 506–519.

Miller, T. R. (2013). *Nurse-Family Partnership home visitation: Costs, outcomes, and return on investment*. Beltsville, MD: HBSA.

Nowak, C., and Heinrichs, N. (2008). A comprehensive meta-analysis of the Triple-P Positive Parenting Program using hierarchical linear modeling: Effectiveness and moderating variables. *Clinical Child and Family Psychology Review*, 11, 114–144.

O'Donnell, J., Hawkins, J. D., Catalano, R. F., Abbott, R. D., and Day, L. E. (1995). Preventing school failure, drug use, and delinquency among low-income children: Long-term intervention in elementary schools. *American Journal of Orthopsychiatry*, 65, 87–100.

Olds, D. L., Eckenrode, J., Henderson, C. R., Kitzman, H., Powers, J., Cole, R., Sidora, K., Morris, P., Pettitt, L. M., and Luckey, D. (1997). Long-term effects of home visitation on maternal life course and child abuse and neglect: Fifteen-year follow-up of a randomized trial. *Journal of the American Medical Association*, 278, 637–643.

Olds, D. L., Henderson, C. R., Chamberlin, R., and Tatelbaum, R. (1986). Preventing child abuse and neglect: A randomized trial of nurse home visitation. *Pediatrics*, 78, 65–78.

Olds, D. L., Henderson, C. R., Cole, R., Eckenrode, J., Kitzman, H., Luckey, D., Pettitt, L., Sidora, K., Morris, P., and Powers, J. (1998). Long-term effects of nurse home visitation on children's criminal and antisocial behavior: 15-year follow-up of a randomized controlled trial. *Journal of the American Medical Association*, 280, 1238–1244.

Olds, D. L., Sadler, L., and Kitzman, H. (2007). Programs for parents of infants and toddlers: Recent evidence from randomized trials. *Journal of Child Psychology and Psychiatry*, 48, 355–391.

O'Neill, D., McGilloway, S., Donnelly, M., Bywater, T., and Kelley, P. (2013). A cost-effectiveness analysis of the Incredible Years parenting programme in reducing childhood health inequalities. *European Journal of Health Economics*, 14, 85–94.

Patterson, G. R. (1982). *Coercive family process*. Eugene, OR: Castalia.

Piquero, A., Farrington, D. P., Welsh, B. C., Tremblay, R. E., and Jennings, W. G. (2009). Effects of early family/parent training programs on antisocial behavior and delinquency. *Journal of Experimental Criminology*, 5, 83–120.

Sanders, M. R., Kirby, J. N., Tellegen, C. L., and Day, J. J. (2014). The Triple-P Positive Parenting program: A systematic review and meta-analysis of a multi-level system of parenting support. *Clinical Psychology Review*, 34, 337–357.

Sanders, M. R., Markie-Dadds, C., Tully, L. A., and Bor, W. (2000). The Triple P-Positive Parenting Program: A comparison of enhanced, standard and self-directed behavioral family intervention for parents of children with early onset conduct problems. *Journal of Consulting and Clinical Psychology*, 68, 624–640.

Sawyer, A. M., and Borduin, C. M. (2011). Effects of multisystemic therapy through midlife: A 21.9-year follow-up to a randomized clinical trial with serious and violent juvenile offenders. *Journal of Consulting and Clinical Psychology*, 79, 643–652.

Schaeffer, C. M., and Borduin, C. M. (2005). Long-term follow-up to a randomized clinical trial of multisystemic therapy with serious and violent juvenile offenders. *Journal of Consulting and Clinical Psychology*, 73, 445–453.

Schweinhart, L. J., Barnes, H. V., and Weikart, D. P. (1993). *Significant benefits: The High/Scope Perry Preschool Study through age 27.* Ypsilanti, MI: High/Scope Press.

Schweinhart, L. J., Montie, J., Zongping, X., Barnett, W. S., Belfield, C. R., and Nores, M. (2005). *Lifetime effects: The High/Scope Perry Preschool Study through age 40.* Ypsilanti, MI: High/Scope Press.

Schweinhart, L. J., and Weikart, D. P. (1980). *Young children grow up: The effects of the Perry Preschool Program on youths through age 15.* Ypsilanti, MI: High/Scope Press.

Sexton, T. L., and Alexander, J. F. (2000). *Functional family therapy.* Washington, DC: U.S. Office of Juvenile Justice and Delinquency Prevention.

Sexton, T., and Turner, C.W. (2010). The effectiveness of Functional Family Therapy for youth with behavioral problems in a community practice setting. *Journal of Family Psychology*, 24, 339–348.

Taxy, S., Liberman, A. M., Roman, J. K., and Downey, P. M. (2012). *The costs and benefits of Functional Family Therapy for Washington, D.C.* Washington, DC: Urban Institute.

Thomas, R., and Zimmer-Gembeck, M. J. (2007). Behavioral outcomes of parent-child interaction therapy and Triple-P positive parenting program: A review and meta-analysis. *Journal of Abnormal Child Psychology*, 35, 475–495.

Tremblay, R. E., Pagani-Kurtz, L., Masse, L. C., Vitaro, F., and Pihl, R. O. (1995). A bimodal preventive intervention for disruptive kindergarten boys: Its impact through mid-adolescence. *Journal of Consulting and Clinical Psychology*, 63, 560–568.

Turner, W., and MacDonald, G. (2011). Treatment Foster Care for improving outcomes in children and young people: A systematic review. *Research on Social Work Practice*, 21, 501–527.

Vitaro, F., Brendgen, M., Giguere, C-E., and Tremblay, R. E. (2013). Early prevention of life-course personal and property violence: A 19-year follow-up of the Montreal Longitudinal-Experimental Study (MLES). *Journal of Experimental Criminology*, 9, 411–427.

Webster-Stratton, C. (1998). Preventing conduct problems in Head Start children: Strengthening parenting competencies. *Journal of Consulting and Clinical Psychology*, 66, 715–730.

Webster-Stratton, C. (2000). *The Incredible Years training series.* Washington, DC: U.S. Office of Juvenile Justice and Delinquency Prevention.

Webster-Stratton, C., Rinaldi, J., and Jamila, M. R. (2011). Long-term outcomes of Incredible Years parenting program: Predictors of adolescent adjustment. *Child and Adolescent Mental Health*, 16, 38–46.

Welsh, B. C., and Farrington, D. P. (2011). The benefits and costs of early prevention compared with imprisonment: Toward evidence-based policy. *Prison Journal*, 91 (3S1), 120–137.

Zara, G., and Farrington, D. P. (2014). Cognitive-behavioral skills training in preventing offending and reducing recidivism. In E. M. Jiminez Gonzalez and J. L. Alba Robles (eds.), *Criminology and forensic psychology* (pp. 55–102). Charleston, SC: Criminology and Justice Publisher.

Chapter 6

Opportunities for public policies to strengthen families and prevent crime

Abigail A. Fagan

Criminologists are increasingly advocating the use of evidence-based interventions to prevent crime (Andrews et al., 1990; Farrington and Welsh, 2007; Sherman et al., 1998). Such programs and practices seek to manipulate the underlying causes of crime: the individual, peer, school, family, and community risk and protective factors that are hypothesized in criminological theories and identified in empirical research to precede and increase the likelihood of offending (Hawkins et al., 1992; Lipsey and Derzon, 1998). To be considered "evidence-based," these interventions should also be evaluated in rigorous scientific studies and demonstrated to reduce crime using valid and reliable measures. Experiments, particularly randomized controlled trials (RCTs) which randomly assign participants to receive an intervention or not, are considered the most rigorous approach to determining what works to reduce crime (Elliott, 2013; Farrington and Welsh, 2005; Weisburd, 2003). Ideally, crime prevention policies will seek to increase the use of interventions that have been tested in multiple RCTs or other rigorous research designs and shown to reduce offending across diverse contexts and populations (Sampson et al., 2013). Family-focused preventive interventions meet these criteria, and, as discussed in this chapter, are worth increased attention from policymakers.

The family context and crime prevention

Several criminological theories emphasize the role of family interactions and parenting practices in directly and indirectly influencing youth delinquency, making the family context an ideal site for crime prevention. Social learning theories (Akers, 2009; Patterson, 1982) contend that parents are the most important role models for young children and that parents who display deviant behaviors and endorse attitudes favoring delinquency help to teach children how to misbehave. Self-control theory (Gottfredson and Hirschi, 1990) posits that parents who actively monitor children's behavior, set and communicate clear expectations that delinquency is not acceptable, and punish transgressions, instill high levels of self-control in children, which will reduce their offending. Social bonding theory (Hirschi, 1969) prioritizes parent/child emotional support and affective communication in helping to prevent delinquency. General strain theory (Agnew, 2006) includes family stressors such as parent/child conflict and child maltreatment among the forms of strain most likely to lead to youth deviance. Finally, life-course theories (Catalano and Hawkins, 1996; Moffitt, 1993; Sampson and Laub, 1993; Thornberry, 1987) acknowledge that multiple family-related risk and protective factors influence delinquency but contend that these factors are most important in shaping children's anti-social behaviors.

Numerous empirical studies have tested these theories and investigated the degree to which family factors impact youth delinquency. Two meta-analyses of this literature (Derzon, 2010; Hoeve et al., 2009) reported mean effect sizes on delinquency ranging from 0.15 to 0.20 for parenting practices including: child maltreatment; parental monitoring, supervision, and discipline of children; parental affection and support; and parental criminal behavior and/or deviant attitudes. While small to moderate in size, these effects are comparable to those found in meta-analyses of other risk factors for delinquency, such as low self-control (Pratt and Cullen, 2000) and exposure to delinquent peers (Pratt et al., 2010).

Based on this empirical evidence, many family-focused interventions have been developed, tested, and shown to be effective in reducing youth delinquency, substance use and/or violence (Elliott, 2013; Institute of Medicine and National Research Council, 2014; Sandler et al., 2011). For example, of the 52 programs on the Blueprints for Healthy Youth Development website (www.colorado.edu/cspv/blueprints/), 20 (38 percent) are family-based interventions. Of the 42 delinquency prevention programs rated as Effective by Crime Solutions (www.crimesolutions.gov/), 20 (48 percent) include programming for parents.

As a whole, these interventions have shown both short- and long-term effects on antisocial behaviors when rigorously tested with families and children of diverse backgrounds. In addition to universal interventions appropriate for use with the general population, effective family-focused programs have targeted low-income families, recently divorced mothers, children living with foster care parents, Hispanic families, and African Americans living in rural areas. Although the content and methods of delivery vary, family-focused interventions have in common the goal of reducing family risk factors and enhancing family protective factors. This typically involves improving parents' ability to set rules and guidelines for children's behavior, monitor children's behaviors, provide appropriate consequences for positive and negative behaviors, communicating effectively and providing warmth and support (Sandler et al., 2011).

Effective programs exist for children of all developmental stages. **Home visitation** programs provide low-income, pregnant women with regular home visits by health care professionals in order to improve the home environment before children are born and for the first few years of life. The goal is to ensure healthy gestation and birth and prevent child maltreatment to give children the best possible start in life. The main goal of **early education programs** is to increase school readiness and improve cognitive skills in early childhood, especially among children from lower income families who may otherwise begin school already at a disadvantage compared to higher income youth (Schindler and Yoshikawa, 2012). These interventions also include outreach to parents to increase their involvement in their children's education.

Parent training programs include a diverse array of interventions which can be implemented with universal or high-risk families and with children of all ages. Those delivered during mid- to late-childhood usually try to reduce early conduct disorder and other antisocial behaviors which predict subsequent involvement in crime (Loeber and Farrington, 2000). Those implemented during adolescence are intended to counteract the growing number of risk factors and shrinking number of protective factors during this period, which result in a heightened risk for initiation and escalation of offending. Regardless of the age at which they are offered, parent training programs try to improve parents' monitoring and discipline of youth, improve parent/child communication and strengthen family bonds and attachment.

Family therapy programs are also delivered during adolescence but are designed for families of youth who have already broken the law. These more intensive services involve weekly meetings between therapists and all members of the family. Although programs are designed for offenders, they are delivered in children's homes or in community-based clinics with the expectation that treating families in their natural environment will improve the relevance and effectiveness of program content.

As mentioned, all of these types of interventions have been tested in high quality studies and shown to reduce antisocial behavior. For example, meta-analyses of home visitation programs (Farrington and Welsh, 2003; Piquero et al., 2009) have shown small to moderate effects on youth misbehavior and delinquency, with effect sizes ranging from 0.24 to 0.30. A similar effect size (0.26) was calculated in a meta-analysis of preschool programs (Farrington and Welsh, 2003), but only five studies were included in the review, indicating the need for more evaluation of the impact of early childhood education programs on crime. Evaluations of parent training programs have shown somewhat stronger effects on delinquency, with effect sizes ranging from 0.36 to 0.42 (Farrington and Welsh, 2003; Lundahl et al., 2006; Piquero et al., 2009). Finally, family therapy programs have been shown to reduce recidivism among youth offenders. For example, evaluations of Multi systemic Therapy have reported average effect sizes of 0.41, indicating a moderate reduction in youth delinquency (Farrington and Welsh, 2003). Similarly, a meta-analysis of eight evaluations of Functional

Family Therapy showed an average effect size of 0.59 (Washington State Institute for Public Policy, 2014).

Importantly, many of these evaluations have conducted tests of mediation to examine if changes in parenting practices are responsible for reductions in delinquency for participants in intervention versus control conditions (Fagan, 2013; Sandler et al., 2011). For example, an evaluation of the FamiliasUnidas intervention for Hispanic parents of 13-year-olds found that participation increased parents' use of positive reinforcement, child monitoring and communication with children, and these outcomes mediated intervention effects on substance use at age 16 (Pantin et al., 2009; Prado et al., 2007). Similarly, a randomized trial of the Positive Family Support – Family Check Up intervention conducted with families of middle school students indicated that those receiving the intervention reported less growth in family conflict from ages 12 to 15 compared to those in the control group, and this improvement mediated reductions in delinquency at age 19 (Van Ryzin and Dishion, 2012).

Although not every family risk and protective factor targeted for change has been shown to be altered by family-based programs, interventions that can quantify such changes are important because they increase confidence that these interventions work as designed. Moreover, they can provide policymakers and practitioners with more convincing evidence that family processes affect delinquency. Policymakers may be reluctant to endorse interventions that will "interfere" in private family matters, but showing that improvements in parenting practices can reduce delinquency and substance use should increase support for these interventions. In addition, evidence that specific program elements (e.g. having parents discuss and practice how to set and consistently enforce rules about behavior) lead to desired changes in behavior can be shared with practitioners to ensure that they fully implement and do not alter these components.

Opportunities for public policy

Significant reductions in crime can only be achieved if the strategies shown to prevent offending are used and if they are delivered to a large enough population to make a difference (Spoth et al., 2013). Fortunately, many effective interventions are now available which can be implemented with families in order to reduce children's involvement in crime. The next step, then, is to convince policymakers and practitioners to make use of these programs (Institute of Medicine and National Research Council, 2014; Piquero et al., 2009). How can we do this?

First, let us consider current progress in the dissemination of family-focused interventions. In 2010, the U.S. federal government launched the Maternal, Infant, and Early Childhood Home Visiting Program (MIECHV) to promote widespread use of effective home

visitation programs (http://mchb.hrsa.gov/programs/homevisiting/index.
html). In 2014, 106 million dollars were given out to agencies in nearly
every state to implement these services. Similarly, in his 2013 State of the
Union address, President Obama called for increased use of early childhood education programs, stating that "we know this works" (www.acf.
hhs.gov/programs/ecd/early-learning/early-learning-initiative). The Early
Learning Initiative provides millions of dollars to states to implement
programs like Head Start and Early Head Start.

We have also seen improvement in the dissemination of family therapy
programs (Greenwood and Welsh, 2012). Likely due to concerns about the
growing population of incarcerated youth offenders and the corresponding
costs to society, calls for reforms to the juvenile justice system have emphasized increased use of community-based treatment services as alternatives
to out-of-home placement and incarceration (National Research Council,
2012). For example, the MacArthur Foundation provides financial support and technical assistance to state juvenile justice systems participating
in the Models for Change initiative to increase the use of evidence-based
prevention and treatment services like family therapy programs (National
Research Council, 2012).

These examples show that policymakers can be persuaded to enact legislation that increases the use of science-based, family-focused interventions. Nonetheless, some caution and additional steps are necessary. Not
all the programs funded by the home visitation and early childhood education initiatives have been demonstrated as effective in reducing crime. For
example, only the Nurse-Family Partnership home visitation program has
shown reductions in children's offending (Bilukha et al., 2005), and the
ability of Head Start to reduce crime has not been established (Schindler
and Yoshikawa, 2012). When substantial variation in effects exists within
program types, it is important that policies designed to reduce crime stip-
ulate the use of *particular* interventions, not *types* of interventions. It is
also important for interventions that *could* affect delinquency and crime to
actually measure these outcomes. This is not routinely done, just as many
crime prevention programs do not often evaluate effects on related problem
behaviors.

Increased funding for family-focused services must also be accompanied by technical support to help communities effectively implement these
programs (Fagan, 2013). Family-focused interventions are not always replicated with implementation fidelity. Instead, deviations from program content and methods are often made during replication which can undermine
the effectiveness of the intervention (e.g. Olds et al., 2002; Washington State
Institute for Public Policy, 2002). Communities need assistance in setting up
monitoring systems and tracking implementation progress. Such support
may come from program developers, non-profit organizations, or state-wide
centers that can be jointly funded and operated by child- or family-serving

agencies and academic institutions (Greenwood and Welsh, 2012; Institute of Medicine and National Research Council, 2014).

Another important task is to increase the dissemination of parent training programs, especially universal programs for adolescents (Fagan, 2013; Institute of Medicine and National Research Council, 2014). It is estimated that only a small proportion of families has ever participated in an effective parent training program (Printz and Sanders, 2007), yet there is currently no large-scale, dedicated effort to increase their use. This oversight is troubling given the potential for these services, which are designed to be implemented with *all* parents, to impact a significant proportion of the population. As discussed, meta-analytic reviews indicate that these programs may produce even larger effects on youth delinquency than programs aimed at younger children. Moreover, there is evidence that many parent training programs are cost beneficial, with financial gains associated with reductions in substance use and crime outweighing participant costs (Washington State Institute for Public Policy, 2014).

Ensuring that parent training interventions are provided "at sufficient scale and reach to significantly reduce the incidence and prevalence of negative....behavioral outcomes in children and adolescents nationwide" (Institute of Medicine and National Research Council, 2014, p. 2) will likely require shifts in both public attitudes about family-based prevention and increases in funding for such initiatives (Fagan, 2013). Universal prevention services can be a "tough sell" because they are intended for populations not yet displaying behavioral problems. When problems are not clearly evident, there is less concern for them. To counter this reluctance to intervene, researchers must more clearly and more often communicate to policymakers and the public that delinquency *can* be prevented – and that the tools for doing so exist. We must also spread the message that even during adolescence, parents can make a difference. Although it is important for parents to encourage teenagers' autonomy, they must still provide monitoring, supervision and emotional support in order to counter the risk factors likely to be faced during this period of life, such as increased exposure to delinquent peers.

Another significant challenge in increasing dissemination of parent training programs is the lack of an influential governmental agency dedicated to this goal. For example, whereas the Department of Education is well equipped to partner with local providers to increase the spread of early childhood education programs, there is no natural federal home for parent training interventions. In 1999–2000, the Office of Juvenile Justice and Delinquency Prevention (OJJDP) launched the Strengthening America's Families initiative with assistance from the Center for Substance Abuse Prevention (CSAP) to fund communities to replicate effective family-focused programs, including parent training interventions (Kumpfer and Alvarado, 2003). Both of these federal agencies have a vested interest in promoting family-based prevention, and a renewed partnership would be much welcomed. Support could also come from the Administration for Children and Families (ACF), a federal agency actually charged with promoting family well-being. Although ACF is helping to implement both the home visitation and early childhood education initiatives, it has not yet taken on the challenge of spreading parent training programs.

At the community level, parent training interventions do not typically require delivery by licensed professionals and can be offered in schools, community centers, doctor's offices, and other youth- or family-serving agencies. This flexibility is both a blessing and a curse. Although services can be offered in multiple contexts, no one agency is necessarily responsible for ensuring widespread and high quality implementation. Nonetheless, local community coalitions (Spoth et al., 2013) or state-level agencies (Greenwood and Welsh, 2012) could provide oversight to ensure that services are well coordinated, well monitored and delivered to diverse families with children of varying ages and needs.

Although these challenges to dissemination will be difficult to surmount, the future is promising. In the past two decades, a relatively large number of family-focused preventive interventions have been developed, tested, and demonstrated as effective for diverse populations, and several policies have been enacted to increase their use in communities. Continuation and extensions of these policies should help to lower rates of crime.

References

Agnew, R. (2006). *Pressured into crime: An overview of general strain theory.* Cary, NC: Roxbury Publishing Company.

Akers, R. L. (2009). *Social learning and social structure: A general theory of crime and deviance.* New Brunswick, NJ: Transaction Publishers.

Andrews, D. A., Zinger, I., Hoge, R. D., Bonta, J., Gendreau, P., and Cullen, F. T. (1990). Does correctional treatment work? A clinically relevant and psychologically informed meta-analysis. *Criminology, 28,* 369–404.

Bilukha, O., Hahn, R. A., Crosby, A., Fullilove, M. T., Liberman, A., Moscicki, E. K., ... Task Force on Community Prevention Services. (2005). The effectiveness of early childhood home visitation in preventing violence: A systematic review. *American Journal of Preventive Medicine, 28,* 11–39.

Catalano, R. F., and Hawkins, J. D. (1996). The Social Development Model: A theory of antisocial behavior. In J. D. Hawkins (ed.), *Delinquency and crime: Current theories* (pp. 149–197). New York, NY: Cambridge University Press.

Derzon, J. H. (2010). The correspondence of family features with problem, aggressive, criminal, and violent behavior: A meta-analysis. *Journal of Experimental Criminology, 6,* 263–292.

Elliott, D. S. (2013). Crime prevention and intervention over the life course: Emerging trends and directions for future research. In C. L. Gibson and M. D. Krohn (eds.), *Handbook of life-course criminology* (pp. 297–316). New York, NY: Springer.

Fagan, A. A. (2013). Family-focused interventions to prevent juvenile delinquency: A case where science and policy can find common ground. *Criminology and Public Policy*, 12, 617–650.

Farrington, D. P., and Welsh, B. C. (2003). Family-based prevention of offending: A meta-analysis. *Australian and New Zealand Journal of Criminology*, 36, 127–151.

Farrington, D. P., and Welsh, B. C. (2005). Randomized experiments in criminology: What have we learned in the last two decades? *Journal of Experimental Criminology*, 1, 9–38.

Farrington, D. P., and Welsh, B. C. (2007). *Saving children from a life of crime: Early risk factors and effective interventions*. New York, NY: Oxford University Press.

Gottfredson, M. R., and Hirschi, T. (1990). *A general theory of crime*. Stanford, CA: Stanford University Press.

Greenwood, P., and Welsh, B. C. (2012). Promoting evidence-based practice in delinquency prevention at the state level: Principles, progress, and policy directions. *Criminology and Public Policy*, 11, 493–513.

Hawkins, J. D., Catalano, R. F., and Miller, J. Y. (1992). Risk and protective factors for alcohol and other drug problems in adolescence and early adulthood: Implications for substance abuse prevention. *Psychological Bulletin*, 112, 64–105.

Hirschi, T. (1969). *Causes of delinquency*. Berkeley, CA: University of California Press.

Hoeve, M., Dubas, J. S., Eichelsheim, V. I., Van der Laan, P. H., Smeenk, W., and Gerris, J. R. M. (2009). The relationship between parenting and delinquency: A meta-analysis. *Journal of Abnormal Child Psychology*, 37, 749–775.

Institute of Medicine and National Research Council. (2014). *Strategies for scaling effective family-focused preventive interventions to promote children's cognitive, affective, and behavioral health: Workshop summary*. Washington, DC: The National Academies Press.

Kumpfer, K., and Alvarado, R. (2003). Family-strengthening approaches for the prevention of youth problem behaviors. *American Psychologist*, 58, 457–465.

Lipsey, M. W., and Derzon, J. H. (1998). Predictors of violent or serious delinquency in adolescence and early adulthood: A synthesis of longitudinal research. In R. Loeber and D. P. Farrington (eds.), *Serious and violent juvenile offenders: Risk factors and successful interventions* (pp. 86–105). Thousand Oaks, CA: Sage Publications.

Loeber, R., and Farrington, D. P. (2000). Young children who commit crime: Epidemiology, developmental origins, risk factors, early interventions, and policy implications. *Development and Psychopathology*, 12, 737–762.

Lundahl, B., Risser, H. J., and Lovejoy, M. C. (2006). A meta-analysis of parent training: Moderators and follow-up effects. *Clinical Psychology Review*, 26, 86–104.

Moffitt, T. E. (1993). Adolescence-limited and life-course persistent anti-social behavior: A developmental taxonomy. *Psychological Review*, 100, 674–701.

National Research Council. (2012). *Reforming juvenile justice: A developmental approach*. Washington, DC: The National Academies Press.

Olds, D. L., Robinson, J., O'Brien, R., Luckey, D. W., Pettitt, L. M., Henderson Jr., C., R., Talmi, A. (2002). Home visiting by paraprofessionals and by nurses: A randomized, controlled trial. *Pediatrics*, 110, 486–496.

Pantin, H., Prado, G., Lopez, B., Huang, S., Tapia, M. I., Schwartz, S. J., ... Branchini, J. (2009). A randomized controlled trial of Familias Unidas for Hispanic adolescents with behavior problems. *Psychosomatic Medicine*, 71, 987–995.

Patterson, G. R. (1982). *A social learning approach. Volume 3: Coercive family practices*. Eugene, OR: Castalia Publishing.

Piquero, A. R., Farrington, D. P., Welsh, B. C., Tremblay, R., and Jennings, W. G. (2009). Effects of early family/parent training programs on antisocial behavior and delinquency. *Journal of Experimental Criminology*, 5, 83–120.

Prado, G., Pantin, H., Briones, E., Schwartz, S. J., Feaster, D., Huang, S., Szapocznik, J. (2007). A randomized controlled trial of a parent-centered intervention in preventing substance use and HIV risk behaviors in Hispanic adolescents. *Journal of Consulting and Clinical Psychology*, 75, 914–926.

Pratt, T. C., and Cullen, F. T. (2000). The empirical status of Gottfredson and Hirschi's General Theory of Crime: A meta analysis. *Criminology*, 38, 931–964.

Pratt, T. C., Cullen, F. T., Sellers, C. S., Winfree, L. T., Madensen, T. D., Daigle, L. E., ... Gau, J. M. (2010). The empirical status of social learning theory: A meta analysis. *Justice Quarterly*, 27, 765–802.

Printz, R. J., and Sanders, M. R. (2007). Adopting a population-level approach to parenting and family support interventions. *Clinical Psychology Review*, 27, 739–749.

Sampson, R. J., and Laub, J. H. (1993). *Crime in the making: Pathways and turning points through life*. Cambridge, MA: Harvard University Press.

Sampson, R. J., Winship, C., and Knight, C. (2013). Translating causal claims: Principles and strategies for policy-relevant criminology. *Criminology and Public Policy*, 12, 587–616.

Sandler, I. N., Schoenfelder, E., Wolchik, S. A., and MacKinnon, D. P. (2011). Long-term impact of prevention programs to promote effective parenting: Lasting effects but uncertain processes. *Annual Review of Psychology* 62, 299–329.

Schindler, H. S., and Yoshikawa, H. (2012). Preventing crime through intervention in the preschool years. In B. C. Welsh and D. P. Farrington (eds.), *The Oxford handbook of crime prevention* (pp. 70–88). New York, NY: Oxford University Press.

Sherman, L. W., Gottfredson, D. C., MacKenzie, D. L., Eck, J., Reuter, P., and Bushway, S. D. (1998). *Preventing crime: What works, what doesn't, what's promising*. Washington, DC: National Institute of Justice.

Spoth, R., Rohrbach, L. A., Greenberg, M. T., Leaf, P., Brown, C. H., Fagan, A., Society for Prevention Research Type 2 Translational Task Force. (2013). Addressing core challenges for the next generation of Type 2 translation research and systems: The translation science to population impact (TSci impact) framework. *Prevention Science*, 14, 319–351.

Thornberry, T. P. (1987). Toward an interactional theory of delinquency. *Criminology*, 25, 863–891.

Van Ryzin, M. J., and Dishion, T. J. (2012). The impact of a family-centered intervention on the ecology of adolescent antisocial behavior: Modeling developmental sequelae and trajectories during adolescence. *Development and Psychopathology*, 24, 1139–1155.

Washington State Institute for Public Policy. (2014). *Benefit–cost results*. Olympia, WA: Washington State Institute for Public Policy.

Washington State Institute for Public Policy. (2002). *Washington State's implementation of Functional Family Therapy for juvenile offenders: Preliminary findings.* Olympia, WA: Washington State Institute for Public Policy.

Weisburd, D. (2003). Ethical practice and evaluations of interventions in crime and justice: The moral imperative for randomized trials. *Evaluation Review*, 27, 336–354.

Chapter 7

Community crime prevention

David Kennedy

Introduction: The dominant role of community crime prevention

Community crime prevention is generally seen as a subordinate and lesser category of programmatic intervention, relative to the larger and more central role played by the criminal justice system. It is the job of police, courts, and corrections to control youth violence, for example, with a supporting role to be played by, for example, a mentoring program operating out of a neighborhood nonprofit organization. In this ordinary view the criminal justice system is official, broad, of high capacity, and bears primary responsibility for producing public safety, while community crime prevention is unofficial, narrow, of marginal capacity, and plays at best a supporting role.

With respect to what are generally considered community crime prevention interventions – particular strategies aimed at individual substantive crime problems, and especially community crime prevention "programs" – this is accurate; such interventions and programs are, relatively speaking, both few and weak compared to the scope and power of the criminal justice system, as will be discussed further. In fact, however, community crime prevention should be considered in much wider and more fundamental terms: and when it is, it assumes a central and dominant place.

Consideration of community crime prevention generally begins with crime as it presents itself – the overall crime rate, or a particular crime problem such as youth violence – and looks at what particular community-based interventions are doing and might do to address that baseline condition. When so considered, those strategies are not usually particularly powerful, either in fact or in prospect, as will be discussed further below. That framework, however, disregards by definition the larger role the overall society plays in *producing* that baseline condition. Crime is not an exogenous condition that is then acted upon by community and criminal justice actions; it is an *endogenous* condition that is both produced and governed largely by community dynamics. If the United States national homicide rate is today somewhat less than 5:100,000, that is because the United States is fundamentally a more violent society than is, say Japan, where it is less than

1:100,000[1]; because despite that fact only a very small part of the American population is at high risk of either committing or suffering homicide; and because the crack cocaine epidemic and associated dynamics that produced a much higher homicide rate in the 1990s have substantially waned. All of those factors – American society, the distribution of risk within that society, and the coming and going of a major drug epidemic – are driven most fundamentally by community, not by criminal justice, processes. Looking at the residual of that process – crime that is in fact committed – and then looking at the marginal additional increment of crime prevention that can be produced by community intervention is to miss the very much larger bedrock contribution of those community processes. Put another way, if it turns out that in Japan deliberate community interventions have little to offer in addressing its already very low homicide rate, and that that job perforce falls to the criminal justice authorities, that is not to say that community crime prevention in Japan is weak; it is to say that community crime prevention in Japan is remarkably powerful, and that the police are left to deal with the very little that is left over.

Scholars have captured this in a variety of rich theoretical and research literatures: for example, as a matter of social organization and disorganization,[2] as the difference between informal and formal social control,[3] and in terms of collective efficacy.[4] There is a strong tendency in these literatures toward the conclusion that community and informal dynamics are more powerful than formal and legal dynamics.[5] These formal findings are in keeping with common-sense experience of how crime works; again in the United States, for example, the crime waves associated with Prohibition, the heroin epidemic of the late 1960s and 1970s, and the crack epidemic of the late 1980s and early 1990s were largely impervious to official action. The first was ended by a statutory change that legalized the social behavior – drinking – that was driving Prohibition's criminality and violence; the second[6] and, according to some evidence, the third by social learning that undercut those epidemics' drug use and illicit markets.[7] In each case the power of official intervention, by both criminal justice and other authorities, was dramatically unequal to the task; in, for example, Baltimore, which was the one major American city where the heroin epidemic did not end largely of its own accord, official action remains unable to control it.[8]

This perspective is strengthened by research showing that – at least for *mala in se* crimes like serious violence – social norms against offending are consistently high across social settings and offending rates can be considered remarkably low, sometimes even in what might appear to be highly challenged and deviant populations. Researchers have found steady attitudes against violence and disorder even in relatively high-crime neighborhoods, where actual exposure to crime appears to lead to lower levels of tolerance.[9] In such neighborhoods very small proportions of the population commit serious violent crime, such that they probably should not be considered violent neighborhoods, but rather relatively ordinary neighborhoods (on these dimensions, at any rate) that include a small and distinctive population of high-risk people.[10] Contrary to popular assertions that what appear to be ordinary social institutions like college campuses in fact represent criminogenic settings, for "rape culture," for example, research shows that most potential offenders do not in fact offend and that a very small percentage of men – under 5 percent – commit about 90 percent of all sexual assaults.[11] Even among high-rate offenders like gang members, research and field experience show regular and ingenious mechanisms to avoid committing violence dictated by gang norms and culture,[12] and the expression of mainstream norms against violence and extreme criminality.[13] There is in fact a growing recognition that even those we think of as criminals mostly *obey* the law: they hurt people rarely, relative to incentive and opportunity; buy most of what they consume; stop at stop signs; etc.[14] And, crucially, research shows that such compliance is not motivated primarily by fear of the law – the prospect of sanction producing deterrence – but by felt respect for the law[15] and, as noted, personal and social norms. (Ordinary people experience this dynamic around speeding; nearly all drivers speed, but nearly all drivers also speed relatively carefully and respectfully, a fact driven not by fear of being stopped and arrested but by a fundamental conviction that one should drive safely. Drivers who speed at dramatically high speeds, weave in and out of traffic, tailgate, and the like are relatively rare, and disliked even by other "offenders.") In fact, voluntary compliance with the law – which is, as has been noted, very high even in what might be regarded as high-crime settings – can itself be regarded as a form of community crime prevention. The law is, at root, a people's statement of some of its most core values: a code of community conduct elevated in a particularly considered, formal, and weighty fashion. Where the law wins out through voluntary compliance – rather than through fear of consequence, actual enforcement, or supervision or incarceration – it can be regarded as the successful application of a special form of social norm.

We should therefore conclude that – contrary to the ordinary view – it is community crime prevention that is the primary producer of crime prevention and public safety, and that the criminal justice system makes an additional important but marginal (in the economic sense of the term) contribution.

The undermining of community crime prevention by official action

It is then important to note the many ways in which formal steps taken to prevent crime – criminal justice system actions – can and in fact do – undermine community crime prevention.

There is a rapidly growing theoretical and research understanding that formal actions can damage individual and collective social capital in ways that promote criminal offending. Clear has found that the damage to the social fabric caused when more than a very small proportion of a community is incarcerated leads to an increase in crime.[16] Incarceration also leads to life-long reductions in income; decreased likelihood of supporting existing family members; decreased likelihood of marriage, increased likelihood of school failure for one's children, and increased likelihood of incarceration for one's children.[17] Incarceration, and concentrations of incarceration at the neighborhood level, can lead to reduced participation in neighborhood crime prevention activity, such as working with community organizations or intervening in criminal and disorderly behavior.[18] Recent research even shows that contacts with the criminal justice system, from being stopped by the police to incarceration, lead to a withdrawal from political participation – such as voting – and civic life in general.[19] (These dynamics seem very likely to have played a part in Ferguson, MO – recently the focus of much American attention around police/community relations – which combined a local criminal justice singularly abusive to its black residents with a black turnout rate in municipal elections of 6 percent.[20]) All these interventions can facilitate criminality at the individual, family, and neighborhood level.

There is also a rapidly growing understanding of how official action can undermine the perceived standing – the legitimacy – of the law and its agents, and lead to offending. Legitimacy research shows clearly that the perception of fair and respectful treatment by agents of the criminal justice system ("procedural justice") weighs more heavily in compliance with the law than does fear of legal consequences. People who obey the law do so, for the most part, because they feel that it is the right thing to do, not because they are afraid of being caught and sanctioned.[21] The main difference between high-crime communities and individuals and others is not core attitudes toward serious offending – all parties generally dislike it – but a lack of respect for and trust in the police and the criminal justice system. Particularly in the most marginalized communities and populations, as perceptions of legitimacy go down, serious crime goes up.[22]

What might seem remarkably small insults to legitimacy can have large consequences. Tyler, Fagan and Geller found that even a single police stop, perceived as unfair, unjust, and disrespectful, could weaken perceptions of police legitimacy, and that below a threshold level of legitimacy, criminal activity doubled.[23] At the neighborhood level, a sufficient proportion of the population with perceptions of illegitimacy can maintain high levels of violence even as the neighborhood improves socially and economically.[24] At an extreme – but one found regularly in American urban areas – perceptions of illegitimacy can lead to pervasive "stop snitching" norms in which even violent offenders are privileged over police. The resulting inability to mobilize the criminal justice system for protection and support can lead to the private use of violence for security and retribution ("self help" violence[25]), and to patterns of cyclical vendetta-like violence.[26]

In the other direction, what might seem remarkably small enhancements in legitimacy can also have large consequences. The Center for Court Innovation's Red Hook Community Justice Center in Brooklyn, NY, for instance, deliberately aims to improve perceptions of justice system legitimacy by enhancing procedural justice, fostering community involvement, and offering community services to defendants. The Justice Center has seen a 10 percent reduction in recidivism among adult criminal defendants over those prosecuted in traditional misdemeanor courts, with a strong indication that procedural justice is the most plausible explanation for the impact.[27]

Programmatic community crime prevention interventions

"Community crime prevention," then, is considerably more fundamental and powerful than is generally understood. When we turn to the portfolio of interventions more traditionally considered community crime prevention, the fundamental issue arises that "community crime prevention" is not a technical term with a clear definition and precise boundaries, but more of a notion: one generally understood to include aspects of community involvement or focus; aspirations toward prevention; and a subordinate role if any for criminal justice actors or, at least, a minimum of actual enforcement. That notion encompasses a vast range of approaches and practice, from major national policy initiatives to small, one-off clinical interventions. Within that huge and heterogeneous portfolio, however, certain strong tendencies can be discerned, particularly for those concerned with the policy and practical implications of the historical and evaluation record.

The weakness of broad "prevention" approaches

One of the strongest and most honorable aspirations behind community crime prevention is to address fundamental "root cause" issues. In the classic statement of the 1967 President's Commission on Law Enforcement and the Administration of Justice:

> Warring on poverty, inadequate housing and unemployment, is warring on crime. A civil rights law is a law against crime. Money for schools is money against crime. Medical, psychiatric, and family-counseling services are services against crime. More broadly and most importantly every effort to improve life in America's "inner cities" is an effort against crime. A community's most enduring protection against crime is to right the wrongs and cure the illnesses that tempt men to harm their neighbors.[28]

Similarly, in an essay on preventing gang homicide, James Alan Fox, one of the nation's most prominent criminologists, wrote that:

> We need to invest in disadvantaged youth through increased funding for preschool enrichment programs like Head Start, for after-school programs like the Boys and Girls Clubs, and for urban schools. These initiatives have been shown to help prevent kids from getting involved in gangs, drugs and crime.[29]

The field and evaluation record has not been kind to such sentiments. The thinking behind the 1967 report, for example, was instantiated in the Johnson Administration's War on Poverty and Great Society initiatives, historically the nation's high-water-mark for deliberate federal intervention in root cause issues. The policies were explicitly aimed at (among other things) crime prevention; were plagued by massive implementation issues[30]; are generally considered epic failures; and manifestly failed to redirect the nation's soaring crime rates. Claims that there are proved broad interventions aimed at serious crime tend to suffer the same fate upon closer examination. The best evaluations of the long-term crime-control impact of Head Start, for example, show that in adulthood both Head Start and non-Head Start populations present low overall rates of offending – about 15 percent – and that black Head Start populations showed a small – about 12 percent – reduction in self-reported criminality, with no distinction in the study between minor and serious violent offending.[31] Even if these results carry over into very different settings – men in neighborhoods with high rates of violent crime tend to have high, not low, overall rates of offending, with those involved in gang crime showing far and away the highest (one criminal history review of gang members in Cincinnati, for example, showed an average of 35 prior charges, with about a third having 10 or more felony priors[32]) – a ten percent or so reduction in crime, which may or may not extend to serious violence and homicide, would hardly constitute a shining success.

The same basic pattern holds for a range of programs intended to have broad preventive effects through early interventions with a general population. Public health violence prevention curricula,[33] drug prevention programs like DARE,[34] gang prevention programs like GREAT,[35] activity-based interventions like Midnight Basketball,[36] and gun buybacks[37] all show little or no impact on the target behavior. Some show iatrogenic impact, making the target behavior worse, as did the United States government's $1.2 billion public-service-advertising National Youth Anti-Drug Media Campaign, which led to an increase in marijuana use[38] (a likely result – well known in other settings – of treating a large general population for what is in fact a low-propensity problem). One of the most recently popular public health community prevention initiatives, stand-alone streetwork to prevent gang violence,[39] in fact has an historical and possibly growing contemporary evaluation record for unintentionally making violence worse.[40]

We should probably not be surprised by these findings. Serious violent crime, especially, is relatively rare on a population basis and – as we have seen – already largely controlled by deep, "natural" community energies. The marginal addition to those deep community energies that can be produced at a general population level by deliberate additional intervention is inevitably small, and will frequently be arrayed against very powerful criminogenic forces, such as gang dynamics.[41] As things stand, we should have modest expectations – and make modest claims – for such broad community crime control approaches.

Targeted community crime prevention approaches: the record and the challenges

Happily, there is no shortage of demonstrably effective community-based initiatives. Most of these have the characteristic of being narrower in scope, often focused on a particular issue such as reentry or gun violence, and/ or being implemented in a relatively specific social and geographic community context. Evaluations can show strong impact: for now-traditional approaches such as neighborhood watch;[42] for relatively new approaches such as reentry initiatives;[43] in family settings;[44] in fundamentally resetting the functioning and public safety context of major public/private spaces;[45] through deliberate criminal justice mobilization of the public[46] and service providers;[47] and more. A review of the literatures on community policing, problem-oriented policing, evidence-based crime prevention, crime prevention through environmental design (CPTED), situational crime prevention, routine activities theory, commercial and industrial security, and the like are replete with examples of effective community-based action. If the frame is expanded to include frameworks and interventions in which community actors work in central partnership with criminal justice agencies, the list grows substantially larger (and impacts on the most serious crime problems).[48]

While this is encouraging, the problem, at present, is twofold. First, nothing resembling a systematic accounting of such interventions exists; one must wander through a wide range of disparate literatures and field experience to get any sense of the state of the art. Second, and arguably more important, there is next to no basic theoretical and empirical understanding of what makes effective interventions work and ineffective interventions (of which there is also a sufficiency) not work, nor what should guide the design and implementation of original interventions. Most evaluations do not assist with this latter set of problems; high-quality evaluations can say whether a given intervention did or did not produce impact, but tend to say nothing whatsoever about how or why.[49]

The result is that the important domain of community crime prevention exists without any real central theoretical or empirical foundation, and what arguably ought to be the important field of community crime prevention practice does not really exist, or exists in only the most vitiated form. Scholars and practitioners familiar with the broader literatures may glean from, say, problem-oriented policing the idea that one should pick a meaningful problem and research it in detail in order to frame a carefully tailored intervention; from situational crime prevention and third-party policing the general precept that one should look for a capable community guardian; and from the procedural justice literature that one should incorporate legitimacy-enhancing measures into any intervention design.[50] At present, however, any such overall theoretical and practical framework is entirely notional rather than actual, and what in fact guides intervention practice is largely dependent on the knowledge and proclivities of the individuals involved.

A lesson here might be drawn from recent practice in the field of evidence-based community corrections, which has developed a well-thought-out framework for mobilizing criminological theory, evaluation research, and experience with organizational design and operational collaborations to drive a new approach to replacing traditional probation and parole supervision with innovative and more effective practice. The field has been driven by a recognition that while having a strong social-science grounding for new practice is important:

> knowledge of these evidence based practices is not sufficient to implement and sustain this new way of doing business. Agencies and systems must have the capacity to undergo a significant shift in their business practices and organizational culture; they require a framework to guide this change.[51]

The field has developed a simple but powerful set of guidelines for shaping new practice (at least two of which – focus primarily on those at highest risk for serious offending, and on the most criminogenic aspects of their situations[52] – seem likely to carry over nicely into any systematic structure for community crime prevention). Until community crime prevention does something similar, it seems clear that it will continue to operate under some considerable number of outdated and disproved guiding principles; fail to fully understand and build on what is in fact a considerable record of success; and fail to fulfill its very considerable potential.

Lessons

All of this would seem to lead to some reasonably clear lessons and next steps:

- First do no harm. Most community crime prevention is not a specially designed and implemented programmatic activity, but the result of the normal functioning of communities. As such it dramatically outweighs the impact of formal authorities and the criminal justice system. Those authorities and that system should take care not to undercut community crime prevention through over-incarceration and other insults to collective efficacy and informal social control, and through the many ways in which criminal justice legitimacy can be damaged.
- The broadest and most ambitious community crime prevention approaches are rarely effective. Claims that there are proved techniques for fundamentally altering community conditions in ways that prevent crime; that investing in current programs is all that is required to produce substantial outcomes; that front-end "prevention" is a pragmatic, operational alternative to back-end "reaction"; and the like are generally not borne out in practice.
- The proved impact of a wide range of more strategic and focused approaches amply demonstrates the power of community crime prevention. Currently the theoretical, evaluation, and field experience with those approaches is spread across a range of scholarly literatures and professional specialties. Integrating them, and beyond that, moving to some more consolidated theory and practice, would greatly advance the field.
- Any meaningful evidence base, and guidance for practice, in this area should include not only evidence about impact but attention to how and why effective interventions work and how they can and should be designed, implemented, managed, and sustained.

Notes

1 Gibbons, J. (ed.). (2013). *Global study on homicide 2013: Trends, contexts data*. United Nations Office on Drugs and Crime. www.unodc.org/documents/data-and-analysis/statistics/GSH2013/2014_GLOBAL_HOMICIDE_BOOK_web.pdf.
2 Shaw, C. R., and McKay, H. D. (1942). *Juvenile delinquency and urban areas: A study of rates of delinquents in relation to differential characteristics of local communities in American cities*. Chicago: University of Chicago Press.
3 Sampson, R. J. (1986). Crime in cities: The effects of formal and informal social control. *Crime and Justice*: 271–311.
4 Sampson, R. J., Raudenbush, S. W., and Earls, F. (1997). Neighborhoods and Violent Crime: A Multilevel Study of Collective Efficacy. *Science* 277(5328): 918–924. www.sciencemag.org/content/277/5328/918.full.
5 See, for example, Kennedy, D. M. (2009). *Deterrence and Crime Prevention: Reconsidering the Prospect of Sanction*. New York: Routledge: 38.
6 Johnson, B., Golub, A., and Dunlap, E. (2000). The Rise and Decline of Hard Drugs, Drug Markets, and Violence in Inner-City New York. Blumstein, A., and Wallman, J. (eds.). *The Crime Drop in America*. New York: Cambridge University Press: 164–206.

7 Ibid.
8 See, for example, Miller, N. (2014, June 2). Baltimore police have a duty to carry naloxone: The prescription medicine can reverse the effects of a heroin overdose, saving lives. *Baltimore Sun.* http://articles.baltimoresun.com/2014-06-04/news/bs-ed-naloxone-baltimore-20140604_1_naloxone-heroin-abuse-drug-users.
9 Sampson, R. J., and Bartusch, D. J. (1998). Legal cynicism and (subcultural?) tolerance of deviance: The neighborhood context of racial differences. *Law and Society Review* 32(4): 777–804.
10 Papachristos, A. V., and Wildeman, C. (2013). Network Exposure and Homicide Victimization in an African American Community. *American Journal of Public Health.* e-View Ahead of Print. doi: 10.2105/AJPH.2013.301441.
11 Lisak, D., and Miller, P. M. (2002). Repeat Rape and Multiple Offending Among Undetected Rapists. *Violence and Victims* 17(1).
12 Garot, R. (2007). Inner-City Teens and Face-Work: Avoiding Violence and Maintaining Honor. Monaghan, L. F., and Goodman, J. E. (eds.). *A Cultural Approach to Interpersonal Communication: Essential Readings* (pp. 294–317). Oxford: Blackwell.
13 Kennedy, D. M. (2011). *Don't Shoot: One Man, a Street Fellowship, and the End of Violence in Inner-City America* (p. 48). New York: Bloomsbury; Papachristos, A. V., Meares, T. L., and Fagan, F. (2012). Why Do Criminals Obey the Law? The Influence of Legitimacy and Social Networks on Active Gun Offenders. *Journal of Criminal Law and Criminology* 102(2).
14 Tyler, T. R. (2006). *Why People Obey the Law.* New Jersey: Princeton University Press.
15 Tyler, 2006.
16 Clear, T. R. (2007). *Imprisoning Communities: How Mass Incarceration Makes Disadvantaged Neighborhoods Worse.* New York: Oxford University Press.
17 Travis, J. (2005). *But They All Come Back: Facing the Challenges of Prisoner Reentry.* Washington, DC: Urban Institute Press.
18 Rose, D., and Clear, T. R. (2002). *Incarceration, Reentry and Social Capital: Social Networks in the Balance.* New York: John Jay College of Criminal Justice.
19 Stanley, Jason. (2014, January 12). Is the United States a 'Racial Democracy'? *New York Times.* http://opinionator.blogs.nytimes.com/2014/01/12/is-the-united-states-a-racial-democracy/?_r=0#more-151303; Weaver, V. (2014). *Arresting Citizenship: The Democratic Consequences of American Crime Control.* Chicago: The University of Chicago Press.
20 Schaffner, B., Van Erve, W., and LaRaja, R. (2014, August 15). How Ferguson exposes the racial bias in local elections. *Washington Post.* www.washingtonpost.com/blogs/monkey-cage/wp/2014/08/15/how-ferguson-exposes-the-racial-bias-in-local-elections/.
21 Tyler, 2006.
22 Kane, R. J. (2005). Compromised Police Legitimacy as a Predictor of Violent Crime in Structurally Disadvantaged Communities. *Criminology* 43; Meares, T. L. (2009). The Legitimacy of Police Among Young African-American Men. *Marquette Law Review* 92.
23 Tyler, T. R., Fagan, J., and Geller, A. (2014). Street Stops and Police Legitimacy: Teachable Moments in Young Urban Men's Legal Socialization. *Yale Law School, Public Law Working Paper* 302.
24 Kirk, D. S., and Papachristos, A. V. (2011). Cultural Mechanisms and the Persistence of Neighborhood Violence. *American Journal of Sociology* 166(4): 1190–1233.
25 Donald Black, Crime as Social Control (1983). *American Sociological Review* 48(1): 34–45.

26 For a gripping account of how a lack of trust in the police, and overall police incapacity, can drive violence, see Leovy, J. (2015). *Ghettoside*. New York: Spiegel and Grau. See also Kennedy, D. M. (2015, February 19). What you think about dangerous inner-city neighborhoods is wrong. *Washington Post*. www.washington-post.com/opinions/book-review-ghettoside-by-jill-leovy/2015/02/19/b7fbb2ae-b 077-11e4-827f-93f454140e2b_story.html.

27 Lee, C.G., Cheesman, F., Rottman, D., Swaner, R., Lambson, S., Rempel, M. and Curtis, R. (2014). *A Community Court Grows in Brooklyn: A Comprehensive Evaluation of the Red Hook Community Justice Center Final Report*. National Center for State Courts.

28 President's Commission on Law Enforcement and the Administration of Justice (1967). The Challenge of Crime in a Free Society (p. 6). United States Government Printing Office.

29 Fox, J. A. (2015, April 10). Better to pre-habilitate children than rehabilitate killers. *Los Angeles Times*. www.latimes.com/opinion/bookclub/ la-reading-los-angeles-fox-ghettoside-20150404-story.html.

30 Moynihan, D. P. (1970). *Maximum Feasible Misunderstanding: Community Action in the War on Poverty*. New York: Free Press.

31 Garces, E., Thomas, D., and Curry, J. (2000). *Longer Term Effects of Head Start. NBER Working Paper Series*. Cambridge: National Bureau of Economic Research.

32 Engel, R. S., Baker, S. G., Tilyer, M. S., Eck, J., and Dunham, M. S. (2008). *Implementation of the Cincinnati initiative to reduce violence (CIRV): Year 1 report*. Cincinnati: University of Cincinnati Policing Institute.

33 Webster, D. W. (1993) The unconvincing case for school-based conflict resolution programs for adolescents. *Health Affairs* 12.

34 Birkeland, B., Murphy-Graham, E., and Weiss, C. (2005). Good reasons for ignoring good evaluation: The case of the drug abuse resistance education (D.A.R.E.) program. *Evaluation and Program Planning* 28: 247–256.

35 The most favorable evaluation of GREAT found no statistically significant impact on self-reported delinquency. Esbensen, F., et al. (2010). Evaluation and Evolution of the Gang Resistance Education and Training (G.R.E.A.T.) Program. *Journal of School Violence*, 10: 53–70.

36 The most positive evaluation of Midnight Basketball found some correlation with reduced property crime but none with violent crime, the program's *raison d'etre*. Hartmann, D., and Depro, B. (2006). Crime Rates Analysis of the Relationship Between Midnight Basketball and Urban Crime Rates. *Journal of Sport and Social Issues* 30: 180.

37 Plotkin, M. (ed.) (1996). *Under Fire: Gun Buy-Backs, Exchanges, and Amnesty Programs*. Washington, DC: Police Executive Research Forum.

38 Orwin, R., et al. (2006). *Evaluation of the National Youth Anti-Drug Media Campaign: 2004 Report of Findings*, Executive Summary. Westat.

39 Cure Violence. http://cureviolence.org/.

40 Klein, M. W. (1969). Gang Cohesiveness, Delinquency, and a Street-Work Program. *Journal of Research in Crime and Delinquency* 6(2): 135–166; Klein, M. W. (2011). Comprehensive gang and violence reduction programs: Reinventing the square wheel, *Criminology and Public Policy* 10(4): 1037–1044; Papachristos, A. V. (2011). Too big to fail: The science and politics of violence prevention. *Criminology and Public Policy* 10(4): 1053–1061.

41 For a discussion of the ineffectiveness and implausibility of prevention approaches more generally with respect to serious crime, see the chapter of Kennedy, D. M. 2011 entitled "Stopping it."

42 Bennett, T., Holloway, K., and Farrington, D. (2008). *The Effectiveness of Neighborhood Watch*. Oslo: Campbell Collaboration.

43 See, for example, Crimesolutions.gov. Program Profile: Auglaize County (Ohio) Transition (ACT) Program. U.S. Department of Justice, National Institute of Justice. www.crimesolutions.gov/ProgramDetails.aspx?ID=130; Crimesolutions. gov. Program Profile: Boston (Massachusetts) Reentry Initiative (BRI). U.S. Department of Justice, National Institute of Justice. www.crimesolutions.gov/ProgramDetails.aspx?ID=42.

44 Crimesolutions.gov. Program Profile: Functional Family Therapy (FFT). U.S. Department of Justice, National Institute of Justice. www.crimesolutions.gov/ProgramDetails.aspx?ID=122.

45 Felson, M., et al. (1994). Redesigning Hell: Preventing Crime and Disorder at the Port Authority Bus Terminal. In R.V. Clarke (ed.) *Preventing Mass transit Crime*. Crime Prevention Studies 6. Monsey, NY: Criminal Justice Press.

46 Mazzerole, L., and Ransley, J. (). *Third Party Policing*. Cambridge: Cambridge University Press.

47 Collins, S. E., Lonczak, H. S., and Clifasefi, S. L. (2015). *LEAD Program Evaluation: Recidivism Report*. Harm Reduction Research and Treatment Lab, University of Washington, Harborview Medical Center.

48 Braga, A. A., and Weisburd, D. L. (2012). The Effects of "Pulling Levers" Focused Deterrence Strategies on Crime. Campbell Systematic Reviews; Papachristos, A. V., Meares, T. L., and Fagan, J. (2007). Attention Felons: Evaluation Project Safe Neighborhoods in Chicago. *Journal of Empirical Studies*, 4(2), 223–272.

49 The U.S. government's crimesolutions.gov, which collects evaluations of crime control interventions according to methodological rigor, offers an excellent illustration of this point. Studies of community crime control efforts – both effective and ineffective – feature amongst its "evidence based" portfolio, but there are absolutely no general insights, lessons, or guidance offered.

50 For a provocative argument on this point directed at policing, but more widely applicable, see Braga, A. A., and Weisburd, D. L. (2013). The Importance of Legitimacy in Hot Spots Policing. *Community Policing Dispatch* 6(9). U.S. Department of Justice, Office of Community Oriented Policing Services.

51 Bogue, B., *et al.* (2009) *Implementing Evidence-Based Policy and Practice in Community Corrections: Second Edition* (p. ix). U.S. Department of Justice, Crime and Justice Institute and National Institute of Corrections.

52 Bogue, 2009 (p. x).

Chapter 8

Situational crime prevention

Rob T. Guerette, Shane D. Johnson and Kate Bowers

Introduction

Situational Crime Prevention (SCP) is an approach to the reduction of crime through alteration of the physical or systemic environment (Clarke, 1997) in such a way that it reduces opportunities for offending. It is based on the recognition that the presence of a motivated offender is simply one component necessary for crime to take place. Rather than attempting to alter individual dispositions – the focus of most other crime prevention strategies – the situational approach seeks to remove and eliminate environmental opportunities for crime. Doing so is viewed as much easier than trying to alter social structural or life course processes which lead to higher risk of offending among some individuals. The approach was developed by researchers who recognized that crime problems tended to concentrate in such a way that implicated the role of opportunity in crime causation. The premise is straight forward: if opportunities are necessary for crimes to occur, then their removal – through physical and situational alterations – stands as a viable way to prevent crime. This chapter discusses in more detail the situational crime prevention framework, its historical origins and theoretical underpinnings, and assesses evaluation evidence of its effectiveness. It offers justifications and recommendations for the adoption of the Situational Crime Prevention approach by policymakers and practitioners.

The situational approach to crime prevention

While conducting research for the British government in the 1970s, researchers Ron Clarke and Pat Mayhew, developed the beginnings of the scientific and creative approach of situational crime prevention (Hough et al., 1980). The approach was inspired by research findings that examined delinquency infractions across juvenile detention facilities. Here it was found that the frequency of offending tended to cluster within specific facilities rather than being equally distributed; something that would not be expected given the ostensible constant presence of criminal dispositions among detention facility juveniles. This finding led them to conclude that it was the situational environments, how the facilities were designed and managed, which largely determined the nature and frequency of offending, not offender dispositions (Clarke and Martin, 1975). Over the next several decades this new thinking spurred the Situational Crime Prevention (SCP) approach through several developmental iterations with the help of many criminologists.

In practice, SCP calls for the systematic process of analyzing, understanding, implementing, and assessing situational tactics designed to reduce crime. This "action research methodology" is very similar to the scanning, analysis, response, assessment (SARA) approach used in Problem-Oriented Policing. In both, the process is important because it helps to ensure that the tactics devised and implemented are relevant to address the situational circumstances responsible for the targeted crime problem. The prescribed actions to be taken within each step of the process are as follows:

- *Problem identification* – Entails the identification of the problem to be addressed. In most cases this requires identification of both the behavior producing the harm and the specific locations and facilities where it is taking place.
- *Analysis of the problem* – This involves both quantitative and qualitative data collection and analysis to thoroughly identify the contributing characteristics within the environment or system where the problem occurs. It also involves searching for evidence on tactics that have worked elsewhere to address similar problems.
- *Formulation and implementation of intervention tactics* – Identification and implementation of suitable situational tactics identified within the 25 techniques of SCP (see below), which are logically relevant to each of the circumstances that were identified in the analysis as facilitating the problem.
- *Determining impact* – Involves an assessment of the impact of those interventions to determine whether they have reduced the occurrence of crime or alleviated the harms of the problem behavior.
- *Dissemination of findings* – Finally, the dissemination of those findings to inform other preventative efforts and to strengthen the knowledge-base of what does and does not work to reduce crime.

While the process of SCP has remained the same since its beginning, the suggested techniques have gone through several iterations and refinements.[1] Today, the framework identifies 25 techniques that can be used to reduce and prevent crime problems. These are organized around five theoretical axioms that work to reduce the opportunities for offending. They include techniques which seek to increase the effort involved in carrying out crime, those to increase the risk involved, those to reduce the rewards of offending, methods of reducing provocations for offending, and techniques to remove excuses for engaging in crime. While these techniques are listed individually, in practice it is common and often advantageous to use "packages" of several SCP measures together to reduce the given crime problem.

The first classification scheme of SCP techniques was published in 1980 (Hough et al., 1980). In this arrangement there were two groups of techniques, one that made it physically harder to commit crime whereas the other manipulated the costs, benefits and material conditions of crime. The first group entailed target hardening and the removal of the targets, tools and methods of crime, while the second consisted of reducing the payoffs, establishing different types of surveillance, and finally environmental management. Recognizing the limited relationship between this arrangement and any theoretical foundations, a second iteration of the SCP framework was articulated by Clarke in 1992.

This drew heavily from the rational choice perspective and incorporated three primary categories within which 12 techniques of prevention were identified. These categories were techniques to increase the effort, increase the risk, or to decrease the rewards involved in committing crime. For instance, tactics identified to increase the effort included target hardening, access control, deflecting offenders, and controlling facilitators of crime. Methods of increasing the risks included screening exits and entry points, establishing formal surveillance, strengthening surveillance by employees, and creating natural surveillance. Finally, methods to reduce the rewards of crime included target removal, property identification, the removal of inducements, and rule setting. A third iteration of the SCP framework, by Clarke and Homel (1997), expanded the number of techniques to 16 and added a fourth dimension which included inducing guilt or shame as a means to reduce or prevent crime. This dimension was informed by criminological research regarding offending stemming partly from Sykes and Matza's (1957) idea of guilt and Bandura's (1978) ideas about forms of self-exoneration and the importance of peer influences, and public shaming. Techniques to remove excuses include setting rules, posting instructions, and controlling drugs and alcohol.

The fourth and most recent iteration of the SCP framework was expanded with the work of Wortley (2001) who identified the importance of precipitation and control strategies in facilitating and, therefore, perhaps preventing crime. This led to the addition of a fifth category of tactics to include methods of reducing provocations for offending. This also brought the number of situational techniques to 25. Examples of techniques added under the category of provocations included methods of reducing frustrations and stress, avoiding disputes, methods of reducing emotional arousal, neutralizing pressure, and discouraging imitation (see www.popcenter.org/25techniques/).

Theoretical underpinnings

Although the SCP framework has been informed by both practice and a variety of criminological theories, it is most centrally grounded in three primary theories of crime events. This includes Rational Choice Perspective (RCP), the Routine Activities Approach (RAA), and Crime Pattern Theory (CPT). The RCP (Clarke and Cornish, 1985; 2001) is primarily a crime event model. It posits that offenders make assessments of the effort, risk and rewards involved in engaging in a given crime event on the basis of available (often incomplete) information. According to this perspective, if the expected effort and risk outweigh anticipated rewards, crime should be less likely to occur. In turn, where the reverse is perceived to be the case, crime should be more likely. The Rational Choice framework helps to explain why some targets are victimized and others are not. Also, more importantly for SCP, the theory helps to understand and identify suitable prevention tactics to offset the ratio of acceptable effort and risk and hence the likelihood of crime. Indeed, three of the five categories (increase the effort, increase the risk, and reduce the rewards) of SCP techniques are derived from the RCP.

The Routine Activities Approach (RAA) (Cohen and Felson, 1979) complements the RCP and identifies three elements necessary (simultaneously) for a crime to occur. These are the absence of a capable guardian, the presence of a suitable target, and the presence of a motivated offender. Since direct contact predatory crimes cannot occur unless all three elements converge in space and time, the theory can help identify possibilities for prevention. For example, practitioners might implement prevention tactics which seek to establish or strengthen capable guardianship; remove, control access to, or make less attractive potential targets; or otherwise control motivated offenders.

Crime Pattern theory (CPT) (Brantingham and Brantingham, 1981, 1995) complements both the RCP and the RAA and helps to explain the geographical distribution of crime. This approach identifies "activity nodes" and "paths" of everyday human behavior which comprise individuals' (including potential offenders) "awareness spaces." According to the theory, offenders are most likely to commit offences – and hotspots are most likely to form – where their awareness spaces intersect suitable opportunities for crime. This theory distinguishes between "crime generators," places which attract potential offenders and victims to an area for non-crime purposes which, in turn, generates opportunities for offending and "crime attractors," locations where offenders go because of known opportunities for offending. CPT is also a foundational theory of the SCP framework since it helps to explain why crime hotspots might form, and hence what might prevent them, and to identify *where* crime prevention tactics could be most useful.

Evidence of effectiveness[2]

The accumulation of over thirty years of evaluation research on situational prevention measures suggests that altering situational environments can effectively reduce crime. This effectiveness has been shown in both individual case studies (see Clarke, 1997) and systematic reviews. A handful of systematic reviews of situational crime prevention evaluations have assessed conclusions reported by study authors, while others have examined outcomes using meta-analysis. The reviews sometimes disaggregate by place and/or intervention types. Still others have examined more narrowly specific intervention types, such as CCTV and street lighting. Reviews of evaluations are always limited by the underlying methodological rigor of the primary evaluation studies on which they are based – those with stronger research designs are viewed with more confidence. Conventionally, randomized experimental designs are largely viewed as the strongest, but these remain rare in the evaluation of SCP for reasons that will be discussed in the next section. The result is that most evaluations of SCP measures have relied on a range of quasi-experimental study designs (see Guerette, 2009).

In a descriptive review of 206 SCP evaluations (Guerette, 2009), it was found that three out of four studies (75 percent, n = 154) concluded that the intervention was effective overall. Twelve percent (n = 24) concluded that the situational intervention was not effective, while 6 percent (n = 12) reported mixed findings, and for 8 percent (n =16) study outcomes were inconclusive. Relying on this same sample of evaluations, another review examined study findings across five common place types (Eck and Guerette, 2012) which resulted in a subsample of 149 evaluations. In that review, notwithstanding some variation, effectiveness was reported by at least 60 percent of the evaluations (see Table 8.1). Though all recreational interventions appeared successful, the small number makes any meaningful conclusion unreliable. Considered differently, situational efforts in public outdoor settings and in residential places had the most failures, but even in those settings ineffective interventions were comparatively small compared to those found to be effective and those with mixed results.

An examination of the success rate of commonly used interventions suggested effectiveness overall, though with some variation across intervention type. Table 8.2 presents interventions that were used in decreasing order of frequency (totals column) and shows the percent of each intervention type demonstrating different outcomes (effective, not effective, mixed, inconclusive). The majority of studies reviewed (79 percent) relied on only 7 of the 25 possible situational intervention techniques. Most were found effective, yet the most commonly used showed the lowest rate of efficacy. This may be due to a tendency for practitioners to use "off the shelf" techniques rather than those tailored to the specific problems.

In separate meta-analytic reviews of the two most common SCP techniques, closed circuit television (CCTV) and street lighting, similar positive findings were found (Welsh and Farrington 2008a, Welsh and Farrington 2008b). Using meta-analytical techniques, a review of 41 evaluations of CCTV found that overall the technique produced moderate significant

Table 8.1 Effectiveness of place-based intervention evaluations by common place types

Place Type	Percent of authors' conclusions (n)			
	Effective	Not effective	Mixed findings	Inconclusive
Residential (39)	77 (30)	10 (4)	10 (4)	3 (1)
Public ways (52)	62 (32)	12 (6)	19 (10)	8 (4)
Retail (25)	88 (22)	4 (1)	4 (1)	4 (1)
Transport (26)	88 (23)	0 (0)	8 (2)	4 (1)
Recreational (7)	100 (7)	–	–	–
Total (149)	77 (114)	7 (11)	11 (17)	5 (7)

Source: Adapted from Eck and Guerette (2012).

Table 8.2 Effectiveness of the most used interventions

Intervention	Percent of a authors' conclusions (n)				
	Totals n (%)	Effective	Not effective	Mixed	Inconclusive
CCTV	25 (37)	59 (22)	14 (5)	24 (9)	3 (1)
Lighting	14 (20)	55 (11)	15 (3)	15 (3)	15 (3)
CPTED	11 (16)	94 (15)			6 (1)
Mixed / other	10 (16)	93 (14)	7 (1)		
Access control	9 (14)	92 (13)			8 (1)
Place management	6 (9)	89 (8)		11 (1)	
Street redesign	4 (6)	67 (4)		17 (1)	17 (1)
Total	79 (118)	74 (87)	7 (8)	12 (14)	6 (7)

Source: Adapted from Eck and Guerette (2012).

reductions in crime, though this too varied by place type. CCTV was found to be most effective when used in parking lots to reduce vehicle-related crime. The findings also revealed that they tended to be more effectively applied in the United Kingdom than in the United States. Using similar methods, a meta-analysis of 13 evaluations of the effects of improved street lighting found that they too achieved significant reductions in crime.

In a recent exercise that compiled evidence from five systematic reviews of SCP, a database was compiled of 110 different intervention effect sizes. A statistical meta-analysis of these demonstrated a reliable positive impact of SCP interventions on crime. In line with other research, there was considerable variation in outcomes depending on the country, year of intervention, specific context, and the type of crime and intervention.

Of course, these findings are far from conclusive partly because the studies reviewed were conducted with varying degrees of methodological rigor. Stronger evaluation designs allow for more confident determinations that it was in fact the situational intervention that was responsible for any observed crime reduction, while weaker evaluation designs leave open the possibility that something else caused the change. The consistency of the findings observed alleviates some concern, but for now we can only take an aggregated and tentative understanding of situational crime prevention effectiveness. Beyond this several challenges exist in the evaluation of SCP outcomes which often limits the methodologies that can be employed.

Methodological issues in SCP evaluation

One issue facing SCP evaluation is that it is a *process* rather than a specific intervention. A fundamental component of this process is that the implementation of situational measures should be tailored to the specific circumstances responsible for a given problem. What works in one location, or in response to one problem, may not work elsewhere under different circumstances. Resultantly, random assignment of interventions, a requirement of classical experiments, is contrary to the intentional process of SCP since such designs call for the blind application of interventions.

Another issue facing SCP evaluation is that many situational prevention schemes rely on several intervention measures together as a prevention "package." For instance, an initiative to reduce residential burglary may include an assortment of tactics such as a media campaign, target hardening measures including the use of security alarms and the fortification of dwelling entry points, and improved lighting, among others. Because of this it is usually not possible to specify the role of any single situational intervention as being, in fact, responsible for any observed reductions in crime. The consequence is that in such evaluations the best that can be concluded is that the package of situational interventions together resulted in any given change. An additional issue which often precludes the use of randomized evaluation designs is that most evaluations of SCP techniques are conducted retrospectively after the intervention has already been implemented, thereby eliminating the possibility for random assignment.

A fourth issue is that despite SCP having a formal theoretical foundation and an applied process for understanding crime problems and formulating situational interventions (Clarke, 1997), many applications of situational prevention efforts and their subsequent evaluation are not informed by the framework. Because of this the situational techniques deployed may not have been accurately suited for the crime problem they sought to address. This creates the possibility of producing false negatives (erroneous conclusions of ineffectiveness) when trying to determine the efficacy of the situational techniques implemented.

A final challenge is that there are a variety of unique issues which situational evaluations must address which further complicates the type of research design used. This includes possibilities of displacement (the movement of crime to other places, times, tactics, targets, or offenses), diffusion of benefits (a reduction in crime surrounding intervention areas), and anticipatory benefits (the premature reduction in crime prior to the implementation of an intervention). Addressing each of these possibilities requires methodological approaches in addition to those common to other evaluations of crime prevention. For instance, to study spatial displacement and diffusion effects requires the use of buffer zones that surround treatment areas. Moreover, it means that comparison areas cannot be adjacent to treatment areas or the areas that surround them. For determining anticipatory benefits a time series design must be utilized in order to reveal any premature reductions in crime before the intervention is implemented.

Implications for policy and practice

For those responsible for reducing crime, either by the crafting crime reduction policy or the practice of prevention, SCP has much to offer. By focusing on reducing opportunities for offending within the environments where crime takes place it offers a more receptive venue for manipulation rather than trying to alter social structures or individual propensities for offending, something that historically has been met with limited success (Martinson, 1976). Some may argue that SCP leads down the road to a "fortress society" yet most community members openly welcome the presence of some physical security measures if it keeps them from becoming victims of crime.[3]

It may also be argued that a reliance on situational prevention measures ignores or distracts from efforts which get to the "root causes" of crime. But the SCP framework promises no more than it can deliver and offers a comparatively quick way of ameliorating serious community crime problems. It also recognizes that much crime is the product of normal human dispositions coupled with easy opportunities for offending, the latter which serves as a causal mechanism for crime. Removing such situational opportunities offers to reduce crime, where no other "root causes" exist. A final, yet common, concern about SCP is that it will simply displace crime to other places and times. But here too over thirty years of research indicates that displacement is the exception rather than the rule, and where some displacement does occur it tends to be less than the volume of crime that was prevented, making the prevention gains still worthwhile (see Guerette and Bowers, 2009; Johnson et al., 2012; 2014).

Because evaluations of SCP tell us more about the effectiveness of the *process* of the approach rather than the universal suitability of any given technique, it is difficult to offer recommendations for the promotion of any specific opportunity reduction tactic. There are, however, several ways that the use of the SCP approach could be advanced through policy and in practice. First, the situational approach could be promoted through government grant programming. For the most part, in the United States at least, opportunity reduction has not been promoted visibly by the government such as through grant programming. Instead, most efforts to incorporate situational prevention measures have been carried out in the private sector with little government guidance. Consequently, there is an opportunity to promote situational prevention more visibly as a formidable method to reducing crime and the harms that are incurred. With proper protocols such programming can help to ensure that the process of SCP will be used to develop relevant prevention packages and to help further the idea that opportunity reduction practices should become central to crime prevention activities by local government rather than something relegated to the private sector.

Second, there also exists an opportunity to establish a government regulatory process which ensures that new products and systems coming on to the marketplace have prevention measures that are built in prior to their release. Several studies of so-called hot products and technologies (such as cell phones, computers, ATMs) reveal a predictable sequence in which the rush to get them to market creates abundant opportunities for crime and that later retrofitting of prevention measures subsequently reduces the criminogenic nature of the product or system (for more on this, see Clarke 1999; Ekblom 1997; Guerette and Clarke, 2003). This predictable tendency has led some to argue that much crime could be prevented with the establishment of protocols which incorporate situational prevention measures as an inherent requirement of product development (Ekblom, 1997; Clarke, 1999). Finally, SCP could become more central as a method for prevention within police departments and within city management, planning and urban development practices. Promoting the establishment of regulations which requires greater police use (including training) of situational crime prevention and which establishes implementation of opportunity reduction in regulations of the development and management of public systems such as at parks, transport systems, roadways, and public housing could also lead to worthwhile reductions in crime. A further challenge is the production of repositories of easily accessible information on which methods work and where possible how this is mediated by particular location conditions. Two current exercises exist to do this by providing research evidence on SCP and other crime prevention strategies through online tools. These are the U.S.-based Crime Solutions website (www.crimesolutions.gov/) and the UK-based Centre for What Works in Crime Reduction (www.college.police.uk/en/20399.htm).

The large volume of evaluation research documenting the effectiveness of situational prevention measures suggests that it is a method of prevention which should be at the forefront of policy and practice. Even with the methodological caveats discussed, situational approaches to crime reduction have a substantial evidence base to support its use. Still, where the evidence base may be weak or absent, there is little chance that relying on situational prevention techniques will make matters worse.

Notes

1 For more on the development of Situational Crime Prevention, see Smith and Clarke (2012).
2 This section was adapted from Bowers and Guerette (2013).
3 For more on the criticisms of SCP and corresponding rebuttals, see Clarke (2005).

References

Bandura, A. (1978). Social learning theory of aggression. *Journal of Communication*, 28(3), 12–29.

Bowers, Kate and Rob T. Guerette (2013). "Evaluation of situational crime prevention." In Gerben Bruinsma and David Weisburd (eds.), *Encyclopedia of Criminology and Criminal Justice*. New York, NY: Springer Press.

Brantingham, P. J., and Brantingham, P. L. (eds.). (1981). *Environmental Criminology* (pp. 27–54). Beverly Hills, CA: Sage Publications.

Brantingham, P., and Brantingham, P. (1995). Criminality of place. *European Journal on Criminal Policy and Research*, 3(3), 5–26.

Clarke, Ronald V. (ed.). (1997). *Situational Crime Prevention: Successful Case Studies*. (2nd edition) Albany, NY: Harrow and Heston Publishers.

Clarke, R. V. G. (1999). "Hot products: understanding, anticipating and reducing demand for stolen goods." Policing and Reducing Crime Unit: Police Research Series Paper 112. London, UK: Home Office.

Clarke, R. V. (2005). "Seven misconceptions of situational crime prevention." In Nick Tilley (ed.) *Handbook of Crime Prevention and Community Safety*, 39–70. UK: Willan Publishing (Routledge).

Clarke, R. V., and Cornish, D. B. (1985). "Modeling offenders' decisions: A framework for research and policy." In M. Tonry and N. Morris (eds.) *Crime and Justice: An Annual Review of Research Vol. 6*, 147–185. Chicago: University of Chicago Press.

Clarke, R. V., and Cornish, D. B. (2001). "Rational choice." In Paternoster, R. and Bachman, R. (eds.) *Explaining Criminals and Crime: Essays in Contemporary Criminological Theory*, 23–42. Los Angeles: Roxbury.

Clarke, R.V. and Homel, Ross. (1997). "A revised classification of situational crime prevention techniques." In Steven P. Lab (ed.) *Crime Prevention at a Crossroads*, Highland Heights, KY, and Cincinnati: Academy of Criminal Justice Sciences and Anderson.

Clarke, R.V., and D. Martin (1975). "A study of absconding and its implications for the residential treatment of delinquents." In J. Tizard, I. Sinclair and R.V. Clarke (eds.) *Varieties of Residential Experience*. London: Routledge and Kegan Paul.

Cohen, L. E., and Felson, M. (1979). Social change and crime rate trends: A routine activity approach. *American Sociological Review*, 588–608.

Cornish, Derek B., and Ronald V. Clarke. (2003). "Opportunities, precipitators and criminal decisions: A reply to Wortley's critique of situational crime prevention." In Martha Smith and Derek B. Cornish (eds.) *Theory for Situational Crime Prevention. Crime Prevention Studies*, vol.16, Monsey, NY: Criminal Justice Press.

Eck, J.E., Guerette, R. T. (2012). "Own the Place, Own the Crime Prevention: How Evidence about Place-Based Crime Shifts the Burden of Prevention." In Rolf Loeber and Brandon C. Welsh (eds.) *The Future of Criminology*, Oxford: Oxford University Press.

Ekblom, P. (1997). Gearing up against crime. *International Journal of Risk, Security and Crime Prevention*, 2, 249–265.

Guerette, Rob T. 2009. The pull, push and expansion of situational crimeprevention evaluation: An appraisal of thirty-seven years of research. *Crime Prevention Studies*, 24, 29–58.

Guerette, R. T., and Bowers, K. J. (2009). Assessing the extent of crime displacement and diffusion of benefits: a review of situational crime prevention evaluations. *Criminology*, 47(4), 1331–1368.

Guerette, R. T., and Clarke, R. V. (2003). Product life cycles and crime: Automated teller machines and robbery. *Security Journal*, 16(1), 7–18.

Hough, J.M., R.V.G. Clarke, and P. Mayhew. (1980). "Introduction." In R.V.G. Clarke and P. Mayhew (eds.) *Designing Out Crime*, London: Her Majesty's Stationery Office.

Johnson, S. D., Guerette, R. T., and Bowers, K. (2014). Crime displacement: what we know, what we don't know, and what it means for crime reduction. *Journal of Experimental Criminology*, 1–23.

Martinson, R. (1976). "What works?–questions and answers about prison reform." Martinson, R., Palmer, T. and Adams, S. (eds.), *Rehabilitation, Recidivism, and Research*, National Council on Crime and Delinquency, Hackensack, NY, 17–54.

Smith, Martha J. and Clarke, Ronald V. (2012). "Situational Crime Prevention: Classifying Tecnniques Using 'Good Enough' Theory." In Welsh, B. C., and Farrington, D. P. (eds.). (2012). *The Oxford Handbook of Crime Prevention*. Oxford University Press.

Sykes, G. M., and Matza, D. (1957). Techniques of neutralization: A theory of delinquency. *American Sociological Review*, 664–670.

Welsh B. C, Farrington D. P. (2008a). Effects of closed circuit television surveillance on crime. *Campbell Systematic Reviews* 2008:17 DOI: 10.4073/csr.2008.17

Welsh B. C, Farrington D. P. (2008b). Effects of improved street lighting on crime. *Campbell Systematic Reviews* 13 DOI: 10.4073/csr.2008.13

Wortley, R. (2001). A classification of techniques for controlling situational precipitators of crime. *Security Journal*, 14(4), 63–82.

Part III

Policing and court sentencing

Introduction

Policing

Thomas G. Blomberg, Julie Mestre Brancale, Kevin M. Beaver and William D. Bales

The criminal and juvenile justice systems comprise the police, adult and juvenile courts, juvenile institutions, jails, and prisons; but the component that is currently in the forefront of American's minds is the police. The 2014 incident in Ferguson, Missouri in which Michael Brown, an unarmed 18 year-old African American man, was fatally shot by a white police officer, sparked massive protests for several weeks and extensive rioting and looting. The subsequent deaths of unarmed African American citizens by the police in New York City, North Charleston, South Carolina and Baltimore, Maryland further elevated the visibility of police policies and practices and resulted in calls for investigations and changes in police policies and practices. As a result, the current need for evidence-based police policies and practices could hardly be more timely or evident.

Charlotte Gill, David Weisburd, and Cody Telep review the evidence on the effectiveness of community policing in Chapter 9. Community policing emerged as a popular police policy reform in the 1990s and is a strategy which places emphasis on bringing the police and the community together as "co-producers" of making communities safe and solving other community problems. The community policing approach diverges from other policing approaches primarily through its emphasis on non-traditional crime-fighting activities of the police such as maintaining order, reducing citizens' fear of victimization, and resolving conflicts. On the negative side, community policing appears to have a limited effect on preventing criminal activity. However, on the positive side, studies have demonstrated that it is effective for some non-crime control outcomes such as increased levels of citizens' satisfaction with the police and an enhanced legitimacy of law enforcement personnel. Despite the evidence indicating community policing is not an effective crime reducing strategy, the authors believe this policy does increase the level of trust and satisfaction with the police among citizens which can help establish, reinforce, and even result in constructive working relationships between police agencies and the communities they serve.

The Problem-Oriented Policing (POP) approach described and assessed in Chapter 10 by John Eck and Kathleen Gallagher is not as concrete as the other policing strategies covered in this section. It is an approach in which science is applied to the work of police officers. In fact, popular approaches to policing such as COMSTAT, intelligence-led policing, evidence-based policing, and hot-spots policing are versions of POP. Based on an exhaustive review of the existing research, the authors conclude that the effectiveness of POP is comparable to standard approaches of policing. However, it is clear from the prior research that this mode of policing is difficult to implement and its sustainability is questionable.

Arguably the most evidence-based police strategy today is hot-spots policing, which Anthony Braga reviews in Chapter 11. The basic rationale and method of hot-spots policing is that specific geographic locations where crime is occurring are targeted by law enforcement since the vast majority of crime in a city occurs in a relatively small number of distinct locations, such as buildings, blocks, clusters of addresses, etc. Braga's exhaustive review of the research evidence on the effectiveness of hot-spot policing demonstrates that this policy is an effective crime control strategy. Also, and very importantly, the research shows that this strategy does not simply displace the crime problem from one location to another, but actually reduces the overall level of crime. The numerous criminological research studies on the effectiveness of hot-spots policing have contributed to police agencies throughout the U.S. and beyond embracing this crime fighting approach.

Policing strategies across the United States are under intense scrutiny from the public and policymakers alike. Among the major public and policy concerns is the poor relationship between law enforcement agencies and predominantly African American communities. The community policing strategy described in Chapter 9 by Gill, Weisburd, and Telep, was found to be capable of helping to build meaningful relationships between residents and their local police departments. Fundamental in doing so is having an effective and open dialogue between the police and community members. Problem-oriented policing (Chapter 10 by Eck and Gallagher) and hot-spots policing (Chapter 11 by Braga) can be used as effective strategies for identifying geographic locations in need of more targeted policing and the most effective scientific approaches for crime control in those areas. Rather than utilizing one policing strategy over another, integrating elements from several practices may be more beneficial in controlling crime by targeting areas, identifying the most appropriate technique for that area, and building more positive relationships between community residents and their law enforcement agencies.

Chapter 9

Community policing

Charlotte Gill, David Weisburd and Cody Telep

Community policing in the United States

Community, or community-oriented, policing is a philosophy or guiding principle of law enforcement that places the police and community together at the forefront of addressing and preventing crime and other community problems as "co-producers" of public safety. Community policing emphasizes three key elements: community partnerships, organizational transformation, and problem-solving (Office of Community Oriented Policing Services, 2012; Skogan, 2006a). The organizational transformation component sets community policing apart from many other crime prevention programs in that the approach requires a philosophical shift throughout the police agency in terms of leadership, structure, information sharing and other factors that allow delegation of decision-making and problem-solving to the street-level officers who directly engage the community (Cordner, 1999; Office of Community Oriented Policing Services, 2012; Trojanowicz et al., 1998).

Community policing became an extremely popular policy in the early 1990s, following decades of challenges to traditional policing models that emphasized reactive approaches to crime problems and short-term outcomes and targets rather than longer-term impacts on police effectiveness, legitimacy, and relationships with the community (e.g. Weisburd and Eck, 2004). During the 1970s, against a backdrop of rising crime and overall dissatisfaction with criminal justice policies and practices (e.g. Martinson, 1974), several studies called into question the effectiveness of two dominant components of the traditional policing model: preventive random patrol and rapid response (Kelling et al., 1974; Spelman and Brown, 1984; Weisburd and Braga, 2006). By the 1990s many scholars believed that the police could do nothing about crime (e.g. Bayley, 1994; Goldstein, 1990; Gottfredson and Hirschi, 1990).

At the same time, advocates of community-oriented policing highlighted the non-crime-fighting elements of police work: order maintenance, fear reduction, service provision, and conflict resolution, and the central role of the community in these activities (e.g. Kelling and Moore, 1988; Reiss Jr, 1971; Sherman, 1997; Skogan and Frydl, 2004; Skogan and Hartnett, 1997; Weisburd and Braga, 2006). Following massive investment in community-oriented policing approaches by the U.S. Department of Justice through the Office of Community Oriented Policing Services, created in 1994, most larger police departments claim to have adopted community policing (Hickman and Reaves, 2001; Mastrofski et al., 2007; Skogan, 2004, 2006b; see Skogan and Frydl, 2004; Weisburd and Eck, 2004), although deployment of full-time community police officers has declined more recently, especially in smaller departments (Reaves, 2010)—perhaps partly as a result of financial pressures created by the economic downturn.

The effectiveness of community policing

The evidence-base for the effectiveness of community policing as a policy is mixed. As its history suggests, community policing was not originally intended as a crime prevention approach, but crime control has been a key outcome measure of community policing initiatives in both research studies and the policy arena (Gill et al., 2014; Klockars, 1985; Skogan, 2006b). Perhaps as a result of this mismatch between intentions and measurement, several narrative reviews (Sherman and Eck, 2002; Skogan and Frydl, 2004; Weisburd and Eck, 2004) and a recent systematic review of controlled studies of community policing from the United States, United Kingdom, and Australia (Gill et al., 2014), have all found that while it may be too extreme to say that community policing "doesn't work," its impact on crime prevention is limited. Further, Gill et al. (2014) find that community policing efforts have little impact on reducing citizens' fear of crime in neighborhoods.

On the other hand, there is much more convincing evidence that community policing is effective for other non-crime control outcomes such as citizen satisfaction with the police and perceptions of legitimacy. In their meta-analysis of 37 community policing studies, Gill et al. (2014) find that community policing is associated with a moderate, statistically significant increase in citizens' ratings of their satisfaction with the police as well as benefits for police legitimacy and citizen perceptions of disorder. These findings are in line with the early emphasis of community policing on the non-crime-fighting roles of the police, such as responding to fear and disorder and building trust with the local community, over the traditional law enforcement role (e.g. Mastrofski et al., 1995).

Challenges of community policing

The mixed findings on the impact of community policing, and particularly its limited effectiveness for crime prevention, have raised questions about the significant investment by the federal government and many police departments around the country in hiring community police officers and developing specialist teams. Both the research on and implementation of community policing are fraught with challenges that may explain some of the limitations in the evidence base.

Gill et al. (2014) note that as a philosophy rather than a concrete strategy or "program" with a specific end goal, community policing may be more difficult to implement successfully compared to other policing innovations that have taken hold, such as hot-spots policing or Compstat (see also Trojanowicz et al., 1998). Some police agencies have reported that the "transformative" nature of community policing has failed to live up to expectations, and that leaders are unsure how to engage the community or obtain buy-in from front-line officers (Mastrofski et al., 2007; Stone and Travis, 2011). There are no criteria or set guidelines for implementing community policing. Morabito (2010) notes that the mission of each agency is assumed to be guided by the local community. The tenet of organizational transformation is therefore key to implementation, but is also the most vaguely defined of the three elements of community policing and perhaps the most difficult to put into practice, since it involves changing whole-department culture and operations rather than comparatively simple changes such as convening a specialist team or redeploying officers.

The lack of guiding principles for implementing community policing means that the approach looks different in any given agency, creating challenges for police leaders and researchers alike. Community policing is often introduced as a diverse set of tactics to be employed by specialist teams or individual officers in defined areas, rather than as a department-wide reorientation toward the community's problems and needs (e.g. Weisburd and McElroy, 1988). Furthermore, the specific tactics that are deployed under the umbrella of community policing vary substantially, over both departments and time, and the level of community engagement and involvement required ranges from active to passive. Weisburd and Eck (2004) note that some of the community-oriented strategies employed over the past few decades include problem solving, foot patrol, newsletters, door-to-door surveys and "knock-and-talks," neighborhood watch, and multi-agency partnerships (Mastrofski et al., 1995; see also Skogan, 2006a). This not only makes community policing "vague and difficult to execute" (Mastrofski et al., 2007, p. 224), but many of the individual tactics that purport to be community-oriented have not been rigorously tested and research has shown some to be ineffective at preventing crime (Eck and Rosenbaum, 1994; Skogan and Frydl, 2004; Weisburd and Eck, 2004).

The resulting heterogeneity in community policing implementation has also proved challenging for researchers trying to determine the effectiveness of the overall policy. Gill et al. (2014) describe a lack of fidelity to the accepted threefold definition of community policing and the "morass of strategies that have come to define the approach," and note that their systematic review can only evaluate community policing as it is understood in practice rather than the "theoretical ideal" (p. 404). The studies of community policing they reviewed were so different that they were unable to draw any conclusions about the optimal strategies or combination of strategies that police departments should adopt.[1] This also raises the question of the external validity of community policing evaluations—what do their findings actually mean for practice when the causal evidence is drawn from a vast range of different strategies implemented in different contexts?

Moving forward: community policing in practice

Despite the lack of clarity around the definition, goals, implementation, and effectiveness of community policing, we think that police agencies should not be discouraged from making the effort to reorient themselves toward the communities they serve. In the United States, the national reaction to recent high-profile police-involved deaths in communities of color, including Michael Brown in Ferguson, MO; Tamir Rice in Cleveland, OH; and Eric Garner and Akai Gurley in New York City, indicates—among many other issues—that crime control cannot and should not be the sole focus of police agencies. Even if the investment in community policing does not match its effectiveness in preventing crime, findings for its effectiveness at building trust and satisfaction with police among citizens suggest that it could be used to help establish, reinforce, and even rebuild positive working relationships between police agencies and communities. In addition to improving police–community relations in the short term, this could ultimately help to reduce crime.

Based on the results of their systematic review, Gill et al. (2014) propose a refined "logic model" for community policing focused around reorienting the police agency to prioritize relationships with the community, which they suggest may be the first step in a process toward longer term benefits. In this model, citizen satisfaction, perceived legitimacy of police, and immediate quality-of-life improvements are the short-term outcomes that need to be realized before longer-term effects such as crime control and fear reduction can occur. Even in areas where police–community relations are non-existent or fractured, such improvements could be accomplished over time. Police departments can be reoriented around community issues through training and moving away from a purely reactive operational model to allow officers time to identify key constituents and start to build relationships. This collaboration with the community may in the short term improve citizens' satisfaction and trust with the police, as indicated by the promising findings for these outcomes. In turn, increased satisfaction and trust can be a precursor to collective efficacy (Sampson et al., 1997), whereby community residents are largely able to self-regulate public safety through informal social controls (Kochel, 2012; Silver and Miller, 2004; Weisburd et al., 2012; Wells et al., 2006). Once this baseline is established and residents are mobilized, police and community can collaborate in problem solving, which has the potential to both reduce crime and fear, and further strengthen collective efficacy and self-regulation.

While the above framework for thinking about the effectiveness of community policing has not been evaluated, it appears that the first step for police agencies is to ensure fidelity to the accepted definition of community policing. This will involve challenging wider organizational cultures that do not fully prioritize community engagement, decentralization of decision-making, or an expanded definition of police work. Agencies and police leaders should not view the approach as simply another tool to be deployed temporarily or by specialized teams. Officers on the ground must feel supported in their problem-solving work with community members, in terms of time, resources, and recognition by peers and leadership. An officer in a smaller agency that takes a progressive approach to community building recently told us that even within a supportive environment other officers questioned whether the youth program she helped to develop was "real police work." A cultural shift toward this broader view of policing requires training, leadership, and a recognition that the permeation of new values throughout the entire agency is a long-term prospect that needs to outlive individual police leaders and supervisors who champion them.

Timing, then, is crucial to the successful implementation of community policing. The proposed logic model described above suggests that community policing may provide stronger long-term benefits, just as deterrence-based approaches like hot-spots policing provide stronger short-term benefits. Yet long-term strategizing is extremely challenging in the political environment of the police department, where chiefs are replaced or re-elected every few years and local captains, sergeants, and beat officers are frequently reassigned to new units and operations. As noted above, a commitment to community policing must be infused throughout the organization and passed along to future leaders and supervisors as well as new recruits, since the development of trust and ultimately collective efficacy and crime prevention that may result cannot develop overnight.

One way to facilitate this longer-term commitment is to focus on the street level officers. Agencies can ensure all patrol officers are trained in principles of problem solving and community engagement from the outset, rather than assigning specialized problem-oriented or community policing/community outreach teams that act somewhat independently of local beat officers, as is often the case. Importantly, those officers need to be given responsibility for smaller geographic units with manageable, identifiable populations so that they can work on identifying the key community members, institutions, and businesses who will contribute to effective partnerships. Officers need to be assigned to these communities for as long as possible within operational constraints, and could use their discretionary time—the periods during which they are not respond-ing to 911 calls—to focus on collaborating with the community (e.g. Weisburd et al., 2015). This can only be done well in an organizational culture where first-line supervisors and higher-level leaders also buy in to the approach and support the officers on the ground through delega-tion of decision-making; direction and facilitation of partnerships and multi-agency collaboration where necessary and appropriate; and devel-opment of performance targets and metrics that emphasize contributions to community collaboration and problem-solving as well as arrest and enforcement.

Conclusion and directions for future research

As the preceding discussion indicates, we believe that while implementing community policing effectively is not easy, it can be done thoughtfully and successfully despite the empirical uncertainty around whether community policing "works" and how. Police agencies should continue efforts to under-stand the problems facing the communities they serve and allocate resources so that officers are best placed to collaborate with citizens to address them. While we offer some broad recommendations for practice, there is also a need for further research as these initiatives move forward.

First, very little research exists that specifically evaluates community policing implementation that adheres to the threefold definition: commu-nity partnerships, problem-solving, and organizational transformation. Following the logic model from Gill et al. (2014), we suggest that the three components are necessary and build on each other—organizational trans-formation is required to support both community partnerships and proac-tive, problem-oriented approaches that are the 'tactical manifestation' of the community policing philosophy (Cordner, 1999; Maguire and Mastrofski, 2000). Case studies and process evaluations that carefully document how successful agencies have facilitated organizational change, and identified key community constituents for collaborative problem-solving, will pro-vide extremely useful guidance to other departments as they make similar adjustments.

Related to this is a need to address the uncertainty in the literature about which tactics should be deployed in a community-oriented context. Is there an optimal set or combination of strategies that works best? Are there specific individuals or institutions within communities who need to be involved in decision-making? Of course, it is likely that the specific nature of community-based problem-solving is driven by the unique needs and com-position of the community in question. Nonetheless, if research can provide some clarity on this issue it may help to reduce the uncertainty and feeling that community policing does not live up to expectations reported by police leaders (Mastrofski et al., 2007; Skogan and Hartnett, 1997).

We suggest, following Scheider et al. (2009), that community policing may be effective when integrated with other evidence-based policing strategies and innovations that do provide crime control gains, including problem-oriented policing, hot-spots approaches, broken windows policing, and Compstat (Kelling and Coles, 1996; see also Willis et al., 2010). For example, Weisburd et al. (2015) describe an in-progress experiment in Brooklyn Park, Minnesota, funded by the Bureau of Justice Assistance's Smart Policing Initiative, in which hot-spots policing is combined with community-building with a focus on increasing collective efficacy in high-crime areas. Small teams of police officers will have responsibility for several small geographic areas, where they will spend their discretionary time identifying key community stakeholders and implementing and following up on problem-solving efforts. Such blending of community collaboration and promising practices for crime prevention could have both short- and longer-term benefits, and ensure that policing is both effective and conducted with the support and involvement of community members rather than imposed upon them—a crucial step forward for police–community relations.

Finally, and perhaps most importantly (albeit challenging during a period of limited research funding), studies of community policing efforts need much longer follow-up periods. Gill et al. (2014) suggest that, if their logic model is accurate, few if any of the studies they reviewed would have covered a sufficient time period to detect both the initial improvements in citizen satisfaction and trust and longer-term benefits for crime prevention and collective efficacy. There is a risk that police departments and policymakers alike could overlook or dial back community policing efforts, thus missing out on its considerable effectiveness for short-term improvements in community relations, because of limited evidence for its influence on crime prevention. However, it is important to emphasize that causal uncertainty in the short-term does not mean that community policing does not provide important benefits in the long term. Long-term studies that capture both the process and impact of community policing could potentially provide concrete data to support this claim.

Overall, despite the considerable uncertainty around the implementation and goals of community policing, recent evidence indicates that when the police prioritize building positive relationships with the community they can impact satisfaction and trust within the community fairly quickly, which may then set the stage for effective problem-solving and public support for other evidence-based initiatives. Even if longer-term crime control gains are not realized, however, increasing trust and legitimacy among citizens are important goals in themselves. Ultimately, we hope that these policy and research recommendations could help to strengthen the evidence-base for community policing so that police and communities can work together to effectively "co-produce" public safety for all involved.

Note

1   Gill et al. (2014) do note that problem-oriented policing approaches that emphasize collaboration with the community in identifying, prioritizing, and solving problems may be promising, given evidence for the effectiveness of problem-oriented policing (e.g. Weisburd et al., 2010).

References

Bayley, D. H. (1994). *Police for the future*. New York: Oxford University Press.

Cordner, G. W. (1999). Elements of community policing. In Larry K. Gaines and Gary W. Cordner (eds.), *Policing perspectives: An anthology* (pp. 137–149). Los Angeles, CA: Roxbury.

Eck, J. E., and Rosenbaum, D. P. (1994). The new police order: Effectiveness, equity, and efficiency in community policing. In Dennis P. Rosenbaum (ed.), *The challenge of community policing: Testing the promises*. Newbury Park, CA: Sage Publications.

Gill, C., Weisburd, D., Telep, C. W., Vitter, Z., and Bennett, T. (2014). Community-oriented policing to reduce crime, disorder and fear and increase satisfaction and legitimacy among citizens: a systematic review. *Journal of Experimental Criminology*, 10(4), 399–428. doi:10.1007/s11292-014-9210-y.

Goldstein, H. (1990). *Problem-oriented policing*. New York, NY: McGraw-Hill.

Gottfredson, M. R., and Hirschi, T. (1990). *A general theory of crime*. Stanford, CA: Stanford University Press.

Hickman, M. J., and Reaves, B. A. (2001). *Community policing in local police departments, 1997 and 1999* (No. NCJ 184794). Washington, DC: U.S. Dept. of Justice, Office of Justice Programs, Bureau of Justice Statistics. Retrieved from www.bjs.gov/content/pub/pdf/cplpd99.pdf.

Kelling, G. L., and Coles, C. (1996). *Fixing broken windows: Restoring order and reducing crime in American cities*. New York, NY: Free Press.

Kelling, G. L., and Moore, M. H. (1988). From political to reform to community: The evolving strategy of police. In J. R. Greene and S. D. Mastrofski (eds.), *Community policing: Rhetoric or reality*. New York, NY: Praeger.

Kelling, G. L., Pate, A. M., Dieckman, D., and Brown, C. E. (1974). *The Kansas City preventive patrol experiment: A technical report*. Washington, DC: Police Foundation

Klockars, C. B. (1985). Order maintenance, the quality of urban life, and police: A different line of argument. In William A. Geller (ed.), *Police leadership in America: Crisis and opportunity* (pp. 309–321). New York, NY: Praeger.

Kochel, T. R. (2012). Can police legitimacy promote collective efficacy? *Justice Quarterly*, 29(3), 384–419. doi:10.1080/07418825.2011.561805.

Maguire, E. R., and Mastrofski, S. D. (2000). Patterns of community policing in the United States. *Police Quarterly*, 3(1), 4–45. doi:10.1177/1098611100003001001.

Martinson, R. (1974). What works? Questions and answers about prison reform. *Public Interest*, 10, 22–54.

Mastrofski, S. D., Willis, J. J., and Kochel, T. R. (2007). The challenges of implementing community policing in the United States. *Policing*, 1(2), 223–234. doi:10.1093/police/pam026

Mastrofski, S. D., Worden, R. E., and Snipes, J. B. (1995). Law enforcement in a time of community policing. *Criminology*, 33(4), 539–563. doi:10.1111/j.1745-9125.1995.tb01189.x

Morabito, M. S. (2010). Understanding community policing as an innovation: patterns of adoption. *Crime and Delinquency*, 56(4), 564–587. doi:10.1177/0011128707311643.

Office of Community Oriented Policing Services. (2012). *Community policing defined*. Washington, DC: U.S. Department of Justice, Office of Community Oriented Policing Services.

Reaves, B. A. (2010). *Local police departments, 2007* (No. NCJ 231174). Washington, DC: U.S. Dept. of Justice, Office of Justice Programs, Bureau of Justice Statistics. Retrieved from www.bjs.gov/content/pub/pdf/lpd07.pdf.

Reiss Jr, A. J. (1971). Systematic observation of natural social phenomena. *Sociological Methodology*, 3, 3–33.

Sampson, R. J., Raudenbush, S. W., and Earls, F. (1997). Neighborhoods and violent crime: A multilevel study of collective efficacy. *Science*, 277(5328), 918–924. doi:10.1126/science.277.5328.918.

Scheider, M. C., Chapman, R., and Schapiro, A. (2009). Towards the unification of policing innovations under community policing. *Policing: An International Journal of Police Strategies and Management*, 32(4), 694–718. doi:10.1108/13639510911000777.

Sherman, L. W. (1997). Communities and crime prevention. In *Preventing crime: What works, what doesn't, what's promising*. Washington, DC: United States Department of Justice, National Institute of Justice. Retrieved from www.ncjrs.gov/works/chapter3.htm.

Sherman, L. W., and Eck, J. E. (2002). Policing for crime prevention. In L. W. Sherman, D. P. Farrington, B. C. Welsh, D. L. Mackenzie, and D. L. MacKenzie (eds.), *Evidence-based crime prevention* (pp. 295–329). New York, NY: Routledge.

Silver, E., and Miller, L. L. (2004). Sources of informal social control in Chicago neighborhoods. *Criminology*, 42(3), 551–584. doi:10.1111/j.1745-9125.2004.tb00529.

Skogan, W. G. (2004). Community policing: Common impediments to success. In L. A. Fridell and M. A. Wycoff (eds.), *Community policing: The past, present, and future* (pp. 159–168). Washington, DC: The Annie E. Casey Foundation; the Police Executive Research Forum.

Skogan, W. G. (2006a). The promise of community policing. In D. Weisburd and A. A. Braga (eds.), *Police innovation: Contrasting perspectives*. New York: Cambridge University Press.

Skogan, W. G. (2006b). *Policing and community in Chicago: A tale of three cities*. New York: Oxford University Press.

Skogan, W. G., and Frydl, K. (eds.). (2004). *Fairness and effectiveness in policing: The evidence*. Washington, DC: National Academies Press.

Skogan, W. G., and Hartnett, S. M. (1997). *Community policing, Chicago style*. New York: Oxford University Press.

Spelman, W., and Brown, D. K. (1984). *Calling the police: Citizen reporting of serious crime*. Washington, DC: U.S. Department of Justice, National Institute of Justice.

Stone, C., and Travis, J. (2011). *Toward a new professionalism in policing*. Washington, DC: U.S. Dept. of Justice, Office of Justice Programs, National Institute of Justice. Retrieved from https://www.ncjrs.gov/pdffiles1/nij/232359.pdf.

Trojanowicz, R. C., Kappeler, V. E., Gaines, L. K., and Bucqueroux, B. (1998). *Community policing: A contemporary perspective*. Cincinnati, OH: Anderson Publishing.

Weisburd, D., and Braga, A. A. (2006). Understanding police innovation. In D. Weisburd and A. A. Braga (Eds.), *Police innovation: Contrasting perspectives.* New York: Cambridge University Press.

Weisburd, D., and Eck, J. E. (2004). What can police do to reduce crime, disorder, and fear? *Annals of the American Academy of Political and Social Science*, 593(1), 42–65. doi:10.1177/0002716203262548.

Weisburd, D., and McElroy, J. (1988). Enacting the CPO role: Findings from the New York City pilot program in community policing. In J. R. Greene and S. D. Mastrofski (eds.), *Community policing: Rhetoric or reality*. New York, NY: Praeger.

Weisburd, D., Davis, M., and Gill, C. (2015). *Increasing Collective Efficacy and Social Capital at Crime Hot Spots: New Crime Control Tools for Police.* Policing 9(3), 265–274. http://doi.org/10.1093/police/pav019.

Weisburd, D., Groff, E. R., and Yang, S.-M. (2012). *The criminology of place: Street segments and our understanding of the crime problem*. New York, NY: Oxford University Press.

Weisburd, D., Telep, C. W., Hinkle, J. C., and Eck, J. E. (2010). Is problem-oriented policing effective in reducing crime and disorder? *Criminology and Public Policy*, 9(1), 139–172. doi:10.1111/j.1745-9133.2010.00617.

Wells, W., Schafer, J. A., Varano, S. P., and Bynum, T. S. (2006). Neighborhood residents' production of order: The effects of collective efficacy on responses to neighborhood problems. *Crime and Delinquency*, 52(4), 523–550. doi:10.1177/0011128705284681.

Willis, J. J., Mastrofski, S. D., and Kochel, T. R. (2010). The co-implementation of Compstat and community policing. *Journal of Criminal Justice*, 38(5), 969–980. doi:10.1016/j.jcrimjus.2010.06.014.

Chapter 10

Problem-oriented policing

Evidence v. framing in implementation success

John E. Eck and Kathleen Gallagher

The problem

Problem-oriented policing (POP) is a normative theory of police administration. It is a comprehensive approach to the police role that departs from
previous policing strategies. It is also the first of a class of policing strategies that puts a premium on empirical examination of police work. In fact,
analytic policing strategies that followed POP – for example, COMPSTAT,
intelligence-led policing, evidence-based policing, hot-spots policing – can
be considered truncated versions of POP. The breadth of POP and its radical departure from standard policing make it distinctive, but this also creates major difficulties in implementing and sustaining a problem-oriented
approach, despite a substantial body of evidence suggesting that POP is
more effective than other policing strategies, including other evidence-based
strategies. An important reason why POP is difficult to implement and
sustain is that it may require a conceptual framework for crime and other
police problems that the police do not typically use.

In this paper, we describe: what problem-oriented policing is and the
nature of police problems; the connection of POP to crime science; evidence
for its effectiveness; difficulties of implementing POP; and evidence that
inappropriate problem framing may be responsible for these difficulties.
We conclude this paper with recommendations for addressing the framing
problem.

What is problem-oriented policing and what is a problem?

In 1979, Herman Goldstein stated that the central difficulty for policing
was that police placed far too much emphasis on the way policing was conducted relative to what they wanted to achieve. He called this the "means
over ends syndrome" (Goldstein, 1979: p. 238). Goldstein suggested that the
police should focus much more on the ends of policing and attach the means
of policing to those ends. Goldstein's radical departure from other's ideas

Table 10.1 Problems must have the CHEERS characteristics

	Examples	
Description	Police Problem	Not A Police Problem
Community – The problem must occur within a community	Minor vehicle collisions in a shopping district	Minor police vehicle collisions in the police parking lot
Harm – Tangible harms from the circumstances have to be specified	Assaults on homeless men	Homelessness
Expectations – The community must expect police to help address it	Sexual assaults	Influenza
Events – A problem contains specific events	Crowds throwing rocks through windows	Bored youth
Repeat – These events must repeat	A series of burglaries	A one-off catastrophic event
Similarity – These events must share some characteristics	Occurring at the same location	An assortment of unrelated events, e.g. "disorder"

of the police role was his suggestion that the police function is to address community problems, so the police should reorient their operations to specifically identify and address them.

This raises the question, "what is a problem?" Goldstein did not specifically define "problem," though he gave numerous examples. Much later, in an effort to operationalize this concept for police practice, Clarke and Eck (2003) developed the CHEERS criteria (Table 10.1). A problem must have each of these six characteristics; any troublesome matter without all six criteria is not a "police problem."

The value of the CHEERS criteria is that they focus police attention on harmful actions in the community that will recur if unaddressed, and separate these problems from states of being (like homelessness) and police administrative issues. The non-problems may need addressing, but not necessarily by the police. However, some of these non-problems may be partially responsible for a police problem – for example, homelessness contributes to other problems: aggressive panhandling by homeless men, death of homeless people in bad weather, and assaults on homeless people.

POP is mostly a normative theory – a suggestion as to how we should organize policing – more so than a descriptive theory. It is normative because it is logically possible to argue that the police should be exclusively about something other than resolving problems – catching "bad guys" or emergency call handling, are examples – and that problem solving is something best left to others. POP is not descriptive in the sense that it portrays policing as currently being mostly about resolving problems. They should be, according to Goldstein, but they often are not. Only in two senses it is descriptive. First, Goldstein implied that if the police focused on problems, they would have more success at resolving them than they would by using standard policing. As we show later, the evidence suggests Goldstein was correct. Second, regardless of what one might prefer the police to do, they get drawn into problem solving as a result of their other functions. In other words, by default police are problem solvers of last resort.

Problem-oriented policing and crime science

Goldstein's (1979) original theory was incomplete. It was a theory of the police function that claimed police should resolve community problems. But it was not a theory of the problems. This is like a theory of civil engineering stating civil engineering should build large-scale physical infrastructure, without having theories of physics, metallurgy, chemistry or fluids which could guide building such structures. Civil engineers might have some success, but it would be very limited and subject to failure.

Eck and Madensen (2012) claim that modern problem-oriented policing is a combination of two sets of theories: Goldstein's original theory and the theories of Crime Science (aka Environmental Criminology) (Clarke, 2010). Crime Science theories describe how many problems (particularly crime and disorder) arise and what can be done to resolve them. They have been widely applied to policing and are the principle tools police use to analyze and resolve problems. Wartell and Gallagher's (2012) examination of crime analysis units suggests that Crime Science frameworks have influenced how police crime analysts approach their work, though this influence is far from pervasive. Like problem-oriented policing, Crime Science theories present a radically new way of thinking. Instead of focusing on offenders, as is the case in standard criminology and in policing, Crime Science demands that other actors also receive as much attention (victims, places, handlers, guardians, and place managers) and that the objective is to understand patterns of crime, rather than search for deep-seeded pathologies of offenders.

Eck and Madensen (2012) call this combination a "lichen theory" after the ubiquitous composite organism comprised of a fungus and an algae or bacteria. The lichen perspective asserts that any theory of policing that claims it can help police become more effective must have a theory of policing combined with a theory of the phenomena the police are addressing (e.g. a theory of police traffic management must not only account for how the police are organized, but also the physics of vehicle traffic).

Does problem-oriented policing work?

As a normative theory, it does not matter whether POP is effective or not. But this is a theory based on pragmatic consideration of policing and justified on the basis that standard policing is ineffective and sometimes harmful (Goldstein, 1979; 1990). Consequently, it matters a great deal whether POP works. More specifically, does it work better than alternatives? This is a difficult question to answer, for two reasons. First, POP implies police apply scientific methods to their work. So any question about POP's effectiveness is like asking science to answer the question, "does science work?" From this perspective the question is less about whether science works in policing, but whether police can apply science. It is conceivable that police are so inept, or politically hamstrung, or organizationally challenged that they cannot routinely apply science to their work. We will show evidence that this might be true.

The second difficulty is that police address many types of problems. By one estimate, there are 66 categories of police problems, each of which may contain numerous subcategories so that under reasonable assumptions there may be more than 3,500 problem types (Eck and Clarke, 2003: p. 25). Policing may be able to handle some problems better than others, so to answer the effectiveness question researchers need to look at multiple police attempts to resolve a very large number of problems. This level of research has not been conducted. Nevertheless, the limited research to date is informative and optimistic.

Numerous evaluations of problem-oriented policing efforts have been conducted. However, the rigor of these evaluations varies tremendously. Weisburd and colleagues (2010) conducted a systematic review and meta-analysis of these. For the meta-analysis they found 10 studies that met their search criterion. With such a small number of cases (compared to the variety of policing problems) great caution must be taken with any result. This is particularly true as it is highly likely that two of the ten studies had substantial implementation troubles,[1] making their conclusions of dubious validity. With these caveats in mind, Weisburd and colleagues concluded that compared to alternative treatments, on average, POP is modestly effective. They also examined 45 pre-post evaluations, over 70 percent of which came from applications for a problem-solving award. Thus, there is a reasonable chance of publication bias: unsuccessful POP efforts may be less likely to be nominated for an award. Forty-three of these cases indicated the problem-solving effort was successful, with an average reduction in target events of 45 percent (Weisburd et al., 2010: page 159).

Though we have to treat these conclusions with caution, we also have to recall that most policing strategies have even less evidence backing them. The only other policing strategy with more evaluations is hot-spots policing, another form of analytic policing. It too is effective (Braga, 2007). This raises the questions, are there any benefits to POP above focusing on hot spots? Or is focusing on high crime spots the "active ingredient" in POP? Three studies help answer these questions. In a study of drug market interventions using problem solving, Weisburd and Green (1995) used hot-spots interventions as a control condition. They found that problem solving at drug hot spots is more effective than just focusing on hot spots.

Another randomized controlled trial of problem-oriented policing indicates that there is more to POP than hot-spots policing. Braga and Bond (2008) found that problem-solving efforts were effective and that the "active ingredient" was situational crime prevention (an approach from the Crime Science paradigm), rather than arrest or social service interventions. A third effort, a meta-analysis focused on measuring the impact of hot spot interventions, was conducted by Braga, Papachristos, and Hureau (2012). This work found that while hot-spot interventions involving traditional policing activities (e.g. patrol and arrest) can reduce crime, when these interventions are paired with POP, they result in even stronger crime drops in target areas. In summary, there is systematic evidence pointing to the conclusion that a problem-oriented policing strategy is effective at reducing crime and disorder. Though based on a rather thin body of evidence, this body is thicker than most bodies of evidence in policing. Further, when compared to a related strategy with more evaluations, problem-oriented policing appears superior.

Difficulties with implementing POP

A large number of studies of problem-oriented policing, over a long period of time, consistently begin by noting the soundness of the strategy, but then go on to show how police find it difficult to operationalize or sustain it over time. Goldstein, himself, noted this in a very early report (Goldstein and Susmilch, 1982). Other notable critiques include Buerger (1994), Clarke, 1997; Read and Tilley (2000), Scott (2000), Eck (2004, 2014), and Maguire et al., (2010).

There are numerous reasons noted for implementation difficulties, including: insufficient political willpower, inadequate training, organizational opposition, weak police leadership, and confusion with other policing strategies (Eck, 2004). However, one reason that has received less attention is the possibility that the mental framework police bring to problem solving may be inappropriate. Recall, there are two theories at work in problem-oriented policing, a normative one and a descriptive one. The first directs attention to problems. The second describes how problems arise and can be resolved. Goldstein and most others have drawn attention to the first theory. The second theory has received very little attention among policing scholars. They, like the police they study, are largely unaware of the revolution in thinking about crime that Crime Science has brought about. Consequently, despite efforts to bridge this knowledge gap (see for example, Clarke and Eck, 2003) police view problems through a standard criminological framework and focus too much on offenders relative to other aspects of crime and disorder problems.

Problem frames and POP

At the start of any problem solving process, police must define the problem (Eck and Spelman, 1987; Goldstein, 1990). This is when the problem gets framed. Problem frames are "general thought structures that allow us to organize shared theories and personal experiences to guide decision-making" (Gallagher, 2014: p. 1). Framing has received considerable attention in the fields of economics, sociology, and communications. Across all fields, however, there is agreement that: (1) multiple frames may be used to define a problem and (2) the particular frame that is selected will influence all later problem-solving activities (Allison, 1969; Kahneman, 2011; Tversky and Kahneman, 1981). Nevertheless, framing has only been studied by a few policing scholars (Bichler and Gaines, 2005; Graziano et al., 2013; Payne et al., 2013; Rossmo, 2009).

If the broad literature on framing is correct, then different police problem frames will lead to different police responses. A recent case study provides an example. Payne and colleagues (2013) worked with a police department that believed it had a crime problem associated with individuals using government housing subsidies. The police frame seemed to be a variant of social disorganization theory – offenders were concentrated in neighborhoods associated with housing subsidies. However, the problem could also be described as a problem with specific rental property owners/managers. Switching the frame from residents to owners made a difference. Ultimately, once reframed the police were able to make headway at reducing calls for service by concentrating on a few property owners whose rental complexes generated exceptionally high numbers of calls.

Gallagher (2014) examined how different problem frames can lead to the use of different police responses. She looked at the extent to which police used Crime Science theories in their problem framing. Gallagher found that officers were aware of Crime Science theories and sometimes used them in problem-solving activities. The use of Crime Science theories during the framing of a problem influenced the types of solutions police selected. In contrast, when a project team conducted weak or limited problem framing activities, or failed to apply theories of Crime Science to the problem, they were more likely to use only traditional police responses (patrol and/or arrest). Officers or project teams who conducted extensive problem framing and considered theories of Crime Science were more likely to incorporate a wide variety of activities into their solutions. Thus, the choice of an explicit frame for a problem had noticeable and important consequences for the outcome of problem-solving projects.

Previous examinations of POP have focused on weaknesses in the implementation process, particularly related to analysis and assessment of the problems (Clarke, 1997; Scott, 2000). Recommendations to improve these weaknesses focus on more and better training and collaborating with outside researchers (Scott, 2000). Gallagher's work suggests that implementation weaknesses are evident from the start of POP projects, with the inappropriate framing of a problem. Given Gallagher's findings, and other work clearly showing Crime Science Theories lead to more effective solutions (Braga and Bond, 2008; Braga et al., 2012), it is clear what sort of framework is needed. This research also suggests that currently popular frameworks from standard criminology, including hot-spots policing, broken-windows theory and social disorganization theory, are possibly detrimental to effective application of problem-oriented policing.

Conclusions

Let us summarize our basic points. First, Goldstein (1979; 1990) proposed a new normative theory of police administration that stated the police function should focus on problems. Second, this theory became tightly bound to a parallel set of theories from Crime Science (aka Environmental Criminology) that describes the origins of crime patterns and methods for prevention. Third, when tested, POP is effective relative to standard approaches to policing and relative to other evidence-based policing strategies. The most likely active ingredients in POP actions are practices drawn from Crime Science. Fourth, despite the effectiveness, POP is difficult to implement and sustain. Finally, a likely reason for implementation problems is the mind-set police bring to problems: the frames they use to define problems are insufficiently based on Crime Science.

This suggests that evidence for effectiveness is not a sufficient condition for the success of a policy. In practice, policies and strategies are implemented by bureaucracies, such as the police. These bureaucracies use frameworks to understand their problems. New ideas that fit old frameworks will be implemented faster, even if there is little or no evidence supporting them, or even in the face of evidence challenging them. This explains why policing is more comfortable with hotspots policing, broken-windows policing, and community policing. These do not challenge the frameworks police (or the public) have. Hotspots policing can be incorporated within existing offender deterrence and incapacitation frameworks widely used within criminal justice policy, and embraced by conservative voters. Community policing fits the pathological neighborhood frameworks taught by criminologists, and embraced by more liberal voters. Broken-Windows Theory, interestingly, fits both frames. Problem-oriented policing fits neither popular framework.

This raises an important question. Should we continue improving policing through a POP strategy? This will probably require addressing the framing question within policing and within the political environment within which police reside. Though POP has persisted for over a third of a century – a long time for a policing strategy – its slow progress suggests we might want to think of alternatives. This brings us to the second question. Would it be easier to create effective sustainable local crime prevention strategies by creating alternative institutions that are built on a Crime Science framework? This would allow the police to continue on with its emergency response function, but leave most prevention to professional experts. Exactly what these alternative institutions would look like is unclear, though Eck and Eck (2012) suggest one alternative: local crime place regulatory agencies applying evidence-based approaches. At first blush, this might seem absurd, but this is exactly what we have done with fire prevention. Fire departments are largely emergency response agencies. Fire prevention is chiefly implemented through the regulation of building codes and insurance companies, with the fire services in support. If the police are unable to deliver sustained evidence-based prevention through a problem-oriented approach, perhaps we should create an institution that can.

Note

1 The Atlanta study (Stone, 1993) grew out of a project administered by Eck while at the Police Executive Research Forum. Personal experience with the difficulties of getting the Atlanta Police Department to enact the agreed upon POP strategy suggests that conclusions about its effectiveness are more likely due to implementation failure than treatment failure. The Minneapolis RECAP study has been reasonably well documented by Michael Buerger in published articles as being riddled with implementation difficulties (see, for example, Buerger, 1994; and Buerger and Mazerolle, 1998). Consequently, we do not know what the results would have been if POP had been implemented as planned.

References

Allison, G.T. (1969). Conceptual models and the Cuban missile crisis. *The American Political Science Review*, 63(3), 689–718.

Bichler, G. and Gaines, L. (2005). An examination of police officers' insights into problem identification and problem-solving. *Crime and Delinquency*, 51(1), 53–74.

Braga, A. A. (2007). Effects of hot spots policing on crime. A Campbell Collaboration systematic review. Retrieved March 26, 2009 from db.c2admin.org/doc-pdf/ Braga_HotSpotsPolicing_review.pdf.

Braga, A. A. and Bond, B.J. (2008). Policing crime and disorder hot spots: A randomized controlled trial. *Criminology*, 46(3), 577–607.

Braga, A.A., Hureau, D. M. and Papachristos, A.V. (2012). An ex post facto evaluation framework for place-based police interventions. *Evaluation Review*, 35(6), 592–626. doi:10.1177/0193841X11433827.

Buerger, M. (1994). The problems of problem-solving: Resistance, interdependencies, and conflicting interests. *American Journal of Police*, 13, 1–36.

Buerger, M. E. and Mazerolle, L. G. (1998). Third-party policing: A theoretical analysis of an emerging trend. *Justice Quarterly*, 15(2), 301–327.

Clarke, R. V. (1997). *Problem-oriented policing and the potential contribution of criminology*. Washington, DC: U.S. Department of Justice, National Institute of Justice.

Clarke, R. V. (2010). Crime Science. In E. McLaughlin and T. Newburn (eds.), *The Sage Handbook of Criminological Theory* (pp. 271–283). Thousand Oaks, CA: Sage.

Clarke, R. V. and Eck, J. E. (2003). *Becoming a problem-solving crime analyst: In 55 small steps*. London: Jill Dando Institute of Crime Science.

Eck, J. E. (2004). Why don't problems get solved? In W. G. Skogan (ed.), *Community policing: Can it work?* (pp. 185–206). Belmont, CA: Wadsworth.

Eck, J. E. (2014). *The status of collaborative problem solving and community problem-oriented policing in Cincinnati*. Cincinnati, OH: School of Criminal Justice, University of Cincinnati.

Eck, J. E. and Clarke, R. V. (2003). Classifying common police problems: A routine activity approach. In M. J. Smith and D. B. Cornish (eds.), *Theory for practice in situational crime prevention*. Crime Prevention Studies, vol. 16. Monsey, NY: Criminal Justice Press.

Eck, J. E. and Eck, E. B. (2012). Crime place and pollution: Expanding crime reduction options through a regulatory approach. *Criminology and Public Policy*, 11(2), 281–316.

Eck, J. E. and Madensen, T.D. (2012). Situational crime prevention makes problem-oriented policing work: The importance of interdependent theories for effective policing. In N. Tilley and G. Farrell (eds.), *The Reasoning Criminologist: Essays in Honour of Ronald V. Clarke*. New York: Taylor and Francis.

Eck, J. E. and Spelman, W. (1987). *Problem-solving: Problem-oriented policing in Newport News*. Washington, DC: Police Executive Research Forum.

Gallagher, K. M. (2014). *Problem framing in problem-oriented policing: An examination of framing from problem definition to problem response* Unpublished doctoral dissertation. University of Cincinnati.

Goldstein, H. (1979). Improving the police: A problem-oriented approach. *Crime and Delinquency*, 25(2), 236–258.

Goldstein, H. (1990). *Problem-oriented policing*. New York: McGraw-Hill.

Goldstein, H. and Susmilch, C. (1982). *Experimenting with the problem-oriented approach to improving police service: A report and some reflections on two case studies*. Madison, WI: Law School, University of Wisconsin.

Graziano, L. M., Rosenbaum, D. P. and Schuck, A. M. (2013). Building group capacity for problem-solving and police-community partnerships through survey feedback and training: A randomized control trial within Chicago's community policing program. *Journal of Experimental Criminology. Published online*, 1–25.

Kahneman, D. (2011). *Thinking, fast and slow*. New York, NY: Farrar, Straus and Giroux.

Maguire, E. R., Uchida, C.D. and Hassell, K.D. (2010). Problem-oriented policing in Colorado Springs: A content analysis of 753 cases. *Crime and Delinquency*. doi:10.1177/0011128710386201.

Payne, T. C., Gallagher, K. M., Eck, J. E. and Frank, J. (2013). Problem framing in problem solving: A case study. *Policing: An International Journal of Police Strategies and Management*, 36(4), 670–682.

Read, T. and Tilley, N. (2000). *Not rocket science? Problem-solving and crime reduction*. London: Home Office, Policing and Reducing Crime Unit.

Rossmo, D.K. (ed.). (2009). *Criminal investigative failures*. Boca Raton, FL: CRC Press.

Scott, M. S. (2000). *Problem-oriented policing: Reflections on the first 20 years*. Washington, DC: U.S. Department of Justice.

Stone, S. S. (1993). Problem-oriented policing approach to drug enforcement: Atlanta as a case study. Unpublished doctoral dissertation, Emory University.

Tversky, A. and Kahneman, D. (1981), The framing of decisions and the psychology of choice. *Science*, 211, 453–458.

Wartell, J. and Gallagher, K. (2012). Translating environmental criminology theory into crime analysis practice. *Policing*, 6(4), 377–387.

Weisburd, D. and Green, L. (1995). Policing drug hot spots: The Jersey City drug market analysis experiment. *Justice Quarterly*, 12, 711–735.

Weisburd, D., Telep, C.W., Hinkel, J.C. and Eck, J. E. (2010). Is problem-oriented policing effective in reducing crime and disorder? Findings from a Campbell Systematic Review. *Criminology and Public Policy*, 9(1), 139–172.

Chapter 11

The science and practice of hot-spots policing

Anthony A. Braga

Introduction

Over the past 30 years, research has demonstrated that crime is not evenly distributed across urban areas; rather it is concentrated in very small places, or "hot spots," that generate half of all criminal events (Pierce et al., 1988; Sherman et al., 1989). A number of police executives and researchers have argued that many crime problems can be reduced more efficiently if police officers focused their attention to these deviant places (Braga and Weisburd, 2010; Eck, 2002; Weisburd, 2008). The appeal of focusing limited resources on a small number of high-activity crime places is straightforward. If crime can be prevented at these hot spots, then citywide crime rates might be reduced. A majority of U.S. police departments currently use hot-spots policing strategies to reduce crime (Police Executive Research Forum, 2008; Weisburd et al., 2003).

Hot-spots policing is not simply the application of police strategies to units of geography (Weisburd, 2008). Traditional policing in this sense can be seen as place-based. Police have routinely defined their units of operation in terms of large areas, such as police precincts and beats. In hot-spots policing, place refers to a very different level of geographic aggregation than has traditionally interested police executives and planners. Places in this context are very small micro units of analysis, such as buildings or addresses; block faces, or street segments; or clusters of addresses, block faces, or street segments (Eck and Weisburd, 1995). When crime is concentrated at such places, they are commonly called hot spots.

This chapter reviews the available research evidence on hot-spots policing. It begins by presenting applied research on the concentration and stability of crime at specific places and highlighting two complementary theoretical perspectives that support the crime control efficacy of the hot-spots policing approach. The next section presents the most recent evaluation evidence on the general impact of hot-spots policing on crime and the specific crime prevention effects of particular types of hot-spots policing strategies used to control high-activity crime places. The importance of incorporating community and problem-oriented policing techniques in the design and implementation of hot-spots policing is then considered.

Theoretical perspectives on hot-spots policing

The concentration and stability of crime at places

Crime is highly concentrated at a small number of specific hot-spot locations within cities. Seminal studies in Boston and Minneapolis revealed that only 5 percent of the addresses in each city generated roughly 50 percent of citizen emergency calls for service to the police (Pierce et al., 1988; Sherman et al., 1989). Even within the worst neighborhoods, these studies suggested that crime clusters at a few discrete locations, leaving blocks of areas relatively crime-free. Further, research by Taylor and Gottfredson (1986) revealed conclusive evidence that links this spatial variation to the physical and social characteristics of particular blocks and multiple dwellings within a neighborhood. The empirical observation that a small number of places generate the bulk of urban crime problems suggested to scholars and crime policy analysts that the police could be more effective in controlling crime if they concentrated their resources in these hot-spot locations (Sherman et al., 1989; Weisburd, 2008; Braga and Weisburd, 2010).

An important issue in the potential benefit of policing places is whether high-rate locations tend to remain high rate for a long time. The "criminal careers" of high-activity places have been found to be relatively stable, suggesting that place-oriented interventions do have potential crime prevention value. Spelman (1995) analyzed calls-for-service at high schools, housing projects, subway stations, and parks in Boston, and found that the risks at these public places remained fairly constant over time. Taylor (1997) also reported evidence of a high degree of stability of crime at place over time, examining crime and fear of crime at 90 street blocks in Baltimore using a panel design with data collected in 1981 and 1994. In Seattle, an analysis of crime trends at specific street segments over a 14-year period suggested that places have stable concentrations of crime events over time (Weisburd et al., 2004). The study also found that a relatively small proportion of places could be grouped as having steeply rising or declining crime trends and this subgroup of places was primarily responsible for overall city crime trends. Weisburd et al. (2004) observed that city crime trends could be better understood as strong changes generated by a relatively small group of micro places over time rather than a general process evenly spread across the city landscape. Similar findings on the concentration and stability of crime at specific places over time have been reported for fatal and non-fatal shootings (Braga et al., 2010) and robberies (Braga et al., 2011) in Boston.

Crime prevention perspectives

The crime control effectiveness of hot-spots policing is supported by two complementary theoretical perspectives: general deterrence and criminal opportunity reduction. Evaluation evidence has found support for both theoretical perspectives. For instance, in the Minneapolis hot-spots patrol experiment, Sherman and Weisburd (1995) claimed evidence of place-specific general deterrence associated with increased police presence in hot-spot areas. Moreover, in Lowell, Massachusetts, Braga and Bond (2008) suggested that the crime reduction impacts observed in their randomized experiment were primarily generated by problem-oriented policing strategies that modified the criminal opportunity structures at crime hot spots.

Deterrence theory posits that crimes can be prevented when the costs of committing the crime are perceived by the offender to outweigh the benefits (Zimring and Hawkins, 1973). General deterrence is the idea that the general population is dissuaded from committing crime when it sees that punishment necessarily follows the commission of a crime. Much of the literature evaluating deterrence focuses on the effect of changing certainty, swiftness, and severity of punishment associated with certain acts on the prevalence of those crimes (see, e.g. Apel and Nagin, 2011; Blumstein et al., 1978; Cook, 1980; Paternoster, 1987). Recent reviews of the deterrence literature suggest that the certainty of punishment is the most important ingredient in generating crime control effects (Durlauf and Nagin, 2011; Nagin, 2013).

Traditional police crime control strategies attempt to deter offenders from committing crimes by increasing their perceptions of the risks of criminal apprehension (and, by extension, enhancing the certainty of punishment). Unfortunately, standard practices, such as random patrol, rapid response to calls for service, and follow-up investigations, do little to change apprehension risks faced by potential offenders (Skogan and Frydl, 2004). By concentrating police presence in high-activity crime places, hot-spots policing strategies are well positioned to substantially increase the certainty of detection and apprehension at places and raise potential offenders' perceptions of risk at places. As such, would-be offenders attracted by criminal opportunities at high crime places are more likely to perceive the risks of crime commission as larger than the benefits of crime commission.

Nagin (2013) identifies a second crime prevention function of police – the role of sentinel in their conventional patrol and monitoring activities – that supports the crime control efficacy of hot-spots policing initiatives. Opportunity theories of crime, such as routine activity (Cohen and Felson, 1979), rational choice (Cornish and Clarke, 1986), and crime pattern theory (Brantingham and Brantingham, 1981), have often been used to understand the place characteristics, situations, and dynamics that cause criminal events to concentrate at particular places. Routine activities theory focuses on the criminal event and posits that criminal events occur when potential offenders and suitable targets converge in space and time in the absence of a capable guardian (Cohen and Felson, 1979). The increased presence of police augments the level of guardianship in targeted places. Heightened levels of patrols prevent crimes by introducing the watchful eye of the police as a guardian to protect potential victims from potential offenders.

Opportunity theories support the use of situational crime prevention and problem-oriented policing strategies by police agencies to reduce crime. Changes in the physical environment may discourage potential offenders from frequenting an area by altering criminal opportunities at a place. Strategies to ameliorate physical incivilities (thereby changing site features and facilities) may diminish the number of easy opportunities at the place and, thus, discourage offenders from frequenting targeted places. Braga and Weisburd (2010) suggest police departments should strive to develop situational prevention strategies to deal with crime hot spots. Careful analyses of problems at crime hot spots seem likely to yield prevention strategies that will be well positioned to change the situations and dynamics that cause crime to cluster at specific locations.

The empirical evidence on hot-spots policing and crime control

A series of careful academic reviews of hot-spots policing evaluations consistently documented that these programs reduced crime in hot-spot areas without simply displacing crime problems elsewhere; in fact, many evaluations revealed a diffusion of crime control benefits from targeted areas to the proximate areas (see Sherman and Eck, 2002; Eck, 2002; Weisburd and Eck, 2004). The U.S. National Research Council's Committee to Review Research on Police Policy and Practices was not ambiguous in its conclusions regarding the effectiveness and importance of hot-spots policing. The committee concluded:

> There has been increasing interest over the past two decades in police practices that target very specific types of criminals, and crime places. In particular, policing crime hot spots has become a common police strategy for addressing public safety problems. While there is only weak evidence suggesting the effectiveness of targeting specific types of offenders, a strong body of evidence suggests that taking a focused geographic approach to crime problems can increase policing effectiveness in reducing crime and disorder.
>
> (Skogan and Frydl, 2004: 246–247)

Campbell systematic review of the effects of hot-spots policing and crime

The most detailed examination of the impact of hot-spots policing on crime is an ongoing systematic review conducted for the Campbell Collaboration. Formed in 2000, the Campbell Collaboration Crime and Justice Group aims to prepare and maintain systematic reviews of criminological interventions and to make them electronically accessible to scholars, practitioners, policy-makers and the general public (www.campbellcollaboration.org). In system-atic reviews, researchers attempt to gather relevant evaluative studies in a specific area, critically appraise them, and come to judgments about what works "using explicit, transparent, state-of-the-art methods" (Petrosino et al., 2001: 21). Rigorous methods are used to summarize, analyze, and combine study findings.

As part of the Campbell Collaboration Crime and Justice Group's efforts to build a scientific knowledge base on effective crime prevention practices, a systematic review has been conducted on an ongoing basis on the crime prevention effects of hot-spots policing programs (Braga, 2001; 2005). The most recent iteration of the Campbell hot-spots policing review identified 19 rigorous evaluations involving 25 tests of hot-spots policing programs (Braga *et al.*, 2014). Ten eligible studies used quasi-experimental research designs (52.6 percent) and nine eligible studies used randomized controlled trials (47.4 percent) to evaluate the effects of hot-spots policing on crime. A noteworthy majority of the hot-spots policing evaluations concluded that hot-spots policing programs generated significant crime control ben-efits in the treatment areas relative to the control areas: 20 of the 25 tests (80 percent) of hot-spots policing interventions reported noteworthy crime control gains associated with the approach. The meta-analysis of main effect sizes found that hot-spots policing strategies generated an overall statistically-significant crime reduction impact. Moreover, the meta-analysis found that hot-spots policing programs that engaged problem-oriented policing interventions to change underlying conditions at crime places gen-erated much larger crime control impacts relative to hot-spots policing pro-grams that simply increased traditional police crime prevention actions such as directed patrol and drug enforcement.

Thirteen hot-spots policing tests examined whether the interventions generated crime displacement or diffusion of crime control benefits (Braga et al., 2014). All 13 displacement and diffusion tests were limited to exam-ining immediate spatial displacement and diffusion effects; that is, whether focused police efforts in targeted areas resulted in crime "moving around the corner" or whether these proximate areas experienced unintended crime control benefits. Nine of the 13 displacement/diffusion tests reported effect sizes that favored diffusion effects over displacement effects. The displace-ment/diffusion meta-analysis suggests a small but statistically significant overall diffusion of crime control benefits effect generated by the hot-spots policing strategies.

What we need to know most: how hot-spots policing programs affect police legitimacy

In a recent essay, Weisburd and Telep (2014) identify a number of areas where new knowledge on hot-spots policing programs must be developed. These include the importance of understanding how hot-spots policing affects police legitimacy, considering the impact of hot-spots approaches on non-spatial displacement, refining our knowledge on what strategies are most effective in addressing hot spots, evaluating whether hot-spots policing will be effective in smaller cities and rural areas, investigating the long-term impacts of hot-spots policing, and considering whether the adoption of hot-spots policing will reduce overall crime in a jurisdiction. While developing new knowledge would be worthwhile in all these areas, the impact of hot-spots policing on police legitimacy stands out as the area where rigorous empirical research is needed the most.

The Braga et al. (2014) systematic review found that only three evaluations considered the impacts of these police programs on community members as well as crime outcomes. In contrast to concerns that hot-spots policing can easily become zero-tolerance and indiscriminate aggressive tactics can drive a wedge between the police and communities (Rosenbaum, 2006; Tonry, 2011), these three evaluations revealed the community members had positive opinions and experiences when subjected to hot-spots policing initiatives. Moreover, in a recent randomized controlled trial, explicitly designed to test the impacts of hot-spots enforcement on community perceptions in three mid-sized California cities, Weisburd et al. (2011) did not find any evidence of "backfire effects" associated with a policing disorder intervention: the hot-spots policing program delivered in this study had no significant impacts on fear of crime, police legitimacy, collective efficacy, or perceptions of crime or social disorder. It is important to note that these four evaluations interviewed or surveyed residents and business owners in hot-spot areas and did not interview individuals arrested, detained, and/or interrogated as a result of these focused police actions. It is possible these individuals may have very different opinions and experiences when compared to community members who do not experience direct law enforcement actions.

The potential impacts of hot-spots policing on police–community relations may depend in good part on the context of the hot spots affected and types of strategies used. An increased enforcement program to control a repeat shoplifting problem in a shopping mall, for instance, may be welcomed by store owners and legitimate customers alike. However, police actions that seek to prevent crime by changing places, such as problem-oriented policing interventions, seem better positioned to generate both crime control gains and positive community perceptions of the police relative to simply increasing police presence and arresting large numbers of offenders. Whatever the impacts, we need to know more about the effects of hot-spots policing approaches on the communities that the police serve. Future evaluations of hot-spots policing programs must make understanding these complex police–community dynamics a high priority.

In contrast to the methodologically rigorous evaluation research on the crime control efficacy of hot-spots policing (Braga and Weisburd, 2010), the general research evidence on community perceptions of appropriate police behavior, procedural fairness and police legitimacy, and related topics is still developing and, as such, not as scientifically strong. However, few observers of American policing would disagree with the statement that police–minority relations remain stressed by ongoing issues involving unwarranted stops, verbal abuse, brutality, and police corruption. As such, it is important to develop a *normative* dimension to the ongoing discussion of hot-spots policing practices. It seems likely that overly aggressive and indiscriminant police crackdowns would produce some undesirable effects, such as increased resentment and fear of police, in targeted hot-spot areas. The potential for negative effects needs to be drawn into our broader analysis of hot-spots policing initiatives precisely because community reactions to police practices have normative significance to wider society. Indeed, the National Research Council's Committee to Review Research on Police Policy and Practices concluded that police practices need to be evaluated in terms of their impact on the legitimacy of the police as well as their crime control effectiveness (Skogan and Frydl, 2004).

Legitimacy is linked to the ability of the police to prevent crime and keep neighborhoods safe. If the public's trust and confidence in the police is undermined, the ability of the police to prevent crime will be weakened by lawsuits, declining willingness to obey the law, and withdrawal from existing partnerships (Tyler, 2006). The political fallout from illegitimate police actions can seriously impede the ability of police departments to engage innovative crime control tactics. While residents in neighborhoods suffering from high levels of crime often demand higher levels of enforcement, they still want the police to be respectful and lawful in their crime control efforts (Skogan and Meares, 2004; Tyler, 2006). Residents don't want family members, friends, and neighbors to be targeted unfairly by enforcement efforts or treated poorly by overaggressive police officers.

The concentration of crime at specific hot-spot locations within neighborhoods provides an important opportunity for police to make connections with citizens who are most vulnerable to victimization and experience fear and diminished quality of life as a result of ongoing and intense crime and disorder problems. Regrettably, these community members are often the same people who view the police with suspicion and question the legitimacy of police efforts to control crime in their neighborhoods. In this sense, residents and business owners in high-activity crime places represent "hot spots" of community dissatisfaction with and mistrust of the police. If police departments are concerned with improving their relationships with community members, the residents and business owners in hot-spot locations seem like a logical place to start. Like crime, poor police-community relationships are not evenly spread throughout city environments (Brunson and Gau, 2014). If the police can win the hearts and minds of long-suffering community members in hot-spot areas, it seems likely to produce larger impacts on the overall legitimacy of police departments in the city than developing stronger relationships with community members in more stable neighborhoods who are more likely to already have generally positive perceptions of police services.

Conclusion

The available scientific evidence suggests that hot-spots policing increases the crime prevention effectiveness of police departments. Basic research reveals that crime is concentrated at very small geographic units of analysis, such as street segments or small groups of street blocks. Such crime hot spots offer stable targets for police interventions, as contrasted with the constantly moving targets of criminal offenders. Evaluation research provides solid experimental evidence for the effectiveness of hot-spots policing and contradicts the assumption that such interventions will just move crime around the corner. Indeed, the evidence available suggests that such interventions are much more likely to lead to a diffusion of crime control benefits to areas nearby. Crime hot spots also provide a focus for policing that can reduce legal barriers to police strategies and lessen the long-term social and moral consequences of traditional police activities that simply seek to arrest people.

Crime hot spots tend to cluster in disadvantaged, minority neighborhoods where police–community relationships can often be characterized by distrust and suspicion. If the police are not viewed as legitimate authorities in such neighborhoods, they will be challenged in developing the community cooperation necessary to deal with serious crime problems. Police actions that seek to prevent crime by changing places are better positioned to generate positive community perceptions of the police relative to simply increasing presence and arresting large numbers of offenders. Community engagement and treating citizens with respect and dignity needs to accompany heightened levels of police activity in small places.

Research accordingly suggests that it is time for police to shift from person-based policing to hot-spots policing. While such a shift is largely an evolution in trends that has begun over the last few decades, it will nonetheless demand radical changes in data collection in policing, in the organization of police activities, and particularly in the overall world view of the police. It remains true today that police officers see the key work of policing as catching criminals. It is time to change that world view so that police understand that the key to crime prevention is in ameliorating crime at problem places.

References

Apel, Robert J. and Daniel Nagin. 2011. General deterrence: A review of recent evidence. In (James Q. Wilson and Joan Petersilia, eds.), *Crime and public policy*. New York; Oxford University Press.

Blumstein, Alfred, Jacqueline Cohen, and Daniel Nagin. 1978. *Deterrence and incapacitation: Estimating the effects of criminal sanctions on crime rates.* Washington, DC: National Academy of Sciences.

Braga, Anthony A. 2001. The effects of hot spots policing on crime. *Annals of the American Academy of Political and Social Science*, 578: 104–125.

Braga, Anthony A. 2005. Hot spots policing and crime prevention: A systematic review of randomized controlled trials. *Journal of Experimental Criminology*, 1: 317–342.

Braga, Anthony A. and Brenda Bond. 2008. Policing crime and disorder hot spots: A randomized controlled trial. *Criminology*, 46: 577–608.

Braga, Anthony A., David Hureau, and Andrew Papachristos. 2011. The relevance of micro places to citywide robbery trends. *Journal of Research in Crime and Delinquency*, 48: 7–32.

Braga, Anthony A., Andrew Papachristos, and David Hureau. 2010. The concentration and stability of gun violence at micro places in Boston, 1980–2008. *Journal of Quantitative Criminology*, 26: 33–53.

Braga, Anthony A., Andrew Papachristos, and David Hureau. 2014. The effects of hot spots policing on crime: An updated systematic review and meta-analysis. *Justice Quarterly*, 31: 633–663.

Braga, Anthony A. and David Weisburd. 2010. *Policing problem places: Crime hot spots and effective prevention.* New York: Oxford University Press.

Brantingham, Paul and Patricia Brantingham, eds. 1981. *Environmental criminology*. Beverly Hills, CA: Sage.

Brunson, Rod K. and Jacinta Gau. 2014. Race, place, and policing the inner-city. In (Michael Reisig and Robert Kane, eds.), *The Oxford handbook of police and policing*. New York: Oxford University Press.

Cohen, Lawrence and Marcus Felson. 1979. Social change and crime rate trends: A routine activity approach. *American Sociological Review*, 44: 588–605.

Cook, Philip J. 1980. Research in criminal deterrence: Laying the groundwork for the second decade. In (Norval Morris and Michael Tonry, eds.), *Crime and justice: An annual review of research*, vol 2. Chicago: University of Chicago Press.

Cornish, Derek and Ronald V. Clarke, eds. 1986. *The reasoning criminal: Rational choice perspectives on offending*. New York: Springer-Verlag.

Durlauf, Steven and Daniel Nagin. 2011. Imprisonment and crime: Can both be reduced? *Criminologyand Public Policy*, 10: 13–54.

Eck, John E. 2002. Preventing crime at places. In (Lawrence Sherman, David Farrington, Brandon Welsh, and Doris MacKenzie, eds.), *Evidence-based crime prevention*. New York: Routledge.

Eck, John E. and David Weisburd. 1995. Crime places in crime theory. In (John E. Eck and David Weisburd, eds.), *Crime and place*. Monsey, New York: Criminal Justice Press.

Nagin, Daniel. 2013. Deterrence in the 21st century: A review of the evidence. In (Michael Tonry, ed.), *Crime and justice: A review of research*, vol 42. Chicago: University of Chicago Press.

Paternoster, Raymond. 1987. The deterrent effect of the perceived certainty and severity of punishment: A review of the evidence and issues. *Justice Quarterly*, 4: 173–217.

Petrosino, Anthony A., Robert Boruch, Haluk Soydan, Lorna Duggan, and Julio Sanchez-Meca. 2001. Meeting the challenge of evidence-based policy: The Campbell collaboration. *Annals of theAmerican Academy of Political and Social Science*, 578: 14–34.

Pierce, Glenn L., Susan Spaar, and LeBaron Briggs.1988. *The character of police work: Strategic and tactical implications*. Boston, MA: Center for Applied Social Research, Northeastern University.

Police Executive Research Forum. 2008. *Violent crime in America: What we know about hot spots enforcement*. Washington, DC: Police Executive Research Forum.

Rosenbaum, Dennis. 2006. The limits of hot spots policing. In (David Weisburd and Anthony A. Braga, eds.), *Police innovation: Contrasting perspectives*. New York: Cambridge University Press.

Sherman, Lawrence and John E. Eck. 2002. Policing for crime prevention. In (Lawrence Sherman, David Farrington, Brandon Welsh, and Doris MacKenzie, eds.), *Evidence-based crime prevention*. New York: Routledge.

Sherman, Lawrence, Patrick Gartin, and Michael Buerger. 1989. Hot spots of predatory crime: Routine activities and the criminology of place. *Criminology*, 27: 27–56.

Sherman, Lawrence and David Weisburd. 1995. General deterrent effects of police patrol in crime hot spots: A randomized controlled trial. *Justice Quarterly*, 12: 625–648.

Skogan, Wesley and Kathleen Frydl, eds. 2004. *Fairness and effectiveness in policing: The evidence*. Washington, DC: The National Academies Press.

Skogan, Wesley and Tracey Meares. 2004. Lawful policing. *Annals of the American Academy of Political and Social Science*,593: 66–83.

Spelman,William. 1995. Criminal careers of public places. In (John E. Eck and David Weisburd, eds.), *Crime and place*. Monsey, New York: Criminal Justice Press.

Taylor, Ralph. 1997. Social order and disorder of street-blocks and neighborhoods: Ecology, micro-ecology, and the systematic model of social disorganization. *Journal ofResearch in Crime and Delinquency*, 34: 113–155.

Taylor, Ralph and Stephen Gottfredson. 1986. Environment design, crime, and prevention: An examination of community dynamics. In (Albert J. Reiss and Michael Tonry, eds.), *Communities and crime*. Chicago: University of Chicago Press.

Tonry, Michael. 2011. Less imprisonment is no doubt a good thing: More policing is not. *Criminology and Public Policy*, 10: 137–152.

Tyler, Tom R. 2006. *Why people obey the law*. Princeton, NJ: Princeton University Press.

Weisburd, David. 2008. *Place-based policing.* Ideas in American policing series, no 9. Washington, DC: Police Foundation.

Weisburd, David, Shawn Bushway, Cynthia Lum, and Sue Ming Yang. 2004. Trajectories of crime at places: A longitudinal study of street segments in the city of Seattle. *Criminology,* 42: 283–322.

Weisburd, David and John E. Eck. 2004. What can police do to reduce crime, disorder, and fear? *Annals of the American Academy of Political and Social Science,* 593: 42–65.

Weisburd, David, Joshua Hinkle, Christine Famega, and Justin Ready. 2011. The possible "backfire" effects of hot spots policing. *Journal of Experimental Criminology,* 7: 297–320.

Weisburd, David, Stephen Mastrofski, Anne McNally, Rosann Greenspan, and James Willis. 2003. Reforming to preserve: Compstat and strategic problem solving in American policing. *Criminology and Public Policy,* 2: 421–456.

Weisburd, David and Cody Telep. 2014. Hot spots policing: What we know and what we need to know. *Journal of Contemporary Criminal Justice,* 30: 200–220.

Zimring, Frank and Gordon Hawkins. 1973. *Deterrence.* Chicago: University of Chicago Press.

Introduction

Court sentencing

Thomas G. Blomberg, Julie Mestre Brancale, Kevin M. Beaver and William D. Bales

Perhaps no other area of the criminal justice system has generated more debate or discussion than court sentencing. Whether it is the appropriate sentence for youthful offenders, the reasons for racial disparities in prison sentences, or the continued use of the death penalty as the ultimate sentence, there is no shortage of polarizing opinions on these and many other aspects related to sentencing decisions. All too often, however, views and opinions related to sentencing issues have been based on commonsensical notions, media depictions, or outdated and erroneous information. This section of the volume provides a counter-balance to this non-scientific approach by focusing on findings generated from empirical research that explores some of the key issues in court sentencing.

Chapter 12, by Celesta Albonetti, on mandatory minimum sentences begins this section. The chapter includes an historical analysis of the development of mandatory minimum sentencing laws to provide context for the development of these laws. The author then examines the outcomes associated with mandatory minimum sentences by noting, among other things, that these laws have led to a dramatic upswing in prison populations, an increase in racial disparities, and an increase in the length of incarceration. The outcomes of mandatory minimum sentences, according to Albonetti's review of the empirical evidence, have been largely negative. The remainder of her chapter deals with some of the ways these negative consequences can be reduced through sentencing policies that are evidence-based and humane.

Chapter 13, by Jeffrey Ulmer and Julia Laskorunsky, then explores one of the salient and problematic issues on court sentencing, namely sentencing disparities. The authors provide some revealing statistics regarding differential incarceration rates by race/ethnicity which document that minorities, particularly African-American males, are disproportionately sentenced to prison. Ulmer and Laskorunsky examine some of the potential reasons that might account for these disparities, including how sentencing policies play a pivotal role in creating and exacerbating racial disparities in sentencing.

Clearly, disparities in sentencing represent a complex and multifaceted phenomenon that lack a straightforward or immediate solution. The authors recognize this and suggest the need for further research studies that can contribute to greater recognition and understanding of sentencing disparities, thereby providing evidence-based policies to reduce these disparities.

Chapter 14, by Kelly Socia and Jason Rydberg, examines sex offender legislation and policies. Sex offender policy has received a significant amount of attention, largely because of the general fear of sex offenders and the perceived risk that they pose to society. Socia and Rydberg examine whether the fear of sex offenders is warranted or whether it has been the result of politics and the media. Based on their examination of the research literature, the authors conclude that the general view of sex offenders and the associated policies that have developed are not consistent with the relevant empirical research. They conclude with the recommendation that sex offender policies should be separated from politics and that relying on empirical research findings would help to increase the effectiveness of sex offender policies and practices.

Chapter 15, by Douglas Marlowe, provides an examination of the primary issues and findings related to drug courts and drug policy. After providing some background information concerning the creation of drug courts, Marlowe focuses upon the empirical research that has evaluated the effectiveness of drug courts. His review of the research literature is centered upon rigorously designed studies that show drug courts have resulted in significant reductions in rearrests. While his conclusion is that drug courts are effective, he also considers some of the intricacies and caveats of these findings by focusing on variability in the effectiveness of these programs and for whom drug courts are most effective. In closing, Marlowe makes a general call for all policies, including drug policies, to be guided by what is discovered in research studies, not by political ideology.

In the section's closing chapter (Chapter 16), Gordon Waldo examines the death penalty by employing the case of Furman v. Georgia for his conceptual framework. Although Waldo begins his chapter by listing a number of reasons why the death penalty should be abolished, his rationale for its abolishment is based upon how it is used in an arbitrary and discriminatory fashion as related to the decision of the Furman v. Georgia case. Waldo reviews a considerable amount of research and discusses findings related to arbitrariness as it pertains to geography, culpability, and judges, among other factors. He reviews the literature on racial discrimination and the death penalty and presents research showing that racial minorities are more likely than whites to receive a death penalty sentence. Waldo concludes his chapter by recommending that the United States abolish the death penalty because it continues to be used in an arbitrary and discriminatory way as documented consistently in the relevant research literature.

Sentencing policies and practices generate a significant amount of attention and debate among the public, policymakers, and researchers. As the chapters in this section demonstrate, there are several areas within the field of criminal justice sentencing that are particularly contentious and devoid of scientific evidence, namely, the use of mandatory minimum sentences (Chapter 12), sex offender sentences (Chapter 14), and the use of the death penalty (Chapter 16). However, drug courts (Chapter 15) provide an example of an evidence-based sentencing option that has been proven to be effective at reducing recidivism. Overall, sentencing disparities (Chapter 13) are widespread in the American criminal justice system and are the result of sentencing policies that have been implemented without the best available research evidence. In sum, to minimize disparities and increase the effectiveness of sentencing policies, rigorous evaluations and reliance upon research evidence is fundamental.

Chapter 12

Mandatory minimum penalties

Evidence-based consequences and recommendations for policy and legal reform

Celesta A. Albonetti

Introduction

During the "war on crime" and "war on drugs" political climate in the 1970s, many states and the federal government instituted mandatory minimum penalties in response to increases in drug and violent crime. At the federal level, statutory mandatory minimum penalties for drug offenses began at a serious level in the 1970s during the Nixon administration. They were expanded to include firearm violations in the mid-1980s with full support of the Reagan administration. The scope and severity of mandatory minimum penalties increased in the 1990s and 2000s with inclusion of child pornography, child exploitation related violations, expansion of drug, firearm, and career criminal enhancements. In the United States, it is an understatement to say that federal and state legislatures used mandatory minimum penalties as the principal response to increases in drug and violent crime rates. After over four decades of a preoccupation with enacting mandatory minimum penalty laws, the Department of Justice, the United States Sentencing Commission, some members of Congress, and some states are reconsidering the efficacy of mandatory minimum statutes, as well as the desirability of hand-cuffing judges' and jury's decision making at the punishment phase of adjudication. Research indicating the dramatic escalation in prison population, the associated financial costs of this escalation and failure of mandatory minimum penalties to reduce recidivism has promoted federal and state legislative changes in the sentencing policies.

This chapter presents: (1) a brief history of implementation of federal and state mandatory minimum penalties; (2) evidence-based findings of the consequences of mandatory minimum penalties; (3) recent policy changes and recommendation aimed at rolling back these consequences; and (4) research-based projections of the effect of these law and policy changes.

Mandatory minimum sentencing policy

In the United States, reliance on mandatory minimum punishment, as a deterrent and a retributive force, dates as far back as the late eighteenth century (USSC, 2011). However, it is not until the 1970s that policymakers placed mandatory minimum penalties as the centerpiece of sentencing policy. Currently, most states have some form of mandatory minimums. Federal statutes provide mandatory minimum penalties for 195 offenses (USSC, 2011).

In the 1970s Congress enacted 36 mandatory minimum penalties. Early in the decade, mandatory minimum statutes focused primarily on murder of a member of Congress, the cabinet or the Supreme Court, and drug violations. Mandatory minimum penalties ranged from life imprisonment to sentence enhancements of between 5 years and 20 years. Later in the decade, Congress shifted focus to enactment of a series of criminal offenses involving child sexual exploitation. Mandatory minimum penalties ranging from 15 to 35 years were enacted for crimes such as engaging in explicit conduct with a child for the purpose of producing visual depictions of such conduct or producing or publishing visual depictions of a child engaging in sexual activity.

During the 1970s, three states took legislative action to address the rising crime rates. In New York, the Rockefeller Drug Laws were enacted in 1973. These laws provided a mandatory minimum sentence of 15 years to life in prison for conviction of selling two ounces or possessing four ounces of heroin, morphine, cocaine, or marijuana. Later in the decade, Minnesota and Pennsylvania created sentencing commissions for the purpose of reforming sentencing practices. The reforms were directed toward meeting goals of increased uniformity, severity, and truth-in-sentencing.

In the mid-1980s Congress passed the Anti-Drug Abuse Act of 1986 that established mandatory minimum penalties for drug offenses: 31 drug-related penalties were created, each carrying a mandatory minimum sentence. This Act instituted the 100:1 powder-to-crack cocaine sentencing ratio that later became the basis of the drug quantity table calculations of the Federal Sentencing Guidelines. Of the statutes carrying a non-life imprisonment sentence, eight assigned a 20-year term of imprisonment or fine or both, four statutes assigned a 10-year term of imprisonment or fine or both, and four carried a 5-year term of imprisonment or fine or both. In the 1980s, Congress substantially increased the number of federal crimes assigned a mandatory minimum penalty and imposed severe punishment for drug-related, sexual exploitation of children, firearm offenses, and criminal enterprise.

During the 1980s, the State of Washington enacted the first truth-in-sentencing law that mandated violent offenders to serve most of the term of imprisonment imposed. Five states developed sentencing guidelines requiring greater uniformity and accountability in sentencing practices. It is not until the mid-1990s that a substantial number of states aggressively adopted truth-in-sentencing laws and three strikes law.

In the 1990s, Congress enacted 21 mandatory minimum penalties and sentence enhancements ranging from one year in prison for stalking to life imprisonment for murder of various federal officials in the act of carrying out their official duties. In 1994, Congress enacted the Violent Crime Control and Law Enforcement Act that provided for federal three strikes laws. In addition, the Act tied federal funds for prison construction to state implementation of truth-in-sentencing policies (Subramanian and Delaney, 2014). Five states had already established truth-in-sentencing laws. One year after passage of the Violent Crime Control and Law Enforcement Act, 11 more states enacted truth-in-sentencing laws. State quickly responded to the federal stimulus to enact such sentencing policies. By the end of the decade, 24 states had enacted three strikes laws, 17 states had created sentencing guidelines, and 29 states had implemented truth-in-sentencing statutes (Subramanian and Delaney, 2014). Since the beginning of the twenty-first century, Congress has passed 31 mandatory minimum penalties and sentence enhancements. Terms of imprisonment range from a mandatory minimum of six months in custody to life imprisonment.

The history of federal mandatory minimum penalties has been one of increased federalization of criminal law and the continued application of decades-long terms of imprisonment. Expansion of offenses carrying a mandatory minimum penalty spread from drug-related crimes and firearm offenses to career criminal enterprise, child sexual exploitation related offenses and sex trafficking of a minor. Attention now turns to evidenced-based findings of the consequences of federal and state reliance on severe mandatory minimum terms of imprisonment.

Evidence-based findings of the consequences of mandatory minimum penalties

Research over the last four decades reveals the costly consequences of federal and state adoption of harsh mandatory minimum sentences and sentence enhancements for drug offenses and weapon offenses. Ample empirical evidence exists, assessing the ramifications of federal and state adoption and expansion of mandatory minimum sentences, drug and weapon sentence enhancements, and three strikes laws and truth-in-sentencing policies. Empirical evidence indicates that these ramifications are multi-pronged. The prongs include dramatic increases in length of imprisonment (USSSC, 1991, 2011; Sutton, 2013; Meierhoefer, 1992; Tonry, 2013), immediate and continued escalation of the prison population (USSC, 1991, 2011; Tonry, 2011), the social and economic costs of this escalation, measured in terms of diminished opportunities for successful re entry into society after lengthy imprisonment, long-term disruption of family relations for low-level drug offenders, prison overcrowding (e.g. Caulkins et al., 1997; Parsons et al., 2015; Levy-Pounds, 2007), and race/ethnicity sentencing disparity tied to differential access to relief from application of mandatory minimums (USSC, 1991, 2011; Albonetti, 2002a, 2002b). The latter consequence is particularly troublesome in light of reform goals of uniformity, proportionality, and truth-in-sentencing. The very legitimacy of the criminal justice system is challenged when evidence indicates practices that shield some offenders from mandatory minimum penalties and sentence enhancements, while providing no such shield to similarly situated defendants.

Research indicates that implementation of federal and state mandatory minimum penalties and truth-in-sentencing policies resulted in immediate increases in prison populations. Parsons et al. describe three decades during which the New York State prison population escalated by almost "sixfold and the number of people incarcerated for drug offenses grew by a factor of nearly 15 – skyrocketing from 1,488 people in 1973 to 22,266 in 1999" (2015:5). Furthermore, Parsons et al. (2015) found substantial racial disparities in the New York state prison population by 2001. They note "For every white male between the ages of 21 and 44 incarcerated for a drug offense, there were 40 African American males, also in the prime of life, behind bars for the same reason" (Parsons et al., 2015:15).

In a special report to Congress, the U.S. Sentencing Commission (hereafter, Commission) indicated the following direct impact of sentencing guidelines and mandatory minimum penalties enacted in 1986. They reported the following:

a)   reduction from 42.42% to 18.9% if offenders receiving probation with no confinement conditions,
b)   the pre-guidelines average prison time served of 15.3 months will increase to 28.7 months with sentences for violent offenses accounting for most of almost doubling of imposed length of imprisonment,
c)   the substantial increase in average length of imprisonment will be accounted for by the Anti-Drug Abuse Act of 1986 and the career criminal provision of the Sentencing Reform Act of 1984.

(USSC, 1991:113)

The Commission projected, "... that the Anti-Drug Abuse Act of 1986 along with a relatively low rate of increases in prosecutions resulted in a doubling of the federal prison population over a ten-year period; from approximately 42,000 inmates in 1987 to approximately 85,000 inmates in 1997" (USSC, 1991:115). The Commission further noted that, "If one looks at the high growth scenario, the increase due to the drug laws is ever more dramatic; from a population of 42,000 to one of approximately 108,000" (USSC, 1991:115). Early Commission projections identified the Anti-Drug Abuse Act of 1986 and to a lesser degree, the career offender provision of the SRA of 1986, as the forces driving the dramatic increase in federal prison population during the late 1980s and the 1990s.

The Commission's report to Congress in 1991 provided unquestionable evidence of the multi-dimensional cost of drug and weapon mandatory minimum penalties. Apparently, Congress was unmoved by the dramatic projected increases in prison population and the associated cost per inmate. The political climate, at both the federal and state level, was steeped in a "get tough with crime" agenda, with little or no interest in rolling back the number and punishment severity of mandatory minimum. In fact, during the decade of the 1990s, federal and state legislatures expanded mandatory minimum penalties.

Twenty years later, the Commission produced a second report on the impact of mandatory minimum penalties on the federal prison population and on the operation of the federal criminal justice system (USSC, 2011). Using data provided by the Bureau of Justice Statistics (BJS), the Commission described the dramatic increase in the federal prison population at the end of each year from 1991 to 2009. Their report indicated that at the end of 1991 the federal prison population was 71,606 inmates and by the end of 2009, the prison population had grown to 208,188 inmates (USSC, 2011, see footnote 445:76). This increase in federal prison population reflects a tripling of the inmate population over the 20-year period, largely due to mandatory minimum provisions.

The Commission (2011) empirically documented substantial changes in the length for offenders convicted of an offense carrying a mandatory minimum penalty for FY 1990 and FY 2010. The report notes that in FY 1990, sentences carrying relative higher mandatory minimum sentences, that is sentences greater than five years imprisonment, accounted for 43.5 percent of the mandatory minimum sentences imposed (USSC, 2011, see Figure 4–7:76). In FY 2010, the percentage of mandatory minimum sentences carrying greater than 5-year imprisonment represented 55 percent of the sentences carrying a mandatory minimum penalty (USSC, 2011, Figure 4–7:76). These findings reveal an 11.5 percent increase in offenses carrying extremely long terms of imprisonment – 10, 15, 20+ years (USSC, 2011). These findings provide further evidence-based understanding of the dramatic impact of federal mandatory minimum penalties over the ten-year period (USSC, 2011).

Increasing punishment severity and reducing judicial discretion are the hallmarks of truth-in-sentencing laws and mandatory minimum penalties in federal and state criminal adjudication. There is ample evidence that the relationship between mandatory minimum penalties and sentence severity is embedded in dynamics of prosecutorial charging decisions (Ulmer et al., 2007; Bjerk, 2005; Loftin et al., 1983; Schulhofer, 1993) and guidelines' mechanisms (substantial assistance departures and safety-valve provision) that allow federal judges to relax applicable mandatory minimum penalties (USSC, 2011; Albonetti, 2002a, 2002b; Greenblatt, 2008).

At the state level, Ulmer et al. (2007) examined prosecutorial discretion to impose eligible mandatory minimums in Pennsylvania during 1998 to 2000. They found that prosecutors actually applied mandatory minimums rarely. They found that in the general sample of offenses, prosecutors applied eligible mandatory minimums in only 18.4 percent of the cases and in only 16.2 percent of drug trafficking cases. They found the highest percent (29 percent) of prosecutorial imposition of eligible mandatory minimum among three-strike cases (Ulmer et al., 2007). Of particular interest, is their finding that negotiated pleas, compared to trial disposition, significantly reduced the likelihood of prosecutors imposing mandatory minimums for the full sample of offenses and for drug trafficking offenses, but not for three-strike offenses (Ulmer et al., 2007). Furthermore, they found that non-negotiated pleas, compared to trial disposition, significantly reduced the likelihood of prosecutors imposing eligible mandatory minimums for only three-strike offenses. Their research in Pennsylvania reveals how mandatory minimum penalties may be used to leverage guilty plea dispositions, thus avoiding both the uncertainty of obtaining a guilty verdict and the associated drain on scarce resources associated with trials.

Turning to research on the effect of mandatory minimum penalties on federal sentencing requires consideration of the effect of two mechanisms of relief from applicable mandatory minimum penalties. Chapter 5 of the Federal Sentencing Guidelines provide for § 5K1.1 substantial assistance departures and § 5C1.1 safety-valve provision, each is a mechanism by which the defendant can avoid application of any mandatory minimum penalty. By receiving one or both of these mechanisms, 46.7 percent of the offenders convicted of an offense carrying a mandatory minimum penalty in FY 2010 avoided being sentenced under the mandatory minimum penalty (USSC, 2011:133). The Commission's (2011) study reveals the sentence advantage to an offender facing a mandatory minimum penalty of receiving a § 5K1.1 substantial assistance departure and/or the § 5C1.1 safety-valve provision. In FY 2010, the average length of imprisonment for offenses carrying a mandatory minimum penalty was 139 months, compared to 63 months for offenders convicted of an offense with no mandatory minimum sentence (USSC, 2011, see Figure 7–12:137). Among offenders facing a mandatory minimum penalty and who receive a § 5K1.1 substantial assistance departure, the average length of imprisonment drops to 91 months. For those qualifying for the § 5C1.1 safety-valve provision, the average length of imprisonment drops to 50 months and drops to 33 months for offenders who received both a § 5K1.1 substantial assistance departure and qualified for the § 5C1.1 safety-valve provision (USSC, 2011, Table 7–12:137). Clearly, the Commission's (2011) report to Congress revealed the sentence advantage provided by substantial assistance departures and the safety-valve provision.

Research (USSC, 2011; Albonetti, 2002a, 2002b, 1997) consistently finds that substantial assistance departures and the safety-valve provision are differentially distributed across offender's race/ethnicity. Specifically, the Commission's report (2011, see Figure 7–8:133) and Albonetti (2002a, 2002b) indicate that African-American offenders are least likely to avoid a mandatory minimum sentence by receiving a § 5K1.1 substantial assistance departure and/or the§ 5C1.1 safety-valve provision. Compared to whites, Hispanics, and other race-ethnicity offenders, African-Americans were the least likely to qualify for the safety-valve provision due criminal history and use of a weapon during the offense (USSC, 2011, see Table 7–8:133). Among offenders convicted of an offense carrying a mandatory minimum penalty in FY 2010, African-Americans had the highest percentage of offenders receiving a § 5K1.1 substantial assistance departure. Yet, research indicates that African-Americans receive the least sentence reduction from the substantial assistance departure (Albonetti, 2002a). Examining the 20-year period from 1991–2009, the Commission's (2011) study indicated that African-Americans consistently experienced the lowest percentage of offenders receiving relief from a mandatory minimum sentence via a § 5K1.1 substantial assistance departure and/or the § 5C1.1 safety-valve provision (USSC, 2011, see Table 7–9:134), the two available mechanisms or avoiding harsh federal mandatory minimum penalties.

Using multivariate regression analysis, Albonetti (2002a, 2002b) and Albonetti and Baller (2010) found that, consistent with congressional intent, low-level, non-violent, first offenders who qualified for the safety-valve provision were shielded from mandatory minimum penalties. Albonetti (2002a) concluded that the safety-valve provision conditioned the direct effect of mandatory minimum penalties on sentence length. The effect of qualifying for the safety-valve provision extended beyond its direct effect on reducing length of imprisonment. Specifically, Albonetti (2002a) found that the safety-valve provision mitigated increases in length of imprisonment associated with African-American offenders, compared to white offenders. These findings point to *direct* and *mitigating* effects on length of imprisonment related to the safety-valve provision. These findings complement the Commission's report (2011) by examining the relationship between mandatory minimum penalties, substantial assistance departures, the safety-valve provision, and sentence length, controlling for guidelines, legally relevant case information, route of case disposition, and other offender characteristics.

Separating drug offenders convicted in 1998–1999 into six groups (African-American males, white males, Hispanic males, African-American females, white females and Hispanic females), Albonetti (2002b) found that African-American males received significantly *lower* sentence reduction from a substantial assistance departure, compared to four of five race/ethnicity-gender groups. Hispanic males and African-American males received similar sentence reductions. These findings indicate that offender's race/ethnicity and gender jointly condition the effect of the safety-valve provision and substantial assistance departure on length of imprisonment. Further research is needed to examine whether these effects interact with the application of eligible mandatory minimum penalties.

Fischman and Schanzenbach (2012) analyzed disparities in length of imprisonment over four periods of time during which judicial sentencing discretion to depart from the Federal Sentencing Guidelines expanded and contracted as a result of Supreme Court decisions in Koon v. U.S., Booker v. U.S., Rita v. U.S., Gall v. U.S., U.S. v. Kimbrough, and the PROTECT Act. Their research examined primarily the relationship between changes in judicial discretion and racial disparities in sentence outcomes. Fischman and Schanzenbach's (2012) analyses revealed that racial disparities in length of imprisonment were reduced when sentencing judges were given greater discretion as a result of the Supreme Court decisions in Koon and Booker. Furthermore, they found that after the Koon decision, providing greater appellate court deference and, thereby greater discretion to judges' decisions to depart from the Guidelines, reduced racial disparities. After the Supreme Court's decisions in Rita, Gall, and Kimbrough clarified the standard of review introduced in Booker, Fischman and Schanzenbach (2012) reported an increase in racial disparities in sentencing. However, they assert that this increase was "due to the increased relevance of statutory minimums under a system of advisory Guidelines. White and Hispanic prison sentences declined after Rita. Black prison sentences did not, except in those cases in which mandatory minimums were less likely to bind" (2012:757). Fischman and Schanzenbach conclude that, "Policymakers interested in redressing racial disparity today should pay much closer attention to mandatory minimums and their effects on prosecutorial and judicial decisions" (2012:761). This conclusion is consistent with previous research on the importance of judicial discretion in applying mandatory minimum penalties (LaCasse and Payne, 1999; Reimer and Wayne, 2011–2012; Albonetti, 2002a, 2002b).

Attention now turns to evidence-based findings of the relative cost-effectiveness of mandatory minimum sentences, compared to other policy approaches aimed at reducing cocaine drug consumption and other drug-related crime. Caulkins et al.'s early research concluded that "Mandatory minimum sentences are not justifiable on the basis of cost-effectiveness at reducing cocaine consumption and drug offenses" (1997:2). Their analysis revealed that treatment programs were more strongly associated with positive outcomes than either non-mandatory sentencing practices or mandatory minimum sentencing schemes. The exceedingly high cost of incarceration accounted for the findings supporting use of drug treatment programs for offenders who were categorized as "heavy" drug users. Caulkins et al. (1997) concluded that it was more cost-effective to use drug treatment than incarceration for cocaine drug users. They maintained that their findings indicate that, regardless of type of drug dealer (high- or low-level), mandatory minimum penalties are less cost-effective than conventional enforcement. Caulkins et al. (1997) asserted that their findings provide a sound basis for shifting some state and federal resources to developing and implementing treatment programs and away from long mandatory minimum sentences as the only real government approach to drug-related offenders.

Caulkins et al.'s (1997) study addressed another policy question: What is the relative cost-effectiveness of treatment, conventional enforcement, and long sentences for heavy cocaine users and the typical drug dealer over a one to 15-year horizon? Caulkins et al. (1997) found that as time horizon is shortened, the effect of treatment, relative to mandatory minimum sentences, is worse. They reasoned that the costs of treatment are immediate and remain, while the benefits realized by offenders as they reduce cocaine consumption are reduced. Finally, Caulkins et al. (1997) concluded that it is more cost-effective for government expenditures to be directed toward arresting, prosecuting, and non-mandatory minimum sentences, compared to mandatory minimum longer terms of imprisonment. Imposing long mandatory minimum penalties seems to be cost-effective only for the highest-level cocaine drug dealers. They suggested that judges should be given discretion to consider the offender's location in the drug distribution hierarchy when imposing mandatory minimum sentences.

Response to evidence-based consequences of mandatory minimum penalties

The U.S. Sentencing Commissions purposed extensive recommendations to Congress regarding mandatory minimum penalties (see USSC, 2011, see Chapter 12, for the complete list). Regarding drug offenses, the Commission proposed two recommendations. First, the Commission recommended expanding the safety-valve provision to include non-violent offenders who receive two or even three criminal history points under the guidelines calculation (USSC, 2011:368). By so doing, a greater percent of black drug offenders would qualify for the provision, resulting in more black offenders eligible for relief from mandatory minimum sentences. Second, the Commission recommended mitigation of the cumulative effect of criminal history by reassessing the scope and severity of the recidivist provisions that double mandatory minimum terms of imprisonment for offenders with a prior felony drug conviction (USSC, 2011:368).

Regarding firearm offenses, the Commission proposed three recommendations. First, the Commission recommended that the enhanced mandatory minimum penalty, assigned for a second or subsequent offense, apply only to prior convictions and carry shorter lengths of imprisonment (USSC, 2011:368). Second, the Commission recommended elimination of the "stacking" requirement provided in 18 U.S.C. § 924(c) (USSC, 2011:368). Third, the Commission recommended clarification of the statutory definitions of the underlying and predicate offenses that trigger mandatory minimum penalties under 18 U.S.C. § 924 (c) and the Armed Career Criminal Act (USSC, 2011:369).

At the federal level recent amendments and congressional laws have been enacted to alleviate severe prison overcrowding and racial disparity in length of imprisonment. In 2010, Congress passed the Fair Sentencing Act that changed the powder to crack cocaine 100:1 sentencing ratio to 18:1.[1] The Act lowered the statutory penalties for crack cocaine offenses, abolished the statutory mandatory minimum penalty for simple possession of crack cocaine and instructed the Commission to amend the guidelines so that aggravating and mitigating circumstances for certain drugs are accounted for in calculating the offense level (*USSC Federal Sentencing Guidelines Manual*, 2014, Appendix C, Amendment 750:1220). By raising the drug quantity threshold that triggers the 5-year and 10-year mandatory minimum sentence, the Amendment 750 restructures sentences for crack cocaine to correspond to sentences imposed for other drugs (*USSC Federal Sentencing Guidelines Manual*, 2014, Appendix C, Amendment 750:1221). Restructuring of the drug quantity table – directly related to the calculation of the offense level in the Sentencing Table – addresses the disproportionate terms of imprisonment associated with convictions for crack cocaine offenses. Also, since black offenders are disproportionately convicted of crack cocaine offenses, Amendment 750 is likely to reduce racial disparities in length of imprisonment among that group of drug offenders.

What is the estimated impact of the Amendment on prison overcrowding? The Commission's data forecasts that Amendment 750 will shorten imprisonment length for approximately 63 percent of crack cocaine offenders sentenced after Nov. 1, 2011(*USSC Federal Sentencing Guidelines Manual*, 2014, Supplement to Appendix C:1221). The Commission estimates that the change in the drug quantity table for crack cocaine offenses will result in an approximately 26 percent reduction in the average length of imprisonment for crack cocaine offenders. By so doing, prison overcrowding is expected to be reduced.

Given the earlier discussed empirical findings of the direct and intervening effect of prosecutorial discretion, it is noteworthy that the Commission cautioned their estimates by acknowledging that changes in prosecutorial practices may alter these estimates. The Commission does not provide estimates of increases or decreases to average sentence length associated with the two-level enhancement provided for offenders who used violence in some form in committing the drug offense. Prosecutorial charging decisions may well affect how the two-level enhancement effects attempts to eliminate prison overcrowding by reducing terms of imprisonment for a substantial number of offenders who are convicted of drug offenses.

As a further attempt to reduce federal prison overcrowding, the Commission enacted Amendment 782 that provides for a two-level decrease in the offense level assigned to the drug quantities that trigger mandatory minimum terms of imprisonment (*USSC Federal Sentencing Guidelines Manual*, Appendix C:1314). The Commission estimated that the two-level decrease would not change the percent of drug offenders who plead guilty and cooperate with the government (*USSC Federal Sentencing Guidelines Manual*, Appendix C: 1316).

The Commission estimates that the Amendment will reduce sentences of 17,457 (approximately 70 percent) inmates currently imprisoned for drug trafficking/manufacturing. In addition the Amendment is expected to reduce the average length of imprisonment by 11 months (62 to 51 months); reflecting a 17.7 percent decrease (*USSC Federal Sentencing Guidelines Manual*, 2014, Supplement to Appendix C: 1316). Further, the Commission anticipates the Amendment will result in a prison population decrease of approximately 6,588 inmates over the first five years of implementation. Linked to this reduction, the Department of Justice testified before the Commission that the Amendment will result in a non-trivial reduction in the current $6 billion federal expenditures yearly on incarceration: Department of Justice estimates that federal prisons are overcrowded by 32 percent with drug trafficking inmates accounting for approximately 50 percent of the 199,810 inmates as of October 2013 (USSC Guidelines Manual, 2014, Supplement to Appendix C. Amendment 782: 1316). The Commission further noted that stakeholder testifying before the Commission indicated that the Amendment would divert funds, otherwise expended for incarceration, to expansion of programs directed toward reducing recidivism, increasing law enforcement activities aimed at crime prevention and public safety (*USSC Federal Sentencing Guidelines Manual*, 2014, Supplement to Appendix C. Amendment 782: 1316).

To further address prison overcrowding, the Commission promulgated Amendment 759 which made retroactive Amendment 750 changes to the drug quantity levels that triggered mandatory minimum penalties for crack cocaine offenders. The Commission reports (USSC Final Crack Retroactivity Data Report, Fair Sentencing Act, 2014) that 13,992 offenders would be eligible for retroactivity review of their current sentence. Of these offenders, 7,710 (54 percent) offenders would be granted a sentence reduction (USSC, Final Crack Retroactivity Data Report, Fair Sentencing Act, 2014, see Table 3). Furthermore, the Commission's analysis indicates that, of the 8,974 offenders considered for a sentence reduction from 2004–2008, black offenders have the greatest percent (85 percent) granted a retroactive sentence reduction (USSC, Final Crack Retroactivity Data Report, Fair Sentencing Act, 2014, see Table 5).

Taken together, federal policymakers have pursued evidence-based reform of the harsh mandatory minimum penalties provided by the Anti-Drug Abuse Act of 1986. If the Commission's estimates are correct, the changes in crack cocaine drug quantity that triggers mandatory minimum sentences will reduce federal prison overcrowding and alleviate some of the racial disparity in sentencing of drug offenders. Moreover, the goal of proportionality in punishment, central to the Sentencing Reform Act of 1984 will be close to being realized, at least for drug offenders.

In recent years, 19 states have enacted reform of mandatory minimum sentencing and three strike laws. For example, in 2009 the Rhode Island legislature repealed all mandatory minimum penalties for drug offenses. Under the old law, drug offenders were sentenced to 10 and 20-years of imprisonment for possession and/or distribution together with fines of $10,000 and $25,000. In 2011 the Ohio legislature replaced mandatory minimum sentences for first-time, non-violent offenders with community service, job training or individualized treatment programs. In addition, Ohio reform provided for more lenient sentences for low-level drug trafficking and possession offenses. Increased use of drug courts to divert low-level drug offenders from imprisonment has appeared in Florida and New York.

According to Families Against Mandatory Minimum [hereafter, FAMM] (2015), in 2014 the Florida legislature enacted reform of its harsh drug trafficking laws by raising the weight for trafficking in prescription pain killers and eliminated mandatory minimums for illegal possession or distribution of Oxycodone pain killers under seven grams. Due to Florida's Constitution, these reforms cannot be made retroactive (FAMM, 2015). After decades of mandatory minimum sentences, including three strikes law, the tide seems to be turning away from rigid sentencing polices toward giving judges greater sentencing discretion. In 2009, New York's legislature repealed mandatory minimum drug penalties, expanded eligibility for drug treatment and increased judicial discretion to individualize sentencing.

In 2012, Missouri reduced its crack-powder cocaine sentence disparity by increasing the amount of crack cocaine that triggers a mandatory minimum penalty. With the reform, the crack-powder disparity decreased from 75:1 to 18:1 (FAMM, 2015). California's three strikes law was modified by requiring the third strike to be a serious or violent felony. This modification was made retroactive and will reduce prison time for approximately 3,500 inmates who are serving life imprisonment (FAMM, 2015). It is estimated that this change will save the state approximately $70-$100 million annually (FAMM, 2015).

In conclusion, after decades of mandatory minimum sentences, including three strikes law, federal and state policymakers have begun to: (1) modify rigid sentencing polices; (2) provide greater opportunities for diversion from imprisonment; and (3) increase the judge's sentencing discretion. It is fair to say that evidence-based findings indicating dramatic escalation in federal and state prison populations, driven by mandatory minimum penalties, and the associated high cost of long terms of imprisonment for low-level, non-violent drug offenders accounts for the relatively recent reforms away from mandatory minimum penalties at both state and federal levels.

Note

1 The Commission implemented congressional directives contained in section 8 of the Fair Sentencing Act of 2010 on a temporary emergency basis with Amendment 748. One year later, the Commission implemented Amendment 750 making the Fair Sentencing Act section 8 directives permanent.

References

Albonetti, Celesta A. 2002a. The effects of the "safety valve" amendment on length of imprisonment for cocaine trafficking/manufacturing offenders: mitigating the effects of mandatory minimum penalties and offender's ethnicity. *Iowa Law Rev.* 87: 401–434.

Albonetti, Celesta A. 2002b. The joint conditioning effect of defendant's gender and ethnicity on length of imprisonment under the federal sentencing guidelines for drug trafficking/manufacturing offenders. *The Journal of Gender, Race and Justice* 6: 39–60.

Albonetti, Celesta A. 1997. Sentencing under the federal sentencing guidelines: Effects of defendant characteristics, guilty pleas, and departures on sentence outcomes for drug offenses, 1991–1992. *Law and Society Review* 31: 789–822.

Albonetti, Celesta A. and Baller, Robert D. (2010). Sentencing in federal drug trafficking/manufacturing cases: A multilevel analysis of extra-legal defendant characteristics, guidelines departures, and continuity of culture. *Journal of Gender, Race and Justice* 14: 41–71.

Bjerk, David. 2005. Making the crime fit the penalty: The role of prosecutorial discretion under mandatory minimum sentencing. *Journal Law and Economics* 48: 591–625.

Caulkins, Jonathan P., C. Peter Rydell, William L. Schwabe, and James Chiesa. 1997. *Mandatory minimum drug sentences: throwing away the key or the taxpayers' money?* MR-827- DPRC RAND.

Families Against Mandatory Minimums. 2015. Available online at famm.org/states-map.

Fischman, Joshua and Max Schanzenbach. 2012. Racial disparities under the federal sentencing guidelines: the role of judicial discretion and mandatory minimums. *Journal of Empirical Legal Studies* 9: 729–764.

Greenblatt, Nathan. 2008. How mandatory are mandatory minimums? How judges can avoid imposing mandatory minimum sentences. *American Journal of Criminal Law* 36: 2–38.

LaCasse, Chantale and A. Abigail Payne. 1999. Federal sentencing guidelines and mandatory minimum sentences: Do defendants bargain in the shadow of the judge? *Journal of Law and Economics* 42: 245–269.

Levy-Pounds, Nekima. 2007. From the Frying Pan Into the Fire: How Poor Women of Color and Children are Affected by the Sentencing Guidelines and Mandatory Minimums. *Santa Clara Law Review* 47 (No. 2, Spring).

Loftin, Colin, McDowall, David and Brian Wiersema. 1983. Mandatory Sentencing and Firearm Violence: Evaluating an alternative to gun control. *Law & Society Review* 12: 287–318.

Meierhoefer, B. 1992. *The General Effect of Mandatory Minimum Prison Terms* (Federal Judicial Center).

Parsons, Jim, Qing Wei, Christian Henrichson, Ernest Drucker and Jennifer Trone. 2015. *End of an era? The impact of drug law reform in New York City.* VERA Institute of Justice.

Reimer, Norman L. and Lisa M. Wayne. 2011–2012. From the practitioners' perch: how mandatory minimum sentences and the prosecution's unfettered control over sentence reductions for cooperation subvert justice and exacerbate racial disparity. *University Pennsylvania Law Rev. PENNumbra* 160:159–177.

Schulhofer, Stephen J. 1993. Rethinking mandatory minimums. *Wake Forest Law Review* 28: 199–222.

Subramanian, Ram and Ruth Delaney. 2014. *Playbook for change? States reconsider mandatory Sentences.* VERA Institute of Justice.

Sutton, Jonathan. 2013. *Mass Incarceration on Trial: A Remarkable Court Decision and the Future of Prisons in America.* New York: The New Press.

Tonry, Michael. 2011. *Punishing Race: A Continuing American Dilemma.* New York: Oxford University Press, Inc.

Tonry, Michael. 2013. Sentencing in America, 1975–2025. *Crime and Justice* 42: 141–187.

Ulmer, Jeffery T., Megan C. Kurlychek and John H. Kramer. 2007. Prosecutorial discretion and the imposition of mandatory minimum sentences. *Journal of Research in Crime and Delinquency* 44: 427–458.

U.S. Sentencing Commission. 2014. *The Federal Sentencing Guidelines Manual.* Washington, D.C.

U.S. Sentencing Commission. 2011. *Special Report to Congress: Mandatory Minimum Penalties in Federal Criminal Justice System.*

U.S. Sentencing Commission. 1999. *Special Report to Congress: Mandatory Minimum Penalties in Federal Criminal Justice System.*

U.S. Sentencing Commission. 2014. *Final Fair Sentencing Act Amendment Retroactivity Data Report.*

Statutes

Anti-Drug Abuse Act, Pub. L. No. 99–5700 (1986)

Anti-Drug Abuse Act, Pub. L. No. 100–690 (1988)

Drug Abuse Prevention and Control Act, Pub. L. No. 91–513 (1994)

Fair Sentencing Act, Pub. L. No. 111–220 (2010)

Prosecutorial Remedies and Other Tools to End the Exploitation of Children Today Act (PROTECT Act), Pub. L. No. 108–21(codified and amended at U.S. 18 §§ 2423(a)-(g), 2246, 2516(1) (c), 1591, 3142(e), 3283, 3559(c), section 401 (2003)

Sentencing Reform Act, Pub. L. No. 98–473 (1984)

Violent Crime Control and Law Enforcement Act H.R. 3355 Pub. L. No. 103–322 (1994)

Supreme court cases

Booker v. U.S. 543 U.S. 220 (2005)
Koon v. U.S. 518 U.S. 81 (1996)
Gall v. U.S. 552 U.S. 38 (2007)
Rita v. U.S. 551 U.S. 338 (2007)
U.S. v. Kimbrough 552 U.S. 85 (2007)

Chapter 13

Sentencing disparities

Jeffrey T. Ulmer and Julia Laskorunsky

Introduction

As we write this, protests roil U.S. cities in the wake of the police shooting of Michael Brown in Ferguson, MO, and the death of Eric Garner at the hands of a New York City police officer. Racial and ethnic disparity in criminal justice has important consequences for the legitimacy of the justice system, especially in the eyes of minorities. The perception that criminal justice institutions are biased against certain minority groups erodes those groups' trust in, and increases their alienation from, courts and government (Tyler and Huo, 2002). The scale of racial and ethnic disproportionality in U.S. imprisonment has also attracted criticism from across the political spectrum. As of 2011, black males represented 36 percent and Hispanic males 21 percent of all state and Federal prisoners (Bureau of Justice Statistics, 2011). These figures far exceed the black and Hispanic male proportions of the U.S. population. This disproportionality is a key source of social disadvantage for minority men and the families, social networks, and communities in which they are embedded (Alexander, 2010). What role does the sentencing stage of the criminal justice decision-making process play in this disproportional punishment of black and Hispanic men?

Research on racial/ethnic and gender disparity in sentencing decisions has a long history. The 1980s and 1990s saw notable advances, in terms of data quality, methodological sophistication and rigor, and theoretical development. Sentencing research has continued apace in the 2000s and 2010s, with more notable developments (see review by Ulmer, 2012).

Several theories, more complementary than competing, explain mechanisms of and variation in race/ethnicity and gender disparity in sentencing. Many of these theories focus on individual cases, defendants, and decision makers. For example, Albonetti's *uncertainty avoidance* and *causal attribution* (1991) perspective argues that sentencing operates in a context of bounded rationality. Albonetti (1991) particularly stressed uncertainty and insufficient information regarding the recidivism risk and rehabilitative potential of offenders. As a means of reducing such uncertainty, decision makers fall back on attributions about reoffending risk and/or rehabilitation potential that can be linked to race and gender, and other social status stereotypes. This can then result in sentencing disparity connected to these statuses. Another proposition is the *liberation hypothesis* (Spohn and Cederblom, 1991), which posits that as the seriousness and/or visibility of the offense or case increases, discretion is tightened and legally relevant variables are decisive, leaving little room for extralegal influences. By contrast, in less serious/visible cases, opportunities for discretion are greater and extralegal variables can influence outcomes more than in serious cases.

The *focal concerns perspective* holds that court actors' definitions of offenders and offenses relative to three focal concerns – blameworthiness, community protection, and practical constraints – determine punishment decisions. The focal concerns perspective also states that both legal and extralegal considerations affect the interpretation and prioritization of focal concerns in courts' discretion (Kramer and Ulmer, 2009). The influence of race, for example, may be conditional on defendant gender, age, social class, legally relevant factors, and especially local contexts.

It has long been recognized that sentencing practices vary, sometimes substantially, between jurisdictions (Eisenstein et al., 1988). This is true of disparity as well, which can be non-existent in one locale and glaring in another. Thus, other theoretical conceptions of sentencing disparity emphasize the influence of the social context surrounding courts and their decision makers. The court community perspective views courts as organizational communities in mutual relation with their larger socio-political environments (Eisenstein et al., 1988; Ulmer, 1997). Court communities foster their own distinctive sentencing norms, which may potentially condition sentencing disparity. More specifically, applications of racial threat theory to sentencing disparity emphasize the nexus of criminal punishment and perceptions of certain minorities or intersectional statuses (e.g. men of color) in surrounding social contexts (Bontrager et al., 2005; Crawford et al., 1998). As "threatening" minority groups grow in size and/or visibility relative to the majority, the majority may fear that minorities will develop greater power or economic resources in the community. More relevant to criminal justice and sentencing, this theory implies that when perceptions of minority group threat are salient, and when criminal justice actors perceive particular groups as more dangerous or morally disrespectable, members of these groups receive harsher punishments at the hands of the criminal justice system, who levers the majority controls.

Research on racial, ethnic, and gender disparity in sentencing

Research on racial disparity in particular has a long history. Hagan and Bumiller's review in the 1983 National Academy of Sciences report *Research on Sentencing: The Search for Reform* (Blumstein et al., 1983) found mixed

evidence for racial disparity in sentencing, but noted that the existing literature had several major shortcomings. The report pointed to: (1) the need
for better measurement of legally relevant variables; (2) the need to study
different and more complex sentencing outcome variables; (3) the need for
larger samples from more varied jurisdictions; (4) the need to investigate the
conditioning effects of social contexts on sentencing and disparity.

Two comprehensive reviews of research up to 2000 (Spohn, 2000; Zatz,
2000) noted that research had improved in quality since the Blumstein et al.
(1983) report. Importantly, both reviews reframed the key question for sentencing disparity beyond simply assessing whether race/ethnicity, gender, or
other social statuses mattered in sentencing, to investigating *when* and *how*
such social statuses matter in sentencing – that is, investigating how the
influence of race, ethnicity, and gender mutually conditioned one another.

In a meta-analysis synthesizing 71 published and unpublished studies,
Mitchell (2005) found that significant racial disparities clustered around
the odds of incarceration; black defendants were more likely than white
defendants to be sent to prison. African-Americans generally received
longer sentences than whites, but this effect was small and highly variable.
Importantly, Mitchell (2005:462) noted "the observed differences between
whites and African-Americans were small, suggesting that discrimination
in the sentencing stage is not the primary cause of the overrepresentation
of African-Americans in U.S. correctional facilities." The review by Ulmer
(2012) regarding direct effects of race in sentencing, which included more
recent studies, agreed with Mitchell's (2005) conclusions.

While research on direct gender effects in sentencing tends to find that
women are sentenced more leniently than men, some studies suggest that
this is not always the case. According to Steffensmeier et al., (1993), judges,
prosecutors, probation officers, and even defense attorneys often argue that
women offenders are typically less likely to be violent. They observe that
women are often involved in crime (especially drug trafficking) in connection with abusive and coercive men, and tend to play more minor roles in
crime. They also believe women to be more amenable to rehabilitation and
less likely to recidivate. Finally, judges express concern about "collateral
damage" incarceration might have on the children of offenders who are
single mothers (Curry et al., 2004).

Race and ethnic disparity is conditional on gender and context

It is important to assess whether overall disparity exists, but as reviews by
Spohn (2000), and Ulmer (2012) and others have noted, there has been
increasing emphasis in the past 20 years on explaining when, where, and
how race and gender differences occur. Albonetti's (1991) attribution
framework, the focal concerns perspective, the liberation hypothesis, and
other views all imply that the effects of defendant social statuses may be

conditioned by situational factors such as offense type and characteristics, or other defendant attributes such as criminal history. Different circumstances likely mobilize different defendant status-based interpretations and attributions of character and focal concerns. In the 2000s and 2010s, major developments in connection with the visions of the Blumstein et al. (1983) and Spohn (2000) and Zatz (2000) reviews include: (1) a focus on how racial disparity is conditional on gender; (2) investigation of how local jurisdictional contexts condition disparity, and (3) how characteristics of individual court community actors condition disparity. We focus our discussion below on these three developments (for a fuller treatment, see Ulmer, 2012).

Gendered racial and ethnic disparity

A relatively consistent finding in the past 20 years is that race and ethnic sentencing disadvantage largely characterizes males more than females. Many recent studies that examine the issue find young black, and to a lesser extent Hispanic, males to be sentenced more severely (a few examples are Steffensmeier and Demuth, 2000; Spohn and Holleran, 2000; Kautt and Spohn, 2002; Kramer and Ulmer, 2009; Steen et al., 2005; Doerner and Demuth, 2009). Interestingly, at least three studies find minority females to be sentenced as or more leniently than white females (e.g. Spohn and Beichner, 2000; Steffensmeier and Demuth, 2000; Kramer and Ulmer, 2009). Others have found that minority males are sentenced more severely conditional on sentencing policy options such as mandatory minimums (Kautt and DeLone, 2006; Kautt and Spohn, 2002). More research along these lines is needed to illuminate how sentencing policies might mobilize or dampen disparities.

Social contexts and sentencing disparity

Several of the theoretical frameworks described earlier predict that disparity likely varies by social contexts. Overall, the recent literature on contextual variation in sentencing shows that local variation permeates many aspects of sentencing, both under sentencing guideline jurisdictions and non-guideline jurisdictions. Studies typically find that most sentencing outcome variation exists at the individual level, and is most strongly predicted by individual level factors. However, not only does sentencing severity (and related outcomes such as guideline departures), vary between local courts and their contexts, but so too do the effects of other important sentencing predictors, including gender and race/ethnicity (see Ulmer, 2012).

Many multilevel sentencing studies find that the effects of race and ethnicity in sentencing decisions do indeed vary significantly across courts, with some support for racial threat theory (e.g. Ulmer and Johnson, 2004).

However, results have been decidedly mixed regarding racial threat theory's ability to explain this variation. That is, race/ethnic effects on sentencing tend to vary widely across contexts, but not always in ways predicted by racial threat theory (see Feldmeyer and Ulmer, 2011). Other studies reveal either no support for racial threat (Weidner et al., 2004; Kautt, 2002), or evidence contrary to racial threat (Britt, 2000).

Researchers are just beginning to scratch the surface of studying the effects of court community composition on sentencing. Farrell et al., (2009) studied the effects of federal district court racial composition on variation in the effects of race on sentencing. They found that district U.S. Attorney's Office black representation was associated with significantly smaller race differences on the odds of incarceration (the more black U.S. Attorney personnel, the less disparity). King et al., (2010) found that greater black representation among county attorneys attenuated racial disparity.

A smaller amount of research has investigated the race and gender of judges as they condition sentencing disparity (e.g. Spohn, 1990; Steffensmeier and Hebert, 1999). Johnson (2006) found that black and Hispanic judges sentenced all offenders, and particularly minority offenders, more leniently than white judges. Furthermore, male judges sentenced female offenders more leniently. Wooldredge (2010) also found wide variation between Ohio judges in the effects of race, gender, or financial means on their sentences. Anderson and Spohn (2010) examined the sentencing decisions of 18 judges in three district courts, and found that judges considered legal and extralegal factors quite differently in their sentencing decisions.

Sentencing disparity and sentencing policy

Policies that change sentencing structures have the potential to affect disparity through changes in actors' discretion and/or through differential impacts of the policies (Ulmer et al., 2015). In the last 45 years, sentencing guidelines have become entrenched in about a third of all U.S. states and the Federal government and mandatory minimum laws became widespread. More recently, another change has begun to affect the structure of sentencing: the expanding adoption of sentencing risk assessments, which has affected judicial decisions and raised ethical concerns about its effects on racial disparities.

Sentencing guidelines

Over fifteen states, as well as the federal criminal justice system, have adopted sentencing guidelines. Guidelines explicitly strove to eliminate unwarranted disparity in sentences based on race, gender, and ethnicity, as well as to create more uniformity across local courts. However, Engen (2009) noted the paucity of research on what happens in the wake of the repeal or relaxation of presumptive sentencing schemes, and called for research that examines how the exercise of discretion is related to the structure of (and changes in) sentencing laws and guidelines.

There is evidence that Pennsylvania's sentencing guidelines seem to have reduced racial and ethnic disparities over time (Kramer and Ulmer, 2009; Ulmer et al., 2015). In addition, an important literature has developed on racial and ethnic disparity under the U.S. Sentencing Guidelines across legal eras. *United States v. Booker* (543 U.S. 220 {2005} and *United States v. Fanfan* 542 U.S. 296 {2004}, hereafter *Booker*) ruled that the U.S. Sentencing Guidelines should be advisory rather than presumptive. Subsequent decisions, especially *Gall v. United States* (128 S. Ct. 586 {2007}) *Rita v. United States* (127 S. Ct. 2456, 2487 2007), and *Kimbrough v. United States* (128 S. Ct. 558 2007) have also expanded federal judges' discretion.

Much scholarly research on federal courts has assessed unwarranted disparity under the pre-*Booker* Guidelines. These studies have often found small to moderate racial and ethnic sentencing differences benefitting whites (e.g. Albonetti, 1997; Mustard, 2001; Steffensmeier and Demuth, 2000; Kautt, 2002). Evidence also suggests that extralegal differences in punishment are tied to departure sentences (Johnson et al., 2008). Some studies have also shown that young minority males in particular were disadvantaged in incarceration decisions and sentence lengths (e.g. Doerner and Demuth, 2009). Also, defendant race has been shown to influence prosecutorial charge reductions, which in turn influence sentencing (Shermer and Johnson, 2010). Race/ethnicity and gender influences on guideline sentencing vary by judge (e.g. Anderson and Spohn, 2010), and Hispanic defendants are punished more severely in federal districts where Hispanics are least numerous, but are not at all disadvantaged in districts with large Hispanic populations (Feldmeyer and Ulmer, 2011).

A United States Sentencing Commission (USSC) report in 2010, which included data up to FY 2009, found that black–white disparity, specifically affecting male defendants, had increased in the post-*Gall* period. A USSC report in 2013 largely confirmed and extended these findings. To be clear, the USSC 2010 and 2013 reports did not claim that *Booker* and *Gall* caused increases in racial disparity, and recognized that other factors not related to the two decisions could be driving these increases. On the other hand, research by Ulmer, Light, and Kramer (2011a; 2011b) have found: (1) Post-*Booker/Gall* black–white disparity in sentence length increased compared to the 2003–2004 period, but generally returned to levels comparable to pre-2003 levels of disparity; (2) Post-*Booker/Gall* race disparity in sentence length is less than in the late 1990s; (3) black males' odds of imprisonment have increased significantly post-*Gall;* (4) Over 40 percent of the sentence length disparity affecting black males is accounted for by immigration cases; and (5) prosecutor initiated departures below guidelines are a greater site of racial disparity than judge-initiated departures in the post-*Booker/Gall* era.

Sentencing guidelines have also had a complex relationship with mandatory minimums and, in more recent years, risk assessment. It is to these other sentencing structures that we now turn.

Mandatory minimums

With the goal of increasing the certainty and severity of sentences imposed, U.S. Congress and all 50 states have adopted mandatory minimum laws by stipulating a minimum period of incarceration for certain offenses (Sorensen and Stemen, 2002). On the Federal level and in a few guideline states, the mandatory minimums override guideline recommendations and, in almost every case, result in a more severe sentence for the offender. According to general consensus, mandatory minimums have contributed to mass incarceration, disproportional imprisonment of minorities, and individual-level disparity (National Research Council, 2014; U.S. Sentencing Commission, 1991; 2011). Furthermore, these laws have been criticized for failing to deliver on their touted crime control effects (Kovandzic et al., 2004; National Research Council, 2014).

Mandatory minimums have been identified as a key locus of racial disproportionality in criminal justice, as they specify minimum sentences for crimes for which minorities are more likely to be arrested and charged, and because the prosecution is more likely to enforce them for minority defendants (Fischman and Schanzenbach, 2012; Kramer and Ulmer, 2009; U.S. Sentencing Commission, 1991). As with guideline factors, mandatory minimums have a differential impact on minority males and help explain their disproportionate incarceration. For example, the most widely publicized mandatory minimum law is California's "three strikes law," which guarantees a minimum of 25 years in prison for an offender convicted of a third felony.[1] African American men make up about 3 percent of California's population; however they make up 44 percent of those in prison for a third strike violation (Chen, 2008). This is largely due to the fact that minority men tend to have more substantial criminal records (Bushway and Piehl, 2011); but there is also evidence that, in some cases, prosecutors are more likely to seek mandatory minimums for similarly situated male and minority offenders (Starr and Rehavi, 2013; Ulmer et al., 2007). Thus, while mandatories and sentencing guidelines were intended in part to reduce disparities by limiting judicial discretion, they may in fact be an example of how laws and policy structures encode differential racial/ethnic impact into punishment (Fischman and Schanzenbach, 2012), and allows for further differential impact through individual level decisions prior to and at the sentencing stage (for example, see Farrell, 2003; Bjerk, 2005; Ulmer et al., 2015).

Mandatory minimum laws provide prosecutors with substantial discretion in determining which offenders end up being sentenced under a mandatory, which allows for the potential of racial, ethnic, and gender disparity. For example, Ulmer et al. (2007) conducted a multilevel analysis of prosecutorial discretion in applying mandatory minimums among mandatory-eligible offenders sentenced for drug crimes or as "three strikes" offenders in Pennsylvania. They found that prosecutors' decisions to apply mandatory minimums were significantly affected by the type and characteristics of offenses and guideline sentence recommendations (the greater the difference between the mandatory and the otherwise applicable guideline sentence, the less likely the mandatory was applied), prior record, mode of conviction (negotiated guilty pleas greatly assisted defendants in avoiding mandatories), and gender. In addition, Hispanic males were more likely to receive mandatory minimums, and blacks were more likely to receive mandatories in counties with greater black populations. Bjerk's (2005) multi-state analysis found that prosecutors used their charge reduction discretion to circumvent three strikes mandatories for some defendants, but that this was moderately less likely to occur for men, Hispanics, and to a lesser extent, blacks. Similarly, Farrell (2003) found that blacks, males, and those convicted by trial were more likely to receive mandatory minimums for firearms offenses in Maryland. Research suggests that prosecutors may be more likely to apply mandatory minimums to minorities (Fischman and Schanzenbach, 2012; Starr and Rehavi, 2013; Kramer and Ulmer, 2009). Other research also shows that prosecutorial discretion in applying mandatory minimums increases racial and gender imprisonment disproportionality (for examples, see Crawford, 2000; Fischman and Schanzenbach, 2012; Starr and Rehavi, 2013).

A National Research Council report called for the re-examination of mandatory minimum laws, which "impose large social, financial, and human costs; yield uncertain benefits; and are inconsistent with the long-standing principles of the jurisprudence of punishment" (2014:10). In 2013, U.S. Attorney General Eric Holder announced that Federal prosecutors would no longer seek mandatory minimum sentences in certain drug cases (Holder, 2013). However, it appears that the mandatory minimums trend has been reversing for some time. According to a Vera Institute of Justice report (Subramanian and Delaney, 2014), 29 states have also limited the use of mandatory minimums and increased judicial discretion since 2000.

As the support for mandatory minimums has declined, states have increasingly turned to considering risk at sentencing. We discuss this emerging area of sentencing policy below.

Sentencing risk assessments

The criminal justice field has used a variety of actuarial risk instruments for decades, yet, the courts have been slow to adopt risk assessment (RA) tools for use at the sentencing stage. However, over the last 20 years, a host of scholars, judges, and sentencing professionals have called for the use of social scientific evidence to promote evidence-based sentencing, or "smart sentencing" (see Etienne, 2009; Marcus, 2009; Virginia Criminal Sentencing Commission, 2001). Increasingly, these tools identify higher risk offenders for detention and lower risk offenders for community sanctions (Skeem, 2013). Currently, twelve states use, or are in the process of integrating, some form of a statewide sentencing risk assessment. Twelve other states consider risk at sentencing some of the time or in certain districts (Starr, 2014; Hannah-Moffat, 2013).[2] Despite the proliferation of sentencing RAs, many questions remain about their potential effects on racial disproportionality – particularly with the "use of demographic, socioeconomic, family, and neighborhood variables to determine whether and for how long a defendant is incarcerated" (Starr, 2014: 806).

Research discussed above shows that judges already consider a variety of factors when making sentencing decisions, including risk of recidivism. The belief that a defendant can avoid future criminal involvement has long been a common justification for a lighter sentence (Wolff, 2008). Presentence investigation reports (PSIs), which often include information on an offender's employment, living situation, and juvenile record, are often available to judges and considered to varying degrees. Hence, states that adopt sentencing RAs are simply transitioning to a different *method* of considering risk – albeit one that is more formalized. Clinical consideration of risk-related variables is unsystematic and based on perceptions of the relationships between general offender characteristics and recidivism. An RA instrument provides the court with a standardized way to place offenders on a risk continuum using risk-related attributes. In some states, the risk level is tied to specific sentence recommendations (e.g. eligibility for diversion).

While judges may already consider risk-related factors at sentencing, formalized risk reflective sentence recommendations signify a departure from a sentencing structure that emphasizes uniformity and "just deserts" (Silver and Miller, 2002) to one placing greater importance on efficient offender management. They can also be at odds with the purpose of sentencing guidelines, which have been adopted in order to increase sentencing uniformity and reduce racial and gender disparity. Risk-based sentencing generally includes the consideration of a variety of offender characteristics, such as employment, gender, and age. The focus shifts from punishing the offender mainly based on their criminal actions to assigning a sentence based on the offender's life-circumstances, as they relate to potential criminality. Thus for many states, sentencing RAs juxtapose two potentially conflicting policy and legal mandates: controlling disparity and managing recidivism.

Some scholars and policymakers have voiced their concerns about the adoption of formalized and quantified risk-based sentencing (Holder, 2014; Hannah-Moffat, 2013; Starr, 2014). Hannah-Moffat warns that "marginalized groups unavoidably score higher on risk instruments because of their increased exposure to risk, racial discrimination, and social inequality"

(2013:281), which may result in greater black/white disparities in sentencing. Research has shown that race and gender explains a significant portion of the variance in recidivism (DeMichele and Laskorunsky, 2013; Kleiman et al., 2007). While states do not use race as a risk factor, other predictive factors such as employment, criminal history, and neighborhood are often highly correlated with race. This results in minority offenders facing greater odds of being categorized as high-risk. Including variables such as gender and age is likely to disadvantage young black men in particular (Starr, 2014). But eliminating factors highly correlated with race, such as criminal history, reduces the predictive validity of the tool (Oleson, 2011).

While minorities are likely to have higher risk scores than white offenders, this does not guarantee that moving to a formalized risk-based sentencing structure would *exacerbate* the current racial and gender disproportionality seen in sentencing. Standard sentencing guideline structures, for example, rely on offense seriousness and criminal history (with an informal consideration of risk), and already result in higher incarceration odds for minorities (Bales and Piquero, 2012). Recent research shows that differences in criminal history explain much of this disproportionality (Bushway and Piehl, 2011; Ulmer et al., 2015). Thus, the potential for increasing sentencing disproportionality must be considered in the context of the status quo. In other words, does using formalized risk-based sentencing increase racial and gender disproportionality – *compared to the current sentencing structures*? This is an essential question which has yet to be empirically explored.

Additionally, it will be important to determine how much effect risk assessment tools will ultimately have on sentencing decisions. In jurisdictions where many of the same variables are already informally considered during sentencing, or in states where the RA instruments do not make specific sentence recommendations (thus leaving room for more discretion) – the impact of RA may be slight or non-existent. Therefore, it is likely that the effects of sentencing RAs, similar to sentencing guidelines, will be dependent on context and location. Finally, none of the states that currently use a risk assessment have conducted a pre- and post-adoption analysis of its effects on racial disproportionality. In light of the issues raised by criminal justice scholars and practitioners, this is an important next step.

Conclusion

A great deal of policy discourse has centered on judges' sentencing-stage discretion as the main problem contributing to disproportional imprisonment and racial/ethnic disparity. Indeed, guidelines and mandatory minimums were developed with the aim of controlling such discretion. However, judicial sentencing-stage discretion may not be the biggest contributor to disproportional punishment of black and Hispanic men. Evidence exists that the majority of racial/ethnic disparity may be determined by processes that come before sentencing, such as: (1) arrest; (2) charging, conviction and the guilty plea agreement process; (3) the determination of eligibility for guideline departures or mandatory minimums; (4) pre-sentence reports and the calculation of the many guidelines sentencing factors; (5) pre-sentence and pre-trial detention; and (6) the assessment of offender risk, either informally or formally (see Ulmer et al., 2015; Rehavi and Starr, 2012; Fischman and Schanzenbach, 2012). If so, a focus on restricting judicial discretion as the primary policy solution to disproportional imprisonment of black and Hispanic men may be misplaced.

First, a conceptual distinction is necessary between *disparity* and *differential impact*. In disparity in sentencing decisions, the culprit is local court sentencing discretion. By contrast, if sentencing structures have differential impact, the "culprit" is less local sentencing discretion, than *codified, formal decision criteria*. As Frase (2013: 263) argues, it is important to differentiate between possible sentencing decision bias and "...disparate impact – the effects of seemingly legitimate, race-neutral factors which more adversely affect racial and ethnic minority offenders." Features of sentencing guidelines, mandatory minimums, and risk assessment tools may help explain racial/ethnic disproportionality in punishment because they incorporate factors that are often highly correlated with race and ethnicity (Baumer, 2013; Hannah-Moffat, 2013).

The debate surrounding the aftermath of racial disparity in the wake of the *Booker* and *Gall* decisions in federal courts raises the issue of how best to control disparity. Is further restricting judicial discretion the solution? A simplistic and tempting answer is yes, but we are doubtful. Further restricting discretion does not seem to us to be the best answer, because as Savelsberg (1992) and many others have argued, sharply restricting judicial discretion can cause as many problems as it solves. The single biggest criticism of the U.S. Sentencing Guidelines of the pre-*Booker/Fanfan* era was that they restricted judicial discretion too much, and removed flexibility seen as necessary to avoid unjust sentences. Further, it is not at all clear that the increased judicial discretion produced by the *Booker* and *Gall* decisions *caused* an increase in black-white disparity under the federal guidelines (Hofer, 2013). Plus, the Pennsylvania experience with guidelines suggests that at least moderate reductions in disparity can be achieved over time under sentencing guidelines that are relatively loose, and that have always been advisory in the *Booker* sense. Perhaps sentencing guidelines best succeed by serving an organizational *norm setting* function, and reduce disparity to the extent that they become embedded in the organizational norms of courts, and are seen as a useful tool to manage uncertainty (Kramer and Ulmer, 2009; Ulmer et al., 2011a).

Perhaps one broad, overall solution to racial and ethnic disparity in sentencing is the power of visibility. In the wake of outcry from many quarters about the recent spate of police shootings of black men, many have called for police to wear body cameras, under the notion that greater visibility of police actions and discretion will reduce disparate treatment of minorities. Perhaps similar logic could apply to court case processing and sentencing. Sentencing guidelines and sentencing commissions have a unique ability to render sentencing outcomes and disparity visible, a point suggested by Savelsberg (1992). Perhaps this visibility could be extended to all criminal justice case processing, from arrest to charging, and sentencing to post-sentencing decisions (parole, probation revocation, etc.). What if sentencing commissions or other agencies took the lead in fostering greater understanding of race, ethnicity, and gender's complex roles in conditioning disparity as a part of their regular training for judges, and what if such training was extended to prosecutors? What if judges and also prosecutors received periodic summaries of their own sentencing, charging, guilty plea, and trial conviction data, broken down by race, ethnicity, and gender? What if risk assessment tools explicitly stated the risk of differential racial/ethnic impact, and evaluations of risk assessment policies were as concerned about disparate impacts as recidivism?

These might seem like relatively weak solutions, but recent research in the psychology of racial bias suggests their efficacy. An intriguing body of experimental evidence shows that racial stereotypes operate to a great extent at a subconscious level, out of individuals' routine awareness (Harris, 2007). However, when people are alerted to the issue of bias (for example, seeing a video or hearing a brief presentation about it), this tends to bring stereotypes and biases into awareness and people typically become more careful not to discriminate (Harris, 2007). The very act of making racial bias visible, even in general terms, may reduce it. Racial/ethnic disparity in sentencing appears to thrive when it is hidden and out of awareness. Making the racial/ethnic proportionality of every step of the criminal justice process visible may be a particularly effective means of reducing it.

Notes

1 Since its enactment in 1994 the law has been scaled back to include options for rehabilitation and require a violent or serious felony for third strike.
2 The states are Arizona, Michigan, Missouri, Ohio, Oklahoma, Pennsylvania, Utah, Virginia, Washington, West Virginia, Indiana, Kentucky, Illinois, New Mexico, North Dakota, Maine, Minnesota, North Carolina, Texas, Wisconsin, California, New York, Florida, and Tennessee. This does not include the use of sex offender risk assessment instruments, which is widespread.

References

Albonetti, C. 1991. An integration of theories to explain judicial discretion. *Social Problems*, 38, 247–266.

——1997. "Sentencing under the federal sentencing guidelines: An analysis of the effects of defendant characteristics, guilty pleas, and departures on sentencing outcomes for drug offenses." *Law and Society Review*, 31, 601–634.

Alexander, M. 2010. *The New Jim Crow: Mass Incarceration in the Age of Colorblindness*. NY: The New Press.

Anderson, A. and Spohn, C. 2010. Lawlessness in the federal sentencing process: a test for uniformity and consistency in sentencing practices. *Justice Quarterly*, 27(3), 362–393.

Bales, W. D., and Piquero, A. R. 2012. Racial/ethnic differentials in sentencing to incarceration. *Justice Quarterly*, 29(5), 742–773.

Baumer, E. P. 2013. Reassessing and redirecting research on race and sentencing. *Justice Quarterly*, 30(2), 231–261.

Bjerk, D. 2005. "Making the crime fit the penalty: The role of prosecutorial discretion under mandatory minimum sentencing." *Journal of Law and Economics*, 48, 591–625.

Blumstein, A., Cohen, J., Martin, S., and Tonry, M. (eds.). 1983. *Research on Sentencing: The Search for Reform*. Washington, DC: National Academy Press.

Bontrager, S., Bales, W., and Chiricos, T. 2005. Race, ethnicity, threat and the labeling of convicted felons. *Criminology*, 43(3), 589–622.

Britt, C. L. 2000. Social context and racial disparities in punishment decisions. *Justice Quarterly*, 17, 707–32.

Bureau of Justice Statistics. 2011. Prison Inmates at Midyear – Statistical Tables.

Bushway, S. D., and Piehl, A. M. (2011). Location, location, location: The impact of guideline grid location on the value of sentencing enhancements. *Journal of Empirical Legal Studies*, 8(s1), 222–238.

Chen, E. Y. 2008. Impacts of "three strikes and you're out" on crime trends in California and throughout the United States. *Journal of Contemporary Criminal Justice*, 24(4), 345–370.

Crawford, C. 2000. "Gender, race, and habitual offender sentencing in Florida." *Criminology*, 38(1), 263–80.

Crawford, C., Chiricos, T., and Kleck, G. 1998. Race, racial threat, and sentencing of habitual offenders. *Criminology*, 36(3), 481–512.

Curry, T., Lee, G., and Rodriguez, F.S. 2004. Does victim gender increase sentence severity? Further explorations of gender dynamics and sentencing outcomes. *Crime and Delinquency*, 50(3), 319–343.

DeMichele, M., and Laskorunsky, J. 2013. *Sentencing Risk Assessment: A Study of the Occurrence and Timing of Re-arrest among Serious Offenders in Pennsylvania*. Prepared for the Pennsylvania Commission on Sentencing.

Doerner, J. K., and Demuth, S. 2009. The independent and joint effects of race/ethnicity, gender, and age on sentencing outcomes in U.S. federal courts. *Justice Quarterly*, June: 1–27.

Eisenstein, J., Flemming, R. and Nardulli, P. 1988. *The Contours of Justice: Communities and Their Courts*. Boston: Little, Brown.

Engen, R. 2009. Assessing determinate and presumptive sentencing: Making research relevant. *Criminology and Public Policy*, 8, 323–336.

Etienne, M. 2009. Legal and practical implications of evidence-based sentencing by judges. *Journal of Criminal Justice*, 1, 43.

Farrell, A., Ward, G., and Rousseau, D. 2009. Race effects of representation among federal court workers: does black workforce representation reduce sentencing disparities? *Annals of the American Academy of Political and Social Science*, 623, 121–133.

Farrell, J. 2003. Mandatory minimum firearm penalties: A source of sentencing disparity. *Justice Research and Policy*, 5, 95–115.

Feldmeyer, B., and Ulmer, J. F. 2011. Racial/ethnic threat and federal sentencing. *Journal of Research in Crime and Delinquency*, 48(2), 238–270.

Fischman, J. B., and Schanzenbach, M. M. 2012. Racial disparities under the federal sentencing guidelines: The role of judicial discretion and mandatory minimums. *Journal of Empirical Legal Studies*, 9(4), 729–764.

Frase, R. 2013. Research on race and sentencing: goals, methods, and topics. *Justice Quarterly*, 30(2), 262–269.

Hagan, J. and Bumiller, K. 1983. Making sense of sentencing: race and sentencing outcomes. in *Research on Sentencing: The Search for Reform*, edited by A. Blumstein, J. Cohen, S. Martin, and M. Tonry. Washington, DC: National Academy Press.

Hannah-Moffat, K. 2013. Actuarial sentencing: An "unsettled" proposition. *Justice Quarterly*, 30(2), 270–296.

Harris, D. A. 2007. The importance of research on race and policing: Making race salient to individuals and institutions within criminal justice. *Criminology and Public Policy*, 6, 5–24.

Hofer, Paul. 2013. The Commission defends an ailing hypothesis: Does judicial discretion increase demographic disparity? *Federal Sentencing Reporter*, 25(5), 311–322.

Holder, E. 2013. Remarks at the Annual Meeting of the American Bar Association's House of Delegates. SF, California.

Holder, E. 2014. Address at the National Association of Criminal Defense Lawyers 57th Annual Meeting and 13th State Criminal Justice Network Conference. PA, Philadelphia.

Johnson, B. D. 2006. The multilevel context of criminal sentencing: Integrating judge and county level influences in the study of courtroom decision making. *Criminology*, 44, 259–98.

Johnson, B, Ulmer, J., and Kramer, J. 2008. The social context of Guideline circumvention: the case of federal district courts. *Criminology*, 46, 711–783.

Kautt, P. M. 2002. Location, location, location: Interdistrict and intercircuit variation in sentencing outcomes for federal drug-trafficking offenses. *Justice Quarterly*, 19, 633–71.

Kautt, P., and Delone, M. 2006. Sentencing outcomes under competing but coexisting sentencing interventions: untying the Gordian knot." *Criminal Justice Review*, 31(2), 105–131.

Kautt, P., and Spohn, C. 2002. Cracking down on black drug offenders? Testing for interactions among offenders' race, drug type, and sentencing strategy in federal drug sentences. *Justice Quarterly*, 19(1), 1–35.

King, R., Johnson, K., and McGeever, K. 2010. Demography of the legal profession and racial disparities in sentencing. *Law and Society Review*, 44(1), 1–32.

Kleiman, M., Ostrom, B., and Cheesman, F. 2007. Using risk assessment to inform sentencing decision for nonviolent offenders in Virginia. *Crime and Delinquency*, 53(1), 106–132.

Kovandzic, T. V., Sloan III, J. J., and Vieraitis, L. M. 2004. "Striking out" as crime reduction policy: The impact of "three strikes" laws on crime rates in US cities. *Justice Quarterly*, 21(2), 207–239.

Kramer, J. H., and Ulmer, J. T. 2009. *Sentencing guidelines: Lessons from Pennsylvania*. Boulder: Lynne Rienne.

Marcus, M. H. (2009). Conversations on evidence-based sentencing. *Chapman Journal of Criminal Justice*, 1, 61.

Mitchell, Ojmarrh. 2005. A meta-analysis of race and sentencing research: Explaining the inconsistencies. *Journal of Quantitative Criminology*, 21(4), 439–466.

Mustard, D. 2001. Racial, ethnic, and gender disparities in sentencing: Evidence from the U.S. federal courts." *Journal of Law and Economics*, 44, 285–314.

National Research Council. 2014. *The Growth of Incarceration in the United States: Exploring Causes and Consequences*. Washington, DC: The National Academies Press.

National Center for State Courts. 2011. Using Offender Risk and Needs Assessment Information at Sentencing. Guidance for Courts from a National Working Group.

Oleson, J. C. 2011. Risk in sentencing: Constitutionally suspect variables and evidence-based sentencing. *SMUL Review*, 64, 1329.

Rehavi, M. Marit and Starr, Sonja B., 2012. Racial disparity in federal criminal charging and its sentencing consequences (May 7, 2012). *U of Michigan Law & Econ, Empirical Legal Studies Center* Paper No. 12-002.

Savelsberg, J. J. 1992. Law that does not fit society: Sentencing guidelines as a neo-classical reaction to the dilemmas of substantivized law. *American Journal of Sociology*, 1346–1381.

Shermer, L. O., and Johnson, B. 2010. Criminal prosecutions: examining prosecutorial discretion and charge reductions in U.S. Federal District Courts. *Justice Quarterly*, 27(3), 394–430.

Silver, E., and Miller, L. L. 2002. A cautionary note on the use of actuarial risk assessment tools for social control. *Crime and Delinquency*, 48(1), 138–161.

Skeem, J. 2013. Risk technology in sentencing: Testing the promises and perils. *Justice Quarterly*, 30(2), 297–303.

Sorensen, J., and Stemen, D. 2002. The effect of state sentencing policies on incarceration rates. *Crime and Delinquency*, 48(3), 456–475.

Spohn, C. 1990. Decision making in sexual assault cases: do black and female judges make a difference? *Women and Criminal Justice*, 2, 83–105.

Spohn, C. 2000. Thirty years of sentencing reform: the quest for a racially neutral sentencing process. In *Policies, Processes and Decisions of the Criminal Justice System*. Vol. 3, *Criminal Justice 2000*. Washington, DC: U.S. Department of Justice, 2000.

Spohn, C., and Cederblom, J. 1991. Race and disparities in sentencing: a test of the liberation hypothesis. *Justice Quarterly*, 8, 305–27.

Spohn, C., and Beichner, D. 2000. Is preferential treatment of female offenders a thing of the past? A multisite study of gender, race, and imprisonment. *Criminal Justice Policy Review*, 11(2), 149–184.

Spohn, C., and Holleran, D. 2000. The imprisonment penalty paid by young unemployed Black and Hispanic male offenders. *Criminology*, 38(1), 281–306.

Starr, S. B. 2014. Evidence-based sentencing and the scientific rationalization of discrimination. *Stanford Law Review*, 66, 803–953.

Starr, S., and Rehavi, M. M. 2013. Mandatory sentencing and racial disparity: Assessing the role of prosecutors and the effects of Booker. *Yale Law Journal*, 123, 2–80.

Steen, S., Engen, R., and Gainey, R. 2005. Images of Danger and Culpability: Racial Stereotyping, Case Processing, and Criminal Sentencing. *Criminology*, 43(2), 435–69.

Steffensmeier, D., Kramer, J., andStreifel, C. 1993. Gender and imprisonment decisions. *Criminology*, 31, 411–446.

Steffensmeier, D., and Hebert, C. 1999. Women and men policymakers: does the judge's gender affect the sentencing of criminal defendants? *Social Forces*, 77, 1163–196.

Steffensmeier, D., and Demuth, S. 2000. Ethnicity and sentencing outcomes in U.S. federal courts: Who is punished more harshly? *American Sociological Review*, 65, 705–29.

Subramanian, R., and Delaney, R. 2014. Playbook for change? States reconsider mandatory sentences. *Federal Sentencing Reporter*, 26(3), 198–211.

Tyler, T. R., and Huo, Y.J. 2002. *Trust in the Law: Encouraging Public Cooperation with the Police and Courts*. NY: Russell-Sage Foundation.

Ulmer, J. T. 1997. *Social Worlds of Sentencing: Court Communities Under Sentencing Guidelines*. Albany: State University of New York Press.

——2012. Recent developments and new directions in sentencing research. *Justice Quarterly*, 29(1), 1–40.

Ulmer, J. T., and Johnson, B. 2004. Sentencing in context: A multilevel analysis. *Criminology*, 42, 137–77.

Ulmer, J. T., Kurlychek, M. C., and Kramer, J. H. 2007. Prosecutorial discretion and the imposition of mandatory minimum sentences. *Journal of Research in Crime and Delinquency*, 44(4), 427–458.

Ulmer, J. T., Light, M. and Kramer, J. 2011a. "Racial disparity in the wake of the Booker/Fanfan Decision: An alternative analysis to the USSC's 2010 Report." *Criminology and Public Policy*, 10(4), 1077–1118.

——2011b. "Does increased judicial discretion lead to increased disparity? The 'liberation' of judicial sentencing discretion in the wake of the Booker/Fanfan Decision." *Justice Quarterly*, 28(6), 799–837.

Ulmer, J., Painter-Davis, N., and Tinik, L. 2015. Disproportional imprisonment of Black and Hispanic males: sentencing discretion, processing outcomes, and policy structures. *Justice Quarterly*, 1–40.

U.S. Sentencing Commission. 1991. *Special Report to the Congress: Mandatory Minimum Penalties in the Federal Criminal Justice System*. Washington, DC: U.S. Sentencing Commission.

——2010. *Demographic Differences in Federal Sentencing Practices: An Update of the Booker Report's Multivariate Regression Analysis*. Washington, DC. United States Sentencing Commission.

——2011. "Statistical overview of mandatory minimum penalties." *Report to the Congress: Mandatory Minimum Penalties in the Federal Criminal Justice System*. Washington, DC: United States Sentencing Commission.

——2013. *Report to Congress on the Continuing Impact of U.S. v. Booker on Federal Sentencing*. Washington, DC: United States Sentencing Commission.

Virginia Criminal Sentencing Commission. 2001. *Assessing Risk among Sex Offenders in Virginia*. Richmond, VA: Crime Sentencing Commission.

Weidner, R., Frase, R., and Pardoe, I. 2004. Explaining sentence severity in large urban counties: a multilevel analysis of contextual and case-level factors. *The Prison Journal*, 84(2), 184–207.

Wolff, M. 2008. Lock 'em up and throw away the key? Cutting recidivism by analyzing sentencing outcomes. *Federal Sentencing Reporter*, 20(5), 320–321.

Wooldredge, J. 2010. Judges' unequal contributions to extralegal disparities in imprisonment. *Criminology*, 48(2), 539–567.

Zatz, M. 2000. The convergence of race, ethnicity, gender, and class on court decision making: looking toward the 21st Century. In *Policies, Processes and Decisions of the Criminal Justice System*. Vol. 3, *Criminal Justice 2000*. Washington, DC: U.S. Department of Justice, 2000.

Chapter 14

Sex offender legislation and policy

Kelly M. Socia and Jason Rydberg

The current state of research, policy, and practice

The current state of sex offender policies and practice is the result of a largely political process devoid of research evidence. In this process, political actors respond to public outrage concerning media-sensationalized tragic cases of rape and murder of young victims by strangers who were convicted sex offenders. As such, the majority of federal, state, and local laws focusing on convicted sex offenders are based on tracking and controlling these offenders after their return to the community, rather than on providing treatment and other rehabilitative services. This trend in favoring protection of the public over treatment and rehabilitation is in line with changes to other correctional policies outside of the sex offender policy sphere (Garland, 2001). Further, many of these policies are based on assumptions about the nature and etiology of sexual offending, rather than research evidence (Maguire and Singer, 2011; Socia and Stamatel, 2010). Unsurprisingly, over the last quarter century a vast number of scholars have questioned the efficacy of these laws. This chapter reviews the following laws: Registration and Community Notification, Residence Restrictions, and Civil Commitment.

Registration and community notification policies

Perhaps the most pervasive of all sex offender policies are those of registration and community notification. While the registration of sex offenders began in California in 1947 (Leon, 2011; Office of the Attorney General, 2014), the majority of state registries were set up immediately prior to or as a result of the federal passage of the 1994 Jacob Wetterling Act. Named after a child who was abducted in 1989 and is still missing (Jacob Wetterling Resource Center, 2014), the Act required states to maintain a registry of convicted sex offenders' information (description, address, etc.). Offenders registered and updated their information with law enforcement within each state. The Act also recommended, but did not require, the public release of this information to the community (i.e., community notification).

In 1994, following the abduction, rape, and murder of Megan Kanka by convicted sex offender Jesse Timmendequas, Megan's Law was passed by New Jersey. Megan's Law required the public release of information contained on the state's sex offender registry (Socia and Stamatel, 2010). Within two years Megan's Law had been implemented by the Federal Government and applied to all state registries ("Megan's Law," 1996; Socia and Stamatel, 2010). Since then, the registration and community notification provisions have been tightly intertwined both in terms of policy and practice, and in terms of research. Related legislation also established the Dru Sjodin National Sex Offender Public Registry ("The Pam Lychner Act of 1996," 1996; U.S. Department of Justice, 2010), and set new baseline requirements for who must register, what information is maintained by the registry, and what information is released to the public (SMART Office, 2014; Socia and Stamatel, 2010; Wright, 2008).

Most studies find that registration and/or community notification policies have not significantly reduced sex crimes, either overall or those committed by convicted sex offenders (Ackerman et al., 2011; Letourneau et al., 2010; Letourneau et al., 2010c; Sandler et al., 2008; Schram and Milloy, 1995; Vasquez et al. 2008; Zgoba et al., 2008). However, some state-level research has found evidence of general or specific deterrence effects of either registration or community notification (e.g., Barnoski, 2005; Duwe and Donnay, 2008; Letourneau et al., 2010b; Prescott and Rockoff, 2011). Aside from effects on crime rates, there is also conflicting evidence on whether these policies have influenced plea bargaining rates (Freeman et al., 2009; Letourneau et al., 2013; Letourneau et al., 2010a).

Research also suggests that the community rarely views the public registry (Anderson and Sample, 2008; Kernsmith et al., 2009), and these policies may result in a false sense of security (Craun and Simmons, 2012; Hughes and Kadleck, 2008; Maguire and Singer, 2011). Further, there are questions as to the accuracy and usefulness of the information contained on the registry (see Ackerman et al., 2012; Tewksbury, 2002).

Research evidence also suggests these laws have resulted in an assortment of collateral consequences for sex offenders and their families. These consequences have included stigmatization and isolation (Tewksbury, 2005; Tewksbury and Lees, 2006; Vandiver et al., 2008), loss of employment opportunities (Levenson and Cotter, 2005a; Tewksbury and Lees, 2006; Tewksbury and Zgoba, 2009), difficulty finding or maintaining housing (Burchfield and Mingus, 2008; Levenson and Cotter, 2005a; Zevitz and Farkas, 2000), and in some cases, harassment and vigilante attacks from the community (Hughes and Kadleck, 2008; Levenson and Tewksbury, 2009; Tewksbury, 2005; Tewksbury and Lees, 2006). Such consequences are typically found to be directly or indirectly correlated with increased recidivism risk (Ainsworth and Taxman, 2013; CSOM, 2007; Roman and Travis, 2004; VCSC, 2001).

Overall, the existing research suggests that registration and notification have not been very successful in their goals of reducing sexual recidivism and victimization. Instead, these laws may actually be *harming* sex offenders' chances of successful reentry, due to the collateral consequences that come from the release of registry information to the community.

Residence restriction policies

Residence restrictions were first enacted in 1995 by Delaware and Florida (Meloy et al., 2008). While some states followed suit over the next decade, there was a surge of these laws at the state, county, and local levels in 2005 following the abduction, rape, and murder of 9-year-old Jessica Lunsford by a drifter who lived nearby (CNN.com, 2005). These laws prohibit registered sex offenders from living within a given distance from a set of locations where children typically congregate (Socia, 2011a, Socia, in press). The distance and prohibited areas vary widely, but *typically* these laws create a "buffer zone" of restricted housing between 500 and 2,500 feet around schools, daycares, parks, and playgrounds (Socia and Stamatel, 2010). Over the past two decades, these laws have spread across the United States, and currently exist at the state, county, and local levels (Meloy et al., 2008; Socia, in press).

Given the overlapping geographic implementation of these laws, there have been instances where a state residence restriction was surpassed by a more restrictive county or local restriction. In some cases this has resulted in court challenges for preemption, with local laws occasionally being overturned by judicial action (e.g. Foderaro, 2008; "G.H. v. Township of Galloway," 2008; "People v. Blair," 2009), or restricted by follow-up legislative action as a result of potential future judicial challenges (e.g. Bain, 2006; Timmins, 2014).

In terms of effectiveness, all of the existing research on residence restrictions suggests that they do not work as intended, and do not protect children from sex offenders (Nobles et al., 2012; Socia, 2012, in press). Indeed, scholars have been consistent in noting this issue and calling for the elimination of these laws (e.g. Barnes, 2011; Socia, 2014; Walker, 2007). This is likely because the scenario that residence restrictions are based on preventing is exceedingly rare (i.e. a convicted sex offender contacting a new, unknown child victim at a child congregation location near the offender's residence) (Duwe et al., 2008; Minnesota Department of Corrections, 2007; Zandbergen et al., 2010). For example, a study in Minnesota found that over the course of 16 years, not a single one of the 224 instances of convicted sex offender recidivism involved all of the elements required for a residence restriction to have stopped the event from occurring (Duwe et al., 2008; Minnesota Department of Corrections, 2007). This is also supported by the finding that the vast majority of known sex crimes against children involve family members or acquaintances, and not strangers prowling in public (Greenfield, 1997; Snyder, 2000). Relatedly, there have been calls for more research on the mechanisms for how sex offenders actually gain access to victims (Davies and Dale, 1996; Leclerc et al., 2009; Leclerc et al., 2011). This is an important consideration for residence restrictions, given that this policy can only be applied to individuals who have already been convicted for a previous sex offense. To date, little is known about the modus operandi of repeat sex offenders following their apprehension by law enforcement.

On the other hand, there have been numerous studies documenting the various collateral consequences that come from these policies. These consequences chiefly involve the lack of unrestricted available and affordable housing that sex offenders face under residence restriction policies (see Chajewski and Mercado, 2009; Socia, 2011a, 2011b; Zandbergen and Hart, 2006). This inability to find suitable housing results in other consequences for both the offender and their family members, such as isolation and stigmatization (Farkas and Miller, 2007; Levenson and Cotter, 2005b; Zandbergen and Hart, 2006), homelessness and/or transience (California Sex Offender Management Board, 2008, 2011; Levenson et al., in press; Rydberg et al., 2014; Socia et al., in press), difficulty accessing employment options and treatment facilities (Barnes et al., 2008; Mulford et al., 2009; Zandbergen and Hart, 2006), and being unable to live with supportive family members (Levenson and Cotter, 2005b). All of these consequences can reduce the chances of successful reentry and increase the likelihood of recidivism (Roman and Travis, 2004).

Overall, and similar to the research on registration and notification policies, the existing research suggests that residence restrictions have not been successful in their goals of reducing sexual recidivism and victimization. Once again, these laws may actually be *harming* sex offenders' chances of successful reentry, due to the collateral consequences that come from the restriction of housing options in the community.

Civil commitment policies

Civil commitment statutes in the United States have been in place for over a century, and their use in targeting dangerous sex offenders has almost an equally long history (Jenkins, 1998; Leon, 2011). Indeed, the original Sexual Psychopath Laws from the 1930s through 1950s were constitutionally banned (Jenkins, 1998), and by the 1980s, most of the earlier civil commitment laws had either "been repealed or fallen into disuse" (Davey and Goodnough, 2007, p. 4; Janus, 2000). However, modern versions of such laws specifically targeting sex offenders were implemented in Washington in 1990 (Ackerman et al., 2011; Farkas and Stichman, 2002; Mears, 2010). Indeed, such laws received increased attention in the 1990s, following a number of brutal crimes involving young children, including the 1995 abduction, rape, and murder of 9-year-old Jimmy Ryce by a local ranch hand in Florida (Davey and Goodnough, 2007; Presley, 1999). Additionally, the 2006 Adam Walsh Act "mandates civil commitment for certain dangerous offenders" at the federal level (ATSA, 2014; Bonnar-Kidd, 2010, p. 413).

Civil commitment statutes targeting sex offenders are grounded in mental health law, which traditionally allow a state to hold an individual with a psychiatric condition who is identified as being a high risk to themselves or others (CSOM, 2008). These individuals are detained in a protective facility that offers rehabilitation and treatment (Ackerman et al., 2011). Over the last 25 years, these statutes have been repurposed to hold convicted sex offenders, identified as having a very high risk to recidivate, past their sentence expiration dates (Ackerman et al., 2011). Currently at least 20 states and the District of Columbia use civil commitment statutes to hold sex offenders (ATSA, 2014). Since these laws are based in the mental health and not the criminal statutes, courts have held that their application does not violate Ex Post Facto protections, including the U.S. Supreme Court (ATSA, 2014; Davey and Goodnough, 2007).

While the exact statistics are hard to find, it is estimated that as of 2006, between 3,000 and 4,500 sex offenders were being held under civil commitment statutes across the United States (Davey and Goodnough, 2007; Gookin, 2007). As of 2010, that number was projected to be approximately 5,200 (Associated Press, 2010). While committed, sex offenders are (ideally) given treatment, and eventually released back into society. However, scholars have raised numerous concerns about these laws, including that the treatment is not consistently provided, it is not effective, that few offenders are ever released, and that civil commitment is inefficient and too costly (Ackerman et al., 2011; Cohen and Jeglic, 2007; Davey and Goodnough, 2007; Janus, 2000).

While generally supported by courts across the country, a Federal judge in Minnesota recently ordered the state to reassess the confinement of approximately 700 civilly committed sex offenders (Karsjens v. MN Department of Human Services et al., 2014). The court noted that no single sex offender had ever been fully discharged from the program, and only two had been conditionally released on indefinite supervision since operations began in 1995. According to Minnesota statutes the standard to be discharged from civil commitment is that:

> ...the committed person is capable of making an acceptable adjustment to open society, is no longer dangerous to the public, and is no longer in need of inpatient treatment and supervision. ... [As well as] whether specific conditions exist to provide a reasonable degree of protection to the public and to assist the committed person in adjusting to the community
>
> (Minn. Stat. § 253D.31).

Such standards seem unlikely to be met when one is being held in a secure facility. This ruling echoes the legal criticisms that led to the disuse of the sexual psychopath statutes in the 1960s and 1970s, noting that they held absurd standards for committed offenders to prove that they had been rehabilitated (Jenkins, 1998; Swanson, 1960).

To date, there is no research directly examining recidivism among sex offenders referred to civil commitment, due to civil commitment essentially representing the detainment of a sex offender in a secure mental health facility, and few such offenders ever having been released back into the community. However, there has been some research exploring exactly how many potential crimes are being *prevented* via civil commitment. Based on actuarial risk projections, Duwe (2014) estimated that civil commitment in Minnesota reduced the sexual recidivism rate by 12 percent. Research has suggested that sex offenders referred for civil commitment in Florida and Wisconsin appear to mirror the legislation's intent, with the majority of offenders demonstrating higher rates of diagnosed paraphilia and scoring higher on actuarial risk assessments than individuals not referred for commitment (Elwood et al., 2010; Levenson, 2004; Lucken and Bales, 2007). However, research has also suggested substantial heterogeneity between states in the characteristics of sex offenders referred for commitment, with Nebraska commitments appearing to be lower risk than commitments from other states (McLawsen et al., 2012).

Alignment of policy and practice with empirical research

The current policies discussed here were created under conditions in which high profile sexual murders placed politicians under public pressure to *do something* about the threat posed by sexual predators (Jenkins, 1998; Sample and Kadleck, 2008). Support for punitive policy has outpaced public support for treatment-oriented strategies (Pickett et al., 2013), with the result being an array of policies aligned with punitive public opinion regarding the management of convicted sex offenders in the community. Survey research has suggested that the public is largely supportive of these policies, believing that all sex offenders, regardless of designated risk level, should be subject to community notification (Levenson et al., 2007). Support for residence restrictions has been widespread (Mancini et al., 2010), and persists regardless of whether the public perceives the policy as being effective in reducing sexual victimization (Levenson et al., 2007; Schiavone and Jeglic, 2009).

There is some question as to how the effectiveness of sex offender policies should be assessed. If the goals of the policies are primarily retributive, then there is little question that they are meeting these objectives. On the other hand, enhancing public safety has been cited as an explicit goal by those developing these policies (e.g. Office of the Attorney General, 1999).

There are two avenues through which this goal should manifest – the general deterrence of sexual offending by unregistered sexual offenders, and the reduction of recidivism risk by previously identified sex offenders. The evidence in support of a general deterrence effect resulting in a reduction of sex offense rates is limited and indirect at best (see Socia, 2012 for an example). This review focuses on the recidivism risk of convicted sex offenders that are subject to the requirements of these policies.

As they are currently implemented, registration, community notification, residence restrictions, and civil commitment do not align with existing knowledge of effective means of reducing recidivism. In the past several decades a great deal of empirical research has been developed on the characteristics of correctional interventions that are effective and ineffective. A key finding of meta-analytic research in this area is that primarily sanction or deterrence-based programs (i.e. those that focus on increasing the severity of punishment and intensity of supervision) result in an average *increase* in recidivism among program participants (Andrews, 1994; Lipsey and Cullen, 2007). In other words, they make offenders *worse*. Conversely, research under the Risk-Need-Responsivity (RNR) model (Andrews and Bonta, 2010) has suggested principles that describe the programs that are the most effective at reducing recidivism. Contrary to sanction-based programs, these programs are largely treatment and service oriented.

Briefly, the *risk principle* requires that the level and intensity of treatment and services should be matched to the sex offender's level of recidivism risk, with the level of risk being determined through validated actuarial risk assessments (see Studer et al., 2011). Existing research suggests that sex offender policies, such as registration, either consistently misapply risk tiers (Zgoba et al., 2012), or treat sex offenders as a homogenous population, regardless of risk level (Lynch, 1998).

The *needs principle* suggests that correctional interventions should target the dynamic risk factors that are highly correlated with sexual recidivism. Meta-analytic research has found that these include deviant sexual interests, anti-social attitudes and values, and intimacy deficits, among others (Hanson and Morton-Bourgon, 2005). There is no evidence to suggest that any of the policies described above address these risk factors in any meaningful sense.

The *responsivity principle* states that the most effective means of reducing recidivism will include structured social learning or cognitive behavioral components that are designed to change behavior and cognition conducive to sexual offending. Additionally, effective programs will be responsive to individual characteristics of sexual offenders that may potentially impact treatment effectiveness. There is no indication that the management-based initiatives described here systematically apply these techniques or make any such distinctions among identified sexual offenders.

In short, the sex offender management policies described above share all of the characteristics of correctional programs that either have no effect on recidivism or result in a net increase in recidivism, and share practically no characteristics with programs that actually improve recidivism outcomes.

Conclusions

Examining sex offender policies and practices in light of the existing research lends itself to certain recommendations concerning revisions and best practices. First, the highly politicized and media-frenzied atmosphere that has spawned or spurred the passage of these laws simply does not lend itself to scientific, even handed, evidenced-based policymaking. Policymaking in the immediate aftermath of a tragic crime may be beneficial in scoring political points with constituents and satiating the public's demand to *do something*. However, as the existing research has found, this has also resulted in many policies that, at best, are largely ineffective, and at worst, are producing many unintended collateral consequences and simply making things worse.

In terms of future best practices, proposed legislation and policies should be given a closer inspection using evidence-based research and input from the scientific community *prior* to being debated and voted on. This will require efforts from policymakers to resist constituent pressures to "do something!" in the immediate aftermath of a tragic, highly-publicized, (and typically extremely rare) crime. More specifically, in order for a criminal justice policy or intervention to be effective there must be a solid understanding of the underlying problem that the policy is designed to address (Weiss, 1997). Prior to designing a response, policymakers should consider information on the nature and extent of sexual offending, rather than treating individual incidents as representative of a broader problem. Without careful and measured scientific analysis of proposed policies, removed from moral panics and election-year politics, it is unlikely that future sex offender legislation and policies will be much more successful than the existing ones.

In terms of existing policies, it seems clear that a number of revisions (or repeals) would be justified in light of the existing research. There is only limited evidence that registration and notification policies have actually affected sex crimes, but there is overwhelming evidence of their collateral consequences. While it seems unlikely that sex offender registration will be repealed wholesale, the public availability of sex offender information should be reconsidered. Specifically, it seems prudent to recommend the public release of information only for the extremely small segment of sex offenders that represent the highest level of (evidence-based) risk to the community, rather than overwhelming the public registries with many thousands of records. Further, the risk levels applied to sex offenders should be based on evidence-based, validated risk instruments, rather than on the specific criminal code that has been violated.

In terms of residence restrictions, these policies were not based on empirical research, have never been supported by research evidence, and have resulted in severe collateral consequences for sex offenders that is harmful to successful reentry and reintegration. To be clear: there is *zero* evidence that these policies have met their intended purpose of stopping sex crimes by registered sex offenders, and much evidence to the contrary. As such, these policies should either be repealed or, at most, be applied on an individual case-by-case basis, rather than as blanket provisions.

Finally, civil commitment can clearly keep some dangerous sex offenders from returning to society. However, these laws should not be used to simply warehouse individuals after their criminal sentence has ended, but rather as a way to provide intensive treatment to individuals who have a realistic potential for future release. As such, civil commitment must link evidence-based risk assessment with viable treatment programs. This not only makes sense empirically, but is consistent with Supreme Court rulings on the appropriateness of such a policy. If this is not feasible, and the majority of civilly-committed sex offenders are unable to meet release conditions even after years of commitment, then these policies should be revised or repealed.

In summary, the proposal and implementation of sex offender legislation and policy cannot continue to be a response to public frenzy or used for political gains. Rather, this process must rely on evidence-based practices in order to achieve its intended goals. If the purpose of such policies is to reduce recidivism, frameworks such as the RNR model make clear suggestions about the characteristics of effective and ineffective responses. Separating the politics from the policies, and interjecting research into the policymaking, would go a long way towards fixing the current state of ineffective and sometimes harmful sex offender legislation and policy.

References

Ackerman, A. R., Levenson, J. S., and Harris, A. J. (2012). How Many Sex Offenders Really Live Among Us? Adjusted Counts and Population Rates in Five U.S. States. *Journal of Crime and Justice*, 35(3), 464–474. doi: 10.1080/0735648X.2012.66 6407.

Ackerman, A. R., Sacks, M., and Greenberg, D. F. (2011). Legislation Targeting Sex Offenders: Are Recent Policies Effective in Reducing Rape? *Justice Quarterly*, 1–30. doi: 10.1080/07418825.2011.566887.

Ainsworth, S. A., and Taxman, F. S. (2013). Creating Simulation Parameter Inputs with Existing Data Sources: Estimating Offender Risks, Needs, And Recidivism. In F. S. Taxman and A. Pattavina (eds.), *Simulation Strategies to Reduce Recidivism: Risk Need Responsivity (RNR) Modeling for the Criminal Justice System* (pp. 115–142): Springer.

Anderson, A. L., and Sample, L. L. (2008). Public Awareness and Action Resulting From Sex Offender Community Notification Laws. *Criminal Justice Policy Review*, 19(4), 371–396. doi: 10.1177/0887403408316705.

Andrews, D. A. (1994). An Overview of Treatment Effectiveness: Research and Clinical Principles. (Department of Psychology, Trans.). Ottawa, Ontario, Canada: Careleton University.

Andrews, D. A., and Bonta, J. (2010). *The Psychology of Criminal Conduct* (5th ed.). New York, NY: Routledge.

Associated Press. (2010). Sex Offender Confinement Costing States Too Much. *CBSNews.com*.www.cbsnews.com/news/sex-offender-confinement-costing-states-too-much/.

ATSA. (2014, August 17, 2010). Civil Commitment of Sexually Violent Predators. Retrieved November 13, 2014, from www.atsa.com/civil-commitment-sexually-violent-predators.

Bain, B. (2006, December 21). Legal Doubts on Sex Offender Limits, *Newsday*. Retrieved from http://find.galegroup.com/gtx/infomark.do?andcontentSet=IAC-Documentsandtype=retrieveandtabID=T004andprodId=SPN.SP04anddocId=CJ1 56198363andsource=galeandsrcprod=SP04anduserGroupName=albanyuandversion=1.0.

Barnes, J. C. (2011). Place a Moratorium on the Passage of Sex Offender Residence Restriction Laws. *Criminology and Public Policy*, 10(2), 401–409. doi: 10.1111/j.1745-9133.2011.00715.

Barnes, J. C., Dukes, T., Tewksbury, R., and De Troye, T. M. (2008). Analyzing the Impact of a Statewide Residence Restriction Law on South Carolina Sex Offenders. *Criminal Justice Policy Review*, 20(1), 21–43. doi: 10.1177/0887403408320842.

Barnoski, R. (2005). *Sex Offender Sentencing in Washington State: Has Community Notification Reduced Recidivism?* Olympia: Washington State Institute for Public Policy.

Bonnar-Kidd, K. K. (2010). Sexual Offender Laws and Prevention of Sexual Violence or Recidivism. *American Journal of Public Health*, 100(3), 412–419. doi: 10.2105/ajph.2008.153254.

Burchfield, K. B., and Mingus, W. (2008). Not in My Neighborhood: Assessing Registered Sex Offenders' Experiences With Local Social Capital and Social Control. *Criminal Justice and Behavior*, 35(3), 356–374. doi: 10.1177/0093854807311375.

California Sex Offender Management Board. (2008). *Homelessness Among Registered Sex Offenders in California: The Numbers, the Risks, and the Response.* Sacramento, CA: California Division of Criminal Justice.

California Sex Offender Management Board. (2011). Homelessness Among California's Registered Sex Offenders: An Update.

Chajewski, M., and Mercado, C. C. (2009). An Evaluation of Sex Offender Residency Restriction Functioning in Town, County, and City-Wide Jurisdictions. *Criminal Justice Policy Review*, 20(1), 44–61. doi: 10.1177/0887403408320845

CNN.com. (2005). Drifter says he held girl three days. Retrieved from CNN.com website: http://www.cnn.com/2005/LAW/06/23/lunsford.report/index.html.

Cohen, M., and Jeglic, E. L. (2007). Sex Offender Legislation in the United States: What Do We Know? *International Journal of Offender Therapy and Comparative Criminology*, 51(4), 369–383. doi: 10.1177/0306624x06296235.

Craun, S. W., and Simmons, C. A. (2012). Taking a Seat at the Table: Sexual Assault Survivors' Views of Sex Offender Registries. *Victims and Offenders*, 7(3), 312–326. doi: 10.1080/15564886.2012.685217.

CSOM. (2007). *Managing the Challenges of Sex Offender Reentry*. Washington, DC: Center for Sex Offender Management.

CSOM. (2008). Legislative Trends in Sex Offender Management: Center for Sex Offender Management.

Davey, M., and Goodnough, A. (2007). Doubts Rise as States Hold Sex Offenders After Prison, *The New York Times*. Retrieved November 13, 2014 from www.nytimes.com/2007/03/04/us/04civil.html?_r=0.

Davies, A., and Dale, A. (1996). Locating the Stranger Rapist. *Med Sci Law*, 32(2), 146–156.

Duwe, G. (2014). To What Extent does Civil Commitment Reduce Sexual Recidivism? Estimating the Selective Incapacitation Effects in Minnesota. *Journal of Criminal Justice*, 42(2), 193–202. doi: 10.1016/j.jcrimjus.2013.06.009.

Duwe, G., and Donnay, W. (2008). The Impact of Megan's Law on Sex Offender Recidivism: The Minnesota Experience. *Criminology*, 46(2), 411–446. doi: 10.1111/j.1745-9125.2008.00114.

Duwe, G., Donnay, W., and Tewksbury, R. (2008). Does Residential Proximity Matter? A Geographic Analysis of Sex Offense Recidivism. *Criminal Justice and Behavior*, 35(4), 484–504. doi: 10.1177/0093854807313690.

Elwood, R. W., Doren, D. M., and Thornton, D. (2010). Diagnostic and risk profiles of men detained under Wisconsin's sexually violent person law. *International Journal of Offender Therapy and Comparative Criminology*, 54(2), 187–196.

Farkas, M. A., and Stichman, A. (2002). Sex Offender Laws: Can Treatment, Punishment, Incapacitation, and Public Safety Be Reconciled? *Criminal Justice Review*, 27(2), 256–283. doi: 10.1177/073401680202700204.

Farkas, M. A., and Miller, G. (2007). Reentry and Reintegration: Challenges Faced by the Families of Convicted Sex Offenders. *Federal Sentencing Reporter*, 20(2), 88–92. doi: 10.1525/fsr.2007.20.2.88.

Foderaro, L. W. (2008, July 16). Trenton Court Says Towns Can't Expand Sex Crime laws, *The New York Times*, p. 2.

Freeman, N. J., Sandler, J. C., and Socia, K. M. (2009). A Time-Series Analysis on the Impact of Sex Offender Registration and Community Notification on Plea Bargaining Rates. *Criminal Justice Studies: A Critical Journal of Crime, Law, and Society*, 22(2), 153–165. doi: 10.1080/14786010902975424.

G.H. v. Township of Galloway, 951 A.2d 221 (N.J. Court of Appeals 2008).

Garland, D. (2001). *The Culture of Control: Crime and Social Order in Contemporary Society*. Chicago: University of Chicago Press.

Gookin, K. (2007). Comparison of state laws authorizing involuntary commitment of sexually violent predators: 2006 Update, revised. Olympia, WA: Washington State Institute for Public Policy.

Greenfield, L. A. (1997). Sex Offenses and Offenders: An Analysis of Data on Rape and Sexual Assault (B. o. J. Statistics, Trans.). Washington: National Institute of Justice.

Hanson, R. K., and Morton-Bourgon, K. E. (2005). The characteristics of persistent sexual offenders: A meta-analysis of recidivism studies. *Journal of Consulting and Clinical Psychology*, 73(6), 1154–1163. doi: 10.1037/0022-006X.73.6.1154.

Hughes, L. A., and Kadleck, C. (2008). Sex Offender Community Notification and Community Stratification. *Justice Quarterly*, 25(3), 469–495. doi: 10.1080/07418820701710941.

Jacob Wetterling Crimes Against Children and Sexually Violent Offender Registration Act, § 14071, Pub. L. No. 103–322 § § 14071 (1994).

Jacob Wetterling Resource Center. (2014). Jacob's Story. Retrieved November 11, 2014, from http://www.gundersenhealth.org/ncptc/jacob-wetterling-resource-center/who-we-are/history/jacobs-story.

Janus, E. S. (2000). Sexual Predator Commitment Laws: Lessons for Law and the Behavioral Sciences. *Behavioral Sciences and the Law*, 18(1), 5–21.

Jenkins, P. (1998). *Moral Panic: Changing Concepts of the Child Molester in Modern America*. New Haven, CT: Yale University Press.

Karsjens v. MN Department of Human Services et al., No. Civil No. 11–3659 (DWF/JJL) (U.S. District Court, D. Minnesota 2014).

Kernsmith, P. D., Comartin, E. B., Craun, S. W., and Kernsmith, R. M. (2009). The Relationship Between Sex Offender Registry Utilization and Awareness. *Sexual Abuse: A Journal of Research and Treatment*, 21(2), 181–193. doi: 10.1177/1079063209332235.

Leclerc, B., Proulx, J., and Beauregard, E. (2009). Examining the Modus Operandi of Sexual Offenders Against Children and Its Practical Implications. *Aggression and Violent Behavior*, 14(1), 5–12. doi: 10.1016/j.avb.2008.08.001.

Leclerc, B., Wortley, R., and Smallbone, S. (2011). Getting into the Script of Adult Child Sex Offenders and Mapping out Situational Prevention Measures. *Journal of Research in Crime and Delinquency*, 48(2), 209–237. doi: 10.1177/0022427810391540.

Leon, C. S. (2011). *Sex Fiends, Perverts, and Pedophiles: Understanding Sex Crime Policy in America*. New York, NY: New York University Press.

Letourneau, E. J., Bandyopadhyay, D., Armstrong, K. S., and Sinha, D. (2010). Do Sex Offender Registration and Notification Requirements Deter Juvenile Sex Crimes? *Criminal Justice and Behavior*, 37(5), 553–569. doi: 10.1177/0093854810363562.

Letourneau, E. J., Armstrong, K. S., Bandyopadhyay, D., and Sinha, D. (2013). Sex Offender Registration and Notification Policy Increases Juvenile Plea Bargains. *Sexual Abuse: A Journal of Research and Treatment*, 25(2), 189–207. doi: 10.1177/1079063212455667.

Letourneau, E. J., Levenson, J. S., Bandyopadhyay, D., Armstrong, K. S., and Sinha, D. (2010a). The Effects of Sex Offender Registration and Notification on Judicial Decisions. *Criminal Justice Review*, 35(3), 295–317. doi: 10.1177/0734016809360330.

Letourneau, E. J., Levenson, J. S., Bandyopadhyay, D., Armstrong, K. S., and Sinha, D. (2010b). Effects of South Carolina's Sex Offender Registration and Notification Policy on Deterrence of Adult Sex Crimes. *Criminal Justice and Behavior*, 37(5), 537–552. doi: 10.1177/0093854810363569.

Letourneau, E. J., Levenson, J. S., Bandyopadhyay, D., Sinha, D., and Armstrong, K. S. (2010c). Effects of South Carolina's Sex Offender Registration and Notification Policy on Adult Recidivism. *Criminal Justice Policy Review*, 21(4), 435–458. doi: 10.1177/0887403409353148.

Levenson, J. S. (2004). Sexual predator civil commitment: A comparison of selected and released offenders. *International Journal of Offender Therapy and Comparative Criminology*, 48(6), 638–648. doi: 10.1177/0306624X04265089.

Levenson, J. S., and Cotter, L. P. (2005a). The Effect of Megan's Law on Sex Offender Reintegration. *Journal of Contemporary Criminal Justice*, 21(1), 49–66. doi: 10.1177/1043986204271676.

Levenson, J. S., and Cotter, L. P. (2005b). The Impact of Sex Offender Residence Restrictions: 1,000 Feet From Danger, or One Step From Absurd? *International Journal of Offender Therapy and Comparative Criminology*, 49(2), 168–178. doi: 10.1177/0306624X04271304.

Levenson, J. S., and Tewksbury, R. (2009). Collateral Damage: Family Members of Registered Sex Offenders. *American Journal of Criminal Justice*, 34(1–2), 54–68. doi: 10.1007/s12103-008-9055-x.

Levenson, J. S., Brannon, Y. N., Fortney, T., and Baker, J. (2007). Public Perceptions About Sex Offenders and Community Protection Policies. *Analysis of Social Issues and Public Policy*, 7(1), 137–161. doi: 10.1111/j.1530-2415.2007.00119.

Levenson, J. S., Ackerman, A. R., Socia, K. M., and Harris, A. J. (2015). Where for Art Thou? Transient Sex Offenders and Residence Restrictions. *Criminal Justice Policy Review*. 26(4): 319–344, doi: 10.1177/0887403413512326.

Lipsey, M. W., and Cullen, F. T. (2007). The Effectiveness of Correctional Rehabilitation: A Review of Systematic Reviews. *Annual Review of Law and Social Science*, 3, 297–320. doi: 10.1146/annurev.lawsocsci.3.081806.112833.

Lucken, K., and Bales, W. D. (2007). Florida's Sexually Violent Predator Program: An Examination of Risk and Civil Commitment Eligibility. *Crime and Delinquency*, 54(1), 95–127.

Lynch, M. (1998). Waste Managers? The New Penology, Crime Fighting, and Parole Agent Identity. *Law and Society Review*, 32(4), 839–870.

Maguire, M., and Singer, J. (2011). A False Sense of Security: Moral Panic Driven Sex Offender Legislation. *Critical Criminology*, 19(4), 301–312. doi: 10.1007/s10612-010-9127-3.

Mancini, C., Shields, R. T., Mears, D. P., and Beaver, K. M. (2010). Sex Offender Residence Restriction Laws: Parental Perceptions and Public Policy. *Journal of Criminal Justice*, 38(5), 1022–1030. doi: 10.1016/j.jcrimjus.2010.07.004.

McLawsen, J. E., Scalora, M. J., and Darrow, C. (2012). Civilly Committed Sex Offenders: A Description and Interstate Comparison of Populations. *Psychology, Public Policy, and Law*, 18(3), 453–476. doi: 10.1037/a0026116.

Mears, B. (2010). Can sex offenders be held after serving their sentences? *CNN Justice*. Retrieved from Cnn.com website: www.cnn.com/2010/CRIME/01/12/scotus.sex.offender.law/.

Megan's Law, 110 Stat. 1345, Pub. L. No. 104–145, H.R.2137 Stat. (May 17, 1996).

Megan's Law: Final guidelines for the Jacob Wetterling crimes against children and sexually violent offender registration act (1999).

Meloy, M. L., Miller, S., and Curtis, K. (2008). Making Sense Out of Nonsense: The Deconstruction of State-Level Sex Offender Residence Restrictions. *American Journal of Criminal Justice*, 33(2), 209–222. doi: 10.1007/s12103-008-9042-2.

Minnesota Department of Corrections. (2007). Residential Proximity and Sex Offender Recidivism in Minnesota (pp. 28). St. Paul, MN.

Mulford, C. F., Wilson, R. E., and Parmley, A. M. (2009). Geographic Aspects of Sex Offender Residency Restrictions: Policy and Research. *Criminal Justice Policy Review*, 20(1), 3–12. doi: 10.1177/0887403408327683.

Nobles, M. R., Levenson, J. S., and Youstin, T. J. (2012). Effectiveness of Residence Restrictions in Preventing Sex Offender Recidivism. *Crime and Delinquency*, 58(4), 491–513.

Office of the Attorney General. (2014). California Megan's Law: Sex Offender Registration and Exclusion Information. Retrieved October 30, 2014, from http://www.meganslaw.ca.gov/sexreg.aspx?lang=ENGLISH.

Pam Lychner Sexual Offender Tracking and Identification Act of 1996, 110 Stat. 3093, Pub. L. No. 104–236 (Oct 3, 1996).

People v. Blair (Albany City Court 2009).

Pickett, J. T., Mancini, C., and Mears, D. P. (2013). Vulnerable Victims, Monstrous Offenders, and Unmanageable Risk: Explaining Public Opinion on the Social Control of Sex Crime. *Criminology*, 51(3), 729–759. doi: 10.1111/1745–9125.12018.

Prescott, J. J., and Rockoff, J. E. (2011). Do Sex Offender Registration and Notification Laws Affect Criminal Behavior? *Journal of Law and Economics*, 54(1), 161–206.

Presley, M. M. (1999). Jimmy Ryce Involuntary Civil Commitment for Sexually Violent Predators' Treatment and Care Act: Replacing Criminal Justice with Civil Commitment. *Florida State University Law Review*, 26, 487–516.

Roman, C. G., and Travis, J. (2004). Taking Stock: Housing, Homelessness, and Prisoner Reentry (J. P. Center, Trans.). Washington, DC: Urban Institute.

Rydberg, J., Grommon, E., Huebner, B. M., and Bynum, T. (2014). The Effect of Statewide Residency Restrictions on Sex Offender Post-Release Housing Mobility. *Justice Quarterly*, 31(2), 421–444. doi: 10.1080/07418825.2012.667141.

Sample, L. L., and Kadleck, C. (2008). Sex Offender Laws: Legislators' Accounts of the Need for Policy. *Criminal Justice Policy Review*, 19(1), 40–62. doi: 10.1177/0887403407308292.

Sandler, J. C., Freeman, N. J., and Socia, K. M. (2008). Does a Watched Pot Boil? A Time-Series Analysis of New York State's Sex Offender Registration and Notification Law. *Psychology, Public Policy, and Law*, 14(4), 284–302. doi: 10.1037/a0013881.

Schiavone, S. K., and Jeglic, E. L. (2009). Public Perception of Sex Offender Social Policies and the Impact on Sex Offenders. *International Journal of Offender Therapy and Comparative Criminology*, 53(6), 679–695. doi: 10.1177/0306624x08323454.

Schram, D. D., and Milloy, C. D. (1995). *Community Notification: A Study of Offender Characteristics and Recidivism* (U. P. Research, Trans.). Seattle: Washington State Institute for Public Policy.

SMART Office. (2014). Legislative History. Retrieved October 30, 2014, from http://ojp.gov/smart/legislation.htm.

Snyder, H. N. (2000). *Sexual Assault of Young Children as Reported to Law Enforcement: Victim, Incident, and Offender Characteristics*. Washington, DC: U.S. Department of Justice, Bureau of Justice Statistics.

Socia, K. M. (2011a). The Policy Implications of Residence Restrictions on Sex Offender Housing in Upstate, NY. *Criminology and Public Policy*, 10(2), 351–389. doi: 10.1111/j.1745-9133.2011.00713.

Socia, K. M. (2011b). *Residence Restriction Legislation, Sex Crime Rates, and the Spatial Distribution of Sex Offender Residences*. (Ph.D. Dissertation), University at Albany, SUNY, Albany, NY. Retrieved from http://proquest.umi.com/pqdweb?did=2365415911andsid=1andFmt=2andclientId=9718andRQT=309andVName=PQD Available from Proquest Dissertations and Theses database database. (3454528).

Socia, K. M. (2012). The Efficacy of County-Level Sex Offender Residence Restrictions in New York. *Crime and Delinquency*, 58(4), 612–642. doi: 10.1177/0011128712441694.

Socia, K. M. (2014). Residence Restrictions Are Ineffective, Inefficient, and Inadequate: So Now What? *Criminology and Public Policy*.

Socia, K. M. (2015). State Residence Restrictions and Forcible Rape Rates: A Multi-State Quasi-Experimental Analysis of UCR Data. *Sexual Abuse: A Journal of Research and Treatment*, 27(2): 205–227. doi: 10.1177/1079063213509412.

Socia, K. M., and Stamatel, J. P. (2010). Assumptions and Evidence Behind Sex Offender Laws: Registration, Community Notification, and Residency Restrictions. *Sociology Compass*, 4(1), 1–20. doi: 10.1111/j.1751-9020.2009.00251.

Socia, K. M., Levenson, J. S., Ackerman, A. R., and Harris, A. J. (2015). 'Brothers Under the Bridge': Factors Influencing the Transience of Registered Sex Offenders in Florida. *Sexual Abuse: A Journal of Research and Treatment*, 27(6): 559–586. doi: 10.1177/1079063214521472.

Studer, L. H., Aylwin, A. S., Sribney, C., and Reddon, J. R. (2011). Uses, misuses, and abuses of risk assessment with sexual offenders. In R. Eher, L. A. Craig, M. H. Miner and F. Pfäfflin (eds.), *International Perspectives on the Assessment and Treatment of Sexual Offenders: Theory, Practice and Research* (pp. 193–212): John Wiley and Sons.

Swanson, A. H. (1960). Sexual Psychopath Statutes: Summary and Analysis. *Journal of Criminal Law, Criminology, and Police Science*, 51, 215–235.

Tewksbury, R. (2002). Validity and Utility of the Kentucky Sex Offender Registry. *Federal Probation*, 66(1), 21–26.

Tewksbury, R. (2005). Collateral Consequences of Sex Offender Registration. *Journal of Contemporary Criminal Justice*, 21(1), 67–81. doi: 10.1177/1043986204271704.

Tewksbury, R., and Lees, M. (2006). Perceptions of Sex Offender Registration: Collateral Consequences and Community Experiences. *Sociological Spectrum*, 26(3), 309–334. doi: 10.1080/02732170500524246.

Tewksbury, R., and Zgoba, K. M. (2009). Perceptions and Coping With Punishment: How Registered Sex Offenders Respond to Stress, Internet Restrictions, and the Collateral Consequences of Registration. *International Journal of Offender Therapy and Comparitive Criminology*, Onlinefirst. doi: 10.1177/0306624x09339180

Timmins, A. (2014, January 29th). House Committee Passes Bill Prohibiting Restrictions on Where Sex Offenders Can Live, *Concord Monitor*. Retrieved from www.concordmonitor.com/home/10425897-95/house-committee-passes-bill-prohibiting-restrictions-on-where-sex-offenders-can-live.

U.S. Department of Justice. (2010). Dru Sjodin National Sex Offender Public Website (NSOPW). Retrieved January 18, 2010, from www.nsopw.gov/.

Vandiver, D. M., Dial, K. C., and Worley, R. M. (2008). A Qualitative Assessment of Registered Female Sex Offenders: Judicial Processing Experiences and Perceived Effects of a Public Registry. *Criminal Justice Review*, 33(2), 177–198. doi: 10.1177/0734016808318448.

Vasquez, B. E., Maddan, S., and Walker, J. T. (2008). The Influence of Sex Offender Registration and Notification Laws in the United States: A Time-Series Analysis. *Crime and Delinquency*, 54(2), 175–192. doi: 10.1177/0011128707311641.

VCSC. (2001). *Assessing Risk Among Sex Offenders in Virginia*. Richmond, VA: Virginia Criminal Sentencing Commission.

Walker, J. T. (2007). Eliminate Residency Restrictions for Sex Offenders. *Criminology and Public Policy*, 6(4), 863–870. doi: 10.1080/07418820701717110.

Weiss, C. H. (1997). *Evaluation: Methods for Studying Programs and Policies. 2nd. sl* (2nd ed.). Upper Saddle River, NJ: Prentice Hall.

Wright, R. G. (2008). From Wetterling to Walsh: The Growth of Federalization in Sex Offender Policy. *Federal Sentencing Reporter*, 21(2), 124–132. doi: 10.1525/fsr.2008.21.2.124.

Zandbergen, P. A., and Hart, T. C. (2006). Reducing Housing Options for Convicted Sex Offenders: Investigating the Impact of Residency Restriction Laws Using GIS. *Justice Research and Policy*, 8(2), 1–24. doi: 10.3818/JRP.8.2.2006.1.

Zandbergen, P. A., Levenson, J. S., and Hart, T. C. (2010). Residential Proximity to Schools and Daycares: An Empirical Analysis of Sex Offense Recidivism. *Criminal Justice and Behavior*, 37(5), 482–502. doi: 10.1177/0093854810363549.

Zevitz, R. G., and Farkas, M. A. (2000). Sex Offender Community Notification: Managing High Risk Criminals or Exacting Further Vengeance? *Behavioral Sciences and the Law*, 18(2/3), 375–391. doi: 10.1002/1099-0798(200003/06)18:2/3<375::AID-BSL380>3.0.CO;2-N.

Zgoba, K. M., Witt, P., Dalessandro, M., and Veysey, B. (2008). *Megan's Law: Assessing the Practical and Monetary Efficiency* (O. o. P. P. The Research and Evaluation Unit, Trans.). Washington: National Institute of Justice.

Zgoba, K. M., Miner, M., Knight, R. A., Letourneau, E. J., Levenson, J. S., and Thornton, D. (2012). *A Multi-State Recidivism Study Using Static-99R and Static-2002 Risk Scores and Tier Guidelines from the Adam Walsh Act*. Washington, DC: U.S. Department of Justice, Office of Justice Programs, National Institute of Justice.

Chapter 15

Drug courts and drug policy

Douglas B. Marlowe

Introduction

Policy development commonly vacillates between endorsement of evidence-based practices and reliance on political or social ideology. Although evidence-based practices can usually unseat false beliefs over time, they also fall victim readily to newly emerging beliefs.

The history of Drug Courts exemplifies this process writ large. Created largely in response to the failed War on Drugs of the 1980s, Drug Courts deliver community-based substance abuse treatment and correctional supervision for drug-addicted individuals in lieu of criminal prosecution or incarceration (National Association of Drug Court Professionals [NADCP], 1997). Since their founding in 1989, more research has been conducted on the effects of Drug Courts than on any other substance abuse treatment or criminal justice program. As reviewed below, a large body of evidence proves not only that Drug Courts work, but how they work and for what types of drug-addicted individuals. Studies have identified specific practices within Drug Courts that double their effectiveness and increase their cost-effectiveness by more than half (Carey et al., 2012; NADCP, 2013; Zweig et al., 2012).

The unprecedented success of Drug Courts made them an exemplar of evidence-based practices for the criminal justice system. Other programs modeled some of their interventions after Drug Courts and achieved similarly favorable results. For example, pre-trial supervision programs such as the 24/7 Sobriety Project (Kilmer et al., 2012), prosecutorial programs such as D.T.A.P. (Drug Treatment as an Alternative to Prison) (Crime Solutions, n.d.), and probation programs such as Project H.O.P.E. (Honest Opportunity Probation with Enforcement) (Hawken and Kleiman, 2009) borrowed elements from the Drug Court model – substance abuse treatment, drug and alcohol testing, and/or gradually increasing sanctions and rewards – and proved effective at reducing crime and substance abuse significantly.

After 25 years of proven accomplishments, Drug Courts now face existential challenges which threaten to undermine their viability and utility.

In their haste to undo the damage wrought by the War on Drugs, policy advocates are ignoring basic lessons derived from Drug Courts and other evidence-based programs, diluting the core ingredients of these programs, and promoting a policy environment which removes some of the requisite conditions for Drug Courts to succeed. If history is any guide (and it always is), the failure of these untested efforts to protect public health and public safety could herald the return of punitive sentencing policies akin to those discredited in the War on Drugs.

Background

More than 80 percent of persons charged with criminal offenses in the U.S. abuse illicit substances (National Center on Addiction and Substance Abuse, 2010) and nearly half are addicted to drugs or alcohol (Fazel et al., 2006; Karberg and James, 2005). Continued substance abuse is associated with a two- to four-fold increase in the likelihood of criminal recidivism (Bennett et al., 2008). Providing substance abuse treatment reduces recidivism substantially (Holloway et al., 2006; Chandler et al., 2009); however, unless they receive intensive supervision and consequences for noncompliance, more than three-quarters of persons referred to treatment by the criminal justice system will refuse to attend treatment or drop out prematurely (Marlowe, 2002; Sung et al., 2004; University of California at Los Angeles, 2007). In fact, the more individuals need treatment and the greater their likelihood of recidivism, the less likely they are to comply with treatment (Olver et al., 2011).

Mandatory sentencing policies such as the War on Drugs have produced similarly minimal gains (Cullen et al., 2011). More than two-thirds of drug-involved inmates commit a new crime within three years of release from jail or prison, approximately half are returned to custody for a new offense or technical violation, and over 80 percent resume illicit drug or alcohol abuse (Durose et al., 2014; Green and Winik, 2010; Marlowe, 2002; Spohn and Holleran, 2002).

Drug Courts were created to enhance compliance with community-based substance abuse treatment. The Drug Court judge leads a multidisciplinary team of professionals, which includes a prosecutor, defense attorney, community supervision officer, and substance abuse and mental health treatment providers (NADCP, 1997). Participants are required to complete substance abuse treatment and other indicated services, undergo random weekly drug and alcohol testing, and attend frequent status hearings in court, during which the judge reviews their progress in treatment and imposes consequences contingent upon their performance. The consequences may include desired rewards (e.g. verbal praise, reduced supervision requirements, or token gifts), punitive sanctions (e.g. writing assignments, community service, or brief jail detention) or modifications to the participant's treatment plan (e.g. transfer to a more intensive level of care).

In pre-adjudication Drug Courts, the criminal charge(s) are withdrawn and the offense may be expunged from the participant's record. Although the offense may not be erased literally from criminal justice databases, expungement entitles the individual to respond truthfully on an employment application or similar document that the arrest or conviction did not occur (Festinger et al., 2005). In post-adjudication Drug Courts, graduates avoid incarceration or reduce the length or conditions of probation.

Effectiveness of drug courts

Seven meta-analyses[1] (Drake et al., 2009; Gutierrez and Bourgon, 2012; Lowenkamp et al., 2005; MacKenzie, 2006; Mitchell et al., 2012; Shaffer, 2010; Wilson et al., 2006), a national multisite study (Rossman et al., 2011) and several systematic reviews (e.g. Belenko, 2002; Government Accountability Office [GAO], 2005; Marlowe, 2011; National Institute of Justice, 2006) have concluded that Drug Courts significantly reduce crime (typically measured by re-arrest rates) by an average of 8 to 14 percent. The studies have included several randomized controlled experiments (Breckenridge et al., 2000; Gottfredson et al., 2003; Harrell et al., 1999; Jones, 2013; MacDonald et al., 2007; Turner et al., 1999) and dozens of quasi-experiments (Mitchell et al., 2012). The effects on recidivism have been determined to last at least three years after entry (Gottfredson et al., 2005; Mitchell et al., 2012; Turner et al., 1999) and one study reported effects lasting more than 14 years (Finigan et al., 2007).

Because these figures reflect averages, they mask substantial variability in the performance of individual Drug Courts. Approximately three-quarters of the Drug Courts that were studied reduced crime significantly (Shaffer, 2006), with the best Drug Courts reducing crime by 35 percent to 50 percent (Carey et al., 2012; Carey and Waller, 2011; Lowenkamp et al., 2005; Shaffer, 2006). A sizeable minority (22 percent) of Drug Courts, however, was determined to have no impact on crime (Shaffer, 2006) and a small proportion (6 percent) were associated with *increases* in crime (Lowenkamp et al., 2005). As will be discussed, studies have revealed that poorly performing Drug Courts typically delivered ineffective or contraindicated services, or targeted their services to the wrong types of individuals who did not require those services (Carey et al., 2012; Gutierrez and Bourgon, 2012; Marlowe, 2012a; Zweig et al., 2012).

A recent national study of 23 adult Drug Courts, called the Multisite Adult Drug Court Evaluation (MADCE), examined a wide range of outcomes beyond recidivism in Drug Courts. In addition to reducing crime, the MADCE found that Drug Courts significantly reduced illicit drug and alcohol use and improved participants' family interactions (Rossman et al., 2011). For example, 29 percent of the Drug Court participants tested positive by saliva testing for illicit drugs and/or alcohol at 18 months post-admission, compared with 46 percent of a carefully matched comparison sample (p < .01).

Drug Courts have also proven to be highly cost-effective. The MADCE and two meta-analyses concluded that Drug Courts produce an average of more than $2 in direct benefits to the criminal justice system for every $1 invested (Bhati et al., 2008; Downey and Roman, 2010; Rossman et al., 2011). These savings reflect tangible cost-offsets resulting from reduced re-arrests, law enforcement contacts, court hearings, use of jail or prison beds, and crime victimization. When more distal offsets were also taken into account, such as savings from reduced healthcare and foster care utilization, studies have reported economic benefits ranging from approximately $2 to $27 for every $1 invested (Carey et al., 2006; Finigan et al., 2007; Lee et al., 2012; Loman, 2004). The net result has been economic savings to local communities ranging from approximately $3,000 to $13,000 per participant (Aos et al., 2006; Carey et al., 2006; Finigan et al., 2007; Lee et al., 2012; Logan et al., 2004; Loman, 2004).

Target population

According to the criminological theory of the *Risk Principle*, intensive programs such as Drug Courts are hypothesized to produce the greatest benefits for high-risk individuals who have more severe antisocial propensities or treatment-refractory histories; however, such programs may be unnecessary or counterproductive for low-risk individuals (Andrews and Bonta, 2010). Low-risk individuals are, by definition, less likely to be on a fixed antisocial trajectory and are predisposed to improve their conduct following a run-in with the law. Therefore, intensive interventions offer small incremental benefits for these individuals but at a substantial cost (DeMatteo et al., 2006). Worse, low-risk individuals often adopt antisocial attitudes and behaviors from associating with high-risk peers, which makes their outcomes worse (Lloyd et al., 2014; Welsh and Rocque, 2014).

The Risk Principle has been validated reliably in Drug Courts. Drug Courts reduce crime approximately twice as much and are 50 percent more cost-effective when they treat high-risk participants as compared to low-risk participants (Marlowe, 2012a). The effects of Drug Courts are particularly pronounced for high-risk individuals who are younger, have more prior felony convictions, have been diagnosed with antisocial personality disorder, or failed previously in substance abuse treatment (Festinger et al., 2002; Fielding et al., 2002; Lowenkamp et al., 2005; Marlowe et al., 2007).

Fidelity to the model

In fiscally challenging times, there is always pressure to do more with less. This pressure raises important questions about whether some of the components of the Drug Court model can be dropped or the dosage reduced without eroding the benefits. The "Key Components" of Drug Courts (NADCP, 1997) are hypothesized to include a frequent schedule of judicial status hearings, weekly drug and alcohol testing, progressively escalating rewards for achievements and sanctions for infractions, and an intensive regimen of substance abuse treatment. Each of these components has been studied carefully and proven to be pivotal for achieving positive outcomes for high-risk, drug-addicted individuals.

Studies involving more than 100 Drug Courts have examined whether the average effect size (ES) for Drug Court increases or decreases significantly depending on how particular services, such as court hearings or treatment sessions, are structured and delivered.[2] Among other findings, these studies found that the ES for Drug Court is nearly double in magnitude when the program adheres to the practices listed below (Carey et al., 2012; Zweig et al., 2012). The evidence supporting these practices is so strong that the field adopted these practices as an enforceable standard of care for Drug Courts (NADCP, 2013).

- Participants appear in court for status hearings no less frequently than every two weeks for the first phase of the program, and monthly thereafter for the remainder of the first year of treatment.
- Participants receive a minimum of 200 hours of cognitive-behavioral addiction counseling over a period of at least 12 months.
- In addition to group counseling, participants receive individual counseling or clinical case management at least twice per week for the first several months of the program.
- Participants are tested for drug and alcohol use no less frequently than twice per week on a random basis for at least the first year of the program.
- Participants receive gradually escalating sanctions for illicit substance use, and jail sanctions for substance use are ordinarily no more than 3 to 5 days in length.
- Participants receive gradually increasing rewards for achievements in the program, such as providing negative drug tests and attending counseling sessions.

The policy environment

With unambiguous proof that Drug Courts protect public safety, improve public health and return substantial cost-savings to taxpayers, one would expect them to be endorsed wholeheartedly by policymakers and the public at large. In fact, endorsement of Drug Courts has followed a circuitous path.

In the early years, critics of Drug Courts were primarily "law and order" advocates who viewed the programs as potentially soft on crime. Proponents tended to be critics of the War on Drugs who favored almost any community alternative to incarceration. The public, for the most part, was unaware of what a Drug Court was or why they were needed. Over the ensuing 25 years, scientific support for Drug Courts gradually caught the attention of policymakers and slowly permeated the public's consciousness. The number of Drug Courts in the U.S. increased from one in 1989 to nearly 3,000 in 2014 (Huddleston and Marlowe, in press) and Drug Courts have been started or are in the planning stages in approximately 30 other countries (Marlowe, 2012b). Financial appropriations for Drug Courts increased in lockstep with their growth in numbers. Despite the 2008 economic recession in the U.S. and concomitant state budget crises, state and federal appropriations for Drug Courts held steady or continued to rise and topped $350 million by 2012 (Huddleston and Marlowe, in press).

Much of this growth was fueled by emerging scientific evidence demonstrating the positive impacts of Drug Courts. Politically conservative groups, who were initially cool to the idea of Drug Courts, took notice of the fact that they reduce crime (an important yardstick for law and order advocates), save money (a critical benchmark for fiscal conservatives), and hold individuals accountable for contributing to their own recovery (a touchstone for social conservatives). Leading conservative think tanks, such as the Texas Public Policy Foundation (n.d.), endorsed Drug Courts as a rational building block for evidence-based drug policy and criminal-justice policy reforms. Victims' rights groups such as M.A.D.D. (n.d.) also endorsed Drug Courts as a responsible approach to dealing with recidivist intoxicated drivers and other public safety threats. Science and policy were firmly in sync.

Drug Courts also fit comfortably into the national narrative in the U.S. about the proper role of the federal government. Local court administration is a function of state and county governments, and some commentators questioned why federal agencies should fund these programs. The simplest response is that the programs work. Rarely has federal seed funding proved to be so demonstrably successful, and rarely have state and local governments picked up the tab after federal funding dried up. As federal seed monies ended, state and county governments continued to fund Drug Courts at consistent or increasing levels, in some cases for decades. It is estimated that each dollar contributed by the federal government has elicited more than $3 of ensuing state and county appropriations; more than $9 when in-kind contributions, such as donated judicial and court clerk time, are taken into account (Huddleston, 2007).

Recently, however, the political zeitgeist has shifted markedly. The abject failure of the War on Drugs, which set the stage for Drug Courts to arise and thrive, has given rise to newer policy proposals which may contribute to the demise of Drug Courts and other evidence-based programs. Most policy analysts agree that the mandatory sentencing provisions of the War on Drugs were ineffective, harmful and costly. Crime rates did not budge, families and communities (especially low-income and racial-minority families and communities) were decimated, and state budgets buckled under enormous correctional expenditures (Jensen et al., 2004). Drug Courts helped to ameliorate these problems but they may have been too little too late (Drug Policy Alliance [DPA], 2011; National Association of Criminal Defense Lawyers, 2009; Justice Policy Institute [JPI], 2011). At the height of their funding, Drug Courts have reached 5 percent to 10 percent of eligible drug-addicted persons (Bhati et al., 2008; Huddleston and Marlowe, 2011). This level of penetration is simply insufficient to undo the devastation wrought by the War on Drugs (Lilley, 2013; Sevigney et al., 2013). Policymakers and the public began to look for simpler, cheaper and faster measures. They found them in the decriminalization and legalization movements.

The logic of decriminalization is (seemingly) simple. If incarceration is ineffective and harmful, then perhaps the best alternative is to reduce or remove criminal penalties altogether. According to this view, the criminal justice system cannot be counted on to reform itself; rather, it is oriented inexorably toward maintaining and extending the status quo (Bach, 2009; Perkinson, 2010). Reform must come from the grassroots and not from innovative justice programming.

This sentiment found company in the views of constituencies seeking to rectify racial and ethnic disparities in the criminal justice system (O'Hear, 2009; Wolf, 2009). The War on Drugs unquestionably burdened racial-minority and poor citizens disproportionately (Jensen et al., 2004; Marlowe, 2013). The answer for some advocates is to dismantle this unfair framework and reduce the possibility of criminal justice system entanglements (Alexander, 2010). Any correctional rehabilitation program, no matter how well intentioned or effective, is viewed by these advocates as part of the problem rather than the solution because it criminalizes "victimless behavior" and treats sickness as deviance (DPA, 2011; Tiger, 2013).

The upshot of these sentiments has been the steady decriminalization of drug-possession offenses in many states, de-felonization of a wide range of theft and property crimes (reducing the crimes from felonies to misdemeanors), and providing "good-time credits" and other sentence reductions irrespective of whether individuals are, in fact, compliant with the conditions of their criminal justice supervision (California Proposition 47, 2014; Couzens, 2013; Vera Institute of Justice, 2012).

Drug Courts cannot function nearly as effectively in this new policy environment as they have in the past. The typical Drug Court curriculum is 12 to 18 months in duration. This is because, as was noted earlier, studies have determined that a minimum of 12 months of treatment (including 200 hours of counseling) is necessary to achieve beneficial results. If the typical sentence for a misdemeanor offense is six to 12 months, and most probationers can have their sentences shortened further via unearned credits, it will be the rare individual who enters a Drug Court voluntarily. The more severely addicted the person and the greater the risk of recidivism, the less likely the person will enter Drug Court (Olver et al., 2011). Intrinsic motivation for treatment is the hallmark of a low-risk individual who is already predisposed to change for the better. It is the serious and recalcitrant offender who needs Drug Court the most but is least likely to recognize this fact.

Science leaves little question that the severity of the presumptive or alternative sentence is critical to the success of Drug Courts and similar criminal justice programs (Carey et al., 2012; Gottfredson et al., 2003; Mitchell et al., 2012; Rossman et al., 2011; Shaffer, 2010; Zweig et al., 2012). Drug Courts work, in part, by applying the leverage of a potential jail or prison sentence to keep unmotivated persons engaged in community treatment. Without this "carrot and stick," retention in treatment is unacceptably poor and recovery dishearteningly rare (Coviello et al., 2012; Gregoire and Burke, 2004; Hser et al., 2001; Kelly et al., 2005; Perron and Bright, 2008).

The destructive pressures facing Drug Courts are, by no means, the product of disillusionment with Drug Courts. Although a minority of commentators continue to challenge the scientific basis for Drug Courts (DPA, 2011; JPI, 2011), these outliers are becoming less and less vocal as proof of Drug Courts' efficacy accumulates. The dangerous waters surrounding Drug Courts were spawned not by critics, but by like-minded groups who similarly detest the punitive impacts of the War on Drugs and the unfair racial disparities it engendered. What these well-intentioned groups fail to understand, however, is that sentiments are not the same as facts, and goals are not the same as methods. Their understandable impatience to undo the damage caused by past policies has led them to turn a blind eye to empirical evidence. No matter how one justifies the course of action, abdicating responsibility for treating and supervising seriously ill and self-destructive persons is not a new policy. It is the absence of a policy.

Conclusion

The most destructive policies are often backed by constituencies with unquestioned moral aims, ardent fervor for positive change, and a great deal of money to spend on political campaigns. When these same constituencies lack knowledge about scientific reasoning, their actions may be unconstrained by logic and unmoved by proof. At present, there is not a shred of evidence to support decriminalization, de-felonization, or similar policy initiatives (Laqueur, 2014). This lack of supporting evidence should give proponents pause for reflection and policymakers and the public cause for concern; it has, however, failed to ebb the pace of reform. Laws are being rewritten at a furious rate with no way to predict or prepare for the consequences (Pennypacker and Thompson, 2014).

When public or private entities seek to build new industries or plants, they are often required to hire independent experts to prepare an environmental impact statement. This process ensures the public is not injured by unintended and unforeseen consequences of the planned course of action. An analogous process should be followed for proposed legislation which could have unforeseen impacts on the policy landscape. Before lawmakers pass sweeping criminal justice reforms, they should be expected to engage independent experts to examine the potential impacts of those reforms on evidence-based programs which are delivering proven benefits to public health and safety. Policymakers would, of course, be free to ignore such impacts and pass the reforms regardless of the effects; nevertheless, they should be required to deliberate about foreseeable impacts before embarking on a course of action.

Ideology should not be permitted to usurp more than 25 years of research on best practices without at least some consideration of the potential repercussions. Taking empirical evidence of effectiveness into account before drafting legislation is the definition of rational policy reform.

Notes

1 Meta-analysis is an advanced statistical procedure that yields a conservative and rigorous estimate of the average effects of an intervention. This process involves systematically reviewing the research literature, selecting only those studies that are scientifically acceptable according to standardized criteria, and statistically averaging the effects of the intervention across the acceptable studies (Lipsey and Wilson, 2001).
2 An effect size (ES) is defined as the average difference in outcomes between the program of interest (in this case, Drug Court) and those of a comparison condition, such as probation (Cohen, 1988). For example, if the recidivism rate is 35 percent for Drug Court participants and 50 percent for traditional probationers, then the ES for Drug Court would be a 15 percentage-point reduction in recidivism.

References

Alexander, M. (2010). *The new Jim Crow*. New York: The New Press.

Andrews, D.A., and Bonta, J. (2010). *The psychology of criminal conduct* (5th ed.). New Providence, NJ: Anderson.

Aos, S., Miller, M., and Drake, E. (2006). *Evidence-based public policy options to reduce future prison construction, criminal justice costs, and crime rates*. Olympia, WA: Washington State Institute for Public Policy.

Bach, A. (2009). *Ordinary injustice: How America holds court*. New York: Metropolitan Books.

Belenko, S. (2002). Drug Courts. In C. G. Leukefeld, F. Tims, and D. Farabee (eds.), *Treatment of drug offenders: Policies and issues* (pp. 301–318). New York: Springer.

Bennett, T., Holloway, K., and Farrington, D. (2008). The statistical association between drug misuse and crime: A meta-analysis. *Aggression and Violent Behavior*, 13, 107–118.

Bhati, A. S., Roman, J. K., and Chalfin, A. (2008). *To treat or not to treat: Evidence on the prospects of expanding treatment to drug-involved offenders*. Washington, DC: The Urban Institute.

Breckenridge, J. F., Winfree, L. T., Maupin, J. R., and Clason, D. L. (2000). Drunk drivers, DWI "Drug Court" treatment, and recidivism: Who fails? *Justice Research and Policy*, 2, 87–105.

California Proposition 47. (2014). *Reduced penalties for some crimes initiative.* Retrieved from http://ballotpedia.org/California_Proposition_47,_Reduced_Penalties_for_Some_Crimes_Initiative_%282014%29.

Carey, S. M., Finigan, M., Crumpton, D., and Waller, M. (2006). California Drug Courts: Outcomes, costs and promising practices: An overview of phase II in a statewide study. *Journal of Psychoactive Drugs, SARC Supplement* 3, 345–356.

Carey, S. M., Mackin, J. R., and Finigan, M. W. (2012). What works? The ten key components of Drug Court: Research-based best practices. *Drug Court Review*, VIII (1), 6–42.

Carey, S. M., and Waller, M. S. (2011). *Oregon Drug Courts: Statewide costs and promising practices.* Portland, OR: NPC Research.

Chandler, R. K., Fletcher, B. W., and Volkow, N. D. (2009). Treating drug abuse and addiction in the criminal justice system: Improving public health and safety. *Journal of the American Medical Association*, 301, 183–190.

Cohen, J. (1988). *Statistical power analysis for the behavioral sciences* (2nd ed.). Hillsdale, NJ: Lawrence Erlbaum.

Couzens, J. R. (2013). Realignment and evidence-based practice: A new era in sentencing California felonies. *Federal Sentencing Reporter*, 25(4), 217–219.

Coviello, D. M., Zanis, D. A., Wesnoski, S. A., Palman, N., Gur, A., Lynch, K. G., and McKay, J. R. (2012). Does mandating offenders to treatment improve completion rates? *Journal of Substance Abuse Treatment*, http://dx.doi.org/10.1016/j.jsat.2012.10.003.

Crime Solutions. (n.d.). *Program profile: Drug Treatment Alternative to Prison (DTAP).* Retrieved from www.crimesolutions.gov/ProgramDetails.aspx?id=89.

Cullen, F. T., Jonson, C. L., and Nagin, D. S. (2011). Prisons do not reduce recidivism: The high cost of ignoring science. *The Prison Journal*, 91, 48S–65S.

DeMatteo, D. S., Marlowe, D. B., and Festinger, D. S. (2006). Secondary prevention services for clients who are low risk in Drug Court: A conceptual model. *Crime and Delinquency*, 52, 114–134.

Downey, P. M., and Roman, J. K. (2010). *A Bayesian meta-analysis of Drug Court cost-effectiveness.* Washington DC: The Urban Institute.

Drake, E., Aos, S., and Miller, M. (2009). Evidence-based public policy options to reduce crime and criminal justice costs: Implications for Washington State. *Victims and Offenders*, 4, 170–196.

Drug Policy Alliance. (2011). *Drug Courts are not the answer: Toward a health-centered approach to drug use.* Los Angeles, CA: Author.

Durose, M. R., Cooper, A. D., and Snyder, H. N. (2014). *Recidivism of prisoners released in 30 states in 2005: Patterns from 2005 to 2010.* Washington DC: U.S. Dept. of Justice, Bureau of Justice Statistics.

Fazel, S., Bains, P., and Doll, H. (2006). Substance abuse and dependence in prisoners: A systematic review. *Addiction*, 101, 181–191.

Festinger, D. S., DeMatteo, D. S., Marlowe, D. B., and Lee, P. A. (2005). Expungement of arrest records in Drug Court: Do clients know what they're missing? *Drug Court Review*, 5(1), 1–21.

Festinger, D. S., Marlowe, D. B., Lee, P. A., Kirby, K. C., Bovasso, G., and McLellan, A. T. (2002). Status hearings in Drug Court: When more is less and less is more. *Drug and Alcohol Dependence*, 68, 151–157.

Fielding, J. E., Tye, G., Ogawa, P. L., Imam, I. J., and Long, A. M. (2002). Los Angeles County Drug Court programs: Initial results. *Journal of Substance Abuse Treatment*, 23, 217–224.

Finigan, M., Carey, S. M., and Cox, A. (2007). *The impact of a mature Drug Court over 10 years of operation: Recidivism and costs*. Portland, OR: NPC Research.

Gottfredson, D. C., Kearley, B. W., Najaka, S. S., and Rocha, C. M. (2005). The Baltimore City Drug Treatment Court: 3-year outcome study. *Evaluation Review*, 29, 42–64.

Gottfredson, D. C., Najaka, S. S., and Kearley, B. (2003). Effectiveness of Drug Treatment Courts: Evidence from a randomized trial. *Criminology and Public Policy*, 2, 171–196.

Government Accountability Office. (2005). *Adult Drug Courts: Evidence indicates recidivism reductions and mixed results for other outcomes* [No. GAO-05-219]. Washington, DC: Author.

Green, D. P., and Winik, D. (2010). Using random judge assignments to estimate the effects of incarceration and probation on recidivism among drug offenders. *Criminology*, 48(2), 357–387.

Gregoire, T. K., and Burke, A. C. (2004). The relationship of legal coercion to readiness to change among adults with alcohol and other drug problems. *Journal of Substance Abuse Treatment*, 26, 35–41.

Gutierrez, L., and Bourgon, G. (2012). Drug Treatment Courts: A quantitative review of study and treatment quality. *Justice Research and Policy*, 14(2), 47–77.

Harrell, A., Cavanagh, S., and Roman, J. (1999). *Findings from the evaluation of the D.C. Superior Court Drug Intervention Program: Final report*. Washington, DC: The Urban Institute.

Hawken, A., and Kleiman, M. (2009). Managing drug involved probationers with swift and certain sanctions: Evaluating Hawaii's HOPE [NCJRS no. 229023]. Washington DC: National Institute of Justice. Retrieved from www.ncjrs.gov/pdffiles1/nij/grants/229023.pdf.

Holloway, K. R., Bennett, T. H., and Farrington, D. P. (2006). The effectiveness of drug treatment programs in reducing criminal behavior. *Psicothema*, 18, 620–629.

Hser, Y., Joshi, V., Maglione, M., Chou, C., and Anglin, M. D. (2001). Effects of program and patient characteristics on retention of drug treatment patients. *Evaluation and Program Planning*, 24, 331–341.

Huddleston, W. (2007). *Statement of West Huddleston, Chief Executive Officer, National Association of Drug Court Professionals, before the House of Representatives Appropriations Committee, Subcommittee on Commerce, Justice, and State*. Retrieved from http://nadcp.org/sites/default/files/nadcp/NADCP_CEO_West_Huddleston_4-24-07_Testimony.pdf.

Huddleston, W., and Marlowe, D. B. (2011). *Painting the current picture: A national report on Drug Courts and other problem solving court programs in the United States*. Alexandria, VA: National Drug Court Institute.

Huddleston, W., and Marlowe, D. B. (in press). *Painting the current picture: A national report on Drug Courts and other problem solving court programs in the United States*. Alexandria, VA: National Drug Court Institute.

Jensen, E. L., Gerber, J., and Mosher, C. (2004). Social consequences of the War on Drugs: The legacy of failed policy. *Criminal Justice Policy Review*, 15, 100–121.

Jones, C. (2013). Early-phase outcomes from a randomized trial of intensive judicial supervision in an Australian Drug Court. *Criminal Justice and Behavior*, 40, 453–468.

Justice Policy Institute. (2011). *Addicted to courts: How a growing dependence on Drug Courts impacts people and communities.* Washington DC: Author.

Karberg, J. C., and James, D. J. (2005). *Substance dependence, abuse, and treatment of jail inmates, 2002* [NCJ 209588]. Washington, DC: Bureau of Justice Statistics, U.S. Dept. of Justice.

Kelly, J. F., Finney, J. W., and Moos, R. (2005). Substance use disorder patients who are mandated to treatment: Characteristics, treatment process, and 1- and 5-year outcomes. *Journal of Substance Abuse Treatment*, 28, 213–223.

Kilmer, B., Nicosia, N., Heaton, P., and Midgette, G. (2012). Efficacy of frequent monitoring with swift, certain, and modest sanctions for violations: Insights from South Dakota's 24/7 Sobriety Project. *American Journal of Public Health*, DOI: 10.2105/AJPH.2012.300989.

Laqueur, H. (2014). Uses and abuses of drug decriminalization in Portugal. *Law and Social Inquiry*. DOI: 10.1111/lsi.12104.

Lee, S., Aos, S., Drake, E., Pennucci, A., Miller, M., and Anderson, L. (2012). *Return on investment: Evidence-based options to improve statewide outcomes.* Olympia, WA: Washington State Institute for Public Policy.

Lilley, D. R. (2013). Drug Courts and community crime rates: A nationwide analysis of jurisdiction-level outcomes. *Journal of Criminology*, http://dx.doi.org/10.1155/2013/571760.

Lipsey, M. W., and Wilson, D. B. (2001). *Practical meta-analysis.* Thousand Oaks, CA: Sage.

Lloyd, C. D., Hanby, L. J., and Serin, R. C. (2014). Rehabilitation group coparticipants' risk levels are associated with offenders' treatment performance, treatment change, and recidivism. *Journal of Consulting and Clinical Psychology*, 82 (2), 298–311.

Logan, T. K., Hoyt, W., McCollister, K. E., French, M. T., Leukefeld, C., and Minton, L. (2004). Economic evaluation of Drug Court: Methodology, results, and policy implications. *Evaluation and Program Planning*, 27, 381–396.

Loman, L. A. (2004). *A cost–benefit analysis of the St. Louis City Adult Felony Drug Court.* St. Louis, MO: Institute of Applied Research.

Lowenkamp, C. T., Holsinger, A. M., and Latessa, E. J. (2005). Are Drug Courts effective? A meta-analytic review. *Journal of Community Corrections*, 15(1), 5–28.

MacDonald, J. M., Morral, A. R., Raymond, B., and Eibner, C. (2007). The efficacy of the Rio Hondo DUI Court: A 2-year field experiment. *Evaluation Review*, 31, 4–23.

MacKenzie, D. L. (2006). *What works in corrections: Reducing the criminal activities of offenders and delinquents.* New York: Cambridge University Press.

Marlowe, D. B. (2002). Effective strategies for intervening with drug abusing offenders. *Villanova Law Review*, 47, 989–1025.

Marlowe, D. B. (2011). The verdict on Drug Courts and other problem-solving courts. *Chapman Journal of Criminal Justice*, 2, 53–92.

Marlowe, D. B. (2012a). *Targeting the right participants for Adult Drug Courts.* Alexandria, VA: National Drug Court Institute.

Marlowe, D. B. (2012b). Drug Court activity in the Americas. In *Report on Citizen Security in the Americas, 2012* (pp. 84–88). Washington DC: Secretariat for Multidimensional Security, Organization of American States.

Marlowe, D. B. (2013). Achieving racial and ethnic fairness in Drug Courts. *Court Review*, 49(1), 40–47.

Marlowe, D. B., Festinger, D. S., Dugosh, K. L., Lee, P. A., and Benasutti, K. M. (2007). Adapting judicial supervision to the risk level of drug offenders: Discharge and six-month outcomes from a prospective matching study. *Drug and Alcohol Dependence*, 88S, 4–13.

Mitchell, O., Wilson, D. B., Eggers, A., and MacKenzie, D. L. (2012). Assessing the effectiveness of Drug Courts on recidivism: A meta-analytic review of traditional and nontraditional Drug Courts. *Journal of Criminal Justice*, 40, 60–71.

Mothers Against Drunk Driving (n.d.). *MADD position statement on alcohol assessment and treatment.* Retrieved from http://www.madd.org/about-us/position-statements/madds-positions-on-alcohol.html.

National Association of Criminal Defense Lawyers. (2009). *America's problem-solving courts: The criminal costs of treatment and the case for reform.* Washington DC: Author.

National Association of Drug Court Professionals. (1997). *Defining Drug Courts: The key components.* Washington, DC: Office of Justice Programs, U.S. Dept. of Justice.

National Association of Drug Court Professionals. (2013). *Adult Drug Court Best Practice Standards.* Alexandria, VA: Author.

National Center on Addiction and Substance Abuse. (2010). *Behind bars II: Substance abuse and America's prison population.* New York: Author.

National Institute of Justice. (2006). *Drug Courts: The second decade* [NCJ 211081]. Washington DC: Office of Justice Programs, U.S. Dept. of Justice.

O'Hear, M. M. (2009). Rethinking Drug Courts: Restorative justice as a response to racial injustice. *Stanford Law and Policy Review*, 20, 463–500.

Olver, M. E., Stockdale, K. C., and Wormith, J. S. (2011). A meta-analysis of predictors of offender treatment attrition and its relationship to recidivism. *Journal of Consulting and Clinical psychology*, 79(1), 6–21.

Pennypacker, P. H., and Thompson, A. (2014). Realignment: A view from the trenches. *Santa Clara Law Review*, 53(4), 991–1038.

Perkinson, R. (2010). *Texas tough: The rise of America's prison empire.* New York: Metropolitan Books.

Perron, B. E., and Bright, C. L. (2008). The influence of legal coercion on dropout from substance abuse treatment: Results from a national survey. *Drug and Alcohol Dependence*, 92, 123–131.

Rossman, S. B., Rempel, M., Roman, J. K., Zweig, J. M., Lindquist, C. H., Green, M., Downey, P. M., Yahner, J., Bhati, A. S., and Farole, D. J. (2011). *The Multi-Site Adult Drug Court Evaluation: The impact of Drug Courts, volume 4.* Washington DC: Urban Institute Justice Policy Center. Retrieved from https://www.ncjrs.gov/pdffiles1/nij/grants/237112.pdf.

Sevigny, E. L., Pollack, H. A., and Reuter, P. (2013). Can Drug Courts help reduce prison and jail populations? *Annals of the American Academy of Political and Social Science*, 647, 190–212.

Shaffer, D. K. (2006). *Reconsidering Drug Court effectiveness: A meta-analytic review* [Doctoral Dissertation]. Las Vegas: Dept. of Criminal Justice, University of Nevada.

Shaffer, D. K. (2010). Looking inside the black box of Drug Courts: A meta-analytic review. *Justice Quarterly*, 28, 493–521.

Spohn, C., and Holleran, D. (2002). The effect of imprisonment on recidivism rates of felony offenders: A focus on drug offenders. *Criminology*, 40(2), 329–357.

Sung, H., Belenko, S., Feng, L., and Tabachnick, C. (2004). Predicting treatment non-compliance among criminal justice-mandated clients: A theoretical and empirical exploration. *Journal of Substance Abuse Treatment*, 26, 13–26.

Texas Public Policy Foundation. (n.d.). *Right on Crime Campaign. Retrieved from* http://www.rightoncrime.com/?s=drug+court.

Tiger, R. (2013). *Judging addicts: Drug Courts and coercion in the justice system.* New York: New York University Press.

Turner, S., Greenwood, P. Fain, T., and Deschenes, E. (1999). Perceptions of Drug Court: How offenders view ease of program completion, strengths and weaknesses, and the impact on their lives. *National Drug Court Institute Review*, 2, 61–85.

University of California at Los Angeles. (2007). *Evaluation of the Substance Abuse and Crime Prevention Act: Final Report.* UCLA Integrated Substance Abuse Programs.

Vera Institute of Justice. (2012). *Realigning justice resources: A review of population and spending shifts in prison and community corrections.* New York: Author.

Welsh, B. C., and Rocque, M. (2014). When crime prevention harms: A review of systematic reviews. *Journal of Experimental Criminology*, 10, 245–266.

Wilson, D. B., Mitchell, O., and MacKenzie, D. L. (2006). A systematic review of Drug Court effects on recidivism. *Journal of Experimental Criminology*, 2, 459–487.

Wolf, R. V. (2009). Race, bias, and problem-solving courts. *National Black Law Journal*, 21, 27–52.

Zweig, J.M., Lindquist, C., Downey, P.M., Roman, J., and Rossman, S.B. (2012). Drug Court policies and practices: How program implementation affects offender substance use and criminal behavior outcomes. *Drug Court Review*, VIII (1), 43–79.

Chapter 16

Did the Gregg decision overcome the arbitrary and discriminatory use of the death penalty so prevalent in Furman?

Gordon P. Waldo

Introduction

There are many reasons to make a recommendation for abolition of the death penalty. Some of the reasons are: (1) the risk of executing innocent people, (2) the absence of evidence for a deterrent effect of the death penalty, (3) the enormous financial cost, (4) the empty promise of "closure" for the victim's loved ones, (5) the "sticky" problems related to the execution of the mentally ill, intellectually deficient, and immature defendants, (6) retribution does not require the use of the death penalty, (7) it is not the "worst of the worst" who are executed, it is those with the "worst lawyers," (8) many secondary victims are created by executions, (9) more crime can be prevented without the death penalty than with it, and (10) the facts that (a) most countries have stopped using the death penalty, (b) most religious organizations oppose capital punishment, (c) the United States is the only major free-world or Christian country using the death penalty, and (d) many prestigious legal, political, educational, and social organizations have taken strong positions opposing the death penalty. To adequately discuss all of these issues, however, would require a lengthy book, not a short chapter.

This chapter will focus instead on the main issues raised in Furman v. Georgia (1972), the arbitrary and discriminatory application of the death penalty. Simply stated, the Furman decision said that the death penalty, as currently applied, was unconstitutional because it was being used in an arbitrary and discriminatory manner. Conversely, a major reason that the Supreme Court reinstated the death penalty in the Gregg v. Georgia decision (1976) was because the new laws had included "guided discretion" provisions adapted from the Model Penal Code and the Court determined that these changes in the statutes had eliminated the problems found in Furman. Writing for the majority Justice Stewart said in the Gregg decision:

> the concerns expressed in Furman that the penalty of death not be imposed in an arbitrary or capricious manner can be met by a … statute that ensures that the sentencing authority is given adequate information

and guidance. ... Georgia did act ... to narrow the class of murderers subject to capital punishment by specifying 10 statutory aggravating circumstances, one of which must be found by the jury to exist beyond a reasonable doubt. ... Georgia's new sentencing procedures require ... specific jury findings as to the circumstances of the crime or the character of the defendant. ... (and) the Supreme Court of Georgia compares each death sentence with the sentences imposed on similarly situated defendants. ... On their face these procedures seem to satisfy the concerns of Furman. ... we hold that the statutory system under which Gregg was sentenced to death does not violate the Constitution.

(*Gregg v. Georgia*, 1976, pp. 8, 9, 11)

The Georgia "guided discretion" death penalty statute that the court carefully examined included: (1) a bifurcated trial, (2) aggravating circumstances, (3) mitigating circumstances, (4) automatic appellate review of all sentences, and (5) a proportionality comparison of all local court decisions by a higher court. Each state developed new statutes that varied in many ways but eventually they all included some variation of "guided discretion." A majority of the justices thought these changes would overcome the problems identified in the Furman decision and approved the Gregg decision on a 7-2 vote. The question to be addressed almost 40 years after the Gregg decision is whether the changes made, which "on their face... seem to satisfy the concerns of Furman (Gregg v. Georgia, 1976, p. 11)," did indeed eliminate arbitrariness and discrimination in the use of the death penalty?

Arbitrariness and the death penalty

Arbitrariness can be found in various forms and at different stages of the death penalty process. It is ironic that Justice Stewart, who voted with the majority and wrote the decision on Gregg that *reinstated* the death penalty, is also the author of one of the most quoted opinions from the Furman decision where he had voted with the majority *against* the death penalty. Justice Stewart had stated in Furman that "these death sentences are cruel and unusual in the same way that being struck by lightning is cruel and unusual. For, of all the people convicted of rapes and murders ... the petitioners are among a capriciously selected random handful upon whom the sentence of death has in fact been imposed" (Furman v Georgia, 1972, p. 34–35). With a stress on its "random" occurrence and "capriciousness" this may be one of the clearest statements of arbitrariness as it relates to the death penalty. But in a different sense "randomness" runs through each of the different types of arbitrariness in that the end product of these various actions can be best described as "random" or "capricious."

Geographic arbitrariness

One form of arbitrariness is a function of geographic variations in the use of capital punishment. In looking at where the death penalty has been used since

1976 it might be surprising to realize that only 2 percent of the counties in the United States have accounted for most of the executions, and 85 percent of the U.S. counties have not had *anyone* executed in more than 50 years (DPIC, Executions by State). More recently, in 2014, *all* of the *executions* came from less than 1 percent of the U.S. counties, only seven states had an execution, and three states (Texas, Missouri and Florida) accounted for 80 percent of the executions (DPIC, Executions by State). Geographically speaking, the North-East has virtually eliminated the death penalty, the Mid-West is making progress, the West uses it very seldom, but the South and South-West are changing very slowly. As of January 1, 2016 Texas has executed 531 people since the Gregg decision, 37 percent of all executions since 1976. Five states, Texas, Florida, Oklahoma, Virginia and Missouri have executed 931 people, 65 percent of all executions since 1976 (DPIC, Executions by State).

Culpability arbitrariness

There are frequently multiple offenders in a murder and it is often the *least* culpable offender that receives a death sentence resulting in "culpability arbitrariness." Offenders with a prior record and experience in the criminal justice system may quickly work out a plea bargain with the prosecutor by casting most of the blame on a less experienced offender who played no role or a minor role in the crime. For example, Patrick Bearup was the only one of four defendants in an Arizona case to receive the death penalty, even though he was not directly involved in killing the victim and was clearly the least culpable. The other three defendants, one of whom instigated the offense, another who beat the victim with a baseball bat, and a third who shot the victim, were all given plea bargains. Two of these participants are likely to be released in five years. A judge who reviewed this case criticized the prosecutor for pursuing the death penalty against a man who "even under the state's theory did not cause the physical death" of the victim, however, the judge did not overturn the death sentence and Bearup is still on death row awaiting execution (Lemons, 2010; Santos, 2013).

Prosecutorial arbitrariness

Political forms of arbitrariness can be found at all levels of the criminal justice system. Prosecutorial arbitrariness is a significant form of arbitrariness and sometimes overlaps with geographic arbitrariness. In 2012 former United States Supreme Court Justice John Paul Stevens said,

> Arbitrariness in the imposition of the death penalty is exactly the type of thing the Constitution prohibits… capital sentencing procedures … (frequently involve) the random or capricious imposition of the penalty, akin to the risk of being struck by lightning. Today one of the sources of such arbitrariness is the decision of state prosecutors – which is not subject to review – to seek a sentence of death. It …may be influenced

by the prosecutor's estimate of the impact of his decision on his chances for reelection or for election to higher office.

(New York Review of Books, 2012)

John Donohue produced a comprehensive and statistically sophisticated report examining the arbitrary and discriminatory manner in which capital punishment had been applied in Connecticut (Donohue, 2013). The study explored the use of the death penalty for 1973–2007. It included all of the 4,686 murders that were committed in Connecticut during this time period. The purpose of the study was to determine whether the system operated in a lawful and reasonable manner without arbitrariness or discrimination affecting the outcome. The findings of this study were instrumental in the Connecticut legislature abolishing the death penalty in 2012.

Donohue says,

> the state's record of handling death-eligible cases represents a chaotic and unsound criminal justice policy. ... (The) death penalty regime does not select from the class of death-eligible defendants those most deserving of execution. At best, the Connecticut system haphazardly singles out a handful for execution. ... arbitrariness and discrimination are defining features of the state's capital punishment regime.
>
> (Donohue, 2013: 1–3)

The major findings of the Donohue study in terms of arbitrariness can be briefly summarized as follows: First, the current death penalty system in Connecticut is very similar to the system in Georgia that the Supreme Court ruled unconstitutional in Furman v. Georgia (1972). Second, the capital-eligible murders in which prosecutors seek the death penalty, and those in which they do not, are not readily distinguishable, they are virtually the same cases. Third, the "worst of the worst" are not the cases selected for execution since many cases that were not selected are equally or even more egregious murders. For example, eight of the nine death sentences handed out were not even on the list of the 15 most egregious cases. Fourth, if the study had focused on all death-eligible murders rather than just those which received the death penalty then the death penalty system would have been shown to be even more arbitrary than that described in the report. Fifth, the regression analysis confirmed the descriptive and qualitative analysis in showing that major geographic differences existed in death sentencing policies and practices across jurisdictions in Connecticut. For example, defendants in Waterbury were much more likely to receive the death penalty than comparable defendants in any other part of the state. Sixth, the regression findings in this study showing that geography is a major determinant of who receives the death penalty are extremely robust in that alternative forms of analysis using different samples and different regression models provided essentially the same results. "Within the class of capital-eligible crimes, these impermissible factors are far more consistent and stronger predictors of capital-charging and sentencing outcomes than are legitimate factors – such as the egregiousness of the crime or the presence of special aggravating factors, which of necessity means that Connecticut's death penalty regime fails to single out 'the worst of the worst' for execution" (Donohue, 2013: 9).

"Geographic arbitrariness" and "prosecutorial arbitrariness" are interrelated, and in small rural counties a third factor, "fiscal arbitrariness" may also be involved. Prosecutors make death penalty decisions based on their own personal beliefs and opinions about the death penalty, and their political ambitions, but in some jurisdictions with a small tax base they have to also consider what the cost of a death penalty case will do to the county budget. Many prosecutors are reluctant to admit that costs affect their decisions about the use of capital punishment, perhaps because of the belief that "you can't put a price on justice," but the reality is that one death penalty case, by itself, can bankrupt most small rural counties (Chammah, 2014). James Farren, the District Attorney of Randall County, Texas recently said, "While … justice is not for sale, if I bankrupt the county, and we simply don't have any money, and the next day someone goes into a daycare and guns down five kids, what do I say? Sorry?" (Chammah, 2014: 2).

Death sentences have declined dramatically at the national level in recent years going from 315 in 1996 to 73 in 2014. The pace of this decline has been even faster in Virginia with death sentences dropping from 10 in 1994 to zero in 2012, 2013, and 2014. In North Carolina they have dropped from 34 in 1995 to 3 in 2014. (DPIC, Death Sentences in the United States From 1977 By State and By Year). There are several reasons for this decline but cost considerations are a major one in many small rural jurisdictions.

> There is every reason to believe that even as Texas retains its reputation as the state most willing to impose the death penalty, the number of actual death sentences will continue to drift downward year by year, remaining only an option for urban counties who can pay for it.
>
> (Chammah, 2014: 8)

Gubernatorial arbitrariness

The Governor plays a role in both the selection of the people to be executed and in the clemency and commutation process. Kubick and Moran studied the relationship between gubernatorial elections and executions in death penalty states controlling for a wide range of variables. They found that states were 25 percent more likely to conduct executions in gubernatorial election years than in other years of the gubernatorial cycle. They also discovered that gubernatorial elections had a larger impact on the probability that black defendants would be executed than on the probability that a white defendant would be executed. They state that the total number of executions conducted is higher in election years than in other years. Furthermore, they found that this relationship between gubernatorial elections and executions also varied by the region of the country and it was strongest in the South where most of the executions occur, once again showing the significance of geographic and prosecutorial arbitrariness. They also say that

> we find some evidence that the existence of politically timed executions reduces the average time that executed defendants spend on death row, which suggests that the increased executions observed in election years may result from an acceleration of the process by which inmates are selected for execution. Taken together, our results indicate that election-year political considerations influence both the timing and racial composition of executions.
>
> (Kubick and Moran, 2003: 24)

An example of how politics might have affected the clemency process is found in Florida. Bob Graham became governor of Florida in 1979. In Graham's first term in office there were six cases considered for execution. Five of the six (83 percent) were granted clemency and their sentences were commuted to life in prison and one of the six (17 percent) was executed. Three reasons were given for the five commutations: one of the five cases that was granted clemency were commuted because of possible innocence; three were commuted because the death sentence was disproportionate in comparison to the sentences of the co-defendants in the case; and one was commuted because the sentence was too harsh for the crime committed (DPIC, Clemency). These are all logical and legitimate reasons why a governor might commute a death sentence to a sentence of life without the possibility of parole (LWOP). In Graham's second term as governor one sentence was commuted early in the term based on possible innocence, but a total of 15 people were executed in this term.

If 83 percent of the cases were granted clemency during the first four-year term of Governor Graham using the three reasons that were given and one was granted early in his second term, one might ask what reasons were given for granting clemency by all of the other governors of Florida in the 29 years since Graham left office? The answer is easy because it is the same for all of the related questions, – *none*! No reason has been given for clemency because no death sentence has been commuted in Florida since early in Bob Graham's second term in office! Although there were legitimate reasons for commuting the sentences of 83 percent of the cases in the first four years, in the next four years of Governor Graham's term fifteen people were executed and one was granted clemency (DPIC, Executions by State; DPIC, Clemency). In total, 90 people have been executed in Florida since anyone was granted clemency although five out of the first six considered had their sentences commuted. One might suggest that these six commuted cases were simply "unusual" and included "special circumstances" and all of the 90 cases since that time were "different," "more heinous," and more clearly deserving of the death penalty, but statisticians would roll their eyes and scoff at the probability of such an occurrence.

Jury arbitrariness

Jurors can be arbitrary in their life and death decisions and as it relates to "death-qualified juries," this is once again related to prosecutorial arbitrariness. Prosecutors have had the option of removing a juror for cause if they were opposed to the death penalty for a long time. Although the process became a little more predictable by virtue of several court decisions placing some limitations on the system, the process is still problematic when it comes to the determination of guilt.

A fairly elaborate study by Cowan et al. examined the impact of death-qualification using a group of 288 adults who met the qualifications for jury service before a Witherspoon exclusion. After watching a video about a trial based on a real case each individual completed a ballot indicating what his or her decision in the case would be. In the death qualified group 78 percent voted guilty to some degree of murder compared to 53 percent of the Witherspoon excludable group who voted guilty, a difference of 25 percent between the two groups (Cowan et al., 1984).

Robert Bohm reviewed the large body of research on death-qualified juries and how they affected death penalty cases and summarized the findings from this research as follows:

> Research shows that death-qualified jurors are less concerned with due process and more inclined to believe the prosecution than are excludable jurors. Death-qualified jurors ... have more misconceptions about the death penalty and the death-sentencing process... Death-qualified jurors are more likely to believe that the focus of the penalty phase of a bifurcated trial should be only on the nature of the crime rather than mitigation, and (they) are more likely to believe that the death penalty deters murder. (Death-qualified jurors) are less likely to believe that innocent people are convicted of capital crimes, that the death penalty is unfair to minorities, and that life without parole really means that a prisoner will not be released from prison. Most troublesome, death-qualified jurors have been found to be more conviction prone.
>
> (Bohm 2012, pp. 48–49)

In other words, the research indicates that the death-qualified jury stacks the deck in favor of conviction and execution, before the first piece of evidence is presented!

Table 16.1 Outcome of death penalty appeals in 6th Circuit Court of Appeals

	For Defendant		Against Defendant	
Republican Appointees				
Ronald Reagan	13	25%	39	75%
George H.W. Bush	4	7%	50	93%
George W. Bush	5	13%	34	87%
Total	22	15%	123	85%
Democratic Appointees				
Jimmy Carter	31	89%	4	11%
Bill Clinton	75	70%	32	30%
Total	106	75%	36	25%

Judicial arbitrariness

While judges can be arbitrary in their individual death penalty sentences, to find an unusual type of "judicial arbitrariness" in the activities of the United States Court of Appeals can be somewhat disconcerting. Apparently, even federal judges with lifetime appointments appear to be affected by politics in making death penalty decisions. An examination by Horn (2007) of the decisions of the U.S. Court of Appeals for the Sixth Circuit on death penalty appeal cases found that these judges voted differently depending on which president had appointed them. Randomly selected three-judge panels of the Court of Appeals normally decide death penalty appeals brought before the court. Sixteen judges are eligible to sit on these three-member panels, with nine republican and seven democratic appointees at the time of this study (Horn, 2007).

Table 16.1 shows that 75 percent of the democratic appointed judges voted in favor of the defendant whereas 15 percent of the republican appointed judges did so. This is a huge 60 percent difference and it seems that life-and-death decisions at this point in the system, which is normally the last level of appeal for most of these cases, often hinge on the defendant's luck of the draw in terms of which judges are selected for their particular three judge panel. A defendant who gets a panel with two of the three judges appointed by a republican president has a far greater chance of being executed than one with two members who were appointed by a democratic president. If, by the luck of the draw, the panel is made up of three republican appointees or three democratic appointees the outcome appears to be a virtual certainty! Nathaniel Jones, a retired U.S. 6th Circuit Court judge said, "It's a roll of the dice. When I look at a lineup of a panel in this kind of case, you can almost go to the bank on what the result is going to be" (Horn, 2007, pp. 2–3). Arthur Hellman, a University of Pittsburgh law professor said, "It looks very much like a lottery. Literally, if someone lives or dies depends on the panel they get" (Horn 2007, p. 3).

Is there racial discrimination in the use of the death penalty?

Research has found that the murderer is much more likely to be charged, convicted and executed if the victim is white. In executions for interracial murders in the United States 93% had a white victim and black defendant (DPIC, Espy Execution File). In Florida, a white person has *never* been executed for the rape or murder of a black person (Radelet, 2001; DPIC, Espy Execution File). In the entire history of the United States *every* rape case that received a death sentence had a white victim and a black defendant (Mandery, 2013 p. 18)!

GAO study

The U.S. General Accounting Office (GAO) reviewed all of the research related to race and the death penalty and found: "a pattern of evidence indicating racial disparities in the charging, sentencing and imposition of the death penalty. In 82 percent of the studies, race of victim influenced the likelihood of being charged with capital murder or receiving the death penalty, i.e. those who murdered whites were... more likely to be sentenced to death.... This finding was remarkably consistent across data sets, states, data collection methods, and analytic techniques" (U.S. Government Accounting Office, 1990, pp. 5–6).

Baldus study

Racial disparity and discrimination occur in virtually all phases of the death penalty process although it may be most egregious in some of the earlier stages. One of the largest and best studies of this period was conducted by Baldus et al. in Georgia and the results were used in the McClesky v. Kemp (1987) Supreme Court decision. The Baldus study examined 2,484 Georgia murder cases from 1973 to 1979, taking into account 230 variables. Baldus used a technique which allowed the researchers to demonstrate the effects of possible explanatory variables (such as the race of the defendant and victim) on outcomes (such as the decision to sentence to death) controlling other variables. Baldus's conclusions were dramatic. Among the most noteworthy: (1) The chances of receiving a death sentence were 4.3 times greater for defendants whose victims were white than for defendants whose victims were black. (2) Of the 128 cases in which the death penalty was imposed, 108 (84 percent) involved white victims. (3) Prosecutors sought the death penalty in 70 percent of the cases involving black defendants and white victims but in only 32 percent of the cases when both the defendant and victim were white. As shown in Table 16.2, when there was a black defendant and a white victim 21 percent of the cases received a death sentence and when both the defendant and victim were white 8 percent received a

Table 16.2 Baldus study of racial discrimination and the death penalty

	% Receiving the Death Penalty	
Black Defendant/White Victim	21%	(50/233)
White Defendant/White Victim	8%	(58/748)
Black Defendant/Black Victim	1%	(18/1443)
White Defendant/Black Victim	3%	(2/60)

death sentence. If both the defendant and victim were black only 1 percent received the death penalty.

The effects of race, however, are not uniform across the spectrum of homicide cases in this study. As might be expected, in the least aggravated cases very few defendants are sentenced to death regardless of race. Also as expected, in the most aggravated cases a high percentage of defendants are sentenced to death regardless of their race or their victim's race. It is in the cases in the middle of the aggravation distribution that race has its greatest influence. In the aggravation mid-range cases death sentences are imposed on 34 percent of the killers of white victims and 14 percent of the killers of black victims. Stating this differently, Baldus et al. said that 20 out of 34 defendants receiving a death sentence for killing a white person would not have gotten the death penalty if their victims had been black instead of white (Baldus et al., 1990).

Justice Lewis Powell Jr. was the swing vote in a 5-4 decision and wrote the majority opinion in Mccleskey v. Kemp 481 U.S. 279 (1987) where the Baldus study results were presented. The majority ruled that although there was clearly racial discrimination in the death penalty system it could not be shown that it directly affected the outcome of this particular case. In other words, unless a defendant can show that there was racial discrimination in their specific case it is irrelevant how much discrimination exists in the death penalty system. After Justice Powell retired his biographer asked him if he would change his vote in any of the cases in which he had participated. "Yes," Justice Powell said, "McCleskey v. Kemp" (Cowan, 2013).

Blume study

Blume et al. reach the same general conclusions as Baldus et al. finding significant disparities based on both race of the defendant and race of the victim. They did an analysis of death row populations in 31 states from 1977 through 1999 and reached the following conclusion:

> Death row's racial disparity, however, is not the result of race-neutral application of the death penalty or a perverse form of affirmative action to favor black defendants. Rather, a racial hierarchy clearly exists. Black

defendants who murder white victims receive death sentences at the highest rate; white defendants who murder white victims receive death sentences at the next highest rate; and black defendants who murder black victims receive death sentences at the lowest rate. The hierarchy stems in part from prosecutors' reluctance to seek death in cases involving black victims, and eagerness to seek death in cases involving black defendants and white victims.

(Blume et al., 2004, p. 167)

Donohue study

The Donohue study discussed earlier in terms of arbitrariness also examined racial discrimination and the death penalty in Connecticut using a sophisticated form of regression analysis. Similar to the Baldus study and the Blume study he found that the death penalty system resulted in racial disparity that did not disappear when controls are introduced for the type of murder, the egregiousness of the crime, and other aggravating factors related to the crime. Donohue also found that capital felony charging decisions by the prosecutor produced additional proof of the racially discriminatory manner in which the death penalty system works. For example, minority defendants who killed whites received more harsh treatment, being charged 25 percent more frequently than those who killed minorities. Donohue emphasized that the regression findings in this study showing that race is a major determinant of who receives the death penalty are extremely robust and varying the forms of analysis and using different samples and different regression models produced similar results (Donohue, 2013).

Racial prejudice and the death penalty

Studies have also been conducted on racial prejudice and the death penalty. Using data from the 1990 General Social Survey Barkan and Cohn examined reasons why more whites than blacks seemed to favor the death penalty in virtually every poll that had ever been conducted. Based on their research they concluded that, "White support for the death penalty in the United States has strong ties to anti-black prejudice....racial prejudice emerges here as a comparatively strong predictor of white support for the death penalty" (Barkan and Cohen, 1994).

Stereotypical 'Blackness' and death sentencing

In a study by Eberhardt et al. photographs of African-American men who had been on trial for murder were shown to a group of research subjects who did not know that these photos were of people who had been on trial for murder. They were asked to rate each photo in terms of how strongly the person appeared to be 'stereotypically black'. The researchers stated that,

> above and beyond the effects of other variables that were controlled, defendants whose appearance was perceived as more stereotypically Black were more likely to receive a death sentence than defendants whose appearance was perceived as less stereotypically Black. (If the victim was white) 24% of those Black defendants who fell in the lower half of the stereotypicality distribution received a death sentence, whereas 58% of those Black defendants who fell in the upper half received a death sentence.
>
> (Eberhardt et al., 2006 p. 384)

In other words, after a real-world conviction more than twice as many defendants who looked "more Black" received a death sentence than those who looked "less Black." "We found that the perceived stereotypicality of Black defendants convicted of murdering Black victims did not predict death sentencing. ... Defendants who were perceived to be more stereotypically Black were more likely to be sentenced to death only when their victims were white" (Eberhardt et al., 2006: 384).

The American Law Institute (ALI)

The ALI is made up of more than four thousand judges, prosecutors, defense attorneys, and law professors, and is the organization that originally developed the Model Penal Code to provide consistent, unbiased, and appropriate punishments for all crimes across states. The ALI developed a model death penalty statute in 1962, (Section 210.6) of the Model Penal Code, which became the model for the new state death penalty laws approved by the United States Supreme Court in Gregg v. Georgia (1976). The ALI recently engaged in a lengthy and exhaustive two-year study of the death penalty process and reviewed virtually every death penalty decision and execution in the United States during this period.

In 2009 the American Law Institute put out the following formal statement related to the death penalty statute in the Model Penal Code. "...the ALI Council.... withdraws Section 210.6 of the Model Penal Code in light of the current intractable institutional and structural obstacles to ensuring a minimally adequate system for administering capital punishment (Liebman, 2009)." The report stated, "Unless we are confident we can recommend procedures that would meet the most important of the concerns, the Institute should not play a further role in legitimating capital punishment" (American Law Institute, 2009: 4).

The ALI worked long and hard at trying to fine-tune the death penalty law but ultimately decided it was an impossible task because the death penalty statute was broken beyond repair. So this prestigious group of lawyers, with combined legal experience of over 160,000 years, did the only responsible thing they thought they could do – they threw up their hands and quit! Michael Traynor, President Emeritus of the ALI said after the decision was announced, "The withdrawal of the model death penalty statute recognizes that it is impossible to administer the death penalty consistently and fairly, and it therefore should not remain a punishment option in this country. The institute could no longer play a role in legitimizing a failed system. How much longer can any of us" (Traynor, 2010)?

Conclusion

The question posed at the beginning of this essay can now be answered. 'Did the Gregg decision overcome the arbitrary and discriminatory use of the death penalty so prevalent in Furman?' Examining all of the research that has been conducted on arbitrariness and discrimination, some of which has been briefly discussed in this chapter, the answer is clearly *no*! Based on this answer, and the answer that would have been obtained if all of the other issues mentioned in the introduction had been examined, the policy recommendation is simple and straightforward; the United States should *abolish the death penalty*.

As a member of the American Society of Criminology for the past 50 years it seems appropriate that the ASC should have the last word: "Be it resolved that because social science research has demonstrated the death penalty to be racist in application ... *the American Society of Criminology publicly condemns this form of punishment, and urges its members to use their professional skills in legislatures and courts to seek a speedy abolition of this form of punishment*" (American Society of Criminology, 1989).

References

American Law Institute, (2009). Report of the Council to the Membership of The American Law Institute On the Matter of the Death Penalty. April 15. Retrieved on July 17, 2014 from http://www.ali.org/doc/Capital%20Punishment_web.pdf.

American Society of Criminology, (1989). Official Policy Position of the American Society of Criminology with Respect to the Death Penalty. Retrieved on December 23, 2014 from https://www.asc41.com/policies/policyPositions.html.

Baldus, David C., George Woodworth and Charles S Pulaski Jr. (1990). *Equal Justice and the Death Penalty: A Legal and Empirical Analysis*, Boston, Northeastern University Press.

Barkan, Steven E., and Steven F. Cohn. 1994. "Racial Prejudice and Support for the Death Penalty by Whites." *Journal of Research in Crime and Delinquency* 31:202–209.

Blume, John, Theodore Eisenberg, and Martin T. Wells. (2004) "Explaining Death Row's Population and Racial Composition." *Journal of Empirical Legal Studies* 1.1: 167.

Bohm, Robert (2012). *Deathquest: An Introduction to the Theory and Practice of Capital Punishment in the United States* (4th edition). Waltham, MA, Anderson Publishing.

Chammah, Maurice (2014). The Slow Death of the Death Penalty. Marshall Project. December 17. Retrieved on December 25, 2014 from: https://www.themarshall-project.org/2014/12/17/the-slow-death-of-the-death-penalty.

Cowan, Claudia, William Thompson and Phoebe Ellsworth (1984). The Effects of Death Qualification on Jurors' Predisposition to Convict and on the Quality of Deliberation. *Law and Human Behavior*. 8, pp. 53–79.

Donohue, John J. III (2013). Capital Punishment In Connecticut, 1973–2007: A Comprehensive Evaluation From 4686 Murders To One Execution. Stanford Law School, National Bureau of Economic Research, June 8. Retrieved on November 14, 2014 from http://works.bepress.com/john_donohue/87.

DPIC, Abolitionist and Retentionist Countries, Retrieved on August 3, 2014 from www.deathpenaltyinfo.org/abolitionist-and-retentionist-countries?scid=30and did=140.

DPIC, Clemency. Retrieved on August 5, 2014 from www.deathpenaltyinfo.org/clemency.

DPIC, Death Sentences in the United States From 1977 By State and By Year. Retrieved on December 26, 2014 from: www.deathpenaltyinfo.org/death-sentences-united-states-1977–2008.

DPIC, Espy Execution File. Retrieved on July 14, 2014 from www.deathpenaltyinfo.org/executions-us-1608-2002-espy-file?scid=8anddid=269.

DPIC, Executions by Race. Retrieved on July 28, 2014 from www.deathpenaltyinfo.org/race-death-row-inmates-executed-1976.

DPIC, Executions by State, Retrieved July 28, 2014 from www.deathpenaltyinfo.org/number-executions-state-and-region-1976.

Eberhardt, Jennifer L.; Davies, P G.; Purdie-Vaughns, Valerie J.; and Johnson, Sheri Lynn (2006). Looking Deathworthy: Perceived Stereotypicality of Black Defendants Predicts Capital Sentencing Outcomes. *Psychological Science*. Vol. 17, No. 5, pp. 383–386. Cornell Law Faculty Publications. Paper 41. Retrieved on September 17, 2014 from http://scholarship.law.cornell.edu/lsrp_papers/41.

Furman v. Georgia 408 U.S. 238 (1972). Retrieved on 3-12-13 from http://laws.findlaw.com/us/408/238.html.

Gregg v. Georgia 428 U.S. 153 (1976). Retrieved on 9-20-14 from http://caselaw.lp.findlaw.com/scripts/getcase.pl?court=USandvol=428andinvol=153.

Horn, Dan (2007). The Politics of Life and Death: An Inmate's Fate Often Hinges on Luck of the Draw. *Cincinnati Enquirer*. April 15. Retrieved on December 22, 2014 from: http://lethal-injection-florida.blogspot.com/2007/04/inmates-fate-often-hinges-on-luck-of.html.

Kubik, Jeffrey and John Moran (2003). Lethal Elections: Gubernatorial Politics and the Timing of Executions. *The Journal of Law and Economics* 46, 1, pp. 1–25.

Lemons, Stephen (2010). Sean Gaines Gets 25 Years in Skinhead Slaying, While Patrick Bearup Remains on Death Row. Dec. 15. *Phoenix New Times*. Retrieved on December 29, 2014 from: http://blogs.phoenixnewtimes.com/bastard/2010/12/sean_gaines_gets_25_years_in_s.php.

Liebman, Lance (2009). "Message From ALI Director Lance Liebman," *American Law Institute*, October 23. Retrieved on September 16, 2013 from: http://www. ali.org/_news/10232009.htm.

Mandery, Evan (2013). *A Wild Justice: The Death and Resurrection of Capital Punishment in America*. New York, W.W. Norton and Company.

New York Review of Books (2012). Justice Stevens on Arbitrariness and the Death Penalty, April 15. Retrieved on December 23, 2014 from: http://standdown.type-pad.com/weblog/ 2012/03/ justice-stevens-returns-to-new-york-review-of-books. html.

Radelet, Michael (2001). Recent Developments in the Death Penalty in Florida. 'Life Over Death' Capital Litigators Training Conference, Florida Public Defender Association, Orlando, Florida, September 7.

Santos, Fernanda (2013). Less Culpable, but with Longer Sentences. *New York Times*, April 5 2013.

Traynor, Michael (2010). The Death Penalty: It's Unworkable. *Los Angeles Times*, February 4. Retrieved on October 12, 2014 from http://articles.latimes.com/2010/ feb/04/opinion/la-oe-traynor4-2010feb04.

Corrections and rehabilitation

Part IV

Corrections and
rehabilitation

Introduction

Community corrections

Thomas G. Blomberg, Julie Mestre Brancale, Kevin M. Beaver and William D. Bales

The field of community corrections is broad in scope and has the difficult mission of overseeing offenders in their communities who otherwise could have been sentenced to a period of incarceration in prison or jail. The range of alternatives to incarceration beyond traditional probation has expanded exponentially over the past few decades to include, among others, day reporting, house arrest, and electronic monitoring. The importance of understanding how correctional agencies can improve the outcomes of offenders placed on community supervision is exemplified by the fact that there were more than twice as many offenders serving a community-based sentence from the court or on post-prison parole than in prison and jail combined in the U.S. in 2013. Specifically, there were 4.7 million individuals on community supervision compared to 2.2 million in prisons, both state and federal or jails (Glaze and Kaeble, 2014). Moreover, the vast majority of offenders sentenced to prison or jail have previously been on some form of community corrections and failed. This section includes two chapters that focus on the best available scientific evidence regarding the effectiveness of various community corrections strategies.

In Chapter 17, Edward Latessa and Myrinda Schweitzer provide a comprehensive review of the scientific evidence on the effectiveness of different community correctional programs. The authors argue that while some level of control is important for offenders on community control, research shows that enhancing punishments is not the solution, but rather identifying offenders' needs and providing intensive treatment is critical. The risk, need, responsivity (RNR) principles developed by Andrews, Bonta, and Gendreau are considered the guiding principles that can address both the treatment and control needs of those on community supervision. The community corrections field has largely embraced the RNR principles by assessing offenders' needs using a standardized and validated instrument. Further, research has found positive effects of an emerging practice known as Strategic Training Initiative in Community

Supervision (STICS). The implementation of this strategy involves training officers in RNR principles and appropriate cognitive approaches to changing offender behavior. Offenders supervised by officers trained in STICS had lower recidivism rates compared offenders supervised by officers not trained in STICS.

Chapter 18, written by James Byrne, provides a discussion of specific community corrections strategies and reviews the current state of research evidence relative to their effectiveness. The use of electronic monitoring and intensive supervision probation programs have experienced rapid growth in popularity and application in recent years; however, empirical evaluations have not kept pace with this rapid growth. While the research evidence needs to be updated, these programs may represent an effective criminal reduction strategy if appropriately targeted and implemented in ways that facilitate positive change in the offender. Specifically, Byrne concludes that if the supervision strategy is focused on reducing the risk of failure through various rehabilitative interventions and treatments the outcomes are positive. Additionally, research has shown that the community context and the availability and quality of treatment related resources in a community have a significant effect on the rates of success and failure of different community corrections strategies.

The use of community corrections has expanded in recent years and has gained popularity from policymakers and practitioners as the era of mass incarceration has begun decline. The best available research evidence on community corrections suggests that it can act as a safe and effective alternative to incarceration if the appropriate offenders are targeted and rehabilitative programming rather than mere control are emphasized. As Chapters 17 and 18 document, the effectiveness of community supervision programs depends on the characteristics of the offender, effective implementation of the supervision method, evidence-based staff training, and the blending of treatment and control. Researchers and policymakers should continue to collaborate in the field of community corrections to further expand the use of RNR testing and in the application of treatment and training programs for offenders. The successful completion of a community corrections sentence and long-term reduction in recidivism appears to depend on individualized treatment plans and consistent implementation of programming; each of which can be strengthened by the collaboration of researchers and practitioners.

Chapter 17

Improving correctional supervision

What does the research tell us?

Edward J. Latessa and Myrinda Schweitzer

Introduction

In recent years, increased attention has been given to the need to reduce prison populations, improve re entry programming and reduce recidivism.[1] Given the large number of offenders under probation and parole, it is important that we utilize research-driven programs and practices, yet despite all of the recent attention given to evidence-based practices, moving the field forward remains a challenge. The focus of this chapter is to briefly examine what is already known from the literature about various supervision practices and their effectiveness, and to provide a roadmap for community supervision agencies wishing to utilize the research in becoming more effective. Prior to delving into these matters, there are several caveats about correctional supervision that should be noted.

First, probation and parole supervision is difficult to study and the methodological challenges of evaluating the effectiveness of probation and parole supervision include difficulties in developing comparison groups, use of multiple interventions, sanctions, and programs, contamination effects, defining and measuring success, and the usual limitations associated with evaluating real world programs (Latessa and Smith, 2011). Second, disaggregating the effects of supervision is very difficult since probation and parole agencies often broker out services to community agencies and programs, the quality of which is often unknown at best and poor at worst (Lowenkamp et al., 2006b). Third, the organization, policies, resources, and oversight of probation and parole agencies varies widely from state to state, as do the roles and responsibilities of supervising officers, which not only makes it more difficult to study, but also limits generalizability.

Despite these issues, the body of research has grown dramatically and many scholars believe that quite a bit has been determined about designing more effective programs and reducing recidivism (Andrews et al., 1990b; Antonowicz and Ross, 1994; Gendreau, 1996; Latessa and Lowenkamp, 2006), and that the knowledge and research about this topic can be transferred into practice that allows supervision agencies to effectively manage as well as reduce risk.

The failure of focusing on control

Perhaps the greatest paradox of correctional supervision is the need to balance control and surveillance with treatment and assistance. Over the years, a great deal has been written about the conflict that exists between these seemingly inconsistent goals and the challenges it poses for supervision agencies. As Clear and Latessa (1993:442) wrote over 20 years ago, "it was assumed that probation/parole supervisors were incapable of managing both roles and therefore faced a dilemma." While Clear and Latessa were optimistic that true professionals could resolve this role conflict, during most of the ensuing years since that article was published, researchers have seen probation and parole agencies focus more on control and surveillance than rehabilitation. More recently, however, the pendulum seems to be swinging back toward the importance of helping offenders change their behavior through evidence-based programs and practices.

The search for the magic caseload size

The predominant approach to correctional supervision is the caseload model in which officers are assigned a number of offenders to supervise. While some agencies utilize workload formulas based on risk and/or other responsibilities (e.g. pre-sentence investigations), the issue of the perceived failure of traditional supervision practices because of large caseloads still remains. Oversized caseloads have often been identified as the obstacle to successful supervision and as the refrain goes, "give us a smaller caseload and we will be more effective." Of course, too large a caseload can have serious consequences for the officer and the Offender. While there may be an upper limit, research has not found the ideal number, and certainly not yet one that demonstrates greater effectiveness (at least in terms of reductions in recidivism).

The search for the ideal caseload size has resulted in numerous studies over the years involving what is generally known as intensive supervision. The history of this intervention also reflects the ideological changes in correctional supervision over the years. The first generation of studies conducted in the 1950s and 1960s were designed to test the assumption that decreased caseloads would lead to increased contacts, improved service delivery and more effective treatment which would then result in reductions in recidivism (Adams, 1967; Latessa and Smith, 2011). There were critics of this research because it did not show the desired outcomes (Adams et al., 1971). Unfortunately, as a result the search for the ideal caseload size seemed to wane.

The large increases in the prison population in the 1980s brought a renewed interest in intensive supervision. However, rather than focus on improving services and reducing recidivism, this rendition was designed to divert higher-risk offenders from prison and to keep them out by significantly increasing contacts and surveillance. In other words, this involved using specific deterrence and punishment to change offender behavior. The second generation of ISP programs are perhaps best exemplified by the Georgia model, where caseloads were reduced even further and two officers were assigned supervision tasks; one traditional probation officer and the other a "surveillance" officer (Erwin and Bennett, 1987). Unlike the earlier studies, this model was clearly focused on control and the underlying belief that ratcheting up surveillance would deter offenders, reduce the prison population, and reduce recidivism. It did none of the above.

Perhaps the study that had the greatest effect on ISP was a randomized study of intensive supervision programs across multiple sites conducted by Petersilia and Turner (1993). They concluded that their findings were consistent with other studies of ISP and that intensive supervision alone was not effective in reducing recidivism.

In response to the growing body of research that found that ISP was not effective in reducing recidivism, the American Probation and Parole Association advocated a more balanced approach that sought to shift the emphasis from a deterrence punitive approach to one that integrated treatment and risk control measures (APPA, nd.). Unfortunately, a randomized study of this model in two states found no significant reductions in recidivism (Latessa et al., 1998).

In summarizing the research on ISP, Latessa et al. (1998) concluded:

- ISP has not been effective in reducing prison populations.
- Most ISP studies have found no significant differences between recidivism rates of ISP offenders and offenders of comparison groups.
- Most studies have not found a relationship between caseload size or number of contacts and effectiveness.
- ISP can often lead to increased technical violations.

Use of technology

Technology has also played a role in the search for other specific deterrence approaches to change offender behavior. Advances in drug testing, electronic monitoring and GPS tracking have all been advocated as interventions that can help manage offenders and reduce recidivism. Rather than review all of the research that has been conducted on these programs, evidence suggests that they should be treated as tools that can be used as part of a strategy to manage *and* reduce risk. For example, electronic monitoring does nothing to change behavior or to target offender risk factors per se; however, it can be used for low-risk offenders who would otherwise be incarcerated with higher-risk offenders (and have their prosocial attributes disrupted), or for higher-risk offenders that are in treatment and whose whereabouts and associates need to be more closely monitored (Latessa,

2000). Likewise, drug testing can be used to support and monitor treatment compliance.

The search continues

Despite fairly consistent findings that indicate correctional interventions that operate primarily on a punishment/deterrence model without some form of human intervention or services are unlikely to be effective in reducing recidivism, the search for supervision models that can change behavior through punishment and sanctions alone continues. The latest version can be seen in Project HOPE, or what Duriez, Cullen and Manchak (2014) refer to as an intervention that promises "crime-reducing powers." By using what Kleiman et al., (2014) call Swift-Certain-Fair (SCF) punishment to violations, the belief is that offenders will modify their behavior and refrain from future criminal conduct. Furthermore, Kleiman et al. (2014) argue that the SCF approach is an alternative to what they call the expensive and time consuming "assess and treat" model. In other words, why bother applying what has been discovered over decades of studying criminal and human behavior when one could simply punish offenders into compliance. While research on the SCF model continues, it is doubtful if this approach will lead to long-term behavioral change and significant reductions in recidivism. As Cullen et al., (2014:77) wrote: "let the buyer beware."

The problem is the belief that somehow punishment alone will deter offenders from continuing to break the law in the future. The underlying assumptions of deterrence are that the offenders are aware of the sanction, perceive it as unpleasant, weigh the cost and benefits of their criminal conduct, assess the risk and, in turn, make a rational choice to break the law. The problem is that most street-level criminals act impulsively; have a short-term perspective, are often disorganized and have failed in school, jobs, and relationships; have distorted thinking; hang around with others like themselves; use drugs and alcohol; and are not rational actors. While punishment alone may bring about some short-term compliance, and can work with low-risk offenders (most of whom don't need much intervention anyway), there is not much evidence that it will lead to long-term reductions in recidivism with higher-risk offenders (those most likely to recidivate). So how can correctional supervision be more effective?

Reducing recidivism and changing behavior

It is rare to read an article or study today on correctional intervention programs that does not refer to the work of Andrews, Bonta, and Gendreau and the risk, need, responsivity (RNR) principles (Andrews and Bonta, 2010; Gendreau 1996). Through the lens of RNR, scholars and practitioners alike have a framework by which they can better study and understand criminal conduct and as well as the effectiveness of correctional programs. Support for these principles has been demonstrated with remarkable consistency across settings and offender populations (Andrews and Bonta, 2010; Smith et al., 2009).

Risk-need-responsivity principles

The *risk principle* asserts that criminal behavior is predictable using actuarial assessments of static (e.g. criminal history) and dynamic risk factors (e.g. pro-criminal attitudes, peers, and substance abuse). Furthermore, previous research has consistently indicated that the most intensive treatment should be delivered to higher risk offenders (Andrews and Bonta, 2010; Lowenkamp and Latessa, 2004; Lowenkamp et al., 2006a) and delivering too much treatment to low-risk offenders may result in increased recidivism (Andrews and Bonta, 2010; Lowenkamp et al., 2006; Lowenkamp et al., 2006b; Lowenkamp et al., 2006c).

The *need principle* highlights the importance of targeting dynamic risk factors, or criminogenic needs, in order to reduce offenders' likelihood of future criminal behavior (Andrews et al., 1990a). These dynamic risk factors are those needs that have demonstrated a correlation to criminal behavior. Criminogenic needs of particular importance are antisocial attitudes, values and beliefs, antisocial peers, and antisocial personality characteristics along with family problems, substance abuse, lack of achievement in education/ employment, and a lack of prosocial leisure activities (Andrews and Bonta, 2010). When criminogenic needs are the target for change, outcomes are consistently positive (Andrews and Bonta, 2010; Lowenkamp et al., 2006b).

Finally, the *(general) responsivity principle* states that effective modes of treatment are those based on behavioral, cognitive, and social learning theories (Gendreau, 1996). These theories focus on how and what the offender thinks as well as make use of key techniques such as modeling, role-playing, and feedback to help the offender develop new ways of thinking and behaving (Spiegler and Guevremont, 2010). Numerous studies have shown the efficacy of cognitive-behavioral interventions with offenders and it is now considered the best approach to changing offender behavior (Lipsey et al., 2007; Lowenkamp et al., 2010). The *(specific) responsivity principle* also suggests that interventions should be tailored to the learning style, motivation level, abilities, and strengths of the individual offender (Andrews and Bonta, 2010). Thus, the *specific responsivity principle* is best met when core correctional practices are used during interactions with offenders. Core correctional practices were first developed by Andrews and Kiessling in 1980 and included five practices (effective use of authority, anti-criminal modeling and reinforcement, problem solving, use of community resources, and interpersonal relationships). Core correctional practices have since expanded to also include effective disapproval, structured learning, cognitive restructuring, and relationship skills (Labrecque et al., 2013).

Real world application of the RNR framework

The correctional treatment literature now contains more than 40 published meta-analyses that consistently demonstrate "what works" (Smith et al., 2009) and the importance of adhering to the RNR framework. In terms of community supervision, the RNR model has made important contributions for *whom* officers target (risk principle) and *what* problem areas they target (need principle). For example, one can rarely find an agency that does not assess offenders' risk to reoffend using a standardized and validated risk tool to identify those higher risk offenders most appropriate for services and supervision (Hubbard et al., 2001). Furthermore, many of these tools include the assessment of dynamic risk factors to help officers identify the targets for change within each offender.

However, as Sperber et al., (2013) poignantly note, knowing which higher-risk offenders should receive more services and supervision in what areas is not the same as knowing how much more service and supervision to provide to higher-risk offenders. Thus, the challenge for community supervision agencies lies within the more subtle aspects of the RNR model – specifically within the areas of dosage and responsivity. How does a community supervision agency ensure that higher-risk offenders receive a greater intensity and duration of quality services compared to lower-risk offenders? Furthermore, what skills should officers' develop in order to target criminogenic need areas using cognitive–behavioral interventions in a way that is most meaningful to each offender? These two questions are perhaps two of the most challenging and least well understood for community supervision agencies. For example, a study of probation in Canada found that officers were not considering the risk level of the offender when making supervision and treatment decisions, nor were they using cognitive-behavioral interventions to target known criminogenic needs (Bonta et al., 2004). Dishearteningly, this study found that officers discussed the offenders' antisocial attitudes in only three percent of the submitted sessions and used cognitive-behavioral interventions less than 25 percent of the time (Bonta et al., 2004).

RNR frameworks for community supervision

In an attempt to implement core correctional practices among officers with offenders in community supervision Chris Trotter (1996, 2006) trained officers in relationship skills, prosocial modeling, effective use of reinforcement and punishment, and problem solving. He then compared the recidivism rates of offenders who were supervised by untrained officers with those supervised by officers who had been trained and found that the recidivism rate for the experimental group was 18 percent lower than the control group over a follow-up period of four years (46 percent vs. 64 percent, respectively) (Trotter, 1996).

To help officers more fully adhere to the RNR model, Bourgon and Bonta, along with their colleagues (2010) developed the Strategic Training Initiative in Community Supervision (STICS) model. STICS is designed to provide a framework for officers to target higher-risk offenders' criminogenic needs using core correctional practices and cognitive-behavioral techniques. The model includes an initial classroom training, ongoing clinical supervision to support skill development, and a refresher workshop one year after the initial training. Officers are trained in the risk-need-responsivity principles, as well as key core correctional practices and mostly cognitive approaches to changing offender behavior. Initial evaluations of the model found very promising results (Bonta et al., 2011; Bourgon and Gutierrez, 2012). The initial study by Bonta and colleagues (2011) found that trained officers spent significantly more time focusing on criminogenic needs and pro-criminal attitudes than untrained officers and significantly less time discussing non-criminogenic needs and conditions of release. This finding shows that the model supports officer adherence to the need principle. Most importantly, the results indicated that offenders supervised by trained officers had lower rates of recidivism (25 percent) in comparison with offenders supervised by untrained officers (40.5 percent) during a two-year follow-up period.

In another evaluation of the STICS model, Bourgon and Gutierrez (2012) found similar reductions in recidivism for offenders supervised by officers who used cognitive-behavioral techniques during contact sessions. Officers who discussed pro-criminal attitudes and cognitions had a one-year recidivism rate of 18 percent compared with a 28 percent recidivism rate for offenders supervised by officers who did not discuss pro-criminal cognitions. Similarly, officers who used cognitive techniques reduced their offenders' risk to recidivate by 18 percent.

In an effort to focus on community supervision officers in the United States, researchers at the University of Cincinnati Corrections Institute (UCCI) developed a similar model known as Effective Practices in Community Supervision (EPICS). The purpose of the EPICS model is to teach community supervision officers how to apply the principles of effective intervention and core correctional practices specifically to community supervision practices. The core correctional practices are organized into an overall framework to assist with the application of specific skills within the context of community supervision.

This overall framework, building off of a risk/need assessment tool, assists with the development and implementation of case management plans to target the criminogenic needs of higher-risk offenders. With the EPICS model, community supervision officers follow a structured approach to their interactions with offenders. Specifically, each session includes four components: (1) Check-In, in which the officer determines if the offender has any crises or acute needs, builds rapport and discusses compliance issues; (2) Review, which focuses on the skills discussed in the prior session, the application of those skills, and troubleshooting of continued problems in the use of those skills; (3) Intervention, where the officer identifies continued areas of need and trends in problems the offender experiences, teaches relevant skills using modeling and role-play techniques, and targets problematic thinking; and finally (4) homework, where the offender receives homework to practice the new thinking or skill along with instructions to follow before the next visit.

The EPICS model is designed to use a combination of monitoring, referrals, and face-to-face interactions to provide the offender with a sufficient "dosage" of treatment interventions, and make the best possible use of time to develop a collaborative working relationship. The EPICS model helps translate the risk, needs and responsivity principles into practice. Specifically, community supervision officers are taught to increase dosage to higher-risk offenders, stay focused on criminogenic needs during contact sessions, and to use a social learning, cognitive-behavioral approach to their interactions. The EPICS model is not intended to replace other programming and services, but rather is an attempt to more fully utilize community supervision officers as agents of change.

The EPICS model includes an implementation strategy that consists of training, coaching, and quality assurance. Officers and supervisors are trained in the EPICS model over the course of three days. Following the training, officers and supervisors participate in at least five coaching sessions designed to provide refresher training on key concepts as well as provide a structured opportunity to develop internal quality assurance and coaching mechanisms.

Early evaluations of the EPICS model show that community supervision officers can adhere to the RNR framework and that this adherence is associated with reductions in recidivism. For example, in the initial pilot of EPICS, officers trained in the EPICS model demonstrated a more consistent use of core correctional practices and spent more time targeting criminogenic needs than untrained officers during contact sessions (Smith et al., 2012). In an evaluation of the implementation of EPICS with juvenile and adult offenders in the state of Ohio, 41 officers and 272 offenders participated in a study to examine the impact of the EPICS model on recidivism. This study found that high-risk offenders who were supervised by officers who adhered to the EPICS model during contact sessions had better outcomes compared to offenders supervised by officers who had low fidelity to the model (Latessa et al., 2013). Across all three measures of recidivism – incarceration, new arrest, and technical violation – the offenders supervised by high-fidelity officers had lower rates of recidivism.

A model similar to EPICS and STICS, Staff Training Aimed at Reducing Re-Arrest (STARR), has been developed and applied within U.S. Federal Probation. An initial study of STARR showed that trained officers were much more likely (44 percent) to target criminogenic needs using cognitive-behavioral techniques than those officers in the untrained group (30 percent). The study also showed significant reductions in recidivism (Robinson et al., 2011).

Summary and conclusions

Over the years, we have seen various attempts to improve the effectiveness of correctional supervision. While many of these efforts have focused on control and surveillance, the empirical research clearly indicates that following the principles outlined in the RNR model show the most promise (Trotter, 1996, 2006; Bonta et al., 2004; Bourgon et al., 2010; Latessa et al., 2013). The challenge has been to translate this model into practice. Recently, we have seen the application of these principles and core correctional practices in various models – STICS, EPICS, and STARR – across community supervision. Through 2014, researchers from UCCI have trained over 85 different groups, including juvenile and adult community supervision agencies, state systems, and small non-profit agencies in the EPICS model. While many agencies have made a commitment to adhering to the RNR model, challenges still remain. First and foremost ensuring fidelity to the model is a consistent challenge across sites. This is not surprising given the body of literature that found programs moving toward evidence-based practices often fail to prioritize implementation fidelity (Andrews and Bonta, 2010; Gendreau et al., 2000). Agencies cite many reasons for this, but most agree it is difficult to prioritize the resources necessary to develop a strong internal capacity to ensure long-term implementation of the model by training internal trainers, investing in skill development for internal coaches, and establishing detailed continuous quality improvement measures that include recidivism. For example, many agencies do not have a staff of researchers to assist with data collection or a specific training unit of officers to participate in the training-of-trainers. Thus these tasks fall on officers, supervisors, and other staff members as "additional responsibilities." Related, administrative staff note challenges associated with adjusting caseload assignment to target higher risk offenders and prioritizing officer skill development through coaching, observing or listening to recordings of audio sessions. Other agencies cite philosophical shift as a barrier to implementation noting that some officers still very much align with increased contacts, monitoring, sanctioning rather than proven behavioral change techniques. Despite these challenges, many agencies are committed to the implementation of an RNR model of community supervision and continue to find ways to enhance fidelity.

Note

1 Efforts include the Second Chance Act, Justice Reinvestment, and work being done by the Council of State Governments, PEW, Urban Institute and others.

References

Adams, S. (1967). Some findings from correctional caseload research. *Federal Probation*, 31(4), 48–57.

Adams, W. P., Chandler, P. M., and Neithercutt, M.G. (1971). The San Francisco project: A critique. *Federal Probation*, 35(4), 45–53.

Andrews, D. A., and Bonta, J. (2010). *The psychology of criminal conduct* (5th ed.). Newark, NJ: LexisNexis.

Andrews, D. A., Bonta, J., and Hoge, R. (1990a). Classification for effective rehabilitation: Rediscovering psychology. *Criminal Justice and Behavior*, 17(1), 19–52.

Andrews, D.A., Zinger I., Bonta, J., Hoge, R.D., Gendreau, P., and Cullen, F. T. (1990). "Does correctional treatment work? A psychologically informed meta-analysis." *Criminology*, 28, 369–404.

Antonowicz, D.H., and Ross, R. R. (1994). "Essential components of successful rehabilitation programs for offenders." *International Journal of Offender and Comparative Criminology*, 38, 97–104.

APPA, (nd.) *A New Direction for Intensive Supervision Programs*. American Probation and Parole Association.

Bonta, J., Bourgon, G., Rugge, T., Scott, T., Yessine, A. K., Gutierrez, L., and Li, J. (2011). An experimental demonstration of training probation officers in evidence-based community supervision. *Criminal Justice and Behavior*, 38, 1127–1148.

Bonta, J., Rugge, T., Sedo, B., and Coles, R. (2004). *Case Management in Manitoba Probation*. (User Report 2004-001). Ottawa: Public Safety and Emergency Preparedness Canada.

Bourgon, G., Bonta, J., Rugge, T., Scott, T., and Yessine, A. K. (2010). The role of program design, implementation, and evaluation in evidence-based "real world" community supervision. *Federal Probation*, 74(1), 2–15.

Bourgon, G. and Gutierrez, L. (2012). The general responsivity principle in community supervision: The importance of probation officers using cognitive intervention techniques and its influence on recidivism. *Journal of Crime and Justice*, 5, 149–166.

Clear, T. R., and Latessa, E. (1993). Probation officer roles in intensive supervision: Surveillance versus treatment. *Justice Quarterly*, 10, 441–462.

Cullen, F. T., Manchak, S. M, and Duriez, S. A. (2014). Before adopting project HOPE, read the warning label: A Rejoinder to Kleiman, Kilmer, and Fisher's comment. *Federal Probation*, 78(2), 75–77.

Duriez, S. A., Manchak, S. M., and Cullen, F. T. (2014). Is project HOPE creating a false sense of hope? A case study in correctional popularity. *Federal Probation,* 78(2), 41–56.

Erwin, B. and Bennett, L. (1987). New dimensions in probation: Georgia's Experience with Intensive Probation Supervision (IPS). *Research in Brief,* Washington, DC: National Institute of Justice.

Gendreau, P. (1996). The principles of effective intervention with offenders. In A.T. Harland (ed.), *Choosing Correctional Options that Work Defining the Demand and Evaluating the Supply* 117–130. Thousand Oaks, CA: Sage Publications.

Gendreau, P., and Ross, R.R. (1987). Revivification of rehabilitation: Evidence from the 1980's. *Justice Quarterly* 4, 349–407.

Gendreau, P., Goggin, C., and Smith, P. (2000). The forgotten issue in effective correctional treatment: Program implementation. *International Journal of Offender Therapy and Comparative Criminology,* 43, 180–187.

Hubbard, D.J., Travis, L. F., and Latessa, E. J. (2001). *Case Classification in Community Corrections: A National Survey of the State of the Art.* Washington, DC: National Institute of Justice; and Cincinnati, OH: Center for Criminal Justice Research, University of Cincinnati.

Kleiman, M. A., Kilmer, B., and Fisher, D. T. (2014). Response to Duriez, Cullen and Manchak: Theory and evidence on the swift-certain-fair approach to enforcing conditions of community supervision. *Federal Probation,* 78(3), 71–73.

Labrecque, R. M., Schweitzer, M., and Smith, P. (2013b). Probation and parole officer adherence to the core correctional practices: An evaluation of 755 offender-officer interactions. *Advancing Practices,* 3, 20–23.

Latessa, E. (2000). Incorporating electronic monitoring into the principles of effective intervention. *Journal of Offender Monitoring,* 13(4), 5–6.

Latessa, E., and C. T. Lowenkamp (2006). What works in reducing recidivism. *St. Thomas Law Journal,* 3, 415–426.

Latessa, E., and Smith, P. (2011). *Corrections in the Community.* Cincinnati: Anderson Publishing.

Latessa, E., Travis, L., Fulton, B., Stichman, A. (1998). *Evaluating the Prototypical ISP.* Cincinnati: Center for Criminal Justice Research, University of Cincinnati.

Latessa, E., Smith, P., Schweitzer, M., and Labrecque, R. (2013). Evaluation of the Effective Practices in Community Supervision model (EPICS) in Ohio. Center for Criminal Justice Research, University of Cincinnati.

Lipsey M.W., Landenberger, N.A., Wilson, S.J. (2007). Effects of cognitive-behavioral programs for criminal offenders. Campbell Systematic Reviews 2007:6 DOI: 10.4073/csr.2007.6.

Lowenkamp, C.T. and Latessa, E.J. (2004). Understanding the risk principle: How and why correctional interventions can harm low risk offenders. *Topics in Community Corrections,* 3–8. National Institute of Corrections, Washington, DC.

Lowenkamp, C.T., Latessa E.J. and Holsinger (2006a). The risk principle in action: What have we learned from 13,676 offenders and 97 correctional programs? *Crime and Delinquency,* 51, 1–17.

Lowenkamp, C., T., Latessa, E., and Smith, P. (2006b). Does correctional program quality really matter? The impact of adhering to the principles of effective intervention. *Criminology and Public Policy,* 5, 575–594.

Lowenkamp, C.T., Pealer, Smith and Latessa (2006c). Adhering to the risk and need principles: Does it matter for supervision-based programs? *Federal Probation*, 70(3), 3–8.

Lowenkamp, C.T., Flores, A.W., Holsinger, A.M., Makarios, M.D., Latessa (2010). Intensive supervision programs: Does program philosophy and the principles of effective intervention matter. *Journal of Criminal Justice*, 38, 368–375.

Petersilia, J., and Tuner, S. (1993). Evaluating intensive supervision probation/ parole: Results of a nationwide experiment. *Research in Brief*, Washington, DC: National Institute of Justice.

Robinson, C. R., Vanbenschoten, S., Alexander, M., and Lowenkamp, C. T. (2011). A random (almost) study of staff training aimed at reducing re-arrest (STARR): Reducing recidivism through intentional design. *Federal Probation*, 75 (2), 57–63.

Smith, P., Gendreau, P., and Swartz, K. (2009). Validating the principles of effective intervention: A systematic review of the contributions of meta-analysis in the field of corrections. *Victims and Offenders*, 4, 148–169.

Smith, P., Schweitzer, M., Labrecque, R. M., and Latessa, E. J. (2012). Improving probation officers' supervision skills: An evaluation of the EPICS model. *Journal of Crime and Justice*, 35, 189–199.

Sperber, K., Latessa, E., and Makarios, M. (2013). Examining the interaction between level of risk and dosage of treatment. *Criminal Justice and Behavior*, 40, 338–348.

Spiegler, M. D., and Guevremont, D. C. (2010). *Contemporary behavior therapy* (5th ed.). Belmont, CA: Wadsworth.

Trotter, C. (1996). The impact of different supervision practices in community corrections: Cause for optimism. *Australian and New Zealand Journal of Criminology*, 29, 1–18.

Trotter, C. (2006). *Working with involuntary clients: A guide to practice* (2nd ed.). Thousand Oaks, CA: Sage.

Chapter 18

Smart sentencing revisited

Assessing the policy/practice implications of research on electronic monitoring and other intermediate sanctions

James M. Byrne

Introduction: intermediate sanctions as a "smart" sentencing strategy

This chapter provides an overview of a group of sentencing options that have been referred to as *intermediate* sanctions, because they offer judges, sentencing commissions, and corrections managers a middle ground between a sentence to traditional probation on the one hand, and incarceration on the other. Intermediate sanctions were first introduced in the late 80s and early 90s as "smart sentencing" strategies(Byrne et al., 1992); and recently, the National Institute of Justice has funded a variety of community corrections initiatives under the heading "smart probation," which flow directly from more recent reviews of the evaluation research on the implementation and impact of intermediate sanctions over the past three decades (e.g. Byrne, 2009). A variety of intermediate sanctions can be identified, including electronic monitoring programs, intensive probation supervision programs, boot camps, residential community corrections programs, split sentencing, day reporting centers, day fines, and community service (Byrne and Taxman, 2005). While national estimates on the utilization of intermediate sanctions certainly vary, it appears that a conservative estimate of the percentage of all offenders sentenced to an intermediate sanction program (front end and back end) is about 10 percent of the current community corrections population (Miofsky and Byrne, 2012).

The focus of this chapter is on intermediate sanctions, but it is important to keep in mind that probation remains the sanction of choice in the United States; it is also the most effective sanction that we have available, assuming that our measure of effectiveness is short-term recidivism reduction. However, long-term declines in the percentage of sentenced offenders who successfully complete their probation terms without committing a new crime or violating a condition of probation can be identified, with success rates falling from over 80 percent in most jurisdictions in the late 60s and early 70s to just over 60 percent today (Byrne and Miofsky, 2009; 2012).

Similarly, researchers have documented the unacceptably high failure rates of offenders receiving prison and jail sentences, which have been stable during this same period (Rosenfeld, 2008). One reason for the drop in overall probation success rates may be increased probation caseloads and the corresponding reduction in time spent interacting with offenders. Over the past 20 years, we have responded to probation crowding by reducing our reliance on active probation supervision, opting instead for either administrative supervision or the use of various electronic reporting mechanisms, such as reporting kiosks (Harris and Byrne, 2007). In 2000, 76 percent of all probationers in the United States were actively supervised; by 2008, the percentage of all probationers on active supervision dropped to 71 percent (Glaze and Bonczar, 2009).

It is in this context of increased demand and diminishing returns from both traditional probation and prison/jail sentences that the potential expansion of intermediate sanctions can and should be viewed. The question is: what does an independent, objective review of the available research on the effectiveness of intermediate sanction reveal? Should current intermediate sanctions strategies be expanded? Or do we need to move sentencing policy in a new direction by developing a new generation of smart sentencing strategies?

The target population for intermediate sanctions: risk vs. stakes

Intermediate sanctions have been a topic of much debate over the past three decades, and there is still disagreement regarding the appropriate target population for these sanctions. It should be recognized that given the target population selected, the necessary key components of intermediate sanctions programs are likely to vary from jurisdiction to jurisdiction. Currently, intermediate sanctions programs target two very distinct offender populations: low-risk, but high-stakes offenders and high-risk, but low-stakes offenders. To the extent that intermediate sanctions are targeting prison-bound offender populations, there seems to be a need to demonstrate that the sanction represents more punishment (and control) than a typical probation sanction. In these instances, offenders placed in intermediate sanctions programs can often be described as *high-stakes* offenders (e.g. sex offenders). When sentencing high-stakes offenders, the probability of recidivism is less important to decision makers than the possibility of recidivism. For these offenders, the surveillance and control features of intermediate sanctions are critical, despite the fact that these offenders often pose very low recidivism risks.

In addition to punishment/control, there is another often mentioned goal associated with the development of intermediate sanctions: risk reduction. To achieve this goal, probation systems complete risk assessments for probationers and the subgroup of high-risk offenders is targeted for place-ment in an intermediate sanction program. According to a recent national review, about 20 percent of the current community corrections population can be classified as high risk to recidivate, while 50 percent fall into the medium-risk and 30 percent low-risk categories (Byrne, 2009). This sub-group of high-risk offenders is specifically targeted for placement in an intermediate sanction program in order to reduce the risk that he/she will commit a new crime. For these offenders, the focus of intermediate sanc-tions programs is on risk reduction through offender lifestyle change (e.g. in the areas of employment, substance use, negative peer associations, etc.). Since the risk of violence while under community supervision is both very low and very unpredictable, it is the risk of offenders committing property crime and/or drug crimes that program developers are primarily attempting to control. The question is: how do we develop strategies that change anti-social lifestyles? Some observers argue that offender lifestyle change is more likely if we focus on surveillance and control (Farabee, 2005), while others argue that offender change is more likely if we focus on offender engage-ment and treatment provision (Cullen, 2007). As the following review demonstrates, the surveillance vs. treatment debate fails to address a key research finding: neither strategy has been demonstrated to be effective by itself. Finding the elusive tipping point between control and treatment is critical, and it will likely guide the development of the next generation of community corrections programs in the United States.

Electronic monitoring

One of the interesting developments in community corrections over the past 25 years (1990–2015) is that as community corrections populations have expanded, the percentage of offenders placed in electronic monitoring pro-grams has remained remarkably low. The most recent national figures on the number of available electronic monitoring devices (GPS and RF) suggest that there were approximately 200,000 electronic monitoring devices avail-able for use monitoring the 4,751,400 persons on probation or parole at year end 2013. Nationally, only 4.2 percent of the community supervision population can be supervised via electronic monitoring, which is about the same proportion of units available in 1990. This raises an obvious ques-tion: why have we not expanded our reliance on this technology? One pos-sible explanation is that the evaluation research conducted on the impact of these programs does not support a policy of widespread utilization (MacKenzie, 2006). However, reviews of this body of research are inconclu-sive (see e.g. Renzema and Mayo-Wilson, 2005; Harris and Byrne, 2007), due in large part to the wide variation in: (1) target populations (drunk drivers, sex offenders, low-risk offenders, high-risk offenders); (2) the pro-grams lumped together in these systematic reviews (short-term surveillance focused vs. programs with separate treatment components); and (3) the overall poor quality of both the programs and the evaluations completed to date (Byrne, 2009; DeMichele, 2014). In their 2005 systematic review of electronic monitoring programs for the Campbell Collaborative, Renzema and Mayo-Wilson (2005: 233) offered the following assessment of the policy implications of the evaluation research they systematically reviewed:

> If E.M. continues to be used as it has been used, shortsighted governments will continue to waste taxpayer dollars for ideological reasons and political gain. Governments that choose to use E.M. in the future ought to use it to enhance other services that have a known effect on crime reduction. Those governments *must* test the marginal effects of E.M., publish the results, and discontinue use of E.M. if it fails to provide quantifiable public benefits. Money spent on E.M. could be spent on empirically tested programs that demonstrably protect our communities.

As Corbett and Marx (1991) commented over 25 years ago, electronic monitoring can most aptly be described as a technology (still) in search of a program. However, there are positive developments to report, particularly in the integration of the treatment and control components of electronic monitoring programs. Gable and Gable (2005) have advocated the use of technology to promote change within a cognitive-behavioral framework. In a similar vein, Pattavina and colleagues (2009; 2010) have argued that the emerging field of persuasive technology (or captology) offers a mechanism for using EM technology in conjunction with cognitive-behavioral treatment strategies. They offer three examples of technology-based applications that can be used to support offender transformation: E-Treat, Ann-e, and the Methamphetamine Remote Recovery Project. Similarly, DeMichele (2014) recently called for a new round of experimental research on community supervision strategies that utilize electronic monitoring as one component in a cognitive transformation strategy. However, De Michele emphasized the limits of electronic monitoring – and by extension, any supervision program or strategy – as an offender transformation strategy: "Currently, what little we know about the lived experience of supervision is negative; individuals dodge supervision officers, are harassed by law enforcement, and have little hope for their future (Goffman, 2009). The intensions here are not to sound the 'nothing works' bell; I am suggesting that we cannot put all our hope into one tool to determine whether it works. Future research should focus on how electronic monitoring contributes to overall cognitive transformations to shape prosocial trajectories." (p. 398)

While the evaluation research on the effectiveness of the current generation of electronic monitoring programs is too limited to draw definitive conclusions, there is some recent evidence that electronic monitoring can be utilized as one component of an effective community control program targeting high-risk offenders (see, e.g. Bales et al., 2010, for a study of the impact of electronic monitoring in Florida; or Turner et al., 2015, for a study of the impact of electronic monitoring with high-risk sex offenders in California). Although we are still searching to find the appropriate mix of control and treatment in these programs, it does seem that if targeted correctly and designed and implemented in ways that support positive transformation, electronic monitoring programs may represent one piece in the desistance puzzle. The key may be to view electronic monitoring technology as support rather than surveillance technology; in this regard, it may be that the positive mentoring relationship that develops between the officer and the offender in the *process* of using this technology that is the most critical component of the next generation of electronic monitoring programs.

Intensive probation supervision

The term "intensive supervision" has been applied in different ways in jurisdictions across the country, but it generally refers to a supervision strategy with four key components: (1) quantity of supervision, (2) style (or quality) of supervision, (3) enforcement of conditions, and (4) response to violations. Since many intensive supervision programs have access to electronic monitoring for at least a portion of their intensive supervision population, it is difficult to distinguish these two sanctioning options. In terms of supervision quantity, intensive supervision programs are designed to provide closer contact between the offender and the probation officer than traditional probation. This component of intensive supervision requires smaller caseloads, especially if electronic monitoring is not a component of the intensive supervision strategy. One facet of smaller caseloads and closer contact between offenders and probation officers is the relationship that develops through this type of engagement (Byrne, 2009). To the extent that this relationship is positive and supportive of individual offender transformation, it could be viewed as a crucial informal social control mechanism (Byrne and Taxman, 2005). However, we have not focused on the impact of the relationship dimension in these intensive supervision programs, especially comparing the effects of people (smaller caseloads as an opportunity to improve informal social controls) vs. thing (e.g. electronic monitoring) technology.

A recent review of the research on the impact of smaller caseloads on probation outcomes conducted by Gill (2010) is worth considering here. Gill identified 14 separate research studies that examined the impact of reduced caseload size on adult probation outcomes: eight studies linked smaller caseload size and increased contacts to higher re-arrest rates, while six linked smaller caseload size and increased contacts to lower re-arrest rates. However, the studies varied considerably in the size of the difference between experimental and control groups in caseload size. In one study, for example, the comparison was 15:1 experimental group vs. 90:1 control group; in another study, the comparison was 20:1 experimental vs. 45:1 control. In terms of this component of intensive probation supervision, it appears that the necessary research has not yet been done.

In terms of style of supervision, much variation is again found from program to program, but in most instances, the supervision strategy is geared toward risk reduction through interventions targeting offender needs in the area of substance abuse, mental health, and employment. In these programs, it is the responsibility of the probation officer to assess the offender's treatment needs, and then to link the offender to the appropriate treatment provider (a classic brokerage model). Evaluation research on the impact of supervision style/quality on offender change supports this component of intensive supervision (Taxman, 2008; Byrne, 2009; Taxman and Pattavina, 2013).

A third component found in intensive supervision programs is more consistent enforcement of conditions. It is anticipated that probation officers will monitor compliance with the conditions of intensive supervision more closely than they would for offenders placed on regular probation supervision. The fourth component of intensive probation supervision is judicial response to technical violations of intensive probation supervision. It can be argued that certainty of judicial response to technical condition violations can potentially act as a specific deterrent. Indeed, this is the argument made by advocates of the Hawaii Project HOPE, where it was reported that increasing the certainty of judicial response to non-compliance with the condition of remaining drug free while on probation resulted in remarkable reductions in drug use, recidivism, and the total time subsequently served in prison (Kleimen, 2009). A multi-site replication RCT evaluation is currently underway, but that has not slowed the development of a new wave of deterrence focused, HOPE-inspired intensive supervision programs in several states (Byrne, 2013).

The essential policy debate regarding this component of intensive supervision can be capsulated as follows. Advocates of treatment-focused interventions for offenders with substance abuse and mental health problems argue that addiction is a disease that requires treatment; advocates of enforcement/control focused interventions for offenders argue that addiction is a choice, and that offender change in decision making can be altered for many substance-using offenders without treatment. Who is correct? While we must await the results of the HOPE replication studies before offering a definitive assessment, it is interesting to note the results of a review of the early research on this issue, conducted by Robert Martinson and colleagues (1976). In the intensive supervision evaluation(see table 1) cited by Martinson,

> the threat of prison resulted in a higher level of compliance with the rehabilitative aspects of intensive supervision, which in turn led to lower

Table 18.1 Success and failure rates for experimentals and controls in percentages by region and risk category (California Special Intensive Parole Unit Studies - SIPU)

Risk Level	Northern Region				Southern Region			
	Experiment		Control		Experiment		Control	
	success*	failure**	success*	failure**	success*	failure**	success*	failure**
Poor Risk	28.0	37.6	26.3	39.9	21.7	30.8	22.7	32.5
Medium-Poor	35.6	29.9	27.9	36.7	35.9	21.1	32.6	27.5
Medium-Good	47.3	28.4	36.5	33.7	44.2	22.5	35.5	26.4
Good Risk	64.3	17.9	59.6	20.2	62.0	11.6	61.2	14.5
Overall†	44.6	28.0	37.2	32.7	40.2	21.7	37.2	25.6

* Success rate defined as the no-arrest rate: one year follow-up period.
** Failure rate defined as the return-to-prison rate.
† differences between the success rates of exp. and control groups are significant (p <.05) only in the *Northern* region
(*source*: Adapted from Lipton et al., 1975:122, Table 8).

recidivism. In other words, the deterrent component of intensive supervision may have had an indirect effect on recidivism through increased compliance with the treatment component of the program. Thus, the results of the early round of intensive supervision programs... suggest that probation and parole policymakers need to develop supervision programs which attempt both to rehabilitate and deter. They certainly do not reveal any glaring flaw in the rehabilitation strategy which would justify the abandonment of this approach to community corrections.

(Miofsky and Byrne, 2012, p. 344)

While there are no systematic, evidence-based reviews of the overall impact of intensive probation supervision available from the Campbell Collaborative, a number of detailed reviews of this body of intensive probation supervision research have been completed (see, e.g. MacKenzie, 2006; Byrne, 2009). These reviews offer strong support for the following two policy recommendations: (1) surveillance-focused intensive probation supervision programs do not reduce recidivism when compared to either probation or prison/jail; (2) the subgroup of intensive supervision programs that focus resources on individual offender treatment – in conjunction with increased surveillance and control – did demonstrate significant, albeit small, overall reductions in recidivism using standard follow-up procedures (1, 2, 3 year re-arrests or reconvictions).

One model of intensive probation supervision that has been advocated in recent years as a "smart probation" strategy by the National Institute of Justice has been referred to as "maximum impact" probation. Jurisdictions develop programs that target high-risk offenders (based on risk assessment), high-risk times for failure (the first few months under supervision), and high-risk places (communities with high levels of concentrated disadvantage, i.e. poverty pocket, high crime areas). While targeting resources in this manner may have a positive impact on offenders and communities, high quality external evaluations of the effectiveness of this new generation intensive supervision strategy have not been completed to date.

One of the underlying assumptions of the Risk, Need, Responsivity (RNR) model popular these days in community corrections is the assumption that probation (and parole) agencies need to target limited resources on high-risk offenders if managers want to maximize community protection for the cohort of offenders under community supervision. Since these offenders are much more likely to re-offend in the first few months of supervision, it may make sense to frontload supervision and resources to these first few "at risk" months. And finally, there is a growing body of research on the importance of place: high crime, high disadvantage communities have a negative impact on offenders that need to be recognized by probation managers, and incorporated into supervision strategies. As I have argued in an earlier review:

We need to evaluate the impact of supervising higher risk offenders using: (1) smaller caseloads, (2) new supervision strategies that emphasize the importance of the relationship that develops between probation officers and probationers in terms of informal social control; and (3) employ new technological innovations for monitoring offenders' movements, drug and alcohol consumption, and progress in treatment

(Byrne, 2009).

However, it is an open question whether we might actually get an even greater overall crime reduction effect if we provided these resources to *medium* rather than high-risk offenders in these same communities. After all, high-risk offenders have very high predicted failure rates, and due to a variety of factors (substance use, mental health, education and employment deficits, location in a high-risk community), they may be less likely to change than medium-risk offenders. One strategy designed to answer this type of question involves the use of simulation modeling techniques to estimate the potential impact of competing policies on corrections outcomes (such as cost, recidivism reduction, and the size of our prison and community corrections system (see e.g. Taxman and Pattavina, 2013).

Boot camps

A third intermediate sanction that has received considerable attention is sentencing adult offenders to a short, but intense, period of incarceration in a setting apart from the state's prison or jail. These boot camp programs – popular through the early 90s in the United States – were typically designed to last from 3 to 6 months, and participation in the boot camp was voluntary. If an offender did not want to participate in a boot camp, that offender would be sentenced using a standard prison sentence. In most programs, offenders were looking at the following choice: a 3–6 month boot camp vs. a 3–5 year prison sentence. While the original boot camp model incorporated many of the elements of a military boot camp, it should be noted that these programs varied considerably, not only in their use of military boot camp features, such as marching and exercise, and group work assignments, but also in the amount of time devoted to education and treatment. While the overall results of the evaluation research supported the conclusion that military-style boot camps were an ineffective sentencing strategy (MacKenzie, 2006), a closer review of these early studies reveals that the treatment-focused boot camp models had the best outcomes in terms of recidivism reduction, especially when the comparison group was prisoners rather than probationers.

It has recently been argued that there may indeed be empirical support for a *therapeutic* boot camp, especially when one considers the evaluation research that compares the traditional prison experience (including longer time served) to the experiences of offenders in these therapeutic boot camps: offenders in the therapeutic boot camps had more positive views of justice system legitimacy than offenders sent to prison (Franke et al., 2010). To the extent that positive changes in offenders' perceptions of justice and legitimacy are viewed as a key step in the identity transformation process, it may make sense to revisit the newer versions of the 1990s boot camp. While the USA has been slow to move back in this direction, other countries are moving to develop boot camp style programs, often targeting young adult offenders. In Australia, for example, the negative evaluation research on the impact of boot camps on adult offenders has not stopped policymakers from designing boot camp programs targeting young adult and juvenile offenders.

Split sentencing

Most discussions of intermediate sanctions do not mention the use of a split sentence as a possible intermediate sanction. Indeed, the utilization of split sentences was not included in the estimates of the size of the intermediate sanction offender population included at the outset of this chapter. However, it makes sense to at least briefly mention this sentencing option. A split sentence is a sentence that begins with a (typically) short period of incarceration followed by a longer period of community supervision; in some jurisdictions, the community supervision portion of the sentence will include placement on intensive supervision, but this is not always the case. According to a recent review, in 2012 almost 20 percent of all offenders under community supervision were identified as split sentence offenders; by comparison, in 1995, only 13 percent of all offenders on probation had received split sentences (Miofsky and Byrne, 2012).

Based on these estimates, the split sentence sanction can be described as the most often used – and fastest growing – intermediate sanction in the United States today. We are using this sentencing strategy more now than in the past. What is the reason for the increased popularity of this sanction? The answer will not be found in a review of the evaluation research, since the necessary research on the impact of split sentencing has not been conducted. Because the split sentence strategy essentially combines traditional probation with a period of incarceration, it does not represent a stand-alone program, such as electronic monitoring, intensive supervision, or a boot camp. With a few exceptions (Byrne and Kelly, 1989), evaluators have simply not evaluated this intermediate sentencing strategy. Because it is not viewed as a standalone sentencing option, the split sentence is often not included in estimates of the extent of the utilization of intermediate sanctions, including – as previously noted – the estimates offered at the outset of this chapter. Older research on the use of split sentences that include a short period of incarceration (1–3 months) followed by a period of intensive probation supervision (1–3 years) suggests that the prison/jail portion of the sentence does have a short term deterrent effect on offenders upon release, but these effects disappear after one month of post release supervision (Byrne and Kelly, 1989). While preliminary, this research does support frontloading both supervision and services for split sentence offenders, a strategy designed to target high-risk times for re-offending.

Other intermediate sanctions: day fines, community service, and residential community corrections

There are other intermediate sanctions that policymakers in the USA need to consider carefully, including residential community corrections programs, day fines, and stand-alone community service programs. It can also be argued that day reporting centers represent yet another intermediate sanction, but since these programs usually operate in conjunction with local jails as early release mechanisms, they will only briefly be mentioned here (but see Parent et al., 1995). While the USA has generally utilized day fines and community service as conditions of probation, other countries utilize these sentencing strategies as stand-alone intermediate sanctions (Subramanian and Shames, 2013; Illescas and Frerich, 2014). The research on the utilization and effectiveness of these sanctions is generally supportive (Villetez et al., 2006; Villetez et al., 2015), which suggests that the USA could easily reduce its reliance on traditional probation (and needless sanction stacking) by utilizing these alternative sanctions in lieu of both traditional probation and prison/jail sentences (Subramanian and Shames, 2013).

Residential community corrections (RCC) programs can target offenders at various points in the criminal justice process from pre-entry, front-end diversion programs to reentry, back-end early release and/or halfway back programs targeting probation and parole violators. Residential community corrections are also known as halfway houses. Unfortunately, no recent surveys of RCC programs have been conducted, so national estimates of the capacity and key characteristics of these programs (and the offenders who pass through them) are not available for review. Latessa and Travis (1992) estimated that in 1988, about 70,000 offenders were placed in RCC programs nationally, which represented about 10 percent of the prison population that year. There are no comparable figures for the current utilization of the various types of RCC programs in operation, but it appears that the RCC movement has been stagnant in recent years, due in large part to the cost of incarceration (Taxman et al., 2007). The early RCC programs varied in target populations, and key program components, but in general, they all provided needed structure and support for those offenders who met the particular RCC program's selection criteria.

There is no definitive systematic evidence-based review of RCC programs, which limits any discussion of the policy implications of this intermediate sentencing strategy (Blomberg, 2011). However, there is one quasi-experimental evaluation study that has received considerable attention. Evaluation research on the effectiveness of residential community corrections programs in Ohio (Lowenkamp and Latessa, 2005) reveals that these programs can have significant, albeit modest, effects on the post-release recidivism of offenders (approximately an 8 percent overall recidivism reduction effect). The potential policy implications of these findings are straightforward: Rather than relying on incarceration, it may be much more cost-effective to expand our residential community corrections infrastructure nationally. For many adult offenders under correctional control, placement in a residential community corrections program offers a viable, front-end alternative to incarceration; it can also be used as a back-end alternative to incarceration for those offenders with technical violation. However, it would be premature to offer this policy recommendation at this time because the necessary research has not been conducted and systematically reviewed.

Conclusions and policy recommendations

A relatively small proportion of all federal and state offenders (perhaps 10 percent) are currently sentenced to an intermediate sanction program in the United States. Based on the research highlighted in this review, it appears that we can reduce our reliance on both traditional probation and imprisonment by expanding the number of available intermediate sanction programs nationally. Sentencing more offenders to one of these intermediate sanctions will likely reduce the overall cost of our corrections system, while improving overall performance, as measured by recidivism reduction (Taxman et al., 2014). Although the focus of intermediate sanction programs developed, implemented, and evaluated in the United States has been on supervision/control based sanctions (electronic monitoring, intensive supervision, boot camps, residential community corrections), there are other, non-supervision-based intermediate sanctions available for review which have been successfully implemented and evaluated internationally, including day fines, and community service (Subramanian and Shames, 2013; Villetez, et al., 2015). Unfortunately, we typically stack these non-supervision sanctions on top of traditional probation sentences, so it is difficult to gauge their respective potential impact as stand-alone intermediate sanctions in this country. And finally, it is apparent from this review that we know remarkably little about the implementation and impact of split sentencing in the United States, despite the fact that it one of this country's fastest growing sentencing strategies.

There are three major policy recommendations that can be offered at this point, despite the limited scope and overall poor quality of the evaluation research on intermediate sanctions. First, we need to utilize our existing eval-uation research to advocate for an increased array of intermediate sanction/sentencing options for judges to consider; and we also need to expand the discretionary zones (allowing for the use of intermediate sanctions) found in federal and state sentencing guidelines, thereby reducing our reliance on mass incarceration (Byrne and Turner, 2010; Clear and Frost, 2014).

Second, the next generation of intermediate sanctions programs will need to be redesigned to focus on both treatment (individual/community) *and* control (formal/informal) if *offender change* is the primary goal of the sanc-tion. *Community-focused* intermediate sanctions programs – including elec-tronic monitoring, and intensive supervision – will need to increase their outpatient treatment capacity, while also utilizing treatment-rich *residential intermediate sanctions* options (e.g. RCC programs, boot camps) for those offenders requiring more control, structure, and in-patient treatment. As we evaluate this new wave of "maximum impact" intermediate sanction options in randomized control trials (RCTs), we need to conduct an assess-ment of whether targeting the subgroup of high-risk offenders offers greater crime reduction benefits than strategies targeting medium-risk offenders. In a similar vein, we need to investigate the impact of programs targeting both high-risk times and high-risk locations. Regardless of targeting strategy, substantial reinvestment in our treatment infrastructure is needed. We need to increase our capacity to treat offenders in both outpatient and residen-tial treatment settings, while fostering participation in treatment through the creative use of both formal and informal social controls. Since some jurisdictions will be more successful in developing balanced treatment and control-based intermediate sanctions, it is critical to develop performance measures that will allow the public to view both high performance and low performance intermediate sanctions programs (Gawande, 2007).

Third, a careful review of the evaluation research on intermediate sanc-tions highlights the limits of these short-term programmatic interventions, and points to a simple, enduring reality: we cannot expect to change offend-ers (or more precisely, to support positive transformation) without chang-ing the communities in which offenders reside. Program developers need to recognize that even the best designed, and fully implemented interme-diate sanction program will likely have only a marginal effect on the life course decisions of the individuals that pass through the program unless community context issues are identified and addressed (Hipp et al., 2010; Kubrin and Stewart, 2006; Kubrin et al., 2007). For example, a number of recent research studies have focused on the impact of community resource availability, quality, and location on the behavior of offenders under com-munity supervision (Byrne, 2008). Strategies designed to improve treatment capacity in high-risk communities appear to be consistent with the view that you cannot change offenders unless you change the communities (e.g. com-munity culture, community resources) in which offenders reside. It appears that the next generation of intermediate sanctions programs will need to be developed based on this basic social ecological framework.

References

Bales, W., Mann, K., Blomberg, T., Gaes, G., Barrick, K., Dhungaga, K., et al. 2010. A Quantitative and qualitative assessment of electronic monitoring (Final Report submitted to the National Institute of Justice for Grant 2007-IJ-CX-0017). Washington, DC, National Institute of Justice.

Blomberg, T. 2011. Confronting crime with science. *Criminology and Public Policy*, 10(1), 1–2.

Bonczar, T. and Glaze, L., 2009. *Probation and Parole in the United States 2008*. Washington, DC: Bureau of Justice Statistics NCJ 228230.

Byrne, J. M. 2008. The social ecology of community corrections: Understanding the link between individual and community change. *Criminology and Public Policy*, 7(2), 263–274.

Byrne, J. M., 2009. *Maximum impact: Targeting supervision on higher risk people, places, and times*. Washington, DC: Pew Charitable Trusts.

Byrne, J. M., 2013. After the fall: Assessing the impact of the great prison experiment on future crime control policy. *Federal Probation*, 77(3), 3–14.

Byrne, J. M., and Kelly, L., 1989. *Restructuring probation as an intermediate sanction: an evaluation of the Massachusetts Intensive Probation Supervision Program*, final report to the Research Program on the Punishment and Control of Offenders, National Institute of Justice, February, 1989.

Byrne, J. and Taxman, F., 2005. Crime control is a choice: Divergent perspectives on the role of treatment in the adult corrections system. *Criminology and Public Policy*, 4(2), 291–310.

Byrne, J. and Miofsky, K., 2009. From preentry to reentry: An examination of the effectiveness of institutional and community-based sanctions. *Victims and Offenders*, 4(4), 348–356.

Byrne, J. and Turner, S. F., 2010. Reforming Federal sentencing guidelines: A modest proposal. *Victims and Offenders*, 5(3), 220–232.

Byrne, J, and Miofsky, K., 2012. New directions in community supervision: Should we target high risk offenders, high risk times, and high isk locations? *European Journal of Probation*, 4(2), 77–101.

Byrne, J., Lurigio, A., and Petersilia, J., 1992. *Smart Sentencing: The emergence of intermediate sanctions*. Newbury Park, Ca: Sage Publications.

Clear, T. and Frost, N., 2014. *The Punishment imperative: the rise and fall of mass incarceration in America*. New York, NY: New York University Press.

Corbett, R. and Marx, G., 1991. No soul in the new machines: Technofallacies in the electronic monitoring movement. *Justice Quarterly*, 8, 399–414.

Cullen, F. T., 2007. Make rehabilitation corrections' guiding paradigm. *Criminology and Public Policy*, 6, 717–728.

DeMichele, M. 2014. Electronic monitoring: It is a tool, not a silver bullet. *Criminology and Public Policy*, 13(3), 393–400.

Farabee, D. 2005. *Rethinking rehabilitation: Why can't we reform our criminals?* Washington, DC: AEI Press.

Franke, D., Bierie, D., and MacKenzie, D., 2010. Legitimacy in corrections: A randomized experiment comparing a boot camp with a prison. *Criminology and Public Policy*, 9(1), 89–117.

Gable, R. K. and Gable, R. S., (2005) Electronic monitoring: positive intervention strategies. Federal Probation, 1(69), 21–25.

Gawande, A. 2007. *Better: A Surgeon's notes on performance*. New York: Picador, Metropolitan Books.

Gill, C. 2010. The effects of sanction severity on criminal conduct: A randomized low intensity probation experiment. *Publically accessible Penn Dissertations*. Paper 121. Available at: http://repository.upenn.edu/edissertations/121.

Glaze, L. E., and Bonczar, T. P. 2009, December. Probation and parole in the United States, 2008 (Fact Sheet U.S. Department of Justice No. NCJ 228230). Retrieved from Bureau of Justice Statistics website: www.ojp.usdoj.gov/bjs/.

Goffman, A. 2009. On the run: Wanted men in a Philadelphia ghetto. *American Sociological Review*, 74, 339–357.

Harris, P. and Byrne, J., 2007. Community corrections and hard technology. In J. Byrne, and D. Rebovich, (eds.), *The new technology of crime, law, and social control*, (pp. 287–327). Monsey, NY: Criminal Justice Press.

Hipp, J., Petersilia, J. and Turner, S., 2010. Parolee Recidivism in California: The effect of neighborhood context and social service agency characteristics *Criminology*, 48(4), 947–979.

Illescas, S. and Frerich, N., 2014. Crime and Justice reinvestment in Europe: Possibilities and Challenges *Victims and Offenders*, 9(1), 13–49.

Kleiman, M., 2009. *When Brute Force fails: How to have less crime and less punishment*. Princeton, NJ: Princeton University Press.

Kubrin, C. E., and Stewart, E., 2006. Predicting who offends: The neglected role of neighborhood context in recidivism studies. *Criminology*, 44,165–197.

Kubrin, C.E., Squires, G., and Stewart, E., 2007. Neighborhoods, race, and recidivism: The community-reoffending nexus and its implications for African Americans. *Race Relations Abstracts*, 32(1),7–37.

Latessa, E. and Travis, L., 1992. Residential community corrections programs, pp.166–181 in Byrne, J., Lurigio, A., and Petersilia, J., editors. *Smart Sentencing: The emergence of intermediate sanctions*. Newbury Park, Ca: Sage Publications.

Lipton, D., Martinson, R., and Wilks, J. 1975. *The effectiveness of correctional treatment: A survey of treatment evaluation studies*. New York: Praeger.

Lowenkamp, and Latessa, E. 2005. Increasing the effectiveness of correctional programming through the risk principle: identifying offenders for residential placement, *Criminology and Public Policy*, 4(2), 265–290.

Mackenzie, D., 2006. *What works in corrections: reducing the criminal activities of offenders and delinquents*. New York, NY, Cambridge University Press.

Martinson, R., Palmer, T., and Adams, S., 1976. *Rehabilitation, recidivism, and research*. Hackensack, NJ: National Council on Crime and Delinquency.

Miofsky, K. and Byrne, J., 2012 "Evaluation research and probation: How to distinguish high performance from low performance programmes" pp.336–357, in Gadd, Karstedt, and Messner, editors, *The Sage Handbook of Criminological Research Methods* (London, UK: SAGE).

Parent, D. J., Byrne, J. M., Tsarfaty, V., Valade, L. and Esselman, J., 1995. *Day Reporting Centers* Volume 1: *Issue and Practices*. Washington, DC: National Institute of Justice.

Pattavina, A. 2009. The use of electronic monitoring as persuasive technology: Reconsidering the empirical evidence on the effectiveness of electronic monitoring, *Victims andOffenders*, 4, 385–390.

Pattavina, A., Miofsky-Tusinski, K. and Byrne, J. 2010. Innovation in community corrections from monitoring technology to persuasive technology. *Journal of Offender Monitoring*, 23(1), 1–5.

Renzema, M. and Mayo-Wilson, E., 2005. Can electronic monitoring reduce crime for moderate to high risk offenders? *Journal of Experimental Criminology*, 1, 215–237.

Rosenfeld, R. 2008. Recidivism and its discontents. *Criminology and Public Policy*, 7(2), b 311–318.

Subramanian, R. and Shames, A., 2013. *Sentencing and Prison Practices in Germany and the Netherlands: Implications for the United States.* New York, NY: VERA Institute of Justice.

Taxman, 2008. No Illusions:Offender and Organizational change in Maryland's proactive community supervision efforts. *Criminology and Public Policy*, 7(2), 275–302.

Taxman, F., and Pattavina, A., 2013. *Simulation strategies to reduce recidivism: Risk, need, responsivity (RNR) modeling for the criminal justice system.* NewYork, NY, Springer.

Taxman, F.S., Perdoni, M., and Harrison, L. 2007. Treatment for adult offenders: A Review of the state of the state. *Journal of Substance Abuse Treatment*, 32(3), 239–254.

Taxman, F., Pattavina, A., and Caudy, M., 2014. Justice reinvestment in the United States: An Empirical assessment of the potential impact of increased correctional programming on recidivism. *Victims and Offenders*, 9(1), 50–75.

Turner, S., Chamberlain, A., Jannetta, J., and Hess, J., 2015. Does GPS improve recidivism among high risk sex offenders? Outcomes for California's GPS pilot for high risk sex offender parolees. *Victims and Offenders*, 10(1), 1–28.

Villetez, P., Killias, M., and Zoder, I. (2006). *The effects of custodial vs. non-custodial sentences on re-offending: A systematic review of the state of the evidence.* Retrieved June 1, 2009 from www.campbellcollaboration.org/doc-pdf/Campbell-report-30.09.06.pdf.

Villetez, P., Gillieron, G., and Killias, M.(2015). *The Effects on Re-Offending ofCustodial vs. non-custodial* sanctions: An updated systematic review of the state of knowledge. The Campbell Library. Retrieved March 30, 2015 from www.campbellcollaboration.org/lib/project/22/.

Introduction

Incarceration

Thomas G. Blomberg, Julie Mestre Brancale, Kevin M. Beaver and William D. Bales

Depriving an individual of their freedom through incarceration is intended to reduce the likelihood of recidivism after release through either mechanisms of deterrence or rehabilitation. However, as the two chapters in this section document, the scientific evidence does not support either a rehabilitation or deterrent outcome for incarceration in prisons or jails. Further, it is shown that while the policies and practices of local jails are largely ignored by researchers, jails are very consequential to the criminal justice system and our reliance upon incarceration.

Chapter 19, by Bales and Garduno, explores an understudied, yet critically important component of the criminal justice system, namely, local jails. They contend that while local jails are a fundamental component of the criminal justice system, criminologists have largely ignored them in research. Eighteen times more individuals enter local jails than state or federal prisons, jails are significantly more expensive to operate than prisons, and every offender who is ultimately convicted and sentenced to probation, house arrest, prison, etc., is initially housed in a local jail. While we know a great deal about prison-based rehabilitation programs and their relative effectiveness in post-prison recidivism, we know very little about the effect of rehabilitation programs in local jails on post-release reentry outcomes. Bales and Garduno conclude that the potential benefits are significant if we make the effort to conduct extensive research on how local jails operate, the effectiveness of the services and programs they provide, and how we can decrease the numerous admissions to our jails while maintaining public safety. If researchers can inform policymakers on local jail strategies that can reduce re-offending by even a minimal amount, given that over 13 million individuals enter local jails in the U.S. each year, the benefit to future crime victims, the police, courts, and correctional systems' policies and practices would be substantial. Also, it is argued that local, state and federal agencies that currently provide funding for research related to state, and federal prisons, juvenile facilities, and community correctional alternatives to incarceration should also support research on jails.

Chapter 20, by Gerald G. Gaes, addresses a fundamental criminal justice policy question that most citizens, lawmakers, and criminal justice practitioners likely believe they know the answer to: "Does a prison term prevent or promote more crime"? Prior research studies have addressed this question as follows: First, by attempting to determine if imprisonment results in a reduction in the likelihood of re-offending because of the fear of future punishment (is it a deterrent?). Second, by attempting to determine if inmates who are exposed to various rehabilitative programs experience a reduction in their likelihood for criminal offending after returning to their communities. Third, by attempting to determine if putting offenders in prison has a "brutalizing" effect, (are inmates more likely to commit crimes post-release?). This "brutalizing" effect may result because the options available to the offender for a conventional lifestyle are severed, they have learned to be a better criminal while in prison, or they are retaliating against what they consider the injustice of their incarceration. After a comprehensive review of the research literature related to the relationship between imprisonment and re-offending, Gaes concludes that we have inconclusive knowledge and, therefore, any recommendation to policy-makers concerning the effects of imprisonment should be considered premature. Clearly, this conclusion means we should be very critical of the mass incarceration policies of the past as well as any and all future use of incarceration.

The chapters in this section have highlighted two conclusions about the use of jails and prisons. First, while the vast majority of all arrested individuals and convicted offenders spend at least some time in a local jail, there is little research evidence on the impact and effectiveness of jails (Chapter 19). Second, while the amount of research conducted on the impacts and effectiveness of imprisonment is much greater, the results are largely inconclusive (Chapter 20). Despite the lack of scientific evidence, jails and prisons are a frequently used correctional strategy as demonstrated over the past three decades by the U.S. reliance upon mass incarceration. However, given the growing retrenchment from mass incarceration by conservative and liberal policymakers alike, it appears that evidence-based policies that support significant reductions in incarceration rates should receive a much more receptive response from lawnmakers in the future.

Chapter 19

Confinement in local jails

Institutions and their clients neglected by criminologists

William D. Bales and L. Sergio Garduno

Introduction

When citizens, politicians and criminologists discuss the imprisonment or incarceration of offenders as a strategy of crime control, to mete out just punishment, etc., they are virtually always referring to state or federal prisons that have the responsibility of carrying out the judgment of the courts to incapacitate felony offenders for some period of time and hopefully reduce their likelihood of re-offending after release. The argument made in this chapter is that the discipline of criminology has all but ignored a critical component of the criminal justice system that also involves incarceration and – unlike prisons which are essentially the last step in the criminal justice system of law enforcement, courts, and corrections – is the nucleus of our system of justice, i.e. the local jail. One of the authors of this chapter has taught an undergraduate corrections course on numerous occasions and a standard question he asks students during the first day of class is, "how many of you have been or know someone who has been in a state or federal prison?" and only a few students raise their hands. This is followed with the question, "how many of you have been or know someone who has been in a local jail?" In contrast to the first question, a relatively significant proportion of students in the class raise their hands.

More specifically, the present chapter describes the key role local jails play in the American criminal justice system. It also draws to the attention of policymakers, practitioners, researchers, and students alike the fact that, unlike prisons, we have limited knowledge and understanding of the practices and policies within local jails, the types and effectiveness of programs that exist to reduce the likelihood of individuals returning to jail, or the behavioral and psychological effects jails have on the people they host. Anyone sentenced by the courts to some form of community supervision or confinement in a prison or local jail began with serving some minimal time in jail upon being arrested and possibly longer if they were denied pre-trial release or could not pay the required bail or bond to be released pending their court disposition. However, little is known about the effect jails have on arrestees who spend time incarcerated waiting for their court arraignment, prior to a plea or trial, sentenced inmates, and offenders on supervision who are charged with violating the terms of supervision. Specifically, we have largely ignored how jails influence their residents' post-release outcomes, such as their likelihood of recidivism, success in securing and maintaining employment, their ability to obtain adequate housing, etc.

Jails, similar to prisons, house individuals who are serving a period of confinement as a result of a court-imposed sentence subsequent to a criminal conviction. However, in contrast to prisons, individuals who are not convicted of a crime are held in jail prior to the disposition of their criminal case in the court because they are denied release through a surety bond or cannot afford the court imposed bond amount. Additionally, local jails house individuals who are under special circumstances such as pending sentencing, awaiting transfer to a state or federal prison, or those detained due to serious mental health issues. While jails play a crucial role in the criminal justice system, and despite the fact that significantly more people enter local jails than prisons every year, the study of their services, programs, and management has been largely neglected by academics, researchers and policymakers. This chapter will address the need to increase the knowledge and understanding of local jails from a public safety, policy, community, and academic perspective. Such understanding should logically improve the quality of how jails are managed, the safety and security of jail staff and inmates, and the behavioral outcomes of released inmates.

What are jails and how do they differ from prisons?

Jails are institutions that serve law enforcement, the courts, and adult correctional systems. It can be argued that local jail facilities are the hub of the U.S. criminal justice system. Jails are correctional facilities that are administered and locally funded by cities or counties, and usually are the first place individuals are taken after being arrested by the police. In 2006 there were 3,271 local and 12 federal jails across the U.S. (Stephan and Walsh, 2011). Regardless of whether arrestees are convicted and sentenced for a crime to a period of time in a local jail or state or federal prison, they all experience time in a local jail. Since jails are the first step in the criminal justice system process after being arrested by the police, they impact a significantly larger number of people than prisons.

The main difference between jails and prisons is that jails are managed at the local level and not at the state or federal levels of government and traditionally house individuals sentenced for minor offenses to a period of confinement for one year or less. In contrast, state and federal prisons are administered at state and federal levels, and house inmates sentenced to confinement for longer periods of time for serious crimes (Welsh, 1995).

Jails, however, also process and house individuals awaiting arraignment, trial, conviction, and sentencing. Local jails may also host state and federal inmates when prisons are overcrowded, when convicted felons are waiting to be transferred to prisons, or when inmates have to temporarily leave a prison system to testify in a local court. Jails also maintain the custody of individuals who violate their pre-trial release, probation, or parole conditions.

The volume of inmates local jails and prisons receive, release and house

While 744,600 individuals had been incarcerated in local jails in the U.S. by midyear 2014 (Minton and Zeng, 2015), state and federal prisons had housed 1,574,741 inmates in 2013 (Carson, 2014). The number of people housed in U.S. jails increased by 17.7 percent (621,149 to 731,208) from midyear 2000 to midyear 2013 (Minton and Golinelli, 2014) while the change in the prison population was significantly lower from 2003 to 2013 (7.2 percent, 1,468,601 to 1,574,741) (Carson, 2014). State prisons released 581,374 inmates in 2012, which represents an 8.6 percent decrease from 2011, and a 3.1 percent decrease from 2000 (Carson and Golinelli, 2013).

While the number of individuals housed in state and federal prison in the U.S. on a given day is about one and one-half times the number of people incarcerated in a local jail on the same day, the number of individuals entering and exiting local jail facilities each year far exceeds the admissions and releases from the prison systems in the U.S. In 2006, one of the years with the highest number of people admitted to prisons, both state and federal prisons combined reported 747,031 new admissions (Carson and Golinelli, 2013). In contrast, 13.6 million individuals were admitted to jails in 2008 (Minton and Golinelli, 2014). In other words, the volume of individuals entering the confinement of local jails in the U.S. is 18 times the number admitted to state or federal prison. Given that the total populations of all of the U.S. prisons combined and all of the local jails combined do not increase significantly from year-to-year, it is accurate to estimate that a similar number of individuals are released as are admitted to these systems. Therefore, there are approximately 1.5 million instances of individuals entering and exiting state or federal prisons in 2008 and 27.2 million entries and exits from local jails, or 18 times what prisons experience. Despite the fact that millions more individuals enter and exit jails than prisons every year, the vast majority of criminologists who conduct correctional and punishment related research devote all or most of their efforts examining prisons and their inmate populations and a modicum amount of their attention is devoted to the operations of jails, the services they provide, and their effect on inmates during and subsequent to their incarceration.

Comparison of one city jail to the 50 state prison systems

To demonstrate the magnitude of local jails relative to state prison systems from the perspective of the number of people impacted by them, we used 2011 comparative numbers of admissions into and the number of individuals incarcerated in the New York City (NYC) jail system relative to the same numbers in the state prison system of New York as well as each of the 50 state prison systems in 2011. It is important to note that state prison systems count their inmate population based on the number of offenders incarcerated on a given day whereas local jails typically quantify their inmate population based on the average daily population over a given period of time due to the tremendous influx of individuals in and out of the jails. Beginning with comparisons in the state of New York, the data shows that the NYC jail system received 87,515 individuals into their jails in fiscal year 2011 (Schriro, 2013). In contrast, the entire prison system in the state of New York received 23,257 inmates, which is approximately one-fourth the volume of the NYC jail system (Carson and Golinelli, 2013). Additionally, the New York state prison system had a population of 55,436 inmates on December 31, 2011 (Carson, 2014). While the average daily population of the NYC jail system was 87,515 (Schriro, 2013), which is 36.7 percent higher. A final comparison is between the inmate population of the NYC jail system and the population of all of the state corrections systems in the U.S. The data show that the inmate population in the NYC jail system alone of 12,790 (Schriro, 2013) inmates in 2011 exceeded the number of inmates incarcerated in 25 of the 50 state prison systems in the U.S. (Carson and Golinelli, 2013). These comparative statistics across prisons and jails clearly indicate that there is a need for criminologists to pay more attention to jails in their research agendas.

Limited knowledge on jails

A central point of discussion in this chapter is the limited existing knowledge about jails in terms of the populations they serve, what policies and practices exist in jails relative to how inmates are managed, the healthcare, educational, and treatment services provided to prepare them for eventual release back to their communities, and the effect of the jail experience on their post-incarceration life. Additionally, the elements that facilitate a larger flow of people into jails than prisons, and their effects on the police, courts, prisons and probation and parole agencies deserve more attention from researchers and policymakers. Jails' widespread geographic locations, their responsibilities of interacting with all actors in the criminal justice system, and the significant flow of people in and out of these facilities, make jails an institution with a larger and more consequential presence to more people and their communities than prisons.

While we know the number of people who are released from prison to parole and can identify those who go back to prison for a technical violation (Glaze and Kaeble, 2014), we largely ignore if the time spent in jail influences a parolee's willingness to meet with their parole officer. We also ignore the extent to which police departments across the nation plan their patrolling activities in neighborhoods with high levels of released jail inmates. We also know that 56 percent of state prisoners have mental health problems (James and Glaze, 2006), but we ignore whether those mental health problems became more or less severe while defendants were in jail.

From a community perspective, we know that families who have an incarcerated parent are more financially strained than before the offender parent was incarcerated, and it is also believed that children lose involvement with the incarcerated parent (Arditti et al., 2003). However, we do not know the extent to which community-based organizations get funded to provide aid and services to the families of incarcerated parents, or the extent to which time spent in jail affects the emotional bond between the incarcerated parent and his or her children. We also ignore the question whether jailed parents act more or less tolerant, affectionate, aggressive, or impulsive with their children and spouse as a result of their incarceration.

Jails also impact local communities from a public health perspective. For example, it is known that some jails offer HIV testing (Beckwith et al., 2011), but we are unaware of how many jails offer that type of testing or the extent to which jails educate inmates about HIV and its modes of transmission. It is unknown to what extent inmates with HIV receive the proper medical care, or how many interrupt their treatment and develop resistance to some medications while incarcerated. We also have no knowledge of how many HIV positive offenders are aware of their health status, and if they are infecting other individuals while in jail and after their release.

Jails serve as a giant net in which offenders are caught and released multiple times. Some offenders get trapped in confinement for long periods of time in prisons, and some others are released from jail immediately after their arrest. As previously stated, jails have a more dynamic flow of people, more lives are affected on a daily basis by jails than by prisons, and jails have a larger net of community resources to whom they can refer ex-offenders for assistance and services for their reintegration into society. However, most empirical research analyzing different aspects of offenders, such as recidivism (Cochran et al., 2012; Mears and Bales, 2009; Bader et al., 2010; Yu et al., 2015; Bales et al., 2005; Richmond, 2014; Spivak and Sharp, 2008), health care (Baillargeon et al., 2000; Belenko and Peugh, 2005; Proctor, 2012; Horsburgh et al., 1990; Harzke et al., 2009; Bernstein et al., 2015), and mental health (Fisher et al., 2014; Adams and Ferrandino, 2008; Gebbie et al., 2008; Wood and Buttaro, 2013; Houser and Welsh, 2014), focuses on prison inmates, and few studies in comparison focus on jail inmates (Lombardo, 1985; Phillips III and Mercke, 2003; Sturges, 2002;

Tartaro and Levy, 2007; Sturges and Al-Khattar, 2009; Lindquist, 2000; Wilson et al., 2011; Greenberg and Rosenheck, 2009; Teplin et al., 1994).

Services available to inmates in local jails

Taking into consideration that 42 percent of people discharged from parole or conditional supervision return to jail, that 16 percent of jail defendants get re-arrested before their case disposition, and that 62 percent of released state prisoners are re-arrested within three years after their release (Beck, 2000), it is not surprising that jails see the same individuals enter and exit these facilities multiple times. The number of people going back to jail might indicate that the criminal justice system, and that society as a whole, is not doing what is needed to keep offenders from engaging in continuous illegal and deviant behaviors. While offenders are in confinement, the state has a unique opportunity to identify and treat some of the factors that contribute to these individuals' offending. The following paragraphs will describe program characteristics of local jails and address some of their limitations.

The capacity that policymakers and jail administrators have to make informed decisions about best practices to manage jails, implement programs, prepare offenders for their post-carceral life, and reduce their risk of recidivism is largely restricted by the limited knowledge there is about what works and does not work for jail inmates. The inability to offer effective programs and services and help offenders satisfy their needs has directly or indirectly contributed to the current levels of recidivism with the already known consequences for local communities.

Freudenberg (2001) states that jails, the same as prisons, have a great influence on communities, especially among low-income and minority urban neighborhoods. Correctional institutions remove and maintain those individuals away from communities who pose a threat to public safety, who are violent, who suffer from substance abuse and addiction, mental illnesses, and infectious diseases. On the other hand, however, correctional systems have the ability to improve the health of urban populations by providing offenders with health care while in confinement, by linking inmates to community services after release, and by assisting ex-offenders in the process of community reintegration. Jail inmates, similar to prison inmates, are a population in need of vocational, mental health, substance abuse treatment, and health and educational services (Petersilia, 2003). While some local jails offer services to help inmates transition successfully into a life out of confinement, the scope, quality and amount of services provided is likely to vary greatly by state, and even by counties within the same state.

Job training and education

The lack of education and job training is prevalent among jail inmates. According to Harlow (2003), only 40 percent of jail inmates in 1997 had a high school diploma or GED. Offenders with low levels of education and job skills will go back to their communities and, in addition to their low literacy level problem, they will encounter reduced wages and the limited legitimate employment opportunities that come with the stigma of a criminal conviction (Western, 2007). Despite the common problem of low job skills among offenders, only 46 percent of jails nationwide offered a work release or pre-release program in 2006 (Stephan and Walsh, 2011). The opportunity for jail inmates to receive a work program would likely be beneficial to them during and after their period of incarceration. However, we do not know the extent to which those programs target the right audience, if they are successful in assisting inmates obtain and maintain a job, and which aspects of those programs work and which do not. We also ignore the number of people who are registered to obtain a GED while in jail.

Substance abuse treatment

The use of alcohol and drugs is a common and serious problem among inmates. In 2002 more than two-thirds of jail inmates abused or were dependent on alcohol or drugs (Karberg and James, 2005). It is logical to expect that released offenders will continue abusing substances after their release if effective treatment and support services are not available to them while in confinement and after their release. Despite drugs and alcohol abuse being serious problems among inmates, only 10 percent of jails nationwide in 2006 offered some type of drug or alcohol treatment programs (Stephan and Walsh, 2011).

As noted before, many offenders enter jails several times, and offenders with substance abuse problems are no exception. In 2002 approximately 415,242 jail inmates had substance abuse problems (Karberg and James, 2005). Those individuals were likely to return to their communities with the same problems if they were not provided with the proper treatment for their addictions and related problems. Inmates who suffered from substance abuse were twice as likely as other inmates to have more prior probation or incarceration sentences than other inmates (Karberg and James, 2005). Research has found that substance abuse is the driving factor behind the recidivism of people with mental illness (Wilson et al., 2011). While the efficacy of substance abuse treatment offered in jails is unknown, it is logical to argue that if more and better substance abuse programs were offered in jails, the number of jail inmates (16.4 percent) who committed an offense to get money for drugs (Dorsey and Middleton, NCJ 165148), or the number of convicted jail inmates who were under the influence of drugs or alcohol while offending (50 percent) would be reduced among repeat offenders (Karberg and James, 2005).

The number of jails offering substance abuse treatment is low relative to the existing demand; and it is unknown if the programs offered target the right audience, and if they are effective in reducing the use of alcohol and drugs. According to only one study conducted by Krishnan et al., (2013), substance abuse treatment does not influence post-release cocaine and opioid use among jail offenders. Although more is known about the effect of substance abuse programs among prison inmates, Petersilia (2003) states that substance abuse programs offered in prisons do not use the most effective methods to treat and help inmates.

Mental health services in jails

Mental health issues are perhaps the most recurrent problems found among local jail inmates. Estimates suggest that around two million people with serious mental illness are booked into U.S. jails every year (Steadman et al., 2009). It is estimated that at midyear 2005 there were 479,000 inmates in local jails with a mental health problem. That number represents 64 percent of all jail inmates. Of those, 76 percent also had substance abuse problems and 44 percent of them had committed a violent offense (James and Glaze, 2006).

The alarming number of individuals with a mental health condition going to jail may be due in part to the deinstitutionalization of the mentally ill after the 1960s, when drug therapies were expected to cure and control many mental illnesses. In recent times, many mentally ill incarcerated individuals are charged with relatively minor crimes that may be symptomatic of their mental illnesses (Etter Sr. et al., 2008). According to Chaiklin (2001), jails now serve as alternative shelters for those with a mental condition. Additionally, while it has been believed that mentally ill inmates tend to be violent, researchers have established that these individuals do not invariably commit violent crimes after they are released into society (Teplin et al., 1994).

The diagnosis of a mental health condition should be considered something serious for the legal, medical and social implications it carries. However, research suggests that jail inmates' mental health assessment conducted by a mental health professional is one of the methods least used by jail administrators to determine inmates' mental health status (Phillips III and Mercke, 2003). Researchers also have developed methods to predict the prevalence of serious mentally ill inmates in jail facilities (Steadman et al., 2009). While this method of prediction should help jail administrators plan and prepare services for those with a mental health diagnosis, its usefulness is in doubt as we ignore the number of jail facilities that offer mental health services, the quality of those services, and their outcomes.

Jail budgets and expenditures

An estimated $26.4 billion dollars were spent in the U.S. in 2011 on jails, juvenile institutions, and the community supervision of offenders. The amount of money spent on corrections represented 1.6 percent of the total local government expenditures between 2005 and 2011 (Kyckelhahn, 2013). While the need for financial resources to build and operate local jails has increased nationwide in recent years, primarily resulting from growth in the jail population, their financial needs have not been met. Jails are locally funded, hence their major source of funding is not derived from state or federal budgets. Jails obtain most of their financial resources through the tax supported budgets authorized by local funding authorities. Despite having limited funding, jail administrators are still expected to operate safe, secure, and adequate jails.

Local budgets and the source of those financial resources destined to jails vary substantially across counties. For example, Arlington County's (VA) budget for the 2015 fiscal year is of $940,887,809 (Arlington County, Fiscal Year 2015). Of that money, nearly $30 million dollars was allocated to the Department of Corrections (Arlington County, Sheriff's Office 2015); which houses an average of 500 inmates per day (Arlington County, Sheriff). Montgomery County (MD) has an allocated budget for the same fiscal year of $4,995,738,414 (Montgomery County, FY15 Budget), from which $71,135,891 was allocated to the county Department of Correction and Rehabilitation (Montgomery County, Correction and Rehabilitation). Montgomery County, MD hosts an average of 530 offenders per month (Montgomery County, 2014). In contrast, Mobile County, AL has a budget of $173,860,256 for the 2015 fiscal year, from which $21,842,371 was allocated to the Sheriff's Metro Jail and Min. Security (Mobile County, 2015). Mobile's County Metro Jail houses an average of 1,500 inmates per day (Mobile County, Sheriff's Office).

According to Welsh (1995), American jails offer poor living conditions and have inadequate or nonexistent medical care, insufficient food services, unsanitary living conditions, vague and discretionary disciplinary procedures, and are operated by poorly trained staff. The increasing number of people going to jails may affect the local expenditures allocated to jails, which in turn may affect the existence and quality of education, health care, and rehabilitation services offered to inmates. Budgets may also affect the quality of jail facilities, the quality of food for inmates, and the salaries and training that guards and staff receive; which ultimately may impact the way custodian and support staff treat inmates (Paoline and Lambert, 2012; Stinchcomb and Leip, 2013). When comparing the estimated $368[1] spent daily by Montgomery County jail on each one of its inmates, with the estimated $40 spent daily on each inmate by Mobile County jail, one could hypothesize that inmates in Montgomery County, MD receive better treatment and services than inmates in Mobile County, AL. However, there is no evidence to suggest that jails with bigger budgets offer better treatment services to their inmates than jails with smaller budgets, or that budgets allocated to jails influence recidivism among released offenders.

Discussion and conclusions

Every year local jails touch the lives of millions of individuals and billions of dollars are spent on these correctional institutions. Jails play a very important role in the criminal justice system by housing defendants and convicted criminals, supervising individuals on probation and parole, and by transferring, and even housing, state and federal inmates. Jails also play an important role in local communities as they maintain under confinement individuals who are considered dangerous or harmful, and who have been removed from their communities by the police. While the roles, responsibilities, and characteristics of jails make them arguably more consequential for American communities than prisons, there is very limited knowledge about the effect of jails on the people they house and supervise and on the communities they serve.

Policymakers are more enthusiastic about the idea that jails should focus on rehabilitation and in serving the needs of those with mental health and substance abuse problems, than on incapacitation deterrence, retribution and detention (Applegate et al., 2003). While their enthusiasm is important, their capacity to serve inmates in need of treatment and services is limited because criminologists, social workers, psychologists, and other professionals pay minimal attention or resources to scientifically determining what works and does not work in jails to help offenders with their needs, and to reduce their level of offending.

Significant taxpayer expenditures and countless hours of human resources are spent on jail treatment and rehabilitation programs every year, and the best answer for a simple question like: "Do programs offered in jails help inmates reduce their dependence to alcohol and drugs?" is, "We don't know." The same answer would apply if asked about the efficacy of work and education programs, mental health services, or any other program offered in local jails. A better answer to the question presented would be forthcoming if more serious research and evaluation was conducted with local jail inmates. As long as we continue to neglect the study of jails and postpone the implementation of evidence-based-practices, local governments will continue to spend millions of dollars on programs that might not work, or that are detrimental to inmates.

It is important for policymakers and researchers alike to realize the potential benefits that research on jails could bring to the criminal justice system and to communities as a whole. Individuals receiving effective mental health treatment while in jail could result in better adjusted inmates and in lower levels of recidivism. Similarly, inmates who benefited from an effective substance abuse treatment intervention while in jail would be less likely to abuse substances again after their release and reduce the likelihood of future offending and an ultimate trajectory to state prison. Additionally, if ex-offenders are consuming less drugs and alcohol, and are psychologically better prepared to deal with the out-of-jail world, they will be less likely to engage in domestic violence, etc., resulting in the police having to apprehend and re-arrest them.

As we continue to drive policies and programs affecting jails based on what is popular or sounds logical, and not evidence derived from empirical scientific studies, we will continue the current path of high recidivism rates and unmeasured consequences that local communities suffer when non-rehabilitated offenders are released from confinement. We believe local, state, and federal agencies that fund criminal justice research, academicians, policy researchers, and practitioners should devote substantially more focus and attention to researching local jails to improve the management and effectiveness of these institutions, reduce the number of individuals sent to jails, and determine best practices and interventions in local correctional systems.

Note

1 This number was obtained by dividing the Department of Correction budget by 365 (number of days in a year), and then by dividing that number by the average number of inmates each correctional facility houses per day.

References

Adams, Kenneth, and Joseph Ferrandino. 2008. Managing mentally ill inmates in prisons. *Criminal Justice and Behavior*, 35(8): 913–927.

Applegate, Brandon K., Robin King Davis, Charles W. Otto, Ray Surette, Bernard J. McCarthy. 2003. The multifunction jail: Policy makers' views of the goals of local incarceration. *Criminal Justice Policy Review*, 14(2): 155–170.

Arditti, Joyce A., Jennifer Lambert-Shute, and Karen Joest. 2003. Saturday morning at the jail: *Implications of incarceration for families and children*, 52(3): 195–204.

Arlington County, Virginia. Budget and Finance. FY 2015 Adopted Budget. Fiscal Year 2015 County Budget Resolution. http://arlingtonva.s3.amazonaws.com/wp-content/uploads/sites/18/2014/08/FY15A_Budget-Summaries.pdf (accessed 29 Dec, 2014).

Arlington County, Virginia. Budget and Finance. FY 2015 Adopted Budget. Sheriff's Office. Department Budget Summary. http://arlingtonva.s3.amazonaws.com/wp-content/uploads/sites/18/2014/06/FY15A_SRF.pdf (accessed 29 Dec 2014).

Arlington County, Virginia. Sheriff, Detention Facility. http://sheriff.arlingtonva.us/detention-facility/ (accessed 29 Dec 2014).

Bader, Shannon M., Robert Welsh, and Mario J. Scalora. 2010. Recidivism among female child molesters. *Violence and Victims*, 25(3): 349–62.

Baillargeon, Jacques, Sandra A. Black, John Pulvino, and Kim Dunn. 2000. The disease profile of Texas prison inmates. *Annals of Epidemiology*, 10(2): 74–80.

Bales, William D., Laura E. Bedard, Susan T. Quinn, David T. Ensley, and Glen P. Holley. 2005. Recidivism of public and private state prison inmates in Florida. *Criminology and Public Policy*, 4(1): 57.

Beck, Allen J. April 13, 2000. State and Federal Prisoners returning to the community: Findings from the Bureau of Justice Statistics. U.S. Department of Justice. Presented at the First Reentry Courts Initiative Cluster Meeting, Washington, DC http://www.bjs.gov/content/pub/pdf/sfprc.pdf (accessed 10 Jan 2015).

Beckwith, Curt G., Lauri Bazerman, Alexandra H. Cornwall, Emily Patry, Michael Poshkus, Jeannia Fu, and Amy Nunn. 2011. An evaluation of a routine opt-out rapid HIV testing program in a Rhode Island jail. *AIDS Education and Prevention: Official Publication of the International Society for AIDS Education*, 23(3 Suppl): 96–109.

Belenko, Steven, and Jordon Peugh. 2005. Estimating drug treatment needs among state prison inmates. *Drug and Alcohol Dependence*, 77(3): 269–281.

Bernstein, Michael H., Savannah N. McSheffrey, Jacob J. van den Berg, Jamie E. Vela, L. A. R. Stein, Mary B. Roberts, Rosemarie A. Martin, and Jennifer G. Clarke. 2015. The association between impulsivity and alcohol/drug use among prison inmates. *Addictive Behaviors*, 42: 140–143.

Carson, E. Ann, and Daniela Golinelli. December 2013. Prisoners in 2012. Trends in Admissions and Releases, 1991–2012. NCJ 243920. U.S. Department of Justice. Office of Justice Programs. Bureau of Justice Statistics. www.bjs.gov/content/pub/pdf/p12tar9112.pdf (accessed 9 Jan 2015).

Carson, E. Ann. September 2014. Prisoners in 2013. NCJ 247282. U.S. Department of Justice. Office of Justice Programs. Bureau of Justice Statistics. www.bjs.gov/content/pub/pdf/p13.pdf (accessed 1 Feb 2015).

Chaiklin, Harris. 2001. Current and prior mental health treatment of jail inmates: The use of the jail as an alternative shelter. *Journal of Social Distress and the Homeless*, 10(3): 255–268.

Cochran, Joshua, Daniel Mears, Sonja Siennick, and William Bales. 2012; 2011. Prison visitation and recidivism. *Justice Quarterly*, 29(6): 888-31.

Dorsey, Tina L., and Priscilla Middleton. NCJ 165148. Drugs and Crime Facts. U.S. Department of Justice. Office of Justice Programs. Bureau of Justice Statistics. http://www.bjs.gov/content/pub/pdf/dcf.pdf (accessed 10 Jan 2015).

Etter Sr., Gregg W., Michael L. Birzer and Judy Fields. 2008. The jail as a dumping ground: the incidental incarceration of mentally ill individuals. *Criminal Justice Studies*, 21(1): 79–89.

Fisher, William H., Stephanie W. Hartwell, Xiaogang Deng, Debra A. Pinals, Carl Fulwiler, and Kristen Roy-Bujnowski. 2014. Recidivism among released state prison inmates who received mental health treatment while incarcerated. *Crime and Delinquency*, 60(6): 811–832.

Freudenberg, Nicholas. 2001. Jails, prisons, and the health of urban populations: A review of the impact of the correctional system on community health. *Journal of Urban Health: Bulletin of the New York Academy of Medicine*, 78: 2.

Gebbie, Kristine M., Roland M. Larkin, Susan J. Klein, Lester Wright, James Satriano, John J. Culkin, and Barbara S. Devore. 2008. Improving access to mental health services for New York state prison inmates. *Journal of Correctional Health Care*, 14(2): 122–135.

Glaze, Lauren E., and Danielle Kaeble. December 2014. Correctional populations in the United States, 2013. NCJ 248479. U.S. Department of Justice. Office of Justice Programs. Bureau of Justice Statistics. xhttp://www.bjs.gov/content/pub/pdf/cpus13.pdf (accessed 8 Jan 2015).

Greenberg, Greg A., and Robert Rosenheck. 2009. Mental health and other risk factors for jail incarceration among male veterans. *Psychiatric Quarterly*, 80(1): 41–53.

Harzke, Amy J., Jacques G. Baillargeon, Michael F. Kelley, Pamela M. Diamond, Karen J. Goodman, and David P. Paar. 2009. HCV-related mortality among male prison inmates in Texas, 1994–2003. *Annals of Epidemiology*, 19(8): 582–589.

Harlow, Caroline Wolf. January 2003. Education and Correctional Populations. NCJ 195670. U.S. Department of Justice. Office of Justice Programs. Bureau of Justice Statistics. http://www.bjs.gov/content/pub/pdf/ecp.pdf (accessed 12 Jan 2015).

Houser, Kimberly A., and Wayne Welsh. 2014. Examining the association between co-occurring disorders and seriousness of misconduct by female prison inmates. *Criminal Justice and Behavior*, 41(5): 650–666.

Horsburgh, C. R., Jr, J. Q. Jarvis, T. McArther, T. Ignacio, and P. Stock. 1990. Seroconversion to human immunodeficiency virus in prison inmates. *American Journal of Public Health*, 80(2): 209–210.

James, Doris J. and Lauren E. Glaze. September 2006. Mental Health Problems of Prison and Jail Inmates. NCJ 213600. U.S. Department of Justice. Office of Justice Programs. Bureau of Justice Statistics. www.bjs.gov/content/pub/pdf/mhppji.pdf (accessed 12 Jan 2015).

Karberg, Jennifer C., and Doris J. James. July 2005. Substance Dependence, Abuse and Treatment of Jail Inmates, 2002. NCJ209588. U.S. Department of Justice. Office of Justice Programs. Bureau of Justice Statistics.

Krishnan, Archana, Jeffrey A. Wickersham, Ehsan Chitsaz, Sandra A. Springer, Alison O. Jordan, Nick Zaller, and Frederick L. Altice. 2013. Post-release substance abuse outcomes among HIV-infected jail detainees: Results from a multisite study. *AIDS and Behavior*, 17(2): 171–180.

Kyckelhahn, Tracey. December 2013. Local Government Corrections Expenditures, FY 2005–2011. NCJ 243527. U.S. Department of Justice. Office of Justice Programs. Bureau of Justice Statistics. http://www.bjs.gov/content/pub/pdf/lgcefy0511.pdf (accessed 12 Jan, 2015).

Lindquist, Christine H. 2000. Social integration and nental well-being among jail inmates. *Sociological Forum*, 15(13): 431–455.

Lombardo, Lucien X. 1985. Mental health work in prisons and jails. *Criminal Justice and Behavior*, 12(1): 17–27.

Mears, Daniel P., and William D. Bales. 2009. Supermax incarceration and recidivism." *Criminology*, 47(4): 1131.

Minton, Todd D., and Daniella Golinelli. May 2014. Jail Inmates at Midyear 2013 – Statistical Tables. NCJ245350 U.S. Department of Justice. Office of Justice Programs. Bureau of Justice Statistics. www.bjs.gov/content/pub/pdf/jim13st.pdf (accessed 9 Jan 2015).

Minton, Todd D., and Zhen Zeng. June 2015. Jail Inmates at Midyear 2014. NCJ 248629. U.S. Department of Justice. Office of Justice Programs. Bureau of Justice Statistics.

Mobile County, Alabama. 2015 Fiscal Year Budget. Mobile County Commission Budget Synopsis FY 2015. www.mobilecountyal.gov/files/budget_book20142015.pdf (accessed 7 Jan 2015).

Mobile County, Alabama. Sheriff's Office. Metro Jail. www.mobileso.com/metro-jail-2/ (accessed 7 Jan 2015).

Montgomery County, Maryland. (Jan 15, 2014). Master Facilities Confinement Study. www.montgomerycountymd.gov/COR/Resources/Files/PDF/MasterFacilities ConfinementStudy-01-15-2014.pdf (accessed 7 Jan 2015).

Montgomery County, Maryland. Operating Budget and Public Services Program. Correction and Rehabilitation. Fiscal Year 2015. https://reports.data.montgom-erycountymd.gov/reports/BB_FY15_APPR/COR (accessed Jan 4, 2015).

Montgomery County, Maryland. Operating Budget and Public Services Program. 2015. FY15 Budget. xhttp://www.montgomerycountymd.gov/OMB/Resources/Files/omb/pdfs/FY15/psp_pdf/psp-highlights.pdf (accessed 7 Jan 2015).

Paoline, Eugene A., and Eric G. Lambert. 2012. Exploring potential consequences of job involvement among jail staff. *Criminal Justice Policy Review*, 23(2): 231–53.

Petersilia, Joan. *When prisoners come home*. 2003. Oxford University Press. New York, NY. United States of America.

Phillips III, Daniel W., and Carrie G. Mercke. 2003. Mental health services in Kentucky jails: A self-report by jail administrators. *Journal of Correctional Health Care*, 10: 1.

Proctor, Steven L. 2012. Substance use disorder prevalence among female state prison inmates. *The American Journal of Drug and Alcohol Abuse*, 38(4): 278–285.

Richmond, Kerry M. 2014. The impact of federal prison industries employment on the recidivism outcomes of female inmates. *Justice Quarterly*, 31(4): 719–745.

Schriro, Dora B. 2013. Department of Correction Mayor's Management Report-FY2013. www.nyc.gov/html/doc/downloads/pdf/MMR-FY2013.pdf (accessed Feb 2, 2015).

Spivak, Andrew L., and Susan F. Sharp. 2008. Inmate recidivism as a measure of private prison performance. *Crime and Delinquency*, 54(3): 482–508.

Steadman, Henry J., Fred C. Osher, Pamela Clark Robbins, Brian Case, and Steven Samuels. 2009. Prevalence of serious mental illness among jail inmates. *Psychiatric services*, 60(6): 761–765.

Stephan, James J., and Georgette Walsh. 2011. Census Of Jail Facilities, 2006. Bureau of Justice Statistics. U.S. Department of Justice. National Institute of Corrections. 2002. Budget Guide for Jail Administrators. http://www.bjs.gov/content/pub/pdf/cjf06.pdf (accessed on 28 Dec 2014).

Stinchcomb, Jeanne B., and Leslie A. Leip. 2013. Expanding the literature on job satisfaction in corrections: A national study of jail employees. *Criminal Justice and Behavior*, 40(11): 1209–27.

Sturges, Judith E. 2002. Visitation at County Jails: potential policy implications. *Criminal Justice Policy Review*, 13(1): 32–45.

Sturges, Judith E., and Aref M. Al-Khattar. 2009. Survey of jail visitors. *The Prison Journal*, 89(4): 482–496.

Tartaro, Christine, and Marissa P. Levy. 2007. Density, inmates assaults, and direct supervision jails. *Criminal Justice Policy Review*, 18(4): 395–417.

Teplin, Linda A., Karen M. Abram, Gary M. McClelland. 1994. Does psychiatric disorder predict violent crime among released jail detainees? A six-year longitudinal study. *American Psychologist*, 49(4): 335–342.

Welsh, Wayne N. 1995. *Counties in Court: Jail overcrowding and Court-Ordered Reform*, Philadelphia: Temple University Press.

Western, Bruce. 2007. Mass imprisonment and economic inequality, *Social Research*, 74: 509–532.

Wilson, Amy Blank, Jeffrey Draine, Trevor Hadley, Steve Metraux, and Arthur Evans. 2011. Examining the impact of mental illness and substance use on recidivism in a county jail. *International Journal of Law and Psychiatry*, 34(4): 264–268.

Wood, Steven R., and Anthony Buttaro. 2013. Co-occurring severe mental illnesses and substance abuse disorders as predictors of state prison inmate assaults. *Crime and Delinquency*, 59(4): 510–535.

Yu, Sung-suk Violet, Hung-En Sung, Jeff Mellow, and Carl J. Koenigsmann. 2015. Self-perceived health improvements among prison inmates. *Journal of Correctional Health Care*, 21(1): 59–69.

Chapter 20

Does a prison term prevent or promote more crime?

Gerald G. Gaes

Introduction

The question seems simple enough, "Does a prison term prevent or promote more crime?" Does it promote crime by breaking up families, by diminishing prosocial and productivity skills, or by exposing inmates to an anti-normative culture? If prison leads to more criminal activity after release, it is said to be criminogenic. Does prison prevent crime either because it gives the person an opportunity to reform, or extracts punishment sufficient to deter future criminality? If it reforms, criminologists say prison rehabilitates. If it deters, we say prison has a specific deterrent effect. In this chapter I try to answer the question I pose; however, not only is the answer complex, criminologists have only started to peel away the layers of complexity.

Two major research branches of criminological research have addressed the impact of imprisonment. One branch examines the effect of incarceration on the individual's life course. The second branch has the rubric mass incarceration. Scholars who research mass incarceration evaluate the impact of the rate at which people are imprisoned in the United States – the highest rate in the world – on broader societal effects. The societal effects encompass a large volume of research and commentary including such topics as general deterrence, political disenfranchisement, racial and ethnic bias, family disintegration, and community disintegration. Readers interested in the causes and effects of mass incarceration should start with the National Research Council report (NRC, 2014). A comprehensive policy discussion of imprisonment should take into account both the effects of imprisonment on individuals, as well as the effects of mass incarceration. In this chapter, I confine my remarks to the effects on individuals.[1] Before I move to the research findings, it is important to lay out the framework for thinking about the problem.

A model of the prison experience: moderating and mediating effects

To answer "Does a prison term prevent or promote more crime?" I use Figure 20.1, a schematic representation of the incarceration process and its position in the life course. The schema broadly distinguishes three types of events: events that occur prior to a current term of prison, including prior prison terms for some people; events that occur within prison; and events that occur once the inmate is released back into the community. Figure 20.1 incorporates factors that moderate and mediate the short- and long-term consequences of imprisonment.

I make the distinction between mediating and moderating effects. This distinction is often misunderstood. Andrew Hayes' book (2013) is an important source in understanding why mediation and moderation matters. He colloquially distinguishes between *whether* a factor such as prison affects an outcome such as committing another crime after release from prison, from factors that affect *how* and *when* prison causes recidivism. The *whether* condition is the causal effect of prison on recidivism. The *when* condition refers to the moderating influence of factors, and the *how* condition represents the mediating influence of factors. A mediator is a process that intervenes between the cause and the outcome. It influences the level of the outcome including whether the outcome actually occurs.

In the context of this chapter, imprisonment could lead to the development of criminal skills when prisoners associate with other inmates. Prison is a causal variable that promotes a secondary process. In this example, the secondary process is the development of criminal skills through exposure to other inmates. In this case, the secondary process mediates recidivism by increasing the likelihood that someone returns to crime after release. What makes the mediation process complex is that there will also be mediators that reduce the likelihood of crime. For example, someone admitted to prison may take the opportunity to develop pro-social, occupational, and other skills that mediate a positive outcome once the person is released from prison. Prison mediators can be affected by aspects of the prison environment, by interactions with other inmates, and by interactions with prison authorities.

According to Hayes, a moderator specifies the boundary condition for the relationship between prison and recidivism. The moderating variable establishes the size and sign of the relationship. For example, imprisonment may increase the likelihood of recidivism for someone with an extensive criminal history, while it may deter those with little or no criminal history. The criminal history moderator does not intervene between the treatment and the outcome. Instead it interacts with the treatment determining the level of the outcome, with the possibility that dependent on certain levels of the moderator there is a zero or very low probability that the outcome will be observed.

Discussion of moderators is another way of introducing the concept of treatment heterogeneity. As Nagin et al., (2009) insightfully argue, the effect of prison is likely conditional on the momentum of events prior to the incarceration. Using the language of experimental design, we say that prison has heterogeneous treatment effects that depend upon the criminal, social, economic and other event-driven histories of individuals that pre-cede their incarceration. In other words, what prison does depends on the backgrounds of who gets imprisoned.[2] In the language of moderators, the effect of prison is dependent on the levels of the moderators. Mediators and moderators can also work in combination, and that is why Hayes uses the terminology of conditional process analysis, alerting us to the many contin-gencies that can modify the effect of treatment or, for the purposes of this chapter, modify the impact of imprisonment.

Why is this distinction between moderators and mediators important? Moderators are key to understanding treatment heterogeneity. Prison has one outcome for one type of person, and different outcomes for people with divergent backgrounds and histories. Mediators point to the mechanisms that have intervening influences, therefore identifying mediators offers the possibility that manipulation of these factors can reduce or prevent return-ing to crime after release from prison. If criminological scholarship on the effect of imprisonment had reached a level of maturity that allowed us to list the moderators, mediators and their effect on the causal relationship of prison and post-release outcomes such as recidivism, this would provide clear policy guidance.

It's important to emphasize why we need a mature, comprehensive under-standing. Assume that the effect of prison depends on the level of prior criminal history increasing the probability of post-release criminality for people with extensive levels of criminal history. Also assume prison has a small criminogenic effect on people with moderate criminal histories, and a deterrent effect for people with little or no criminal history. Such knowledge would allow us to allocate post-release supervision strategies more appro-priately – currently this is called the risk principle owing to Andrews et al., (1990) and others. Next assume that we know the mediators of prison for each of the three different criminal history paths just described. For people with extensive criminal histories who are imprisoned, presume we know that a psychological intervention such as cognitive-behavioral restructuring (Lipsey et al., 2007) has a marginal effect on reducing crime. For people with moderate criminal histories, cognitive restructuring has a large effect on reducing criminal history, and for those with no criminal history, cogni-tive restructuring has no effect. Knowing moderators and mediators allows us to anticipate outcomes and design appropriate interventions in an *effi-cient* manner. If we knew that people with moderate criminal histories were deterred by prison alone, it would be inefficient to assign them to expensive prison interventions. Unfortunately, our knowledge is limited.

Figure 20.1 includes many of the factors appearing in the criminological and correctional research literature. In the first box of Figure 20.1, I have shown many of the characteristics of people that are used to group subsets of individuals on their crime trajectories (Nagin, 2005). Whether or not a person receives prison for criminal behavior, if that person is male, has a

Events in the Life Course

| Prior to a Current Prison Term | Events Occurring within Prison | Post-Release Events |

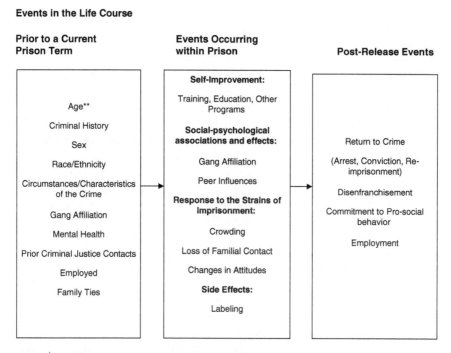

Figure 20.1 The experience of prison in the life course

prior criminal history, and a gang affiliation, he will have a higher likelihood of committing another crime. This list of precursors is not exhaustive, but it makes the pedagogical point that one's history has momentum into the future, and that as moderators, prison may have different effects for different combinations of these factors.

In the second box are the events that occur in prison. Neither is this an exhaustive list. Rather it is intended to provoke thought about the intricacies of the prison environment. Important prison ethnographies document the complexity of the incarceration experience. These works emphasize the total institution where a separate society emerges with unique characteristics of prison institutionalization and depict the strained relationships between inmates and prison staff. The earliest and most influential of these ethnographies are *The Prison Community* (Clemmer, 1940), and *The Society of Captives: A Study of a Maximum Security Prison* (Sykes, 1958). Clemmer and Sykes laid a foundational theory of inmate society and culture from which almost all subsequent ethnographies are derivative. Examples of these latter works include: *Hacks, Blacks, and Cons* (Carol, 1974), *Stateville: The Penitentiary in Mass Society* (Jacobs, 1977), *Asylum* (Goffman, 1961), *Lifers: Seeking Redemption in Prison* (Irwin, 2009), and *In the Mix: Struggle and Survival in a Women's Prison* (Owen, 1998). These books provide insight into the texture of inmate experience, and the structure within which prison staff and inmates interact. They provide context for empirical studies that seek to evaluate factors that moderate or mediate the effect of imprisonment on post-release outcomes.

There is also a rich literature on many of the program events that occur in the second box of Figure 20.1 shown as events that promote self-improvement. There are many meta-analyses such as those of MacKenzie (2006) that use statistical assessment of the research findings as well as other insightful reviews of prison programs. This research literature compares people participating in prison programs with those that do not, and if the study is done well, the two groups are equivalent on all factors that are related to program participation and the outcome. However, these program evaluation studies do not address what would happen in the absence of prison. One way to think about this is to form another hypothetical in which we could randomly assign people who commit a crime into three groups. The three groups are composed of people with equivalent background characteristics and equivalent characteristics of their crime. These people are randomly assigned to receive a non-prison sanction such as probation, a prison sanction with a specific type of prison program, and a prison sanction without the specifically designed program. We further assume, and this is a very big assumption, that the prison environment is equivalent for everyone assigned to the two prison groups, with the exception that one group receives the specially designed prison program throughout the incarceration.

I make a conjecture about some possible outcomes of this three group design. If both prison groups decrease recidivism relative to the non-prison group, and the two prison groups have the same average outcome, then we could conclude prison has a deterrent effect and program participation has no mediating effect. An alternative conjecture follows. If the prison group in which inmates receive specific programming has recidivism rates lower than the non-prison group, and prison without interventions has higher recidivism rates than the non-prison sanction group, that leads us to the conclusion that prison in the absence of programming is criminogenic. However, there are prison interventions that not only suppress the impact of incarceration, but also lead to more favorable outcomes than probation as an alternative outcome. I raise these issues to show how important it is to understand how nuanced and difficult it is to answer the question, "Does a prison term prevent or promote more crime?" I do not diminish the efforts of meta-analysts and prison program evaluators that have devoted a great deal of scholarship to evaluate prison programs. My goal is to introduce an element of caution and skepticism so that naïve consumers of the research have some idea of the fragility of the current level of knowledge, and more importantly to clarify the work ahead for criminologists to dig deeper into the issues.

One last caveat. Almost all of the research on the effect of incarceration is based on observational studies, not experiments. People who commit serious crimes or who have extensive criminal histories are unlikely to be allowed to participate in an experiment in which half are given a community sanction and the other half a prison sanction. Such an experiment would be unjust and unethical. This makes analysis of the impact of imprisonment much more difficult. That is a conversation for methodologists and statisticians. Indeed, there have been some remarkable improvements in the last 60 years in analyzing observational studies as if they were experiments owing to the work of scholars such as Cochran et al., (Cochran, 1965; Rosenbaum and Rubin, 1984; Rosenbaum, 2002; Heckman and Vytlacil, 2007a, 2007b; Roy, 1951) and many others. Having explored the troublesome contingencies of understanding whether prison prevents or promotes, I turn to a summarization of what we know.

Summary of the research on the effect of a term of prison and prison time served

What does the research tell us? There have been major reviews of the literature on the effect of imprisonment by Nagin et al. (2009), Villetaz et al. (2006) and Gendreau et al. (1999) and Smith et al. (2002). Each of these builds on their predecessors. The Nagin et al. review is the most recent, and in my estimation the most careful and comprehensive. I first summarize what these reviews indicate about the impact of a term of prison including prison length of stay. I do this in chronological order. Then I turn to some of my own work.

Gendreau et al. (1999) used meta-analysis to review and code 50 studies published in the period 1958 to 1999. A follow-up by Smith et al. (2002) covered many of the same primary studies but also included intermediate sanctions, as well as other contingencies such as adult versus juvenile subpopulations. I will not cover the follow-up study since it shows similar results to the 1999 meta-analysis. The Villetaz et al., and Nagin et al., reviews are more recent. The Gendreau et al. (1999) meta-analysis evaluated two research issues. They examined correlations of length of time in prison and recidivism, and whether a term of prison as opposed to some community sanction was correlated to recidivism. They found the following:

- On average when comparing people with longer lengths of stay in prison (LOS), the longer term prisoners spent, on average, 30 months and people with the shorter terms spent, on average, 12.9 months. There was a 3 percent absolute increase in the proportion of people recidivating when they had longer versus shorter terms of prison (29 percent v. 26 percent).[3]
- There was no change in recidivism for people who had a term of imprisonment versus those that received a community sanction.

- For those who had higher risk levels, people who spent a longer time in prison had a 2 percent higher level of recidivism than those with shorter sentences.
- For those who had lower risk levels, people who spent a longer time in prison had a 5 percent higher level of recidivism than those with shorter sentences.
- Risk level had no impact on the relationship between a term of prison versus community sanctions and recidivism.

Assessing the effect of prison length of stay in a meta-analysis is very difficult. There is probably a non-linear relationship between length of stay and recidivism. This makes it difficult to discover the relationship with a statistical summarization such as meta-analysis. Gendreau et al.'s assessment of risk as a condition of the relationship between imprisonment and recidivism is a type of moderation analysis. Their results suggest, at a meta-analytic level, there may be prison treatment heterogeneity – namely, the effect of prison depends on the risk levels of people who are imprisoned. However, as I have already indicated, people with very long lengths of stay are more likely to have more extensive criminal records, and are therefore more likely to commit a new crime than people with shorter lengths of stay. It is difficult to tease this out with a meta-analysis even though Gendreau et al. use risk level as a proxy. Risk level assessment itself could cover volumes of scholarship. However, risk is most often dependent on sex, age and prior criminality. Males, younger people and those with extensive criminal histories are more likely to commit crime.

Villetaz et al. (2006) also used meta-analysis to examine the relationship between a term of prison and an alternative community sanction. Their research appeared as a Campbell Collaboration report which ensures a rigorous methodology. To give the reader some sense of the rigor in which this study was conducted, it is important to realize the authors reviewed more than 3,000 research abstracts. Only 23 studies met the minimal conditions of a Campbell Review. This allowed the authors to assess 27 relationships between a term of prison and recidivism. The authors of the review summarized their results and found:

- In 11 of 13 results, a term of prison was associated with a higher level of recidivism than an alternative sanction.
- Two comparisons show a lower level of recidivism after a term of prison.
- In the other 14 comparisons, there was no difference in recidivism between the two groups.
- Using only experimental studies or natural experiments, five studies, there was no difference in post-release recidivism between people given a term of prison and those with a community supervision sanction.

In their discussion of the results, Villetaz, Killias, and Zoder also recognize potential dependencies of the relationship between a term of prison and recidivism on moderators. They are not systematic in this discussion, but do point to potential interaction effects between prison and offender risk and other types of offender characteristics.

The review by Nagin et al. (2009) is the most comprehensive and expansive in explaining how moderators will affect prison–recidivism relationship. They also take pains to separate regression studies based on observational data from quasi-experimental studies using designs that mimic an experiment, and from studies that are experiments or natural experiments. Rather than conduct meta-analysis, Nagin, Cullen, and Jonson argue that the studies are too disparate in their quality to treat as a consistent source of data for statistical summarization.

Before summarizing their findings, it is important for the reader to understand what Nagin, Cullen and Jonson believe to be the strongest threat to the validity of observational studies, namely the lack of precision in controlling for the age of the offender.

> We give age this special status for control because offending rates are highly age dependent and because the post-sanction outcome variable, offending rate or recidivism probability, necessarily must be measured over age. Therefore, we regarded it as very important in analyses of observational data to compare the post-sanction offending rate of an imprisoned individual with that of one or more non-imprisoned individuals who are the same age.
>
> (Nagin et al., 2009, p. 138)

Age takes on this special status as a variable that can confound our understanding of the relationship between prison and recidivism. This is because offending prior to and after imprisonment is age dependent, and differences in the age composition of people who received a term of prison and those who don't could easily bias any differences between the two groups. After considering many qualifications of the evidence, Nagin, Cullen and Jonson reach the following conclusions:

- Most of the studies imply a null or criminogenic effect of a term of prison on recidivism.
- Because of lack of controls especially for age, and because many of the studies do not reach conventional statistical significance, they could not reach a scientifically valid conclusion for most of the regression-based studies.
- However, the best quasi-experimental studies mostly find a null or criminogenic effect.
- It is possible that prison has both a deterrent and criminogenic effect depending on characteristics of the person confined.

- They could not reach a conclusion for the effect of length of prison stay on post-release outcomes.

Inferential limitations

The paper by Nagin, Cullen, and Jonson (2009) is an extremely important piece of scholarship covering the many theoretical and methodological problems inherent in decomposing the effects of imprisonment. However, I would like to bring up one important dimension of the problem that I have not seen thoroughly discussed on this issue even though it is implied by their discussion of treatment heterogeneity. As many scholars have noted, the primary methodological problem in studying the effects of imprisonment is that punishment is proportional to the seriousness of the crime, and in almost every jurisdiction it is also proportional to the level of a person's prior record of criminality. People who are imprisoned are more likely to have more serious past and current crimes than people given alternative sanctions. People who commit serious crimes are more likely to receive longer sentences than those with less serious crimes when they have equivalent past levels of criminality. As I have already indicated, this makes analyzing the effect of imprisonment a difficult inferential problem. In the language of experimental design, it is difficult to construct a control group. Almost all analyses of prison effects make an inference about average treatment effects.[4] However, you never see, at least among the many papers I have read, a discussion of the extent to which the treatment effect may only be relevant to a subset of people receiving a prison sanction. I recently collaborated on a paper (Gaes et al., in press) which shows that using different matching procedures to construct a realistic "control group," only a small subset of people getting a prison sanction can be matched with people who do not receive a prison sanction. This is especially true when you use exact matching to find a control group of people who are not imprisoned, and the matching characteristics are composed of a wide range of data that include dimensions of the sentencing factors that judges take into account when determining a sentence. We find prisoners who can be matched to those receiving a community sanction such as probation have less extensive criminal histories and less serious current offenses for which they are being punished. In other words, the inferences we make about the effect of imprisonment may only pertain to a circumscribed and much less risky subset of people who are incarcerated. The causal analysis results have no implication for the most serious and risky offenders who are imprisoned.

The effect of prison security level

One of the moderating and mediating influences of imprisonment that has been studied is the security level that a person is assigned to serve out their prison term. One way to interpret the security level is to think of it as a level of punishment. The higher the security level someone is assigned to, the more harsh the prison environment. This includes the security procedures that are in place, but it also includes the composition of the inmate population. Maximum security prisons have the harshest conditions, and the most violent and predacious inmates. There are several studies which have examined the impact of the level of security on post-release recidivism (Chen and Shapiro, 2007; Gaes and Camp, 2009; Lerman 2009a, b).[5] Does the strain of the harsher environments contribute to post-release criminality? Several theoretical mechanisms suggest that this strain and harshness can exacerbate the disposition to commit crimes after release from prison. Chen and Shapiro propose potential competing theoretical perspectives. One perspective is that a more severe level of punishment will deter future criminality. Alternatively, higher prison security levels expose inmates to prisoners who are more disposed to crime, elevating their own criminal human capital. They also argued that harsher prison environments depreciate work skills and increase the likelihood that when released potential employers of these inmates will be less likely to hire a former high security inmate. This latter effect is called labeling. Lerman's research is unique because she was able to use a strong quasi-experimental design to evaluate security level placement on prison acculturation. She found that the higher security level contributed to the adoption of anti-social norms. Acculturation only occurred for inmates who had no prior criminal or gang involvement. Her study is one of the few to statistically analyze some of the potential factors that moderate and mediate the impact of prison security level on both in-prison and post-release outcomes. Both Chen and Shapiro and Lerman used a strong quasi-experimental design called regression discontinuity. Gaes and Camp capitalized on an experimental design in which inmates were randomly assigned to a lower and higher security level prison even though they had the same classification levels of risk. Both Chen and Shapiro and Gaes and Camp found that higher security levels were associated with a higher likelihood of recidivating.

Community release conditions

People released from prison encounter a myriad of different conditions. Some are closely supervised, including GPS ankle bracelets, so that their precise movements can be tracked. Others have minimal conditions of post-release supervision. Still others receive no community supervision sometimes because they have reached the expiration of their sentence and there is no legal authority to monitor their activity. These are factors that occur after the effects of prison have taken place so they do not impact how prison affects the outcomes. However, they do independently affect outcomes such as recidivism. If the research design does not take into account potential differences in post-release supervision, effects attributable to prison may instead be the result of different post-release community supervision conditions. Are released prisoners and those placed on probation subject to the same levels of supervision? It is not clear to what extent the research on the effect of imprisonment has been compromised by a failure to equate or at least assess community supervision conditions. However, future research should recognize the importance of the equivalency.

Future research, current policy implications

Consistent with the theme of this book, the closing section of this paper addresses research questions that still must be addressed to advance our understanding of the effect of imprisonment, and based on what we already know, to explore the implications for corrections policy.

Based on my review of the research up to this point, it should be obvious that our knowledge about a term of imprisonment is limited. However, a fair summary of the research to this point indicates that *most* of the best methodological research shows that a term of prison compared to an alternative sanction, such as probation, has either no impact or a small criminogenic effect on post-release criminality. There are, however, circumstances such as imprisoning low-risk offenders where a specific deterrent effect occurs. Our knowledge is limited by the fact that there has not been a thorough assessment of treatment heterogeneity – namely prison may have different impacts on different subpopulations. Even the best studies typically fail to examine how the impact of a term of prison may only be relevant to a limited subpopulation of prisoners, such as those who have the lowest risk levels to commit future crime. There is even less of an understanding about the length of a term of prison. Finally, prison effects are mediated by the acculturation of prisoner normative values, but these are dependent on past criminal trajectories. It is important to understand that because we have not had a systematic investigation of mediating and moderating factors, for some levels of past and current criminality, there are probably jurisdictions where we will observe a deterrent effect of prison and possibly a deterrent effect of prison time served. For example, Gaes et al. (in press) found both no effect and a specific deterrent effect for imprisonment in Florida. In that paper, the authors argue that the different effects depend on the degree of past criminality. For prisoners with low levels of criminal history, no effect was found. For prisoners with higher levels of criminal history found a specific deterrent effect was found.

Because the space for this chapter was limited, I have not discussed the incapacitation effect of imprisonment. No matter whether prison has a deterrent or criminogenic effect on post-release outcomes, while someone is in prison, their potential criminality will have no effect on their community. This is called incapacitation. Therefore, if prison does have a null or criminogenic effect, the total volume of crime over the life course of the individual may be reduced by imprisonment. One of the few studies to examine these issues simultaneously is Bhati and Piquero (2008).

Given the limitations of the current research on imprisonment, the policy advice should be circumspect. However, if incremental changes are made to reduce the use of prison and to lower the amount of time someone serves a prison term, there should be marginal effects on community safety and significant savings in criminal justice monetary costs. A jurisdiction can start with those people who are at the margins of the prison versus probation decision. In determinate sentencing systems, guidelines can be adjusted to reduce the proportion of people who receive a prison term – placing them under community supervision instead. Incremental changes in prison length of stay can also be made. For example, a jurisdiction could lower time served by several months, especially for the less serious crimes. If imprisonment has, on average, a criminogenic effect in a given jurisdiction, then there will be a reduction in post-release crime, but only an incremental reduction. If prison has a null effect, then there may be a small incremental increase in crime because people will not be incapacitated during that small incremental period they are back in the community. If prison has a specific deterrent effect, then there will also be a small incremental impact on crime in the community.

There is a large body of research on the relationship between the national level of imprisonment over time and crime rates. There are too many studies to review or cite in this brief chapter. They also have disparate estimates of the incapacitation effect on crime rates. However, a fair summary of these studies is that given the large increases in prison utilization in the United States, increases in imprisonment beyond a level achieved years ago have had, at best, a small and perhaps even a negligible effect on crime. Raphael's (2014) commentary on the impact of sentencing reform is a good example of this type of research. As economists would say, increases in prison utilization have had diminishing returns on the impact on crime. Backing away from this high level of incarceration by lowering the use of prison and/or the length of time served will have a small impact on crime rates – whether crime goes up or down. Even people who argue that imprisonment should only be evaluated from a principle of proportional punishment should not object to reducing the use of prison. If the argument is that crime should be punished solely based on the penalty the offender deserves, then community sanctions can be a reasonable and justifiable form of justice for many offenders. The public policy goal of reduced prison utilization conforms to the research on individual level effects of imprisonment, the large body of research on mass incarceration, as well as the tenets of scholars and advocates who argue that a term of prison should be based solely on promoting justice.

Returning to the original question, "Does a prison term prevent or promote more crime? It most likely does both. Until we disentangle the factors that moderate and mediate the effects of imprisonment, the public policy choices ought to be guided by cautious, incremental changes to sentencing practices.

Notes

1 The other important caveat is that I focus on the offender in this article and not the victim of the crime. This is not because I have no empathy for the victim. It is because victimization is an important dimension and deserves its own treatment including amount of harm to the victim. Punishment in the form of imprisonment almost always takes into account the harm done to a victim, so it is also implicit in the analysis of the effects of a term of prison. When I discuss imprisonment outcomes such as post-release criminality that discussion also implicitly takes into account future victimization.

2 Gendreau, Coggin, and Cullen (1999) emphasize differences in imprisonment effects due to level of risk, one form of dependency. However, Nagin, Cullen and Jonson are systematic in their exposition of treatment heterogeneity.

3 Gendreau, Goggin, and Cullen (1999) report both weighted and unweighted average effect sizes. The weighting depends on the sample sizes. Since weighted effect sizes are understood by analysts to be more reflective of the average findings, I only report those results. The reader should be aware, however, that weighted and unweighted results were sometimes different.

4 Methodologists distinguish between average treatment effects and average treatment effects of the treated. The latter is the subgroup of people offered treatment and who accept treatment. The former subgroup is the average effect on the entire population under study. This distinction is not important to the current discussion.

5 Katz et al. (2003) also evaluate the harshness of prison conditions using aggregated data at the state level. Their proxy for harshness is the death rate in prison. They use crime rates in the community as their outcome. They found that the higher the prison death rate, excluding executions, the lower the crime rate across the states. They interpret this to mean that the harshness of prison has a deterrent effect. We exclude this study from our discussion because it is based on aggregate data, and because the crime rate they used would include both elements of specific deterrence and general deterrence. The discussion in this chapter focuses on specific deterrence – whether prison prevents the given individual from committing crime once they are released, not general deterrence – whether prison also prevents criminality among people who are not confined.

References

Andrews, Don A., James A. Bonta, and Robert D. Hoge. (1990). Classification for effective rehabilitation: Rediscovering psychology. *Criminal Justice and Behavior*, 17: 19–52.

Bhati, Avinash, and Alex R. Piquero. (2008). Estimating the mpact of ncarceration on subsequent offending trajectories: Deterrent, criminogenic, or null Effect? *Journal of Criminal Law and Criminology*, 98(l): 207–54.

Carroll, Leo. (1974). *Hacks, Blacks, and Cons*. Lexington, MA: Lexington Books.

Cochran, W. G. (1965). The planning of observational studies of human populations (with discussion). *Journal of the Royal Statistical Society*, Series A (128): 134–155.

Chen, M. K., and Shapiro, J. M. (2007). Do harsher prison conditions reduce recidivism? A discontinuity-based approach, *American Law and Economics Review*, Advance Access, published June 12, 2007.

Clemmer, Donald. (1940). *The Prison Community*. New York, NY: Holt, Rinehart and Winston.

Gaes, Gerald G., Bales, William, and Scaggs, Samuel. (in press) The effect of imprisonment on reoffending: An analysis using exact, coarsened exact, and radius matching. *Journal of Experimental Criminology*. Conditionally accepted.

Gaes, Gerald G. and Camp, Scott D. (2009). Unintended consequences: Experimental evidence for the criminogenic effect of security level placement on post-release recidivism. *Journal of Experimental Criminology*, 5(2): 139–162.

Gendreau, P., Goggin, C. and Cullen, F. (1999). *The Effects of Prison Sentences on Recidivism*. Ottawa, ON: Solicitor General Canada.

Goffman, Erving. (1961). *Asylums: Essays on the Social Situation of Mental Patients and Other Inmates*. New York: Doubleday.

Hayes, Andrew (2013). *Introduction to Mediation, Moderation, and Conditional Process Analysis: Regression-based Approach*, New York: The Guilford Press.

Heckman, J., and E. Vytlacil. (2007a). Econometric evaluation of social programs, Part I: Causal models, structural models and econometric policy evaluations. In *Handbook of Econometrics, Vol. 6B*, ed., J. Heckman and E. Leamer. Amsterdam: North Holland Press.

Heckman, J., and E. Vytlacil. (2007b). Econometric evaluations of social programs, Part II: Using the marginal treatment effect to evaluate social programs, andto forecast their effects in new environments. In *Handbook of Econometrics, Vol. 6B*, ed., J. Heckman, and E. Leamer. Amsterdam: North-Holland Press.

Irwin, John. (2009). *Lifers: Seeking Redemption in Prison*. New York, NY: Routledge.

Jacobs, James B. (1977). *Stateville: The Penitentiary in Mass Society*. Chicago, IL: University of Chicago Press.

Katz, Lawrence, Steven D. Levitt, and Ellen Shustorovich. (2003). Prison Conditions, Capital Punishment, and Deterrence. *American Law and Economics Review*, 5(2): 318–43.

Lerman, A. (2009a). The people prisons make: effects of incarceration on criminal psychology. In S. Raphael, and M. A. Stoll (eds.), *Do Prisons Make us Safer? The Benefits and Costs of the Prison Boom*. New York: Russel Sage.

Lerman, A. (2009b). *Bowling Alone (With my Own Ball and Chain): Effects of Incarceration and the Dark Side of Social Capital*, Princeton University.

Lipsey, Mark W., Landenberger, Nana A., and Wilson, Sandra J. (2007) Effects of cognitive-behavioral programs for criminal offenders. *Campbell Systematic Reviews*, 2007:6.

MacKenzie, Doris Layton (2006). *What Works in Corrections: Reducing the Criminal Activities of Offenders and Delinquents*. New York: Cambridge University Press.

Nagin, Daniel S. (2005). *Group-based Modeling of Development*, Cambridge: Harvard University Press.

Nagin DS, Cullen FT, Jonson CL (2009). Imprisonment and reoffending. In M. Tonry (ed.), *Crime and Justice: A Review of Research* (Vol. 38, pp. 115–200). Chicago: University of Chicago Press.

National Research Council (2014). *The growth of incarceration in the United States: Exploring causes and consequences / Committee on Causes and Consequences of High Rates of Incarceration*, Jeremy Travis and Bruce Western, editors, Committee on Lawand Justice, Division of Behavioral and Social Sciences and Education. National Research Council of the National Academies.

Owen, Barbara. (1998). *"In the Mix": Struggle and Survival in a Women's Prison.* Albany, NY: State University of New York Press.

Raphel, Steven (2014). How do we reduce incarceration rates while maintain public safety? *Criminology and Public Policy*, 13(4): 579–597.

Rosenbaum, P. (2002). *Observational Studies.* 2nd edition. New York: Springer-Verlag.

Rosenbaum, P., and D. Rubin. (1984). Reducing bias in observational studies using subclassification on the propensity score. *Journal of the American Statistical Association*, 7: 516–24.

Roy, A. (1951). Some thoughts on the distribution of earnings. *Oxford Economic Papers*, 3: 135–46.

Smith P., Goggin C., Gendreau P., (2002). *Effets de l'incarcération et des sanctionsintermédiaires sur la récidive: effets généraux et différences individuelles*, Ottawa, Solicitor General of Canada.

Sykes, Gresham M. (1958). *The Society of Captives: A Study of a Maximum Security Prison.* Princeton, NJ: Princeton University Press.

Villetaz, Patrice, Martin Killias, and Isabel Zoder. (2006). *The effects of custodial vs. non-custodial sentences on re-offending: A systematic review of the state of knowledge*. Campbell Systematic Reviews. The Campbell Collaboration.

Introduction

Reentry and recidivism reduction programs

Thomas G. Blomberg, Julie Mestre Brancale, Kevin M. Beaver and William D. Bales

In recent years, there has been a considerable amount of research examining various in-prison treatment and training strategies and prisoner reentry and recidivism reduction programs. This section of the volume assesses some of this research and focuses upon several of the most promising evidence-based strategies.

In Chapter 21, Faye Taxman and Kimberly Kras discuss reentry from prison back to the community. The authors address a large number of important topics, including the ability to secure lawful stable employment, the difficulty in finding appropriate housing, the importance of social support networks, and the need for substance abuse treatment, among others. Their review of the existing research literature on prisoner reentry leads them to the conclusion that the most effective type of reentry program is one that includes probation and parole and follows the risk-need-responsivity framework. Programs that adhere to this sort of risk-need framework tend to achieve significant reductions in recidivism and thus are among the most promising evidence-based recidivism reduction programs.

Chapter 22, by Pamela Lattimore and Kelle Barrick, examines the effects of prison programming upon recidivism. The authors first review some of the literature related to prisoner reentry and its connection to recidivism. They then discuss the "what works" research, with a particular emphasis placed on the programs and treatment modalities that have consistently shown significant reductions in recidivism. Based upon their review of the research literature, Lattimore and Barrick contend that determining "what works" in prison programming is challenging due, in part, to practical issues and methodological/statistical limitations. They recommend a series of changes in the way that evaluation research is conducted and/or interpreted in order to facilitate a more meaningful and accurate interpretation of the findings that pertain to evidence-based prison programming policies and practices.

Carolyn Hoyle and Roxana Willis author Chapter 23, which deals directly with the challenges of integrating restorative justice into the criminal justice system. As Hoyle and Willis point out, restorative justice has been written about extensively, but its ability to be integrated into criminal justice policy has been lacking. In their chapter, they present a case study to detail some of the potential reasons why restorative justice has not taken on a more meaningful policy presence in the criminal justice system. They conclude by advocating for restorative justice to be more fully melded into criminal justice policy given its promise for a more just and effective criminal justice system.

Chapter 24, written by George Pesta and Thomas Blomberg, focuses upon the effectiveness of juvenile justice education programs for incarcerated delinquents. The authors begin their chapter by highlighting the strong empirical relationship between educational achievement and the lowered likelihood of juvenile delinquency. Because of this relationship, it seems reasonable that juvenile justice programs that seek to increase levels of education would have great promise in delinquency reduction. Pesta and Blomberg provide an historical context to juvenile justice education programs and use Florida's juvenile justice educational system as an empirical illustration of the value of emphasizing education in juvenile justice residential programs to reduce recidivism. The authors conclude that juvenile justice education programs can be effective in reducing recidivism, particularly when implemented correctly and when evaluated rigorously and regularly.

Policymakers and practitioners have begun to search for correctional strategies that are "smart on crime." At the forefront of this new era of "smart" criminal justice is identifying and implementing effective reentry and recidivism reduction programs. The majority of released inmates recidivate soon after they return to the community; therefore successful monitoring of post-release through probation or parole and the employment of a risk-need-responsivity framework promises to produce the greatest reductions in recidivism (Chapter 21). Effective in-prison programs vary considerably based on the characteristics of the offenders and implementation of the program (Chapter 22). Therefore, researchers and policymakers should collaborate to conduct rigorous evaluations and implement programs based on the needs of specific inmates. While the research on in-prison programming for adults is characterized by contingent findings, the research regarding recidivism reduction among juveniles is more clear, quality education while incarcerated is an effective strategy for reducing recidivism among juveniles (Chapter 24). Restorative justice techniques (Chapter 23), while not used as frequently as the other reentry and recidivism reduction programs discussed in this chapter, should be considered as potentially promising strategies for the criminal justice system and, therefore, subject to comprehensive research and evaluation.

Chapter 21

Reentry from incarceration to community

A convergence of practices based on scientific evidence to enhance citizenship

Faye S. Taxman and Kimberly R. Kras

Introduction

With over 20 percent of the U.S. adult population having some involvement in the justice system, the number of people reentering society from being in jail and/or prison is reported to be approximately 850,000 in 2013 (Glaze and Kaeble, 2014). Reentry is a process of transition from incarceration to the community, with the most effective outcomes resulting from assisting the individual in restoring citizenship. Citizenship implies regaining rights and privileges upon completion of a felony sentence, but also reinstatement into public life and defining for the individual their role in society (see Uggen et al., 2006). Regaining citizenship also is part of the identity transformation process toward desistance, or the exit from a life of crime (Maruna, 2001). These elements of reentry have been highlighted in recent calls to address the mass incarceration policies (see Travis et al., 2014) that have alienated individuals from society and created brick walls for reintegration (Taxman, 2004).

Reentry planning can assist in acquiring the needed skills and behavioral changes; however reentry practices vary according to the jail/prison system and local community corrections agencies. Reentry planning and reestablishment into the community has the potential to impact the process of recycling offenders through the justice system. With over 70 percent of those leaving prison being re-arrested within five years (Durose et al., 2014), concerns over the recycling rate (or recidivism rate) are justifiable. Reentry practices can impact the degree to which formerly incarcerated individuals resume their lives in the community. The challenge is to reduce barriers of reentry in order to build systems that facilitate those returning the community to be productive citizens, thereby reducing recidivism rates.

The transition process for reentry

During a period of incarceration, an individual is removed from the activities that affect daily living (i.e. acquiring food, shelter, clothing, employment, family relationships, parenting). However, the demands of everyday life are not erased when incarcerated since most offenders have a presence in the community, have children and families, accrue child support and other debts, care for loved ones, and address a myriad of life issues. These life arenas are important reentry considerations for programs that assist the returning offender in retaining the role as a productive citizen. Preparation for reentry into the community may be difficult because the incarcerated person needs to maintain some continuity of existence, as well as build linkages before release. This chapter explores what is known about reentry to build citizenship in regard to housing, employment, social support, substance use treatment, and community supervision. The chapter concludes with an agenda to advance knowledge in the building of citizenship as part of reintegration.

Housing

Housing is a critical and immediate concern for individuals, and it presents significant ongoing challenges for offenders released from prison (Visher and Courtney, 2007). Lack of a viable housing plan, housing shortages, and reduced economic capital contribute to reentry difficulties for offenders. In addition, those with the felony label or parolee status are generally considered "least eligible" for housing aid (Travis, 2005), and recent evidence suggests property owners are reluctant to rent to individuals with any criminal record (Clark, 2007; Thacher, 2008). Offenders are financially stymied from obtaining their own housing (i.e. apartment, single room) due to poor credit, limited employment records, and constrained wage prospects (Bradley et al., 2001; Graffam et al., 2008; Harris et al., 2010). Barriers to housing typically include legal restrictions, such as sex offender residence restrictions (Huebner et al., 2014) and limited housing subsidies available to felons (Roman, 2004). Together, both legal and non-legal barriers to housing further increase the need for parolee housing assistance programs (for a review, see Legal Action Center, 2009).

Emerging research emphasizes the importance of stable, independent housing to assist offenders in successfully reintegrating into the community (Roman and Travis, 2006). The "housing first" movement prioritizes housing above all other needs to stabilize a person in the community before addressing other issues, such as substance abuse or criminal cognitions. Research demonstrates positive outcomes for homeless and mentally ill populations (Henwood et al., 2011; Tsemberis et al., 2004), as well as chronic alcoholics (Collins, et al., 2012). Few studies are conducted with individuals reentering from prison, but the convergence of public health evidence with individuals with behavioral health disorders provides sufficient evidence to heighten the importance of housing as a stabilizing factor. For example, Padgett and colleagues (2011) compared a population of homeless and mentally ill individuals assigned to either a housing first program or a treatment only program. Housing first participants had reduced substance use and increased adherence to their substance abuse program, compared to the treatment only group who were more than three times as likely to use drugs and go AWOL from their substance abuse program. Other program evaluations suggest the housing first model has great promise for individuals with dual diagnosis, including substance abuse disorders and mental health challenges (Padgett et al., 2006; Tsemberis et al., 2004) or those with alcohol dependence (Collins et al., 2012).

The reentry literature indicates that offenders with a stable residence are better integrated into the community (Clear, 2007). Housing enables the development of social networks and social capital, thereby assisting the offender in regaining citizenship. The primary source of housing for offenders upon release is typically family or friends; but this option is neither always available nor stable (Makarios et al., 2010; Huebner and Pleggenkuhle, 2013). Approximately 10 to 20 percent of offenders are released from prison without a home plan and this problem is even greater in urban areas (Rodriguez and Brown, 2003; Roman and Travis, 2006). In general, pre-release programming specifically related to housing infrequently occurs, with less than half of cases released into the community receiving assistance (Roman and Travis, 2006). In piloting housing programs, the most successful are those that provide access to additional services. For example, the Washington State's Reentry Housing Pilot Program (RHPP) evaluation found that participants who resided in program housing and had wraparound services were less likely to commit new crimes as compared to a control group who did not receive housing or other services (Lutze et al., 2014).

Transitional housing, such as halfway houses, provides temporary shelter to facilitate a seamless move from prison to community (Petersilia, 2003) and improve correctional outcomes (Fontaine et al., 2012; Wright et al., 2013). For example, Worcel and colleagues (2008) found that individuals who resided in transitional housing had increased self-sufficiency, such as attaining driver's licenses and eventually securing independent housing. Other housing studies have shown reduced recidivism for substance abuse and sex offenders (Lowenkamp and Latessa, 2005; Latessa et al., 2010; Jengeleski and Gordon, 2003; Willison et al., 2010). Despite research and clinical evidence, there remains a dearth in housing programs for reentering individuals, and the current practices of correctional departments and housing agencies vary greatly in terms of their effect on outcomes.

Employment

Employment is often highlighted as the next most important feature of successful reintegration for offenders (Petersilia, 2003; Baer et al., 2006) since it provides the needed finances to be self-sufficient. Offenders encounter many barriers to employment that some reentry programs seek to overcome, such as lack of job training, criminal history, the stigma of a felony conviction, and being a minority (Pager, 2003; Western, 2008). While employers might be willing to hire someone with a criminal record, the type of conviction does affect the inclination to hire an individual (Atkin and Armstrong, 2011). For example, sex offenders seeking employment may find the nature of their crime impacts the ability to obtain employment more than merely having a conviction (Kras et al., 2014; Brown et al., 2007). Most reentry programs rely on vocational and educational programs to improve offenders' marketable skills (Petersilia and Reitz, 2012; Brazzell et al., 2009).

Despite concerns about employment for offenders upon release, there are few programs, and even fewer studies, with mixed evidence of the effectiveness of employment training programs on employment and recidivism. Positive effects on employment and recidivism were shown in an evaluation of the EMPLOY program (Minnesota) that provides offenders with pre-release employment programming followed by one year of employment assistance in the community. Offenders who completed the program showed a reduced risk of recidivism compared to a matched group of offenders who did not participate in the program. Furthermore, the EMPLOY offenders had increased odds of gaining employment by 72 percent, had higher wages and more work hours than non-participating offenders (Duwe, 2012).

Some limited improvements in employment were found in an evaluation of the Center for Employment Opportunities (CEO) program, but no changes occurred in recidivism rates (Redcross et al., 2011). Using a quasi-experimental design, the comparison group received general employment assistance while the treatment group received intensive job skills training and temporary jobs. While employment rates for the treatment group increased from 50 percent to 80 percent in the first year post-release, the gains in employment did not sustain over a two-year period where the treatment group had similar employment levels as the comparison group. While employment rates showed increases during the first year, the re-arrest rates were similar for both groups. In a randomized control trial of the Milwaukee Safe Streets Initiative, a pre-release employment program with post-release assistance, Cook et al. (2014) found increased employment and wage earnings during the first year of release and reductions in likelihood of re-arrest; however, there was no difference in the reincarceration rate.

Recent meta-analyses of reentry employment programs in the community suggest they have negligible effects on recidivism (Visher et al., 2005; Drake et al., 2009).[1] However, a recent series of studies suggest emphasizing behavioral change as a function of employment programs, rather than recidivism, may yield better results (Apel, 2011). For example, the Serious and Violent Offender Reentry Initiative (SVORI) provided employment services to its participants, but only 40 percent reported working each month. Participants in employment services in the SVORI study did not show reductions in recidivism and in some cases were negatively associated with other aspects of successful integration (Lattimore et al., 2012). Having employment services did not improve the quality or pay of employment for SVORI participants, but life skills training helped those who were not employed prior to incarceration to obtain a job. This finding is consistent with other scholars who posit that work alone may not improve recidivism (Bushway and Apel, 2012), but programs including cognitive and behavioral approaches might impact the person's ability to work and to be a productive citizen. In a review of prisoner reentry programs, Petersilia and Reitz (2012) concluded that such programs are critical for increasing employment and reducing recidivism, but only if accompanied by individual change (also see Latessa, 2012). Although employment programs have varied success in reducing recidivism, being employed may signal to others that the reentering individual is making progress in assuming a citizenship role (Bushway and Apel, 2012).

Social support networks

During the period of reentry, offenders typically rely on family, friends, and other members of their community to support their transition. Social support networks may provide instrumental assistance with housing, financial aid, transportation, and clothing in addition to a variety of expressive (emotional) forms of support. Social support can provide the bonds and conventional attachments to pro-social others, both close-knit and within the larger community. Such supports may buffer the chronic nature of stressors, such as those associated with re entry experiences like financial problems, housing issues, and substance abuse (Pettus-Davis et al., 2011). In a study of parolees, Hochstetler and colleagues (2010) found that increased social support upon release reduced feelings of hostility and psychosocial problems. A recent study by Wallace and colleagues (2014) showed that even though pre-prison familial support did not affect mental health after release, having positive family support upon return from prison did improve mental health functionality such as psychosocial well-being and distress.

Positive social support for offenders is associated with positive stabilization in the community such as stable housing, increased employment, and reduced recidivism (Petersilia, 2003; Visher et al., 2009; Bahr et al., 2010). Many offenders identify family support as one of the most important factors in desistance and positive behavior change (Visher and Travis, 2003; Solomon et al., 2006; Naser and LaVigne, 2006; Visher and Courtney, 2007; Mallik-Kane and Visher, 2008; Mills and Codd, 2008) with expressive support being critical (Nelson et al., 1999). Visher and Courtney (2007) found that 63 percent of offenders felt family support would be the most important factor in avoiding the return to prison. Family support plays a key role in assisting the offender in developing social capital within their community by connecting them to employment opportunities, encouraging positive behavior change, and providing access to conventional activities that encourage citizenship (Flavin, 2004; Berg and Huebner, 2011; Visher et al., 2008).

Positive, pro-social relationships with a spouse or intimate partner are important for offender success since they can provide conventional bonds needed to desist from crime (Laub and Sampson, 2003; King et al., 2007). A recent study found that married offenders had significantly lower levels of subsequent criminal activity and drug use than unmarried offenders (LaVigne et al., 2004; see also Visher et al., 2009; Solomon et al., 2006). Friends can be a source of informal social control providing positive instrumental and expressive support, such as employment connections and improved self-esteem (Mallik-Kane and Visher, 2008). Successful parolees are more likely to engage in positive activities with friends that contribute to desistance (Warr, 1998; Bahr et al., 2010). But friendships can be complicated since many friends are part of a criminogenic social network (Warr, 1998; Laub and Sampson, 2003; Visher and Travis, 2003; LaVigne et al., 2004; Cobbina et al., 2012). Social support programs that assist offenders in establishing pro-social relationships can improve the odds of success upon release (see Pettus-Davis et al., 2015).

Social support has been highlighted as an important component of successful reentry in the community and many transitional programs included in other programs. Few programs have focused solely on this particular element of the offenders' reintegration process. But some evaluations of holistic reentry processes demonstrated positive associations between social support and outcomes. In the Minnesota Comprehensive Reentry Program (MCORP) program, Duwe (2012) found that participants in the program were more likely to report a broader social support network as compared to the comparison group.

A common theme in the research literature is that social network connections while in prison tend to produce more successful reintegration of offenders. Visits in prison are associated with reductions in recidivism (Barrick et al., 2014; Cochran, 2014; Bales and Mears, 2008; Jiang and Winfree, 2006; Duwe and Clark, 2013). For example, the Circles of Support and Accountability (COSA) designed for sex offenders, provides returning sex offenders with a support network of community members with instrumental and expressive support and accountability of offender behavior. Offenders in COSA have reduced recidivism and failure on parole compared with those who do not participate in such programming (Wilson et al., 2009).

Social support, while it makes intuitive sense, is difficult to build in programming. Some reentry programs have tried to operationalize positive social supports, especially expressive and instrumental support (Pettus-Davis et al., 2014/2015), but there lacks consensus on how best to achieve these relationships. While social support is a crucial resource for returning offenders who rely on these actors to provide other components of re entry, the dearth of programming to re-establish and enhance these supports is an area that warrants further research.

Substance abuse treatment

With over 80 percent of offenders reporting to have some involvement with illicit drugs, providing substance abuse treatment services during prison and after release from prison can reduce recidivism (Taxman et al., 2007). Numerous meta-analyses have documented the positive results from Therapeutic Community programming and cognitive-behavioral therapy (CBT) on reducing recidivism as compared to other counseling or treatment approaches (Mitchell et al., 2007; Lipsey et al., 2007; Prendergast et al., 2002). While findings support the efficacy of substance abuse treatment for offenders, the most important part of treatment is providing services in the community after release. Studies have found that drug treatment in prison without aftercare is not effective, but when aftercare is provided there are reductions in recidivism (Mitchell et al., 2007).

While substance abuse treatment is effective in reducing recidivism, it is important that the treatment be evidence-based. It needs to be of sufficient duration (at least 90 days if not closer to 18 months), target higher risk offenders, include anger management therapy, and have an evaluator included in the program (see Lipsey et al., 2007 for a discussion of effective components of effective programming). Of course, providing effective treatment, and the right type of treatment for offenders, is the major challenge. Taxman et al. (2013), using a survey of programs in prison and in the community, found that the system has the capacity to provide substance abuse treatment services to about 10 percent of the offenders. More importantly, those services provided did not meet the standards identified by the evidence-based practices and treatment literature (see the National Institute on Drug Abuse, 2006). The services were insufficient in the types of services available, the duration, and the use of clinical staff. Essentially those services were more likely to provide psychosocial educational services instead of clinical, therapeutic services. Simulation models have found that when offenders are provided with the appropriate services in the community, recidivism rates can be significantly reduced (Taxman et al., 2014).

Substance abuse treatment programs stabilize the person to allow for the transition from prison to the community, may be beneficial for offenders in maintaining the sobriety needed to achieve success in other elements of reentry, such as establishing housing, obtaining and maintaining employment, and rebuilding social support relationships. Addressing substance use behaviors is associated with restoring citizenship in communities because the "clean" individual moves closer to pro-social functioning and accessing conventional roles in society.

Parole supervision or reentry supervision

Overall, parole supervision has been found to be ineffective in terms of reducing recidivism or program failures (technical violators; Petersilia and Turner, 1993; Taxman, 2002; Taxman, 2008). Typical supervision models, which emphasize surveillance and sanctions, have not assisted offenders in addressing their myriad of needs. One model of supervision that has been effective is the Risk-Need-Responsivity (RNR) framework (Andrews and Bonta, 2006; Taxman, 2008; 2009). Drake (2011) found that supervision following the RNR framework reduced recidivism by 16 percent as compared to standard supervision with treatment which reduced by 10 percent. The RNR framework has five components: use of a valid risk and need assessment instrument, use of a case plan that specifies treatment and programming appropriate to the risk and need profile of the individual, use of cognitive behavioral therapy, use of rewards (over sanctions) to incentive offenders, and use of a strong working relationship between the officer and offenders that promotes fair and just processes. The RNR framework provides for individualized supervision that focuses on addressing the specific risks and needs of an offender, including issues related to substance abuse treatment, housing, employment, and social supports This supervision model has potential for improving the reentry process for offenders because it accounts for the varied experiences, challenges and strengths of each. Transitions to the community that are supported by criminal justice agents trained in the RNR principles (see Taxman, 2008 and Oleson et al., 2012 for reviews on the challenges of training probation and parole officers) should better equip the offender in handling challenges, solving problems, and reinserting himself into the fabric of society.

Conclusion

For reentry to be successful, and returning offenders to have a chance at restoring citizenship, the research evidence suggests that programs and services need to be individualized, integrated, and seamlessly transitioned from prison to the community. While offenders can regain the components of citizenship (the right to vote, licensure for employment, and access to public assistance) after completing their sentence, the elements of being a citizen in the community are harder to reestablish. Reentry practices, parole supervision, and transition services should use the RNR framework since it provides the best potential effort to advance positive outcomes by emphasizing the needs and responses of individual offenders. Reentry programming, such as effective substance abuse treatment services (preferably beginning in prison followed by aftercare) that address the challenges inhibiting full participation in the community are necessary. These treatment services should emphasize individual behavior change, have a sufficient duration of care, and be in sufficient quantity so that offenders can access appropriate services. Added to this basic framework is the need to ensure that appropriate supports are available including housing, social supports, employment, and other needs like mental health. For the transition process from prison to the community to be successful, supervision strategies, treatment services, and communities need to focus on aspects of the transition that enable desistance. Desistance is most successful when the individual reentering the community assumes an identity of a citizen, and not one of a criminal. By addressing the reentry needs of offenders they have a better opportunity to adopt a conventional role. Citizenship has the greatest potential to facilitate reduced recidivism.

Note

1 Scholars note the studies used in the meta-analysis are old and may not reflect current employment practices and trends in employability of ex-offenders (Visher et al., 2005).

References

Andrews, D. and Bonta, J. (2006). *The Psychology of Criminal Conduct*. (4th edition) Newark, NJ: LexisNexis.

Apel, R. (2011). Transitional jobs program: Putting employment-based reentry programs into context. *Criminology and Public Policy*, 10(4), 939–942.

Atkin, C. A., and Armstrong, G. S. (2011). Does the concentration of parolees in a community impact employer attitudes toward the hiring of ex-offenders?. *Criminal Justice Policy Review*, doi: 0887403411428005.

Baer, D., Bhati, A., Brooks, L., Castro, J., La Vigne, N., Mallik-Kane, K., and Winterfield, L. (2006). *Understanding the Challenges of Prisoner Reentry: Research Findings from the Urban Institute's Prisoner Reentry Portfolio*. Washington, DC: The Urban Institute.

Bahr, S.J., Harris, L., Fisher, J.K., and Armstrong, A.H. (2010). Successful reentry: What differentiates successful and unsuccessful parolees? *International Journal of Offender Therapy and Comparative Criminology*, 54, 667–692.

Bales, W.D., and Mears, D.P. (2008). Inmate social ties and the transition to society: Does visitation reduce recidivism? *Journal of Research in Crime and Delinquency*, 45, 287–321.

Barrick, K., Lattimore, P. K., and Visher, C. A. (2014). Reentering women: The impact of social ties on long-term recidivism. *The Prison Journal*, September 2014, 94(3), 279–304.

Berg, M. T., and Huebner, B. M. (2011). Reentry and the ties that bind: An examination of social ties, employment, and recidivism. *Justice Quarterly*, 28(2), 382–410.

Bradley, K. H., Oliver, R.B. M., Richardson, N. C., and Slayter, E. M. (2001). *No place like home: Housing and the ex-prisoner*. Policy Brief: Community Resources for Justice.

Brazzell, D., A. Crayton, D. A. Mukamal, A. L. Solomon, and N. Lindahl. 2009. *From the Classroom to the Community: Exploring the Role of Education During Incarceration and Reentry.* Washington, DC: The Urban Institute, Justice Policy Center.

Brown, K., Spencer, J., and Deakin, J. (2007). The reintegration of sex offenders: Barriers and opportunities for employment. *The Howard Journal,* 46, 32–42.

Bushway, S. D., and Apel, R. (2012). A signaling perspective on employment-based reentry programming. *Criminology and Public Policy,* 11(1), 21–50.

Clark, L. M. (2007). Landlord attitudes toward renting to released offenders. *Federal Probation,* 71(1), 20–30.

Clear, T. (2007). *Imprisoning Communities: How Mass Incarceration Makes Disadvantaged Neighborhoods Worse.* New York Oxford University Press.

Cobbina, J. E, Huebner, B.M., and Berg, M.T. (2012). Men, women and postrelease offending: An examination of the nature of the link between relational ties and recidivism. *Crime and Delinquency,* 58, 331–361.

Cochran, J.C. 2014. Breaches in the wall: Imprisonment, social support, and recidivism. *Journal of Research in Crime and Delinquency,* 51(2), 200–229.

Collins, Malone, Clifasefi, Ginzler, Garner, et al., (2012). Project-based housing first for chronically homeless individuals with alcohol problems: Within-subjects analyses of 2-year alcohol trajectories. *American Journal of Public Health,* 102(3), 511–519.

Cook, P. J., Kang, S., Braga, A. A., Ludwig, J., and O'Brien, M. E. (2014). An Experimental Evaluation of a Comprehensive Employment-Oriented Prisoner Re-entry Program. *Journal of Quantitative Criminology,* 1–28.

Drake, Elizabeth, Steve Aos, and Marna Miller. (2009). Evidence-based public policy options to reduce crime and criminal justice costs: Implications in Washington State. *Victims and Offenders,* 4, 170–196.

Drake, E. K. (2011). *"What works" in community supervision: Interim report.* Document No. 11-12-1201. Olympia: Washington State Institute for Public Policy.

Durose, Matthew R., Cooper, Alexia D. Cooper, and Snyder, Howard. (2014). *Recidivism of prisoners released in 30 states: Patterns from 2005–2010.* Washington, DC: Bureau of Justice Statics, U.S. Department of Justice.

Duwe, G. (2012). Evaluating the Minnesota comprehensive offender reentry plan (MCORP): Results from a randomized experiment. *Justice Quarterly,* 29(3), 347–383.

Duwe, G., and Clark, V. (2013). Blessed be the social tie that binds the effects of prison visitation on offender recidivism. *Criminal Justice Policy Review,* 24(3), 271–296.

Flavin, J. (2004). Employment counseling, housing assistance... and Aunt Yolanda?: How strengthening families' social capital can reduce recidivism. *Criminology and Public Policy,* 3(2), 209–216.

Fontaine, J., Gilchrist-Scott, D., Roman, J., Taxy, S., and Roman, C. (2012). *Supportive Housing for Returning Prisoners.* The Urban Institute, Justice Policy Center.

Glaze, L.E. and Kaeble, D, (2014). *Correctional Populations in the United States, 2013.* U.S. Department of Justice, Bureau of Justice Statistics.

Graffam, J., Shinkfield, A. J., and Hardcastle, L. (2008). The perceived employability of ex- prisoners and offenders. *International Journal of Offender Therapy and Comparative Criminology,* 52(6), 673–685.

Harris, A., Evans, H., and Beckett, K. (2010). Drawing blood from stones: Legal debt and social inequality in the contemporary United States. *American Journal of Sociology*, 115(6), 1753–1799.

Henwood, B. F., Stanhope, V., and Padgett, D. K. (2011). The role of housing: A comparison of front-line provider views in housing first and traditional programs. *Administration and Policy in Mental Health and Mental Health Services Research*, 38(2), 77–85.

Hochstetler, A., DeLisi, M., and Pratt, T.C. (2010). Social support and feelings of hostility among released inmates. *Crime and Delinquency*, 56, 588–607.

Huebner, B. M., Kras, K. R., Rydberg, J., Bynum, T. S., Grommon, E., and Pleggenkuhle, B. (2014). The effect and implications of sex offender residence restrictions: Evidence from a two-state evaluation. *Criminology and Public Policy*, 13(1), 139–168.

Huebner, B. M. and Pleggenkuhle, B. (2013). Residential location, household composition, and recidivism: An analysis by gender. *Justice Quarterly*, doi: 1 0.1080/07418825.2013.827231.

Jengeleski, J. L., and Gordon, M. S. (2003). The Kintock Group, Inc. Employment Resource Center: a two-year post-release evaluation study. *Journal of Correctional Education*, 27–30.

Jiang, S., and Winfree, L.T. (2006). Social support, gender, and inmate adjustment to prison life: Insights from a national sample. *The Prison Journal*, 86, 32–55.

King, R.D., Massoglia, M., and MacMillan, R. (2007). The context of marriage and crime: gender, the propensity to marry, and offending in early adulthood. *Criminology*, 45, 33–65.

Kras, K. R., Pleggenkuhle, B., and Huebner, B. M. (2014). A new way of doing time on the outside: Sex offenders' pathways in and out of a transitional housing facility. *International Journal of Offender Therapy and Comparative Criminology*, doi 0306624X14554194.

Latessa, E. (2012). Why work is important, and how to improve the effectiveness of correctional reentry programs that target employment. *Criminology and Public Policy*, 11(1), 87–91.

Latessa, E. J., Lovins, L. B., and Smith, P. (2010). *Follow-up Evaluation of Ohio's Community Residential Correctional Facility and Halfway House Programs Outcome Study*. Final Report. Cincinnati: School of Criminal Justice, University of Cincinnati.

Lattimore, P. K., Barrick, K., Cowell, A., Dawes, D., Steffey, D., Tueller, S., and Visher, C. A. (2012). Prisoner reentry services: What worked for SVORI evaluation participants. Washington, DC: National Institute of Justice.

Laub, J. H., and Sampson, R. J. (2003). *Shared Beginnings, Divergent Lives: Delinquent Boys to Age 70*. Harvard University Press.

La Vigne, N. G., Visher, C., and Castro, J. (2004). *Chicago Prisoners' Experiences Returning Home*. Washington, DC: The Urban Institute.

Legal Action Center. (2009). *After prison: Roadblocks to reentry*. A Report on State Legal Barriers Facing People with Criminal Records: 2009 Update.

Lipsey, M. W., Landenberger, N. A. and Wilson, S. J. (2007). Effects of cognitive-behavioral programs for criminal offenders. *Campbell Systematic Reviews*. Retrieved from http://campbellcollaboration.org/lib/project/29/.

Lowenkamp, C.T. and Latessa, E.J. (2005). Increasing the effectiveness of correctional programming through the risk principle: Identifying offenders for residential placement. *Criminology and Public Policy*, 4, 263–290.

Lutze, F. E., Rosky, J. W., and Hamilton, Z. K. (2014). Homelessness and reentry a multisite outcome evaluation of Washington State's reentry housing program for high risk offenders. *Criminal Justice and Behavior*, 41(4), 471–491.

Mallik-Kane, K., and Visher, C.A. (2008). Health and prisoner reentry: How physical, mental, and substance abuse conditions shape the process of reintegration. *Urban Institute, Justice Policy Center*.

Makarios, M., Steiner, B., and Travis, L. F. (2010). Examining the predictors of recidivism among men and women released from prison in Ohio. *Criminal Justice and Behavior*, 37(12), 1377–1391.

Maruna, Shadd. (2001). *Making Good: How Ex-Convicts Reform and Rebuild Their Lives*. Washington, DC: American Psychological Association.

Mills, A., and Codd, H. (2008). Prisoners' families and offender management: Mobilizing social capital. *Probation Journal*, 55, 9–24.

Mitchell, O., Wilson, D. B., and MacKenzie, D. L. (2007). Does incarceration-based drug treatment reduce recidivism? A meta-analytic synthesis of the research. *Journal of Experimental Criminology*, 3(4), 353–375.

National Institute on Drug Abuse, (2006). *Principles of Drug Abuse Treatment Criminal Justice*. Bethesda, MD: National Institute on Drug Abuse. Doi: http://www.drugabuse.gov/publications/principles-drug-abuse-treatment-criminal-justice-populations/principles

Naser, R.L., and LaVigne, N.G. (2006). Family support in the prisoner reentry process: Expectations and realities. *Journal of Offender Rehabilitation*, 43, 93–106.

Nelson, M., Deess, P., and Allen, C. (1999). *The first month out: Post-incarceration experiences in New York City*. Vera Institute of Justice.

Oleson, J. C., VanBenschoten, S., Robinson, C., Lowenkamp, C. T., and Holsinger, A. M. (2012). Actuarial and clinical assessment of criminogenic needs: identifying supervision priorities among federal probation officers. *Journal of Crime and Justice*, 35(2), 239–248.

Padgett, D. K., Gulcar, L., and Tsemberis, S. (2006). Housing first services for people who are homeless with co-occurring serious mental illness and substance abuse. *Research on Social Work Practice*, 16(1), 74–83.

Padgett, D. K., Stanhope, V., Henwood, B. F., and Stefancic, A. (2011). Substance use outcomes among homeless clients with serious mental illness: comparing housing first with treatment first programs. *Community Mental Health Journal*, 47(2), 227–232.

Pager, D. (2003). The mark of a criminal record. *American Journal of Sociology*, 108(5), 937–975.

Petersilia, Joan. (2003). *When Prisoners Come Home*. New York: Oxford University Press.

Petersilia, J. and S. Turner. (1993). *Evaluating Intensive Supervision Probation/Parole: Results of a Nationwide Experiment*. Washington, DC: National Institute of Justice.

Petersilia, J., and Reitz, K. R. (eds.). (2012). *The Oxford Handbook of Sentencing and Corrections*. Oxford University Press.

Pettus-Davis, C., Howard, M.O., Roberts-Lewis, A., and Scheyett, A.M. (2011). Naturally occurring social support in interventions for former prisoners with substance use disorders: Conceptual framework and program model. *Journal of Criminal Justice*, 39, 479–488.

Pettus-Davis, C. Howard, M.O., Murugan, V., Roberts-Lewis, A., Scheyett, A.M., Botnick, C., andVance, M.(online first, 2014/2015). Acceptability of a social support intervention for reentering prisoners. *Journal for Society of Social Work and Research*.

Prendergast, M. L., Podus, D., Chang, E., and Urada, D. (2002). The effectiveness of drug abuse treatment: a meta-analysis of comparison group studies. *Drug and Alcohol Dependence*, 67(1), 53–72.

Redcross, C., Millenky, M., Rudd, T., and Levshin, V. (2011). More than a job: final results from the evaluation of the Center for Employment Opportunities (CEO) transitional jobs program. *OPRE Report*, 18.

Rodriguez, N. and Brown, B. (2003). *Homelessness among People Leaving Prison*. Vera Institute of Justice. Available at: www.vera.org.

Roman, C. G. (2004). *Taking stock: Housing, homelessness, and prisoner reentry*. Urban Institute, Justice Policy Center.

Roman, C. and Travis, J. (2006). Where will I sleep tomorrow? Housing, homelessness, and the returning prisoner. *Housing Policy Debate*, 17, 389–418.

Solomon, A.L., Visher, C.A., LaVigne, N., and Osborne, J. (2006). *Understanding the Challenges of Prisoner Reentry: Research Findings from the Urban Institute's Prisoner Reentry Portfolio*. Urban Institute, Justice Policy Center.

Taxman, F.S. (2002). Supervision: Exploring the dimensions of effectiveness. *Federal Probation*, 66(2), 14–27.

Taxman, F.S. (2004). The offender and reentry: Supporting active participation in reintegration. *Federal Probation*, 68(2), 31–35.

Taxman, F.S. (2008). No illusion, offender and organizational change in Maryland's proactive community supervision model. *Criminology and Public Policy*, 7(2), 275–302.

Taxman, F.S., Perdoni, M.L., and Harrison, L.D. (2007). Drug treatment services for adult offenders: The state of the state. *Journal of Substance Abuse Treatment*, 32(3), 239–254.

Taxman, F.S., Perdoni, M., and Caudy, M. (2013). The plight of providing appropriate substance abuse treatment services to offenders: Modeling the gaps in service delivery. *Victims and Offenders*, 8(1), 70–93.

Taxman, F.S., Pattavina, A., and Caudy, M. (2014). Justice reinvestment in the US: The case for more programs. *Victims and Offenders*, 9(1), 50–75.

Thacher, D. (2008). The rise of criminal background screening in rental housing. *Law and Social Inquiry*, 33(1), 5–30.

Travis, J. (2005). *But they all come back: Facing the challenges of prisoner reentry*. The Urban Institute, Justice Policy Center.

Travis, J., Western, B. and Redburn, S. eds. (2014) *The Growth of Incarceration in the United States: Exploring Causes and Consequences*, Washington, DC: The National Academies Press.

Tsemberis, S., Gulcar, L., and Nakae, M. (2004). Housing first, consumer choice, and harm reduction for homeless individuals with a dual diagnosis. *American Journal of Public Health*, 94 (4), 651–656.

Uggen, C., Manza, J., and Thompson, M. (2006). Citizenship, democracy, and the civic reintegration of criminal offenders. *The Annals of the American Academy of Political and Social Science*, 605(1), 281–310.

Visher, C.A., and Travis, J. (2003). Transitions from prison to community: understanding individual pathways. *Annual Review Sociology*, 29, 89–113.

Visher, C.A. and Courtney, S.M.E. (2007). *One year out: Experiences of prisoners returning to Cleveland. Returning Home: Understanding the Challenges of Prisoner Re-entry.* The Urban Institute, Justice Policy Center.

Visher, C. A., Winterfield, L., and Coggeshall, M. B. (2005). Ex-offender employment programs and recidivism: A meta-analysis. *Journal of Experimental Criminology*, 1(3), 295–316.

Visher, C. A., Debus, S., and Yahner, J. (2008). *Employment after prison: A longitudinal study of releases in three states.* Urban Institute, Justice Policy Center.

Visher, C.A., Knight, C.R., Chalfin, A., and Roman, J.K. (2009). *The impact of marital and relationship status on social outcomes for returning prisoners.* The Urban Institute: Justice Policy Center.

Wallace, D., Fahmy, C., Cotton, L., Jimmons, C., McKay, R., Stoffer, S., and Syed, S. (2014). Examining the role of familial support during prison and after release on post- incarceration mental health. *International Journal of Offender Therapy and Comparative Criminology*, doi: 0306624X14548023.

Warr, M. (1998). Life-course transitions and desistance from crime. *Criminology*, 36(2), 183–216.

Western, B. (2008). Criminal background checks and employment among workers with criminal records. *Criminology and Public Policy*, 7(3), 413–417.

Willison, J., Roman, C.G., Wolff, A., Correa, V. and Knight, C.R. (2010). *Evaluation of the Ridge House Residential Program: Final Report.* U.S. Department of Justice.

Wilson, R. J., Cortoni, F., and McWhinnie, A. J. (2009). Circles of Support and Accountability: A Canadian national replication of outcome findings. *Sexual Abuse: A Journal of Research and Treatment*, 21(4), 412–430.

Worcel, S.D., Burrus, S.W.M., and Finigan, M.W. (2008). *Study of Substance-Free Transitional Housing and Community Corrections in Washington County, Oregon.* U.S. Department of Justice.

Wright, K. A., Pratt, T. C., Lowenkamp, C. T., and Latessa, E. J. (2013). The systemic model of crime and institutional efficacy: An analysis of the social context of offender reintegration. *International Journal of Offender Therapy and Comparative Criminology*, 57(1), 92–111.

Chapter 22

The effects of prison programming

Pamela K. Lattimore and Kelle Barrick

Introduction

Until recently, the U.S. experienced an unprecedented increase in the number of offenders leaving prison. The annual number of releases surpassed half a million for the first time in 1997 and steadily increased to 734,144 in 2008; prison releases began declining over the next few years to 637,411 in 2012 (Carson and Golinelli, 2014). Moreover, many offenders released from prison will recidivate and return to prison. On the high end, research suggests that more than half (55.5 percent) of prison releasees in a given year will be reincarcerated within five years (Durose et al., 2014). Rhodes and colleagues (2014: 18) argue that the event-based methods used to generate these reincarceration rates, which allow an offender to enter the sample each time he is released during the observation window, "exaggerates the failure of offenders, because of the inherent bias of over-representing high-risk offenders." Using an alternative offender-based sample, which only includes one release for each prisoner, Rhodes et al. found that only one-in-three prisoners were reincarcerated within 12 years of release. However, their research averaged state-level recidivism rates which may have resulted in an alternative source of bias in which individuals in low incarceration rate states – which have relatively few prisoners, releases, and recidivists – contributed disproportionately to their findings. Regardless of the specific reincarceration rate, prisons continue to release over half a million offenders annually and experts agree that recidivism rates are too high (National Research Council, 2008).

In this context, it is not surprising that identifying means of reducing recidivism through effective reentry programming for prisoners has been the focus of recent Federal efforts, beginning with the Serious and Violent Offender Reentry Initiative (SVORI) that funded grants in 2002 and, more recently, a variety of grant programs funded through the Second Chance Act (nearly $450 million authorized during fiscal years 2010–2015). Given the inevitable return to society for many prisoners and high expected recidivism rates, researchers have recently focused on the process of desistance among released prisoners in an effort to identify effective ways to help reintegrate offenders into the community and reduce the likelihood that they will eventually return to criminal activity. The first section of this chapter summarizes the extant literature on the effectiveness of various prisoner reentry programs at reducing recidivism, the second section describes several considerations important to interpreting and understanding these research findings, and the third section concludes with recommendations for policy and future research.

Literature review

Released prisoners face numerous obstacles in successfully reintegrating into the community, including limited education and vocational training and experience, substance abuse problems, physical and mental health problems, strained family relations, and the stigma associated with a criminal record (Broner et al., 2010; Petersilia, 2003; Travis and Visher, 2005). Individuals transitioning from prison to the community thus express high levels of need for a wide variety of services, including those associated with basic practical needs, such as housing, transportation, and employment (Lattimore et al., 2008; Petersilia, 2003). Reentry programming and services are designed to facilitate offenders' transition from prison and, ultimately, reduce recidivism. Much reentry programming is premised on a "standard" correctional program logic model, presented in Figure 22.1, which moves from: obtaining resources; to implementing services targeted at specific needs, such as drug treatment or employment services; to either direct effects on recidivism or indirect effects on recidivism through improvements in other (intermediate) outcomes, such as staying sober and securing employment. Yet, the evidence supporting the effectiveness of such programs, particularly those targeting practical needs, is equivocal.

Reviews of the "what works" literature for adult and juvenile offenders, as well as several meta-analyses of studies on institutional- and community-based interventions and treatment programs for these populations, have suggested that human service-oriented programs are more effective at reducing the likelihood of recidivism than control or deterrent approaches such as surveillance and contact-driven supervision (Cullen and Gendreau, 2000; Fonagy and Kurtz, 2002; Lipsey and Cullen, 2007; MacKenzie, 2006). For example, intensive supervision probation/parole (ISP) by itself does not reduce recidivism (MacKenzie, 2006), but there is evidence that ISP that includes a strong treatment component can reduce recidivism (Aos et al., 2006; Petersilia and Turner, 1993). Moreover, in their review of recidivism studies, Lipsey and Cullen (2007) report that rehabilitation programs consistently result in reductions in recidivism; however, there is substantial variability across different types of rehabilitation. The most promising programs and services include cognitive-behavioral therapy

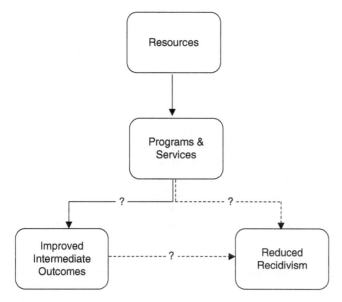

Figure 22.1 "Standard" correctional reentry logic model

and services tailored to address criminogenic risks and needs. Indeed, there is evidence to suggest that cognitive-behavioral approaches and programs that target criminogenic factors and individual needs and that focus on individual-level change may be most effective at reducing recidivism among adults and juveniles (Andrews and Bonta, 2003; Andrews et al., 1990; Aos et al., 2006; Fonagy and Kurtz, 2002; Landenberger and Lipsey, 2005; Lipsey, 1995; Lipsey and Cullen, 2007; MacKenzie, 2006). Some research has suggested that programs that use a multimodal approach or include multiple different services are more effective than single-service programs or programs that use one mode of treatment (Fonagy and Kurtz, 2002; Lipsey, 1999).

While research fairly consistently finds supports for services targeting individual change, there is less evidence supporting the effectiveness of more practical services, such as prison work programs, life skills, and other basic transitional services. In Lipsey and Cullen's (2007) review, vocational and employment programs were among the least effective services. This is somewhat consistent with our findings in a long-term follow-up on SVORI participants, where we found participation in educational programming had a small positive (non-significant) effect on recidivism outcomes (Lattimore et al., 2012). However, interestingly, nearly all study participants endorsed "needing more education" over their self-assessed need for a variety of other services and supports (e.g., substance abuse treatment or help finding housing) (Lattimore et al. 2009). Overall, the SVORI evaluation findings suggest that whereas services oriented toward individual change, including substance abuse treatment and cognitive-focused services, had modest beneficial effects, services oriented toward practical needs, including reentry preparation, life skills programs, and employment services, did not improve outcomes and, in some cases, were associated with higher levels of recidivism (Lattimore et al., 2012).

Greater support for the effectiveness of individual change services are consistent with emerging support for cognitive and identity transformation theories of desistance (e.g., Giordano et al., 2002; Paternoster and Bushway, 2009) in which individuals transform themselves into non-offenders. Absent this transformation, programming that focuses on structural or instrumental factors like employment skills and assistance finding housing or transportation may be of limited use in reducing recidivism. In support of these theories, interviews with 304 individuals from a 1989 therapeutic community evaluation revealed that the vast majority of offenders who had successfully desisted from both crime and drug use reported that they first underwent an identity transformation that was motivated by the realization that they needed to change to avoid an undesirable future, such as dying in prison (Bachman et al., 2012). In light of this evidence, it may be useful to consider an alternative correctional programming logic model that explicitly considers the process of transformation and accounts for potentially different mechanisms for change for practical and individual change services (Figure 22.2).

This model allows for improvement in intermediate outcomes, such as sobriety and employment, as a result of practical services, such as substance abuse treatment or job skills programs; but explicitly recognizes the potential for individual change services to foster identity transformation, which may also be promoted by improved intermediate outcomes (e.g. having a job may generate social bonds that foster transformation from criminal thinking to working). Multiple opportunities for desistance follow in this more complex model – either as a direct result of improvement in intermediate outcomes or as a result of transformation encouraged by individual change services or as a result of improvements in intermediate outcomes.

The question marks on the arrows in Figures 22.1 and 22.2 highlight the testable hypotheses within these models. In the following section, we address considerations concerning the challenges posed in assessing "what works" in prison programming.

Considerations

Competing models of change that reflect different mechanisms of potential change but that also explicitly recognize a potential lack of symmetry between the factors associated with recidivism and those associated with desistance pose one of the challenges in assessing "what works" in prison

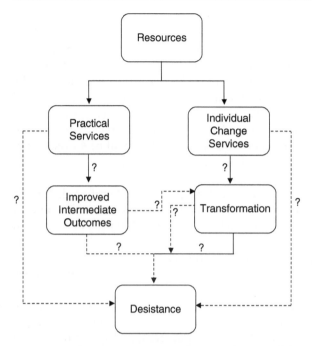

Figure 22.2 Alternative correctional reentry logic model

programming. These considerations are in addition to the long-recognized comorbidity of deficiencies and needs among correctional populations that have led to multi-faceted "programs" aimed at producing improvements in intermediate outcomes traditionally correlated with criminal behavior and, thus, recidivism. Here we discuss issues that complicate the ability to find "what works" in prison programming: indirect effects, incomplete implementation, and, potentially, low base rates.

The models above highlight the expected mechanisms of change in reducing recidivism or promoting desistance. If either of these outcomes are predicated on indirect effects there are potentially serious implications for the effect size that can reasonably be expected from correctional programming. Specifically, expectations of large reductions in recidivism should be tempered when programs and services are expected to have indirect effects.

Thus, consider the following example from Lattimore et al., (2010: 261):

> For example, consider the hypothetical relationships between (1) a prisoner job training program and finding a job post release and (2) having a job and recidivating. Suppose the employment program boosts post-release employment by 20 percent and that without the program 50 percent of released prisoners would find a job. A 20 percent

improvement means that 60 percent of program participants will find employment. So, if you randomly assigned 100 of 200 individuals to receive the program, you would expect that 50 of those in the control group and 60 of those in the treatment group would find employment. Now, suppose that being employed reduces the recidivism rate by 20 percent and that the recidivism rate for the unemployed is 50 percent. With these parameters, the recidivism rate for the employed will be 40 percent. So, what is the effect of the employment program on recidivism? 2.2 percent! Under this scenario, there will be 45 recidivists in the control group and 44 in the treatment group!

In this hypothetical example, the statistical power to identify a difference in *employment* outcomes (60 percent versus 50 percent) is 29 percent (assuming sample sizes of 100 in each group; alpha 0.05).[1] The statistical power to identify a difference in *recidivism* outcomes (44 percent versus 45 percent) is 5 percent. Doubling the size of the samples increases power to 52 percent for the employment outcome but makes little difference in the power of our recidivism test (which increases to 5.5 percent from 5.2 percent). One could argue whether the assumptions are valid – although a case can certainly be made that a 20 percent boost in employment for individuals with low skills, little education, and a criminal record would signify a successful program. Even if we were to assume that having a job decreased recidivism by 50 percent, we would still achieve only a 6.67 percent reduction in recidivism: the control group would have 50 employed and 37.5 recidivists – 25 of the unemployed control subjects and 12.5 of the employed control subjects; the treated group would have 60 employed and 35 recidivists – 20 of the unemployed treated subjects and 15 of the employed treated subjects. With a sample size of 100 in each group, the statistical power is 6.6 percent. With 200 in each group, the statistical power is 8.1 percent. If we boost alpha to 0.2, the statistical power for this scenario jumps only to 25.9 percent.

An additional challenge to finding "what works" involves partial implementation of programs that are being evaluated. As summarized concisely by Lipsey and Cullen (2007: 311), "a treatment that is not delivered cannot have effects." Partial or problematic implementation may include either incomplete or inadequate treatment of the treatment groups and "contamination," or partial treatment of the control group. This problem may be particularly acute when studying correctional programs, where the evaluation occurs as a new program is being implemented and treatment as usual generally involves some intervention.

We can glimpse the potential impact of partial implementation of treatment/partial treatment of control subjects by examining data from the multi-site evaluation of the Serious and Violent Offender Reentry Initiative (SVORI). In Lattimore and Visher (2013), we examined the potential impacts

Table 22.1 Hypothetical treatment effects

Treatment	Treated (%)		Observed Recidivism Rate (Untreated Rate = 20%)			Treatment Effect*
	SVORI	Non-SVORI	SVORI	Non-SVORI	Difference	
Cognitive behavior therapy	52%	36%	19.28%	19.50%	–1.13%	–6.90%
Substance abuse treatment	48%	38%	19.34%	19.48%	–0.71%	–6.40%
Vocational education	17%	4%	19.77%	19.94%	–0.90%	–9.80%
General education	53%	43%	19.27%	19.41%	–0.71%	–8.30%

Source: Adapted from Lattimore and Visher (2013)
Note: Table includes estimates for the incomplete treatment of the Treatment Group and partial treatment of the Comparison Group. Treatment effects assume untreated recidivism rate of 20 percent.
* Estimates from Drake et al. (2009).

of four treatments using treatment effect estimates based on meta-analyses from Drake et al. (2009). Table 22.1 reproduces Table 5 from Lattimore and Visher (2013: 304).

For the SVORI evaluation, interviews were conducted with 1,697 men (863 participated in SVORI programs, 834 were matched comparisons; see Lattimore et al., 2009) about 30 days prior to their release from prison. Respondents were asked whether they had participated in a variety of different types of programs and services during their incarceration. Here, we focus on the four shown in Table 22.1, where cognitive-behavior therapy was measured as "received training to change criminal behavior," substance abuse treatment was measured as "received any substance abuse treatment," "participated in job training program" was a proxy for vocational training, and "received any educational services" was a proxy for the general education measure. The first two columns show the types of treatment and treatment effect estimates ranging from about 6 percent to 10 percent from Drake et al. (2009). The next two columns show that larger percentages of the SVORI group than the non-SVORI group reported receiving the programs during their incarceration, but the differences were substantially smaller than 100 percent versus 0 percent.[2] The next two columns show the (hypothetical) recidivism rates for the SVORI and non-SVORI groups assuming an untreated recidivism rate of 20 percent and that there were no other influences on post-release recidivism. The final column shows that the percentage reduction in recidivism observed between the two groups would be in the 1 percent or so range – unlikely to be detected even if true.

Another example illustrates the difficulty in finding "what works." Even if we were to observe 100 percent treatment of the treated group and 0 percent treatment of the control group – the difference in observed recidivism would be small if the actual untreated recidivism rate is 20 percent (low base rate). In this case, with the treatment effects shown in Table 22.1, the untreated groups would have a 20 percent recidivism rate – and the treated groups would have recidivism rates of 18 percent (vocational education) to 18.7 percent (substance abuse treatment). With the sample sizes observed in the SVORI evaluation (i.e. >800 in each group) and alpha = 0.05, the statistical power to detect the greatest difference (18 percent versus 20 percent) is 18 percent.

Of course, with higher base rates, other things being equal, the statistical power increases. Under the assumptions of the SVORI sample sizes, alpha = 0.05, we can estimate the statistical power for untreated recidivism rates of 50 percent and 80 percent. If the untreated recidivism rate is 50 percent, the effect of substance abuse treatment is a 6.4 percent improvement in recidivism, the treatment group will have a recidivism rate of 46.8 percent, and the statistical power to detect this difference will be 26.1 percent. At an 80 percent untreated recidivism rate, the statistical power would be a respectable 71 percent.

Conclusions

As illustrated above, the ability to determine "what works" in prison programming is challenged by at least three considerations – the underlying theory that may depend upon indirect effects; the practical issues associated with implemented programs in the real world, where partial implementation and treatment of the control group are often the reality; and low base rates in critical outcome measures. Low base rates for recidivism are particularly likely for low-risk populations but for any population when follow-up periods are short or if the recidivism measure is incarceration rather than arrest. The interaction of these factors during even rigorous evaluations poses unknown effects on our ability to identify "what works."

Assuring that evaluation studies is sufficiently powered to accommodate and overcome these factors are critical for the research community – but as illustrated above this may be difficult and in most cases will certainly be expensive. Short of having the resources to conduct 10-year studies that provide ample time for full implementation, large samples, and long-term follow up, the research community, practitioners, and policymakers may want to take another look at the high bar they have set for themselves in assessing "what works" in prison programming. The consequences of failing to address this are not negligible. Specifically, we may be inadvertently harming the corrections field if promising practices are prematurely "killed" by a rush to find "what works" in terms of statistically significant reductions in recidivism. It may be time to relax alpha or at least explicitly identify beta and acknowledge that often there may be a meaningfully large chance that we are saying a program had no effect when in fact it may have. Finally, almost always in corrections, programs are being compared to treatment as usual rather than to nothing. Under these circumstances, no differences in outcomes can reasonably be interpreted as meaning that the program being tested did as well as (but not better than) treatment as usual. (This is the standard the Federal Drug Administration uses in approving new drugs for market – the new drug works as well as the old drug.) One may argue that in that case, treatment as usual should prevail. But agencies may have other reasons for using the "new" program (lower costs, fits with new philosophy) and, perhaps, should be able to do so without concern that the new program doesn't "work."

Notes

1 Statistical power calculations from www.dssresearch.com/KnowledgeCenter/toolkitcalculators/statisticalpowercalculators.aspx.
2 Note that any treatment should be predicated on need. The characteristics of these study samples suggest that most, if not all, "needed" these types of services (see Lattimore et al., 2009).

References

Andrews, D. A., and Bonta, J. (2003). *The psychology of criminal conduct* (4th ed.). Newark, NJ: Lexis/Nexis.

Andrews, D. A., Zinger, I., Hoge, R. D., Bonta, J., Gendreau, P., and Cullen, F. T. (1990). Does correctional treatment work? A clinically relevant and psychologically informed meta-analysis. *Criminology*, 28, 369–404.

Aos, S., Miller, M., and Drake, E. (2006). *Evidence-based public policy options to reduce future prison construction, criminal justice costs, and crime rates* (Report No. 06-10-1201). Olympia: Washington State Institute for Public Policy.

Bachman, R., Kerrison, E., O'Connell, D. and Paternoster, R. (2012). *Roads Diverge: Long-Term Patterns of Relapse, Recidivism, and Desistance for a Cohort of Drug Involved Offenders.* Prepared for the National Institute of Justice.

Broner, N., Lattimore, P. K., and Steffey, D. M. (2010). Mental health needs and services receipt of reentering offenders: A multi-site study of men, women and male youth. In H. A. Dlugacz (ed.), *Re-entry planning for offenders with mental disorders: Policy and practice* (pp. 12–41). Kingston, NJ: Civic Research Institute.

Carson, E.A. and Golinelli, D. (2014). *Prisoners in 2012: Trends in Admissions and Releases, 1991–2012 (NCJ Publication No. 243920).* Washington, DC: U.S. Department of Justice, Office of Justice Programs, Bureau of Justice Statistics.

Cullen, F. T., and Gendreau, P. (2000). Assessing correctional rehabilitation: Policy, practice, and prospects. In J. Horney (ed.), *Criminal justice 2000: Vol. 3. Policies, processes, and decisions of the criminal justice system* (NCJ Publication No. 182410, pp. 109–175). Washington, DC: U.S. Department of Justice, Office of Justice Programs, National Institute of Justice.

Drake, E.K., Aos, S., and Miller, M.G. (2009). Evidence-based public policy options to reduce crime and criminal justice costs: Implications in Washington State. *Victims and Offenders*, 4, 170–196.

Durose, M.R., Cooper, A.D., and Snyder, H.N. (2014). *Recidivism of Prisoners Released in 30 States in 2005: Patterns from 2005 to 2010 (NCJ Publication No. 244205)*. Washington, DC: U.S. Department of Justice, Office of Justice Programs, Bureau of Justice Statistics.

Fonagy, P., and. Kurtz, A. (2002). Disturbances of conduct. In P. Fonagy, M. Target, D. Cottrell, J. Phillips, and Z. Kurtz (eds.), *What works for whom? A critical review of treatments for children and adolescents* (pp. 106–192). New York: Guilford.

Giordano, P.C., Cernkovich, S.A. and Rudolph. J.L. (2002). Gender, crime, and desistance: Toward a theory of cognitive transformation. *American Journal of Sociology* 107(4):990–1064.

Landenberger, N.A. and Lipsey, M.W. (2005). The positive effects of cognitive-behavioral programs for offenders: A meta-analysis of factors associated with effective treatment. *Journal of Experimental Criminology* 1:451–476.

Langan, P. A., and Levin, D. J. (2002). *Recidivism of prisoners released in 1994 (Bureau of Justice Statistics Special Report No. NCJ 193427)*. Washington, DC: U.S. Department of Justice, Office of Justice Programs, Bureau of Justice Statistics.

Lattimore, P.K. and Visher, C.A. (2013). The impact of prison reentry services on short-term outcomes: Evidence from a multi-site evaluation. *Evaluation Review* 37, 3–4, 274–313. doi:10.1177/0193841X14523004.

Lattimore, P. K., Visher, C.A., and Steffey, D. M. (2008). Pre-release characteristics and service receipt among adult male participants in the SVORI Multi-site Evaluation. Research Triangle Park, NC: RTI International. Available from http://www.urban.org/UploadedPDF/1001218_SVORI_evaluation.pdf.

Lattimore, P. K., Steffey, D. M., and Visher, C.A. (2009). *Prisoner reentry experiences of adult males: Characteristics, service receipt, and outcomes of participants in the SVORI multi-site evaluation*. Research Triangle Park, NC: RTI International.

Lattimore, P.K., Steffey, D.M., and Visher, C.A. (2010). Prisoner reentry in the first decade of the twenty-first century. *Victims and Offenders* 5, 3, 253–267. Available from http://dx.doi.org/10.1080/15564886.2010.485907.

Lattimore, P. K., Barrick, K., Cowell, A. J., Dawes, D., Steffey, D. M., Tueller, S. J., and Visher, C.A. (2012, February). *Prisoner reentry services: What worked for SVORI evaluation participants?* Prepared for National Institute of Justice.

Lipsey, M. W. (1995). What do we learn from 400 research studies on the effectiveness of treatment with juvenile delinquency? In J. McGuire (ed.), *What works: Reducing reoffending: Guidelines from research and practice* (pp. 63–78). West Sussex, England: Wiley.

Lipsey, M. W. (1999). Can rehabilitative programs reduce the recidivism of juvenile offenders? An inquiry into the effectiveness of practical programs. *Virginia Journal of Social Policy and Law*, 6, 611–641.

Lipsey, M. W., and Cullen, F. T. (2007). The effectiveness of correctional rehabilitation: A review of systematic reviews. *Annual Review of Law and Social Science*, 3, 297–320.

MacKenzie, D. L. (2006). *What works in corrections? Reducing the criminal activities of offenders and delinquents*. New York: Cambridge University Press.

National Research Council of the National Academies (Committee on Community Supervision and Desistance from Crime, Committee on Law and Justice, Division of Behavioral and Social Sciences and Education). (2008). *Parole, desistance from crime, and community integration*. Washington, DC: National Academies Press.

Paternoster, R. and Bushway, S. (2009). Desistance and the "feared self": Toward an identity theory of criminal desistance. *The Journal of Criminal Law and Criminology* 99(4):1103–1156.

Petersilia, J. (2003). *When prisoners come home: Parole and prisoner reentry*. New York: Oxford University Press.

Petersilia, J., and Turner, S. (1993). Intensive probation and parole. In M. Tonry (ed.), *Crime and justice: A review of research* (Vol. 17). Chicago: University of Chicago Press.

Rhodes, W., Gaes, G., Luallen, J., Kling, R., Rich, T., and Shively, M. (2014). Following incarceration, most released offenders never return to prison. Crime and Delinquency. DOI: 10.1177/0011128714549655.

Travis, J., and Visher, C. (eds.). (2005). *Prisoner reentry and crime in America*. Cambridge, UK: Cambridge University Press.

Chapter 23

The challenge of integrating restorative justice into the "deep-end" of criminal justice

Carolyn Hoyle and Roxana Willis

Restorative justice is one of the most over-theorised, and yet under-practised, areas of criminal justice. Despite evidence-based research to suggest that restorative justice can produce high levels of victim satisfaction and reduce rates of recidivism, especially among violent offenders, for the most part restorative justice remains on the periphery of criminal justice responses. But the trend to restrict restorative justice to lower-level offences is especially peculiar in light of widespread political support to advance restorative policy and legislative reform, and embed restorative interventions in the criminal process.[1] By presenting a case study from Northamptonshire, UK, this chapter will examine why restorative justice seems to be stuck in the "shallow-end" of criminal justice, despite apparent political will to extend it further. "Shallow-end" will be used to refer to lower-level offences, such as low-level theft and minor disputes, and "deep-end" will refer to crimes treated as more severe by the legislator, such as assaults that cause injury or death, most sexual crimes, and high-value fraud or property offences (Hoyle, 2010).

Born out of discontent with deep-rooted failings of traditional criminal justice, restorative justice was hailed as a new way to respond to conflict. Idealised accounts of ancient forms of justice, where victims steered their own cases, began to emerge. Christie's seminal thesis about "conflict as property" stolen by states and lawyers gained currency (1977), and Zehr notably described restorative justice as an alternative "lens" (1990); a new paradigm of justice for the twenty-first century with more promise and potential than retributive justice. Such optimism continued to influence two opposing definitional strands of thought: maximalist restorative justice scholars proposed a transformed legal system where every measure would aim to repair harm caused by offending behaviour; and purist scholars appealed for an entirely separate system of justice, in which "state" and abstract notions of "society" would take a back seat. This chapter revisits an earlier normative position adopted by one of the authors: that restorative justice can comfortably coexist within traditional criminal justice processes, and that state involvement is required for restorative justice to jump into deep-end cases (Hoyle, 2010). This will be critically assessed through an English case study that while particular has relevance for schemes across the world.

The chapter starts by outlining the concept of "restorative justice," and gives a brief overview of evidence-based research on restorative programmes. This is followed by an historical exploration of the Northamptonshire case, where restorative approaches are beginning to dip into the deep-end of criminal justice. The chapter concludes by reflecting on the apparent challenges and enabling factors stemming from the case study.

Restorative justice and evidence-based research

The following frequently cited definition of restorative justice is provided by Tony Marshall: "Restorative justice is a process whereby parties with a stake in a specific offence collectively resolve how to deal with the aftermath of the offence and its implications for the future" (1999). This definition is central to the purist model of restorative justice, which emphasises the value of face-to-face deliberative encounters between primary stakeholders in an offence; namely victims, offenders, and their respective communities-of-care (i.e. people with close relational ties to victims and offenders) (McCold, 2000). In this model, the state (i.e. society and government agents who represent it), and wider communities (i.e. communities delineated by geographical space), are defined as secondary stakeholders (McCold and Wachtel, 1998). According to this account, unlike primary stakeholders who are directly affected by an offence, secondary stakeholders are only vicariously affected. Therefore, secondary stakeholders do not need to be involved in the restorative justice face-to-face process, though they may have a supportive role to provide means and mechanisms for restorative justice to take place. Permitting the direct involvement of abstract entities in restorative justice, such as society and the wider community, is said to pave the way for states to steal the conflict from primary stakeholders. Hence, continuing Christie's metaphor, purist scholars treat disputes as rightfully "owned" by primary stakeholders.

Other restorative advocates, sometimes associated with the maximalist position, are not so ready to dismiss the role of wider community participation in the restorative justice process. Bazemore and Schiff, for example, suggest a number of pro-social benefits of direct wider community involvement (2005). These benefits include the potential for victims and offenders to strengthen weak relationships with law-abiding acquaintances or strangers, described in terms of "bridging" social capital. Consequently, the opportunity for community building is said to arise; and as a result, the potential for collective efficacy – where people with weak relational ties are prepared to do things for each other – may increase. Bazemore explains that instead of a *"government hands-off* approach," the intention is to create a "*community hands-on* approach,"[2] where the government maintains an active, albeit reformed, role in the criminal justice process (Bazemore, 1999, p. 130). From this perspective, the conflict can be viewed as "owned" by the wider community, which comprises victims, offenders, their supporters, and others in a geographically delineated space (i.e. other people in the neighbourhood, or town) (Bazemore and Schiff, 2005, p. 82).

In contrast to these accounts, some scholars are open to a more significant role for the state in restorative justice (Zedner, 1994; Young and Hoyle, 2003). In 1998 McCold attempted to develop a consensual definition of restorative justice between supporters, using a modified Delphi technique (McCold, 1998). While agreement emerged that "professionals" should not own the conflict, one of the most contentious areas was about the role the state ought to play. Some advocates suggested that the judicial system owns the dispute, while others proposed that the community does (conceived of as either "community-of-care" or a wider community beyond the specific offence). Walgrave, in support of state involvement in restorative justice, even claims that a state element is a *sine qua non* for the restorative processes, and that without it, there is no restorative justice (2008). Scholars who recognise an essential public element to restorative justice may view society as owning criminal conflicts, which encompasses the wider community and/or communities-of-care, victims, and offenders.

Alongside discussion about what restorative justice is, a rigorous empirical base about what restorative justice may do as compared to criminal justice counterparts has begun to emerge. For the most part, these studies involve face-to-face processes, and tend to assess effectiveness through rates of participant satisfaction and/or rates of recidivism. Research has consistently found high rates of victim and offender satisfaction as a result of taking part in restorative programmes.[3] Moreover, recent studies indicate that restorative justice may also have a positive impact on reducing recidivism, for at least some types of offences. Sherman and Strang, for example, have carried out two systematic reviews of restorative processes, finding significant reductions in repeat offending in property and violent offences, with restorative responses to more serious offences, involving violent crime, producing the lowest levels of reoffending (Sherman and Strang, 2007; Sherman *et al.*, 2014). More modest results were found in Shapland *et al.'s* investigation of reconviction rates of adult offenders in the UK, which included randomised controlled trials within a two-year period, showing fewer reconvictions of offenders involved in restorative conferencing, compared to the control group (2008). Like Sherman and Strang's research, Shapland *et al.'s* (2008) study indicated that higher-level violent offences were less likely to result in reconviction than property crimes, following a restorative intervention. Notably, in these higher-level cases, restorative justice was used alongside traditional criminal justice interventions.

Empirical research therefore indicates that restorative justice is capable of reducing rates of recidivism, and increasing rates of participant satisfaction, particularly where face-to-face processes are used, in deep-end offences, and alongside traditional criminal justice sanctions. This chapter, which sets out to explore how policy and practice is influenced by evidence-based research, will focus on recidivism as a measure of efficacy since this feature is often appealed to in political discourse, and is where the evidence-base lies. This is not to suggest that restorative justice offers no alternative valuable outcomes, such as positive impacts on victims' and/or offenders' wellbeing, nor is it to say that rate of recidivism is the most appropriate measure by which the efficacy of restorative justice ought to be assessed. (Both issues sit beyond the scope of this chapter.) However, this chapter does suggest that the seminal work upon which restorative justice is based, which envisages restorative justice as a new paradigm of justice, is not in harmony with emergent evidence-based research. The following case study is built on a year-long ethnography in Northamptonshire, UK, and it examines how the application of restorative justice reflects seminal theory and empirical research.

Case study: visions of a "restorative county"

In September 2013, the Northamptonshire Police and Crime Commissioner announced plans to transform Northamptonshire into a "Restorative Practices County" (Sarkis, 2013). Such restorative ambitions are reflective of the history of this East Midlands county. Northamptonshire provides an early example of restorative approaches in the UK: reparative youth diversion programmes were implemented there under the Juvenile Liaisons Bureau as early as 1981, before the concept "restorative justice" was widely understood (Blagg, 1985; Hinks and Smith, 1985); and it is said to be the first place in England and Wales to trial restorative approaches for adult offenders, establishing two parallel pilot programmes, from 1986 until 1989, under the Adult Reparation Bureau (Dignam, 1990; Smith, 2011). While the motivation for these pioneering initiatives was to reduce the strain on the county's backlogged courts, the ideological motivation was framed in terms of avoiding criminalisation, particularly of young people, wherever possible as a way to avoid generating criminal personas and reoffending (Bell et al., 1999). Set up as "reparative" initiatives, these early programmes reflected modern-day restorative justice ideals. In 1986, for example, Blagg outlined the following criteria for a juvenile's case to be deemed suitable for reparation by the Juvenile Liaisons Bureau: "First was the offence admitted? Was it an offence that could be resolved? Was the offender willing to participate? Was the proposed form of reparation appropriate, that is, in keeping with the scale of the offence? Did the victim agree to the idea and feel comfortable with the proposal?" (1985, p. 91).

A canopy of practices which resemble present-day restorative processes was offered as part of the 1980s reparation programmes. These included compensation; direct reparation (where the offender carries out an activity for the victim in order to repair the harm); indirect reparation (where the offender works on a community project, sometimes chosen by the victim); shuttle mediation (where a facilitator delivers messages back and forth between conflicting parties who do not wish to meet face-to-face); letters of apology to the victim; and face-to-face meetings with victims to encourage apologies. The Juvenile Liaisons Bureau and the Adult Reparation Bureau were multi-agency structures, which predominantly received referrals from the police (Bell *et al.*, 1999, 95), though a handful of referrals to the Adult Reparation Bureau programmes were from the Magistrates Court (Dignam, 1990).[4] As diversionary measures, both programmes targeted shallow-end cases, and were predominately implemented to avoid further prosecution. The Juvenile Liaisons Bureau was eventually integrated into a multi-agency Diversion Unit, which continued to implement diversionary restorative approaches for young people, leaving the Youth Service to concentrate on young people processed through the court (Bell et al., 1999). In the late 1990s, the Diversion Unit was dismantled, and the Youth Service was replaced by what is now known as the Youth Offending Service (YOS) under the New Labour Government's 1998 *Crime and Disorder Act*. Like its predecessor, YOS is the statutory body in England and Wales charged with the responsibility of responding to young offenders processed through the criminal justice system.

Northamptonshire YOS has become a leading institution for restorative approaches in Northamptonshire and beyond. It was awarded "green light" status for its restorative approaches from the Ministry of Justice in 2013, and was among the first organisations to receive Quality Mark accreditation from the Restorative Justice Council in 2014.[5] The Northamptonshire YOS aims to implement restorative justice at all levels, and at all stages, of the youth justice process. Like the Juvenile Liaisons Bureau, restorative interventions implemented by YOS include shuttle mediation, a letter of apology, direct reparation, indirect reparation, and restorative conferencing (i.e. face-to-face meetings with victims and offenders to encourage apologies and other symbolic or material reparation). Unlike the Juvenile Liaisons Bureau, YOS cases are processed through the criminal justice system, and most come under the remit of the YOS at the post-sentence stage, though there is also some diversionary work within the YOS. All young people given a Referral Order by the Youth Court are required to attend a Referral Order Panel, which consists of between two and three community volunteers, and a YOS worker, who meet with the young person every three months (usually for between six and twelve months) to review the progress of their order, and their compliance with programmes and interventions that are attached to their Referral Order. These panels were introduced as a national attempt to integrate restorative practices into the youth justice system, and hence victim presence was included as a core feature. However, in reality victim turnout is low-to-nil, and so it is contestable to what degree these panels actually resemble a form of community, rather than restorative, justice (Rosenblatt, 2015).

The two most common forms of restorative interventions implemented by the Northamptonshire YOS during the research period were shuttle mediation and indirect reparation in the wider-community, and the least common form was face-to-face conferencing. When face-to-face conferences did occur, these were facilitated by experienced members of YOS staff, and involved victims, offenders, and a member from each party's community-of-care. The dozen or so restorative conferences that took place since Northamptonshire YOS's inception tended to be for shallow-end offences, such as criminal damage, minor assaults, and theft. One conference, held at the victim's request, involved a burglary of a dwelling which took place while the homeowner was asleep, and hence could be seen as an aggravated offence. Northamptonshire YOS has also recently branched into pre-sentence restorative justice, with three cases being referred by the Magistrates Court between September 2014 and December 2014. Again, these were for shallow-end offences, comprising shop theft, criminal damage, and a low-level assault. While managerial staff at YOS are prepared to use restorative conferencing for all types of offences, even in controversial areas such as domestic violence[6] and sexual assaults[7] if found to be appropriate, for them, it is vital for the process to be victim-led.

In addition to the progressive restorative attitudes within the YOS, two pilot projects were independently trialled in Northamptonshire between 2013 and 2014. The first of these pilots was supported by a Northamptonshire Advisory Group, which, like the above-mentioned Diversion Unit, is a multi-agency public- and third-sector collaboration in Northamptonshire. The first pilot was overtly proactive, and centred on restorative approaches in schools. The term "restorative practice" was adopted in order to distinguish this as early intervention and crime prevention, as opposed to "restorative justice", which is said to be a reactive process following the commission of a particular offence (Wachtel, 2015). The pilot thus targeted shallow-end cases from the outset, with no scope to enter the deep-end. Within its six-month activation period, the pilot received two referrals from schools, and carried out one restorative conference, before it concluded in June 2014, when funding ended.

The second pilot was set up in close collaboration with Northamptonshire Police by the Corby Borough Council, which is a town in Northamptonshire where one of the first of the Youth Justice Bureaus was established. The pilot took the form of a Neighbourhood Resolution Forum (NRF) – community-based national pilots in England that involved local volunteers as facilitators in restorative conferencing at the community level. While it did not secure national funding for the pilot scheme, and was therefore established with local sources, Restorative Solutions hailed the Corby NRF as a leading programme of its type, ranking it among the highest rates of referrals and conferences taking place in the country (receiving 74 referrals and completing 39 forums during 18 months of operation).[8] The NRF's high referral rate echoes the success of the earlier Juvenile Liaisons Bureau and Adult Reparation Bureau programmes (Dignam, 1990, p. 2; Blagg, 1985, 1990). Similarly, the type of cases referred to NRF were shallow-end offences, as a way to divert young offenders from the criminal justice process.

A small number of cases handled by the NRF involved shallow-end *adult* offences. Most referrals were made by the police, but some came from schools, care homes, the Borough Council, and one case was referred directly by a parent in the community. Cases predominately involved face-to-face conferencing with wider community members acting as facilitators. A handful of cases was dealt with by shuttle mediation facilitated by the coordinator employed by the scheme. Towards the end of August 2014, funding for the pilot finally came to an end, and despite local interest and attempts to keep the NRF alive, lack of investment led to its closure.

Following these multiple initiatives, "Restorative Northamptonshire" was formed in September 2014. Like the Juvenile Liaisons Bureau, and the subsequent Diversion Unit, "Restorative Northamptonshire" is a multi-agency approach between public- and third-sector partners. Restorative Solutions were competitively selected as the lead contractor, and Groundworks, a local civil society organisation, became the sub-contractor. Restorative Northamptonshire aims to become a central hub for restorative justice in Northamptonshire, working with education, housing, criminal justice, and community and voluntary sector agencies to deliver restorative *practices*. Rather than outsourcing, the aim is for partner agencies to be able to call on Restorative Northamptonshire for guidance and advice, so that trained individuals within institutions can go on to deliver restorative justice internally. Experienced facilitators within Restorative Northamptonshire are available to support facilitation in complex and sensitive cases, and particularly deep-end cases. While to some extent Restorative Northamptonshire echoes what existed more than 30 years ago – especially with the emphasis on prevention, and hence diversion – the model has nevertheless progressed substantially, because there is now scope for restorative justice to move closer to the deep-end.

Despite only operating for three months at the time of writing, and not officially "open for business," Restorative Northamptonshire has already been consulted by a number of local agencies, and two restorative conferences have been held. One conference was referred by the police, and involved a sensitive police complaint. The second case concerned a homicide, specifically manslaughter, which was initiated by the victim's family, and subsequently referred to Restorative Northamptonshire through the police. The offender in this case had been sentenced by the court, and was serving a term of imprisonment when he was asked to take part in the conference. The restorative conference was therefore hosted in prison, and held in addition to the traditional criminal justice sanctions. An experienced employee of Restorative Solutions and a police officer, who is a member of Restorative Northamptonshire's network of volunteers, facilitated the conference, which was considered to have been a success by those involved. A further homicide case is in the early stages of preparation, again victim-initiated. This accordingly indicates that, following more than 30 years of good intentions in Northamptonshire, and the UK more widely, evidence of restorative justice dipping into the deep-end of criminal justice is finally beginning to emerge.

The challenge of branching into the deep-end

The Northamptonshire case study raises interesting points for discussion, especially when considered alongside the latest empirical research on restorative justice. Despite evidence to suggest that restorative justice may be particularly effective at reducing rates of recidivism for deep-end offences, and in spite of historical aspirational policy in Northamptonshire to extend restorative ideas more widely, for the most part restorative justice has remained on the periphery of criminal justice responses to offending. This is most apparent with the earlier diversionary programmes (namely the Juvenile Liaisons Bureau and the Adult Reparation Bureau), and the latest pilot projects (which include the school-based scheme and the Corby NRF). These measures were designed to respond to shallow-end offences from the outset, which suggests that while political ideology has been to expand restorative approaches, and often with the aim to reduce rates of criminalisation and reoffending, the vision on the ground has been to limit this approach to "softer" (for which we may read "easier" and certainly less controversial) cases, leaving traditional criminal justice to respond to deep-end offending. The explicit policy emphasis on restorative *practices*, and hence preventative and early intervention strategies for shallow-end conflicts and offences, is indicative of this trend. In this instance, dichotomised ideas about restorative justice as a radically different mode of justice, free from the shackles of the state, have arguably fostered restorative rhetoric and peripheral (though nevertheless valuable) programmes in practice, rather than the overhaul of traditional criminal justice systems.

In contrast to the diversionary and pilot restorative justice programmes in Northamptonshire YOS has demonstrated potential to enter the deep-end. However, the most widely recognised form of restorative justice (i.e. face-to-face restorative conferencing, in which both victims and offenders take part) has been adopted in only a limited number of cases, and mainly for shallow-end offences. This is surprising, since Northamptonshire YOS affords a central place for restorative justice in its organisational structure and day-to-day activities. Indeed, management say they are open to facilitating restorative conferencing for potentially all types of conflict, should the victim want this, and staff within Northamptonshire YOS are highly skilled facilitators, keen and able to facilitate deep-end conferences if required. Furthermore, aside from pre-sentence restorative justice led by the courts, for the most part YOS are their own gatekeepers, and thus have access to all manner of deep-end cases.

One reason for the low number of conferences in the Northamptonshire YOS may be the time constraints within which the YOS operates. Nationwide low victim turnout on Referral Order Panels, for example, demonstrates how government targets and timeframes may not accord with victims' needs and aspirations for involvement in the response to "their" crimes (Crawford, 2007). Comparable difficulties have emerged during the implementation of pre-sentence restorative justice, since courts are bound by targets and tight time-frames, leaving a short window of opportunity for agencies to attempt to facilitate pre-sentence conferences. This is a prime example of the tension between respecting individuals' rights to have a case heard in a timely fashion, and providing adequate space for victims and offenders to come to restorative justice when they are ready to do so. State intervention in response to crime provides victims of deep-end offences time to take part in restorative conferences at a time that suits their needs. However, mechanisms to balance restorative interventions alongside criminal justice sanctions requires greater attention.

An alternative reason for the limited number of face-to-face conferences facilitated by Northamptonshire YOS could be risk-averse cultures within public-sector institutions. The YOS implements a rigorous preparatory process in the build-up to a conference, and perhaps deep-end cases that present higher degrees of risk fail to make it through. In such situations, some commentators may even suggest that the state has stolen the conflict. However, it is precisely this attention to risk which makes public institutions appropriate providers for deep-end cases: these institutions can be held to account and implement legal safeguards for all participants. This was demonstrated in an English case in July 2013, which involved Trafford YOS being sued for a breach of the *Victims' Code* (Mellor and Martin, 2013). A staff member in Trafford YOS was found to have placed undue pressure on a victim and their family to take part in a restorative conference, leading to a Local Government Ombudsman investigation, subsequent fines, and an apology. Legislation, such as the Victims' Code (and the accompanying forthcoming statute), thus provides victims, as well as offenders, with rights, which can be enforced against criminal justice agencies. However, agencies outside of the public-sector are not subject to these same requirements. Rather than taking away from the restorative justice process, legal frameworks that provide protection for participants' rights can enhance the programmes on offer, and increase the potential for restorative justice in deep-end cases.

Northamptonshire's emergent deep-end conferences have primarily been carried out through Restorative Northamptonshire. Restorative Northamptonshire demonstrates a number of enabling factors. First, although it is headed by third-sector institutions, it works in close collaboration with public-sector agencies, and the police in particular. One member of staff employed within Restorative Northamptonshire, for example, is a retired Police Inspector, who has the trust of local forces, and who has a track record of implementing successful restorative interventions under one of the above-mentioned pilot programmes. Second, expert facilitators from Restorative Solutions were able to be called on to support the more complex homicide cases, which demonstrates that deep-end restorative conferences can be successfully implemented when trained experts are included in the process. Third, the restorative conference which took place did so within the traditional criminal justice framework, and alongside criminal justice sanctions. Finally, all these deep-end cases have been victim-led.

Accordingly, traditional criminal justice processes and state involvement can create opportunities for victims of deep-end crimes to take part in restorative justice conferences without victims fearing that this will be the only response to the offending behaviour. Negative public opinion that restorative justice is a "soft option" often refers to offenders being able to "say sorry," to "get away" with crime. An English newspaper in October 2014, for example, responded to Hull Police Force plans to extend restorative justice to cases of more serious offending with the headline: "Sex and drug criminals told to say sorry as Humberside Police extends 'restorative justice'" (Campbell, 2014). The article proceeded to explain that offenders were able "to avoid further punishment" by apologising to their victims. Predictably, such reporting resulted in 94 per cent of the Facebook commenters on the article giving negative, and mostly outraged, responses,[9] although more balanced, similarly negative public responses emerged in response to the "What Would You Do?" Facebook campaign, set up for Restorative Justice Week 2014 in the UK.[10] Moving away from the idea of restorative justice as an all-or-nothing solution, and towards the notion that restorative justice is a comfortable ally of traditional criminal justice, would provide victims and the public with assurances that restorative justice does not represent the corrosion of what is widely considered as just.

Northamptonshire offers a prime example of a place with the political will and vision to advance restorative justice ideas. However, viewing restorative justice as something alternative to traditional criminal justice has for the most part confined restorative justice to the outskirts of the criminal justice system, despite its potential to be taken much further. While this has produced commendable community-based initiatives, parsimony needs to be considered. Restorative conferences require time and resources, and it is questionable for how long such energy can be spent on the shallow-end, if the goal is to reduce reoffending. Accepting a clearer role for the state in restorative justice theory, and finding a place for restorative justice within the criminal justice framework, would enable restorative justice to wade into the deep-end where it has the potential to flourish and deliver justice to all.

Acknowledgements

The authors would like to thank the following practitioners in Northamptonshire for their invaluable support and feedback during the development of this article: Darren Carson, Lynn Chapman, Liz Fowler, Cath Hickman, Mike Hodgson, Mandy Rowlatt, and Gary Williams. Thanks too to Alpa Parmar for helpful comments on a first draft.

Notes

1 Over the past few years the British government has produced various reports and position papers encouraging a greater use of restorative justice in both pre-sentence and post-sentence processes, and has placed pre-sentence restorative justice in the Magistrates Courts on a statutory footing for the first time (Crime and Courts Act 2013 (sch. 16(2)). Magistrates are to be given new roles and responsibilities, including the oversight of out-of-court disposals and "Neighbourhood Justice Panels"; (see, for example, Ministry of Justice, Swift and Sure Justice: The Government's Plans for Reform of the Criminal Justice System (2012); Ministry of Justice, Restorative justice past and future (2013). Available at: www.gov.uk/government/news/restorative-justice-past-and-future; Ministry of Justice, Reducing reoffending and improving rehabilitation (updated 2014). Available at: www.gov.uk/government/policies/reducing-reoffending-and-improving-rehabilitation).
2 Emphasis author's own.
3 For example, M S Umbreit, R B Coates and B Kalanj, (1994) *Victim Meets Offender: The Impact of Restorative Justice and Mediation* (Criminal Justice Press/ Willow Tree Press); David Miers and others, (2001) *An Exploratory Evaluation of Restorative Justice Schemes* (Home Office: Crime Reduction Research Series Paper 9,); Paul McCold and Benjamin Wachtel, (1998) *Restorative Policing Experiment: The Bethlehem Pennsylvania Police Family Group Conferencing Project* (Pipersville, PA: Community Service Foundation,); C. Hoyle, R. Young and R. Hill, (2002) *Proceed with Caution: An Evaluation of the Themes Valley Police Initiative in Restorative Cautioning* (Joseph Rowntree Foundation); John Braithwaite, (2002) 'Does restorative justice work?' in Gerry Johnstone (ed.), *A Restorative Justice Reader: Texts, sources, context* (Willan Publishing), 398; Jeff Latimer, Craig Dowden and Danielle Muise, (2005) 'The Effectiveness of Restorative Justice Practices: A Meta-Analysis' 85(2) *The Prison Journal*. Mark S. Umbreit, Robert B. Coates and Betty Vos, (2002)*The Impact of Restorative Justice Conferencing: A Review of 63 Empirical Studies in 5 Countries* (Center for Restorative Justice and Peacemaking: University of Minnesota,); Joanna Shapland and others, (2007) *Restorative justice: the views of victims and offenders. The third report from the evaluation of three schemes* (Ministry of Justice Research Series 3/07,).
4 Magistrates Courts are courts of first instance in England and Wales, which tend to handle lower-level cases. Cases are heard by two or three magistrates, who are trained community volunteers and who sit alongside a district judge.

5 The Restorative Justice Council is a third-sector organisation in the UK that advocates for national adoption of restorative practices, and monitors quality assurance of these programmes. More information available at: www.restorativejustice.org.uk/.

6 See for example, Julie Stubbs, (2007) Beyond Apology?: 'Domestic Violence and Critical Questions for Restorative Justice', *Criminology and Criminal Justice* 7(2), 169–87; Donna Coker, (2002) 'Transformative Justice: Anti-subordination processes in cases of domestic violence', in H Strang and J Braithwaite (eds.) *Restorative Justice and Family Violence*, Cambridge University Press, pp. 128–52. Keenan M, 'Sexual Trauma and Abuse: Restorative and Transformative Possibilities?' University College Dublin School of Applied Social Science http://researchrepositoryucdie/handle/10197/6247 accessed 22nd January 2015.

7 Kathleen Daly, (2006) 'Restorative Justice and Sexual Assault: An Archival Study of Court and Conference Cases', *British Journal of Criminology*, 46(2), 334–56; Annie Cossins, (2008) 'Restorative Justice and Child Sexual Offences: The theory and the practice', *British Journal of Criminology*, 48, 359–78.

8 Similar to the Restorative Justice Council, Restorative Solutions is a not-for-profit community interest company in the UK which supports the third- and public- sector to implement restorative approaches. More information available at: www.restorativesolutions.org.uk/.

9 Accessed at: www.facebook.com/HullDailyMail/posts/873126159366228.

10 In response to the question "what would you do?": "i would never meet a person that puts a gun to my head never"; "I would probably break his legs"; "No!!!". Accessed at: www.facebook.com/whatwouldyoudo.rj.

References

Bazemore G, (1999) 'In Search of a Communitarian Justice Alternative: Youth Crime and the Sanctioning Response as a Case Study' in Carney DE (ed.), *To Promote the General Welfare: A Communitarian Legal Reader* (Lexington Books).

Bazemore G and Schiff M, (2005) *Juvenile Justice Reform and Restorative Justice: Building theory and policy from practice* (Willan Publishing).

Bell A, Hodgson M and Pragnell S, (1999) 'Diverting Children and Young People from Crime and the Criminal Justice System' in Goldson B (ed.), *Youth Justice: Contemporary Policy and Practice* (Ashgate).

Blagg H, (1985) 'Reparation and Justice for Juveniles: The Corby Experience' 25 *British Journal of Criminology*.

Campbell J, (2014) 'Sex and drug criminals told to say sorry as Humberside Police extends "restorative justice"' http://www.hulldailymail.co.uk/Sex-drug-criminals-told-say-sorry-Humberside/story-23147835-detail/story.html accessed 22nd January 2015.

Christie N, (1977) 'Conflict as Property' [17(1)] *British Journal of Criminology*.

Crawford A, (2007) 'International Trends in Restorative Justice: Situating restorative youth justice in crime control and prevention' *Acta Juridica*.

Dignan J, (1990) *An Evaluation of an Experimental Adult Reparation Scheme in Kettering, Northamptonshire* (Centre for Criminological and Legal Research, University of Sheffield).

Hinks N and Smith R, (1985) 'Diversion in Practice: Northants Juvenile Liaison Bureaux' 32:2 *Probation Journal*.
Hoyle C, (2010) 'The Case for Restorative Justice' in Cane P (ed.), *Debating Restorative Justice* (Hart).
Marshall TF, (1999) *Restorative Justice: An Overview* (Home Office, London).
McCold P, (1998) 'Restorative Justice – Variations on a Theme' in Walgrave L (ed.), *Restorative Justice for Juveniles: Potentialities, Risks and Problems* (Leuven University Press).
McCold P, (2000) 'Toward a Holistic Vision of Restorative Justice: A Reply to the Maximalist Model' 3(4) *Contemporary Justice Review*.
McCold P and Wachtel B, (1998) 'Community is not a place: a new look at community justice initiatives' 1 *Contemporary Justice Review*.
Mellor DJ and Martin J, (2013) *Report by the Parliamentary Commissioner for Administration (the Ombudsman) and the Local Government Ombudsman to Ms A MP on the results of an investigation into a complaint made by Mr and Mrs C and T* (Parliamentary and Health Service Ombudsman) Access at: www.gov.uk/government/uploads/system/uploads/attachment_data/file/246474/0565.pdf.
Rosenblatt F. (2015) *The Role of Community in Restorative Justice, Routledge*, forthcoming.
Sarkis A, and others, (2013) *Victims' Voice: Report of the Northamptonshire Victims' Commissioner* (The Northamptonshire Police and Crime Commissioner).
Shapland J, and others, (2008) *Does restorative justice affect reconviction? The fourth report from the evaluation of three schemes* (Ministry of Justice Research Series 10/08).
Sherman L and Strang H, 2007 *Restorative Justice: The Evidence* (The Smith Institute).
Sherman L and others, (2014) 'Are Restorative Justice conferences Effective in Reducing Repeat Offending? Findings from a Campbell Systematic Review' *Journal of Quanitative Criminology*.
Smith R, (2011) 'Developing restorative practice: contemporary lessons from an English juvenile diversion project of the 1980s' *Contemporary Justice Review* 14(4): 425–438.
Wachtel T, (2015) 'Defining Restorative' wwwiirpedu/pdf/Defining-Restorativepdf accessed 22nd January 2015.
Walgrave L, (2008) *Restorative Justice, Self-interest and Responsible Citizenship* (Willan Publishing).
Young R and Hoyle C, (2003) 'Restorative Justice and Punishment' in McConville S (ed.), *The Use of Punishment* (Willan Publishing).
Zedner L, (1994) 'Reparation and Retribution: Are They Reconcilable?' 57 *Modern Law Review*.
Zehr H, (1990) *Changing Lenses* (Herald Press).

Chapter 24

Juvenile justice education

George B. Pesta and Thomas G. Blomberg

Introduction

Education and delinquency are correlated through various relationships. Delinquent youth often have histories of poor school performance, low-attachment to school, lower literacy levels, and higher rates of learning and behavioral disabilities when compared with their non-delinquent peers. Inversely, prior empirical literature on delinquency and education has consistently reported that successful school performance and strong school attachment are protective factors in preventing delinquency. Furthermore, research has focused upon the relationship among school attachment, academic achievement and desistence from delinquency. In this research, education has been demonstrated to serve as an effective intervention policy and practice for some juvenile justice involved youth. Specifically, educational achievement for incarcerated delinquent youth has been found to serve as a "turning point" in reducing post-release recidivism.

Empirical research regarding juvenile justice education

Research consistently documents that higher levels of education and lower levels of juvenile crime tend to be highly correlated. For example, high levels of literacy are consistently associated with lower rates of juvenile delinquency, re-arrest, and recidivism (Center on Crime, Communities, and Culture, 1997). Longitudinal studies of adolescents and young adults that have examined the effects of education on criminal activity also provide support for a negative relationship between various education-related measures and delinquency. Arum and Beattie (1999) found that total years of education, high school grade point average (GPA), and the student-to-teacher ratio of one's high school significantly reduced the likelihood of incarceration among a national sample of juveniles. Similarly, Bernburg and Krohn (2003) studied a sample of high-risk juveniles in Rochester, NY, and found that graduating from high school significantly decreased the likelihood of involvement in serious criminal activity. Overall, the research supports the hypothesis that educational success leads to a reduced likelihood of criminal activity and increased opportunities for college and professional careers; while educational failure reverses these relationships.

Youth in juvenile correctional facilities are among the most educationally disadvantaged in our society (Pfannenstiel, 1993). But research evidence suggests that providing opportunities and assistance for youth to acquire educational skills is an effective approach to the prevention of delinquency and the reduction of recidivism. Furthermore, an educational program intervention is not likely to produce negative or unwanted effects. When successfully implemented, juvenile justice education programs have been shown to produce positive outcomes in behavior, future education, and employment after release (Elliott, 1994; Jensen and Howard, 1998; Foley, 2001). In fact, incarcerated youth, despite their history of school failure, disabilities, and poorly developed academic skills can make significant achievement gains with intensive instruction in a short period of time (Drakeford, 2001; Malmgren and Leone, 2000).

Given the inverse relationship between educational performance and delinquency, some policies and practices have led to the use of education as an intervention for juvenile justice involved youth. This research has focused on the relationship between education and desistance from criminal activity among incarcerated juveniles. Studies that have focused on the education–recidivism link for juvenile offenders support the general finding that education reduces recidivism. Specifically, education as measured by the attainment of a high school diploma or its equivalent, academic achievement, and attachment to school post-release has, in varying degrees, been found to be effective in reducing the likelihood of recidivism (Ambrose and Lester, 1988; Blomberg et al., 2011; Bullis et al., 2002; Lipsey and Wilson, 1998).

For example, in their meta-analysis of intervention programs for committed youth, Lipsey and Wilson (1998) found that programs focusing on educational achievement and structured learning can reduce recidivism among juvenile offenders. Ambrose and Lester (1988) found that incarcerated juvenile offenders with a high school diploma or equivalent were significantly less likely to recidivate during the first year following release.

Blomberg et al. (2011) assessed the potential links between educational achievement, post-release schooling, and re-arrest for a cohort of 4,147 incarcerated youths from 115 Florida juvenile institutions and followed them for two years post-release. The authors reported that when most youths enter a residential commitment program, they are far behind their peers in terms of grade level and test performance. However, the authors found that committed youths with higher levels of educational achievement while incarcerated were more likely to return to school after release. Further, those who attended school regularly post-release were less likely to be re-arrested within 12 and 24 months. In addition, among the youths who were re-arrested, those who attended school regularly following release were arrested for significantly less serious offenses.

Bullis, Yovanoff, Mueller, and Havel (2002) conducted a five-year longitudinal study of committed juvenile offenders in Oregon. The authors found that youth who were participating in school after their release were less likely to recidivate. However, less than one half of the youth were working or in school six months after release. The proportion dropped to less than one third at 12 months post-release. Thus, although participation in school affected recidivism, few juvenile offenders became engaged in school following their release from commitment, and even fewer remained engaged in school over time.

Despite the demonstrated link between educational performance and delinquency, studies that have compared the quality of education in juvenile justice institutions to that of public schools have found education in juvenile justice facilities to be substandard. Many juvenile institutions suffer from deficiencies in oversight and accountability and a lack of consistency across states and localities in the delivery of education services for juvenile justice involved youth. In addition, in many juvenile residential settings education is often forced to compete with other custody, care and treatment programming for funding, resources, space and time. Unfortunately, the lack of quality in juvenile justice education programs is a historical problem that can be traced back to the beginning of the modern juvenile justice system.

History of juvenile justice education

The quality of juvenile justice education programs throughout the country has historically been substandard (Blomberg and Lucken, 2010; Pesta, 2012; Rothman, 2002). In 1899, the first juvenile court was established in Cook County, IL and within a few decades, most other states had established juvenile court systems. The Progressives, who stimulated the juvenile court movement, advocated a model of individual diagnosis, treatment, and education. However, this model was never effectively implemented in the education of juvenile justice involved youth. In addition, differing implementation practices at the state and local levels resulted in fragmented and disparate juvenile justice treatment and education systems throughout the country.

Rothman (2002) traced the history of juvenile residential institutions during America's Progressive Era and concluded that the progressives failed to treat and educate juveniles. Although the progressives sought to provide a more scientific and individualized approach to treatment and education of juvenile offenders, the implementation of their ideals fell far short of their rhetoric (Blomberg and Luken, 2010; Rothman, 2002). Juvenile justice education was intended to be based upon each youth's abilities and interests. However, in reality, most state juvenile institutions remained punitive, and the education and/or vocational training that was offered was typically related to institutional maintenance or menial labor. To illustrate, a juvenile training school superintendent in the early 1900s asked the question, "When is a school not a school?" He went on to answer, "When it is a school for delinquents. Because the child has shown by her anti-social attitudes how much she is in need of more education, she is put in a training school where she will get less" (Rothman, 2002, p. 261).

Despite the inability of training schools to provide an adequate academic and/or vocational curriculum that addressed the needs of the students they were designed to serve, training schools remained the predominant institution for delinquent youth throughout the twentieth century. In their study of residential commitment programs across several states, Westat (1991) found that instruction was most commonly accomplished by providing youth with packets of materials and worksheets, which limited group, student and teacher interactions. Most material was based on repetitive instructional methods of drill and practice. In addition, the study found that transition services aimed at assisting youth with returning-to-school and post-release employment varied widely across institutions and were often non-existent. Similarly, the Research Triangle Institute (1999) conducted a study that consisted of multiple site visits to residential programs in nine states. The study found that the purposes of the educational programs within juvenile justice institutions varied widely across the sites. Like the Westat study eight years earlier, the researchers found a consistent lack of transition services and follow-up.

A legal response to substandard juvenile justice education surfaced during the late twentieth century, as evidenced by the initiation of numerous class-action lawsuits in federal courts concerning education in juvenile justice institutions. Beginning in the 1970s with the Oregon juvenile justice system, and continuing today, the U.S. federal courts began deciding cases regarding the education and treatment of juveniles in confinement. From 1977 to 2005 federal courts decided more than 50 class-action cases relating to education services in states' juvenile justice systems. Litigation is often brought about, on behalf of incarcerated youth, by legal advocacy organizations throughout the country (Pesta, 2012; Warboys, 1999; Leone, 2005).

Most cases have targeted post-adjudication residential facilites and juvenile detention centers however, some cases have also been filed against government entities responsible for jails and prisons as juveniles who are transferred to the adult court and adult facilities retain their public education rights. The most commonly cited federal laws in juvenile justice education litigation are the Individuals with Disabilities Education Act (IDEA) and Section 504 of the Rehabilitation Act of 1978 (504). IDEA requires that eligible children and youth with disabilities receive a free and appropriate public education including special education and related services. Section 504 is a federal civil rights statute that prohibits discrimination against persons with handicaps by any program or activity that receives federal funds, including public school systems and correctional facilities (Pesta, 2012).

This litigation regarding education is often accompanied by complaints of poor conditions of confinement that violate the 8th and/or 14th Amendments to the U.S. Constitution. Although there is a lack of research on the impact of litigation on juvenile justice education services, most scholars agree that the courts have played a significant role in reforming prisons and juvenile facilities (Jacobs, 1980; Dilulio, 1990; Feeley and Rubin, 2000). It should also be noted that litigation and complaints investigated by the Civil Rights Division of the U.S. Department of Justice under the Civil Rights of Institutionalized Persons Act (CRIPA) continue to occur in jails and juvenile facilities throughout the country.

In addition to the litigation and court intervention that has influenced juvenile justice education reform, federal education requirements enacted through standards-based reform initiatives such as Goals 2000 have also had an impact. In particular, in 2002, the enactment of the No Child Left Behind Act (NCLB) posed unprecedented challenges for the reform of the country's juvenile justice schools. NCLB mandated that juvenile justice schools meet the same high standards as all other elementary and secondary public schools, focusing on teacher qualifications, state curriculum standards for core academic courses, testing requirements and the implementation of scientifically-based practices. Moreover, Title I, Part D focused upon institutions for neglected and delinquent youth containing specific provisions for juvenile justice schools, including an emphasis on youth returning to school upon release from institutions, providing transition services, and conducting program evaluations (The Juvenile Justice NCLB Collaboration Project, 2008, Pesta; 2012).

Under NCLB's general provisions for all schools, teachers were required to meet highly qualified standards, which included holding a bachelor's degree, having a professional license, and showing competency in the academic subjects they taught. States and schools were also required to meet common curriculum standards for core academic courses. To measure performance on curriculum standards, NCLB included school testing requirements that mandated a 95 percent student participation rate and demonstrated progress based on each state's annual school achievement testing. Additionally, under Title I, Part D, all juvenile justice schools were monitored for student performance in the areas of maintaining and improving educational achievement, accruing school credits for grade promotion, making a successful transition back to school after release or completing high school while incarcerated (The Juvenile Justice NCLB Collaboration Project, 2008). Although NCLB and Title I, Part D began to articulate standards and expected outcomes for the education of detained and incarcerated youth, states and jurisdictions implemented the requirements inconsistently and the law lacked consequences for failure to meet specific standards and outcomes.

Overall, juvenile justice education has historically lacked professional scrutiny and accountability (Leone and Cutting, 2004; Mechlinski, 2001). Clearly, there are many problems associated with implementing account-ability measures and high-quality academic programs in juvenile justice edu-cational facilities. Meeting these requirements is difficult for many juvenile justice schools due to several factors, including their relatively small size, the short lengths of stay of the students, high student mobility, and the students' disproportionate educational deficiencies compared to their public school counterparts. Leone and Cutting (2004) identify some of the challenges as being characteristic of the incarcerated youth population, the individualized operation of the facilities, and the limited connection between the juvenile justice facility and local public schools. In addition, many juvenile facilities often suffer from overcrowding, have limited financial resources, inadequate space, unqualified teachers and ineffective governance (Leone et al., 1986). Furthermore, during national focus groups, state juvenile justice education leaders expressed common difficulties for reforming their respective state systems. In particular, these state leaders expressed concerns over:

1. Competing with traditional public schools to recruit and retain highly qualified teachers,
2. Lack of planning and coordination with local schools and school dis-tricts to better transition youth into juvenile facilities and back to school after their release, and
3. Difficulty in maintaining and measuring student educational progress due to high student mobility, short lengths of stay and a lack of fit with traditional school accountability systems (The Juvenile Justice NCLB Collaboration Project, 2006).

Despite these inherent barriers and difficulties, an illuminating example of educational reform for juvenile justice involved youth occurred in Florida.

Florida's juvenile justice education system: a case illustration

Florida, like most other states, suffered decades of neglect in its juvenile justice education system. As a result, and after many years of investigation and public interest in Florida's juvenile training schools, in 1983 Florida's juvenile justice system came under the scrutiny of the federal court sys-tem when a class-action lawsuit was filed on behalf of a 14-year-old boy, known as Bobby M., and three other children. Among numerous mandates, the litigation resulted in the removal of dependent youth from the state's major juvenile training schools, the closing of the state's largest training school for girls and a reduction in the population of the state's two largest training schools for boys. In addition, the courts handed down three consent decrees including one that focused solely on educational services throughout Florida's juvenile justice system.

Under the education provisions of the consent decree Florida was required to provide special, vocational, and alternative educational services at least equivalent in quality and quantity to what youth would receive in a traditional public school. In addition, Florida was required to ensure that all youth were provided with a free and appropriate public education including special education and related services in the least restricted environment (Pesta, 2012).

The litigation and resulting consent decree lasted more than a decade and the Florida Legislature responded with several reform acts, including the creation of a new state agency for the administration of juvenile justice and a mandate for the creation of a state juvenile justice education quality assurance system. To fulfill this mandate and to address the state's ongoing deficiencies, in 1998, the Florida Department of Education (DOE) contracted with the Florida State University (FSU) College of Criminology and Criminal Justice to operate a statewide project known as the Juvenile Justice Educational Enhancement Program (JJEEP). For 12 years, from 1998 to 2010, JJEEP developed and operated a comprehensive accountability system for all of Florida's juvenile justice schools. The accountability methods developed took into account the processes of the juvenile justice system, such as the relatively short lengths of stay of the juvenile offenders, high mobility rates, small schools with no economy of scale, a security-rich environment, and concentrated groups of poor educationally performing youth, while encompassing the major educational reforms of the time.

To address the task of elevating the quality of educational services statewide and to ensure that juvenile justice schools embraced and implemented effective educational reforms, JJEEP developed comprehensive and interrelated functions that would monitor, assist, and guide the implementation of evidence-based reforms. Overall, JJEEP's methods were aimed at elevating the field of juvenile justice education through four main functions including:

1. Conducting annual quality assurance (QA) reviews of the educational programs in Florida's juvenile justice facilities.
2. Providing technical assistance (TA) to improve the various educational programs.
3. Conducting research that identified and validated promising educational practices.
4. Providing recommendations to the Florida DOE and the Legislature to guide state policy relating to juvenile justice education (JJEEP, 2010).

Quality Assurance consisted of developing and annually revising educational program standards, developing and maintaining review methods, and conducting annual onsite reviews of all juvenile justice schools throughout Florida. JJEEP's strategy for annual system improvement and informing the QA standards with the best evidence available included annually raising the bar by using evidence-based research, soliciting input from practitioners in the field, and incorporating federal and state educational requirements. The QA standards were used to measure program performance, enforce educational requirements such as Florida public school requirements, IDEA, NCLB, and Title I, Part D and improve the quality of education in all of Florida's juvenile justice schools. The QA standards focused upon the following areas:

- Student assessment and planning to identify and address youths' individual needs.
- Teacher qualifications including certification, in-field teaching status, specialized training, and retention.
- Transition services including transition planning, student exit portfolios, communication with receiving schools and follow-up services.
- Enhanced curriculum and instruction that provided opportunities for academics, remediation and career development and addressed the individual needs of students and prepared them for graduation or a return to school.
- Local school district oversight, program evaluation, and a focus on student outcomes such as academic gains, student progression and return to school upon release (JJEEP, 2010).

JJEEP's quality improvement model was also supported by TA which was designed to help juvenile justice schools meet the annually elevating QA standards. Methods of TA included: (1) training peer-reviewers from school districts and juvenile justice providers throughout the state to assist in conducting reviews and providing technical assistance, (2) providing schools with written recommendations, (3) developing corrective action plans and conducting follow-up visits for low-performing schools and (4) hosting an annual conference dedicated to research, policy and best-practice in juvenile justice education.

To ensure that the QA and TA processes remained relevant and effective, research activities were designed to inform these functions. To meet this objective, JJEEP created a research agenda that was intended to influence policy and practice in juvenile justice education. Primary research methods included continuous literature reviews in the education of juvenile justice involved youth, case studies of high- and low-performing schools, correlated research on school performance, and post-release longitudinal studies of students returning to the community and school from juvenile justice residential programs.

The final function of JJEEP was to inform public policy regarding program performance and research. This was accomplished through annual recommendations to the Florida DOE and the Legislature, presentations to the U.S. Congress, and presentations at high-profile national conferences. In response, education policy also influenced the QA process. In particular, NCLB enhanced the QA standards and validated many of JJEEP's expectations for juvenile justice schools.

From these 12 years of experience operating one of the country's largest juvenile justice education accountability systems some promising practices have emerged. First, juvenile justice involved youth have varying and often intense educational needs. They exhibit disproportionate emotional, social and educational deficiencies which are simultaneously related to lower school attachment and educational attainment as well as delinquency. In addition, learning and behavioral disabilities and below average IQs are prevalent among juvenile justice involved youth often ranging from 32 to 43 percent (JJEEP, 2006; Leone et al., 2003; Quinn et al., 2005). Juvenile justice involved youth are also more likely than their public school counter parts to have poor school grades, be over age for grade placement and perform below average on norm referenced and standardized tests (Nelson et al., 2004; Wang et al., 2005).

However, juvenile justice education programs can confront, and in many cases counteract, these risk factors through a series of educational and treatment strategies. These services include diagnostic and continual assessment, tailored student educational planning, individualized instruction and intense academic curricula that address remediation and credit recovery and prepare youth for graduation or a return to school. Additionally, youth may benefit from a low student-to-teacher ratio and the use of highly qualified teachers, teaching in their area of certification.

Despite a juvenile justice education program's best efforts, given many juveniles' young age and educational deficiencies upon entry into a juvenile justice program, and the program's relatively short length of stay, the majority of youth in the juvenile justice system are too young and/or too far behind in school to complete their secondary education while incarcerated. This results in the majority of the youth exiting juvenile justice facilities in need of further education in order to complete high school. This finding has led practitioners and researchers alike to examine the process by which youth are released from residential care and attempt to reenter their home, work and school settings. Based on community reintegration research, it is evident that there is a need for education-related transition services including transition planning, student exit portfolios, communication with receiving schools and follow-up support services. Despite calls for supportive aftercare services, aftercare programing is often limited to forms of probation and/or conditional release which tend to favor monitoring and compliance. Furthermore, local school jurisdictions throughout the country often require youth returning from juvenile justice institutions to attend alternative schools. Though this practice has not been extensively evaluated, critics question its motive and effectiveness.

Research on community reintegration and school reentry has identified numerous difficulties and barriers that can prevent youth from successfully transitioning back to school after their release from a juvenile justice facility. Some barriers include lack of family, school and social supports, lack of academic skills and being too far behind in school, negative peer association, substance use, experiencing a lack of consistency across varying school systems, and even direct school resistance and stigma (Baltodano, Platt and Roberts, 2005; Unruh, 2005; Unruh and Bullis, 2005). Despite these barriers or risk factors, JJEEPs longitudinal research as well as other community reentry studies found that engagement in school and school attendance post-release reduced the likelihood of recidivism (Bullis et al., 2004; Unruh et al., 2009; Bullis et al., 2002; Blomberg et al., 2011 Blomberg et al., 2012;).

Specifically, JJEEP's research examined the extent to which educational achievement, as measured by credits earned and grade advancement, predicted if youth would return to school upon release. In addition, the research examined if attending school after release predicted the likelihood that youth would recidivate at 12 and 24 months post-release and the severity of the re-offense. The findings concluded that educational achievement did predict a return to school post-release, that higher attendance in school after release resulted in a lower likelihood of recidivism, and among those who did recidivate, those with higher attendance tended to commit less serious offenses (Blomberg et al., 2011 Blomberg et al., 2012).

Ultimately, JJEEP was recognized by the U.S. Office of Juvenile Justice and Delinquency Prevention (OJJDP) as an exemplary program and was funded to provide assistance to other states throughout the country regarding quality and accountability of education practices for incarcerated delinquent youth. This funding enabled JJEEP to host a series of national conferences and work directly with state leaders in juvenile justice education. The meetings, and subsequent targeted assistance to several states, focused upon the implementation of best-practices for the education of juvenile justice involved youth.

Conclusion

In conclusion, what is salient is that juvenile justice youth exhibit numerous risk factors and disproportionate educational deficiencies when compared with their peers in public school. In addition, this disenfranchised population tends to be underserved, lacking the advocates that would ensure they receive the consistent and high quality services needed to treat their many risk factors. Over the decades this has resulted in a system of neglect.

Despite this, educational achievement is a critical element in delinquency prevention and delinquency desistence.

Most juvenile facilities today offer some level of educational services on a fairly consistent, if not always high-quality, basis. Academic, career and technical and social skills classes are typically offered on a regular schedule and often parallel the local public school schedules. Many states offer education to incarcerated youth on a year-round basis. Most Florida facilities offer five hours per day of education, Monday through Friday, for 240 to 250 days per year. Although this does not guarantee that the best teachers are working in juvenile facilities, since the passage of the No Child Left Behind Act, it is increasingly more common to find teachers in juvenile facilities to be professionally certified and teaching classes in their area of certification. Juvenile facilities range in size from 20 or so youth to a few hundred. Depending on the security level of the facility, classrooms may be located in stand-alone educational buildings or, to decrease movement in more high-risk programs, they are directly connected to each dorm, module or cell block. Learning objectives vary by facility but most often focus on standard courses for high school credit, remediation, GED preparation, basic career and technical education and even soft-skills classes for employability and social skills. Though still limited, more recent pedagogy has some facilities offering online and distance learning opportunities through virtual high schools and industry certification preparation programs. Privatization of the educational services is becoming more common throughout the United States with approximately 60 percent of the educational programs in Florida's juvenile facilities being privately operated.

Although the JJEEP program in Florida demonstrated a successful method for large scale system reform, in 2010 the Florida Legislature and DOE chose to no longer support the program. With years of demonstrated success and well-documented measurable impact, one has to ask why a successful reform program was eliminated. Likely, following the financial crisis of 2008, faced with increasing state budget shortfalls and continuing educational accountability pressures resulting from the high stakes testing movement, DOE focused their efforts on mainstream youth in traditional public schools. Bureaucratic maintenance limited the Florida DOE priorities standardizing the oversight of the state's 67 school districts that include over 3,600 schools serving over 2.5 million students. Driven by demands of efficiency to show improvement throughout the education system, it is easy for populations with little political capital or powerful advocates, such as incarcerated youth, to become displaced in the larger policy agendas and bureaucratic priorities and become left behind.

Despite continuous setbacks, juvenile justice education has recently gained new attention at both the federal and state of Florida levels. In 2012, the U.S. Department of Education published a juvenile justice "Education Reentry Model" guidebook. In addition, the Department held a summit with juvenile advocates, practitioners and researchers in Washington DC to discuss the role of education for juvenile justice involved youth. The meeting resulted in recommendations for improving education and reentry services for juvenile justice involved youth. In Florida, the 2014 Legislature passed and signed into law a state statute that will provide new governances, accountability and standards for Florida's juvenile justice educational programs. To address the historical neglect in the field of juvenile justice education and ensure sustained reform throughout the field, several recommendations should be considered.

1. Juvenile justice education programs should undergo rigorous and regular evaluations.
2. Developing common juvenile justice education program standards based upon compliance with the Individuals with Disabilities Education Act (IDEA), the No Child Left Behind Act (NCLB) and identified best-practices.
3. Establishing a national research laboratory for the study of the education and reentry of juvenile justice involved youth for the purpose of conducting, collecting and disseminating research and evidence-based practices in the field.
4. Expanding federal data reporting requirements including the development of common measures and methods for evaluating and improving student outcomes such as academic achievement while incarcerated, educational participation post-release, employment and recidivism.
5. Establishing a publicly accessible national longitudinal data set of juvenile justice involved youth.
6. Developing college curricula that prepares core content area teachers to work effectively with juvenile justice involved youth.

References

Ambrose, D. M. and Lester, D. (1988). Recidivism in Juvenile Offenders: Effects of Education and Length of Stay. *Psychological Reports*, 63: 778.

Arum, R. and Beattie, I. R. (1999). High School Experience and the Risk of Adult Incarceration. *Criminology*, 37(3): 515–540.

Baltodano, H., Platt, D., and Roberts, C. (2005). Transition from Secure Care to the Community: Significant issues for youth in detention. *The Journal of Correctional Education*, 56(4): 372–388.

Bernburg, J. G. and Krohn, M. D. (2003). Labeling, Life Chances, and Adult Crime: The Direct and Indirect Effects of Official Intervention in Adolescence on Crime in Early Adulthood. *Criminology*, 41(4): 1287–1318.

Blomberg, T. G., and Luken, K. (2010). *American Penology*. New York: Aldine De Gruyter.

Blomberg, T. G., Bales, W. D., and Piquero, A. R. (2012). Is Educational Achievement a Turning Point for Incarcerated Delinquents Across Race and Sex? *Journal of Youth and Adolescence*, 41: 202–216.

Blomberg, T. G., Bales, W. D., Mann, K., and Piquero, A. R. (2011). Incarceration, Education and Transition from Delinquency. *Journal of Criminal Justice*, 39: 355–365.

Bullis, M., Yovanoff, P., and Havel, E. (2004). The Importance of Getting Started Right: Further Examination of the Facility-to-community Transition of Formerly Incarcerated youth. *Journal of Special Education*, 38: 80–94.

Bullis, M., Yovanoff, P., Mueller, G., and Havel, E. (2002). Life on the "outs": Examination of the Facility-to-Community Transition of Incarcerated Adolescents. *Exceptional Children*, 69: 7–22.

Center on Crime, Communities, and Culture. (1997). *Education as crime prevention* (Occasional Paper Series No. 2). New York: Author.

Center for Criminology and Public Policy Research; Florida State University. (2008). *The Juvenile Justice No Child Left Behind Collaboration Project: Final Report 2008*. Tallahassee: Center for Criminology and Public Policy Research.

Dilulio, J. J. (1990). The Old Regime and the Ruiz Revolution: The Impact of Judicial Intervention on Texas Prisons. In J. J. Dilulio, *Courts, Corrections and the Constitution* (pp. 51–72). New York: Oxford University Press.

Drakeford, W. (2001). The Impact of an Intensive Program to Increase the Literacy Skills of Youth Confined in Juvenile Corrections. *Journal of Correctional Education*, 53(4): 139–144.

Elliott, D. S., (1994). Serious Violent Offenders: Onset, Developmental Course, and Termination. The American Society of Criminology 1993 presidential address. *Criminology*, 32: 1–21.

Feeley, M. M., and Rubin, E. L. (2000). *Judicial Policy Making and the Modern State*. Cambridge: Cambridge University Press.

Foley, R. M. (2001). Academic Characteristics of Incarcerated Youth and Correctional Education Programs: A Literature Review. *Journal of Emotional and Behavioral Disorders*, 9(4): 248–259.

Jacobs, J. B. (1980). The Prisoners' Rights Movement and Its Impacts. *Crime and Justice*, 2: 429–470.

Jensen, J. M., and Howard M. O. (1998). Youth Crime, Public Policy, and Practice in the Juvenile Justice System: Recent Trends and Needed Reforms. *Social Work*, 43(4): 324–334.

Juvenile Justice Educational Enhancement Program. (2006). *2005 Annual Report to the Florida Department of Education*. Tallahassee, FL: Florida State University.

Juvenile Justice Educational Enhancement Program. (2010). *2009–2010 Annual Report to the Florida Department of Education*. Tallahassee, FL: Florida State University.

Juvenile Justice NCLB Collaboration Project (2008). *2008 Final Report*. Tallahassee, FL: Florida State University.

Leone, P. (2005). *Class Action Litigation Involving Special Education Claims for Youth in Juvenile and Adult Correctional Facilities*. College Park: National Center on Education, Disability, and Juvenile Justice.

Leone, P. E. and Cutting, C.A. (2004). Appropriate Education, Juvenile Corrections, and No Child Left Behind. *Behavioral Disorders*, 29(3): 260–265.

Leone, P.E., Price, T. and Vitolo, R.K. (1986). Appropriate Education for All Incarcerated Youth Meeting the Spirit of P.L 94–142 in Youth Detention Facilities. *Remedial and Special Education*, 7(4): 9–14.

Leone, P.E., Christle, C.A., Nelson, C.M., Skiba, R., Frey, A., and Jolivette, K. (2003). School Failure, Race, and Disability: Promoting Positive Outcomes, Decreasing Vulnerability for Involvement with the Juvenile Delinquency System. *EDJJ: The National Center on Education, Disability, and Juvenile Justice*.

Lipsey, M. W. and Wilson, D. B. (1998). Effective Intervention for Serious Juvenile Offenders: A Synthesis of Research. In R. Loeber and D. P. Farrington (eds.), *Serious and violent juvenile offenders: Risk factors and successful interventions* (pp. 313–345). Thousand Oaks, CA: Sage.

Malmgren, K. and Leone, P. E. (2000). Effects of a Short-Term Auxiliary Reading Program on the Reading Skills of Incarcerated Youth. *Education and Treatment of Children*, 23: 239–247.

Mechlinski, M. J. (2001). School Improvement in Correctional Education. *Journal of Correctional Education Association*, 52(3): 115–118.

Nelson, J. R., Benner, G. J., Lane, K. L., and Smith, B. W. (2004). Academic Achievement of K-12 Students with Emotional and Behavioral Disorders. *Exceptional Children*, 71: 59–73.

Pesta, G. B. (2012). Court Intervention and Institutional Reform: The Bobby M. Case and Its Impact on Juvenile Justice Education in Florida. Florida State University. *Electronic Theses, Treatises and Dissertations*. Paper 5108.

Pfannenstiel, J.C. (1993). Teaching Techniques Determine Students' Success or Failure. *Corrections Today*, 55(1): 70–73.

Quinn, M. M., Rutherford, R. B., Leone, P. E., Osher, D. M., and Poirier, J. M. (2005). Youth with Disabilities in Juvenile Corrections: A National Survey. *Exceptional Children*, 71(3): 339–345.

Research Triangle Institute. (1999). *Study of Local Agency Activities Under the Title I, Part D, Program*. Washington DC: U.S. Department of Education.

Rothman, D. J. (2002). *Conscience and Convenience*. Hawthorne: Aldine De Gruyter.

Unruh, D. (2005). Using Primary and Secondary Stakeholders to Define Facility-to-Community Transition Needs of Adjudicated Youth with Disabilities. *Evaluation and Program Planning*, 28: 413–422.

Unruh, D., and Bullis, M. (2005). Facility-to-community Transition Needs for Adjudicated Youth with Disabilities. *Career Development for Exceptional Individuals*, 28(2): 67–79.

Unruh, D., Gau, J., and Waintrup, M. (2009). An Exploration of Factors Reducing Recidivism Rates of Formerly Incarcerated Youth with Disabilities Participating in a Re-entry ntervention. *Journal of Child and Family Studies*, (18): 284–293.

Wang, X., Blomberg, T.G., and Li, S.D. 2005. Comparison of the Educational Deficiencies of Delinquent and Nondelinquent Students. *Evaluation Review*, 29(4): 291–312.

Warboys, L. (1999). *Court Cases and Agency Rulings on Special Education in Juvenile and Adult Correctional Facilities: A Special Education Clearinghouse*. San Francisco: Youth Law Center.

Werner, J. (2001–2002). No Knight in Shining Armor: Why Courts Alone, Absent Public Engagement, Could Not Achieve Successful Public School Finance Reform in West Virginia. *Columbia Journal of Law and Social Problems*, 61–82.

Westat, Inc. (1991). *Unlocking Learning; Chapter 1 in Correctional Facilities. Final Report*. Rockville: U. S. Department of Education.

Introduction

Special populations

Thomas G. Blomberg, Julie Mestre Brancale, Kevin M. Beaver and William D. Bales

This section examines specialized populations within correctional systems that provide unique, difficult, and costly challenges to those who oversee them, those who prosecute and punish them, as well as policymakers who make decisions relating to who is incarcerated and for how long. These special populations are not new to the correctional system; however, they are more pronounced and consequential particularly, as a result of the "mass incarceration" movement that has occurred over the past several decades. Research relating to these populations is important because correctional systems will be impacted for years to come as these types of inmates increase and thus, will require increases in the number of staff with specialized skills and the need for more program and related resources. The three special prison populations examined in this section include inmates with mental illnesses, women and particularly mothers in prison, and elder prisoners. The section concludes with a chapter that identifies the unique challenges of Native American populations for tribal-based criminal justice systems.

In Chapter 25, Authur Lurigio examines the significant number and growth in people with serious mental illness (PSMI) in U.S. prisons and discusses the unique and difficult challenges these individuals face while incarcerated and when they reenter their communities. The actual prevalence rate of PSMI in our prison systems varies depending upon the source of the data; however, research indicates that approximately 8–19 percent of the inmate population is afflicted with significant psychiatric or functional disabilities and another 15–20 percent will require some form of psychiatric intervention prior to their prison release. After an assessment of deficiencies in the level of mental health services in correctional systems, Lurigio makes three primary policy related conclusions/recommendations based on his review of the scientific evidence. First, the current standard of care for the mentally ill inmate is inadequate. Second, PSMI affects females more than males and, with their growing presence in our prison system, the demand for increases in gender-responsive correctional mental health services is needed. Third, more effort is needed to improve the post-prison outcomes of PSMI inmates through proper transition planning for the special services these inmates require to be successful, especially given that their risk for re-arrest, drug abuse relapse, violence, etc. are higher than non-PSMI prison releases

Chapter 26, by Meda Chesney-Lind and Marylyn Brown, focuses on the policy implications of the increasing numbers of females incarcerated in our prison system and the consequences relative to parenting. The evidence is clear that during the past several decades of unprecedented increases in the U.S. prison population, females generally, and females with children specifically, have been impacted significantly more than their male counterparts. Policymakers, and those making the decisions relating to who enters our prisons and for how long, need to consider the research evidence relating to the challenges women face during and after imprisonment. Specifically, the authors suggest that practitioners who work directly with female inmates use modified risk and assessment instruments that incorporate gendered variables. Research has shown that correctional rehabilitation methods designed for men are less successful in helping women remain crime-free when released. Additionally, the authors recommend the implementation of policies and practices that help to build, strengthen, and maintain relationships between incarcerated mothers and their children.

Chapter 27, by Karol Lucken, examines one of the most notable special populations in U.S. prison, the elderly. The research findings are indisputable that there has been an unprecedented growth in the number and proportion of the total prison population in the U.S. who are older and these individuals, relative to their younger counterparts, require special accommodations and more health care, which has consequences in terms of prison staffing, equipment, and increased funding. With our deterministic punishment policies, longer prison sentences, life without parole, etc. becoming popular in most states over the past 30 years, it is no surprise that the prison population is graying at an alarming rate. The author recommends that states give greater consideration to early release programs for elderly inmates given that their likelihood of re-offending is extremely low relative to their younger counterparts.

In Chapter 28, Roy Janisch describes the unique criminal justice system challenges faced by Native American tribal groups. Criminal justice on Native American reservations is often characterized by complex jurisdictional issues related to Congressional resolutions passed without the consent of the concerned tribes, and a lack of funding for tribal law enforcement, corrections, and judicial systems. Many Native American tribes are plagued with extremely high rates of substance abuse and crime and have largely ill-equipped criminal justice systems. Coupled with these challenges is the lack of empirical research on Native American crime and justice. The author recommends forming meaningful and lasting partnerships between researchers and Native American tribal authorities as a means to begin the development of evidence-based solutions to the crime and justice issues facing Native American tribes.

Imprisonment as a punishment strategy began with the belief that the typical inmate was likely to be a healthy young male in his late teenage or early adult years. However, over time, the characteristics of the inmate population have changed. It is not uncommon for a single prison to house young, old, mentally ill, physically disabled, and diseased inmates. Also important, is that the number of female inmates has been steadily growing. This changing nature of the inmate population has been attributed to the Get Tough on crime movement that began in the 1980s and resulted in an era of mass incarceration. As the chapters in this section have demonstrated, operating a prison under the assumption that all inmates are relatively healthy, young men is not a correct or effective correctional strategy. Mentally ill inmates (Chapter 25), female inmates (Chapter 26), and elderly inmates (Chapter 27) each present their own set of challenges for the correctional system. They require specialized housing units, medications, supervision, reentry programs, etc. When faced with a growing percentage of special inmate populations, policymakers and practitioners must realize that traditional prison inmate characterizations are no longer applicable. Further, criminal justice on Native American reservations presents a unique challenge for policymakers, practitioners, and researchers (Chapter 28). In an effort to remedy the debilitating rates of crime and substance abuse, as well as developing effective evidence-based criminal justice strategies for Native American tribal communities, researchers and practitioners should embrace partnerships that seek to apply, implement, and evaluate evidence-based validated policies and programs.

Chapter 25

Inmates with serious mental illnesses

Current knowledge and challenges for practice

Arthur J. Lurigio and Andrew J. Harris

Prisons have become de facto psychiatric treatment facilities. Along with jails, they are now major providers of behavioral healthcare services in the United States (American Psychiatric Association, 2000; Torrey et al., 2014). The large number of people with serious mental illnesses (PSMI) in U.S. prisons has sorely taxed the capacities of the correctional system (Metzner and Dvoskin, 2006). Accordingly, prison administrators are struggling with the inherent tension between maintaining institutional order and meeting the treatment and therapeutic demands of inmates with serious mental illnesses (SMI) (Lovell et al., 2001). Similarly, local mental health clinics are adapting their care in response to the multifarious problems of PSMI as they leave prison and reenter the community (Council of State Governments, 2002).

This chapter examines the topic of PSMI in prisons, and is divided into three sections. The first explores the presence of PSMI in the country's prison population. The second describes the administrative, operational, and management protocols that affect the housing and treatment of PSMI in prison but often fall short of evidence-based and best practices. The final section suggests directions for research and policy aimed at managing inmates with SMI more humanely and responding to their needs for services, care, and safety more effectively.

The nature and extent of PSMI in prisons

Overview

For more than four decades, PSMI have been falling outside the country's social safety net – a net that has been steadily shrinking – and simply "landing in the criminal justice system at an alarming rate" (Council of State Governments, 2002: 4). Gross racial and economic disparities in mental health and addiction services as well as increasingly punitive crime control polices have intensified the flow of more and more PSMI into the criminal justice system (Lurigio, 2012). At every interception point in the process – from arrest to prosecution, to conviction, to sentencing – policies and procedures have been instituted to identify, assess, and treat PSMI who often suffer from a skein of behavioral healthcare and other problems in living (Council of State Governments, 2002).

Environmental influences. The disproportionate representation of PSMI in the criminal justice system in general, and in prisons in particular, is attributable to a variety of factors. Striking people in late adolescence and early adulthood, SMI diminishes school and job performance, causing those afflicted to drift down to the lowest levels of the socioeconomic ladder and leading to entrenched poverty and economic despair, which are precursors to crime and violence. The stress of living in poverty can precipitate the symptoms of SMI among those vulnerable to such disorders. Exerting pressures on PSMI to engage in criminal behaviors, impoverished environments are both pathogenic (i.e. precipitating and exacerbating mental illness) and criminogenic (i.e. providing many opportunities for crime but few for legitimate pursuits).

The conditions that typify underclass neighborhoods also affect poor persons with no SMI (e.g. joblessness, gang influences, failed educational systems, and housing instability). PSMI can gravitate toward illicit drug use and criminal associates who eschew pro-social values and lead them toward crime and criminal lifestyles. Poor areas are also sites for concentrations of law enforcement resources, which increase the likelihood of arrest for both PSMI and those with no SMI (Lurigio, 2012). Thus, criminally involved PSMI and people with no SMI share many socioeconomic and other characteristics (e.g. youthfulness, unemployment, poverty, lack of education, substance use). They both live in the same criminogenic neighborhoods where the presence of police and the likelihood of arrest are high, creating a gateway into the criminal justice system (Lurigio, 2011). In short, the social ecology of poverty leads to crime and mental illness, exacerbates both, and contributes to the inflow of PSMI into prisons.

Drug policies. The nation's drug control policies are the driving force behind the growing proportion of PSMI in prison (Lurigio and Swartz, 2000). Since the 1980s, the war on drugs has fueled the prison population in the United States. An overwhelming emphasis on law enforcement strategies to combat illegal drug possession and sales dramatically increased the country's arrest and incarceration rates. Both the sustained war on drugs and the high rate of comorbidity between substance use and other psychiatric disorders have fostered the rising numbers of PSMI in the nation's prisons (Lurigio et al., 2009). People with co-occurring substance use and other psychiatric disorders are more likely than those with only one disorder to be arrested, convicted, or incarcerated. They are also more likely to recidivate (i.e. return to jails, prisons, or hospitals following release) (Mueser et al., 2003). Fragmented drug and psychiatric treatment systems fail to afford fully integrated care for persons with such co-occurring disorders, thereby compounding their psychiatric problems and elevating even further their risk for arrest and incarceration (Lurigio and Swartz, 2000).

Prevalence estimates

Epidemiological research on the prevalence of PSMI in prisons has been limited due to the prohibitive cost of such studies and the difficulty of accessing representative samples of correctional facilities and inmates. Hence, most investigations of PSMI in prisons have been conducted within single states (Lamb and Weinberger, 1998; Pinta, 1999; Veysey and Bichler-Robertson, 2002). Nonetheless, the federal government has funded cross-jurisdictional studies on the prevalence of PSMI in the correctional population (Council of State Governments, 2002). Although these national studies were vitiated by their reliance on non-validated self-reports, they helped illuminate the relationships between SMI and a wide variety of social, demographic, and criminal justice variables. The findings of these studies suggest strongly and consistently that the mentally ill are overrepresented in prisons.

National surveys. The Bureau of Justice Statistics (BJS) performed two national surveys measuring the prevalence of mental illness within correctional populations, generating nationwide estimates of the percentages of PSMI in prisons and jails and on probation supervision. The first BJS study found that at midyear 1998, an estimated 283,800 mentally ill offenders were incarcerated in the country's prisons and jails. A total of 16 percent of those surveyed in each population reported either a lifetime mental disorder or an overnight stay in a mental hospital. Similarly, approximately 16 percent, or an estimated 547,800 probationers, reported either a lifetime mental disorder or an overnight stay in a mental hospital (Ditton, 1999).

Based on information from personal interviews, state prison inmates with a mental disorder were more likely than other inmates to be incarcerated for a violent offense (53 percent and 46 percent, respectively) and to be under the influence of alcohol or drugs at the time of their instant offense (59 percent and 51 percent, respectively). They also were more than twice as likely as other inmates to have been homeless in the 12 months before their arrest (20 percent and 9 percent, respectively). More than three-quarters of mentally ill inmates had been sentenced to prison, jail, or probation at least once prior to their current sentence. Since admission, 61 percent of mentally ill inmates in state prison and 41 percent of mentally ill detainees in local jails reported having received treatment for a mental health problem, including counseling, medication, or other mental health services (Ditton, 1999).

Also, using an interview protocol, the second BJS study found that at midyear 2005, 24 percent of jail detainees exhibited symptoms of a psychotic disorder, compared with 15 percent of prison inmates (James and Glaze, 2006). The rates for depression among detainees and inmates were 30 percent and 23 percent, respectively (James and Glaze, 2006). In terms of the aggregated symptoms of the mental health disorders assessed in the second BJS study, "jail inmates had the highest rate of symptoms of a mental health disorder (60 percent), followed by state (49 percent), and federal prisoners (40 percent)" (p. 3). Additionally, approximately 24 percent of state prisoners, 21 percent of jail inmates, and 14 percent of federal prisoners were found to have "a recent history of a mental health problem" (p. 2).

Other studies have shown that the overall prevalence of SMI in correctional populations is significantly higher than in the general (non-incarcerated) population. For example, a review of research through the mid-1990s concluded that approximately 10–15 percent of inmates met the criteria for SMI, which greatly exceeded prevalence estimates of PSMI in the country's general population (Lamb and Weinberger, 1998). At that time, national studies indicated that approximately 5 percent of the U.S. population met the criteria for SMI, and 3 percent met the criteria for serious and persistent mental illnesses (Kessler et al., 1996). One investigation showed that 8–12 percent of inmates suffer from a serious mental disorder such as schizophrenia, bipolar disorder, and major depression (DiCataldo, Greer, and Profit, 1995). Still other research found that 8–19 percent of prisoners are afflicted with significant psychiatric or functional disabilities and another 15–20 percent of inmates will require some form of psychiatric intervention during their incarceration (Metzner, 1993). Estimates suggest that 30–50 percent of prison inmates meet the diagnostic criteria for antisocial personality disorder (Pinta, 1999).

The National Commission on Correctional Health Care sponsored a study entitled the "Health Status of Soon-to-Be-Released Inmates," examining the prevalence of SMI in prisons (Veysey and Robertson-Bichler, 2002). The researchers adopted the methodology of the National Comorbidity Survey (NCS), a nationwide epidemiological study of psychiatric disorders, first conducted in the early 1990s. In contrast to the BJS studies, which relied solely on survey data, the Commission's researchers estimated the prevalence of mental disorders through clinical evaluations (Veysey and Robertson-Bichler, 2002).

The Commission's clinical approach to data collection directly compared the rates of SMI in correctional settings with those in the country's general population. The analyses focused on the six diagnoses that were included in the NCS: schizophrenia and other psychotic disorders, major depression, bipolar disorder, dysthymic disorder (a depressive illness of lower intensity but greater chronicity than major depression), post-traumatic stress disorder, and anxiety disorders. In each of these categories, prevalence estimates were calculated for both jail detainees and prison inmates and compared with the community prevalence rates that had been determined by the NCS.

The percentages of most types of mental illnesses were found to be significantly higher in correctional populations than in the general population (Veysey and Bichler-Robertson, 2002). Certain diagnoses were particularly elevated in correctional settings as compared to the general population, including schizophrenia and psychotic disorders (up to four times more prevalent), bipolar disorder (up to three times more prevalent), and post-traumatic stress disorder (up to two times more prevalent).

Gender differences. Investigations have consistently found higher rates of mental disorders among female than male inmates (Blitz et al., 2006). For example, in the BJA study, approximately 73 percent of women and 55 percent of men in state prison reported mental health problems (James and Glaze, 2006). Another study found that 24 percent of women in prison had a history of psychiatric treatment, 70 percent had a history of substance use disorders, and 60 percent had a history of depression, which were all significantly higher than the percentages of men in prison with such histories (Singer et al., 1995). The percentages of female prisoners who reported symptoms of mood disorders (43 percent), anxiety disorders (42 percent), and psychotic disorders (11 percent) also were all significantly higher than the percentages of women in the general population who reported symptoms of such disorders (Parsons et al., 2001).

Mentally ill inmates' needs

Inmates with SMI present a complex assortment of social problems, clinical complexities, and service needs (Hills et al., 2004; James and Glaze, 2006). For example, several studies have found high rates of co-occurring substance use disorders among inmates with SMI (Lurigio, 2001). In addition, inmates with mental health problems are twice as likely as those without mental health problems to report homelessness during the past year. They are also three times more likely to report being unemployed in the month before arrest and to report a history of physical or sexual abuse, and two times more likely to report a history of foster home placement (James and Glaze, 2006).

The management and treatment of inmates with SMI is complicated by the co-occurrence of personality disorders, including borderline (predominant among women) and antisocial (predominant among men) personality disorders – both of which are characterized by violent, self-destructive, and other risky behaviors that are especially troubling and troublesome to correctional administrators (Nee and Farman, 2005). In summary, inmates with SMI present a daunting array of concomitant problems, including substance use disorders, homelessness, unemployment, histories of trauma, and personality disorders.

Correctional practices for PSMI

The influx of inmates with SMI has forced prison administrators to revisit their standard operating procedures and expand their program options.

Beyond their need for basic psychiatric care, inmates with SMI place significant strains on the security, safety, and custodial functions of prisons, which must depart from their traditional practices in order to respond to the special demands of mentally ill incarcerees (American Psychiatric Association, 2013). The following sections briefly review four major areas of prison operations that affect inmates with SMI: psychiatric treatment, disciplinary procedures, suicide, and classification and capacity management.

Psychiatric treatment

Service availability. Inmates with SMI require a variety of services, including mental health screening, intake assessment and classification, treatment, and discharge and reentry planning (Council of State Governments, 2002). Unlike jails, prisons must be prepared to deliver long-term services to the mentally ill. A 1988 survey of mental health services in prisons, conducted by the Center for Mental Health Services (CMHS), found that only 2.5 percent of inmates were receiving psychiatric care while incarcerated (Swanson et al., 1993), which was well below the estimated rates of 10–20 percent of prisoners who required such services.

More than 10 years after the CMHS survey, mental health programs have become more common in state prisons but remain relatively low. For example, a national survey of state correctional facilities found that varying percentages of the inmates in confinement facilities were receiving mental health care at midyear 2000. Nearly 10 percent were receiving psychiatric medications, 13 percent were participating in counseling or therapy, and less than 2 percent were receiving care in a dedicated mental health unit. The percentage of inmates who were receiving psychiatric medications ranged from 5 percent to 20 percent (Beck and Maruschak, 2001).

With respect to prison policies, more than 90 percent of correctional administrators reported in the CMHS survey that they routinely screen or assess inmates at intake for mental health problems. Approximately 80 percent reported that they offered medication and therapy for inmates with SMI, and nearly two-thirds reported that they provided 24-hour mental health services. The existence of mental health policies to govern these services was most common in maximum-security facilities and least common in minimum-security facilities (Beck and Maruschak, 2001).

As noted above, among prison inmates with mental illness, the first BJS survey (midyear 1998) found that 60 percent overall had received mental health services while in federal or state prison or jail (Ditton, 1999). Nearly 70 percent of female inmates and 60 percent of male inmates with mental illness reported that they had received mental health treatment in state prison. One-quarter reported having been admitted to a mental hospital or treatment program in their lifetime. Half reported that they had taken psychiatric medication, and 44 percent reported having received counseling or therapy in their lifetime (Ditton, 1999).

Legal mandates. Prisons must provide inmates with adequate medical treatment, which includes adequate mental health care (American Civil Liberties Union, 2013; Metzner et al., 1998). Under the Eighth Amendment, the failure to afford medical care to inmates constitutes cruel and unusual punishment. To meet the standard of cruel and unusual punishment, officials must display "deliberate indifference to serious medical needs of prisoners" (Collins, 2001: 30). The Supreme Court's recognition of a prisoner's right to mental health treatment is patent; however, what constitutes "deliberate indifference" and "serious medical needs" is not (Collins, 2001). Therefore, the Supreme Court's attention to this issue does little to guarantee that prisoners with SMI will receive adequate mental health services. Nonetheless, the U.S. Supreme Court has authorized prisons to administer involuntary treatment (antipsychotic and other psychiatric medications) to inmates with SMI (*Washington v. Harper*, 1990). A recent survey reported that 31 states currently permit the administration of such treatments (Torrey et al., 2014).

Levels of care. For prisoners who need mental health services, the basic question is what level of treatment is considered acceptable (Collins, 2001). For example, does merely prescribing psychiatric medication constitute sufficient treatment? Or must an inmate receive counseling, psychotherapy, and psychiatric rehabilitation as well? If so, how many of these services should they receive? Although the Supreme Court has ruled that prisoners should receive mental health care, no specific legal parameters have been established to specify the nature and extent of "acceptable" services.

Effective psychiatric treatment enhances the safety of correctional facilities (Cohen and Dvoskin, 1992; DiCataldo et al., 1995). Nonetheless, correctional staff and administrators might view the procurement of mental health services as secondary to the broader mission of population control (Hills et al., 2004). Many correctional departments have invested considerably in the improvement of mental health services; however, national surveys have found significant variation in the quality of such services among institutions (Adams and Ferrandino, 2008; Torrey et al., 2014). Specifically, a small subset of prisons provides comprehensive psychiatric services, whereas others struggle to meet even minimal standards of psychiatric care, which range from core constitutional mandates to industry-defined best practices to evidence-based practices (Manderscheid et al., 2004). One study found that only 40 percent of prison inmates on psychiatric medication before imprisonment were prescribed medication after incarceration, suggesting the demand for better identification of treatment need at intake (Reingle, Gonzalez and Connell, 2014).

Disciplinary procedures

Incarcerees with SMI can experience extreme difficulty conforming their actions to the strict and formal rules of the prison environment as well as the informal rules of the prison culture (Lovell and Jemelka, 1998). Such difficulties can lead to disciplinary infractions, victimization by other inmates, or self-harm (American Civil Liberties Union of Colorado, 2013). Prison inmates with mental health problems are more likely than those without such problems to be involved in disciplinary incidents (e.g. assaults and rule violations) (Ditton, 1999). Moreover, prison inmates with SMI are twice as likely as those without SMI to be injured in a fight while incarcerated (James and Glaze, 2006). As Lovell et al. (2001: 84) state:

> Some mentally ill offenders require ongoing medical supervision, cannot understand and follow rules, cannot exercise the discretion required for safe living among other offenders, and can disturb other offenders. Some mentally ill inmates are erratic and unpredictable, and both prisoners and staff place a high value on predictability.

Prison rules are rarely formulated to accommodate the signs and symptoms of mental illness. Therefore, prisoners with SMI can struggle to comply with prison rules and codes of conduct due to the profound cognitive and emotional deficits that frequently accompany SMI (Kondo, 2003). "Their idiosyncratic behaviors often alienate them from other offenders (thereby leaving them isolated), create housing dilemmas and management difficulties for correctional staff, and may lead to liability issues for correctional administrators" (Fagan, 2003: 7).

Prison officials use disciplinary measures to punish mentally ill prisoners even though such prisoners are often unable to control their actions (Lovell and Jemelka, 1998); such punitive actions "serve no legitimate purpose and raise serious constitutional concerns" (American Civil Liberties Union of Colorado, 2013: 13). Segregation (solitary confinement) is used to punish prisoners with SMI, and can greatly aggravate their psychiatric symptoms (Coid et al., 2003; Lovell and Jemelka, 1996; Torrey et al., 2014). The exertion of disciplinary measures against inmates with SMI, whose actions are a direct expression of their illnesses, can worsen their mental health problems, decrease their chances for release, and prolong their prison sentence (American Psychiatric Association, 2013). Inmates with SMI spend an average of 15 more months in prison than those without SMI, and can be denied parole due to their disciplinary record (Human Rights Watch, 2003). Moreover, placing inmates in solitary confinement costs twice as much as placing them in general population (American Civil Liberties Union of Colorado, 2013).

Prisoners with SMI are placed in disciplinary segregation (segregated housing units) at a higher rate than prisoners without SMI (American Civil Liberties Union of Colorado, 2013; Haney, 2003). According to one study, the use of mental health services before entering prison was unrelated to whether an inmate was placed in disciplinary segregation (Coid et al., 2003). However, both men and women prisoners in disciplinary segregation were repeatedly denied psychological treatment while in prison. Nonetheless, female inmates placed in disciplinary segregation were overall more likely to receive mental health services while incarcerated than female inmates who were never placed in disciplinary segregation (Coid et al., 2003).

Regarding their current mental health status, both male and female prisoners in disciplinary segregation were more likely to be diagnosed with antisocial and paranoid personality disorders (Coid et al., 2003). Female prisoners in disciplinary segregation were more likely to be diagnosed with narcissistic personality disorder compared with women who were not segregated. Moreover, prisoners in segregation were more likely to have higher rates of substance use disorders and psychopathy than prisoners in the general prison population (Coid et al., 2003), which suggests the need for special prison programs to treat inmates with co-occurring disorders.

At the line-staff level, the lack of correctional officer protocols and training can produce unintended consequences such as the exacerbation of psychiatric symptoms and the escalation of relatively minor infractions into more serious and potentially dangerous incidents. At the system level, correctional institutions usually respond to alleged behavioral violations by initiating a two-phase process: a disciplinary hearing that investigates the violation and the imposition of sanctions commensurate with the severity of the violation. Depending on the seriousness of the incident, sanctions can range from the loss of privileges, such as visitation or canteen, to the use of long-term segregation (i.e. 23-hour cell confinement) (e.g. Federal Bureau of Prisons, 2011).

Correctional agencies' responses to rule infractions can be highly deleterious to mentally ill incarcerees (Morgan et al., 1993; Torrey et al., 2014). Disciplinary procedures in prisons generally ignore the role that SMI plays in the commission of infractions as well as the extent to which environmental or clinical interventions could prevent those infractions and decrease the need for sanctions (e.g. inmate segregation) that are harmful to inmates' psychiatric conditions (American Civil Liberties Union of Colorado, 2013). These factors, and the high rates at which inmates with SMI become involved in disciplinary problems, have produced an over-representation of the mentally ill in disciplinary segregation units (Kupers, 1999). "Courts and the U.S. Department of Justice have agreed that the Constitution forbids subjecting prisoners with serious mental illnesses to prolonged solitary confinement" (American Civil Liberties Union of Colorado, 2013: 1). A recognition of the pernicious effects of prolonged solitary confinement on inmates' mental health also has led to a raft of litigation (e.g., *Bowring v. Godiva*, 1977; *Coleman v. Wilson*, 1995; *Langley v. Coughlin*, 1988; *Laamon v. Helgemoe*, 1977; *Ruiz v. Estelle*, 1999; *Wilson v. Seiter*, 1991) and the incorporation of behavioral management strategies and mental health techniques into prison disciplinary procedures (Haney, 2009; Kupers, 1999).

Inmate suicide

Suicide and self-injury are common in prison due to the high rate of offenders with SMI and the paucity of mental health treatment (Bland et al., 1990). The majority of mentally ill incarcerees who commit suicide had a diagnosable mental illness, which suggests that proper identification and treatment can help decrease the suicide rate in prison (Metzner and Hayes, 2006), which is at least one-and-a-half times higher than in the country's general population (Hayes, 1995). From a legal and operational standpoint, the ability to prevent suicides and attempted suicides is commonly regarded as the touchstone for evaluating a correctional system's overall responsiveness to offenders' mental health problems. Many correctional institutions have been found negligent in this area, with "high-profile" suicides frequently prompting a thorough review of mental health services in prisons (Hills et al., 2004).

Comprehensive mental health services are a vital component of suicide prevention efforts in correctional facilities. Best practices also recommend the engagement of correctional officers in suicide prevention activities, such as identifying suicide risk, monitoring suicidal inmates, and responding immediately to incidents of suicidal ideation, gestures, or attempts (Hills et al., 2004). Therefore, the successful implementation of suicide prevention programs in correctional settings requires specialized training for correctional officers (who represent the "front line" of suicide prevention), for medical and mental health staff (who must be able to implement procedures for the prompt identification, evaluation, and referral of suicidal inmates), and for all correctional staff (who might discover a suicide in progress and must know how to administer emergency medical interventions in such circumstances). In addition, suicide prevention programs should contain protocols for immediate assessment and intervention when warranted by risk factors or behavioral warning signs (Lester, and Danto, 1993).

Suicide prevention in prisons should begin at inmates' first contact with the criminal justice system. Information about an individual's risk for suicide should be communicated from one stage of the criminal justice process to the next – from police officers at arrest and booking to jail admission/intake staff at pre-trial detention to judges and prosecutors at sentencing and to correctional and mental health personnel at admission to prison. Crisis housing units in prisons permit the continuous monitoring of inmates at risk for suicide and are usually located in infirmaries or intake areas. Finally, regular evaluations of suicide prevention protocols help correctional agencies identify gaps and weaknesses in such efforts, and should consist of guidelines for debriefing staff after incidents of suicide or suicide attempts and modifying suicide prevention practices as needed (Hayes, 1999).

Classification and capacity management

The special problems of inmates with SMI have expanded correctional administrators' responsibilities in the areas of classification and capacity management (Hills et al., 2004). For example, dedicated therapeutic housing units have been built to accommodate the clinical and rehabilitation needs of inmates with SMI; however, the demand for specialized housing has frequently collided with the imperatives of mounting incarceration rates, budgetary pressures, and facility overcrowding (Scott-Hayward, 2009). Besides the direct costs of designing, constructing, and staffing specialized units, the reservation of cells for PSMI has reduced the number of beds available for inmates in the general population and has placed significant constraints on the allocation of limited space in overcrowded facilities (Human Rights Watch, 2003).

Moving forward

This chapter presented a variety of issues concerning inmates with SMI and the attendant challenges that they bring to the nation's prisons. Several key points emerged from the discussion. First, legal and accreditation standards establish a general framework for the delivery of (at least) minimally adequate mental health services. Nevertheless, correctional mental health planners must move beyond these basic standards to address a broader set of clinical and programmatic considerations. Services for incarcerees with SMI should begin with symptom management and pursue a whole-life approach to treatment that acknowledges the diverse problems of mentally ill prisoners and the substantial barriers they will face after release. Prisons should never unduly rely on solitary confinement as an alternative for managing the behavior of inmates with SMI (American Civil Liberties Union of Colorado, 2013).

Second, gender-based differences in the rates and types of mental illnesses have crucial implications for correctional programming and operations (Earthrowl and McCully, 2002). In most areas of correctional practice, prisons have been male-centric in their orientation (Bloom et al., 2005); however, now that women constitute a steadily growing proportion of the incarcerated population, the demand has increased for gender-responsive correctional mental health services that are trauma-informed, empowerment-driven, and family-focused (Henderson and Brown, 1998; World Health Organization, 2009).

Third, the coordination of behavioral healthcare services in prisons is critical in meeting the multifaceted needs of inmates with SMI (Weisman et al., 2004). Such coordination entails case management and treatment planning inside and outside the institution as well as a full range of experienced staff, including psychiatrists, psychiatric nurses, psychologists, and mental health technicians. Integrated care provides the best mechanisms for responding holistically to the problems of PSMI in correctional institutions. Practitioners should focus their attention on ameliorating criminogenic factors and not simply on treating the psychiatric symptoms of PSMI in prison. The best approach for working with mentally ill inmates is an intensive and broad set of service modules (e.g. integrated philosophies, services, and outcomes). A greater investment must be made in treating co-occurring disorders and trauma. More funding should be allocated for all services, especially those that can promote recovery and reduce future criminal involvement.

Fourth, prison-based mental health practices should concentrate on reentry. Community reintegration begins at the front door of the prison. Correctional practitioners must respond to the immediate needs of incarcerees, but they should also help inmates envision life in the community as they become formerly incarcerated people. Along these lines, successful outcomes depend upon the community's capacity to overcome the complex range of impediments faced by released inmates with SMI through the implementation of integrated treatment, supervision, and support programs. The lack of efforts to ensure seamless transitions into the community are associated with the exacerbation of psychiatric symptoms and an increased risk for rearrests, substance use relapse, hospitalization, suicide, and violent behavior (Osher et al., 2002).

Finally, as demonstrated by numerous studies and commissions that have investigated PSMI in the criminal justice system, collaboration between the correctional and mental health systems is a fundamental component of virtually all successful programs for mentally ill offenders (Council of State Governments, 2002). Correctional facilities are a vital link in the broader continuum of mental health services. Hence, information-sharing protocols and consistent standards of practice in correctional institutions and community-based mental health programs are essential ingredients in the overall success of programs for inmates with SMI.

References

Adams, K. and Ferrandino, J. (2008). Managing mentally ill inmates in prisons. *Criminal Justice and Behavior* 35(8), 913–927. DOI: 10.1177/0093854808318624.

American Civil Liberties Union of Colorado. (2013). *Out of sight, out of mind.* Retrieved January 16, 2015 from http://aclu-co.org/wp-content/uploads/files/imce/ACLU-COReportonSolitaryConfinement.pdf.

American Psychiatric Association. (2013). *Position statement on segregation of prisoners with mental illness.* Washington, DC: American Psychiatric Association.

American Psychiatric Association. (2000). *Psychiatric services in jails and prisons.* 2nd edition. Washington (DC): American Psychiatric Association.

Beck, A. J., and Maruschak, L. M. (2001, July). *Mental health treatment in state prisons, 2000* (Bureau of Justice Statistics Special Report, NCJ 188215). Washington, DC: U.S. Department of Justice.

Bland, R. Newman, S. Dyck, R. and Orn, H. (1990). Prevalence of psychiatric disorder suicide attempts in a prison population. *Canadian Journal of Psychiatry*, 35(4), 407–413.

Blitz, C. L., Wolff, N., and Paap, K. (2006). Availability of behavioral health treatment for women in prison. *Psychiatric Services*, 57(3), 356–360.

Bloom, B., Owen, B., and Covington, S. (2005). *Gender-responsive strategies for women offenders*. Longmont, CO: National Institute of Corrections.

Cohen, F., and Dvoskin, J. (1992). Inmates with mental disorders: A guide to law and practice. *Mental and Physical Disability Law Reporter*, 16(4), 339–346.

Coid, J.W., Singleton, S., Bebbington, P., et al. (2003). Psychiatric morbidity in prisoners and solitary cellular confinement, I: Disciplinary segregation. *Journal of Forensic Psychiatry and Psychology* 14(1), 298–319.

Coleman v. Wilson. (1995). 912 F Supp. 1282, 1320–21. (E.D. Cal).

Collins, William C. (2001). *Correctional law for the correctional officer*. 3rd Ed. Lanham, MD, American Correctional Association.

Council of State Governments (2002). *Criminal Justice/Mental Health Consensus Project*. New York, Council of State Governments.

DiCataldo, F., Greer, A., and Profit, W.E. (1995). Screening prison inmates for mental disorder: An examination of the relationship between mental disorders and prison adjustment. *Bulletin of the American Academy of Psychiatry and the Law*, 23(4), 573–585.

Ditton, P. (1999). *Mental health and treatment of inmates and probationers*. Washington, DC: U.S. Department of Justice, Bureau of Justice Statistics.

Dunn v. Voinovich (1995). Case No. C1–93–0166 (S.D. Ohio).

Earthrowl, M., and McCully, R. (2002). Screening new inmates in a female prison. *Journal of Forensic Psychiatry*, 13(2), 428–439.

Fagan, T. J. (2003). *Negotiating correctional incidents: A practical guide*. Lanham, MD: American Correctional Association.

Federal Bureau of Prisons. (2011). *Inmate discipline program*. Washington, DC: U.S. Department of Justice.

Haney, C. (2003). Mental health issues in long-term solitary and "supermax" confinement. *Crime and Delinquency*, 49(1), 124–156.

Haney, C. (2009). The social psychology of isolation: Why solitary confinement is psychologically harmful. *Prison Service Journal UK (Solitary Confinement Special Issue)*, 181(3), 12–20.

Hayes, L. (1999). *Suicide prevention in juvenile correction and detention facilities: A resource guide for performance-based standards for juvenile correction and detention facilities*. Washington, DC: Council of Juvenile Correctional Administrators.

Hayes, L., (1995). Prison suicide: An overview and a guide to prevention. *The Prison Journal*, 75(4), 431–455.

Henderson, D., Schaeffer, J., and Brown, L. C. (1998). Gender-appropriate mental health services for incarcerated women: Issues and challenges. *Family Community Health*, 21(3), 42–53.

Hills, H. Siegfried, C. and Ichowitz, A. (2004). *Effective prison mental health services: Guidelines to expand and improve treatments*. Washington, DC: National Institute of Corrections.

Human Rights Watch. (2003). *Ill Equipped: U.S. prisons and offenders with mental illness*. Washington, DC.

James, D.J., and Glaze, L. E. (2006). *Mental health problems of prison and jail.* Washington DC: U.S. Department of Justice, Government Printing Office.

Kessler, R., Nelson, C., McGonagle, K., Edlund, M., Frank, R., and Leaf, P. (1996). The epidemiology of co-occurring addictive and mental disorders: Implications for prevention and service utilization. *American Journal of Orthopsychiatry*, 66(1), 17–31.

Kondo, LeRoy L. (2003). The tangled web: Complexities, fallacies and misconceptions regarding the decision to release treated sexual offenders from civil commitment to society. 23 *Northern Illinois University Law Review* 195.

Kupers, T. (1999). *Prison madness: The mental health crisis behind bars and what we must do about it.* San Francisco: Jossey-Bass.

Lamb, H., and Weinberger, L. (1998). Persons with severe mental illness in jails and prisons: A review. *Psychiatric Services*, 49(4), 483–492.

Langley v. Coughlin (1988). 715 Supp. 522, 540 (S.D. NY).

Lester, D., and Danto, B.L. (1993). *Suicide behind bars: Prediction and prevention.* Philadelphia, PA: Charles Press.

Lovell, D., and Jemelka, R. (1996). When inmates misbehave: The costs of discipline. *The Prison Journal*, 76(2), 165–179.

Lovell, D., and Jemelka, R. (1998). Coping with mental illness in prison. *Family and Community Health*, 21(3), 54–66.

Lovell, D., Allen, D., Johnson, C., and Jemelka, R. (2001). Evaluating the effectiveness of residential treatment for prisoners with mental illness. *Criminal Justice and Behavior*, 28(1), 83–104.

Lurigio, A. J. (2001). Effective services for parolees with mental illness. *Crime and Delinquency*, 47(3), 446–461.

Lurigio, A.J. (2011). People with serious mental illness in the criminal justice system: Causes, consequences, and correctives. *Prison Journal*, 91(1), 66–86.

Lurigio, A.J. (2012). Responding to the needs of people with mental illness in the criminal justice system: An area ripe for research and community partnerships. *Journal of Crime and Justice*, 35(1), 1–12.

Lurigio, A. J., and Swartz, J. A. (2000). Changing the contours of the criminal justice system to meet the needs of persons with serious mental illness. In J. Horney (ed.), *NIJ 2000 Series: Policies, processes, and decisions of the criminal justice system* Vol. 3 (pp. 45–108). Washington, DC: National Institute of Justice.

Lurigio, A.J., Rabinowitz, M., and Lenik, J. (2009). A century of losing battles: The costly and ill-advised war on drugs in the United States. *Justice Policy Journal*, 6(2), 1–46.

Manderscheid, R. W., Gravesande, A., and Goldstrom, I. D. (2004). Growth of mental health services in state adult correctional facilities, 1988 to 2000. *Psychiatric Services* 55(8), 869–72.

Mears, D.P. (2004). Mental health needs and services in the criminal justice system. *Journal of Health Law and Policy*, 4(2), 255–284.

Metzner, J.L. (1993). Guidelines for psychiatric services in prisons. *Criminal Behavior and Mental Health*, 3(4), 252–267.

Metzner, J.L. and Dvoskin, J.A. (2006). An overview of correctional psychiatry. *Psychiatric Clinics North America*, 29(6), 761–772.

Metzner, J.L. and Hayes, L. (2006). Suicide prevention in jails and prisons. In R. Simon and R. Hales (eds.) *Textbook of suicide assessment and management* (pp. 139–155). Washington, DC: American Psychiatric Publishing.

Metzner, J.L., Cohen, F., Grossman, L., and Wettstein, R. (1998). Treatment in jails and prisons. In R. M. Wettstein (ed.), *Treatment of offenders with mental disorders* (pp. 211–264). New York: Guilford.

Morgan D.W., Edwards A.C., and Faulkner L.R. (1993). The adaptation to prison by individuals with schizophrenia. *Bulletin of the American Academy of Psychiatry and the Law*, 21(4), 427–433.

Mueser, K. T., Noordsy, D.L., Drake, R.E., and Fox, L. (2003). *Integrated treatment for dual disorders: A guide to effective practice*. New York: Guildford Press.

Nee, C., and Farman, S. (2005). Female prisoners with borderline personality disorder: Some promising treatment developments. *Criminal Behavior and Mental Health*, 15(1), 2–16.

Osher, F., Steadman, H. J., and Barr, H. (2002). *A best practice approach to community re-entry from jails for inmates with co-occurring disorders: The APIC model*. Delmar, NY: The National GAINS Center.

Parsons S., Walker L., and Grubin D., (2001). Prevalence of mental disorder in female remand prisons. *Journal of Forensic Psychiatry*, 12(1), 194–202.

Pinta, E., (1999). The prevalence of serious mental disorders among US prisoners. *Correctional Mental Health Report*, 34(1), 44–47.

Reingle Gonzalez, J.M., and Connell, N. M. (2014). Mental health of prisoners: Identifying barriers to mental health treatment and medication continuity. *American Journal Public Health*, 104(12), 2238–2333.

Ruiz v. Estelle (1999). 37 F. Supp. 2d 855, 915 (D.D. Tex).

Scott-Hayward, C. S. (2009). *The fiscal crisis in corrections: Rethinking policies and practices*. New York: Vera Institute of Justice.

Singer, M., Bussey, J., Song, L., and Lunghofer, L., (1995). The psychosocial issues of women serving time in jail. *Social Work*, 40(1), 103–113.

Swanson, J., Morrissey, J.P., Goldstrom, I., Rudolph, L., and Manderscheid, R.W. (1993). Demographic and diagnostic characteristics of inmates receiving mental health services in state adult correctional facilities: United States, 1988. *Mental health Statistical Note*, 209, 1–20.

Torrey, E. F., Zdanowicz, M. T., Kennard, A.D., Lamb, H. R., Eslinger, D. F., Biasotti, M.C., and Fuller, D. A. (2014). *The treatment of persons with mental illness in prisons and jails: A state survey*. National Sheriffs' Association and Treatment Advocacy Center.

Veysey, B., and Bichler-Robertson, G. (2002). Prevalence estimates of psychiatric disorders in correctional settings. *In Health status of soon-to-be-released inmates: A report to Congress, Volume 2*, 57–80. Chicago: National Commission on Correctional Health Care.

Weisman, R. L., Lamberti, J. S., and Price, N. (2004). Integrating criminal justice, community healthcare, and support services for adults with severe mental disorders. *Psychiatric Quarterly*, 75(1), 71–85.

Wilson v. Seiter, (1991) 501 U.S. 294, 304.

World Health Organization. (2009). *Declaration on women's health in prison: Correcting gender inequity in prison health*. Copenhagen: Regional Office for Europe, World Health Organization.

Chapter 26

Women's incarceration and motherhood

Policy considerations

Meda Chesney-Lind and Marilyn Brown

Introduction

The dramatic expansion in the incarceration of women has highlighted the insidious impact of criminal justice policy overreach on the fabric of society. Arrest, prosecution, and incarceration are now entrenched as remedies to social problems ranging from homelessness to addiction. And, the very communities where the greatest concentration of poverty and associated problems are found have been the ones hardest hit by these policies – poor, urban communities of color. Perhaps to a greater extent than the mass incarceration of men, the jailing of increasing numbers of women reveals the devastating convergence of punitive criminal justice and social welfare policies, making the most vulnerable families and communities even more fractured. In this chapter, we explore the unique aspects of women's imprisonment against a complex policy backdrop that encompasses both the phenomenon of mass incarceration and social welfare policies that impact women and their children.

Trends in women's incarceration

Over the past several decades, feminist scholars have documented women's increasing involvement in the criminal justice system, both in terms of patterns of offenses as well as policy responses by justice agencies and other stakeholders. The imprisonment of women is one of the most troubling aspects of mass incarceration in the late twentieth and early twenty-first centuries. Fueled largely by the war on drugs, women's incarceration increased 800 percent in roughly the last three decades of the last century. Even at what might be described as the end of the imprisonment boom (between 1995 and 2009), the number of women in prison increased by 90 percent (West and Sabol, 2010).

Despite a leveling off and even slight reductions in the overall imprisoned population since 2008, annual growth rates of female incarceration still outpace those of males. Between 2012 and 2013, the population of females

Table 26.1 Estimated percent of sentenced prisoners under state jurisdiction by offense and gender, December 31, 2012

Most Serious Offense	Total Inmates	Male	Female
Violent	53.8%	55.0%	37.1%
Property	18.8%	18.1%	28.2%
Drug	16.0%	15.4%	24.6%
Public Order	10.7%	10.8%	8.9%
Other/unspecified	0.8%	0.7%	1.2%
Total number of sentenced inmates	1,314,900	1,225,900	89,000

Source: Adapted from Carson, 2014.

imprisoned under state and federal authorities grew by 2.8 percent, compared with a meager 0.2 percent increase for males (Carson, 2014). Another way to look at this pattern is to note that between 2012 and 2013, the female prison population increased in 36 states, compared to only 28 states showing an increase in the male prison population. Included among the states increasing their female prison population were states like Arkansas (up 26 percent), Vermont (up 21 percent), and New Hampshire (up 15 percent) (Carson, 2014: 1).

Despite the expansion in women's imprisonment, there are still marked gender differences in the types of offenses resulting in incarceration. In state prisons in 2012, women were far less likely than men to be imprisoned for violent offenses, but far more likely to be serving time for drug and property crimes, as shown in Table 26.1.

Looking at it another way, roughly 63 percent of women in 2012 were serving time for non-violent offenses in state prisons, compared with 45 percent of men. Tougher penalties made drug offenders an increasingly larger part of the imprisoned population, with women particularly impacted. Prosecutorial practices, augmented by proliferating determinate sentencing laws, which included breaks for offenders who cooperated by providing information, often left women out. Referred to as the "girlfriend problem," women could avoid a harsher mandated penalty by informing on a partner involved in their drug case. However, women tend to bring less information to the table compared with men and are less likely to inform on an intimate (Mauer, 2013).

And, although the story of women's incarceration is largely about drugs and property crime (often in the service of their addiction), racial disparities have long been a significant part of the picture. The war on drugs has long been described as a "war against black women" (Bush-Baskette, 2013) in recognition of the disparate incarceration of black (as well as Hispanic) women. Recently, though, things have shifted in important ways. As an example, in the year 2000, black women were incarcerated in state and federal prisons at six times the rate of white women, definitely confirming the racial aspects noted by Bush-Baskette. However, by 2009 that ratio had declined by 53 percent, to 2.8:1. This shift was a result of both declining incarceration of African American women and rising incarceration of white women. The disparity between Hispanic and non-Hispanic white women declined by 16.7 percent during this period (Mauer, 2013: 2).

Much of this shift is likely explained by policy changes enacted by certain jurisdictions (e.g. New York) to reduce reliance on incarceration (including reducing technical violations parole, increasing re entry services, and encouraging participation in treatment diversion programs) all of which would have dramatically reduced women's incarceration (Mauer, 2013:4). Sadly, though, other states (e.g. Oklahoma, which incarcerates more women than any other state, and Iowa) have not shifted their drug polices (and the drugs involved are different as well). As a result, rural states, many with harsh drug penalties, have seen increases in women's incarceration for methamphetamine as well as prescription drug offenses. The net result is that women's imprisonment numbers have not dropped as dramatically as one would hope, and low-income white women are now being victimized by aggressive anti-drug policing and prosecutorial practices that were once only seen in low-income African American communities.

Over classified; over policed

The last few decades have shown a dramatic increase in the use of classification instruments to assess the risk of recidivism of individuals on probation and parole. Increasingly, these instruments have also been used to assess individuals for classification within the confines of prison (minimum, medium, maximum). The most prominent of these instruments, the LSI-R, was developed based on research involving large numbers of male offenders and only a small number of female offenders (Pollock, 2014).

A lengthy debate has ensued about whether or not instruments developed out of research on largely male populations can adequately predict recidivism (see Pollock, 2014). A number of studies have shown that the instrument is about as good at predicting female recidivism as male recidivism. Van Voorhis and colleagues, though, developed a gender-specific trailer to add to the scale (which includes items such as past victimization and drug use, as well as evidence of depression), and they found that the gender-responsive scales were significantly better at prediction than the gender neutral instrument (Van Voorhis et al., 2008). In addition, key aspects of the male-centered risk instrument (criminal thinking) were weak predictors for women (Pollock, 2014: 250).

These somewhat arcane methodological disputes begin to have real impact on women in prison, since these gender neutral instruments are also used to "classify" inmates and determine the degree of supervision they will experience in prison. There is no question that the same classification instruments, whether the LSI-R or others, are used in virtually all states to classify both male and female inmates (Koons-Witt and Crittenden, 2014). Small numbers of female inmates (relative to their male counterparts) mean fewer housing options, and male centric classification systems (which can automatically classify "violent" offenders to maximum security without considering the context of the behavior) all produce large numbers of women being held in higher security than was warranted (Koons-Witt and Crittenden, 2014: 229). Finally, the many mental and physical health problems that women present, along with the responsibilities that come with being a custodial parent, put pressure on systems ill-equipped to deliver gender-responsive programming.

These risk instruments have also surfaced in criminal justice reform efforts, notably the high profile Justice Re-investment initiatives (JRI) in the U.S. and elsewhere globally. Stubbs (2014), reviewing these global efforts to reform adult criminal justice systems, notes that while JRI work both in the U.S. and Australia tends to be very data driven, there is virtually no concern about either gender or ethnic minorities. This raises the issue of whether these reform efforts, themselves, might endorse problematic approaches to women and ethnic minorities (Stubbs, 2014). Specifically, JRI constructs risk instruments as central to their emphasis on scientific "best practices" despite evidence that they are problematic, at best, for women. To the degree that reform efforts direct services to those in the system and those seeking to re enter communities based on these limited and gender skewed measures, there is an additional concern that women's unique needs, like those associated with family, significant others, and the burdens of parenting, will be neglected.

Parenting concerns of incarcerated women

Mass incarceration and attendant state correctional policies have had an unprecedented impact on the family, especially on those families headed by women. Between 1991 and 2007, maternal incarceration rose 122 percent compared to a 77 percent increase in the incarceration of fathers. Over half (53 percent) of individuals held in state and federal prisons at midyear in 2007 were parents of children under age 18 (Glaze and Maruschak, 2008). This represents an increase of nearly 80 percent since 1991. The report also estimates that 1,706,600 minor children (2.3 percent of the U.S. resident population under 18) have an incarcerated parent.

While the number of children with an incarcerated father in prison increased by 77 percent between 1991 and 2007, the number of children with a mother in prison increased by 131 percent (Glaze and Marushack, 2008). Substantial numbers of both gender parents appear to have been involved with their children prior to incarceration, with women being far more likely to be the custodial parent. When mothers are incarcerated, children often go to one of her relatives (rather than a father) to be cared for – or into the foster care system where they may eventually be placed for adoption.

Separation from children is one of the major pains of imprisonment experienced by incarcerated women. In 2000, the majority of mothers in state and federal prisons lived with their children prior to their current sentence (Mumola, 2000). When a woman is arrested, her children are frequently placed with family members who are unexpectedly thrust into the role of caregiver. As Sandra Enos (2001) writes in her ethnography of imprisoned mothers, women go to great lengths to preserve their maternal identities and roles but are dependent on often precariously situated relatives. Children and their caregivers, in these cases, are subject to increased economic strain, the possible introduction of non-parental figures into the household, residence changes, and changes in schools – all creating some degree of additional risk to the child (Phillips et al., 2006)

Many state facilities are located far from urban families, often limiting or even foreclosing the possibility of regular visitation. Travel distances and related expenses are the primary reasons for low visitation rates, according to a study by the General Accounting Office (1999). Visitations happen far less frequently for mothers compared to fathers (Enos, 2001). In 1997, more than half of incarcerated mothers reported having no visits from children during their time in prison, keeping in touch mainly by phone calls (27 percent) or by letters (35.6 percent) (Mumola, 2000). The cost of prison phone calls, generally made on a collect basis, is borne by families who are often struggling economically as they try to care for additional children now in their charge (Collica, 2010).

Policies impacting imprisoned mothers

State and federal law enacted in the 1990s placed imprisoned women in the cross-hairs of harsher criminal justice and similarly punitive social welfare policies (Bloom and Brown, 2011). A conservative Congress passed the Adoption and Safe Families Act (ASFA) in 1997, responding to reports of children languishing in foster care for years, while parents struggled toward reunification. The political environment offered little sympathy, much less appropriate resources, for mothers who might be struggling with addiction, poverty, mental illness, and domestic violence. With cuts in community services and state welfare support in general, these issues became seemingly intractable in families who were simply attempting to stay together and reunite with children in foster care. ASFA changed the orientation of child welfare from a focus on reunification to one of permanency planning, accelerating the time frame for the termination of parental rights. Once it was determined that a child was in care for 15 of the previous 22 months, the state was required to proceed to terminate parental rights and place children for adoption. Unable to participate in reunification service plans created by child welfare case workers, incarcerated women are at very high risk of having their parental rights terminated. Imprisoned women are seldom able to participate as required in case planning or obtain the services necessary to comply with child welfare mandates.

As Halperin and Harris (2004) note, even when case workers attempt to facilitate reunification from behind bars, imprisoned mothers are seldom able to attend court hearings or communicate well with their child's case worker. Interagency collaborations between child welfare and correctional systems constitute, a "policy vacuum," pitting case workers against an unfamiliar prison system (Bloom and Brown, 2011). Until recently, child welfare case workers had little experience dealing with the correctional systems (Beckerman, 1998). As closed institutions, entrenched barriers inherent in the structure of prisons restrict communication with the outside world. When an incarcerated mother's children are placed in foster care, child welfare case management and planning are subverted to the discipline and regulation of the prison bureaucracy.

Mothers who attempt to maintain their parental rights from prison, as well as their children's case managers, are often both operating in uncharted territory. Often, the two institutions work at cross-purposes, speaking different languages and adhering to different mandates. In their study of the intersection between the child welfare and criminal justice systems, Simmons and Danker-Feldman (2010) of the San Francisco Dependency Court, found that only 7 percent of incarcerated parents scheduled to appear in the proceedings actually attended. The authors point out that despite notices to appear and the relatively short distance between jail and court, such parents only rarely attended these important hearings. These authors also found that incarcerated parents were far less likely to receive services specified in court-ordered case plans, plans that (in most cases) were developed without their participation. This study, although small, sheds light on why terminations of parental rights and placement of children for adoption increased so much among this group after the passage of ASFA (Allard and Lu, 2006).

In their study of 38 states, Wright and Seymour (2000) found very few had policies in place that were directed at children of incarcerated parents placed in foster care. States themselves have little data on children in their system who were impacted by parental incarceration. Among a handful of states, various estimates on such children were offered, ranging from 1.6 percent to nearly 30 percent. These data provided little in the way of demographics, the type of program in which children were enrolled (child protective services, independent living, adoption services), or length of stay, making an understanding of the scope of the issue difficult. States like New York require child welfare agencies to be diligent in keeping children connected with their incarcerated parents, including arranging visits. In California, state law requires courts to order reunification services to these parents with a range of options such as telephone calls, visitation assistance, and services to the caregivers on the outside (Wallace, 2012). However, making correctional and child welfare systems work together in the best interest of both parent and child has mostly eluded policymakers.

The convergence of these policy impacts on poor families of color is best elucidated by Dorothy Roberts, who has written at length about how government agencies police and punish these families. Roberts (2012) has documented the systemic overlap among populations in both correctional and foster care systems, which she argues is responsible for increasing marginality among women and children of color. Mass incarceration has decimated many African American and Hispanic communities, severing the networks that once sustained families during hard times. The retraction of the social safety net coupled with cuts in addiction and mental health treatment at the community level have all increased risks related to crime in poor neighborhoods. Against this reality, Roberts argues that the most egregious "injury" that mass incarceration inflicts on the black community is the imprisonment of black mothers (Roberts, 2012: 1480).

Prison parenting

Maternal incarceration is, of course, not new in the American experiment with the prison. Women's reformatories dating back to the nineteenth century not only incarcerated parenting women but their chief means of regulating female inmates was reinforcing the identities of mother and spouse (Bosworth, 1996; Carlen, 1983; Hannah-Moffat, 2001). In the first decades of the twentieth century, prison nurseries were fairly common in the United States, but declined in number toward the mid-twentieth century, according to a review by Goshin and Byrne (2009). Up until that time, state prisons might simply return pregnant inmates to local lockups or to some "co-residence" alternative until some months after birth. States frequently had legal provisions to keep new mothers and infants together. However, during the 1970s, such policies were retrenched over a number of concerns including security, liability, program management, and potential adverse impacts on child health.

As the women's prison population has increased, there has been a resurgence of support for prison nurseries. As of August 2010, nine states had prison nurseries (ranging from New York, to California, to West Virginia), and most of these programs allowed a mother to parent her infant for a finite period of time in a special unit in the facility. All of the programs also provided the women who participated with information on child development and helped women with parenting skills. The oldest of these prison nurseries, and the best known, is the prison nursery at Bedford Hills Correctional Facility for Women, in New York, which was opened in 1901.

Prison nursery programs vary in length and other characteristics, but generally serve only women who are pregnant upon entering prison, roughly 4 percent of state prisoners and 1 in 33 federal prisoners (Maruschak, 2008). Women who have violent offenses or offenses related to the family are not permitted to participate in these programs. Infants may co-reside with mothers for periods from 30 days to 30 months, upon which time the dyads are separated if the woman is not being discharged from prison (Goshin and Byrne, 2009).

There is fairly good research to suggest that such facilities do increase attachment of babies to their mothers (Byrne et al., 2010), and also that such programs reduce prison misconducts and recidivism among women who participate in them (Carlson, 2001). However, these programs have detractors, including James Dwyer, who argues that prison is no place for children and that prison origins only exacerbate the normativity of incarceration for minority families (Dwyer, 2014). Despite his flat rejection of caring for children in prison (and his troubling assertion that placing such children for adoption is preferable), the image he holds up of a potential "prison to prison" pipeline for black families, at the very least, gives one pause.

For women serving long sentences, the potential benefits of these programs may be forestalled by the inevitable, albeit deferred, separations. Some prison nursery programs that closed also mentioned a concern for the mental health of children housed in prisons as well as the trauma associated with separation from mothers with long sentences. That said, many who review the characteristics of women in prison suggest that a far better approach would be to create community residential centers for pregnant and parenting women who would otherwise be in prison. However, they also note that this population of low-level, non-violent prisoners (usually serving short sentences) could just as well be living in community programs with their children.

Indeed, a study prepared for the Women's Prison Association (Villanueva, 2009) concludes that the determinants of women's incarceration (mental health issues, addiction, lack of education and skills, and poverty) might be better dealt with in the community. Especially given that most female prisoners are at low risk to the community, providing supportive living situations for them and their children would be less costly to society and ultimately less damaging to the family. To state the obvious, the majority of incarcerated mothers have children already, even if they are pregnant upon admission to prison. While prison nurseries play a role in addressing the needs of some mothers and infants, by themselves, they fail to move us far enough forward in dealing with the entirety of imprisoned women's maternal concerns.

Conclusion

Women continue to be sentenced to U.S. prisons, and their rate of increase tends to outstrip the male rate. They also continue to be sentenced to these facilities despite far less serious offense profiles when compared to their male counterparts. Despite decades of research on the characteristics of justice-involved women, correctional management practices often over-classify females, which poses a barrier to supervising them in the community. Reducing reliance on prison in the first place would reduce the need for prison nurseries and, indeed, help the greater number of women who already have children on the outside. Leveraging community-based resources to assist justice-involved women in addressing their issues could help keep families together.

Even decades into mass incarceration, the prisons that sprung up to incarcerate women in unprecedented numbers seem ill equipped to deal with the special needs and issues associated with female imprisonment. Women's pathways into prison are often characterized by high levels of trauma, depression, and violent victimization, and these aspects of women's involvement in crime and drug abuse mean that they bring unique policy challenges to women's prisons. The continued reliance on "gender neutral" risk and classification instruments is highly problematic to women prisoners, given that they have very different treatment needs and issues, particularly around addiction and mental health, but also around family (Davidson and Chesney-Lind, 2009). In brief, for men, re-uniting with family means stability and less recidivism, for women it means many challenges (including relationships with criminalized men), and/or reuniting with children who have problems of their own due to their mother's incarceration. Idealized notions of motherhood do little to help now stigmatized and economically marginalized women successfully navigate re entry.

References

Allard, Patricia and Lynn D Lu. 2006. *Rebuilding Families, Reclaiming Lives*. New York: Brennan Center for Justice, New York University School of Law.

Beckerman, Adella. 1998. "Charting a Course: Meeting the Challenge of Permanency Planning for Children with Incarcerated Mothers." *Child Welfare* 77(5):513–29.

Bloom, Barbara and Marilyn Brown. 2011. "Incarcerated Women: Motherhood on the Margins." Pp. 52–66 in *Razor Wire Women: Prisoners, Activists, Scholars and Artists*, edited by J. M. Lawston and A. E. Lucas. Albany: SUNY.

Bosworth, Mary. 1996. "Resistance and Compliance in Women's Prisons; Towards a Critique of Legitimacy." *Critical Criminology* 7(2):5–19.

Bush-Baskette, Stephanie R. 2013. "The War on Drugs as a War against Black Women." Pp. 175–83 in *Girls, Women, and Crime: Selected Readings*, edited by M. Chesney-Lind and L. Pasko. Thousand Oaks, CA: Sage.

Byrne, Mary W., Lorie S. Goshin and Sarah Joestl. 2010. "Intergenerational Transmission of Attachment for Infants Raised in a Prison Nursery." *Attachment and human development* 12(4):375–93.

Carlen, Pat. 1983. *Women's Imprisonment: A Study in Social Control.* Boston: Routledge and Kegan Paul.

Carlson, J.R. 2001. "Prison Nursery 2000: A Five Year Review of the Prison Nursery at the Nebraska Correctional Center for Women." *Journal of Offender Rehabiliation* 33:75–97.

Carson, E. Ann. 2014. "Prisoners in 2013." Washington, DC: Bureau of Justice Statistics, U.S. Department of Justice.

Collica, Kimberly. 2010. "Surviving Incarceration: Two Prison-Based Peer Programs Build Communities of Support for Female Offenders." *Deviant Behavior* 31(4):314–47.

Davidson, Janet T. and Meda Chesney-Lind. 2009. "Discounting Women: Context Matters in Risk and Need Assessment." *Critical Criminology* 17:221–45.

Dwyer, James G. 2014. "Jailing Black Babies". *Utah Law Review: William and Mary Law School Research Paper No. 09-239.* (3):Available at SSRN: http://ssrn.com/abstract=2231562.

Enos, Sandra. 2001. *Mothering from the Inside: Parenting in a Women's Prison.* Albany, NY: SUNY.

General Accounting Office. 1999. "Women in Prison: Issues and Challenges Confronting U.S. Correctional Systems." GAO/GGD-00-22. Washington, DC: United States General Accounting Office.

Glaze, Lauren E. and Laura M. Maruschak. 2008. "Parents in Prison and Their Minor Children." Washington, DC: Bureau of Justice Statistics, U.S. Department of Justice, Office of Justice Programs.

Goshin, Lorie Smith and Mary Woods Byrne. 2009. "Converging Streams of Opportunity for Prison Nursery Programs in the United States." *Journal of offender rehabilitation* 48(4):271–95. doi: 10.1080/10509670902848972.

Halperin, Ronnie and Jennifer L. Harris. 2004. "Parental Rights of Incarcerated Mothers with Children in Foster Care: A Policy Vacuum." *Feminist Studies* 30(2):339–52.

Hannah-Moffat, Kelly. 2001. *Punishment in Disguise: Penal Governance and Federal Imprisonment of Women in Canada.* Toronto: University of Toronto Press.

Koons-Witt, Barbara and Courtney Crittenden. 2014. "Gender Responsive Practices." Pp. 225–40 in *Criminal Justice Policy*, edited by S. Mallicoat and C. Gardner. Thousand Oaks, CA: Sage Publications.

Maruschak, Laura M. 2008. "Medical Problems of Prisoners." Washington, DC: Department of Justice, Bureau of Justice Statistics.

Mauer, Marc. 2013. "The Changing Racial Dynamics of Women's Incarceration." Washington, DC: The Sentencing Project.

Mumola, Christopher J. 2000. "Incarcerated Parents and Their Children." Washington, DC: Bureau of Justice Statistics, U.S. Department of Justice.

Phillips, Susan D., Alaattin Erkanli, Gordon P. Keeler, E. Jane Costello and Adrian Angold. 2006. "Disentangling the Risks: Parent Criminal Justice Involvement and Children's Exposure to Family Risks." *Criminology and Public Policy* 5(4):667–72.

Pollock, Joy. 2014. *Women's Crime, Criminology, and Corrections.* Long Grove, IL: Waveland Press.

Roberts, Dorothy. 2012. "Prison, Foster Care, and the Systemic Punishment of Black Mothers." *UCLA Law Review* 59(6):1474–501.

Simmons, Charlene and Emily Danker-Feldman. 2010. "Parental Incarceration, Termination of Parental Rights and Adoption: A Case Study of the Intersection between the Child Welfare and Criminal Justice Systems." *Justice Policy Journal* 2014 (Dec. 6):1–37.

Stubbs, Julie. 2014. "Downsizing Prisons in an Age of Austerity? Justice Reinvestment and Women's Imprisonment". *Onati Socio-Legal Series* UNSW Law Research Paper No. 2013–46 (Forthcoming).

Van Voorhis, P., E. J. Salisbury, E. M. Wright and A. Bauman. 2008. "Achieving Accurate Pictures of Risk and Identifying Gender-Responsive Deeds: Two New Assessments for Women Offenders." Washington, DC: U.S. Department of Justice, National Institute of Corrections.

Villanueva, Chandra Kring. 2009. "Mothers, Infants, and Imprisonment: A National Look at Prison Nurseries and Community-Based Alternatives." Women's Prison Association Institute on Women and Criminal Justice. NYC.

Wallace, Kristen S. 2012. "The Adoptions and Safe Families Act: Barrier to Reunification between Children and Incerated Mothers." New York City: National Resource Center for Permanency and Family Connections.

West, H.C. and S.J. Sabol. 2010. "Prisoners in 2009." Washington, DC: Bureau of Justice Statistics, U.S. Department of Justice.

Wright, L.E. and C.B. Seymour. 2000. "Working with Children and Families Separated by Incarceration: A Handbook for Child Welfare Agencies." Washington, DC: Child Welfare League of America.

Chapter 27

Aging and dying in prison

At the intersection of crime, costs, and health care

Karol Lucken

Introduction

Correctional systems in the U.S. are facing both moral and fiscal challenges as greater numbers of offenders are aging and dying in prison. This problem has received growing attention from legislators as well as professionals and scholars in the field of corrections, social work, and health care. It has also aroused the interest of Human Rights Watch and the American Civil Liberties Union (ACLU).

The policy question uniting these diverse groups reflects competing demands that are not easily reconciled. Specifically, how does government balance the demands of elder inmate health care, public safety, and limited resources? The dialogue surrounding this question has been informed by research documenting key features of this inmate population problem (e.g. size of the population, types and extent of illness, estimated costs) and correctional system responses to this problem (e.g. housing, treating, and releasing this population). This chapter focuses on these key features, revealing domains of consensus and conflict among scholars and practitioners.

To provide context, the chapter briefly reviews the scope and purported causes of this correctional trend. This is followed by a more in-depth discussion of the specific health care needs and costs associated with this inmate population. Finally, state and federal responses to the problems of care and costs are examined. The evidence associated with these bodies of work forms the basis for the policy recommendations discussed in the conclusions.

The scope and origins of a correctional problem

The elderly inmate is generally defined as one over the age of 55 or 50 years (Aging Inmate Committee, 2012). While this age group still represents a comparatively small portion of the total inmate population, they are its fastest-growing and most expensive segment. In 2010, there were 246,600 prisoners over age 50 nationwide, constituting approximately 16 percent of the U.S. prison population (ACLU, 2012). It is projected that if current sentencing and other demographic trends continue, one-third of the inmate population will be over the age of 50 by 2030 (Rikard and Rosenberg, 2007). Various experts estimate that the number of elder inmates over the age of 55 is expected to reach 400,000 by 2030, representing a 4,400 percent increase since 1981 (ACLU, 2012).

This correctional trend has been evolving for quite some time. Between 1981 and 1991, the number of inmates over 55 nationwide increased by 50 percent (Flynn, 1993). Between 1992 and 2001, the number of elderly inmates in state and federal facilities increased 173 percent, from 41,586 to 113,358 (Anno et al., 2004). Between 2000 and 2005, the number increased again by 33 percent. Between 1999 and 2012, the number of state and federal prisoners over the age of 55 increased from 43,300 to 131,500, constituting a change of 204 percent (Pew, 2014).

Though certain states have experienced a more significant strain than others, namely Florida, Texas, and California, this overall increase has not been driven by a few states.[1] Between 2007 and 2011, the percentage of older inmates in state facilities rose in at least 40 states, with an overall average increase of 7.1 percent (Pew, 2014). There are also 11 states in which at least 17 percent of the inmate population is over 50. West Virginia (20 percent), New Hampshire (19.8 percent), Massachusetts (19.4 percent), Florida (17.9 percent), Texas (17.7 percent), Nevada (17.2 percent), Michigan (17.2 percent), Hawaii (17 percent), and California (17 percent) are among them (ACLU, 2012).

This nationwide phenomenon has been attributed to several factors. Aside from the common-sense reasoning that people are simply living longer, crime rates among the elderly have been cited as one source of the increase. The role of elder crime in producing this trend is unclear, however. For example, Aday and Krabill (2013) report that between 1998 and 2009, elder arrests for serious offenses such as robbery, aggravated assault and burglary increased by 193, 109, and 159 percent respectively. Yet, Soderstrom (1999) notes that, offenders over the age of 50 are still only responsible for 3.6 percent of violent crime.

It is not certain how many of these elder arrests resulted in convictions, but it is likely that the sentencing policies of the get-tough era would have sent more convicted offenders to prison for longer periods of time. The abolishment of or reduction in the use of discretionary parole and the enactment of three-strikes, mandatory minimum, habitual offender, and truth-in-sentencing laws have increased sentence length and/or decreased chances of early release or release altogether. Between 1986 and 1995, life without parole sentences more than doubled from 7,399 to 17,853; the number of life sentences imposed also increased from 26,178 to 64,686 (ACLU, 2012). Sentences of 20 years or more grew exponentially as well, from 51,256 to 163,881. Taking a longer view of this trend, between 1984 and 2008, the number of state and federal inmates serving life sentences increased from 34,000 to 140,610 (ACLU, 2012). Of these 140,610 inmates, almost 30 percent are ineligible for parole (Aging Inmate Committee, 2012).

Correctional health care needs and costs

The health care implications of this population surge are substantial. In *Estelle v Gamble* (1976) and *DeShaney v Winnebago County Social Services Department* (1989), the U.S. Supreme Court affirmed the state's duty to provide a community standard of care for inmates. This includes the duty to provide acute care, chronic care, dental care, psychiatric care, and long-term services, and to meet general medical and nutritional needs (Kerbs and Jolley, 2009). In sum, correctional health care extends to physical, mental, and functional aspects of daily living.

Physical health refers to traditional conditions such as chronic diseases (e.g. cancer, high blood pressure, heart disease) or acute care arising from unforeseen injuries or temporary conditions. Though definitions vary by state, mental health care refers to psychiatric conditions such as depression, schizophrenia, and anxiety, or non-psychiatric issues such as substance abuse. Functional health care encompasses activities of daily living (e.g. bathing, eating, dressing) and what is known as prison activities of daily living (ADLs, e.g. standing in line, hearing staff commands, other institutional orders) (Aday and Krabill, 2013).

Each of these health care needs is shaped by the inmate's history of substance abuse, alcoholism, poor health habits, and untreated medical conditions. Consequently, the health status of the elderly entering the correctional system is far worse than their non-offending counterparts. Anno et al. (2004) estimate the aging process of an inmate is accelerated by nearly 12 years due to poor health history and prior risky behaviors. The stressors of prison life are also likely to aggravate pre-existing conditions and facilitate a rapid decline in health (Rubenstein, 1982).

The physical health problems experienced by elderly inmates are not unique; they include incontinence, respiratory difficulties, cancer, ulcers, hypertension, diabetes, and cardiovascular disease. It is estimated that, on average, 45 percent of inmates over 50 have a chronic physical health problem; that figure increases to 82 percent for those over the age of 65 (Sterns et al., 2008). Some older prisoners experience an average of three serious or chronic physical health problems (Kerbs and Jolley, 2009). A study of elderly federal inmates found that each inmate averages approximately 24 medical events per year (Aging Inmate Committee, 2012).

The typical mental health problems of the elderly inmate include, but are not limited to, anxiety and depression (Booth, 1989; Meeks et al., 2008; Aday, 1994). A BJS report indicates that 40 percent of state prisoners over 55 met the criteria for a mental disorder, while 52.4 percent of federal inmates over 55 met the criteria (James and Glaze, 2006). Wilson and Barboza (2010) estimate that over 3,500 inmates have symptoms of dementia. Still others claim that elder inmates experience fewer symptoms of depression, psychic pain and loneliness than younger inmates. Kelsey (1986) and Colsher et al. (1992) found little evidence of psychotic or other serious psychological impairment. However, in an environment that esteems toughness, problems that expose vulnerabilities may go unreported and undiagnosed. Psychological conditions might also manifest in ways that are less detectable, such as engaging in isolation and withdrawing from activity (Sterns et al., 2008).

Functional health care involves day-to-day "normal" accommodations for the elderly, such as providing prosthetic devices, glasses, dentures, hearing aids, special shoes, or wheelchairs. Aday's research shows 39 percent of elder male inmates and 88 percent of elder female inmates have vision problems. Additionally, 72 percent of elder male inmates and 32 percent of elder female inmates have hearing problems (Aday and Krabill, 2013). This research also shows that 60 percent of elderly male inmates require ground level housing and 53 percent require a flat terrain for walking. Reportedly, more than half of elder female inmates (59 percent) have difficulty standing up for longer than 15 minutes (Aday and Krabill, 2013). A small study in California found elderly inmates have twice the rate of difficulty with ADLs as the elderly in society (Abner, 2006).

An obvious implication of these various afflictions is that the cost of housing an elderly inmate ($70,000) far exceeds that of a non-elderly inmate ($23,000) (Durham, 1994; Rossell, 1991). The National Institute of Corrections (NIC) puts the annual cost of incarcerating the aging prisoner at a low of $34,135 and a high of $102,405 (ACLU, 2012). Applying NIC's middle estimate of $68,270 to the total number of U.S. inmates over the age of 50 (246,600) means roughly $16 billion is potentially needed to care for these inmates on an annual basis (ACLU, 2012).

To put this in a different perspective, between 2007 and 2011, total spending on all correctional health care nationally increased by a median of 13 percent (Pew, 2014). What is significant about this overall spending increase is that institutions with a higher share of elder inmates had higher per-inmate health care spending. The 10 states with the largest share of inmates over 55 had 37 percent higher per-inmate spending than the 10 states with the smallest share of elder inmates (Pew, 2014). Much of this disproportionate expense stems from health conditions requiring off-site facility treatment, which entails extra expenditure for transportation and staffing. For example, off-site medical expenses for inmates over 50 cost North Carolina $18.1 million in 2006. These external care costs constituted 72 percent of all health care costs spent on aging prisoners (ACLU, 2012). Aging prisoners in Florida also accounted for 34 percent of all off-site/

outsourced care, though they represent 18 percent of the total prison population (ACLU, 2012).

Policy and program responses

States and the federal government have employed a number of strategies to battle the pressures of correctional health care and exorbitant costs. One strategy has been privatization, which entails the traditional tactic of outsourcing health care services. Another, albeit far less common, strategy is to employ the relatively new technology of telemedicine. This enables long-distance electronic based health care that reduces the need for costly transportation to off-site medical facilities (Ferri, 2013; Pew, 2014).

Strategies that reflect the unique circumstances of the aging and dying have been adopted by states and the federal government as well. Correctional systems have recognized that the normal stressors or deprivations of prison life can become insurmountable in old age. Some research has shown that elder inmates are more vulnerable to harassment, extortion, and theft and/or fear victimization more which can aggravate existing physical and mental conditions. Research has also shown that inmates' greatest fear is to grow old and die in prison apart from loved ones (Aday, 2006; Byock, 2002; Crawley and Sparks, 2005). The specter of prison as a "permanent home" in which one will die can make the prison experience especially agonizing. Consequently, inmates with life sentences have expressed the strong desire to die as a free man and defined their confinement as a lonely and almost unbearable struggle (Crawley and Sparks, 2005).

One of the ways correctional systems have been sensitive to both costs and the plight of the elder inmate is through centralized housing arrangements. Special or geriatric housing exists in over half of the states (Aging Inmate Committee, 2012) and can include selected clustering, specified units, separate prisons, or secure nursing facilities (Aday and Krabill, 2013). As of 2008, six states had dedicated prisons for the elderly, nine had exclusive use medical facilities, five had dedicated secure nursing home facilities, and eight had hospice facilities (Ferri, 2013). The FBOP has designed geriatric units for the elderly who are no longer able to function without constant, specialized medical care.

Florida, Ohio, and Nevada are among a group of states (e.g. Pennsylvania, Alabama, Georgia, Virginia, and Lousiana) that have embarked on more innovative programming within these facilities (Aday and Krabill, 2013). Florida has developed exclusive chronic care clinics that provide more holistic and presumably cost-effective ways of handling geriatric conditions. Ohio has developed geriatric programs and courses for memory improvement, diet and wellness, medication management, and Medicare/Medicaid enrollment (Aday and Krabill, 2013). The Structured Senior Living Program at the

Northern Nevada Correctional Center has been widely praised as a model worthy of replication due to its impact on inmate well-being (Kopera-Frye et al., 2013). This separate unit offers geriatric-tailored physical, social, and mental activities. This includes required daily hygiene, room and facility cleanliness, instruction on financial planning and scams, nutrition, as well as cultural (e.g. art, writing, reading, crafts) and fitness activities (Aday and Krabill, 2013).

Hospice care is yet another response to the changing demographics of the correctional environment. Hospice units are available in roughly 25 state systems and may be housed in separate units or buildings or part of the regular inmate infirmary. Some states have a single centralized location for such a unit, while others, such as New York, have multiple units throughout the state (Anno et al., 2004). Still other states have integrated hospice services with dementia-related services for inmates with Alzheimer's, Parkinson's, or Huntington's disease (e.g. New York) or created facilities tailored exclusively to these maladies (e.g. Virginia). Angola Prison in Louisiana and the Federal Medical Center at Fort Worth have a long and respected history of delivering palliative care (National Prison Hospice Association, 2014). To encourage other states to replicate their efforts, The National Hospice and Palliative Care Organization has launched a Quality Guidelines Initiative. This initiative seeks to assist correctional systems in setting up new end-of-life-care programs or ensuring quality care in existing ones (The National Hospice and Palliative Care Organization, 2009).

Early release has also been adopted as an alternative to continued confinement for certain elderly or terminal inmates. An estimated 43 states have provisions for what has been officially or colloquially termed compassionate release or medical or elderly/geriatric parole, release, or furloughs (Anno et al., 2004). The terms and processes underlying these types of release vary by state, but they generally allow for the release of terminally ill inmates or those who can show they are no longer a societal threat physically or cognitively (see Vera Institute of Justice, 2010). However, nowhere is release granted automatically by virtue of age or health condition alone. Release exists as a privilege that may be granted by the state upon the inmate's request.

What is striking about these release provisions is that they are widespread, but rarely utilized. The reasons for this underutilization are certainly political (Ferri, 2013; Vera Institute of Justice, 2010) but equally procedural. The release application and review process is hampered by several factors, principally narrow medical eligibility requirements, difficulty assessing medical condition and life expectancy, complicated applications, and access to suitable housing upon release (Pew, 2014). To illustrate, in Hawaii, barely half of the prisoners approved for release between 2009 and 2012 were ever actually released (ACLU, 2012). In Colorado, between 2001 and 2008, only three inmates were released into the state's compassionate release program

(Maschi, 2012). Between 2001 and 2007, Virginia released four inmates (Vera Institute of Justice, 2010). Oregon has never released more than two inmates in a given year and no inmate has ever been released by these means in Oklahoma (Maschi, 2012). Similar disuse exists in Maryland, where only 10 inmates were released on medical parole between 2004 and 2010 (Aging Inmate Committee, 2012). Even in California, where federal judges ordered a prison population reduction of 40,000, only three elderly/terminal inmates were granted release in 2009 (Buckley, 2010). In Alabama, where prisons are also well over capacity, only four inmates were released in 2009. In fact, the review process can be so cumbersome that inmates may die while waiting. Since 2005, at least 16 New York inmates have died while waiting for the parole board to render a decision regarding their release (Buckley, 2010). In 2009, 35 Alabama prisoners died while their applications were being reviewed (Buckley, 2010).

The FBOP also has a particularly complex process for granting release. A federal judge grants the release, but this final decision is preceded by many other layers of decision making, The process begins with a referral from a prison warden, which is followed by a referral from a regional FBOP director, and finally a referral to the court from the Director of the FBOP (Human Rights Watch, 2012). The circumstances allowing for such release must be deemed "extraordinary and compelling" (Human Rights Watch, 2012). In 2007, the U.S. Sentencing Commission defined this criterion as (1) suffering from a terminal illness or (2) a debilitating condition that prevents self-care within a correctional facility and for which conventional treatment affords no substantial improvement. The definition also extends to an inmate that has encountered the death or incapacitation of the only family member able to care for a minor child. Between 2000 and 2011, FBOP's Central Office reviewed 444 requests for compassionate release that had been approved by wardens and regional directors. The FBOP approved 266, or 60 percent (Human Rights Watch, 2012). Between 2002 and 2008, the FBOP, via a federal judge, released 22 inmates a year (Ferri, 2013).

Conclusions

It is estimated that by 2050, the number of individuals in society over age 65 will be in excess of 88 million (Kopera-Frye et al., 2013). This means that, caring for the elderly and dying is likely to be an ongoing challenge for correctional systems. Dealing with this challenge requires consideration of a host of factors, including the numbers of elder inmates involved, the crimes they have committed, their risk of recidivism, the time served and remaining on their sentence, their health care needs and costs, and their living situation upon release.

Strategies that take these various factors into account have been proposed or implemented nationwide, but to widely varying degrees. As discussed, outsourcing health care services, telemedicine, designated elderly programs, facilities, and units, and early release are the most commonly recommended or acted upon solutions to the problem. Though not detailed here, some states have also taken the more proactive step of repealing "get-tough" laws that fuel the growth of an aging inmate population. Nevertheless, because some of these strategies are still being debated (e.g. separate housing versus mainstreaming) and/or underutilized (early release), substantial numbers of infirm and terminal inmates remain in custody at considerable expense to taxpayers.

While evidence-based practices relating to these strategies have yet to emerge, research that can aid policy decisions is widely available.[2] Evidence suggests telemedicine, consolidated housing, and early release could be greatly expanded without compromising public safety or inmate care. For example, telemedicine has shown promise as a means of reducing costs and improving age-sensitive care. Costs are reduced because it lessens the need for transportation to other facilities and is cheaper than traditional in-prison physician consultations (Curtin, 2007). It has also been shown to improve psychiatric care by increasing inmate access to medication and regular monitoring and decreasing crisis unit transports and waiting times to evaluation (Curtin, 2007). Additionally, telemedicine is age sensitive because elderly inmates experience less disruption or loss of a preferred housing assignment when diagnostic and other services are provided at the prison facility (Ferri, 2013). Finally, as Ferri (2013) observes, such technology can be located in one consolidated elderly unit where its use would be maximized and costs, consequently, minimized.

This notion of cost-savings due to economies of scale has been used to justify the practice of centralized housing in states with large numbers of elder inmates. Yet the advantages of dedicated facilities go beyond economics to include age, health, and managerial concerns. According to the National Institute of Corrections, consolidated housing allows for greater predictability and less fragmentation in service provision, greater gerontology expertise of staff, uniformity in the relaxation of procedures and rules and ultimately greater safety and humane living conditions for the elderly and dying (Anno et al., 2004; Ferri, 2013).

Assuming political barriers can be overcome, evidence suggests early release could be utilized on a far greater scale without detriment to public safety, the legitimacy of the sentence imposed, or state expenditures. The most consistent finding in criminological research is the decline in criminal behavior with age. To quote Brame and Piquero (2003), "the association between age and involvement in criminal behavior is a resilient empirical regularity in criminology." Bushway et al. (2011) show that, nationally, only a little over 2 percent of 50 to 54 year olds have been arrested. This arrest rate declines to nearly 0 for those over the age of 65. Langin and Levin (2002) have also found that only 17 percent of prisoners aged 45 and over were returned to prison for new convictions. This is compared to a 30 percent return rate for those between the ages of 18 and 24. Further, the New York Department of Corrections found that, between 1985 and 2007, only 7 percent of released prisoners between the ages of 50 and 64 were returned for a new conviction after 3 years. That figure dropped to 4 percent for the 65 and older age group (cited in ACLU, 2012). Under New York's compassionate release program, only 3 of the 364 inmates released since 1992 have returned to prison and for non-violent offenses (Buckley, 2010). The work of The Project for Older Prisoners (POPS) lends added support to the feasibility of early release. This group has advocated the release of 500 older prisoners, none of whom returned to prison (Aday and Krabill, 2013).

On the well-founded assumption that public safety is not jeopardized by early release, it is then necessary to use a sentencing profile (Goetting, 1984) to identify inmates whose release would not offend the public conscience or the integrity of the sanction imposed. For example, one category in this profile involves those who were incarcerated for the first time late in life; clearly this group would be inappropriate for early release. A second category consists of those who are career criminals or recidivists who have been incarcerated continually before and after age 50; this category of offender may only be suitable for early release under very limited circumstances, such as imminent death due to terminal illness. A final category consists of those who were incarcerated much earlier in life and have served at least 20 years of their sentence and grown old in prison. This group would be most suitable for early release, given the combination of age, time served, and/or medical condition.

The potential for significant cost-savings from the release of the grown-old-in-prison category can be illustrated using the elder inmate population over 50 as of 2012 and the NIC mid-range estimate of the annual cost of incarcerating an aging prisoner as of 2012 ($68,270).[3] For example, in Mississippi, 15 percent (n=427) of their elder inmates over 50 have served at least 20 years and grown old in prison. In Ohio, 19 percent (n=1,375) of elder inmates over 50 fall in this category. In Florida, 6 percent (n=1,078) are in this category. In both New Hampshire (n=15) and Texas (n=823), 3 percent of elder inmates fall into this category. Calculating costs for a high and low figure state, Ohio spends $93,871,250 (1,375 x $68,270) and New Hampshire spends $1,024,050 (15 x $68,270) each year to retain these inmates. The cost of supervising any inmate on parole or other correctional release is estimated to be $3.50 to $13.50 per day/offender (Pew, 2014) or what would amount to $1,277 to $4,927 per year/offender. If these inmates were supervised in the community then, Ohio, for instance, would only spend $1,755,875 to $6,774,625 ($1,277/$4,927 x 1,375 inmates) annually versus $93.8 million annually for prison. The annual community-supervision cost to New Hampshire would be $19,155 to $73,905 for their 15 released inmates versus $1 million in annual incarceration costs.

The feasibility of early release with or without supervision must also be judged by the real possibility or perception of cost displacement. Releases of this kind indeed have implications for federal entitlement programs such as social security and medicare and other social services administered at the state and local level. Cost assessments are needed to determine the various effects of this budgetary transfer. Offender reentry research would do well to fill this void; the current focus on younger and higher risk offenders should be expanded to include offenders who are quite the opposite.

Notes

1 States with the highest actual numbers of inmates over 50 are California (27,680), Texas (27,455), Florida (17,980), and the Federal Bureau of Prisons/FBOP (25,160) (ACLU, 2012).
2 Ferguson (2012), a professor of medicine at the University of Massachusetts Medical School's Health and Justice Programs, argues that the absence of best practices has impeded the delivery of quality cost-effective health care. He contends this can be overcome with the academic medical community's greater involvement in inmate health care.
3 2012 figures on inmates over 50 who have served at least 20 years obtained from ACLU report.

References

Abner, C. (2006, November/December). Graying prisons: States face challenges of an aging inmate population. *State News*, 49 (10), 8–12 (available at www.csg.org/knowledgecenter/docs/sn0611GrayingPrisons.pdf).

Aday, R.H. (1994). Golden years behind bars: Special programs and facilities for elder inmates. *Federal Probation*, 82: 47–54.

Aday, R.H. (2006). Aging prisoners' concerns toward dying in prison. *OMEGA*, 52(3): 199–216.

Aday, R.H. and Krabill, J.J. (2013). Older and geriatric offenders: Critical issues for the 21st century. In L. Gideon (ed.), *Special needs offenders in correctional institutions*. (pp. 203–232). Thousand Oaks, CA: Sage Publications.

Aging Inmate Committee (2012). Aging inmates: Correctional issues and initiatives. *Corrections Today*, August-September, 85–87.

American Civil Liberties Union (2012). *At America's expense: The mass incarceration of the elderly*. New York, NY: American Civil Liberties Union.

Anno, B.J. Graham, C., Lawrence, J.E. and Shanksy, R. (2004). *Correctional health care: Addressing the needs of elderly, chronically ill, and terminally ill inmates*. Washinton, DC: U.S. National Institute of Corrections.

Booth, D. E. (1989). Health status of the incarcerated elderly: Issues and concerns. *Journal of Offender Counseling Services and Rehabilitation*, 13: 193–213.

Brame, R and Piquero, A. (2003). Selective attrition and the age-crime relationship. *Journal of Quantitative Criminology*, 19: 107–128.

Buckley, C. (2010, January 29). *Law has little effect on early release for inmates.* The New York Times. Retrieved from www.nytimes.com/2010/01/30/nyregion/30parole.html?_r=2and.

Bushway, S.D., Tsao, H.S. and Smith, H.L. (2011). *Has the U.S. prison boom changed the age distribution of the prison population?* Retrieved from National Addiction and HIV Data Archive Program at www.icpsr.umich.edu/icpsrweb/NAHDAP/biblio/resources?paging. startRow=1andcollection%5B0%5D=DATAandauthor%5B0%5D=Bushway%2C+Shawn+D.

Byock, I.R. (2002). Dying well in corrections: Why should we care? *Journal of Correctional Health Care*, 12: 27–35.

Colsher, P.L., Wallace, R.B., Loeffelholz, P.L. and Sales, M. (1992). Health status of older male prisoners: A comprehensive survey. *American Journal of Public Health*, 82: 881–84.

Crawley, E. and Sparks, R. (2005). Older men in prison: Survival, coping, and identity. In A. Liebling and S. Maruna (eds.) *The effects of imprisonment.* UK: Willan Publishing.

Curtin, T. (2007). The continuing problem of America's aging prison population and the search for a cost-effective and socially acceptable means of addressing it. *Elder Law Journal*, 15: 473.

Durham, A.M. III. (1994). *Crisis and reform: Current issues in American punishment.* Boston: Little, Brown.

Ferguson, W.J. (2012). Disseminating innovations in correctional health: A necessary step to recognition in academe. *Journal of Correctional Health Care*, 18(2): 158–160.

Ferri, C.N. (2013). A stuck safety valve: The inadequacy of compassionate release for elderly inmates. *Stetson Law Review*, 43(1): 197–243.

Flynn, E. (1993). The graying of America's prison population. *Prison Journal*, 72: 77–98.

Goetting, A. (1984). The elderly in prison: A profile. *Criminal Justice Review*, 9(14): 14–24.

Human Rights Watch (2012). *The answer is no: Too little compassionate release in U.S. federal prisons.* New York, NY: Human Rights Watch.

James, D. and Glaze, L. (2006). *Mental health problems of prisons and jail inmates.* NCJ 213600. Washington, DC: U.S. Department of Justice. Bureau of Justice Statistics.

Kelsey, O.W. (1986). Elderly inmates: Providing safe and human care. *Corrections Today*, 48(May): 56.

Kerbs, J.J. and Jolley, J.M. (2009). Challenges posed by older prisoners: What we know about America's aging prison population. In R. Tewksbury and D. Dabney (eds.) *Prisons and jails: A reader* (pp. 389–411). New York, NY: McGraw Hill.

Kim, K. and Peterson, B. (2014). *Aging behind bars: Trends and implications of graying prisoners in the federal prison system.* Washington DC: Urban Institute.

Kopera-Frye, K., Harrison, M.T., Iribarne, J., Dampsey, E., Adams, M. Grabreck, T., McMullen, T. Peak, K. and McCown, W.G. (2013). Veterans aging in place behind bars: A structured living program that works. *Psychological Services*, 10(1): 79–86.

Langin, P.A. and Levin, D.J. (2002). *Recidivism of prisoners released in 1994* (NCJ 193427). Washington DC: Bureau of Justice Statistics.

Maschi, T. (2012, August 23). *The state of aging: Prisoners and compassionate release programs.* Retrieved from www.huffingtonpost.com/tina-maschi/ the-state-of-aging-prisoners_b_ 1825811.html.

Meeks, S., Sublett, R., Kostiwa, I., Rodgers, J.R., and Haddix, D. (2008). Treating depression in the prison nursing home: Demonstrating research to practice transitions. *Clinical Case Studies,* 7(6): 555–574.

National Hospice and Palliative Care Organization (2009). Quality Guidelines: For Hospice and End-Of-Life Care in Correctional Settings. Retrieved from www. nhpco.org.

National Prison Hospice Association (2014). A Model for the Future? Retrieved from http://npha.org/npha-articles/models/a-prison-hospice-model-for-the-future/.

Pew Charitable Trusts (2014). *State prison health care spending.* Washington DC: The Pew Charitable Trusts.

Rikard, R.V. and Rosenberg, E. (2007). Aging inmates: A convergence of trends in the American criminal justice system. *Journal of Correctional Health Care,* 13(3): 150–162.

Rossell, N.R. (1991). *Older inmates.* Tallahassee: Florida House of Representatives.

Rubenstein, D. (1982). The older person in prison. *Archives of Gerontology and Geriatrics,* 1: 287–296.

Soderstrom, I.R. (1999). Is it still practical to incarcerate the elderly offender: In C.B. Fields (ed.) *Controversial issues in corrections* (pp. 72–80). Needham Heights, MA: Allyn and Bacon.

Sterns, A.A., Lax, G., Sed, S., Keohane, P., and R.S. Sterns (2008). Growing wave of older prisoners: A national survey of older prisoner's health, mental health, and programming. *Corrections Today,* 70(4): 70–72, 74–76.

Vera Institute of Justice (2010). *It's about time: Aging prisoners, increasing costs, and geriatric release.* Vera Institute of Justice. New York.

Wilson, J. and Barboza, S. (2010). The looming challenge of dementia in corrections. *CorrectCare,* 24(2): 12–14. Chicago, IL: National Commission on Correctional Health Care.

Chapter 28

Native American criminal justice

Toward evidence-based policies and practices

Roy F. Janisch

Introduction

The Native American community in the United States comprise nearly 600 diverse tribal groups; each made up of unique structures, political organizations, and histories. Tribal criminal justice systems also vary greatly from one Native American group to the next. Some justice systems are modeled after the U.S. system while others favor an approach with a strong Native American cultural foundation. However, despite the vast differences that exist between tribal communities, common similarities among them include debilitating rates of poverty, unemployment, drug and alcohol abuse, and crime.

Native American tribes have unique relationships with the U.S. federal government as domestic dependents of the U.S. who have the authority to govern themselves. However, a series of Supreme Court cases and Congressional decisions have greatly limited the sovereignty of Native American tribal governments. When applying its policies to Native Americans, the federal government has seldom asked the Native people for their input on the issues facing them. Complex jurisdictional issues, inconsistency of applying the rule of law in Native American communities, and a lack of cultural understanding has created confusion and misunderstanding between the U.S. and Native Americans and has contributed to a series of social problems plaguing tribal communities, namely increasing crime rates and an ill-equipped justice system.

United States Federal policy towards addressing crime in Indian Country, specifically within Native American Reservation communities, should be made more commensurate with other populations in the country in order for them to approach the levels of justice they deserve. The most direct approach to addressing the shortcomings in these communities is to research, redefine, implement, and fund those activities which will place Native American criminal justice systems on more even footing with the rest of American society. A consistent sound policy approach utilizing an evidence-based strategy is necessary for strengthening law enforcement, courts, detention, and correctional rehabilitation programs within Indian communities.

Historical context

In 1953, without the consent of the impacted tribes, the U.S. Congress officially declared a policy of assimilation for Native Americans when it passed House Concurrent Resolution 108 (HCR-108) and Public Law 280 (PL280), effectively eroding tribal governments' authority and autonomy (Canby, 1988). The passage of PL 280 changed and attempted to clarify the criminal justice jurisdictional authority of the U.S. federal government and Indian nations. For crimes committed within Indian Territory, jurisdiction depends on the Native American status of offenders and victims and the magnitude of the offense. HCR-108 transferred authority to individual states and relieved the federal government of their responsibility over Native American assets while simultaneously reducing the overall spending for Native American criminal justice services.

As a result of HCR-108, states were suddenly required to provide police officers, judges, correctional staff, and infrastructure to tribes. Many did not have funding to do so, thus leaving a dearth of criminal justice services for Native American communities and jeopardizing public safety in the process (Naughton, 2007). Additionally, as noted by Jimenez and Song (1998), the resolutions resulted in a breakdown in the administration of justice to such a degree that Native Americans are being denied due process and equal protection of the law.

Crime and criminal justice in Indian country

A 1997 report conducted by the U.S. Department of Justice found there to be "a public safety crisis in Indian Country"; more recent accounts have demonstrated that this has not changed (Perry, 2004). The self-reported rate of violent crime and victimization among Native Americans is more than twice the national average, and well above that of any other racial or ethnic group in the U.S. (Ibid.). Further, alcohol is much more likely to have been consumed by the offender. Native Americans also represent a disproportionate percent of inmates in prisons and jails across the country.

Jurisdictional issues create challenges for the criminal justice systems in many Native American communities. Often there is a need to answer a series of factual questions to determine jurisdiction. For example, the identity of the victim, offender, the nature of the offense, and the location of the crime all must be determined and verified. Establishing the aforementioned characteristics often causes undue delays in investigations and degradation of evidence and the memories of eyewitnesses. Aside from questions about jurisdiction, the raw number of law enforcement officers and their practices have also been deemed less than adequate to properly ensure public safety and successful criminal investigation in Native American communities.

Native American law enforcement

While the majority of law enforcement agencies in Indian country are tribally administered, the federal government (through the Bureau of Indian Affairs) retains responsibility to investigate certain major crimes that are legally defined as being beyond the jurisdiction of an Indian nation and to enforce laws where no tribal agency exists. In 2011, the U.S. Department of Justice reported that there were 191 tribal law enforcement agencies, 151 of which were tribally administered. The vast majority of tribal police departments are small, many employing fewer than nine officers (Wakeling et al., 2001). These agencies rarely have more than one officer on duty at a time and frequently struggle with providing adequate coverage to their communities. The larger police departments more closely resemble the medium-to-large U.S. police departments outside of Indian country. For example, all tribal police officers in the larger departments are high school graduates and the majority are graduates of certified law enforcement training programs (Ibid). The general functions of Native American police departments also closely resemble those of non-Native departments, namely, routine patrol, responding to citizen calls, criminal investigations, traffic patrol, and various court related duties.

Native American police departments face many challenges that are unique to the populations they serve and the physical size of the land that is under their jurisdiction. The small size of many Native police departments and the vast size of the tribal reservations create many barriers to effective policing. For example, within Indian country, there are less than 3,000 law enforcement officers, which is less than two officers per 1,000 residents. This rate does not account for the non-resident and non-Indian populations served on reservations, including visitors to casinos and tourists. Of the 25 largest tribal law enforcement agencies, all had at least one casino operating within their jurisdiction.

The violent crime epidemic currently plaguing Native American tribes also presents challenges for tribal police departments. For example, although the Wind River Reservation in Wyoming faces a violent crime rate that is 3.58 times the national rate, its police department employs just six to seven officers to patrol the entire 2.2 million acre reservation (Naughton, 2007). Non-Native American urban areas with similar crime rates have police departments that employ between 3.9 and 6.6 officers per 1,000 residents and a much smaller land area. In addition, on some tribal reservations, there may be 100 or more miles of harsh terrain between department offices and remote areas, requiring hours before a responding officer can reach a victim or crime scene. For example, while the Navajo Nation Department of Law Enforcement polices 22,000 square miles in Utah, Arizona, and New Mexico, the comparably staffed Reno, Nevada Police Department covers just 60 square miles.

The number of law enforcement personnel and their ability to adequately patrol Indian country, both in measures of geography and service population, falls far short of the national average. U.S. Department Of Justice (DOJ) has recommended that 4,300 officers, almost double the current number, are needed for tribal police departments to provide basic public safety. However, per capita spending is approximately 60 percent less than the national average, leaving most tribal police departments grossly underfunded.

Police in Indian country also operate within and must learn to navigate a complex jurisdictional system (Wakeling et al., 2001). Jurisdiction often depends on the nature of the criminal event and the identity of the victim and offender. Therefore, prior to making an arrest and conducting a full investigation into a criminal event, police officers must answer a series of questions to establish jurisdiction. Once jurisdiction has been determined, Native American police departments must also answer to multiple authorities, both tribal and federal.

Native American court systems

There are four main types of courts operating in Indian country: Code of Federal Regulations (CFR) Courts, tribal courts, traditional justice systems, and intertribal courts. According to Goldberg (2004), CFR Courts are remnants of a late nineteenth-century court system designed during the era of assimilation for American Indians. CFR Courts were originally used to undermine traditional sources of law and authority, and to suppress traditional cultural and religious practices. Between the 1880s and 1934, CFR Courts operated on about two-thirds of all reservations but have since largely been replaced by tribal courts. Creel (2011) reported that today, CFR Courts serve as the justice system for a small number of tribes that have not yet established a tribal court to exercise criminal jurisdiction.

Tribal court systems are the judicial system of choice for the majority of tribes. While most tribal courts are based on a Western model of justice, many report using traditional methods and/or forums for dispute resolution (Brandfon, 1991). Traditional courts are marked by non-adversarial and culturally distinct forms of dispute resolution and may take the form of peacemaker courts or councils of elders, and may use sentencing circles (Department of Justice, 2005). For example, the Peacemaking Division of the Navajo Nation court system has been operating as a division of the Navajo Nation's judicial system since 1982. It is not intended to replace the Navajo Nation's formal court system, but to provide an alternative forum for resolving certain types of disputes. Navajo peacemaking is a participatory, community-led, consensus-based dispute resolution system. The goal is to heal and renew the victim's physical, emotional, mental, and spiritual well-being. It also involves deliberate acts by the offender to regain dignity and trust, and to return to a healthy physical and emotional state (NIJ, 2007). These principles are similar to the principles of restorative justice that are gaining popularity in communities around the world today.

An emerging court system in Indian country is the intertribal court system. The participating tribes pool their economic, personnel, and administrative resources to form and operate intertribal court systems.

Criminal detention on Native American reservations

Tribal jails are overcrowded, in disrepair, and lack the staffing and funding needed to meet the demands of the criminal justice system (U.S. Government Accountability Office, 2011). Most tribal detention facilities were constructed to house offenders for a very short period of time; therefore, half of Indian nations surveyed in 2011 by the Government Accountability Office noted that they lacked adequate detention space to house offenders convicted in tribal court. Due to inadequate resources on many reservation communities, tribal courts are left to make difficult decisions regarding offenders. Courts must decide whether to forego sentencing, to release inmates to make room for more serious offenders, or subcontract to local non-Native jurisdictions.

According to the Tribal Crime Collection Activities report published, in 2014, the *Survey of Jails in Indian Country* (SJIC) is BJS's only national data collection that provides an annual source of data on the estimated 79 Indian country jails and detention facilities. The report showed that the number of jails or detention centers operating in Indian country increased 14.5 percent, from 1998 to 2012. At midyear 2012, a total of 2,364 inmates were confined in Indian country jails – a 5.6 percent increase from midyear 2011.

Toward evidence-based Native American criminal justice

This chapter has chronicled the limited amount of available information on Native American criminal justice. Aside from descriptive government reports, very little empirical research exists that evaluates the effectiveness of the criminal justice policies and practices in operation in Indian country. Currently, there exists no single system permitting collection and analysis of aggregate Native American crime and prosecution data across tribes. Crime statistics are drawn from three different jurisdictions: federal, state, or tribal. The FBI's Uniform Crime Report (UCR) contains offense data from all three, but only counts crimes reported to law enforcement for those agencies that volunteer those data. The numbers presented by the FBI include only cases subject to federal jurisdiction. A clearer picture of the crime data in American Indian communities is a crucial objective.

Given the limited amount of evidence-based research regarding crime and justice among Native American populations, it is imperative that researchers develop strong relationships with Native American communities. Tribes regularly blame federal agencies for the poor state of policing in Indian country; not only are the resources provided by federal agencies inadequate, but federal policies are driven by a misreading of tribes' real needs and priorities. Efforts to increase evidence-based practices entail field evaluations with appropriate design and methodology, data collection, and analyses. Additionally, the dissemination of data, and applying research to practice in meaningful ways should include the input of the Native American communities. This will facilitate meaningful partnerships between researchers while addressing community needs and allow greater cultural participation. Reliable technical assistance and financial support for Indian nations to address violence in their communities using the best available research knowledge is essential.

Community policing practices that are routinely, and more frequently, being implemented in U.S. urban areas may be an effective method of policing and crime control in Indian country. Police departments may be able to join community issues with departmental values and implement effective policies. Such an effort would lend credibility to the modern police function while showing respect for important tribal traditions. Incorporating research evidence regarding the practices and goals of restorative justice into tribal or traditional Native American court systems will ensure the practices are operating with fidelity and integrity. Moreover, drug courts provide another effective evidence-based strategy that may prove useful as a supplemental Native American court function. Ultimately, what is most needed is for the criminological research community to embrace a research and criminal justice partnership with Native American tribes.

References

Brandfon, F. (1991). Tradition and Judicial Review in the American Indian Tribal Court System. *UCLA Law Review*, 38: 991.

Canby, W.C. (1988). *American Indian law in a nutshell*. (p. 27) Saint Paul, MN: West Publishing.

Creel, B. (2011). Tribal Court Convictions and the Federal Sentencing Guidelines: Respect for Tribal Courts and Tribal People in Federal Sentencing, 46, *U.S.F. Law Review* 37: 83.

Goldberg, C. (2004). Overview: U.S. Law and Legal Issues, in *The Native North American Almanac* 470–473 (Duane Champagne, ed., 2001), in Justin B. Richland and Sarah Deer, *Introduction to Tribal Legal Studies*, 62.

Jimenez, V. J. and Song, S. C. (1998). Concurrent Tribal and State Jurisdiction Under Public Law 280. *The American University Law Review*, 47:1627–1707.

Naughton, R. (2007). State Statutes Limiting the Dual Sovereignty Doctrine: Tools for Tribes to Reclaim Criminal Jurisdiction Stripped by Public Law 280?, *UCLA Law Review*, 55: 489, 498–99. Available at: http://www.uclalawreview.org/pdf/55-2-5.pdf.

NIJ (2007). Harvard Project on American Indian Economic Development, Honoring Nations 1999 Honoree: New Law and Old Law Together, 1. Available at http://www.hpaied.org/images/resources/publibrary/New Law and Old Law Together.pdf.

Perry, S. W. (2004). *American Indians and Crime*. U.S. Department of Justice, Office of Justice Programs: Washington, DC. United States Department of Justice (2005) See Wakeling et al. (2001).

U.S. Government Accountability Office. (2011). *Indian Country Criminal Justice: Departments of the Interior and Justice Should Strengthen Coordination to Support Tribal Courts*, Report No. GAO-11–252, 28. Available at www.gao.gov/new.items/d11252.pdf.

Wakeling, S. et al., (2001). U. S. Department Of Justice, Policing on American Indian Reservations: A Report to the National Institute of Justice (9). Available at www.ncjrs.gov/pdffiles1/nij/188095.pdf.

Part V

Conclusion

Conclusion

Introduction

The future of criminology and criminal justice policy

Thomas G. Blomberg, Julie Mestre Brancale, Kevin M. Beaver and William D. Bales

The field of criminology and criminal justice policy is in the midst of significant change. The public, policymakers, practitioners, and criminologists are increasingly aligned in calls for evidence-based research to guide criminal justice policy and practice. The scientific discipline of criminology and the applied field of criminal justice policy and practice have begun to converge and it is the obligation of criminologists to ensure this continues. As the chapters in this book have illustrated, while the search for causality in criminology will and should continue, best available research knowledge should be used to direct, implement, and alter criminal justice policies and practices where appropriate. The implementation of an increasingly evidence-based criminal justice system will lead to policies that are more effective, efficient, and cost-effective. In the chapters that follow, several salient issues concerning the future of criminology and criminal justice policy will be identified and discussed.

In Chapter 29, Marie Gottschalk addresses what society should do and what needs to be understood in order to move beyond reliance on mass incarceration. Gottschalk argues that the practice of mass incarceration must be understood within the larger political, economic, and institutional context in which it developed, has been sustained, and to which it is relevant. Specifically, why has the U.S. criminal justice system been so vulnerable to political pressures? By examining mass incarceration with a broad contextual focus, the competing and contradictory views of key political actors and the obstacles to forging a powerful and evidence-based decarceration movement become more evident.

A highly influential source of information about crime and justice in the U.S. is the media. An analysis of the culture of society, especially focusing on the criminal justice system, would be incomplete without serious consideration of the influence of the media. In Chapter 30, Ray Surette and Kimberly Kampe highlight the many ways in which the media influences and often drives criminal justice issues and their policy responses. The participatory component of the media is growing and evolving every day; individuals can use social media to post accounts and pictures that have the ability to spread nationwide in a matter of minutes thereby opening the criminal justice system to increased public and political scrutiny and involvement. Thus, it is necessary that crime and justice information be presented to the public and policymakers as accurately as possible rather than through media portrayals that are far too often sensational. With the evolving nature of new forms of media that will continue to influence public opinion and, in turn, criminal justice policy for the foreseeable future, it is critical for criminologists to actively engage the public, journalists, and policymakers with sound and understandable evidence regarding both the problems and associated solutions for our evolving criminal justice system.

Next to ensuring and protecting public safety, criminal justice policies should be cost-effective and accountable. Natasha Frost, Carlos Monteiro, and Beck Strah (Chapter 31) note that criminal justice reform efforts have increasingly focused on ways to encourage the development of accountable and effective policies and practices. Various justice reinvestment approaches being undertaken across the U.S. represent some of the more promising and comprehensive attempts to enact sweeping criminal justice reforms. To the extent that future justice reinvestment initiatives are able to return the focus to reinvesting in local communities that was so central to earlier crime reduction visions, these initiatives should be able to achieve their dual objectives of a reduced reliance on incarceration and safer communities.

New and innovative research methodologies and perspectives have been integral to the development of criminology as a science. In Chapter 32, Kevin Beaver and Joseph Schwartz present the utility of biosocial research findings for progressive criminal justice policy and practice. They point out that when used appropriately, biosocial research can guide the implementation of effective treatment and rehabilitation programs that can ultimately lead to a reduction in criminal offending and increased public safety. The authors contend that there are two main ways that biosocial research can be integrated into criminal justice policies. First, the genetic basis to criminal behavior can be used to develop specific offender-based criminal justice polices. Second, the identification of environmental influences on criminal behavior can result in the creation of more effective and efficient criminal justice policies related to these known environmental influences.

In the book's final chapter, Alfred Blumstein discusses how best to use criminological research in criminal justice policy. While the tradition in the physical and medical sciences is to defer to the randomized controlled trial (RCT) as the strongest test of a treatment, in the context of the criminal justice system, where life and liberty are at stake, there are severe limits to the feasibility and acceptance of RCTs. Because of the inherent complexities of evaluation research in the criminal justice field, replication is almost always a necessary part of accumulating adequate evidence. If one is to argue for a program's effectiveness, then it must have been shown to be effective in a variety of settings under the control of a variety of managers. An important part of the process of bringing evidence into the shaping of policy requires the building of links between local criminal justice organizations and criminologists.

These chapters collectively demonstrate that the future of criminological research and criminal justice policy will likely reflect a broader social context in which sound bites, ideologically driven criminal justice reform, and proposals without compelling research justification will no longer be the rule. Rather, it appears that research will be relied upon more as we continue to confront crime. Further, it seems that criminal justice policy decisions will increasingly be characterized by more non-partisan rather than bi-partisan processes in which research evidence will be center stage. Considering some of the criminal justice policy recommendations being made in 2015 by a number of presidential candidates, the common denominator is not party affiliation but rather the realization that the criminal justice policies of the past have not worked and have resulted in unprecedented financial costs. As a result, it is no longer about getting tough on crime, but rather getting smart on crime as related to what works. For example, Tea Party Conservative Rand Paul supports the restoration of voting rights for nonviolent felons, Republican Scott Walker supports drug courts and Democrat Hillary Clinton supports mandatory police body cameras and new sentencing guidelines for nonviolent offenders (*Time*, May 18, 2015: 40–41).

Most important, what all of the criminal justice policy reforms have in common is research support. Moreover, throughout states and in Congress, among both liberals and conservatives, there has been an emerging consensus for more offender treatment, reduced reliance on mandatory-minimum sentences, limiting solitary confinement, providing more alternatives to prison for low-level nonviolent offenders, increasing education and job training programs in prisons, etc. In sum, and as aptly concluded by Dagan and Teles (2014), retrenchment from "getting tough" on crime is as orthodox today among conservatives as it was to establishing it by them a few decades ago.

It is abundantly clear that criminologists and their research will play a growing criminal justice policy role in the future. The chapters included in this volume demonstrate the substantial body of valuable research evidence on the criminal justice system that have specific policy and practice relevance. This body of current and future research evidence should and, no doubt, will play a bigger role in advancing criminology and criminal justice policy. It is no longer a matter of criminology as a science versus criminology as an applied discipline – it is a matter of both.

Reference

Dagan, David and Steven M. Teles. (2014). Locked in? Conservative Reform and the Future of Mass Incarceration. *The ANNALS of the American Academy of Political and Social Science*, 651(1): 266–276.

Chapter 29

Mass incarceration, the carceral state, and evidence-based research

Marie Gottschalk

Evidence-based research is the mantra today across many areas of public policy, including penal policy. But as Todd Clear emphasized in his 2009 presidential address to the American Society of Criminology, the "evidence-based policy paradigm is, at its core, extraordinarily conservative" (Clear, 2010: 6). The "what works" model generally rests on a narrow understanding of what counts as evidence. It deifies program evaluations based on multiple randomized trials or controlled experiments – the so-called gold standard of research. Such a narrow construction of evidence centered on what has already been shown to work fosters what Clear calls a "kind of slavery to the present" (Clear, 2010: 6). It also contributes to a denigration of other kinds of knowing and evidence that are not the results of controlled experiments, including policy studies, case studies, qualitative research, and historically oriented research (Clear, 2010: 7). This is especially a problem in the case of mass incarceration, one of the country's leading public policy issues.

Punishment in any society is never a purely rational act. It is a means to regulate deviance, but it is also an expressive act "in which society talks to itself about its own moral identity," explains Philip Smith (2008: 29, 37), channeling Durkheim. Analyzing that conversation needs to be part of what we consider evidence-based research, even if that conversation cannot be easily quantified or subjected to multiple randomized trials. A narrow view of evidence-based research favors investigating subjects that can be precisely measured, like recidivism rates and racial disparities in punishment. It slights messier subjects that are sometimes better analyzed through expert interpretation, not expert measurement – such as the underlying role of institutions, culture, and politics in impeding or advancing certain penal policies and in fostering racial and other disparities in punishment.

The wide swaths that mass incarceration cuts through U.S. society and polity contrast sharply with the narrowness of the dominant research agenda on this pressing public issue. Measuring the recidivism rates of various programs and interventions has been a central pillar of research on mass incarceration. So has measuring racial disparities in punishment. Allowing these concerns to dominate the research agenda ends up minimizing the problem and minimizing the solutions. It marginalizes two of the most important research questions related to this pressing public issue: What are the political, social, and economic consequences of having so many people – especially so many people of color – subject to state surveillance in an ostensibly democratic country? And what can and should be done to radically reduce the U.S. incarceration rate to where it was for most of the twentieth century? The focus on measuring racial disparities in punishment often comes at the cost of more fine-grained analyses of the underlying sources of these disparities. It also tends to come at the cost of minimizing or ignoring how other disadvantaged groups, including Latinos and poor whites, have been significantly harmed by the carceral state, even if not to the extent that African-Americans have been hurt (Gottschalk, 2015: 119–38).

Promising new research on mass incarceration has embraced this wider set of questions and issues. This work has tended to enlist a more encompassing understanding of what counts as evidence-based research. It includes historical-institutional case studies on the rise of mass incarceration at the state and national levels, as detailed below, and scholarship that sets U.S. penal policies and practices in a comparative context with other developed countries. The wider political, social, and economic consequences of mass incarceration are another fruitful area of scholarly interest.

This chapter begins with an analysis of what's wrong with an evidence-based approach to research on mass incarceration that is preoccupied with recidivism rates. It then critiques the dominant approach to analyzing racial disparities in punishment. It concludes with a discussion of some promising new vistas in research on mass incarceration and the emergence of the carceral state that take a much more encompassing view of the problem and of what counts as evidence.

The slippery concept of "recidivism"

As in many areas of research on criminal justice, how policymakers define the problem and define the policy options has driven much of the research agenda. Reducing the recidivism rates of released offenders has become a leading penal policy goal. It has become the pre-eminent yardstick by which to judge the success or failure of justice reinvestment, reentry, and other criminal justice reform initiatives. It has displaced broader public-safety goals and more encompassing visions of how to improve the quality of life in the neighborhoods and communities that have bore the brunt of mass incarceration. We have a plethora of research on how specific penal and criminal justice programs and interventions affect recidivism rates but relatively little on how broader social, economic, and political trends and interventions affect general trends in crime.

Government funding reinforces the bias toward a narrowly conceived evidence-based research agenda preoccupied with recidivism rates.

Historically, research on crime and criminal justice has been underfunded. The Department of Justice was the last cabinet agency to set up a research program (Blumstein, 2009: 3). Much of the federal research money in this area has gone to fund evaluations of programs. Basic research on a wide range of other subjects is grossly underfunded (Blumstein, 2009: 3; Clear, 2010: 15). The Second Chance Act, the signature criminal justice legislation of the George W. Bush administration, reinforced the tendency toward a narrow research agenda defined by program evaluations and recidivism rates. A major goal of the measure, whose full name is the Second Chance Act of 2007: Community Safety Through Recidivism Prevention, was to fund programs that would slash the recidivism rate in half within five years (Civic Impulse, 2015: 664).

Evaluating each penal intervention by putting it on the evidence-based, cost–benefit scales to determine whether it reduces crime while saving public money reinforces the tight linkage in the public mind between punishment and crime. It is at odds with some of the most compelling research findings of the last decade or so about the relationship between punishment and crime. We have long known that crime rates move up and down quite independently of punishment practices. More recent research has helped pinpoint the precise relationship between incarceration rates and crime rates.[1] A recent National Research Council study concluded that the "average crime reduction effect of incarceration is small, and that the size of the effect diminishes with the scale of incarceration" (Travis et al., 2014: 337).

The country's purportedly high recidivism rates have raised public alarm, even as crime rates have fallen to historic lows not seen since the Eisenhower administration. Many commentators, public officials, and researchers have focused public attention on the key findings from a 2002 Bureau of Justice Statistics study that about two-thirds of released prisoners are re-arrested within three years, and four in ten are returned to prison in that time (Langan and Levin, 2002).[2] In doing so, they have fostered the mistaken public belief that many of the people released from prison go on to become serious repeat offenders and are the main drivers of crime rates.

Public officials and policymakers have valorized recidivism rates as the key indicator of the return that states and taxpayers are receiving for their investments in the corrections system. But recidivism is a "notoriously slippery concept that is difficult to operationalize and reliably measure" (Hannah-Moffat, 2010: 12). It has been "variably defined as rearrest, reconviction, or reincarceration, and does not always refer to the original offence(s)" (Hannah-Moffat, 2010: 12). One analysis counted nine different definitions of recidivism in a survey of 90 studies of recidivism in the United States (Maltz, 2001: 61–62).

The two-thirds figure is frequently invoked in discussions of mass incarceration without noting that this is the re-arrest rate, not the rate at which released offenders are returned to prison for committing new crimes. Often left unsaid is that the number of people who are sent back to prison for committing a new serious crime is trivial compared to the overwhelming majority who are imprisoned for committing a minor crime or a technical parole violation, such as a dirty urine test, a curfew infraction, or a missed appointment with a parole officer (Gottschalk, 2015: 101–04).

The recidivism-crime connection

This fixation on recidivism rates in research on penal reform fosters the misperception that released offenders are the primary drivers of crime rates and that reducing recidivism rates is the best way to reduce crime rates. But using the re-arrest rates of released offenders to gauge wider crime trends is problematic for many reasons.

The re-arrest rate of released offenders does not tell us much about what is driving the crime rate. It is well established that arrest rates are as much a function of police activities as they are of criminal activities. People subject to greater police attention, notably young minority men, residents of high crime areas, and people with prior criminal records, tend to be arrested more often (Sampson and Lauritsen, 1997).

People released from prison are arrested at a far higher rate than the general population even after adjusting for age, race, and other factors. But they are responsible for only a small fraction of all the crimes committed each year (Langan and Levin, 2002, 5–6; Rosenfeld et al., 2005 91–92). The overall impact of released prisoners on the crime rate is "nontrivial but small," according to Rosenfeld et al. (2005: 88).

Experts on crime and punishment often use the metaphor of a broken thermostat to explain the stubbornly persistent view among members of the general public that crime rates are out of control and rising, despite ample evidence that they have been falling for years. All the research and public attention on the purportedly high recidivism rates of released offenders does nothing to fix this broken thermometer. Spectacular crimes committed by released offenders that lead the nightly news further distort public understandings of the degree to which released offenders drive the crime rate. Instead of clarifying this relationship, public officials often fuel these misunderstandings (Gottschalk, 2015: 105–06).

The capacity of prison-based and reentry programs to significantly reduce recidivism rates remains a central research concern despite consistent evidence-based research findings that the best programs tend to have only a modest effect on recidivism rates. Even for the best programs, recidivism rate reductions tend to be in the 10–15 percent range and often are evident in only certain demographic groups. Program effects of this size might reduce a re-arrest rate from 60 percent to 50 percent (Western, 2007: 353). In short, the leading research to date has consistently shown that desistance "does not come in the shape of a 'prison program'" (Maruna and Toch, 2005: 171).

Designating a reduction in recidivism rates as the primary point of attack against mass incarceration flies in the face of what Clear and Austin call the "iron law" of prison populations (Clear and Austin, 2009). Simply put, the number of people in prison depends primarily on how many people are sent to prison and how long they stay there. Prison programs are incidental.

The fixation on the recidivism rates of individual offenders as the main evidence-based gauge of the correctional system is problematic for other reasons. It ignores the fact that larger political, social, and economic forces – not penal policies alone – drive recidivism and crime rates. Just as students' scores on standardized achievement tests are not just a factor of school and teacher performance, recidivism rates are not merely a consequence of penal policies and prison and reentry programming. Large numbers of returning parolees tend to be associated with increases in a neighborhood's crime rate. But research on how neighborhood and community characteristics affect recidivism rates has been scant.[3]

The single-minded focus on recidivism has diverted the research and public gaze away from other important yardsticks by which to gauge the performance of the criminal justice system. For example, research support for studying the quality of life for offenders while they are in prison and once they are released is scant compared to support for analyzing whether certain programs reduce recidivism or not. Virtually no public attention has been paid to disquieting research findings that the mortality rates for released prisoners are dramatically higher than for the general population, even after adjusting for factors like age, gender, and socioeconomic background (Rosen et al., 2008; Pratt et al., 2010; Spaulding et al., 2011; Binswanger et al., 2007). In the first two years following release, the adjusted rate of death for former prisoners was 3.5 times higher than the rate for the general population (Binswanger et al., 2007). The risk of death in the first two weeks after release is astronomical – nearly 13 times higher than the adjusted mortality rate for the general population (Binswanger et al., 2007). Even many years after release, moderately higher rates of mortality persist for people who have served time (Spaulding et al., 2011; Patterson, 2013, 526).

Racial disparities and evidence-based research

In addition to recidivism, racial disparities in punishment have been another central focus of research on mass incarceration. Many criminologists and other experts on crime and punishment recoil from drawing parallels between the causes and consequences of mass incarceration and "the new Jim Crow," a term popularized by Michelle Alexander (2010). Nonetheless, many of them have been preoccupied with assessing the racial disparities of the criminal justice system. For example, analyzing racial disparities has become something of a cottage industry for the U.S.

Sentencing Commission. These efforts have made some important contributions to our understanding of mass incarceration (see Gottschalk,
2015, 123–30). But the preoccupation in criminology and other disciplines with measuring racial disparities has come at an increasingly
higher cost. It has impeded our understanding of some key developments in American politics and public policy not only with respect to
mass incarceration, but also other leading social, political, and economic
problems.

Much of the research on racial disparities in incarceration has fallen
into what Adolph Reed and Merlin Chowkwanyun characterize as the
trap of "interpretive pathologies" (Reed and Chowkwanyun, 2011: 150).
Researchers have devised ever more sophisticated statistical models to measure the extent of black–white disparities in criminal justice and other realms
like education, employment, health care, and income. But the deep and complex sources of those disparities and how to alleviate them often go largely
unexamined beyond broad-brushed assertions of "institutional racism,"
deep-seated white racial animus toward blacks, or the "long and unbro-
ken arc of American racism" (Reed and Chowkwanyun, 2011: 150). Also
left largely unexamined is "the extent to which particular inequalities that
appear statistically as 'racial' disparities" may in fact be embedded in other
political, social, and economic social relations (Reed and Chowkwanyun,
2011: 151). Furthermore, much of this work focuses nearly exclusively on
disparities between whites and blacks, largely ignoring other racial and ethnic groups, including Latinos. It also downplays socioeconomic disparities
in incarceration and other punishments.

Methodological rabbit hole

Shortly before his death, David Baldus summed up in 2010 the findings of
decades of research on racial disparities and punishment. He concluded that
Gary Kleck's analysis, based on a comprehensive review of published data
on racial bias in criminal sentencing and of execution rates by race from the
1930s to the 1970s, still largely held up for the post-1980 period as well.
Quoting Kleck, Baldus concluded that, leaving aside the early capital rape
cases in the South, there was no convincing evidence of "general or widespread overt discrimination against black defendants, although there is evidence of [such] discrimination for a minority of specific jurisdictions, judges,
crime types, etc" (Kleck, 1981: 799, quoted in Baldus 2010: 3). Baldus then
posed an often overlooked puzzle: why, despite substantial evidence of persistent anti-black prejudice in the white population generally and among
those involved in the criminal justice system, is there little evidence of statewide sentencing disparities for black defendants?

Baldus suggested that statewide studies of racial disparities in sentencing
might be misleading because they may be failing to account for differences

in the policies and practices of local jurisdictions, most notably at the county level. "[A]nti-black discrimination or other race effects in some counties may be neutralized by pro-black or no discrimination in other counties," thus cancelling out the statewide effects, according to Baldus (Baldus, 2010: 10).

Findings like these should spur greater interest in examining the specific institutional, political, social, and economic factors at the local, state, and national levels – of which racial animus is but one – to better understand both what fuels variations in punitiveness and what are the best political and public policy solutions to reduce the incarceration rate. But much of the research on racial disparities has gone in a different direction, down a methodological rabbit hole. The focus continues to be on devising ever more complex models to capture the omitted variables and the confounding variables so as to measure ever more precisely what accounts for racial disparities in punishment.[4] This parallels the seemingly unending search for ever more sophisticated statistical models to quantitatively identify and measure what caused the exponential growth in the U.S. incarceration rate and to settle the question of what impact the escalation in the incarceration rate has had on the crime rate. As a consequence, "the emphasis on disparity has taken away from direct research on the policies themselves" and from how to reverse the prison boom (Forst and Bushway, 2010: 23). This "excessive focus" in detecting unwarranted disparities has come at the cost of examining fundamental questions about how and why certain laws, policies, and sentencing regimes brought about harsher penalties across the board – regardless of race or ethnicity (Engen, 2009: 332–33).

In light of the persistent and deeply troubling racial and ethnic disproportionality of the U.S. inmate population, identifying and addressing the sources of these disparities in punishment should continue to be a main focus of research. In particular, we need greater attention to how "indirect race effects may be embedded" in "seemingly legitimate race-neutral" factors in processing (such as pre-trial detention and the quality of defense counsel) and sentencing (such as a defendant's prior criminal record, and employment status) (Frase, 2001). We also need a better understanding of how race interacts with other factors like socioeconomic status and geography (especially rural versus urban) in determining who receives what punishments. But too much of the research attention and resources have been shoehorned for too long into a relatively narrow set of questions, many of them premised on some aspect of more precisely measuring racial disparities in punishment.

The focus on developing ever more sophisticated models and experiments to measure racial disparities and racial prejudice in the operation of the criminal justice system diverts intellectual energy and resources from other critical issues. It has also helped to perpetuate the mistaken view that the problem of mass incarceration is a problem confined primarily to African-Americans and members of other minority groups, and that the emergence of colorblind racism is the main source of the problem. According to this view, mass incarceration is only a problem for whites and the larger society to the extent that they must bear the increasingly heavy economic costs of sustaining such an expansive and expensive penal system – and they might not be getting their money's worth in terms of enhancing public safety. But even if every African-American were released from U.S. prisons and jails today, the United States would still have a mass incarceration crisis. The incarceration rate for whites in the United States is about 400 per 100,000. This is about two to two and a half times the total incarceration rates of the most punitive countries in Western Europe and about five to six times the rate of the least punitive ones (Gottschalk, 2015: 5).

New research frontiers on mass incarceration and the carceral state

There certainly is a need for ongoing research on recidivism and racial disparities in punishment. But this work, if it continues along the same path, will not contribute much to understanding how to reverse the prison boom and dismantle the punitive scaffolding that extends far beyond the prison gate. Some of the most promising new research on mass incarceration takes a more expansive and nuanced view of the problem and of possible solutions. It also takes a more holistic view of what counts as evidence-based research.

Historical scholarship on national debates over race, crime, and punishment suggests that deeper institutional, ideological, and historical developments that predate the prison boom by decades set the stage for the takeoff of punitive law-and-order politics in the 1960s and the rise of the carceral state (Murakawa, 2014; Muhammad, 2010; Gottschalk, 2006). State-level case studies on the deeper causes and consequences of mass incarceration (Lynch, 2010; Chase, 2009; Schoenfeld, 2009; Perkinson, 2010; Campbell, 2011a, 2011b; Barker, 2009; Page, 2011; Miller, 2008) bolster such claims. Mass incarceration is a national phenomenon that has left no state untouched. All 50 states have seen their incarceration rates explode since the 1970s. But the state-level variation in incarceration rates is still enormous, far greater than what exists across the countries of Western Europe. This great variation and the fact that crime control in the United States is primarily a local and state function, not a federal one, suggest that local, state, and perhaps regional factors might be critical in explaining why some states have been more punitive than others.

The Great Recession has raised expectations that the United States will begin to empty its jails and prisons because it can no longer afford to be the world's warden.[5] The new state-level studies are a sober reminder that gaping budget deficits will not necessarily reverse the prison boom because a penal system is not only deeply embedded in a state's budget but also in its political, cultural, institutional, and social fabric. Fine-grained state-level case studies can help illuminate why some states may be better able than others to reduce their prison populations in the future.

Emergence of the carceral state

The wider political, economic, and social consequences of mass incarceration are another important and growing area of scholarly and public interest. Evidence suggests that having such a large penal system embedded in a democratic polity has enormous repercussions that reverberate throughout the political system and beyond. Mass incarceration bears down on many central issues in contemporary American politics, everything from broad questions about how we conceptualize the American state to more specific ones concerning voting rights, voter participation, public opinion, and changing conceptions of citizenship.

Fifteen years ago, a small group of scholars and activists began embracing the term mass incarceration to refer to the unprecedented explosion in the size of the U.S. jail and prison population since the mid-1970s. At the time, it was an obscure concept. Today, high school and college students across the country are taking courses on mass incarceration. Numerous church and community groups have been reading Michelle Alexander's *The New Jim Crow: Mass Incarceration in the Age of Colorblindness* (2010). Public figures spanning the political spectrum from Grover Norquist to Eric Holder to Rachel Maddow now identify mass incarceration as a leading public issue. So does *Sesame Street*. In 2013, the popular children's show introduced the first Muppet who has an incarcerated parent.

The general public has been slowly waking up to the idea that the United States is the world's warden, incarcerating more people in absolute and proportional numbers than any other country. Meanwhile, some scholars and activists have started to popularize a new concept: the carceral state (Gottschalk, 2006, 2015; Beckett and Murakawa, 2012; Murakawa, 2014; Lerman and Weaver, 2014). Or what I like to call "the prison beyond the prison."

Embedded in an ostensibly democratic state, the carceral state operates an extensive and unprecedented system of surveillance and punishment through a set of institutions, including police departments, prosecutors' offices, corrections departments, and the courts, that are increasingly unaccountable to the wider polity. The carceral state metes out an enormous and growing array of penal and non-penal sanctions. It surveils and controls wide swaths of people, many of whom have never been charged or convicted of a crime. The brunt of the carceral state falls hardest on the most dispossessed groups, including the poor, people of color, the mentally ill, and immigrants. But in levying more punishments and controls on these groups, the carceral state has begun to deform the wider polity and society in significant ways.

The carceral state has become a key governing institution in the United States and a major source of political, social, and economic inequalities. It is no longer just a problem largely confined to the prison cell and prison yard and to poor urban communities and minority groups – if it ever was. The U.S. penal system has grown so extensive that it has begun to metastasize. It has altered how key governing and public institutions operate, everything from elections to schools to social programs like public housing and food stamps.

The political development of the carceral state challenges the common understanding of the U.S. state. The United States has developed an awesome power and an extensive apparatus to monitor, incarcerate, and execute its citizens that is unprecedented in modern U.S. history and among other Western countries. This development raises deeply troubling questions about the health of democratic institutions in the United States and the character of the liberal state. As Mary Bosworth notes, "Imprisonment is, by nature, an articulation of state power" (Bosworth, 2010: 22).

The emergence of the carceral state is also cause to rethink our understanding of the U.S. welfare state. Examined more closely, what we may be seeing is not so much the contraction of the welfare state as its absorption by the carceral state, which has become the primary regulator of the poor and a main conduit of social services for the poor and disadvantaged. Wacquant argues that it is untenable to analyze social and penal policy in isolation from one another because they are so enmeshed today and have been for a long time (Wacquant, 2009: 13). He and others (Beckett and Western, 2001) have documented how the carceral state has expanded at the expense of the welfare state. State regulation of the poor did not recede in the United States in the 1990s. It merely shifted course. The government significantly increased its role in regulating the lives of poor, uneducated men and women by sweeping more and more of them up into the criminal justice system's growing dragnet. By a number of measures – expenditures, personnel, congressional hearings, and legislation – the law enforcement apparatus has been growing while social welfare provision has been contracting.

The enormous political consequences of mass incarceration are a blossoming area of scholarly interest. Felon disenfranchisement raises fundamental questions about how we define (and redefine) citizenship (Manza and Uggen, 2006; Uggen, Manza, and Thompson, 2006; Hull, 2006; Pettus, 2005; Ewald, 2002; Brown-Dean, 2004). It also may be a decisive factor in some close elections (Manza and Uggen, 2006: 192–96; Burch, 2012).

The impact of the carceral state on political participation extends far beyond official barriers to voting like felon disenfranchisement statutes. New research suggests that incarceration and other kinds of contact with the criminal justice system have a ripple effect on political and civic participation. A criminal conviction may be a more significant factor in depressing voter turnout among offenders and ex-offenders than formal legal barriers to voting (Burch, 2013; Hjalmarsson and Lopez, 2010). Contact with the criminal justice system, including everything from being stopped by the police to serving time in prison, appears to have a cumulatively negative effect not just on voter registration and turnout, but also on involvement in civic groups, trust in the government, and belief in the legitimacy of the criminal justice systems and other government institutions (Lerman and Weaver, 2014; Peffley and Hurwitz, 2010: 189; Bobo and Thompson, 2006; Burch 2013). Goffman's (2014) ethnographic study of "life on the run" in a poor neighborhood in Philadelphia is a chilling account of how the expansive systems of policing and supervision that have accompanied the rise of the carceral state have fostered a pernicious climate of fear and suspicion that penetrates all aspects of daily life, including intimate and family relations, labor force participation, and access to medical care.

Mass incarceration raises other troubling and largely unexplored issues about political participation and citizenship. Fixated on the staggering increase in the number of people behind bars, analysts have paid less attention to the political and social implications of the stunning escalation in the number of people consigned to legal and civil purgatory who are not fully in prison or fully a part of society. These include the estimated 5 million people who are on probation or parole or under some form of community supervision (Glaze et al., 2010), the millions of people who are subjected to "civil death" due to a criminal conviction, and the numerous people subjected to other restrictions, such as banishment orders (Beckett and Herbert, 2010).

The relationship between the rise of the carceral state and the criminalization of immigration enforcement is another important area of emerging scholarly and public interest (Bosworth and Kaufman, 2011; Aas and Bosworth, 2013; Gottschalk, 2015, ch. 10). In a remarkable development, Latinos now represent the largest ethnic group in the federal prison system. This is a consequence of the dramatic rise in immigration raids and prosecutions for immigration violations, and the drop in federal prosecutions of other crimes (Gorman, 2009). The criminalization of immigration policy is just one example of how the "technologies, discourses, and metaphors of crime and criminal justice" have been migrating to all kinds of institutions and public policies that seem far afield from crime fighting (Simon, 2007: 4).

Evidence is mounting that the carceral state fundamentally impedes not only the political advancement of the most disadvantaged people in the United States, but also their economic advancement. As Bruce Western soberly concludes in his careful analysis of wage, employment, education, and other socioeconomic data, mass imprisonment has erased many of the "gains to African-American citizenship hard won by the civil rights movement" (Western, 2006: 191). The criminal justice system is increasingly serving as a gateway to a much larger system of stigmatization and permanent marginalization (Alexander, 2010: 12). In short, the country's penal system is no longer just the creation of the larger political, social, and economic forces that shape U.S. society. It has become "one of those causal or shaping forces" (Haney, 2008: 90).

The enormous growth in political, social, and economic inequality in the United States due to the carceral state and other factors has remained invisible or understated because people who have been captured by the state in prison and jail are not captured in standard social surveys. Years ago when the incarceration rate was much lower, excluding prisoners and ex-felons from the U.S. Census, the Current Population Survey, and other major social surveys that track the health and welfare of American society did not have such major consequences. But with the tremendous growth in the size of the prison population since the 1970s, the failure to accurately and fully incorporate felons and ex-felons into key indicators like trends in unemployment, wage inequality, high school completion, voter turnout, mortality, and morbidity has enormous implications and is seismic. This practice casts doubt on the validity of these major federal surveys and on the validity of social scientific research based on these surveys. By failing to account for the impact of mass incarceration, these surveys are helping to foster illusions of progress by African-Americans and other historically disadvantaged groups. Researchers who do incorporate the incarcerated population into their analyses of trends in major indicators of inequality paint a picture of widening inequalities. Their findings are strikingly at odds with conventional narratives that stress a narrowing of the black–white gap in critical areas like wages, employment, education, political participation, and health indicators (Western and Beckett, 1999: 1052; Western, 2006: 87–90; Pettit, 2012; Ewert et al., 2014; Manza and Uggen, 2006: 176–77; Sykes et al., 2014: 5).

Mass imprisonment within a democratic polity and the hyper-incarceration of certain groups are unprecedented developments. The consolidation of this new model in the United States has spurred interest in comparative work on crime control and penal policy. Scholars have been identifying distinctive cultural, historical, constitutional, institutional, and political factors that may render some countries more susceptible to get-tough policies (Whitman, 2003; Zimring, 2003; Zimring et al., 2001; Garland, 2001; Lacey, 2008; Cavadino and Dignan, 2006; Downes, 2007; Garland, 2010; Tonry, 2007; De Giorgi, 2006; Tonry and Bijleveld, 2007; Gottschalk, 2006, 2015). Single-country case studies comprise some of the best evidence-based research in this area.

Research that situates the U.S. carceral state in a comparative framework suggests that fundamental differences in how the polity and economy are organized explain vast differences in penal policy among industrialized countries. Nicola Lacey and others argue that countries with neoliberal, first-past-the-post electoral systems (notably the United States and Britain) create a reinforcing political and economic environment that fosters more punitive and exclusionary penal policies. Countries that have coordinated market economics and more consensual electoral systems with proportional representation (such as Germany) tend to be less punitive for they are more conducive to inclusionary and welfarist policies (Lacey, 2008; 2010: 203–239; Cavadino and Dignan, 2006; De Giorgi, 2006).

Thanks to comparative and U.S.-focused work on the political economy of penal policy, we are beginning to acquire a better understanding of the relationship between economic factors and penal policy (Sutton, 2004; Gilmore, 2007; Lacey, 2008; Gottschalk, 2015). In particular, a much more sophisticated understanding is emerging of who benefits economically and who doesn't from the carceral state. This work challenges the narrowly economistic view, popular for a long time among many anti-prison activists, that attributes the origins of mass incarceration primarily to the private interests that profit from building prisons, running prisons, and exploiting prison labor.

Interest in the political factors and public policy choices that have propelled other countries or individual jurisdictions to drastically cut their incarceration rates or otherwise pursue less punitive policies is growing (Gartner et al., 2011; Webster and Doob, 2014; Brodeur, 2007: 49–51; Lappi-Seppälä, 2007: 234; Graham, 1990; Roberts and Gabor, 2004). The experience of other industrialized countries may shed some light on how to dampen the enthusiasm in the United States for putting so many of its people under lock and key and the watchful eye of the government. An underlying theme of much of the work on comparative penal policy is that stable incarceration rates and penal policies cannot be taken for granted (Brodeur, 2007: 84; Webster and Doob, 2007; Johnson, 2007).

Differences in country-specific institutional, socioeconomic, and cultural factors dominate explanations for variations in punitiveness. But transnational factors are not incidental (Downes, 2007, 118). Some contend that mounting transnational pressures stemming from migration, neoliberalism, economic and political integration, and the "war on terror" are likely to exert significant upward pressure on the incarceration rates of other developed countries (De Giorgi, 2006; Wacquant, 2009; McLennan, 2001: 416; Strange, 2006; Bosworth, 2010). Others suggest that domestic institutions and conditions and the accelerated political and economic integration of Europe) may moderate these pressures (Snacken, 2007; Newburn, 2007; Lacey, 2008: 167; Padfield, 2004).

Conclusion

Stung by the hyperpoliticization of penal policy since the 1970s and the denigration of scientific evidence during the George W. Bush administration, many criminologists, policymakers, and penal reform advocates have sought refuge in the illusionary promise that a focus on a narrow, quantifiable goal like recidivism provides an escape from politics (Loader and Sparks, 2011,

127–44). They have sought refuge in producing state-of-the-art, ostensibly apolitical, evidence-based research centered largely on how to help government agencies or other groups reduce crime. Treating the mass incarceration problem in a narrowly instrumental way as a crime problem "appears to forget that in a liberal democracy it matters not only that crime is prevented and detected, but also *how* that happens," explain Ian Loader and Richard Sparks (2011, 107, original emphasis).

A research agenda based on a narrow understanding of what counts as evidence-based research will inevitably yield too timid an agenda to tackle the problem of the carceral state. So will a preoccupation with "what works." "What works" has a poor track record when it comes to engineering important shifts not just in penal policy, but all kinds of public policy (Tonry and Green, 2003; Hood, 2002: 153–7). In fact, a major public policy research puzzle is why good scientific often loses out in the contest against bad public policy. Just look at the policy history of the enactment of the country's toughest three-strikes law in California in 1993–94. Legislators and the public enthusiastically backed that measure despite solid evidence-based research at the time that the law would spark an expensive explosion in the state's prison population without greatly reducing the crime rate (Zimring et al., 2001).

Mass incarceration and the carceral state must be understood within the larger political, economic, and institutional context in which they are deeply embedded. It is critical to examine not just the actions and preferences of critical political actors and policymakers with respect to penal policy but also the objectives these actors pursue simultaneously in other key realms of politics and economics. It also is important to situate the problem of the carceral state within the main political and economic currents that shape American politics and the U.S. political economy today. Using such a broader lens brings penal policy better into focus. It reveals the competing and contradictory views and impulses of key political actors and policymakers that stand in the way of dismantling the carceral state. It also reveals the enormous obstacles to forging a powerful political movement that fundamentally challenges the carceral state and other gaping political and economic inequalities in the United States today.

Crime control strategies are profoundly political because they both reflect and direct the distribution of power in society (Scheingold, 1998: 857). Loader and Sparks rightfully beseech criminologists to recognize that all aspects of crime and punishment are inherently political for they lie at the "heart of matters of state, authority, and sovereignty" and are central to how we think about what constitutes a good and fair society (Loader and Sparks, 2011: 60, 108). Even the choice to pursue narrow models of evidence-based research is not entirety apolitical.

The fixation on technocratic, expert-driven solutions to the problem of the carceral state denies the fundamental role that politics, emotion, and culture play in meting out punishment, defining good and bad penal policy, and shaping the research agenda. It implies that the United States stumbled down the path to mass incarceration because of the lack of good evidence-based research at the time or because the politicians and the policymakers largely ignored the experts on crime and punishment. This unjustifiably absolves the scholarly community of some responsibility for the emergence of the carceral state.

To help reverse the prison boom, we do not just need better evidence-based research or a more encompassing understanding of what counts as evidence. We also need a reckoning with why research on criminal justice in the United States has been so vulnerable to political pressures. We need to better understand why experts on criminal justice in the United States, especially criminologists, are so much more dependent on policy-making institutions and political agencies for their funding and legitimacy compared to many of their counterparts elsewhere. As Joachim Savelsberg (1994) and others have noted, research findings based on funding provided by the state are more likely to reflect the concerns of the state (Savelsberg et al., 2002).

Notes

1 For a quick summary of research in this area, see Austin et al., 2007, 13–14.
2 A follow-up Bureau of Justice Statistics Study released in 2014 reported three-year recidivism rates that were comparable to the pioneering 2002 BJS study (Durose et al., 2014, 15, table 16).
3 For some exceptions, see Hipp and Yates, 2009, 619–54; Kubrin and Stewart, 2006, 165–97; Mears et al., 2008, 301–40; Peterson and Krivo, 2010.
4 See, for example, Mitchell, 2005.
5 For a skeptical view of whether the economic crisis marks the beginning of the end of mass incarceration, see Gottschalk, 2015, ch. 2.

References

Aas, Katja Franko and Bosworth, Mary, eds. 2013. *The Borders of Punishment: Migration, Citizenship, and Social Exclusion.* Oxford: Oxford University Press.

Alexander, Michelle. 2010. *The New Jim Crow: Mass Incarceration in the Age of Colorblindness.* New York: The New Press.

Austin, James et al. 2007. *Unlocking America: Why and How to Reduce America's Prison Population.* Washington, DC: JFA Institute.

Baldus, David C. 2010. "Racial Discrimination in Capital and Non-Capital Sentencing with Special Reference to the Evidence in Murder and Rape Prosecutions." Paper presented at Symposium on Crime and Justice: The Past and Future of Empirical Sentencing Research, S.U.N.Y. at Albany School of Criminal Justice September.

Barker, Vanessa. 2009. *The Politics of Imprisonment: How the Democratic Process Shapes the Way America Punishes Offenders.* New York: Oxford University Press.

Beckett, Katherine and Western, Bruce. 2001. "Governing Social Marginality: Welfare, Incarceration, and the Transformation of State Policy." *Punishment and Society*, 3(1): 43–59.

Beckett, Katherine and Herbert, Steve. 2010. *Banished: The New Social Control in Urban America*. New York: Oxford University Press.

Beckett, Katherine, and Murakawa, Naomi. 2012. "Mapping the Shadow Carceral State: Toward an Institutionally Capacious Approach to Punishment." *Theoretical Criminology*, 16(2): 221–44.

Binswanger, Ingrid A. et al. 2007. "Release from Prison – A High Risk of Death for Former Inmates." *The New England Journal of Medicine*, 356(5): 157–65.

Blumstein, Alfred. 2009. "What Role Should ASC Take in Policy Advocacy? *The Criminologist*, 34(3): 1, 3–4.

Bobo, Lawrence D. and Thompson, Victor. 2006. "Unfair by Design: The War on Drugs, Race, and the Legitimacy of the Criminal Justice System." *Social Research*, 73(2): 445–472.

Bosworth, Mary. 2010. *Explaining U.S. Imprisonment*. Thousand Oaks, CA: Sage.

Bosworth, Mary and Kaufman, Emma. 2011. "Foreigners in a Carceral Age: Immigration and Imprisonment in the United States," *Stanford Law and Policy Review*, 22(2): 429–54.

Brodeur, Jean-Paul. 2007. "Comparative Penology in Perspective." In Michael Tonry, ed. *Crime, Punishment, and Politics in Comparative Politics – Crime and Justice: A Review of Research 36*. Chicago: University of Chicago Press, 49–51.

Brown-Dean, Khalilah L. 2004. "One Lens, Multiple Views: Felon Disenfranchisement Laws and American Political Inequality." Ph.D. dissertation. Ohio State University.

Burch, Traci R. 2012. "Did Disenfranchisement Laws Help Elect President Bush? New Evidence on the Turnout Rates and Candidate Preferences of Florida's Ex-Felons." *Political Behavior*, 34(1): 1–26.

Burch, Traci R. 2013. *Trading Democracy for Justice: Criminal Convictions and the Decline of Neighborhood Political Participation*. Chicago: The University of Chicago Press.

Campbell, Michael C. 2011a. "Ornery Alligators and Soap on a Rope: Texas Prosecutors and Punishment Reform in the Lone Star State." *Theoretical Criminology*, 16(3): 1–23.

Campbell, Michael C. 2011b. "Politics, Prisons, and Law Enforcement: An Examination of 'Law and Order' Politics in Texas," *Law and Society Review*, 45(3): 177–99.

Cavadino, Michael and Dignan, James. 2006. *Penal Systems: A Comparative Approach.*, 4th ed. London: Sage.

Chase, Robert. 2009. Civil Rights on the Cell Block: Race, Reform, and Violence in Texas Prisons and the Nation, 1945–1990. University of Maryland at College Park, Ph.D. diss.

Civic Impulse. 2015. H.R. 1593 – 110th Congress: Second Chance Act of 2007. Retrieved from www.govtrack.us/congress/bills/110/hr1593 (retrieved March 10, 2015).

Clear, Todd R. 2010. "Policy and Evidence: The Challenge to the American Society of Criminology." *Criminology*, 48(1): 1–26.

Clear, Todd and Austin, James. 2009. "Reducing Mass Incarceration: Implications of the Iron Law of Prison Populations," *Harvard Law and Policy Review*, 3(2): 307–24.

De Giorgi, Alessandro. 2006. *Re-thinking the political economy of punishment: Perspectives on post-Fordism and penal politics.* Aldershot, England: Ashgate.

Downes, David. 2007. "Visions of Penal Control in the Netherlands." In *Crime, punishment, and politics in comparative politics – Crime and justice: A review of research* 36, ed. Michael Tonry: 93–125. Chicago: University of Chicago Press.

Durose, Matthew R., Cooper, Alexia D., and Snyder, Howard N. 2014. "Recidivism of Prisoners Released in 30 States in 2005: Patterns from 2005 to 2010," *Bureau of Justice Statistics Special Report.*

Engen, Rodney L. 2009. "Assessing Determinate and Presumptive Sentencing – Making Research Relevant," *Criminology and Public Policy*, 8(2): 332–33.

Ewald, Alec C. 2002. "'Civil Death': The Ideological Paradox of Criminal Disenfranchisement Law in the United States." *Wisconsin Law Review*, 2002(5): 1045–138.

Ewert, Stephanie, Sykes, Bryan L., and Pettit, Becky. 2014. "The Degree of Disadvantage: Incarceration and Inequality in Education," *The ANNALS of the American Academy of Political and Social Science*, 651: 24–43.

Forst, Brian, and Bushway, Shawn. 2010. "Discretion, Rule of Law, and Rationality," Symposium on Crime and Justice: The Past and Future of Empirical Sentencing Research, S.U.N.Y. at Albany School of Criminal Justice.

Frase, Richard S. 2001. Comparative Perspectives on Sentencing and Research. In *Sentencing and Sanctions in Western Countries*, ed. Michael Tonry and Richard S. Frase: 259–92. Oxford, UK: Oxford University Press.

Garland, David. 2001. *The Culture of Control: Crime and Social Order in Contemporary Society.* Chicago: University of Chicago Press.

Garland, David. 2010. *Peculiar Institution: America's Death Penalty in an Age of Abolition.* Cambridge: Belknap Press of Harvard University Press.

Gartner, Rosemary, Doob, Anthony N., and Zimring, Franklin E. 2011. "The Past as Prologue? Decarceration in California Then and Now. *Criminology and Public Policy*, 10(2): 291–325.

Gilmore, Ruth W. 2007. *The Golden Gulag: Prisons, Surplus, Crisis, and Opposition in Globalizing California.* Berkeley: University of California Press.

Glaze, Lauren E., Bonczar, Thomas P., and Zhang, Fan. 2010. "Probation and Parole in the United States, 2009." *Bureau of Justice Statistics Bulletin.*

Goffman, Alice. 2014. *On the Run: Fugitive Life in an American City.* Chicago: University of Chicago Press.

Gorman, Anna. 2009. "Latinos Make Up a Growing Bloc of Federal Offenders." *Los Angeles Times*. February 19, A10.

Gottschalk, Marie. 2006. *The Prison and the Gallows: The Politics of Mass Incarceration in America.* Cambridge: Cambridge University Press.

Gottschalk, Marie. 2015. *Caught: The Prison State and the Lockdown of American Politics.* Princeton: Princeton University Press.

Graham, John. 1990. "Decarceration in the federal republic of Germany: How practitioners are succeeding where policy-makers failed." *British Journal of Criminology*, 30(3): 150–70.

Haney, Craig. 2008. "Counting Casualties in the War on Prisoners," *University of San Francisco Law Review*, 43(1): 90.

Hannah-Moffat, Kelly. 2010. "Actuarial Sentencing: An 'Unsettled" Proposition," paper presented at Symposium on Crime and Justice: The Past and Future of Empirical Sentencing Research, S.U.N.Y. at Albany School of Criminal Justice.

Hipp, John R., and Yates, Daniel K. 2009. "Do Returning Parolees Affect Neighborhood Crime? A Case Study of Sacramento," *Criminology*, 47(3): 619–54.

Hjalmarsson, Randi, and Lopez, Mark. 2010. "The Voting Behavior of Young Disenfranchised Felons: Would They Vote if They Could?," *American Law and Economics Review*, 12(2): 265–279.

Hood, Roger. 2002. "Criminology and penal policy: The vital role of empirical research," in Anthony Bottoms and Michael Tonry, eds., *Ideology, Crime and Criminal Justice: A Symposium in Honor of Sir Leon Radzinowicz*, Portland: Willan, 153–7.

Hull, Elizabeth A. 2006. *The Disenfranchisement of Ex-Felons*. Philadelphia: Temple University Press.

Johnson, David T. 2007. "Crime and Punishment in Contemporary Japan." In *Crime, Punishment, and Politics in Comparative Politics – Crime and Justice: A review of Research* 36, ed. Michael Tonry. Chicago: University of Chicago Press, 371–423.

Kleck, Gary. 1981. "Racial Discrimination in Sentencing: A Critical Evaluation of the Evidence with Additional Evidence on the Death Penalty," *American Sociological Review*, 46(6): 799.

Kubrin, Charis E. and Stewart, Eric A. 2006. "Predicting Who Reoffends: The Neglected Role of Neighborhood Context in Recidivism Studies," *Criminology*, 44(1): 165–97.

Lacey, Nicola. 2008. *The Prisoners' Dilemma: Political Economy and Punishment in Contemporary Democracies*. Cambridge, UK: Cambridge University Press.

Lacey, Nicola. 2012. "Political Systems and Criminal Justice: The Prisoners' Dilemma After the Coalition," *Current Legal Problems*, 65(1): 203–239.

Langan, Patrick A. and Levin David J., 2002 "Recidivism of Prisoners Released in 1994," *Bureau of Justice Statistics Special Report*, June.

Lappi-Seppälä, Tapio. 2007. "Penal Policy in Scandinavia." In *Crime, Punishment, and Politics in Comparative Politics – Crime and Justice: A Review of Research* 36, ed. Michael Tonry. Chicago: University of Chicago Press, 217–95.

Lerman, Amy E., and Weaver, Vesla M. 2014. *Arresting Citizenship: The Democratic Consequences of American Crime Control*. Chicago: University of Chicago Press.

Loader, Ian and Sparks, Richard. 2011. *Public Criminology?* London and New York: Routledge.

Lynch, Mona. 2010. *Sunbelt Justice: Arizona and the Transformation of American Punishment*. Stanford: Stanford University Press.

Maltz, Michael. 2001. *Recidivism*. Orlando: Academic Press.

Manza, Jeff and Christopher Uggen C. 2006. *Locked Out: Felon Disenfranchisement and American Democracy*. New York: Oxford University Press.

Maruna, Shadd and Toch, Hans. 2005. "The Impact of Imprisonment on the Desistance Process," in Jeremy Travis and Christy Visher, eds., *Prisoner Reentry and Crime in America*. New York: Cambridge University Press, 139–78.

McLennan, Rebecca. 2001. "The New Penal state: Globalization, History, and American Criminal Justice, c. 2000." *Inter-Asia Cultural Studies*, 2: 407–19.

Mears, Daniel P. et al. 2008. "Social Ecology and Recidivism: Implications for Prisoner Reentry," *Criminology*, 46(2): 301–40.

Miller, Lisa L. 2008. *The Perils of Federalism: Race, Poverty and the Politics of Crime Control*. New York: Oxford University Press.

Mitchell, Ojmarrh. 2005. "A Meta-analysis of Race and Sentencing Research: Explaining the Inconsistencies," *Journal of Quantitative Criminology*, 21(4): 439–66.

Muhammad, Khalil Gibran. 2010. *The Condemnation of Blackness: Race, Crime, and the Making of Modern America*. Cambridge: Harvard University Press.

Murakawa, Naomi. 2014. *The First Civil Right: Racial Proceduralism and the Construction of Carceral America*. New York: Oxford University Press.

Newburn, Tim. 2007. "Tough on Crime": Penal Policy in England and Wales. In *Crime, Punishment, and Politics in Comparative Politics – Crime and Justice: A Review of Research* 36, ed. Michael Tonry, Chicago: University of Chicago Press, 425–70.

Padfield, Nicola. 2004. "Harmonising of Sentencing: Will it Encourage a Principled Approach?" In *Crime and Crime Control in an Integrated Europe*, ed. Kauko Aromaa and Sami Nevala. Helsinki: Heuni.

Page, Joshua. 2011. *The Toughest Beat: Politics, Punishment, and the Prison Officers Union in California*. New York: Oxford University Press.

Patterson, Evelyn J. 2013. "The Dose-Response of Time Served in Prison on Mortality: New York State, 1989–2003," *American Journal of Public Health*, 103(3): 523–28.

Peffley, Mark, and Hurwitz, Jon. 2010. *Justice in America: The Separate Realities of Blacks and Whites*. New York: Cambridge University Press, 189.

Perkinson, Robert. 2010. *Texas Tough: The Rise of America's Prison Empire*. New York: Metropolitan Books.

Peterson, Ruth D. and Krivo, Lauren J. 2010. *Divergent Social Worlds: Neighborhood Crime and the Racial-Spatial Divide*. New York: Russell Sage Foundation.

Pettit, Becky. 2012. *Invisible Men: Mass Incarceration and the Myth of Black Progress*. New York: Russell Sage Foundation.

Pettus, Katherine I. 2005. *Felony Disenfranchisement in America: Historical Origins, Institutional Racism, and Modern Consequences*. New York: LFB Scholarly Publishing.

Pratt, Daniel et al. 2010. "Suicide in Recently Released Prisoners: A Case-Control Study," *Psychological Medicine*, 40(5): 827–35.

Reed, Adolph, Jr., and Chowkwanyun, Merlin. 2011. "Race, Class, Crisis: The Discourse of Racial Disparity and Its Analytical Discontents," in Leo Panitch, Gregory Albo, and Vivek Chibber, eds., *Socialist Register 2012: The Crisis and the Left*. New York: Monthly Review Press. 150.

Roberts, Julian V., and Gabor, Thomas. 2004. "Living in the Shadow of the prison: Lessons from the Canadian Experience in Decarceration. *British Journal of Criminology*, 44: 92–112.

Rosen, David L., Schoenbach, Victor J., and Wohl, David A. 2008. "All-Cause and Cause-Specific Mortality Among Men Released from State Prison, 1980–2005," *American Journal of Public Health*, 98(12): 2278–84.

Rosenfeld, Richard, Wallman, Joel, and Fornango. Robert. 2005. "The Contribution of Ex-Prisoners to Crime Rates," in Jeremy Travis and Christy Visher, eds. *Prisoner Reentry and Crime in America*. New York: Cambridge University Press: 80–104.

Sampson, Robert, and Lauritsen, Janet. 1997. "Racial and Ethnic Disparities in Crime and Criminal Justice in the United States," in Michael Tonry, ed., *Ethnicity,*

Crime, and Immigration: Comparative and Cross-National Perspectives, Chicago: University of Chicago Press, 311–74.

Savelsberg, Joachim J. 1994. "Knowledge, Domination, and Criminal Punishment." *American Journal of Sociology*, 99(4): 911–43.

Savelsberg, Joachim J., King, Ryan, and Cleveland, Lara. 2002. "Politicized Scholarship? Science on Crime and the State." *Social Problems*, 49(3): 327–48.

Scheingold, Stuart A. 1998. "Constructing the New Political Criminology: Power, Authority, and the Post-liberal State." *Law and Social Inquiry*, 23: 857–95.

Schoenfeld, Heather. 2009. "The Politics of Prison Growth: From Chain Gangs to Work Release Centers and Supermax Prisons, Florida, 1955–2000." Ph.D. dissertation, Northwestern University.

Simon, Jonathan. 2007. *Governing Through Crime: How the War on Crime Transformed American Democracy and Created a Culture of Fear*. New York: Oxford University Press.

Smith, Philip. 2008. *Punishment and Culture*. Chicago: University of Chicago Press.

Snacken, Sonja. 2007. "Penal Policy and Practice in Belgium." In *Crime, Punishment, and Politics in Comparative Politics – Crime and Justice: A Review of Research 36*, ed. Michael Tonry, Chicago: University of Chicago Press, 127–215.

Spaulding, Anne C. et al. 2011. "Prisoner Survival Inside and Outside the Institution: Implications for Health-Care Planning" *American Journal of Epidemiology*, 173(5): 479–87.

Strange, Carolyn. 2006. "Pain and death: Transnational perspectives." *Radical History Review*, 96: 137–150.

Sutton, John R. 2004. "The Political Economy of Imprisonment in Affluent Western Democracies, 1960–1990." *American Sociological Review*, 69(2): 170–189.

Sykes, Bryan et al. 2014. "Mass Incarceration and Racial Inequality in Political Participation: U.S. 1980–2012," mimeo.

Tonry, Michael, ed. 2007. *Crime, Punishment, and Politics in Comparative Politics – Crime and Justice: A Review of Research 36*. Chicago: University of Chicago Press.

Tonry, Michael and Green, David A. 2003. "Criminology and Public Policy," in Lucia Zedner and Andrew Ashworth, eds., *The Criminological Foundations of Penal Policy: Essays in Honour of Roger Hood*, Oxford: Oxford University Press, 485–525.

Tonry, Michael and Bijleveld, Catrien eds. 2007. *Crime and Justice in the Netherlands – Crime and Justice: A Review of Research 35*. Chicago: University of Chicago Press.

Travis, Jeremy, Western, Bruce, and Redburn, Steve, eds., 2014. *The Growth of Incarceration in the United States: Exploring Causes and Consequences*, Washington, DC: National Academies Press.

Uggen, Christopher, Jeff Manza, and Melissa Thompson. 2006. "Citizenship, Democracy, and the Civic Reintegration of Criminal Offenders." *The Annals of the American Academy of Political and Social Sciences*, 605: 281–310.

Wacquant, Loïc. 2009. *Punishing the poor: The Neoliberal Government of Social Insecurity*. Durham: Duke University Press.

Webster, Cheryl Marie and Doob, Anthony N. 2007. "Punitive Trends and Stable Imprisonment Rates in Canada." In *Crime, Punishment, and Politics in Comparative Politics – Crime and Justice: A Review of Research 36*, ed. Michael Tonry. Chicago: University of Chicago Press, 297–369.

Webster, Cheryl Marie and Doob, Anthony N. 2014. "Penal Reform 'Canadian style': Fiscal Responsibility and Decarceration in Alberta, Canada." *Punishment and Society*, 16(1): 3–31.

Western, Bruce. 2006. *Punishment and Inequality in America*. New York: Russell Sage Foundation.

Western, Bruce. 2007. "The Penal System and the Labor Market," in Shawn D. Bushway, Michael A. Stoll, and David F. Weiman, eds. *Barriers to Reentry? The Labor Market for Released Prisoners in Post-Industrial America*. New York: Russell Sage Foundation: 335–60.

Western, Bruce, and Beckett, Katherine. 1999. "How Unregulated is the U.S. Labor Market? The Penal System as a Labor Market Institution," *American Journal of Sociology*, 104: 1052.

Whitman, James Q. 2003. *Harsh Justice: Criminal Punishment and the Widening Divide between America and Europe*. Oxford: Oxford University Press.

Zimring, Franklin. 2003. *The Contradictions of American Capital Punishment*. New York: Oxford University Press.

Zimring, Franklin, Hawkins, Gordon and Kamin, Sam. 2001. *Punishment and Democracy: Three Strikes and You're out in California*. Oxford: Oxford University Press.

Chapter 30

The media and criminal justice policy and practices

Ray Surette and Kimberly Kampe

Introduction

"Crime – and the criminal justice system's response to crime – has long fascinated the public" (Roberts, 1992, p. 99). Whether they are related to punishments for offenders, the morality involved in levying sentences, the extent to which offenders are responsible for their behavior, or the determination of which behaviors are deserving of punishment, many of the publicly debated topics in our society are crime and justice issues. It is important to understand the details of current criminal justice policies, but it is also important to examine the influences that drive these policies. Among other influences, the media are a powerful source of policy effects (Hobbs and Hamerton, 2014; Silverman, 2012). Studies have found that the public's image of criminality is significantly shaped by media portrayals, which in turn makes media influence an important factor in how criminal behavior is defined and addressed (Gerbner et al., 1979; Graber, 1979; Surette and Otto, 2001). A significant interactive relationship between the criminal justice system, its policies, and the mass media has long been acknowledged (Surette, 2015). In modern society, the media are omnipresent and are clearly "not neutral, unobtrusive social agents providing simple entertainment or news" (Surette, 2015, p. 2). This means that society cannot avoid the influence of the media and the vision of reality they create. How a society views crime and justice echoes that society's values, relationships, worldviews, and ideologies. One result is that criminal justice practices are often adopted by the criminal justice system and the public after gaining legitimacy through mass media portrayals. In a similar fashion, policies that fail to find support in the mass media tend to be forgotten in the minds of the public and fail to be legitimized (Surette and Otto, 2001). With these media, crime, and justice interactions in mind, this chapter will explore the nature of the interactions between media and criminal justice policy and practice and offer recommendations that reflect the current state of knowledge and research for criminal justice policy-makers and practitioners.

Drawing their interpretations from media portrayals, the public has little factually accurate knowledge about crime and the criminal justice system (Roberts, 1992; Surette, 2015; Dowler, 2003; Graber, 1980; Greer, 2009). Members of the public do not correctly know the extent or limitations of their own rights as citizens; and they incorrectly estimate crime statistics, recidivism rates, and the average length of prison sentences (Roberts, 1992). Along these lines, research conducted by Hough and Roberts (1998) found that nearly four out of five respondents felt that violence was involved in 30 percent or more crimes (the actual rate is about 6 percent). Further, when looking at public opinion and sentencing, respondents consistently felt as though criminal justice agencies were too lenient in their handling of offenders (Applegate et al., 1997). In addition to perceiving a need for the criminal justice system to be more punitive, the public also underestimates the severity of the sentences handed down by the criminal justice system and tend to suggest more lenient sentences than those actually being imposed (Hough and Roberts, 1999). These mismatches are problematic for a criminal justice system that rests on public support for legitimacy and community cooperation (Hough, 2010). In addition to generating support or opposition for distinct criminal justice policies, media-driven public opinion influences criminal justice policy through voting behavior, moral panics, and social movements (Surette, 2015). Thus, the lack of accurate criminal justice information disseminated to the public through the media is an important source of crime-related public opinions and subsequent justice policy creation.

In sum, the media are key for the ways in which people view crime, criminals, criminal justice system agents, and criminal justice system responses to crime (Marsh and Melville, 2009; Roberts, 1992; Surette, 2015; Barak, 1994). The importance of the media would be less worrisome if crime and justice content was varied and balanced in the media. However, the portrayed content is persistently pervasively distorted with regard to the nature of crime and how the criminal justice system responds (Marsh and Melville, 2009). The media consistently present a picture of crime and justice that emphasizes predatory violent criminality with the result that the public support more punitive criminal justice policies for a justice system that is already more punitive than the public desires (Surette, 1994; Applegate et al., 1997). Crime news has played a prominent role in this process.

Crime news and criminal justice

Over the history of the American mass media, shifts in news coverage of crime have paralleled shifts in the way that society views crime while not reflecting shifts in actual crime levels (Surette, 2015). During the eighteenth century, for example, newspapers focused on high profile trials and crimes. During this period crime was perceived as sin that must be punished; and the social function of a trial, therefore, was to degrade the status of the criminal sinner (Drechsel, 1983). In this light the newspaper reporting of trials forwarded both the expiation of sin and the deterrence of crime by emphasizing the costs of committing a crime/sin for individual offenders (Drechsel, 1983). By the nineteenth century, crime had been separated from sin, with crime becoming a secular matter and the criminal justice system slowly shifting so that criminal investigation and the compiling of evidence began to gain predominance (Flanders, 2011). When a person's soul was not on the line, it also became easier to use crime stories for entertainment. Coverage of crime thereby began to be constructed as individual melodramas and mysteries to be solved rather than the result of societal shortcomings (Rothman, 1971). By the latter part of the nineteenth century, print media had set the standard explanations and stereotypes of crime and justice that still dominate news media crime portraits to this day. The media-constructed crime portraits that came to dominate how crime and justice stories were presented were established with radio and news reels in the early twentieth century. Thereafter crime news reflected the profit-driven nature of the media and crimes were constructed in the news along status quo supporting infotainment storylines with offenders presented as a criminal sub-species preying upon society (Drechsel, 1983; Surette, 2015).

In this crime and justice commodification process, and in order to gain large audiences, news media presented unique and unusual crime stories that could be constructed in entertaining narratives and mass marketed. The result was a focus on the sensational and heinous crimes, with crime stories in the news media often playing out as though they were solely created for the purposes of pure entertainment. Here again, the social impact was public support for more punitive punishments for crime and more aggressive law enforcement policies. When the dominant media portrait is of a predatory offender committing violent crimes in constant battle with the criminal justice system, non-punitive policies come across as naïve (Gorelick, 1989). When offenders are consistently portrayed not as wayward citizens who have made regrettable mistakes but as relentless predators, rehabilitation policies are disparaged (Surette, 1994). In that you very rarely find the regretful offender and usually find an innate predator in news about crime, the ultimate criminal justice policy push from the media construction of crime and justice is away from rehabilitation and toward punishment (Surette, 2015).

Setting the social problem agenda

An additional avenue through which the media affects criminal justice policy is by influencing the rank of crime on the public agenda. According to the social constructionist perspective, a particular social condition becomes a social problem when it is raised to a level of collective attention that people begin to think of the condition as a serious problem. For crime and justice, social constructionism attempts to show how deviant behaviors are criminalized, how deviant persons are identified, and how institutions deal with crime (Surette, 2015). In this perspective, social problems are the negotiated and created products of collectively accepted definitions which exist separately from objective social conditions (Blumer, 1971). Therefore, social conditions that come to be labeled as recognized social problems are not solely the result of social dysfunction, but are the end product of a condition being recognized and validated as a social problem, sometimes in direct opposition to relevant statistical evidence. Hence, crime has at times increased its rank on the social problem agenda during periods of falling crime rates (Altheide, 2002). Consequently, a pernicious social condition does not socially exist until it is recognized, labeled, and accepted as a social problem. Only when recognized do societies begin to take steps to address the issue and associated social policies emerge (Barak, 1994).

Which social conditions become social problems depends upon public interest and the emergence of effective claims-makers to champion the issue in the media. When the issue is criminal justice related, the media is invariably involved in determining which social behaviors are criminalized (Surette and Otto, 2001). The process for crime and justice issues follows five steps (CF Jensen and Gerber, 1998; Kitsuse and Spector, 1973). In the first step, a condition is seen by a few people as being a problem for society, the incipiency stage. In the second step, coalescence, for some issues formal and informal organizations support the claims of media sophisticated claims-makers and raise public awareness and concern. Third, in the institutionalization stage, criminal justice agencies begin to see the problem as significant and an opportunity to garner resources and respond (Jenkins, 1994). The fourth step is fragmentation, where the issue begins to lose urgency and news value as newer issues emerge and compete. The fifth and final stage is either the eventual discrediting of the issue as a serious social problem or its legislative legitimization and adoption as a permanent issue that needs to be dealt with by the criminal justice system (demise or criminalization). Each step in this criminalization process is fueled by media attention. The media provides a forum for issues to be discussed, for problems to find a foundation, and for raising the visibility of issues and attracting champions to argue for their criminalization and the need for a justice system response (Surette and Otto, 2001). Media attention leads to a public outcry for action on the part of the government. In the end, the media breathe life into criminal justice-related problems that would otherwise have been short-lived.

New media, crime, and justice

In addition to the above considerations, new forms of media have created a paradigm shift in the criminal justice policy and media relationship. New media allow for on demand access to content at any time, from any location, on multiple digital devices; and unlike traditional legacy print, sound and visual media, new media also allow for interactive user feedback resulting in the "democratization" of media content (Lievrouw and Livingstone, 2006). The most important result has been the shift in media consumers from passive receptors of content to actively involved participants in a new media virtual and digital world (Surette, 2013). Contemporary new media provide both a medium for the formation of virtual communities around shared media content interests and the means for socialization into these virtual communities (Hjarvard, 2013).

There are a number of social changes that are a result of new media; and inevitably, some of these impacts are felt in the criminal justice system. Interaction with media-generated content is leading to a mediated reality replacing directly experienced reality, and more personal interactions and face-to-face communication being replaced by social networking. New media users are able to communicate at any time from any place as well as enabling the access of information in an on-demand decentralized fashion. Media information flows in multiple directions with traditional content producers and new media users having the ability to contribute to the creation of mediated knowledge (Hjarvard, 2013).

New media have also supplanted involvement in real-world face-to-face interaction socialization (Lievrouw and Livingstone, 2006). Thus, people are less likely to have face-to-face social encounters and are more likely to seek attention through new media outlets. A contemporary social group is broad but shallow; and how a person defines themselves, as well as how they are defined by others, is largely determined through new media interactions (Hjarvard, 2013). Furthermore, new media changes the ways in which people gain knowledge about the world. First, new media provides vast amounts of information on a wide range of topics. Second, crime and justice-related media content is now readily available and shared among large groups of people. Third, audience members actively participate in the content creation process by posting videos and commentary. Together, these changes have affected the ways in which society receives and processes information about crime, and justice, and their related policies. As a result new media has a profound influence on the political process (Surette, 2015). Politicians are able to garner votes by reaching out through new electronic avenues while simultaneously potential voters are able to easily gain access to a wealth of information about politicians and issues through websites and blogs (Socha and Eber-Schmid, n.d.).

Not only does new media have the potential to impact views about crime and justice, they also have the potential to impact criminality (Surette, 2015). For example, new media provides a method for terrorists to recruit new members and disseminate their message to a large audience. Fraud, stalking, and bullying are additional examples of traditional crimes that have evolved into cybercrimes. Another effect of new media on criminality is the use of social media as a stage to perform a criminal act as a social statement to garner attention or for self-promotion (Surette, 2015). New media also impacts crime victims. Having replaced personal contact with online social groups, some victims of crime seek solace in online communities, which makes them vulnerable to digitized victimization, and social media forums have been used in a number of examples to further humiliate crime victims with victim shaming resulting in a number of social media induced suicides (Surette, 2015). Lastly, new media provides a social marketing platform for different social groupings to bring forth issues that they feel are deserving of criminal justice policy attention (Silverman, 2012). With this history and these effects in minds, a set of recommendations for criminal justice policymakers and practitioners are suggested for a new media crime and justice world.

Recommendations for practitioners

1: Conduct rigorous research and criminal justice practice evaluations

The first and an obvious recommendation is to support and encourage efforts to add to the relevant knowledge base in order to increase understanding of the media, crime, and justice relationship. There has been little research into what characteristics make it most likely that an issue will gain traction within the contemporary media echo chamber. There is widespread agreement that the media focuses on unusual crimes that tend to be particularly shocking and uses them as exemplars of perceived social problems. But in most cases, these crimes are one of many that have similar characteristics. Research needs to look into the characteristics and circumstances which lead to some cases garnering more attention than others and the process by which certain crimes receive enough media attention to lead to policy changes.

2: Raise your media consciousness

Noting the idiosyncratic local nature of the criminal justice system-media relationship, which social problems receive attention and are addressed with action will vary greatly across jurisdictions (Pritchard, 1986; Protess et al., 1985). Individual criminal justice professionals are recommended to become aware of the potential avenues and nuances of media influence on criminal justice policy. Social problems are dynamic and their structural components are both concrete and perceptual, necessitating any actions that are taken to be of a similar nature. Both the objective conditions in the real world and the public perception of those conditions must be simultaneously addressed. It is a responsibility of those who work and legislate in criminal justice to challenge misinformation in those instances where real world conditions and public perceptions of those conditions significantly differ. Criminal justice policymakers and practitioners are recommended to become students of their local crime, justice and media environment as its history and idiosyncrasies will predict the role that the media they must individually deal with will play. A better understanding of the fluctuating social dynamics, the role of the media in these changes, the emergence of associated social issues, and the crafting of social responses of how to best respond to these issues is needed.

3: Recognize that punitive effects are the most common result of media attention

The media's coverage of crime and the criminal justice system is driven more by market forces and entertainment values than by the reporting of factual information about crime rates and criminal justice issues (Beale, 2006). The relentless focus of the media on sensational and heinous crimes unduly raises public concern regarding predator criminals (Surette, 1994). Usually, this portrayal of crime leads the public to desire more punitive criminal justice system policies (Andreasen, 2006). One reason that a stronger direct linear relationship between the media and criminal justice policies has not been found may be due, in part, to the media's portrayal of crime as an act rather than an issue, which leads the public to misunderstanding crime and criminal justice policies, and open to manipulation by media skilled claims-makers (Barak, 1994) In addition, how one views crime and justice is often interconnected with how one views general society (Sacco, 1982; Stroman and Seltzer, 1985). Thus, it becomes important for criminal justice professionals to comprehend the effects of the media on views of overall social conditions. It is likely that these media-influenced perceptions fuse with pre-existing social experiences and attitudes which then impact the rank of crime on the public agenda and, eventually, lead to support for criminal justice policies which are usually punitive in nature (Bortner, 1984; Lichter, 1988). The message that is generally promoted is one of fear, intolerance, and the need to punish those who deviate from social norms (Altheide, 2002; Carlson, 1985).

Further, the skewed portrayal of crime and predatory criminal presented by the media also leads to increased fear of crime, which again leads to support for more punitive policies (Barak, 1994; Beale, 2006). Although it may be understood that there is a relationship between the media's distorted portrayal of crime, criminals, and criminal justice that leads media consumers to support more punitive policies, it does not appear to be often taken in account. Therefore, it is recommended that criminal justice policymakers and practitioners become self-aware of this general punitive drive and recognize and resist unwarranted over-reactions to sensationalized crimes. One tool for modifying the media-induced punitive reaction is to better instruct the public regarding unintended consequences that accompany media attention to crime (Surette, 2015).

4: Become aware of unintended consequences of media

In many situations where the media play a role in emerging criminal justice issues, counterproductive results may occur, especially where crime reduction is the goal (Surette, 1992). For example, a Canadian study of an extensive media-based crime prevention campaign found that, although many in the media audience reported receiving the information and understanding the content of the message, a decrease in crime prevention behaviors followed. The extensive media-based crime prevention campaign. The counterproductive unanticipated result was due to a lack of salience of campaign themes and messages for the target audience (Sacco and Silverman, 1981). Early media anti-drug campaigns provide related examples which share the goal of making issues more salient by providing detailed information regarding how easy it was to achieve a drug high and led to the unintended consequence of increased drug abuse. Audience members who were previously uninformed of specific drug abuse practices such as inhaling fumes from commercial home products (huffing) to get high were unintentionally educated in the practice (Leukefeld, 1991). Another unintended media effect is an "anticipatory effect" in which the causal order of media coverage and criminal justice practice appear to reverse so that criminal justice personnel preemptively react to anticipated media coverage (Surette, 1992). At times, policy responses are in anticipation of what policymakers expect public opinion will be after media shaping. Although there may be no tangible media coverage at the time, policymakers may act upon, or fail to act upon, an issue based on their perception that media coverage will be forthcoming and will play a role in shaping public opinion (Campbell and Ross, 1968; Surette, 1992). Similarly, "announcement effects" occur when offenders change their behaviors in conjunction with an advertised criminal justice enforcement change (Surette, 1992). Criminal justice professionals need to be aware that offender behavior changes may only reflect the effect of media coverage and not a street level impact of a new practice. As such announcement effects are short lived, changes in offenses will be temporary. These unintended, unexpected outcomes of the media–criminal justice policy relationship are not uncommon; and criminal justice personnel are recommended to be sensitive to their existence. The most pernicious effect is the emergence of continuous moral panics directed at types of crimes and offenders.

5: Become aware of media-generated moral panics and new media's role

Previously the impact of crime and criminal justice-related stories was short-lived, but today these stories often become lengthy moral panics due to a media amplification effect. New social media outlets such as Facebook and Twitter pick up stories and continuously repeat them in a new media echo chamber where discussions of crime and justice are subjective and driven by statements of fear and outrage (Surette, 2015). This creation of moral panics within the new media social reality supports a faulty systems frame which sees crime as the result of a failure of agents of social control and promotes punitive policies to compensate for a perceived lenient and inefficient system (Green, 2009). Fear of crime is one of the ways in which public disinformation impacts criminal justice. Although there are varying estimates of the level of fear of crime in American society, most agree that the level of fear exceeds the actual risk of crime (Lab, 2014). When the media focuses on rare and heinous crimes, especially local ones, fear rises (Altheide, 2002). In today's dynamic crime, justice, and media environment, it is difficult for individuals to perceive the influence that new media has on the life cycle of social issues. The impact of new media on public opinion regarding deviant versus criminal behavior, and how media influenced public opinion leads to changes in criminal justice policy, are seldom acknowledged and less often addressed. It is recommended that those in the criminal justice system strive to understand the mechanisms and dynamics though which new media generates moral panics and work to close off reasoned public debate (Surette, 2013).

6: Become a news-making criminologist

A final recommendation is for criminal justice individuals to actively embrace and engage in crime news creations as a way to influence policy (Barak, 1994). According to Barak (2007), "newsmaking criminology refers to the conscious efforts and activities of criminologists to interpret, influence, and shape the representation of 'newsworthy' items about crime and justice" (p. 192). There exists a historical reluctance for criminal justice practitioners to interact with the media and the public has been left to the influence of distorted entertainment products and haphazard news content (Surette, 2015). However, in many other disciplines, there are mass-mediated discussions wherein professionals in the field lend their viewpoints and provide their expertise. In public discourses regarding crime and justice, though, criminologists have generally remained silent (Barak, 2007). While a few criminologists have consistently made their voices heard, for example James Alan Fox and Alfred Blumstein, they rarely drive a news story in the media; and they are mostly used to provide sound bites that add credence and legitimacy to the version of the crime and justice story that is being portrayed (Barak, 2007). Further, these criminologists are rarely seen on any news program or talk show where principal exchanges take place. Historically the case has been that mass media outlets tend to rely on state agents and politicians when collecting their information and shaping their views on crime and justice (Barak, 2007).

It is recommended that criminal justice professionals and practitioners become directly involved in the public discourse surrounding crime and justice issues. Newsmaking criminology is a call for these individuals to become "public intellectuals" and to take sides based on their knowledge and experiences (Barak, 2007). In our postmodern society, where technology and mass communication are central to the accumulation, legitimization, and dissemination of information, these mass communication media outlets provide a readily accessible framework for influencing change (Barak, 2007). Because these outlets may also be used to provide the public with disinformation, it is essential that newsmaking criminologists become involved in the process to dispel some of the myths surrounding crime and justice and to encourage a progressive, informed discourse. This will ultimately hopefully lead to the adoption of crime and justice policies based on an informed perspective rather than the current emotionally driven process (Barak, 2007).

Conclusion

The influence of media on crime and justice will continue. While in the past people feared the surveillance of an overreaching government, individuals are now posting personal information that allows for others to watch their private moments (Surette, 2013). Self-surveillance and performance crime have grown in the associated twenty-first century celebrity culture (Penfold-Mounce, 2009; Surette, 2015). With new media also having a participatory component, the criminal justice system has been opened to further public scrutiny and involvement. How offenders, victims, and police react to crime; how crimes are committed and investigated; how the courts operate and process cases; how sentenced prisoners behave and corrections operate have all been altered by contemporary media forces (Surette, 2015: 228). Thus, it is important that we understand public involvement in a new media world of crime and justice. Crime and justice information needs to be presented to the public as accurately as possible and media portrayals of crime should present neutral coverage that does not sensationalize. Criminal justice professionals should contribute to that goal.

The future is one in which there will be an increase in the interactions between the media, crime, justice, and policy. Failure to acknowledge the role that the media plays in the formation of criminal justice policy will allow the media to unaccountably influence the policy process. It is not only important to understand that the media plays a part in the formation of policy, but it is also important for society to understand that the media play a role. Media criminal justice policy effects impact how tax dollars are spent, how components of society perceive each other, and how society interacts (Surette, 2015). With the evolving of new forms of media, media will continue to impact public opinion and, in turn, criminal justice policy for the foreseeable future.

References

Altheide, D. (2002). *Creating fear*. Hawthorne, NY: Aldine de Gruyter.

Andreasen, A.A. (2006). *Social marketing in the 21st century*. Thousand Oaks, CA: Sage Publications.

Applegate, B. K., Cullen, F. T., and Fisher, B. S. (1997). Public support for correctional treatment: The continuing appeal of the rehabilitative ideal. *The Prison Journal*, 77(3), 237–258.

Barak, G. (2007). Doing newsmaking criminology from within the academy. *Theoretical Criminology*, 11(2), 191–207.

Barak, G. (ed.). (1994). *Media, process, and the social construction of crime: Studies in newsmaking criminology*. New York, NY: Garland Publishing.

Beale, S.S. (2006). The news media's influence on criminal justice policy: How market-driven news promotes punitiveness. *William and Mary Law Review*, 48(2), 397–481.

Blumer, H. (1971). Social problems as collective behavior. *Social Problems*, 18(3), 298–306.

Bortner, M.A. (1984). Media images and public attitudes toward crime and justice. In R. Surette (ed.), *Justice and the media*. Springfield, IL: Charles C. Thomas.

Campbell, D. T., and Ross, H. L. (1968). The Connecticut crackdown on speeding: Time-series data in quasi-experimental analysis. *Law and Society Review*, 33–53.

Carlson, J. (1985). *Prime time law enforcement*. New York, NY: Prager Publishers.

Conklin, J.E. (1975). *The impact of crime*. New York, NY: Macmillan.

Dowler, K. (2003). Media consumption and public attitudes toward crime and justice: The relationship between fear of crime, punitive attitudes, and perceived police effectiveness. *Journal of Criminal Justice and Popular Culture*, 10(2), 109–126.

Drechsel, R. (1983). *News making in the trial courts*. New York, NY: Longman.

Flanders, J. (2011). *The invention of murder*. London, UK: Harper Collins.

Gerbner, G., Gross, L., Signorielle, N., Morgan, M., and Jackson-Beeck, M. (1979). The demonstration of power: Violence profile no. 10. *Journal of Communication*, 29, 177–196.

Gorelick, S. M. (1989). "Join our war": The construction of ideology in a newspaper crimefighting campaign. *Crime and Delinquency*, 35(3), 421–436.

Graber, D.V. (1980). *Crime news and the public*. Westport, CT: Prager Publishers.

Graber, D. (1979). Evaluating crime fighting policies. In R. Baker and F. Meyer (eds.), *Evaluating alternative law enforcement policies*. Lexington, MA: Lexington Books.

Green, D.A. (2009). Feeding wolves: Punitiveness and culture. *European Journal of Criminology*, 6(6), 517–536.

Greer, C. (2009). Crime and media: Understanding the connections. In C. Hale, K. Hayworth, A. Wahidin, and E. Wincup (eds.), *Criminology* (3rd ed.). Oxford, UK: Oxford University Press.

Hjarvard, S. (2013). *The mediatization of culture and society*. New York, N.Y.: Routledge.

Hobbs, S. and Hamerton, C. (2014). *The making of criminal justice policy*. New York, NY: Routledge.

Hough, M. (2010, July 1). Modernization and public opinion: Some criminal justice paradoxes. *Contemporary Politics*, 9(2), 143–155.

Hough, M., and Roberts, J.V. (1998). *Attitudes to punishments: Findings from the British Crime Survey. Home Office research study 179*. London: Home Office.

Hough, M., and Roberts, J.V. (1999). Sentencing trends in Britain. *Punishment and Society*, 1(1), 11–26.

Jenkins, P. (1994). *Using Murder: The social construction of serial murder*. Hawthorne, NY: Aldine de Gruyter.

Jensen, E.L., and Gerber, J. (1998). *The new war on drugs: Symbolic politics and criminal justice policy*. Cincinnati, OH: Anderson Publishing.

Kitsuse, J.I., and Spector, M. (1973). Toward a sociology of social problems: Social conditions, value judgments, and problems. *Social Problems*, 20(4), 407–419.

Lab, S.P. (2014). *Crime prevention: Approaches, practices, and evaluations* (8th ed.). Waltham, MA: Anderson Publishing.

Leukefeld, C. (1991). The role of the National Institute on drug abuse and in drug abuse prevention research. In L. Donohew, H. Sypher, and W. Bukoski (eds.), *Persuasive communication and drug abuse prevention*. Hillsdale, NJ: Lawrence Erlbaum Associates.

Lichter, S. (1988). Media power: The influence of media on politics and business. *Florida Policy Review*, 4, 35–41.

Lievrouw, L.A., and Livingstone, S. (eds.). (2006). *Handbook of new media: Social shaping and social consequences*. London, UK: Sage Publications. Retrieved from http://eprints.lse.ac.uk/21502/1/Introduction_to_the_updated_student_edition_(LSERO).pdf.

Marsh, I., and Melville, G. (2009). *Crime, justice and the media*. New York, NY: Routledge.

Penfold-Mounce, R. (2009). *Celebrity culture and crime*. London, UK: Palgrave.

Prichard, D. (1986). Homicide and bargained justice: The agenda-setting effect of crime news on prosecution. *Public Opinion Quarterly*, 50, 143–159.

Protess, D., Leff, D. Brooks, S. and Gordon, M. (1985), Uncovering rape: the watchdog press and the limits of agenda setting. *Public Opinion Quarterly*, 49, 19–37.

Roberts, J.V. (1992). Public opinion, crime, and criminal justice. *Crime and Justice*, 16, 99–180.

Rothman, D. (1971). *The discovery of the asylum*. Boston, MA: Little, Brown.

Sacco, V. (1982). The effects of mass media on perceptions of crime. *Pacific Sociology Review*, 25(4), 475–493.

Sacco, V., and Silverman, R. (1981). Selling crime prevention: The evaluation of a mass media campaign. *Canadian Journal of Criminology*, 23, 191–201.

Silverman, J. (2012). *Crime policy and the media: The shaping of criminal justice, 1989–2010*. New York, NY: Routledge.

Socha, B., and Eber-Schmid, B. (n.d.). What is new media?: Defining new media isn't easy. *New Media Institute*. Retrieved from www.newmedia.org/what-is-new-media.html.

Stroman, C., and Seltzer, R. (1985). Media use and perceptions of crime. *Journalism Quarterly*, 62, 340–345.

Surette, R. (1990). The media and criminal justice public policy: Future prospects. In R. Surette (ed.), *The media and criminal justice public policy: Recent research and social effects*. Springfield, IL: Charles C. Thomas.

Surette, R. (1992). Methodological problems in determining media effects on criminal justice: A review and suggestions for the future. *Criminal Justice Policy Review*, 6(4), 291–310.

Surette, R. (1994). Predator criminals as media icons. In G. Barak (ed.), *Media, process, and the social construction of crime: Studies in newsmaking criminology*. New York, NY: Garland Publishing.

Surette, R. (2013). Why has the criminal justice system become another source of entertainment for the American public? In *ABC-CLIO Praeger Pop Culture Universe*. Retrieved from www.abc-clio.com/ABC-CLIOCorporate/product.aspx?pc=POPAW.

Surette, R. (2015). *Media crime and criminal justice: Images, realities, and policies*. Stamford, CT: Cengage Learning.

Surette, R. and Otto, C. (2001). The media's role in the definition of crime. In S. Henry, and M.M. Lanier (eds.), *What is crime? Controversies over the nature of crime and what to do about it*. Lanham, MD: Rowman and Littlefield Publishers, Inc.

Chapter 31

Cost-effective and accountable criminal justice policy

Natasha A. Frost, Carlos E. Monteiro and Beck M. Strah

Introduction

What are the most effective policies for reducing crime and curbing recidivism? How can we hold offenders accountable and enhance public safety? For decades, the answer to these types of questions has tended towards enhancing control over active offenders through increased use of incarceration and more stringent forms of community supervision (Clear and Frost, 2014). Get-tough crime policies passed throughout the 1970s, 1980s, and 1990s resulted in unprecedented numbers of people living under the control of the American criminal justice system as the new millennium dawned. Although there have been slow but steady declines in the total correctional population over the past several years, the United States still had an estimated 6,899,000 adults under some form of correctional control as of year-end 2013 (Glaze and Kaeble, 2014). The number of lives touched by these get-tough policies far exceeds the number of offenders, as the families of those caught up in the criminal justice system also suffer some of the consequences. The number of children under the age of 18 with an incarcerated parent, for example, has risen sharply over the last several decades, with particularly sharp increases beginning in 1990. Between 1991 and 2007, the number of children with a mother in prison increased by 131 percent (Glaze and Maruschak, 2008), and recent figures suggest that roughly 2.7 million children currently have a parent incarcerated (Western and Pettit, 2010). We have amassed enough evidence about the effects of incarceration on children and families to know that this level of criminal justice intervention and control does not bode well for the future (Massoglia and Warner, 2011; Wakefield and Wildeman, 2014).

For several decades, there was remarkable political consensus on the utility of get-tough policies, with many of the most punitive policies garnering notable bi-partisan support. However, in recent years, a new mantra of criminal justice has been gaining currency in political circles. The edict that we must be "tough on crime" is slowly being supplanted by a clarion call to be "smart on crime" or "right on crime" (Greene, 2003; Right on Crime,

2010). The policies of the get-tough era are increasingly seen as inefficient, unjust, and at times counter-productive. Perhaps most importantly, our attempts to legislate our way out of crime, particularly through increasing use of incarceration, have been very expensive. The financial burden associated with mass incarceration has been well documented. Since 1982, correctional expenditures have nearly quadrupled, making it the second largest expenditure behind Medicaid (Henrichson and Delaney, 2012; Kyckelhahn, 2012). In 2006, federal and state jurisdictions across the country spent $68 billion on correctional expenditures and by 2008 that number had grown to $75 billion (Bureau of Justice Statistics, 2008; Schmitt et al., 2010). More recently, researchers have highlighted the additional, but often overlooked costs related to employee health insurance, pensions, and inmate hospital care that are not commonly factored into the accounting and have argued that America's experiment in mass incarceration has actually cost taxpayers far more than most estimates suggest (Henrichson and Delaney, 2012). There had been a time when it seemed that no price was too much to pay for public safety; but the growing body of evidence, suggesting that some of these policies are not only expensive but also in many ways counter-productive, has led to a reconsideration of their utility (Clear, 2007; Clear and Frost, 2014; Gottschalk, 2010).

As jurisdictions across the country grapple with fiscal crises and budget shortfalls, the legislative, executive, and judiciary branches of state and federal governments have begun to look for ways to roll back some of the most punitive policies of the "get tough" era, and many of these efforts expressly target reducing prison populations. The emerging sentiment is perhaps most clearly expressed in the "Declaration of Principles" put forward by the Right on Crime initiative (led by some of the country's most conservative thinkers and politicians). The opening paragraphs of the Declaration of Principles expressly acknowledge that while fiscal matters are perhaps the driving motivation for criminal justice reformers on the right of the political spectrum, concerns about accountability and effectiveness are also paramount: "Conservatives are known for being tough on crime, but we must also be tough on criminal justice spending. That means demanding more cost-effective approaches that enhance public safety" (Right on Crime, 2010). Since 2011, 17 states have closed (or taken steps to close) correctional facilities as a result of successful efforts to reduce prison populations (Porter, 2013). These more recent prison closures resulted in a prison capacity reduction of over 35,000 beds between 2011 and 2013. Moreover, at least 17 states are currently working on legislation to reduce prison populations, usually through redrafting penal codes to reintroduce flexibility into sentencing (Chettiar and Stamm, 2012; Gill, 2013). Around the country, efforts to revise or repeal mandatory minimum sentences that often result in lengthy prison sentences are well underway. Since 2000, at least 29 states have taken legislative action to roll back or repeal mandatory sentences, with the vast majority of these reforms initiated in the past five years (Subramanian and Delaney, 2014).

Of course, all of this activity related to retreating from some of the most punitive policies of the past few decades requires careful thought around what should replace them. Key to this emerging conversation are concerns around accountability and effectiveness – with a desire to make seismic shifts in the way we approach criminal justice without compromising public safety. The preamble to Right on Crime's Declaration of Principles offers a concise summary of the emergent sentiment: "Conservatives correctly insist that government services be evaluated on whether they produce the best possible results at the lowest possible cost, but too often this lens of accountability has not focused as much on public safety policies as other areas of government" (Right on Crime, 2010). Although the Right on Crime initiative couches its appeal for criminal justice reform in fiscal terms, it makes a direct appeal to considerations of evidence and effectiveness. Moreover, criminal justice reform initiatives are not just unfolding among a handful of the "more progressive" states. Crucially, some of the most expansive penal reform initiatives are coming from what would have traditionally been considered the most punitive of states across the southern sunbelt (Clear and Frost, 2014).

What works: evidence-based policy

Much of this criminal justice reform activity has ridden the wave of the evidence-based policy movement that has been growing in importance over the past two decades. The dawn of the evidence-based era in the mid-1990s made the identification of both effective and ineffective programs critical for policymakers and practitioners, who began eyeing the fiscal and social costs of ineffective crime prevention strategies with increasing concern. The call for results-oriented policy and practice was officially pronounced in a 1996 Federal law that mandated the U.S. Department of Justice to "employ rigorous and scientifically recognized standards and methodologies" to determine effectiveness of the estimated $3 billion in funded crime prevention programs (Sherman et al., 1998). In 1997, a federally commissioned evaluation of roughly 500 crime prevention programs was presented to Congress, with conclusions detailing the types of programs that work effectively, the types that don't work effectively, and the types that show promise (Sherman et al., 1997). In the years since, scholars and practitioners alike have sought to develop a more comprehensive understanding of what works (and what doesn't) in the areas of policing (Bayley, 1998), crime prevention (Farrington and Welsh, 2008; Welsh and Farrington, 2001) and crime control (MacKenzie, 2006). Based in part on the demands of national funders, federal, state and local agencies as well as non-profits and capital investors are looking to employ strategies and adopt programs that already have a substantial evidence-base.

Pay for success and social impact bonds

In an effort to promote innovation and experimentation while remaining focused on effectiveness, much of the more recent federal funding provided to states and localities for criminal justice initiatives explicitly ties accountability measures to the distribution of funds. Take for example the millions of dollars distributed under the federal Second Chance Act legislation (P.L. 110–199), which since 2008, has funded initiatives designed to enhance public safety through improving outcomes for people returning to communities from prison. Over $250 million dollars in Second Chance Act funding have been awarded through more than 600 grants to 49 states between 2009 and 2013 (The Council of State Governments Justice Center, 2014b). Although the Second Chance Act became law in 2008, the 2012 re-authorization explicitly tied funding to effectiveness and accountability through prioritizing funding for those initiatives that adhere to the "pay for success" model.

Pay for success models, initially developed in the United Kingdom, emphasize payments for performance in terms of demonstrable outcomes rather than payments for completion of an activity, and have tended to take the form of Social Impact Bonds (SIBs). In one of the early reports assessing the feasibility of the Social Impact Bond model for scaling up programs related to juvenile and criminal justice in the United States, Callanan, Law, and Mendonca (2012) define a Social Impact Bond as "a multi-stakeholder partnership in which philanthropic funders and impact investors – not governments – take on the financial risk of expanding preventive programs that help poor and vulnerable people. Nonprofits deliver the program to more people who need it; the government pays only if the program succeeds" (p. 7). The SIB model has four central tenets: (1) collaboration among multiple stakeholders, (2) a focus on results, (3) allocation of risk, and (4) the alignment of incentives (Callanan et al., 2012). Perhaps not surprisingly, social impact bonds – or pay for success models – have become popular very quickly among funders.

Justice reinvestment

Although federal funding has emphasized accountable and effective criminal justice policy for almost two decades, the 2012 appropriation for Second Chance Act (SCA) grant funding explicitly prioritized the distribution of SCA funding to the use of a Pay for Success model. While enthusiasm persists for Second Chance Act programs, excitement has recently begun to shift to a new model for reducing our reliance on incarceration while maintaining the focus on public safety: justice reinvestment. Justice reinvestment was initially offered as a somewhat utopian vision of what could happen if some of the billions of dollars currently invested in incarceration were reinvested in the communities that are hardest hit by the use of incarceration. Susan Tucker and Eric Cadora (2003) first formally introduced the idea of justice reinvestment in a policy paper written for the Open Society Institute, noting that "the goal of justice reinvestment is to redirect some portion of the $54 billion America now spends on prisons to rebuilding the human resources and physical infrastructure – the schools, healthcare facilities, parks, and public spaces – of neighborhoods devastated by high levels of incarceration" (p. 3). Over the decade since Tucker and Cadora first offered justice reinvestment as an alternative vision, it has emerged as one of the most popular new ideas in criminal justice reform. More recently, Clear (2011) has described justice reinvestment as "as a broad strategic plan of action; incarceration rates are purposefully reduced through new sanctioning policies and practices, and the money saved by doing so is invested in local communities hard hit by crime and cycles of incarceration" (p. 587). Central to this vison was the notion of rebuilding communities as a long-term strategy for preventing crime.

Just as former Attorney General Janet Reno was in many ways pivotal to expanding the popularity of a new emphasis on prisoner reentry during the 1990s, President Obama's former Attorney General, Eric Holder was central to the rapid spread of justice reinvestment projects around the country. Holder emphasized Justice Reinvestment strategies during many of his public appearances, broadly describing justice reinvestment as strategies that "have directed funding away from prison construction and toward evidence-based programs and services, like treatment and supervision, that are designed to reduce recidivism" (U.S. Department of Justice, 2013). In the 2015 Omnibus Appropriations bill, Congress authorized an appropriation of 68 million dollars to fund grants through Second Chance Act and 27.5 million to fund Justice Reinvestment Initiatives (The Council of State Governments Justice Center, 2014b). Over the past several congressional appropriation bills, Second Chance Act funding has been slowly but steadily declining, just as Justice Reinvestment Initiative (JRI) funding has been increasing. Justice reinvestment has been gaining in popularity, precisely because it resonates so well with contemporary concerns in criminal justice reform (Clear and Frost, 2014). As an approach, justice reinvestment offers a way to reduce prison populations and reduce costs, diverting some portion of the savings to the very communities that have suffered the most under the punitive policies of the previous era. This reinvestment in communities is expected to help interrupt the community-to-prison cycle and promises to do so through an emphasis on community development (Anglin, 2004). Such a model has an intuitive appeal among philanthropists and capital investors concerned about social impact.

In its early conception, justice reinvestment was very much focused on, and embedded within, the community development model (Anglin, 2004; Tucker and Cadora, 2003). In its realization, however, the focus has shifted to reinvesting the correctional dollars saved into other government-based criminal justice and social service agencies (Clear and Frost, 2014). In other words, savings realized through a reduced reliance on incarceration have frequently been diverted to community corrections (often through increased investments in probation) rather than to the community itself (La Vigne et al., 2010; LaVigne et al., 2014). Nonetheless, justice reinvestment's emphasis on reducing incarceration-related spending and reinvesting the savings realized has led to a fairly rapid diffusion of the idea around the country. Part of the appeal of justice reinvestment is its focus on data-driven, evidence-based approaches to crime reduction (Clement et al., 2011). Justice reinvestment is frequently marketed as "reinvesting in what works," explicitly bringing together some of the more politically popular ideas of our time: evidence-based crime prevention, accountability, and fiscal responsibility. As of January 2015, the Bureau of Justice Assistance reported that 24 states and 17 local jurisdictions were receiving funds through its justice reinvestment initiative (Bureau of Justice Assistance, 2015). Moreover, 20 states had launched justice reinvestment initiatives with the assistance of the Council of Government's Justice Center (The Council of State Governments, 2014).

Justice reinvestment has taken many different forms across the states that have launched initiatives, and indeed, this has been part of its appeal. Every state, every locality, has its own set of circumstances and justice reinvestment approaches can be directly tied to those circumstances. A simple schematic offered by The Council of State Governments describes the justice reinvestment approach as a four-step process (The Council of State Governments Justice Center, 2014a). First, jurisdictions are directed to "look at the big picture" using state-specific data from criminal justice agencies to identify the cost-drivers. Once the cost-drivers have been identified, stakeholders craft state-specific policy solutions to address those drivers. The states and localities receive implementation assistance to ensure that good policy translates into good practice. As a final step toward increased accountability, data on outcome measures are regularly collected and assessed to ensure that recidivism is being reduced, costs are being averted, and savings are being appropriately reinvested.

Although each state's story will unfold in a slightly different way, in a justice reinvestment assessment report recently published by the Urban Institute, the authors identified some of the more frequently reoccurring cost-drivers (LaVigne et al., 2014). Common cost-drivers across justice reinvestment states included: (1) probation and parole revocations, particularly for violations of the technical conditions of supervision; (2) sentencing policies and practices that underutilized diversion programs or resulted in lengthy terms of confinement; (3) insufficient or inefficient use of community corrections, with some states lacking the infrastructure to efficiently and effectively deliver supervision services in the community; and (4) inefficiencies in parole processing, with lengthy delays in the transition from incarceration to less expensive community supervision driving up costs.

As similar cost-drivers occurred across many jurisdictions, LaVigne et al. (2014) identified a number of policy approaches that have been integral to the various justice reinvestment strategies used across jurisdictions. Some of these strategies included using risk-needs assessments to classify offenders to services appropriate to their risk, expanding the use of earned time and good time credits for those incarcerated, and adopting intermediate/graduated sanction approaches for those under supervision in the community. Other common broad-based reforms included incorporating accountability measures to ensure that providers use evidence-based practices, expanding the use of specialized and problem-solving courts and offering expanded community treatment options (LaVigne et al., 2014). Although most of these reform initiatives are too new to be fully assessed, the report projects savings of as much as 4.6 billion dollars across the 17 justice reinvestment states assessed. These savings are to be realized through averted prison operating and building costs that would have been expected without the reforms (LaVigne et al., 2014).

The underlying appeal of the justice reinvestment movement is its emphasis on individualized assessments of problem areas within different states. North Carolina's justice reinvestment initiative involved adopting a series of policies aimed at addressing the major drivers of the state's correctional population. An assessment of data related to North Carolina's prison population cost-drivers indicated that probation and parole revocations made up more than half of all prison admissions, with a majority of revocations occurring due to technical violations, rather than new crimes. Through its 2011 Justice Reinvestment Act, North Carolina instituted sweeping criminal justice reforms that included allowing for swift and certain responses to probation violations, shifting admissions to jails rather than prisons, and providing enhanced supervision and services for offenders deemed to be at greater risk of reoffending (Council of State Governments Justice Center, 2014). North Carolina's justice reinvestment efforts also shifted fiscal resources to allow for the hiring of additional parole and probation officers charged with enhanced supervision of at-risk offenders, such as those with mental illness and substance dependency issues or with histories of serious offending (Austin et al., 2013; Eckholm, 2014).

Lastly, one of the key changes in North Carolina's correctional approach involved ensuring that every offender convicted of a felony would receive up to a year of post-release supervision (Council of State Governments Justice Center, 2014). In essence, the goal of North Carolina's justice reinvestment strategy has been to reserve prison space for high-risk and violent offenders, while ensuring that low-level offenders are held accountable in ways that are consistent with public safety.

While similar problems with probation and parole violations troubled Delaware's correctional population management efforts, other concerns including a burgeoning pre-trial population, and an average prison sentence that was greater than the national average, also motivated stakeholders to take action (Delaney, 2014). Delaware's justice reinvestment initiatives included the implementation of pre-trial risk assessments to better assist judges in making informed "detain or release" decisions, the use of risk but also *needs* assessments before sentencing, and the establishment of increased incentives for program completion. One of the critical sentencing reforms in Delaware's justice reinvestment effort was the rejection of an antiquated policy requiring judges to hand out consecutive sentences for offenders convicted of multiple offenses (Delaware.gov, 2014). Community supervision efforts in Delaware were also targeted, with greater emphasis on expanding and aiding community reentry resource centers (LaVigne et al., 2014).

As these two state examples demonstrate, justice reinvestment approaches seek to reduce the exorbitant costs of incarceration through analyzing cost drivers associated with growing prison populations, then crafting policy approaches that will result in cost-savings without compromising public safety. Cost-savings are realized primarily through analysis of state-specific data to identify the inefficiencies in the criminal justice process. Once inefficiencies have been identified, stakeholders come together to develop policy approaches to address those inefficiencies in the hopes of developing more effective and accountable criminal justice policies and processes. Performance measures are a key component of assessing the new approaches, with reduced recidivism being a key outcome measure in many of the early assessments (Austin et al., 2013; LaVigne et al., 2014).

Justice reinvestment initiatives have been embraced across the political spectrum, in part due to their focus on data-driven assessments, evidence-based programs, implementation assistance, and accountability in the form of performance indicators. Moreover, justice reinvestment initiatives encourage the very public–private partnerships that have become increasingly popular as federal agencies have moved toward pay for success models. Indeed, the federal Justice Reinvestment Initiative (JRI) that has funded many state criminal justice reform efforts is itself a public–private partnership between the U.S. Department of Justice and the Pew Charitable Trusts (Bureau of Justice Assistance, 2015). Despite its growing popularity, some of the earliest proponents of the justice reinvestment approach have cautioned that the current JRI initiatives "will not achieve the dual objectives of sustained reductions in state correctional populations and stronger, safer communities" for a number of reasons (Austin et al., 2013). While the current initiatives often involve sweeping legislative reforms, usually at the state-level, these reforms have rarely targeted serious and violent offenders. Even a cursory look at prison population statistics makes clear that any real sustained reductions in prison populations will require a willingness to substantially reduce length of stay for those who have committed more serious crimes of violence. Moreover, the savings associated with the current JRI initiatives have rarely been reinvested in improving conditions in local communities. Although there is nothing inherently wrong with reinvesting savings in less costly and often equally effective criminal justice interventions, these sorts of investments do little to break the cycle of crime and violence through addressing some of the root causes of crime. In their critique of the current JRI, Austin and colleagues (2013) have offered suggestions for how to realign the justice reinvestment model to better ensure that it stays true to its original objective of reducing our reliance on incarceration while improving public safety in some of our most vulnerable communities.

From the early "What Works?" evidence-based movement through the pay for success and justice reinvestment initiatives of the current era, criminal justice reform efforts have increasingly focused on ways to encourage the development of accountable and effective criminal justice policy. Although somewhat removed from the early vision of what justice reinvestment might entail, the various justice reinvestment approaches being undertaken across the United States today represent some of the more comprehensive attempts to enact sweeping criminal justice reforms. To the extent that future justice reinvestment initiatives are able to return the focus to reinvesting in local communities that was so central to the early vision, these initiatives might be able to achieve their dual objectives of a reduced reliance on incarceration and safer communities.

References

Anglin, R. V. (2004). *Building the Organizations that Build Communities*. Washington, DC: Department of Housing and Urban Development.

Austin, J., Cadora, E., Clear, T. R., Dansky, K., Greene, J., Gupta, V., Young, M. C. (2013). *Ending Mass Incarceration: Charting a New Justice Reinvestment* Washington, DC: The Sentencing Project.

Bayley, D. H. (1998). *What Works in Policing*. New York: Oxford University Press.

Bureau of Justice Assistance. (2015). Justice Reinvestment Initiative. Retrieved 1/2/2015, 2015, from www.bja.gov/programs/justicereinvestment/index.htmlx.

Bureau of Justice Statistics. (2008). *Justice Expenditure and Employment Extracts*. (NCJ 224394). Washington, DC: U.S. Department of Justice.

Callanan, L., Law, J. and Mendonca, L. (2012). From Potential to Action: Bringing Social Impact Bonds to the U.S. Retrieved December 26, 2014, from McKinsey and Company. http://mckinseyonsociety.com/downloads/reports/Social-Innovation/McKinsey_Social_Impact_Bonds_Report.pdf.

Chettiar, I., and Stamm, A. (2012). States take sizeable steps in 2012 to end overincarceration. Article retrieved from the website of the American Civil Liberties Union (ACLU): www.aclu.org/blog/states-take-sizeable-steps-2012-end-overincarceration.

Clear, T. R. (2007). *Imprisoning Communities: How Mass Incarceration Makes Disadvantaged Neighborhoods Worse*. New York: Oxford University Press.

Clear, T. R. (2011). A private-sector, incentives-based model for justice reinvestment. *Criminology and Public Policy*, 10(3), 585–608. doi: 10.1111/j.1745-9133.2011.00729.

Clear, T. R., and Frost, N. A. (2014). *The Punishment Imperative: The Rise and Failure of Mass Incarceration in America*. New York, NY: New York University Press.

Clement, M., Schwarzfeld, M., and Thompson, M. (2011). The National Summit on National Reinvestment and Public Safety: Addressing Recidivism, Crime, and Corrections Spending. New York: Council of State Governments Justice Center.

Council of State Governments Justice Center. (2014). Justice Reinvestment in North Carolina: Three Years Later. New York: Council of State Governments Justice Center.

Delaney, R. (2014). Delaware Governor recognizes benefits of JRI in State of the State, Pushes for more reform.

Delaware.gov. (2014). Governor signs criminal justice reforms into law.

Eckholm, E. (2014, September 14). North Carolina Cuts Prison Time for Probation Violators, and Costs. *New York Times*.

Farrington, D. P., and Welsh, B. C. (2008). *Saving Children from a Life of Crime: Early Risk Factors and Effective Interventions*. New York: Oxford University Press.

Gill, M. M. (2013). Turning off the spigot: How sentencing safety valves can help states protect public safety and save money. *Federal Sentencing Reporter*, 25(5), 349–358.

Glaze, L., and Kaeble, D. (2014). Correctional Populations in the United States, 2013. Washington, DC: U.S. Department of Justice, Bureau of Justice Statistics.

Glaze, L., and Maruschak, L. M. (2008). *Parents in Prison and their Minor Children*. Washington, DC: U.S. Department of Justice.

Gottschalk, M. (2010). Cell blocks and red ink: mass incarceration, the great recession and penal reform. *Daedalus*, 139(3), 62–73.

Greene, J. (2003). *Smart on Crime: Positive Trends in State-Level Sentencing and Correctional Policy*. Washington, DC: Families Against Mandatory Minimums.

Henrichson, C., and Delaney, R. (2012). *The Price of Prisons: What Incarceration Costs Taxpayers*. New York, NY: VERA Institute of Justice.

Kyckelhahn, T. (2012). State Corrections Expenditures, FY 1982–2010. Washington, DC: U.S. Department of Justice, Bureau of Justice Statistics.

La Vigne, N. G., Neusteter, S. R., Lachman, P., Dwyer, A., and Nadeau, C. A. (2010). *Justice Reinvestment at the Local Level: Planning and Implementation Guide*. Washington, DC: Urban Institute.

LaVigne, N., Bieler, S., Cramer, L., Ho, H., Cybele, K., Mayer, D., Samuels, J. (2014). *Justice Reinvestment Initiative State Assessment Report*. Washington, DC: Urban Institute.

MacKenzie, D. L. (2006). *What Works In Corrections: Reducing the Criminal Activities of Offenders and Delinquents* New York: Cambridge University Press.

Massoglia, M., and Warner, C. (2011). The consequences of incarceration. *Criminology and Public Policy*, 10(3), 851–863. doi: 10.1111/j.1745-9133.2011.00754.

Porter, N. D. (2013). *On the Chopping Block 2013: State Prison Closures.* Washington, DC: The Sentencing Project.

Right on Crime. (2010). *Statement of Principles.* Austin, TX: Texas Public Policy Foundation.

Schmitt, J., Warner, K., and Gupta, S. (2010). *The High Budgetary Cost of Incarceration.* Washington, DC: Center for Economic and Policy Research.

Sherman, L. W., Gottfredson, D., MacKenzie, D. L., Eck, J., Reuter, P., and Bushway, S. (1997). *Preventing Crime: What Works, What Doesn't, What's Promising.* Washington, DC: U.S. Department of Justice, National Institute of Justice.

Sherman, L. W., Gottfredson, D. C., MacKenzie, D. L., Eck, J., Reuter, P., and Bushway, S. (1998). *Research in Brief: Preventing Crime: What Works, What Doesn't, What's Promising.* Washington, DC: National Institute of Justice.

Subramanian, R., and Delaney, R. (2014). *Playbook for Change? State Reconsider Mandatory Sentences.* New York, NY: VERA Institute of Justice.

The Council of State Governments. (2014). Justice Center. Retrieved December 26, 2014, 2014, from http://csgjusticecenter.org/.

The Council of State Governments Justice Center. (2014a). About Justice Reinvestment. Retrieved 12/30/2014, 2014, from http://csgjusticecenter.org/jr/about/.

The Council of State Governments Justice Center. (2014b, November 16, 2014). Department of Justice Announces 78 New Second Chance Act Grantees. Retrieved from http://csgjusticecenter.org/nrrc/posts/department-of-justice-anno unces-78-new-second-chance-act-grantees/.

Tucker, S. B., and Cadora, E. (2003). Justice reinvestment: To invest in public safety by reallocating justice dollars to refinance education, housing, healthcare, and jobs. *Ideas for an Open Society. Occasional Papers Series.* New York: Open Society Institute.

U.S. Department of Justice. (2013). *Attorney General Eric Holder Delivers Remarks at the Annual Meeting of the American Bar Association's House of Delegates.* Retrieved from www.justice.gov/opa/speech/attorney-general-eric-holder-delivers-remarks-annual-meeting-american-bar-associations.

Wakefield, S., and Wildeman, C. (2014). *Children of the Prison Boom: Mass Incarceration and the Future of American Inequality.* New York, NY: Oxford University Press.

Welsh, B. C., and Farrington, D. P. (2001). Toward an evidence-based approach to preventing crime. *The ANNALS of the American Academy of Political and Social Science,* 578(1), 158–173.

Western, B., and Pettit, B. (2010). Incarceration and social inequality. *Daedalus,* 139(3), 8–19.

Chapter 32

The utility of findings from biosocial research for public policy

Kevin M. Beaver and Joseph A. Schwartz

Introduction

The biosocial perspective has quickly become one of the leading areas of research within the field of criminology. During the past decade, there has been a tremendous amount of scholarship examining the various ways in which biosocial factors are associated with criminal involvement, delinquency, criminogenic traits, and other forms of antisocial behavior. Despite the vast amount of biosocial research produced over a relatively short period of time, there remain significant concerns regarding this line of inquiry. Of all the criticisms leveled against biosocial research, perhaps those dealing with public policy implications have been the most acrimonious and tenacious. Critics can often be heard arguing that biosocial findings will inevitably lead to a new eugenics movement, that they will justify the use of even more punitive sanctions, and that they will shift attention away from treatment and rehabilitation to harsher forms of incarceration and punishment (Beaver, 2013). Following this line of reasoning, biosocial studies, and those scholars conducting such research, are either knowingly or unknowingly advocating for the implementation of oppressive policies designed to subjugate criminal offenders.

These critiques regarding the policies that could stem from biosocial research, however, are largely unfounded and likely originate from a lack of understanding of the biosocial perspective and a misperception regarding the meaning of biosocial findings. In this chapter, we attempt to correct these misconceptions. To do so, we argue that concerns of biosocial findings being used to legitimize oppressive criminal justice policies is misplaced, and, to the contrary, findings from biosocial research can be used in such a way as to support progressive public policies. Further, we point out that when used appropriately, biosocial research can guide the implementation of effective treatment and rehabilitation programs and that this research can ultimately lead to a reduction in criminal offending thereby promoting public safety. Toward this end, our chapter is divided into two sections. First, we review the key findings from biosocial research. Second, we discuss how these biosocial findings can be used to guide the development of public policies aimed at reducing criminal offending.

Key findings from biosocial research

Although biosocial research is quite heterogeneous in terms of the goals, analytical techniques, and research designs employed, a main interest is partitioning variance in criminal and antisocial outcomes (Barnes et al., 2014; Beaver, 2013). In biosocial research, variance is partitioned into genetic and environmental components, with each component expressed as a proportion or percentage of the amount of variance explained. The genetic component is typically referred to as heritability and captures the proportion of variance in the outcome measure that can be explained by genetic influences.

When it comes to debates regarding how the findings from biosocial research could be used in the development of public policy, much of the disagreement centers upon the use of heritability estimates. A large part of the reason why heritability estimates are so contentious in the discussion of criminal justice policy is because heritability estimates are commonly misunderstood by criminologists and other social scientists. Heritability does not represent a fixed, immutable estimate, but rather, such estimates can wax and wane depending on social context, maturational development, and other situational-specific factors. When heritability estimates change depending on the environmental context, this is typically referred to as a gene–environment interaction. Studies testing for gene–environment interactions have increased at an exponential rate during the past five years or so and the results of these studies have provided some evidence indicating that some genetic effects are moderated, in part, by certain environmental stimuli. The results flowing from this line of research also indicate the inverse, wherein some environmental influences are moderated by genetic predisposition.

The variance that is not accounted for by genetic influences is attributable to environmental sources (and error). Unlike most criminological theories and research which lump all environmental influences together, biosocial research delineates two types of environments: shared environments and nonshared environments. Shared environments are those environments that are the same between siblings and that result in greater levels of similarity between siblings from the same household. Common examples of shared environments are family-wide factors (e.g., SES, parental educational achievement, etc.) as well as neighborhood-level and school-level influences. Nonshared environments, in contrast, are environments that differ between siblings and produce between-sibling differences. Peer groups, sibling-specific parenting influences, and idiosyncratic experiences, are just a few examples of some specific nonshared environments.

A number of different research designs are available to partition variance into these three components, including blended-family designs and adoption designs. The most commonly used research design, however, is the twin-based research design. With the twin-based research design, pairs of monozygotic (MZ) twins and dizygotic (DZ) twins are compared. MZ twins are genetic clones of each other while DZ twins share approximately 50 percent of their distinguishing DNA. MZ and DZ twins, however, are assumed to share environmental experiences that are comparable in similarity. Since MZ twins share twice as much genetic material, a finding indicating that MZ twins more closely resemble one another relative to DZ twins would indicate a significant genetic effect on the examined outcome. Heritability estimates therefore increase as the similarity of MZ twins increases relative to DZ twins. The remaining variance is then partitioned between shared environmental and nonshared environmental components depending on whether the environmental influence is producing similarities between siblings (twins) or dissimilarities between siblings (twins). As long as the assumptions of twin-based research designs are upheld – and there have been mathematical models proving that they are (Barnes et al., 2014) – then the estimates generated from twin studies are highly reliable, valid, and generalizable.

There have been hundreds of studies that have examined the biosocial foundations to criminal and antisocial behaviors using twin-based research designs (Beaver, 2013). The precise estimates for the variance components fluctuate across these studies depending on the characteristics of the sample, the outcome measure being studied, and other study-specific factors. Four meta-analyses have been published, however, in an effort to synthesize the estimates from all of these studies and the results of these meta-analyses have been remarkably similar (Ferguson, 2010; Mason and Frick, 1994; Miles and Carey, 1997; Rhee and Waldman, 2002). The results indicate that genetic factors explain approximately 50 percent of the variance, shared environmental influences have been found to explain approximately 15 percent of the variance, and nonshared environmental influences (plus error) have been found to explain around 40 percent of the variance. These findings are highly robust and dovetail with the results generated using other research designs. In addition, these findings are similar to those reported with other behavioral outcomes (Plomin et al., 2013), and they also converge with laws of behavior genetics (Turkheimer, 2000). There are few findings within the social sciences that are so consistent and thus, there should be confidence in using these findings to help structure criminal justice policies, a topic to which we turn to in the next section.

Integrating biosocial findings into criminal justice policies

The existing findings from biosocial studies can be used to guide the development and implementation of criminal justice policies that are geared towards preventing the emergence of delinquency during adolescence, rehabilitating offenders, and reducing recidivism. There are two main ways that biosocial research can be integrated into criminal justice policies. First, the genetic basis to criminal behavior can be used to develop specific criminal justice polices. Second, the identification of environmental influences on criminal behavior can result in the creation of more effective and efficient criminal justice policies. Both of these approaches will be discussed in more detail, beginning first with the ways in which genetic findings relate to criminal justice policy.

The belief that since the structure of DNA cannot be changed, this makes the identification of genetic influences on criminal behavior dangerous, is wholly misguided. Although DNA *structure* does not change, the *effects* that emanate directly from DNA can be altered via environmental context in a process known as gene–environment interaction. Gene–environment interactions are particularly important because they specify the conditions under which genes will exert their most significant influence and, at the same time, also specify for whom environmental influences are likely to exert their most significant influence. This latter point is particularly important when considering the influence of rehabilitation programs. There is now a solid knowledge base indicating that certain programs can be quite effective at reducing recidivism for some offenders. One of the more tantalizing issues, however, is trying to figure out which offenders are the most likely to respond to specific treatment programs and why.

A body of research has been directed at addressing exactly this issue which has resulted in the creation of what is known as the responsivity principle (Smith et al., 2009). The responsivity principle recognizes that all offenders possess different characteristics and these characteristics may be partially responsible for moderating program effectiveness. As a result, treatment programs should be somewhat tailored to each offender, or at the very least, offenders should be funneled into treatment programs that best suit their individual needs and are most likely to result in change. To illustrate, males and females tend to respond to the same treatment programs in very different ways; females may benefit greatly from one program whereas the same program may be relatively ineffective for males. In such a case, gender would be considered a responsivity factor. A list of responsivity factors has been crafted and includes factors such as age, gender, race, and even mental abilities. Programs that take into account responsivity factors tend to be significantly more effective at reducing recidivism compared with those programs that do not.

The logic of responsivity can easily be extended to include gene–environment interactions. Recall that with gene–environment interactions genetic effects can account for heterogeneity in response to environmental stimuli. As it relates to responsivity, certain genotypes might be responsible for explaining why one offender responds to a program positively, why another offender is unaltered by the program, and yet another offender responds to that same program negatively. Genes, therefore, might be another responsivity factor that could help to increase program effectiveness. Of course, the genes-as-responsivity factors supposition hinges on being able to identify specific genes that act as responsivity factors. If these genes could be identified, then offenders could be genotyped for them and, depending on the results of the genetic testing, be funneled into programs that would maximize their potential for reducing recidivism. At this point, however, there are only a handful of genes that have been consistently linked to criminal involvement in a gene–environment framework (Beaver, 2013). Adding to this issue, genes that are implicated in the development of criminal behavior within the confines of a gene–environment interaction framework may differ from the genes that are involved in gene–environment interactions that predict recidivism. Empirical research is needed to examine gene–environment interactions as they relate to program effectiveness. Until more empirical evidence is accrued, the genes-as-responsivity factors hypothesis remains nothing more than conjecture.

Genetic influences do not always operate within the framework of a gene–environment interaction (Beaver et al., 2014), which begs the question of whether these genetic findings have any application to progressive policies. The answer is "yes," particularly when the findings are merged with another principle of effective intervention: the risk principle. Whereas the responsivity principle examined why there is variation in response to treatment programs, the risk principle provides information about which offenders are the most amenable to meaningful behavioral changes. Studies have revealed that high-risk offenders are the most likely to reap the rewards of rehabilitation programs while low-risk offenders may actually become more criminal if processed through a rehabilitation program (Smith et al., 2009). Against this backdrop, actuarial risk assessment tools were developed and used as a way to identify the risk level of each offender. Programs that adhere to the risk principle would pass over low-risk offenders and select high-risk offenders to be included in their programs.

What is particularly interesting about the risk principle is that the risk assessment tools can continuously be improved upon by including additional questions that are able to more finely delineate the risk level of each offender. If a new risk factor or risk level is identified, then it can simply be added to an existing risk assessment instrument and the resulting outcome should be a more reliable assessment tool. Importantly, risk assessment tools include both dynamic risk factors, such as exposure to delinquent peers and employment status, and static risk factors, such as gender. When viewed in this way, genetic information could be integrated into risk assessment tools by genotyping offenders for genes that are known to predict risk level. This genetic information would not be used in isolation, but rather in combination with the risk factors that are currently included on these risk assessment instruments. As with the responsivity principle, however, the extent to which genetic information could help to more accurately identify a given offender's level of risk is dependent on identifying genes related to risk level. Although there are genes that have been uncovered that predict criminal involvement (Beaver, 2013), to date there have not been any studies examining risk level as it relates to the intersection of criminal recidivism and rehabilitation programs. Future research is needed to address this issue more fully in order to provide information that could potentially lead to more precise evaluations of offender risk. In addition, keep in mind that high-risk offenders, including those that are at highest genetic risk, would be the ones who are the most likely to benefit from rehabilitation programs. Far from being oppressive, genotypic information about risk level could actually open up more opportunities for treatment for those offenders who possess the greatest levels of genetic risk.

The second way that biosocial findings can be integrated into criminal justice policies is by focusing on environmental influences on criminal involvement. There is a belief that biosocial research focuses only on the genetic basis to criminal and antisocial outcomes and thus biosocial findings are limited to the enactment of policies that are focused on genetic influences. In reality, however, nothing could be further from the truth. As the findings of biosocial studies reveal, approximately one half of the overall variance in criminal outcomes is the result of environmental influences, with most of this environmental variance explained by nonshared environments. What this finding necessarily means is that programs targeting nonshared environmental risk factors are likely to be more effective than those targeting shared environmental risk factors. Given that criminological research fails to distinguish between shared and nonshared environments, and that most criminological research focuses exclusively on shared environments (Harris, 1998; Pinker, 2002; Wright and Beaver, 2005), it is not surprising that the majority of prevention and treatment programs focus on shared environmental factors believed to produce crime and delinquency. And, given that shared environmental factors only account for about 10–15 percent of the variance in crime and delinquency, it is not all that surprising that such programs are not very effective at reducing recidivism (Hiscock et al., 2008).

Funneling scarce resources to prevention and treatment programs built upon (environmental) findings that are culled from sub-par studies is a recipe for disaster; money is wasted, program effectiveness is low, and public safety is compromised. This is precisely the current state-of-affairs for many treatment and prevention programs. If, however, these scarce resources were channeled into programs that were guided by rigorous research showing that nonshared environmental factors, not shared environmental factors, should form the crux of such programs, such programs should be comparatively quite effective at reducing recidivism and preventing crime and delinquency. As was the case with genes and their influence on public policy, the key is to identify specific nonshared environments that are related to the development of crime and delinquency. A small but growing body of research has focused on examining potential nonshared environments associated with crime and delinquency (Beaver, 2013). The results of these studies have not been successful at uncovering a broad swath of nonshared environmental risk factors, though a small number of such environmental influences have been identified. Some of these nonshared environments are quite common in criminological research, such as exposure to delinquent peers, but others, such as prenatal environments, are rarely integrated into criminological research. Clearly, much more research is needed in this area in order to identify specific nonshared environmental factors that can be used to guide the creation of prevention and treatment programs. As for now, though, research strongly suggests that programs focusing on shared environmental resources are wasting resources whereas those that focus on nonshared environments, such as prenatal environments, are significantly more effective (Olds, 2007).

Conclusions

Despite the tremendous amount of biosocial findings produced, the biosocial criminological perspective is still in its infancy. Owing to its newness in the field of criminology, along with the knee-jerk reaction that biosocial research leads to inhumane policies, there has not been much scholarship devoted to the manner in which biosocial criminology can inform public policy. In this chapter, though, we have detailed the ways in which biosocial findings can be integrated into criminal justice policy by focusing on genetic influences, gene–environment interactions, and nonshared environmental effects. Although we have provided the conceptual foundation that can be used for biosocially informed criminal justice policies, there still remains much to be uncovered in order for such policies to become a reality and in order for them to achieve maximum levels of effectiveness. Specifically:

- More research needs to be devoted to examining the genes that are associated with antisocial behaviors and traits. To date, not much is known about which specific genes are involved in the etiology of crime and delinquency. Future research that focuses on candidate genes as well as genome-wide associations will be useful in this regard.
- Research is needed to examine the potential genes that might: (1) predict recidivism and (2) moderate program effectiveness at reducing recidivism. No research to date has explored these possibilities in an empirical, large-scale study.
- More research is needed that attempts to identify specific nonshared environments that are involved in the development of crime, delinquency, and other antisocial behaviors. The vast majority of current research focuses on shared environments which only provide a small snippet of information regarding the origins of criminal and delinquent

behavior. Refocusing attention on the nonshared environment will most certainly provide information about the etiology of crime and delinquency and, at the same time, insight into what prevention and treatment programs can target for change to reduce crime, delinquency, and recidivism.

The current state of the evidence on the biosocial underpinnings to antisocial behaviors can be used to begin to inform criminal justice polices in a cautious and judicious fashion. As answers to the above gaps in the literature are discovered, they too can be added into policies on a widespread basis. If integrated successfully, then it is not unreasonable to believe that these policies can become even more effective than they are today.

References

Barnes, J. C., Wright, J. P., Boutwell, B. B., Schwartz, J. A., Connolly, E. J., Nedelec, J. L., and Beaver, K. M. (2014). Demonstrating the validity of twin research in criminology. *Criminology*, 52, 588–626.

Beaver, K. M. (2013). *Biosocial criminology: A primer* (2nd edition). Dubuque, IA: Kendall/Hunt.

Beaver, K. M., Barnes, J. C., and Boutwell, B. B. (2014). The 2-repeat allele of the MAOA gene confers an increased risk for shooting and stabbing behaviors. *Psychiatric Quarterly*, 85, 257–265.

Ferguson, C. J. (2010). Genetic contributions to antisocial personality and behavior: A meta-analytic review from an evolutionary perspective. *The Journal of Social Psychology*, 150, 160–180.

Harris, J. R. (1998). *The nurture assumption: Why children turn out the way they do*. New York, NY: Free Press.

Hiscock, H., Bayer, J. K., Price, A., Ukoumunne, O. C., Rogers, S., and Wake, M. (2008). Universal parenting programme to prevent early childhood behavioural problems: Cluster randomised trial. *British Medical Journal*, 336, 318–321.

Mason, D. A., and Frick, P. J. (1994). The heritability of antisocial behavior: A meta-analysis of twin and adoption studies. *Journal of Psychopathology and Behavioral Assessment*, 16, 301–323.

Miles, D. R., and Carey, G. (1997). Genetic and environmental architecture on human aggression. *Journal of Personality and Social Psychology*, 72, 207–217.

Olds, D. L. (2007). Preventing crime with prenatal and infancy support of parents: The Nurse-Family Partnership. *Victims and Offenders*, 2, 205–225.

Pinker, S. P. (2002). *The blank slate: The modern denial of human nature*. New York, NY: Viking.

Plomin, R., DeFries, J. C., Knopik, V. S., and Neiderhiser, J. M. (2013). *Behavioral genetics* (6th edition). New York, NY: Worth.

Rhee, S. H., and Waldman, I. D. (2002). Genetic and environmental influences on antisocial behavior: A meta-analysis of twin and adoption studies. *Psychological Bulletin*, 128, 490–529.

Smith, P., Gendreau, P., and Swartz, K. (2009). Validating the principles of effective intervention: A systematic review of the contributions of meta-analysis in the field of corrections. *Victims and Offenders*, 4, 148–169.

Turkheimer, E. (2000). Three laws of behavior genetics and what they mean. *Current Directions in Psychological Science*, 9, 160–164.

Wright, J. P., and Beaver, K. M. (2005). Do parents matter in creating self-control in their children? A genetically informed test of Gottfredson and Hirschi's theory of low self-control. *Criminology*, 43, 1169–1202.

Chapter 33

Bringing evidence into criminal justice policy

Alfred Blumstein

Introduction

It has been impressive to see the widespread desire for "evidence-based policy" in many aspects of the operation of the criminal justice system. That is certainly a much more desirable approach than the ideology-based policy that has dominated so many of the policies that have been enacted over the past several decades. That raises the question of the strength or validity of various forms of evidence and the degree to which they provide helpful guidance for setting appropriate policy.

Also, in a field like criminal justice, where there are multiple objectives and a variety of important constraints, formulating intelligent policy choices must inevitably go beyond even the best available evidence, and that complexity has certainly opened the door to the control by ideology.

The role of evidence is based on the validity of the statement "treatment or policy X causes a change in outcome Y in the context of environmental variables Z." The strength of such a statement will inevitably depend on the rigor of the test of the evidence. The tradition in science is to defer to the randomized controlled trial (RCT) as the strongest test of such a treatment, but even that test can have important flaws and limitations. Furthermore, in the context of the criminal justice system, where life and liberty are at stake, there are severe limits to which a randomized trial is feasible or acceptable. There are many other forms of evidence, where a treatment could be implemented without a comparable control, or where assignment to treatment group or comparison group is done by some means other than at random. There are many opportunities to collect observational data in the context of existing or innovative practices and those opportunities should certainly be pursued.

The issue becomes complex because the results can differ considerably depending on the context: the subjects treated, the jurisdiction and its traditions and constraints, the outcome measures used, and the skills and methodologies of the data collectors. And an association between an X and a Y could be a little more than correlation rather than reflecting a causal effect.

Because of these inherent complexities, challenge and replication is almost always a necessary part of accumulating adequate evidence.

Contrast with the medical field

A useful contrast to the use of evidence in criminal justice is its use in the medical field. Science is a strong tradition that pervades all levels of training in medicine and all decisions are supposed to be based on scientific evidence. Extensive RCTs are required for all new drugs, with double-blind control where the administering physician and the patient are both supposed to be unaware of whether the patient is receiving the drug or the placebo. Even here, the drug may have side effects that provoke its patients into dropping out of the experiment, thereby distorting the results of even this "gold standard" form of evidence.

In contrast, decisions within the criminal justice field fail to have this strong evidentiary discipline. In particular, the dominant traditions are those of the legal profession, where science has at best a secondary role and strength and persuasiveness of the argument as presented to the decision-maker are closer to the tradition. In the three branches of government, the legal tradition is clearly the case in the judiciary. In the legislature, the political appeal, particularly to the public's concern for safety, can easily lead to policies that respond to the public's limited perception that "punishment works" regardless of the context in assessing the effectiveness of various policies.

In the executive branch, the Department of Justice is inevitably dominated by lawyers most comfortable with following legal traditions; the U.S. Department of Justice that has never had an assistant secretary for science and technology. But that tradition has begun to change slowly with the creation in 2010 by Attorney General Eric Holder of a Science Advisory Board for the Office of Justice Programs, which includes the National Institute of Justice and the Bureau of Justice Statistics and provides grant support predominantly for state and local criminal justice operations. But that Board has no line authority or interaction with other parts of the Justice Department and its limited role could well be diminished by any successor attorney general.

Complexities of the evidence models

The difficulty of providing strong evidence of a treatment effect is highlighted by the difficulty of isolating the effect of any particular treatment X from the many other factors that can affect crime or factors associated with crime. Some of the more salient factors include individual factors such as demography, education, employment status and opportunities, cognitive effects of lead, and socioeconomic status, and environmental factors such as peer networks, family structure, gun availability, and drug markets, and the varying criminal justice environments such as policing, legislation, probation and parole supervision, and court decisions. Isolating the particular effects of some specific treatment X in this complex environment is clearly a difficult challenge.

Where it is possible, an RCT is certainly one approach to this issue. RCTs work best in the context of evaluating treatments applied to individuals. It is often feasible to identify a reasonable set of candidates eligible for a particular treatment and then randomly partition those eligibles into a treatment and a control group, but since there is no "blind" like a placebo, if members of the two groups interact, then some of the treatment might be transmitted to members of the control group. To get around this, one might create groups of eligibles in different settings and then randomly select the treatment and control groups from among the settings.

Even in this best-case scenario, we see complications introduced. The complications become more severe as we try to introduce randomization into operational situations. To the extent that they involve a more lenient police response to a defined crime situation, each situation is likely to be somewhat different and some that were intended as treatment may be too severe to warrant leniency and others that were intended as controls may be too minor to be dealt with as the more severe control. As a result, decisions by the police officers out there to do their assigned jobs could well distort the results of the experiment.

One feature of experimental trials is the limited number of variables that could be introduced as "blocks" in the experiment. In the simplest experiment, there is no blocking and all members of the treatment and control groups are dealt with similarly. On the other hand, one might want to separate members of each group based on some characteristic like gender or employment status to see if the treatment works differently with these different groups. There are obviously limits to how many of these different blocks can be incorporated into an experiment, so one would want to be quite sure of what blocking is called for. That warrants extensive analysis of operational situations beforehand to be confident that the most appropriate blocking has been carried out.

To the extent that the appropriate treatment will be different for different subgroups, then a failure to introduce blocking into the experiment would lead to recommending the same treatment for all groups. This was an important aspect of the classic Minneapolis domestic-violence experiment that contrasted police response of arrest compared to counseling (Sherman and Berk, 1984). The reported results indicated that arrest worked better at reducing recidivism. The results were widely reported in the *New York Times* and elsewhere, and were received with enthusiasm by police and even enacted into statutes in many jurisdictions. Subsequent analyses by Sherman indicated that the better treatment would depend very much on whether the offending partner was employed, but that was reported only years later.

With that knowledge, it would have been important to have run the initial experiment blocking on employment status. It is difficult to know whether there might have been other characteristics that would similarly differentiate the appropriateness of counseling or arrest.

The complex choice environment

The difficulty of making policy choices lies not only in the complexity of the causal relationship between treatment and outcome, but in the complexity of the desired outcomes. At the simplest level, there are two principal outcomes of interest: crimes and costs. Estimating the costs of any treatment is relatively easy and likely to be similar in different contexts, but estimating the crime reduction will be quite complex and likely to be quite different in different settings since different settings will have different values of the array of crime-related factors illustrated above. Thus, in any particular setting where one has an estimate of the crime reduction effectiveness of a variety of treatments, one must weigh their costs against an estimated value of the crimes reduced.

Also, different treatments will have different effects on different kinds of crime. For example, incarceration could well be quite effective in incapacitating a rapist, who is likely to take his rapes off the street when sent to prison. On the other hand, however, incarcerating a drug seller is likely to be *in*effective in averting drug transactions because the drug market will simply respond to the external demand for the drug by recruiting a replacement; this concern was an important theme of my 1992 Presidential Address to the American Society of Criminology (Blumstein, 1993). Indeed, it is entirely possible that the replacement could well be more prone to commit other crimes than his predecessor; those replacements were much younger and much less restrained in their use of the guns they needed to protect themselves against street robbers, and that gave rise to a major increase in homicide rates by young people, a doubling between 1983 and 1993 for all ages of 20 or under (Blumstein, 1995).

Another important influence on policy choices relates to the public acceptability of those choices. The public's desire for their legislatures to "do something" about the growing drug problem was undoubtedly an important influence on the dramatic rise of incarceration during the 1980s and 1990s. And the public's naïve view about the uniform effectiveness of incarceration provided continuing support for the increasingly punitive sanctions (e.g. mandatory minimum sentences) being imposed, even in the face of the strong arguments that the sanctions would not be effective. In the current period, there seems to be widespread agreement about the desirability of reducing those legislated sanctions, but a reluctance to do so because of legislators' concerns about being seen as "soft on crime" if the sanctions were lifted.

Also serving as a limit on many aspects of public policy that might serve to reduce crime are the constraints imposed by constitutional amendments. In particular, the 2nd, 4th, 5th, 6th, 8th, and 14th Amendments all serve as particular constraints on actions that might otherwise increase the effectiveness of the criminal justice system in reducing crime, but would be precluded as violations of one or more of these protections of individual liberty and privacy.

All of these considerations affecting choices involving the weighing of costs and benefits and the need for public approval and avoiding constitutional constraints, make criminal-justice policy choices much more complex than the choices in other realms of policy. They also provide the opportunity for a decision-maker to justify a policy choice based on less than adequate evidence.

Research approaches to provide evidence

The principal research question is one of estimating the effect of treatment X on outcome measure Y in the presence of a variety of contextual factors, Z1, Z2, etc. As indicated earlier, the "gold standard" is the RCT that compares a treatment to a control with random assignment between treatment and control in order to avoid selection effects biasing the results. There are many operational situations, however, that preclude the possibility of an RCT. It is the unusual judge who would consider flipping a coin or even referring to a random-numbers table in making a sentencing decision. As indicated earlier, it would be desirable to introduce blocking into an RCT, but it is important to identify those contextual variables, Z, to which the outcome is most sensitive to serve as blocks in the experiment.

It is clear that an RCT will have the strongest internal validity but not necessarily the strongest external validity in terms of its applicability in a setting other than the one where the RCT was conducted. If similar RCTs were conducted in a diversity of settings with similar results, that would certainly strengthen the argument for its general applicability. It is usually the case that mounting an RCT is likely to be much more expensive than other approaches using traditional statistical analyses like regression. Such approaches using available data from different settings provide a very useful opportunity for sorting among the most relevant covariates for identifying variables that would be strong candidates for blocking in a subsequent RCT.

Statistical analysis using the variety of regression methods is also appropriate for providing initial estimates of effect sizes for particular treatments that have been carried out in a variety of settings and evaluated in each of those settings. Meta-analysis (Lipsey et al., 2000) has been developed as a means of integrating a variety of evaluations in different settings to provide estimates of the range of effect sizes and particularly salient covariates.

In recognition of the large number of situations that preclude an RCT, a wide variety of quasi-experimental methods have been developed that also provide very useful tools for evaluation. These could include a shift in the patterns of an outcome variable following the introduction of a treatment. Where one cannot randomly select treatments from controls, it is possible to provide statistical matching in selecting a control sample from the population of eligibles using methods such as propensity scoring.

There are many programs that have been implemented and evaluated carefully. The Blueprints project at the University of Colorado has set very high standards of evaluation and replication of programs targeted at youth. CrimeSolutions.gov provides a listing of hundreds of programs that have been evaluated as "effective" if they have been well evaluated and replicated, "promising" if there has been a positive evaluation, or "no effects" if there have been multiple evaluations showing no significant effect. The Campbell Collaboration identifies particular problem areas and collects the variety of studies that address each such area and assesses the quality of the evidence of the array of programs in that area. Thus, it is clear that there exists a rich variety of catalogs, each with its own methodology and standards of assessment, which have been compiled and can provide guidance in selecting programs that are at least promising and, in many cases, demonstrated to be effective.

It should be clear that the strong scientific principle of replication is a necessary part of providing evidence of a program's effectiveness. Replication of a particular program in a variety of settings highlights the generalizability of any assessment of a program's effectiveness. It is also particularly important for testing the performance of a program in a setting that goes beyond the intensity, commitment, and enthusiasm – as well as the potential data-collection bias – of the program's innovator. If one is to argue for a program's effectiveness, then it must have been shown to be effective in a variety of settings under the control of a variety of managers, and that can only be accomplished with replication.

Strengthening the link between evidence and policy

It should be clear that estimating strong criminal-justice treatment effects is a complex process that inherently admits evidence that can vary widely in its quality and in its applicability to any particular setting. We have strong methods like RCT, but those are often not applicable, and other strong quasi-experimental methods that can provide strong indications. An important part of the process of bringing evidence to the shaping of policy requires the building of links between local policy organizations and academics, particularly criminologists.

It becomes important as an innovation is introduced to bring academics who will participate in the evaluation into close collaboration early in the process. They can provide guidance based on what is known in the research literature, scanning the various catalogs presenting evaluation results to assess their applicability to the local situation, and they can be most helpful as participants in the design and execution of the local evaluation.

One other useful role of academics is as visiting fellows or embedded participants in policy organizations. Individuals in such a role can build understanding of the policy process so that they can make their research more relevant and more applicable. They can bring to the organization existing knowledge in the criminological literature and especially insights from the emerging literature. And when they return to their academic activities, it will be with a knowledge and awareness of the kinds of problems and issues of concern in the policy environment, and so their subsequent research is more likely to address those policy issues with a sensitivity to the issues of policy concern.

Perhaps most important is the necessity to build the relevant research enterprise. That research literature can provide insights into programmatic innovations that are likely to be effective. The insights into the importance of crime "hot spots," for example, has had a major effect on strategies and styles of policing and their effectiveness in dealing with violent crime. The Committee on Law and Justice of the National Research Council of the National Academy of Sciences has been the source of considerable useful evaluation of the research literature in a variety of areas, and most importantly where there are conflicting research findings that need sorting out.

Unfortunately, the federal support for criminal justice research is extremely limited compared to research investments in other areas. The budgetary support for the National Institute of Justice and the Bureau of Justice Statistics is in the order of $100 million to cover all issues of interest to state and local criminal justice agencies. Those budgets are miniscule compared to the $600 million allocated to the Bureau of Labor Statistics just for research and measurement of labor markets. In sharp contrast, the National Institute of Health has an annual budget of $30 billion. Research investment in NIJ and BJS several times their current budgets is certainly warranted. That expansion is particularly appropriate in view of the growing recognition of the importance of evidence-based policy and the realization that progress in research and statistics is particularly important for facilitating those efforts.

References

Blumstein, Alfred. 1993. Making Rationality Relevant: The American Society of Criminology 1992 Presidential Address. *Criminology*, 31(1): 1–16.

Blumstein, Alfred. 1995. Youth Violence, Guns, and the Illicit-Drug Industry. *Journal of Criminal Law and Criminology*, 86(1): Fall.

Lipsey, Mark, and Wilson, David. (2000), *Practical Meta-Analysis*. Sage.

Sherman, Lawrence W., and Richard A. Berk. 1984. The Specific Deterrent Effects of Arrest for Domestic Assault. *American Sociological Review*, 49(1): 261–72.

Index